W9-CSD-302

The National Question
in Yugoslavia

The National Question
in Yugoslavia

ORIGINS, HISTORY, POLITICS

IVO BANAC

Cornell University Press

ITHACA AND LONDON

PUBLICATION OF THIS BOOK WAS ASSISTED BY A GRANT FROM
THE PUBLICATIONS PROGRAM OF THE NATIONAL ENDOWMENT
FOR THE HUMANITIES, AN INDEPENDENT FEDERAL AGENCY.

First published 1984 by Cornell University Press.
Published in the United Kingdom by Cornell University Press Ltd., London

International Standard Book Number 0-8014-1675-2
Library of Congress Catalog Card Number 83-45931
Printed in the United States of America
*Librarians: Library of Congress cataloging information
appears on the last page of the book.*

*The paper in this book is acid-free and meets the guidelines
for permanence and durability of the Committee on Production
Guidelines for Book Longevity of the Council on Library Resources.*

To my mother

Annæ autem dedit partem unam tristis,
quia Annam diligebat.

Contents

Contents

Maps and Tables

Maps and Tables

Preface

Before charter flights and motels it was the legend of romantic barbarianism and heroic chivalry that shaped the European image of the South Slavs—an image that markedly resembles the tales of the Wild West. Alberto Fortis's dramatic description of the hajduks, or brigands, of Dalmatia includes this tidbit: "The objects of their rapine are bovine animals and sheep, which they transport to their lairs to feed themselves and to supply them with hide for shoes." In 1914, John Reed saw the war-ravaged Serbs as the "strong virile stock of a young race not far removed from the half-savagery of a mountain peasantry." A considerably less perceptive young Irishman, Patrick the O'Doneven, viewed these lands and societies as a version of Ireland's West Country skillet, "filled with simmering 'stirabout' that crackles to explosion in places where it boils . . . forced to keep on spluttering by the fire beneath, which is never allowed to go out." Outlaws, rustlers, mountain men, mules, hostile clans—

And then, there was the notorious national question, a term that, from the Western point of view, conveyed the very essence of Eastern Europe. The Russian domains commanded prior attention, but after them it was surely the complicated nationality problems of the South Slavic regions that, to Westerners, best exemplified the East European national question. The fact of recognition, however, did not necessarily imply understanding; indeed, profound misunderstanding was more often the result. The South Slavs themselves were aware that their perennial struggles for national equality—struggles fought both internally and externally—had only reinforced the Western inclination to treat them with condescension or, indeed, scorn. The "petty local feuds" among these "bits and refuse of peoples" (*Völkerabfälle*—the phrases only by chance belong to Friedrich Engels) interfered with the grand moves of European cabinets and, as Bismarck scornfully put it, were "not worth the healthy bones of a single Pomeranian grenadier."

Faced with such sentiments, South Slavic intellectuals came to believe that one had to have an equivalent history to understand. If the very idea of a national question seemed baffling, particularly to the English-speaking world, surely this was because the terminology that detailed the (unpleasant) matters between two or among several nationalities bore no relation to the situation in countries where the dominant consciousness of nationhood was not the product of a shared history of subjugation to alien rulers. The nation-empires of the West, which themselves often dominated others, did not really comprehend what it meant to live in a "house of bondage." The decision to study the question of South Slavic national aspirations from the inside, and not as a perplexing phenomenon that repeatedly set Europe aflame, was taken by these intellectuals as the mark of a kindred spirit. R. W. Seton-Watson therefore "understood" the South Slavs because he was a Scotsman. Frano Supilo, visiting Edinburgh in January 1917, viewed the Scottish capital as another Zagreb. Supilo clearly saw at least two national societies in Britain. He had on his own (South Slavic) spectacles.

In this book I have tried to look at the national question of Yugoslavia with a clearer eye, focusing on the first two and a half years (1918–1921) of the history of the Kingdom of the Serbs, Croats, and Slovenes. (Since this first common South Slavic state was even then unofficially referred to as Yugoslavia, I shall follow this practice throughout for the sake of simplicity.) Much effort has gone into this study, but, even if I am said to have failed in all other respects, I hope that my readers will gladly recognize that they were not glancing through the wrong end of perspective glass, by which the views and concerns of the protagonists were in any sense minimized.

The national question has to do with the conditions (by definition inade-quate) for the free and independent development of nations and national communities—inadequate, because were it otherwise the question would not exist. Though even Switzerland has its Jura problem, the national question is presumed missing in those happy lands that either are uninational or at least are spared dissension between different groups. Neither can be said of Yugoslavia. To this day, its political and social life is dominated by a particularly complex, long-standing, and troublesome nationality problem. The concept is therefore essentially negative. It describes inharmonious rela-tions among various nationalities, characterized by the supremacy of one group (or a coalition of groups) and the resistance (violent or passive) of the others. And since tolerance for one's neighbor is regarded as a virtue even when it is not practiced (and perhaps especially then), the standing East European euphemism for the national question is the cumbersome phrase "problems (or aberrations) in internationality relations," or sometimes sim-ply the last two words.

The purpose of this book is to provide the first complete study of the origins of the tragic sequence in Yugoslavia that precipitated a long period of interwar instability, brought untold suffering to her peoples during the course of the Second World War, and continues to test the wisdom of her leaders.

No single book could possibly provide a worthy appraisal of the whole history of Yugoslavia's national question, and I therefore chose to concentrate on the period that set the pattern for the subsequent development of the problem. This is, in short, a genetic study, which traces and analyzes the history and characteristics of the South Slavic national ideologies, connects these trends with Yugoslavia's flawed unification in 1918, and ends with the adoption of the centralist constitution of 1921. It will not take readers through the labyrinthine byways of the two interwar decades, nor will it guide them through the dramatic wartime struggles and the postwar socialist experiment. But none of these developments, each in its own way connected with the new twists in the national question, can be understood without the prelude that contained all the seeds of future disorders. The aim is therefore to provide the single book that will serve as a learned introduction to the national problems of interwar, wartime, and present Yugoslavia.

Although the contrasts in the material culture of Yugoslavia's various peoples represented a serious obstacle to harmonious unity, the national question cannot be attributed to rivalries over distribution of wealth or to the choleric temperament of entire nations. On the contrary, mutually exclusive national ideologies have been most responsible for the tensions between particular nationalities, contributing more to these tensions than the attempts by various of Yugoslavia's political groups to encourage and perpetuate particular forms of national inequality. This book therefore focuses on these ideational questions, illustrating how the delusive aspects of national ideologies have influenced both personal and group consciousness and in that way helped to shape events.

Since it is my considered judgment that relations between the Serbs and the Croats are central to any discussion of Yugoslavia's national question, I have examined certain topics at greater length than others, among them the characteristics of Serb and Croat national ideologies, the meaning attached to Yugoslavist unitarism among the Croats and the Serbs, and the role of the Radić phenomenon in the movement for Croat sovereignty. Throughout, though many of the matters I discuss are still subject to widely varying interpretations, I have made every effort to present a truthful—if not necessarily detached—picture of events. Evidence itself exerts its power over historians and pushes them to assume stands according to the values that they profess.

The contents of the book reflect the present stage of scholarship and should be viewed in part as an attempt to combine the findings of several generations of historians, mainly from Yugoslavia, into a newly interpreted whole. Surprisingly, although most studies on various aspects of Yugoslavia's history must deal in one way or another with the national question, this is the first general study of the subject. Therefore, in addition to voluminous amounts of published sources and documents of the period, I have made careful use of

13

the inquiries of those colleagues who best advanced the knowledge of inter-war Yugoslavia's political, diplomatic, and economic history, even though their purpose may not always have been to comment on the various aspects of the national problem. Many of the themes I introduce, those of a social and, especially, intellectual and cultural nature, have never been studied before, and they necessitated primary research carried out in various depositories and research institutions of Yugoslavia. I should point out that few investigators have had the occasion to examine so broad a range of periodical literature for inquiry into the period under consideration. This rich source mitigated the loss or inaccessibility of documentary collections relating to the activities of certain prominent individuals and political groups.

This work has gone through several major revisions and now bears little resemblance to its early versions. When I started work on my dissertation at Stanford some years ago I had an entirely different subject in mind, but gradually I realized that my original topic was only a small part of the huge and complex national problem in Yugoslavia, and in due course it was the national problem that consumed all my attention and became my main subject. Though I do not recommend this style of work, I am infinitely indebted to those institutions and individuals who made the long quest possible.

I am especially grateful for the grants from the International Research and Exchanges Board and the Fulbright-Hays Commission, Stanford University, and the A. Whitney Griswold Faculty Research Fund at Yale. I am glad to acknowledge the generous assistance of the staffs of the University and National Library (Sveučilišna i nacionalna knjižnica), the Archives of Croatia (Arhiv Hrvatske), the Institute for the History of the Workers' Movement of Croatia (Institut za historiju radničkog pokreta Hrvatske), and the Lexicographical Institution (Leksikografski zavod), all of Zagreb, and of the Hoover Institution and the Stanford University Libraries at Stanford University and the Sterling Memorial Library at Yale. The Frederick W. Hilles Publication Fund of Yale University provided a grant that met the expenses of the maps included in this book; I thank the Hilles Publication Fund Committee for its generous support. The assistance of a good many other persons, too numerous to be mentioned individually, including dear friends and members of my immediate family, is also sincerely appreciated.

I should, however, like to single out several persons to whom I am under a special obligation. Walter and Hildegard Oerter probably have no idea what their help and friendship meant to me in a particular moment of distress connected with this project. I do—and thank them again in this fashion. I am extremely grateful for the valuable suggestions of several colleagues, especially John Ackerman of Cornell University Press, Jeffrey Brooks of the Department of History at the University of Chicago, and Norman Naimark of the Department of History at Boston University, who read all or parts of the several versions of my manuscript. I warmly appreciate the patience and consummate artistry of Shirley Taylor, who edited the manuscript for publication with fearful intelligence. I also owe much to Branimir Babić, my master mapmaker, Mary Whitney and Florence Thomas, who took the burden of typing the final draft, José Roberto Martínez, the postman of Dark Hollow Road, and Nikola Svilokos, the master of Tinicum scriptorium.

Over the years I have benefited from the totally selfless support of three persons, whose roles in the shaping of this manuscript are complementary. There is a point in the research of every topic when an author's interest, with all the elements of the story resolved, begins to sag. Ivo J. Lederer, whose style always carved out my way, seized me by the scruff of the neck at that point and has held me to my task ever since. Few scholars can match Jozo Tomasevich's determination in following up the very faintest historical tracks. I have profited enormously from the vast learning that he acquired in decades of most disciplined *studijanje i ričerkavanje,* as he will best note after reading this book. The entire volume would have been impossible without the invaluable aid, inspiration, and encouragement of Wayne S. Vucinich of the Department of History at Stanford, my mentor and veritable uncle, who taught me all the intricacies of *muderisluk.* Finally, a special recognition to my wife, Manana, who has long been oppressed by historical sciences. *ſaC oVo Dan InoCh neprIstah trudeCi: prIaſnu tVoiu MoCh i druXbu XeLeci.*

IVO BANAC

New Haven, Connecticut

A Note on Transliteration, Terminology, and References

The systems of transliteration from Cyrillic to Roman alphabets, each in its specific way, are notoriously difficult of solution. Though I retained a simplified version of the Library of Congress system for Russian, I prefer the linguistic system in transliterating paleo-Cyrillic and South Slavic Cyrillic alphabets. The merits on each side may appear equal, but the linguistic system's diacritics, also used in the Croatian and Slovenian Roman alphabets and Romanized Serbian, certainly command—or ought to command—prior choice in works dealing with the South Slavs. In linguistic transliteration the various Balkan Cyrillic alphabets put on almost identical Roman garb, eliminating as nearly as possible the artificial differences that derive from the systems of transliteration themselves—the differences among these alphabets and between them and the South Slavic Roman scripts. Moreover, to heighten the scriptory unity of the South Slavic languages, I abandoned the substitution of the Cyrillic x with the Roman x in the linguistic transliteration from Bulgarian, my preference being the Roman h. Therefore "Hristov" and not "Xristov," which, I trust, will please Messrs. Hristovskis and Hristićes.

In the course of writing this book, after some prior experiments, I felt a special obligation to help establish proper English usage for the South Slavic national appellations. Against the anarchy that obtains in this area, I prefer a definite morphological system, which, in part, is derived from H. W. Fowler's rule for Arab, Arabian, Arabic. For nouns, I prefer Slovene(s), Croat(s), Serb(s), Bulgar(s). The noun Croatian(s) is used only for the inhabitants of the pre-1918 counties of Croatia proper (Zagreb, Bjelovar-Križevci, Varaždin, Modruš-Rijeka, Lika-Krbava) with Medjimurje; Serbian(s) and Bulgarian(s) for the inhabitants of pre-1912 Serbia and Bulgaria (in all three cases with exceptions). For adjectives, Slovene, Croat, Serb, and Bulgar refer to *people* (irrespective of and as opposed to specific territory). Therefore, Slovene women, Croat leader, Serb movement, Bulgar aspirations. The adjectives Slovenian, Croatian, Serbian, and Bulgarian refer to the *land,* the *language,* and other concepts that assume a long history. Therefore, Slovenian mountains, Croatian language, Serbian history, Bulgarian literature. The same adjectives refer to any aspect of Croatia proper, Serbia proper, and Bulgaria proper (as above, with exceptions). Therefore, Croatian Sabor, Serbian army, Bulgarian cadets, and so on. This system is not perfect, but it certainly eliminates many problems in an area noted for confusion and, occasionally, plain willfulness.

Unless noted otherwise, the emphasis in quotations is taken directly from the sources. All translations, unless otherwise noted, are my own. Throughout, the reader will encounter many statistical references that are not specially footnoted. All references to the numerical strength of national, religious, and linguistic groups in the immediate post-1918 period are drawn or negotiated from the preliminary results of Yugoslavia's 1921 census—Direkcija državne statistike u Beogradu, *Prethodni rezultati popisa stanovništva u Kraljevini Srba, Hrvata i Slovenaca 31. januara 1921. godine* (Sarajevo, 1924). All references to the electoral performance of political parties, groups, and candidates in the elections for the Constituent Assembly (November 28, 1920) are derived or calculated from the official publication of electoral results—*Statistički pregled izbora narodnih poslanika Kraljevine Srba, Hrvata i Slovenaca* (Belgrade, 1921).

Abbreviations

BMORK	Bəlgarski makedono-odrinski revoljucionni komiteti (Bulgar Macedono-Adrianopolitan Revolutionary Committee)
Cemiyet	İslam Muhafazai Hukuk Cemiyet (Society for the Preservation of Muslim Rights)
DS	Demokratska stranka (Democratic Party)
HPS	Hrvatska pučka stranka (Croat People's Party)
HPSS	Hrvatska pučka seljačka stranka (Croat People's Peasant Party), the official name of Radić's party from 1904 to 1920
HRSS	Hrvatska republikanska seljačka stranka (Croat Republican Peasant Party), the official name of Radić's party from 1920 to 1925
HSK	Hrvatsko-srpska koalicija (Croato-Serb Coalition)
HSP	Hrvatska stranka prava (Croat Party of Right)
HZ	Hrvatska zajednica (Croat Union)
JDL	Jugoslovenska demokratska liga (Yugoslav Democratic League)
JMO	Jugoslavenska muslimanska organizacija (Yugoslav Muslim Organization)
JO	Jugoslavenski odbor (Yugoslav Committee)
KK	Komiteti i Mbrojte Kombëtare e Kosovës (Committee for the National Defense of Kosovo; the Kosovo Committee)
KONARE	Komiteti Nacional Revolucionar (National Revolutionary Committee)
KPJ	Komunistička partija Jugoslavije (Communist Party of Yugoslavia)
NRS	Narodna radikalna stranka (National Radical Party)
PNP	Privremeno narodno predstavništvo (Interim National Legislature)
SLS	Slovenska ljudska stranka (Slovene People's Party)
SRPJ(k)	Socijalistička radnička partija Jugoslavije (komunista) (Socialist Workers' Party of Yugoslavia [Communist])
SSDP	Srpska socijaldemokratska partija (Serbian Social Democratic Party)
SSP	Starčevićeva stranka prava (Starčević's Party of Right)
SZ	Savez zemljoradnika (Alliance of Agrarian Workers)

Abbreviations

TMORO	Tajna makedono-odrinska revoljucionna organizacija (Secret Mac-edono-Adrianopolitan Revolutionary Organization)
VMK	Vərhovnija makedonski komitet (Supreme Macedonian Committee)
VMRO	Vətrešna makedonska revoljucionna organizacija (Internal Macedonian Revolutionary Organization)
VMRO (ob.)	VMRO (obedinena) (VMRO [United])

PART I

Antecedents and Antipodes

To Be Reckoned among Nations

The perception that humanity is divided by national and linguistic characteristics is as ancient as recorded history. The sacred history of the Israelites (Deut. 32:8) holds that the Most High divided the nations and separated the sons of Adam. Contemporary social scientists—sharing in our present loss of a common allusion—are far more likely to be familiar with Stalin's five necessary characteristics of a nation (common territory, economic life, language, and psychological makeup, as well as certain national specifics in culture) than with the biblical attributes of the People of God (*ho laos*). For Israel was a community of blood, language, worship, and fate. It had common institutions and a defined sacred territory. Though products of selection, the Israelites bore the marks of the hallowed people that were not necessarily at variance with the experiences of their neighbors. The non-Israelites, the peoples (*ta ethnē*), could recognize themselves in Israel's national experience.

There is no question that the ability to distinguish between one's own national community and other national communities was unimpaired, unambiguous, suprasocial, and—one might add—remarkably accurate long before modern nationalism. Yet, for reasons that need not be examined here, the conventional historical point of view frequently rebels at the suggestion that the lasting sense of national loyalties ought not be paired with the spirit of nationalism. Like the bourgeoisie, its supposed social carrier, nationalism seems to have been gestating through the ages, to be born by a Caesarean gash in the course of the French Revolution.

At the beginning of this inquiry the misunderstandings connected with practically all aspects of nationhood must therefore be cleared, and the terminology defined. Certainly the most ambiguous and muddled term that requires a clear explanation is that of the *nation* itself. Contemporary American usage assigns this term to a vast variety of phenomena, though largely territorial and political. When a roving reporter is said to have crisscrossed

21

the "far-flung corners of the nation," it is clear from the context that he did not become a spiritual astronaut who investigated the uncharted byways of his countrymen's collective personality. He simply went about a particular country. Or, when we hear that the "oil-producing Persian Gulf nations" of Kuwait, Saudi Arabia, Bahrain, Qatar, and the Emirates are of one mind on a particular question, the term *nations* certainly refers to states. All of these states are Arab, and state sovereignty apparently does not affect their consciousness of belonging to a large community of people which views itself as the Arab nation.

Nations and states generally do have common territories, but their frontiers are not necessarily the same. And since nations must not be confused with states, the much misused term *nation-state* makes sense only if the territory of a nation corresponds exactly to the territory of a state. In Europe, at least, state frontiers more often than not divide nations. The Spanish-Portuguese frontier and the waters that encircle Iceland and Malta are perhaps the only genuine national frontiers in Europe. This does not of course mean that Portugal, Iceland, and Malta are the only European nation-states. Most European countries with numerically insignificant national minorities may well qualify, though none are as uninational as the three cited examples.

Moreover, some nations may be split among several almost entirely minority-free states. Germans are an absolute majority in the two Germanies, Austria, Switzerland, and Liechtenstein, and form significant minorities in several other European countries. Other nations—the Albanian case is particularly poignant—may have one state that forms their national nucleus or matrix (the term *matrix-state* is applied in such cases), though its members are important minorities in neighboring states. Still other nations have no state of their own but form a minority within one (Bretons) or more states (Basques, Kurds). Then there is the category of *multinational states*—particularly germane to this study, since Yugoslavia is an excellent example of a state that contains many nations, none in this case with an absolute majority.

My definition of the term *nation* is not, then, readily fixed by political criteria. *Cultural* attributes, above all language, are decisive. Because modern national ideologies place great stock in the ability of language to provide an instant national identity, we tend to forget that even from the earliest times language was a frequent synonym for a national community. Yahweh was praised "by all tongues" in recognition of the multinational mystery of the world. The term *barbarian* indicated those outside the linguistic frontiers of the Hellenic world. And in the South Slavic annals, the turn of phrase of Priest Martinac from Grobnik, who in 1493 noted with sorrow that the Turks "fell upon the Croatian language," clearly conveys an attack upon a people.

In principle, though a single language may be shared by two or more nations, a single nation cannot be multilingual. English is indeed the language of a group of nations, either partially assimilated by or the extensions of England, but the English nation speaks only its own English language. The exceptions to this principle are most often a result of centuries of assimilation (as in the Irish case), of unique historical circumstances (the Swiss example), or of colonial experience. Considering the importance of language to national identity, it is not surprising that saving (or shaping) the national language is the first priority of nationalism. National movements are often mistaken for linguistic movements, but clearly, the Québecers, for example, are fighting for more than the equality of the French language.

Besides the cultural criteria of nationhood, which also include the customs, character, and psychology of each people, nations are also founded on certain *historical* premises. Every nation is a product of specific development. The autocephalous Serbian church or the continuity of Croatian parliamentary life, vested in the Sabor (assembly) and in the figure of the Ban (prorex or viceroy), are examples of separate institutions that become the foci of national consciousness. Traditions of statehood, or simply the memories of past sovereignty, are often vested in such institutions.

It is highly significant that, among the South Slavs, the national identity of the Bulgars, Croats, and Serbs was acquired, though not firmly fixed, long before the development of modern nationalism. These three nations maintained a collective memory of their medieval statehood, and this memory survived in various forms—in the consciousness of national elites but also in part in popular imagination—despite interruptions or reductions in full state independence. As a result, the measure of state-historical tradition separates these old South Slavic nations from the Slovenes, who acquired a national consciousness only in the nineteenth century, and especially from the Montenegrins, Macedonians, and Bosnian-Hercegovinian Muslims, who are the products of twentieth-century mutations in South Slavic national affinities and are, indeed, still in the process of formation. Since the ideological underpinnings of these new South Slavic nations were seemingly incomplete without a state tradition, modern Slovenes therefore looked upon the early seventh-century Carantanian principality as their prototypal state and the proof of their continuous nationhood, and theorists of Montenegrin and Macedonian national uniqueness augmented their claims with reference to eleventh-century Doclea (Duklja) and the Western Bulgarian empire of Samuil.

Religion, too, has been a significant mark of various nations, though not always in the clumsy way posited by its critics. To this day the religious Jews maintain ancient Israel's community of worship (*qāhāl/ekklēsía*) in which, by a curious osmosis, their unreligious fellows also partake. In fact, the nonobservant Jews present a good example of how cultural and historical properties of religion help maintain national identity in secular surroundings. It is well known that the Poles, for example, are overwhelmingly Catholic, but it is often overlooked that the Catholic contribution to Polish national character is an aspect of the unchurched Poles' national culture, whether they realize it or not and even if they may be recently Polonized or descend from a different religious tradition. Much the same could be said, with reservations, about several South Slavic nationalities, notably the Slovenes. On the other hand, the integrity of a nation need not be compromised by religious sectarianism. Of course, this depends on the size of a religious community—the handful of Italian Protestants are generally thought of as somehow less Italian than their Catholic countrymen. All other things being equal, however, the *Deutschtum* of a Calvinist from Mannheim, a Lutheran from Oldenburg, or a Catholic from Bavaria is no longer an issue, though in the past the patriotic standing of their forefathers certainly was challenged.

There are cases, however, where the nationality-based strife is assumed to be religious. The Irish case is the textbook example. The Orangemen are indeed Protestants, but they are also the descendants of seventeenth-century Scottish and English settlers, whom the English throne charged with making the Croppies lie down. Though the Orangemen look upon themselves as Irish—and are certainly so looked upon by the English—their troubled relations with Ireland's indigenous Catholic majority are the result as much of national as of religious antipathies. The suppression of the old Irish religion was perhaps only the most obvious aspect of cultural, linguistic, and social repression, which created a specific national consciousness based on the particular disadvantage and the sense of epic grievance.

Inevitably, it seems, the dependence on a national culture creates emotional bonds that reinforce nationhood. This emotional attachment, or simply *patriotism,* has always been universally regarded. Though Ithaca was not a rich or powerful dwelling place, Odysseus held to it despite the euphoria induced by the fruit of lotus, which made his men forget the homeland. And Christ, the Man of Sorrows, who repeatedly manifested compassion for the people, cried only over Jerusalem. The emotional side of nationhood may be a byproduct of socialization, but it is more than that, and some of its aspects are of a sacred or privileged character that defy ordinary analysis.

Nations are therefore defined by cultural criteria, a set of characteristics which here also includes a peculiar historical consciousness, emotional allegiance, as well as earmarks of institutional and, in certain cases, religious separateness. They are moreover a historical category. Like all living organisms they have a parentage, infancy, and maturity. New nations can evolve from the old ones, and, as is unhappily obvious in this century of genocide, nations can come to an end. The universality of genealogy, that most fundamental form of history, is evidence that humanity always had an idea, however rudimentary, that nationhood was historical and evolutionary and that it resembled a family history. Abraham literally means the "father of many" nations. And Vinko Pribojević, the Dominican polyhistor of Hvar (15th to 16th centuries), though he was not certain whether Illyrius, supposedly the immediate ancestor of the Slavs, was a son of Cadmus or of the Cyclops Polyphemus, had no doubts that Illyrius was ultimately descended from Thyras, the seventh son of Japheth.[1] The vision may have been naive, but it expressed the popular belief that individuals begot families, clans, tribes, and peoples.

Nationhood implies a certain hierarchy of social formations. In the South Slavic case we know that after coming to the Balkan peninsula, the Slavs lived in a free tribal society, referred to by Constantine VII Porphyrogenitus (905–959), the Byzantine emperor-historian and one of the chief sources on the early South Slavic developments, as *hai Sklabēniai*. But these "Sclavinias" clearly belonged to what could be called a subnational category. Their inhabitants formed *families, clans,* and *tribes.* They were also certainly a *people,* which Porphyrogenitus called Slavic, though he knew of the more exact national names, including the Serb and Croat. For some of the Sclavinias, one could apply that appalling term *ethnic group.* But they were not exactly a nation, either individually or as a totality.

Much depends on the precise definition of these subnational terms. In English, for example, until the middle of the last century, the ethnic designation conveyed the Gentiles, exactly as it did in the Greek version of the scriptures, and was even taken to be the source of the word *heathen.* Nowadays it is used indiscriminately to cover practically every phenomenon connected with nationhood. It also has a seamy side. Just like the Soviet Russian term *natsmeny,* the acronym for national minorities, it is manifest evidence of inferiority. Its proper role should be to convey a well-defined regionalism within a national community. The Lalas, those proverbial Serbs of the Banat with tulip designs on their motley pants, and the Šops of Bulgaria, are ethnic groups. But the Serbs and Bulgars are not. These last are first of all peoples, which means that members of each group have certain common characteristics in actual outward fact. These are moreover identical to the necessary attributes of nationhood, described above. When one adds to this the ideology of national consciousness, one has modern nations.

Another term that should by right fit in the terminology of the subnational phenomena is *nationality.* Karl Deutsch concluded that it was most often used for those peoples obviously on their way to achieving political, economic, or cultural autonomy.[2] A nationality is therefore higher than a people but is not quite a nation. This valuation may well discharge a specific function in some highly abstract scheme, but it seems unduly vague for our purpose. The term should not be abandoned, however; it has admirable potential as the exact synonym for nation, especially since it is difficult to accustom the Western ear to the notion that nation is not the same as state.

1. Vinko Pribojević, *De origine successibusque Slavorum,* 2d ed. (Zagreb, 1951), pp. 61–62.
2. Karl W. Deutsch, *Nationalism and Social Communication,* 2d ed. (Cambridge, Mass., 1966), p. 17.

An additional difficulty is to find the proper adjectival form for the concept of nation (and now nationality). Today, we speak of "the national question" (leaving aside the usage as any problem that concerns a nation—gasoline shortages, for example). Until recently, the term *race* conveyed a nationality. The adjectival form *racial question* nowadays means the problem of color, not necessarily of nationhood. To adopt the adjective *ethnic* or the corresponding term *ethnicity* (for nationhood) would be to surrender to the confused—as opposed to the sensible—neologists. The gravity of this problem of course depends on the context.

There are in addition certain qualifying terms that belong to the terminology of the intermediary stage between the absence of any sort of common national characteristics and modern nationhood. The term *cultural nation,* for example, implies that a group possesses all the characteristics of nationhood except national consciousness. But the term seems rather inadequate, because it suggests that common history, origin, language, and the rest are not in themselves sufficient to define a nation. Furthermore, the term is not flexible enough to accommodate changes in historical circumstances. When applied to the precapitalist period, when nations, like the early proletariat in Marx's theory, existed more "in themselves" than "for themselves," it makes some sense. But if used to describe the situation after the beginning of the age of nationalism, when national ideologies gripped much of Europe, it seems inappropriate and will be shunned in this study.

Certain other attributes of the term *nation* are not merely inadequate or incomplete (like *cultural nation*) but result from ideological distortion. The outworn Central European distinction between historical and unhistorical nations, for example, reflects the partiality of legalistic feudal discernment for those nations that had an independent state in the Middle Ages as distinct from those that did not. The term *political nation* indicated the nobility, the only political class of historical nations; but because *political nation* also implies that domicile in a particular polity, rather than national culture, is the determinative criterium of nationhood, in recent times the designation has increasingly found its way into the thesaurus of integralist terminology. In nineteenth-century Hungary, for example, the Slovaks, Serbs, and Romanians, and some other non-Magyar groups, officially were regarded as Magyars by nationality, because the ruling ideology foresaw only one political nation in Hungary—the Magyar nation. Needless to say, besides implying a strict interpretation of the doctrine of national sovereignty (and sovereignty was supposedly indivisible), this tenet was an open assertion of the will to assimilate—in this case, to Magyarize.

All the considerations enumerated so far should help us to define nationalism. As we have seen, national consciousness is often confused with nationalism. This leads to two possible errors. One is the tendency to see nationalism everywhere and at all times. Every hint of a certain essence—

26

what the Germans call *Völkertum*—whereby human cultures, and therefore also nations, differ from one another, beginning with the story of the Tower of Babel, is seen as a manifestation of nationalism. Or, second, the accurate belief that nationalism is a modern phenomenon is used as an argument to deny the possibility of national consciousness in the premodern periods.

In fact, though nationalism is predicated on national consciousness, the two are not identical. Nor is nationalism a special political movement that alternately defends or promotes the integrity of a nation, though this is much closer to the truth. Both national consciousness and national movements existed long before nationalism. Strictly speaking, nationalism should only indicate an ideology, a comprehensive, modern world view, distinguished by its all-inclusive penetration of national consciousness into every going pursuit.

Nationalist ideology emerged during one of the most complex structural crises of European history, when the old order of particularistic and hier- archical estates gave way to a more democratic and dynamic system. New habits and necessities had to evolve on the basis of a new interpretation of human experience, a task which the ideology of nationalism performed admi- rably. The concepts of nationhood—nationally differentiated elements of consciousness, which evolved in small intellectual circles over the cen- turies—as a result became widely diffused. The very idea of nation became democratic as it embraced the lower classes, notably the peasantry, the group which, from the point of view of German romanticism, was the most authen- tic and therefore the most "national" expression of the *Volksgeist*. More- over, nationalism promoted new integrations in national societies, dispelled many old barriers between kindred regions, and occasionally even created a new national consciousness.

The old national consciousness was not necessarily concerned with specif- ic cultural or political goals. Nationalism always is, and it frequently seeks to introduce national criteria into purely private or everyday concerns. The old national consciousness also was not preoccupied with the political tools necessary for the maximization of national welfare. It took the world of nations as a reality, sometimes even as an aspect of the mystery of sin, since the confounding of languages at Babel was after all the punishment for human pride. The ideology of nationalism seeks to change the world. It promotes the idea of fraternity, interdependence, and common purpose among conationals and sometimes tends to channel social disputes onto the plane of relations with other national communities.

The diapason of nationalist thought is very wide, but its essence is the vision of a new order in national relations. The romantic nationalism of the early nineteenth century, especially the mode of teaching encountered among the Herderian Slavic "awakeners," viewed the world of nations as a beauti- ful garden. Like flowers planted by the Creator, each nation-person had its characteristics. But the fragrance of a rose could not—and therefore ought not—be artificially bred into the autumnal chrysanthemum. Each nation-flower had its separate place in the divine plan. Unlike *assimilationism,* romantic nationalism rejected all attempts to increase the nation by incorporating extraneous national elements: a nation can only be happy if it finds its own individual voice, its national spirit, and if that spirit is corrupted it will be led far afield from its national mission. The most characteristic voice of the nation is its language, and therefore the most authentic frontiers are linguistic. This benign ideology envisioned universal peace and harmony when every last national community obtained its national state.

Another national ideology commenced from the notion that relations among nations are not harmonious at all and that they resemble a kind of naturalism that is not far from downright predacity. This variant of nationalism is usually called integral, because it insists on the "completeness" of the nation in question. Depending on specific circumstances, it is explicitly assimilationist and dangerous to the integrity of neighboring nations. Integral nationalism emerged in the second half of the nineteenth century as part of the complex process of liberal decline and adapted itself to the positivist spirit of the age, but its roots go back to Jacobin planned ethnocide, whereby the minority nationalities and languages of France, as typical manifestations of "feudalism," had to disappear. Patriots spoke French, counterrevolutionaries, Basque and Breton. Only the French nation could exist in France. To insist on minority rights was treason.[3]

The link between benign and aggressive national ideologies—and those which assume the elements of both—is the determination to achieve the goal of national integration. The object of national movements is therefore the promotion of the national idea, which in turn transforms the commonplace of national identity into the all-important, even metaphysical, distinction. The Czech historian Miroslav Hroch has determined three stages of modern national integration especially appropriate for the small (and frequently dominated) European peoples. In the first stage a group of "awakened" intellectuals starts studying the language, culture, and history of a subjugated people. In the second stage, which corresponds to the heyday of national revivals, the scholars' ideas are transmitted by a group of "patriots," that is, the carriers of national ideologies, who take it upon themselves to convey national thought to the wider strata. In the last stage the national movement reaches its mass apogee.[4]

---

3. For a fine presentation of this attitude see H. E. Chehabi, "Ethnic Diversity in European Democracies: Four Intellectual Perspectives and a Normative Model" (unpublished article, Yale University, 1980), pp. 4–13.

4. Miroslav Hroch, *Die Vorkämpfer der nationalen Bewegung bei den kleinen Völkern Europas: Eine vergleichende Analyse zur gesellschaftlichen Schichtung der patriotischen Gruppen* (Prague, 1968), pp. 24–25.

Hroch's sequence aptly sums up the course of national revivals among the South Slavs, and his shrewd confidence in the worth of identifying the social composition and regional distribution of his patriots should also be seconded. But though it certainly makes a great deal of difference for the content of a national ideology that one half of its promoters was almost evenly divided between public administrators and clergymen, as was the case in Croatia during the Illyrianist phase (1836–1848) of the national revival,[5] it is far more important to examine how faithfully each national ideology reflects the great issues of a nation's history. To argue otherwise would be to give credence to vulgar theories that view every ideology as a crude manipulation mounted by special interests.

In order to be accepted an ideology must proceed from reality. Nationalism can attempt to deal with the conditions of its group's subjugation, but it cannot manufacture the conditions. And though members of a patriotic elite may be more sensitive to a nation's inferior position than are most of their compatriots, it does not follow that they willfully exaggerate national grievances nor that these do not affect the lower class. Expansionist elements in a national ideology are only infrequently a reflection of narrow caste interests; rather, they are usually brought forth from a latent, mass-based, idea of national prerogatives or superiority.

This range of agreement distinguishes nationalism from constricted class ideologies. Though various schools of socialism historically have equated nationalism with bourgeois ideology, social ownership of the means of production has not necessarily promoted internationalism. Indeed, the influence of national ideologies may have lessened in the capitalist world, while in the socialist countries, nourished with collectivist motifs, nationalism has perhaps even increased.

The social standing of the promoters of national ideologies is an important, but not the most important, consideration. The fact that Ljudevit Vukotinović (1813–1893), an important Croat revivalist writer, was a county judge is far less significant than the question of how accurately his ideas and actions reflect the historical memories of the Croats in the context of their nineteenth-century aspirations. This nationalist nobleman, for example, found it necessary to ''translate'' his Hungarian surname Farkas into Vukotinović (*farkas* = *vuk* = wolf). The ritualistic significance of this deed, made all the more dramatic if evaluated from the viewpoint of the nobility's protective-

5. Based on my analysis of the membership of Matica Ilirska, the Croat cultural and patriotic foundation, in 1838–1843, calculated from a list in Jakša Ravlić, ''Povijest Matice hrvatske,'' *Matica Hrvatska, 1842–1962* (Zagreb, 1963), pp. 260–263. Of the 217 members in those years, 26.85 percent were administrators and public servants, 22.22 were clergymen, 17.59 belonged to the free professions (mainly lawyers), 14.35 were craftsmen and merchants, 7.41 were teachers, and 10.65 percent identified themselves only by their noble titles, though noblemen were also represented in some of the other stations. There were no students, peasants, or workers.

ness of titled appellations, cannot be explained by Vukotinović's social position. Other gentry jurists in similar circumstances did not "nationalize" their names, but Vukotinović was imbued with a powerful ideology that required change not only in his spiritual environment but even in his most elementary self-identity. Wise in his own conceit, he wanted everybody to know to which pack he belonged.

The ideology of nationalism shaped the outlines of modern national integrations. It also imparted a sensitivity for the extension of national rights as opposed to the rights of individuals and social classes, which were argued more forcefully by the other modern ideologies. Above all, it found its fulfillment in national self-rule and invariably promoted state independence either through a separation of national territory from a larger multinational state (*secessionism*) or through incorporation of kindred territory within the already established matrix-state (*irredentism*). Modern state organization owes much to its political insights. As part of the modern trend toward self-determination (political, social, national), it challenges the most ancient premises of rulership. Who could argue with conviction that the divine right of the Holy Roman emperors was limited to their German subjects alone? Small wonder that the large, illiberal, and multinational empires sensed their most elementary enemy in the ideology of nationalism.

Certain elements in nationalism make it an adversary of liberal multinational societies as well. The legitimacy of a multinational state can only be maintained if it balances nationality interests against one another within a supranational party system. Nationalism generally promotes harmony within a specific national group; in parliamentary multinational systems it tends to promote the formation of political parties on the basis of nationality, thereby consolidating a given nationality, but not the parliamentary system or the multinational state. If a multinational society is authoritarian, chances are even better that the political class will be rooted in one national community—and the oppositional leadership in another.

The problem of modern multinational states is central to this inquiry precisely because these politics so often challenge the widely accepted—and as widely subverted—principle of national self-determination. Repeatedly, the ruling elite indulges in overbearing violations of national equality in favor of one—usually the most numerous—constituent nationality (*hegemonism*), promotes supranational ideologies (often ersatz nationalism), or suggests, at least, the benefits of union, sometimes implying that the national criteria are an inferior means of political organization.

One would have to search far and wide to find a political elite that sees the wisdom of stability to be derived from the breakup of a multinational state. They prefer to deal with the uncertainties inherent in maintaining the troubled status quo. When the national movements of constituent nationalities (regardless of whether they develop among large nations or among small minorities) succeed in upsetting state integrity, the dominant political forces manifest an inclination toward authoritarianism.

Of the various remedies against instability that multinational states have tried, the least successful seem to be those that depart most radically from the principle of self-determination: *centralism* is less successful than *local autonomy,* and the latter, if constituted on a geographical rather than national basis, is less successful than nationally based *federalism* (though these terms are not always precise and their political weight depends on the attitudes of political practitioners). All remedies, however, seem inadequate from the standpoint of political pluralism. In the words of a leading political sociologist:

> The basic assumption of the democratic political process is that today's minority might in the future either become a majority by convincing those in the present majority to agree with them, or hope to become a majority as a result of slow changes in the social structure. . . . The situation is quite different in the case of ethnic, cultural, or linguistic minorities, unless they can hope to assimilate the majority or unless decisions on the policies affecting them are delegated to self-governing local bodies, where they would constitute the majority. Unfortunately, even that might not be a solution in societies in which the national minority that is a majority at the local level faces a large-scale minority in its own region without any hope of assimilating it. . . . In fact, we would say that the principle of nationality . . . is not likely to lead to stable democracies.[6]

The dilemma is an eminently modern one, and in this century the long history of the South Slavs culminated in a particularly poignant case.

Lands and Identities

> Populorum pauca effatu digna aut facilia nomina.
>
> Little is worth mentioning about these peoples, nor are their names without difficulty.
>
> Pliny the Elder

Though one need not agree with Pliny on the worth of Liburnian Illyrians, he was clearly not the first observer to despair of being able to keep track of Balkan lands and peoples. If the representation of the lands that constituted Yugoslavia in 1918–1919 (see map 1-1) seems astonishing, it must be point-

6. Juan J. Linz, *The Breakdown of Democratic Regimes: Crisis, Breakdown, and Reequilibrium* (Baltimore, 1978), pp. 61–62.

1-1. Constituent areas of Yugoslavia

ed out that the dominant political contours give no indication of historical movement. The history of the Balkans is the history of migrations—not just of peoples, but of lands. The original Serbia was far from the Danube, the political center of Croatia was on the Adriatic, the "little land of Bosnia" (*to khōrion Bosona*) of Constantine Porphyrogenitus was a small canton at the source of the Bosna River, and the term Slovenia emerged as a geographical and national designation only in the nineteenth century.

Unlike the Germanic peoples, who traversed the Balkan peninsula for centuries on their way to Italy and the west, the Slavs came to the Balkans as permanent, largely agrarian, settlers. Their advent can be divided into several stages. Beginning with the first decades of the sixth century they aided various nomad invaders in forays over the borders of the Byzantine Empire. But their greatest incursion started in the 580s when they entered the peninsula as tribal footmen in the Avar host, helping to devastate imperial cities throughout the Balkans, the fate that Constantinople narrowly escaped in 626.

During the almost half a century of migrations, either under the Avar overlordship, as in the western Balkans, or independently, the Slavs covered the entire peninsula, from its Alpine fringes to the Peloponnesus. These were undifferentiated Slavs, who identified themselves only with the common Slavic name or according to the local—pre-Slavic—toponyms. Almost certainly, wherever the general Slavic appellation survived into modernity, as in the national names of the Slovenes and Slovaks and as in the name of the Croat province of Slavonia, the people or land in question did not have a strong state tradition in the early Middle Ages or thereafter.

There were in fact many Slavonias (or Sclavinias, as Constantine Porphyrogenitus had it) throughout the Balkans, proof of the staying qualities of the Slavs, which made it possible for them to establish themselves as permanent settlers in the new lands. For though they came to the Balkans as the larger part of the Avar military expedition, the Slavs were primarily sedentary. The free tribal organization suited their rustic character. The Slavs were self-governing in their extended families and districts (*županije*), and their tribal organization was sufficiently strong to abolish Byzantine rule in the Balkans, leaving only the coastal Adriatic cities, Salonika, and Constantinople itself to the imperial authority. But the Slavs did not have marked state-building skills. The construction of the first South Slavic states was accomplished under the auspices of subsequent invaders, who gave rise to the three South Slavic matrix-nationalities. These were the Croats, Serbs, and Bulgars.

Constantine Porphyrogenitus, the main source on early South Slavic history, relates that the Croats came to the Adriatic coast from "beyond Bavaria" under the leadership of five brothers and two sisters. They then killed and subjugated the Avars and took possession of the land. In another passage, the emperor-historian promotes his own style of Byzantine legitimacy by claiming that the Croat newcomers sought the protection of Emperor Heraclius (ruled 610–641), who then charged them with expelling the Avars. The Serbs sought Heraclius's tutelage somewhat later and received from him land for settlement in the theme of Salonika. They were unhappy with their new situation and wandered off beyond the Danube. Heraclius then summoned them to settle some of the coastal lands desolated by the Avars.[1] The Bulgars, a Turkic people, unlike the Slavic Croats and Serbs, moved south of the Danube in 679 and soon created a state, in which the numerically small Proto-Bulgar element in due course became completely assimilated with the Slavic majority but left it its state structure and national name.

Though one need not insist on the martial nature of the Croats and Serbs (the Bulgar case is a much clearer example of a typical steppe host), in all three cases a new wave of migrants, coming after the Slavicization of the peninsula, succeeded in organizing a new tribal alliance and, as a result of the political-state structure that developed, imposed its own appellation on the Slavic tribes in its own immediate area of settlement and much beyond. Just as the Bulgar state spread the Bulgar name to the Aegean littoral and into Macedonia, so also the Croat and Serb states, emerging respectively as sovereign principalities in the late ninth and twelfth centuries, created traditions of nationhood where previously there had been only tribal agriculturists.

Bulgaria was the first major South Slavic state. The height of its power came under Simeon at the turn of the eighth century. The ebb and flow of Bulgarian statehood need not concern us here except as it involved Macedonia, an ancient Balkan territory that became the political, ecclesiastical, and cultural center of Bulgaria under Samuil (ruled 976–1014). The Byzantine-Bulgar rivalry over Macedonia continued during the reign of the Bulgar Asen dynasty (1187–1258). In the fourteenth century, Macedonia was captured by the expanding Serbian state, and it remained within the Serbian orbit until the Ottoman conquest. The nineteenth- and twentieth-century "Macedonian question" was in a sense a replaying of the old contest. The three emerging Balkan states of Serbia, Greece, and Bulgaria each claimed the whole territory. After the Second Balkan War of 1913, waged by the Balkan allies against Bulgaria over the share in the Macedonian spoil, taken from the Ottomans in 1912, Macedonia was divided among the three states. Defeated Bulgaria received the smallest portion, the so-called Pirin Macedonia; Greece obtained the Aegean littoral of Macedonia, centered round Salonika; and Serbia acquired the large territory around the upper flow of the Vardar, to which the Strumica district accrued after Bulgaria's defeat in the First World War.

1. Constantine Porphyrogenitus *De adm. imp.* 30.61–71; 31.6–20.

The territory of modern Macedonia corresponds roughly to the area of ancient Macedon. Since the seventh century, this land has been overwhelmingly Slavic and, moreover, the cradle of Slavic literary activity. If one discounts the far-fetched Greek arguments about the Hellenic character of "Slavophone" Macedonians, the real question is to which Slavic nationality do they properly belong. The Macedonian dialects in the area north of Skopje show a similarity to Serbian Prizren and Timok idioms, but Serbian claims to Macedonia really rest on the effects of Serbian cultural influences dating from Serbian penetration of Macedonia in the thirteenth and fourteenth centuries and continuing through the work of a Serbian ecclesiastical organization that obtained in northern Macedonia under the Turks until the eighteenth century. The Bulgarian claims are far more substantial. The nineteenth-century national awakening in Macedonia was undoubtedly a Bulgar affair, though it posited the question of Macedonian autonomy. After 1918, the status of Macedonia is the question of the Bulgarian—as opposed to the separate Macedonian—status of the region.

The nucleus of medieval Croatia was the coastal territory from the mouth of Raša in Istria to the Cetina River. In the interior its confines went as far east as the Vrbas River in present-day Bosnia. Three mountain districts on the plateau north of the Velebit mountain (Gacka, Lika, Krbava), nowadays collectively Lika, were governed separately by an official called the Ban. In addition to these core territories, Croat groups and political influence were noticeable in all the Adriatic Sclavinias and in diminutive Bosnia. Porphyrogenitus mentions a part of the Croats that "split off and took control of Illyricum and Pannonia."[2] The former territory probably refers to Doclea (Duklja), an Adriatic Sclavinia extending from the Bay of Kotor to slightly north of Durrës, an area that another medieval source refers to as Red Croatia. Pannonia, on the other hand, is almost certainly the central interior area between the Sava and Drava rivers, better known as Slavonia. Zagreb (first mentioned in 1093) became its principal center. There is no doubt that these areas had their own *arkhontes* (princes), but the nature of the "friendly contact" between the Doclean prince and Croatia proper remains unclear. As for Slavonia, it was brought within the Croat state during the reign of King Tomislav (ruled about 910–928), who waged continuous wars against the Magyars, the new nomad proprietors of the central Danubian plains. With the emergence of royal Hungary, the status of Slavonia remained an issue in Croat-Hungarian relations.

Though an enduring concern, the periphery of the Croat state did not engage the Croat rulers as much as the Adriatic cities and fortified adjacent islands. Some of these centers, such as Porphyrogenitus's Aspálathos (Split) and Raúsion (Dubrovnik), were Roman refugee colonies, which grew as

2. Ibid., 32.1–29.

shelters for the displaced Latin speakers from the hinterland. These were the last vestiges of Roman Dalmatia, a province that under Augustus extended from the Adriatic to slightly south of the Sava. To the chagrin of the rustic Slavic principalities, the coastal, urban, and urbane Latin community managed to preserve its Dalmatian Romance idiom and municipal autonomy under nominal Byzantine rule and became the taskmaster, transmitting to the Slavs the craft of constructing civil government and jurisprudence in the ancient Roman tradition.

The role of the Adriatic cities as political intermediaries need not be exaggerated. Ready-made Byzantine civic models reached the Bulgars and to a lesser extent the Serbs directly from Constantinople; and the Croats were also influenced by Western (Frankish) statecraft. Nevertheless, the determination to hold the coastal cities was a tribute to their acculturative endurance. The Croat rulers, for one, regularly tried to seize these outposts or to bargain with Byzantium over their control. The Dalmatian cognomen in the title of Croat kings signified the claim to these municipalities. When the Dalmatian cities and islands (with the exception of Dubrovnik) definitely passed into Venetian hands in the early fifteenth century, the concept of Dalmatia's influence contracted and expanded with the ebb and flow of Venetian control over the eastern Adriatic shores. Simultaneously, however, the fifteenth century marks the upper limits of the complete Croatization of Latin enclaves. From an indicator of alien presence, the Dalmatian appellation became yet another Croat regional term.

After the Croat crown by right of inheritance passed into the Árpád house of Hungary at the turn of the eleventh century, the three historical Croat lands of Croatia, Dalmatia, and Slavonia continued their parallel existence. To be sure, the Hungarian influence was most palpable in Slavonia, where the Hungarian kings exercised direct royal authority and appointed separate Slavonian Bans, but this advantage was in due course offset by the growth of totally autonomous secular and ecclesiastic grandees, who, even when Magyar by nationality, found it in their interest to protect Slavonia's distinguishing features. In Croatia proper, the princely dynasts were totally oblivious to royal prerogatives. The king established no counties, collected no taxes, and bestowed no estates in Croatia. Moreover, until their reversals in the fourteenth century, the princes of Bribir, who made the title of Croatian Bans hereditary in their family, dominated Bosnia and Hum (the early name for Hercegovina).

The Venetian expansion in Dalmatia and especially the Ottoman conquest of Bosnia occasioned the slow migration of Croat nobility toward the north and effected a lasting change in the political map of Croatia. The term was more and more extended northward, as Zagreb, the center of old Slavonia, increasingly assumed the authority of an all-Croat capital. The sixteenth-century Ottoman conquests reduced the unoccupied Hungarian and Croat lands to a thin strip of hills and fields from the Tatras to the Adriatic. The new Habsburg dynasty defended these areas by creating a protective cordon, the so-called Military Frontier, a martial zone under the direct rule of the Habsburg War Council and which was denied to the Croat civil authorities.

At the end of the seventeenth century, when the Habsburg armies finally drove the Turks out of Central Europe, Civil Croatia meant the old Slavonian environs of Zagreb and its narrow extension toward the Adriatic. Civil Slavonia consisted of territories farther to the east, ending close to the confluence of the Sava and the Danube. The expanded Military Frontier, embracing the whole of Lika, lands immediately south of the Kupa (Kordun, Banija), and extending along the frontiers of the Ottoman paşalıks of Bosnia and Belgrade, separated Croatia from Slavonia in a vertical prong north of the Una-Sava confluence. After the Military Frontier was dissolved and the area fell under the authority of the Croatian Ban (1881), Croatia-Slavonia assumed its familiar contours (see map 1-1). In similar fashion, Habsburg Dalmatia, reconstructed after the Napoleonic wars, received its final shape with the joining of the old Venetian Dalmatia and the Bay of Kotor to the territory of the former Republic of Dubrovnik, abolished by the French in 1808. In the west, Venetian coastal possessions in Istria were added to the old Habsburg holdings on the same peninsula, bringing still more Croats under Habsburg rule.

Croatia's exodus from the Adriatic to the northwest was repeated in a still more radical form by Serbia. Though Porphyrogenitus located the Serbs in several Adriatic Sclavinias and in the little land of Bosnia, his Serbia was identical with Raška (Rascia), the old Serbian heartland centered on Ras, a town near today's Novi Pazar. From this base in the Ibar valley, medieval Serbia started expanding in the late twelfth century under the dynasty founded by Stefan Nemanja. Together with Stefan Prvovjenčani, his son and the "first-crowned" king of Serbia, Nemanja conquered the lands to the east of Raška as far as the Morava valley, as well as the littoral from the Cetina to the mouth of the Drin. Under the succeeding Nemanjićes, Serbia expanded farther to the east. Stefan Uroš II Milutin (ruled 1282–1321) dominated most of Macedonia, and his holdings extended to the Danube, east of Belgrade. Simultaneously, Serbia lost Hum to the expanding Bosnian state. The epogee came during the reign of Stefan Dušan (1331–1355), who commanded a vast empire from the Danube to Aetolia in central Greece and from the middle flow of the Drina to western Thrace.

The capital of Dušan's empire was Skopje, the site of his imperial coronation in 1346 and a logical geographical center of a realm intent on becoming the master of the Balkan peninsula. After Dušan's death, Serbia broke up into a plethora of dynastic principalities, making itself vulnerable to the imposition of Ottoman supremacy. Increasingly, under the vassal despots of the Lazarević and Branković lineages, Serbia began shifting toward the

Danube, as if to escape the Ottoman grip. The court of Stefan Lazarević (ruled 1389–1427), who staggered between the Ottomans and Hungary, was at Belgrade, a former Hungarian fortress that became a truly Serbian city only in the nineteenth century. The area that is now usually referred to as Serbia proper, that is, the territory of independent Serbia before the Balkan wars (see map 1-1), came to be the principal Serbian area only during the period of the Despotate.

Ottoman conquest of Serbia, completed in 1459, prompted great migrations, but the decisive Serbian migratory current to the north of the Danube came after the Habsburg reconquest of Hungary at the turn of the seventeenth century. Habsburg generals penetrated deep into the Ottoman Balkans, rousing the Christian subject peoples to uprising. But with the prospect of liberation deferred, the insurgents and their families drew back before Ottoman reprisals. Serbian homesteads in the Sandžak of Novi Pazar, Metohia, and Kosovo, which the subsequent generations of Serbs named Old Serbia, as well as in northern Macedonia and Serbia proper, were literally uprooted, as the Serbs (along with some Christian Macedonians and Albanians) rushed to Hungary, establishing their oases as far north as Szentendre, on the upstream side of the Danube from Buda. The greatest Serb concentrations were in southern Hungary, in the districts of Baranja, Bačka, and the Banat of Temesvár, and in eastern Slavonia. Srijemski Karlovci in the Slavonian Military Frontier became the see of Serbian Orthodox metropolitans; and Novi Sad, the principal Serb cultural center.

Though these lands were peopled with many other nationalities, settled by the Habsburgs in the same areas at approximately the time of the great Serb migration, the Serbs stamped the new Danubian centers of their settlement with their national impress. Southern Hungary was the location of Serb national awakening of the eighteenth and nineteenth centuries. Throughout this period the Serbs clamored for an autonomous entity of their own in this area, for a principality (*vojvodina*), ruled by a *vojvoda* of their own blood, and for a brief time, in 1849–1860, after the Serbs took arms against the Hungarian insurgents, the dream seemed possible. But Serb integration of the area took place only after the establishment of Yugoslavia, when the territory north of the Drava and the Danube became the *okrug* of Vojvodina in 1921.

Both the Serbs and the Croats contributed to the exceptionally complex national composition of Bosnia. The original territory of Bosnia, Porphyrogenitus's little land, was situated at the source of the Bosna River. Porphyrogenitus listed it, almost as an afterthought, at the end of the chapter on the Serbs. In an earlier chapter on the Croat conquest of Dalmatia, he included Chlebíana (Livno), Pléva (Pliva), and Pesénta (Psat), all in present-day western Bosnia, among the Croat counties (*županije*). Other comments in the same chapter may be interpreted to mean that the whole of Bosnia was a part of Croatia, but Croat territory certainly extended to the Vrbas.[3]

Despite these and other contradictions in Porphyrogenitus's account, there is no question that the original Bosnia was on the periphery of Serbia and Croatia and yet withstood any efforts those states may have made to impose their state traditions. Indeed, although the Serbs and Croats participated in Bosnia's earliest national integrations and continued to do so into the modern period, the growth of Bosnia's pronounced regional character may derive from the strong presence of the undifferentiated Slavs from the first migration. An alternative interpretation is to view Bosnia as a nationally polarized Croat-Serb state, which, like many other peripheral medieval states with mixed population (Savoy, Burgundy), fostered a state-preserving regional consciousness.

Bosnia's national consolidation was complicated after the expansion of original Bosnia. In the early thirteenth century, at the end of Ban Kulin's reign, the Bosnian principality included the lands at the upper flows of the Bosna (the district of Usora) and farther east to the mouth of the Drina. In the west, the little land was bulging into purely Croat areas and was simultaneously developing a pronounced regional character. Under the Kotromanić dynasty, Bosnian rulers exploited the weaknesses of their neighbors to build the last major South Slavic medieval state. Stjepan II Kotromanić (ruled 1314–1353) seized Hum and gained an exit to the Adriatic. He also expanded the so-called *Partes inferiores* of his state, gaining new Croat population. The increasing Croat presence in Bosnia, not merely in the newly acquired regions but in the old heartland, can be inferred from the predominance of ikavian idioms. But this territorial expansion into Croat and Serb regions did not dilute Bosnian regional consciousness: on the contrary, the spread of state authority reinforced it. Stjepan II referred to his retainers as *dobri Bošnjane* (well-born Bosnians), an example of how political affiliations influenced ethnogenesic trends.

Bosnian regional consciousness received an incalculable surge during the reign of Stjepan's son Tvrtko I (ruled 1353–1391). Tvrtko, the greatest of all Bosnian rulers, assumed the royal title and laid claim to the thrones of Serbia, Dalmatia, and Croatia, and thus his Bosnia included all the old Dalmatian cities (except Zadar and Dubrovnik) and their hinterland from the Velebit range to the Bay of Kotor. But in addition to these remarkable successes there was another reason for the growing affirmation of Bosnian regional feeling. Since Kulin's times, Bosnia had become fertile ground for

3. For contradictions in the work see Relja Novaković, "Još o nekim pitanjima teritorijalnog prostranstva Srbije i Hrvatske sredinom X stoljeća," *Historijski zbornik*, vols. 19–20 (1966–1967), pp. 265–293.

the growth of a new dualist sect, akin to the neo-Manichean communities of the Bulgarian Bogomils and the related heretical sectaries of the West (Patarins, Catharists). The nature of the cult and doctrines of the Church of Bosnia, as its adherents—or *krstjani* (Christians)—called their congregation, is still not precisely understood, but there is no doubt that the *ecclesia Bosnensis* represented a religious assertion of Bosnian individuality. This nativist blend of Catholic church organization and heretical doctrine survived a number of crusades launched by the Croat-Hungarian kings, whose Catholic ardor frequently amounted to no more than an ill-disguised attempt to subjugate a rising state. The real threat to the heretical church was the territorial expansion of Bosnia and its acquisition of new Catholic and Orthodox subjects, the latter in Hum and portions of Raška seized by Tvrtko. From the middle of the fourteenth century, Catholic missionary activity in Bosnia, as a result of the activities of the incoming Franciscan monks, was much more systematic, peaceable, and, ultimately, highly successful.

For a time, even after the Catholic inroads, the Church of Bosnia still had a powerful ally in the Bosnian nobility. This was certainly an advantage in the first two decades of fifteenth century, when the powerful lords undermined the royal authority in all respects. The term "Bosnia" increasingly conveyed not so much the state as the assembly of great dynasts, powerful lords like Stipan Vukčić Kosača, whose ducal title (*herceg*) gave rise to Hercegovina, the new name for his possessions in old Hum. As the Ottoman danger approached, however, the Bosnian nobility began to see the wisdom of espousing the Catholic cause, since it was only the Catholic countries, notably Hungary, that could be looked to for aid. During the last years of the Bosnian kingdom, the king and the dynasts clearly favored the Franciscan missionaries, before whom, it has been said, the heretics melted away "like wax before a fire."[4] The *krstjani* did not vanish entirely, though the church itself did. When the Turks conquered Bosnia in 1463 and beheaded the last Kotromanić, the Church of Bosnia had less reason to fear the Ottomans than the policies of Bosnian kings and lords. Though a few heresiarchs joined the flood of Bosnian exiles, most of the ordinary followers turned to the Muslim religion of the conqueror, leaving the Bosnian state tradition in the hands of the Bosnian Franciscans, who alone ministered to what remained of the Catholic flock.

The Ottoman conquest of the Balkans created a wave of "ethnic cyclones," which further complicated the existing national settlement. Not only did thousands flee before the Turks, but the establishment of Muslim oases in the Balkans brought forcible deportations (*sürgün*) and colonization of Turkoman nomads (*yörük*). Though small Slavic groups in Bulgaria, Macedonia, and Kosovo converted to Islam (Pomaks in the Rhodope Moun-

---

4. Sima Ćirković, *Istorija srednjovekovne bosanske države* (Belgrade, 1964), p. 319.

tains, Torbeši, Gorani), conversions were relatively infrequent. Most of the Muslims in the Ottoman Balkans were transplanted Anatolians. The great exceptions were the large communities of Bosnian and Albanian Muslims. In both cases, conversions to Islam were massive and protracted. By the end of the seventeenth century, three-quarters of Bosnia's population were Muslim.

The Ottomans did not, apparently, promote Islam by forcible means: the economic and political advantages to be gained by joining the state religion were sufficiently compelling. The profession of Islam enabled the feudatory to enter into the new elite; peasant converts were exempted from the special poll tax (*cizye*). In Bosnia, the special circumstances of political anarchy and discontent among the *krstjani* (and perhaps some of their theological affinities for Islam) were also important. But though the *krstjani* apparently converted en masse, there is ample evidence that canonical Christians, especially Catholics, also converted in large numbers.

The progress of Islam in Bosnia and the notion—encouraged by the Bosnians themselves—of being the vaumure of the Ottoman fortress assured this region a special status in the Ottoman state. Unlike the other conquered Balkan lands, Bosnia was not pulled asunder into a cluster of arbitrary administrative divisions, nor were its towns settled with Anatolian migrants. The *eyalet* (province) of Bosnia was in fact expanded to include old Croat heartlands on the Adriatic coast, its hinterland, and parts of Slavonia. The central portion of old Raška, later organized into a special *sancak* (banner, district), the Sandžak of Novi Pazar, also belonged to Bosnia, and its heavily Islamicized population thought of itself as Bosnian. The contraction of the Ottoman Empire at the turn of the seventeenth century, followed by the decisions of the Congress of Berlin (1878) left Bosnia-Hercegovina (as it became in 1878) with the frontiers that were effective in 1918 (see map 1-1). But Bosnia still included such towns as Bihać, one of the sites of medieval Croat assemblies and never a part of medieval Bosnia.

The continuity of Bosnian regional consciousness was also maintained by several circumstances that made Bosnian society atypical of Ottoman possessions. The Muslims in Bosnia were taxed less and governed themselves more than other Ottoman subjects; Bosnian fiefs became hereditary, and the notables, a genuine hereditary nobility. Unlike the Muslims in the eastern Balkans, who were largely bilingual, few Bosnian Muslims knew Ottoman Turkish. They spoke "Bosnian" and made a careful distinction between themselves and the handful of Ottoman officials in their midst. To Ottoman Christian subjects, all Muslims were Turks—indeed, the Bosnian Muslims often referred to themselves as Turks by virtue of their "Turkish faith"—but where they were the *Turci*, the Anatolians were the *Turkuše*. The Ottoman way of dividing peoples by religious community is the key to Bosnian national mutations. The Catholics maintained links with Croatia. The growing Orthodox community established ties with Serbia. Together with the

Muslims, they accepted and maintained their regional appellation. More-over, in those areas where the pre-Bosnian national traditions survived, the Muslims simultaneously kept up a memory of their Croat or Serb origin. The humanist Antun Vrančić (1504–1573), bishop and privy counsellor at the court of Ferdinand I, found it perfectly natural in 1559 to bolster his entreaty to Hasan, the *sancak bey* of Hatvan (Hungary), with a reminder of their common ancestry (*Croatici generis propinquitas*).[5]

The other lasting effect of Ottoman conquest on the South Slavic eth-nogenesis—even more important than the creation of a notable Bosnian Muslim community—was the full-scale dislocation of Christian groups. Ot-toman raids, plunder, slaving forays, as well as the devastation caused by constant wars, uprooted large numbers of Serbs even before the Great Migra-tion of 1690. The direction of Serb migrations was to the north of the Danube and occasionally to the northwest. Croat refugees from enlarged Bosnia and the old Croat heartlands fled to Venetian Dalmatia, the independent Republic of Dubrovnik, and Bačka, and smaller groups went as far as distant Burgen-land, on the borders of Styria and Hungary, and the Molise area of Italy.

Most migrants left on their own, but occasionally, especially when it involved the distrusted Catholic minority in frontier areas, they were de-ported or resettled by the Turks, who made it a practice to encourage new settlements whenever land became depopulated. The Turks were particularly eager for a return of order in strategic areas close to the Habsburg frontier. They found their most reliable settler material in the Orthodox Balkan Vlachs, the descendants of hinterland Romans who survived the sixth- and seventh-century Slavic onslaught by retreating to the peninsula's high moun-tain passes. Rather like the unlatinized ancestors of the Albanians, these Romance speakers also stemmed from the indigenous pre-Roman Illyrian population of the western Balkans, though, unlike the Albanians, they had lost their Illyrian language after the Roman conquest. These hinterland Ro-mans evolved into highland herdsmen, who for centuries led a primitive, nomadic life, moving their flocks with the succession of seasons in search of better pasture.

The hinterland Romans called themselves *Aromuni,* but for the Slavs they were the Vlachs (after the Germanic *Walh* for Latin and Celtic foreigners). In the early Middle Ages the Vlachs were heavily concentrated in central Greece (Great Wallachia in Thessaly) and the Carpathian ranges. Though their association with the Slavs usually led to Slavicization, some remnants still survive in isolated highland districts (the Aromuns of Macedonia and eastern Serbia, the Ćići in Istria), or, until relatively recently, as multilingual

5. Antun Vrančić, "Ad Hassan-begum zangziacchum hatvanensem," in *Hrvatski latinisti,* vol. 2 of *Pet stoljeća hrvatske književnosti,* ed. Veljko Gortan and Vladimir Vratović (Zagreb, 1969), p. 637.

urban traders (Hellenized Cincars in Greece, Macedonia, and Serbia). The Romanians were the most important exception. By the time of their historical emergence in the twelfth century, they had Romanized the Slavic lowlanders between the Carpathians and the Danube and were on their way to establishing their principalities in Wallachia and Moldavia.

The Vlachs of medieval Croatia had their separate estate organization, and some of their more enterprising members, such as Butko Brančić, the *voj-voda* of the Vlachs in Lika, even married into the nobility of the Dalmatian cities.[6] But unlike the "Vlachs of the banate of the Kingdom of Croatia" (*Wolachi banatus regni Croacie*), who were Catholics, the Vlachs in Ottoman service were Orthodox and came for the most part from the interior of the Balkans. The Turks used these mobile and adaptable herdsmen to repopulate the emptied frontier zones and defend the mountain passages. They incorporated them into hereditary privileged Christian groups (*martolos, voynuk*) and settled them in northwestern Bosnia and parts of old Croatia (the *sancaks* of Lika, Bihać, and Klis). Many then crossed over into Venetian and Habsburg territories and played a key role in the Croatian-Slavonian Military Frontier.

Apart from their redoubtable contribution to the defensive institutions of two hostile empires, the Vlach inflow is notable because of the changes it produced in the religious map of the western Balkans. Though Orthodoxy thrived in portions of the old Bosnian kingdom (the estates of the Pavlović princes in eastern Bosnia and in parts of Hum), it made the first significant inroads there only with the Ottoman conquest. Moreover, Orthodoxy was established in the Croat lands, far away from its old confines. Since the majority of South Slavic Orthodox Christians in the western Balkans belonged to the Serbian Patriarchate of Peć (sanctioned by Süleyman the Magnificent in 1557), the Orthodox Slavicized Vlachs in time acquired Serb national consciousness through their church organization. As a result, the process of Vlach assimilation created Serb pockets among the heterodox Croats, and these pockets subsequently had a great bearing on relations between Serbs and Croats.

One school of scholarly opinion would have us believe that the term "vlach" (always lower case) carried no specific national connotations but was applied to all nomadic Balkan herdsmen and that therefore the Orthodox herdsmen of the western Balkans are true Serbs.[7] But as Ivan Božić has pointed out, the process of Vlach Slavicization was not necessarily completed in the fifteenth century. The contemporaries made a "clear distinction

---

6. Nada Klaić, *Povijest Hrvata u razvijenom srednjem vijeku* (Zagreb, 1976), p. 608.

7. This tendency is evident in the works of Milan Vasić, the foremost specialist on the privileged Christian military groups in the western Balkans under the Ottomans. See Milan Vasić, "Etnička kretanja u Bosanskoj krajini u XVI vijeku," *Godišnjak Društva istoričara Bosne i Hercegovine*, vol. 13 (1962), pp. 233–249.

between the Vlachs (Morlachi) and those Slavs whose descent did not exclude Vlach admixture.''[8] Ultimately, of course, it matters not at all whether
a large group of Serbs was or was not of predominantly non-Slavic origin: no
South Slavic group is entirely free of Vlach components. What does matter is
the accurate reconstruction of national consolidation—in short, the understanding of the assimilatory potential of a given nationality. This was a great
issue in the shaping of South Slavic national ideologies.

Ivan Božić has also traced the Vlach contribution to the shaping of Montenegro, another Serb regional enclave. The name Crna Gora (literally, Black
Mountain) was first used in the fourteenth century for a part of old Doclea
(the Zeta area of the Serbian Nemanjić state), originally a small district
extending from the hinterland of the Bay of Kotor to Lake Skadar (Shkodër).
In the fifteenth century, Montenegro was ruled by the Crnojević family.
After the Ottoman conquest the land was devastated and depopulated. There
followed a steady inflow of Vlach herdsmen from Hercegovina organized in
their pastoral cantons (*cathone, katun*). The interblending of the highland
newcomers and the remaining peasants living in the sedentary lowland village (*villa*, in Venetian sources) produced a territorially constituted tribal
society; to this community the ''village brought a feeling for legal order,
while the *katun* introduced the blood feud, respect for the word of honor,
hospitality, and the cult of brotherhood by adoption.''[9]

The rise of Montenegro began in the early eighteenth century, when the
primacy of authority in Old Montenegro passed into the hands of Orthodox
metropolitans residing at the Cetinje monastery. The Montenegrins rid themselves of Ottoman overlordship under the leadership of the Cetinje prelates,
whose hierarchical station became fixed in nepotal succession from the Petrović clan of the Njeguši tribe. But it was only in the nineteenth century that
the territory of Old Montenegro expanded first to the nearby Brda (Highlands) and then into eastern Hercegovina, the Zeta valley, and the littoral
from Bar to the south of Ulcinj. The Petrović dynasty was secularized in
1851, and the Principality (later Kingdom) of Montenegro was recognized as
independent at the Congress of Berlin. By that time, its control extended to
the Tara River and embraced many Serb tribesmen, who did not necessarily
think of themselves as Montenegrins.

Montenegrin statehood contributed to the increase of Montenegrin regional consciousness, but it did not necessarily lessen the feeling that Montenegro
was the bastion of the Serbs, the ''Serbian Sparta.'' Though it may be, as
some claim, that the Serb appellation had only a religious significance, a
synonym for Orthodoxy, the appelation was ubiquitous.[10] Like the Serbs of

8. Ivan Božić, ''Svijet ratničkih družina i stočarskih katuna,'' in *Crna Gora u doba oblasnih
gospodara*, vol. 2, pt. 2, *Istorija Crne Gore*, ed. Milinko Djurović (Titograd, 1970), p. 349.

9. Ibid., p. 370.

10. See Savo Brković, *O postanku i razvoju crnogorske nacije* (Titograd, 1974), pp. 82–85.

Croatia-Slavonia, Dalmatia, and Bosnia-Hercegovina, the Montenegrins had lost sight of their complex origins and thought of themselves as Serbs. Furthermore, the eighteenth- and nineteenth-century repopulation of Serbia proper was to a great extent the handiwork of Montenegrin and Hercegovinian migrants. The two foremost leaders of the Serbian Revolution, Karadjordje Petrović (1752–1817) and Miloš Obrenović (1789–1860), were of this stock—Karadjordje stemmed from the Vasojevići clan of the Lim valley and Miloš from the Bratonožići in the Brda. Though these areas were not a part of Old Montenegro, their inhabitants were products of identical national processes that shaped the Montenegrin clans. The contemporary claims over the separate Montenegrin nationhood are on the whole a result of interwar Serbian misrule in Montenegro (though this does not mean that a new, strictly Montenegrin, national ideology could not have effected a qualitative change in Montenegrin national consciousness since 1918).

The Ottoman conquest was the last in the chain of events that made the South Slavs an island separated from the East European Slavic mainland. The Germans were the first wedge in the uninterrupted Slavic territory that extended from the Baltic to the Adriatic after the sixth-century migrations. During the eighth-century Bavarian colonization of the east, most of the eastern Alpine regions, previously solidly Slavic, were assimilated and Germanized. The remaining Slavic population was subjected to German rule. The emergence of the marks of Carniola, Carinthia, and Styria in the eleventh and twelfth centuries provided the framework for the subsequent development of the Alpine Slavs. Though conscious of their general Slavic significance, their principal loyalties remained provincial until the nineteenth century.

The Alpine peasant world, largely untouched by the Balkan migratory currents, was left to its own devices without its national elite, but it was able to survive centuries of uneven Germanization that included several perilous turns. Though the sixteenth-century Slovene religious reformers had no clear idea of a Slovene national community (they used the Slovene appellation both as the synonym for all the Slavs and as a regional term for the Styrian and Carinthian Slavs, to whom they countered the Carniolans), the Protestant use of Slovene vernacular elements could have led to an early form of Slovene national affirmation.[11] Instead, the Habsburg Counter-Reformation scotched this potential trend. Moreover, during the period of absolutism, the Habsburgs replaced the German noble autonomists in the Slovene lands with loyal imperial retainers of various backgrounds. In light of these obstacles, the nineteenth-century Slovene national awakening appears as an achievement of seemingly supernatural scale.

11. Ferdo Gestrin, "Organizacija crkve. Početak slovenske književnosti," in vol. 2 of *Historija naroda Jugoslavije*, ed. Branislav Djurdjev, Bogo Grafenauer, and Jorjo Tadić (Zagreb, 1959), pp. 376–377.

The second rampart in the human barrier that split the Slavic settlement was the Magyars. After their ninth- and tenth-century conquest of the Carpathian basin, they absorbed the Slavic population in an assimilative process that continued into the twentieth century. The rise of the Romanians in the Danubian principalities completed the division of the Slavic settlement. In the south of the Balkan peninsula, however, despite the hiatuses in Greek settlement that on occasion lasted for centuries, the northern Hellenic protrusions in Thessaly and Macedonia have remained remarkably constant since the time of the Dorian migration of the eleventh century B.C. Hence, if the fluctuating Romance-Slavic line in Aquileia and Istria is discounted, the human garland round the Balkan Slavs was drawn together by the Albanian expansion that attended the Ottoman conquest.

The original territory of the Albanians, in the high mountains from Krujë to the Šar range, represented the contraction of unlatinized Illyrians, who eluded the Roman assimilatory faculties.[12] The situation of the Arbëni, as the early Albanians called themselves, was not changed with the coming of the Slavs, who covered the present-day Albania in the sixth and seventh centuries, but in the thirteenth century, especially after Charles d'Anjou formed his *Regnum Albaniae* in 1272. The Albanian highland chiefs evolved into feudal nobility, and the men of their military companies increasingly assimilated or expelled the fettered Slavic peasants from Durrës to Vlorë and beyond. These Albanian chiefs offered a stout resistance to the Turks in the early days of Ottoman conquest but ultimately came to accept the new sovereign and, on the Bosnian pattern, brought the vast majority of their countrymen to Islam. The new religion brought the Albanians a status similar to that of the Bosnian Muslims and a consequent expansion in all directions. After the seventeenth- and eighteenth-century Serb migrations, the Albanians moved into depopulated Kosovo, Metohia, and western Macedonia and made these areas overwhelmingly Albanian.[13]

The flow of peoples also aggravated the linguistic situation, which became one of the most complex sources of intellectual contest, especially among the Serbs and Croats. Their ancestors brought to the western areas of the Balkan peninsula the basic elements of subsequently fully developed Serbian and Croatian dialects, which may have reflected the still more ancient Slavic isoglosses. Medieval Croats spoke three dialects, čakavian, kajkavian, and old western štokavian, which belonged to the western South Slavic group. The names of these dialects derived from the characteristic pronouns *ča, kaj,* and *što,* all meaning "what." Čakavian was originally spoken in Istria, immediately south of the Kupa and to the west of the Una and Cetina rivers. Its area included all the islands northwest of Mljet, although a čakavian

12. Zef Mirdita, "Problem etnogeneze Albanaca," *Encyclopaedia moderna,* vol. 5 (1970), no. 13, p. 39.
13. Petar Skok, *Dolazak Slovena na Mediteran* (Split, 1934), pp. 167–170.

substratum apparently existed as far south as Dubrovnik. Kajkavian dominated the length of the Kupa and also the large trapezium formed by the river's upper reaches, the field of Lonja, the Ilova, and portions of the areas bordering the Drava, Mura, and Sutla rivers. This was the area of early medieval Slavonia, with Zagreb, a diocesan see since 1093, its center. In the lands that constitute present-day Slavonia and Bosnia-Hercegovina (in the latter, roughly those portions west of the Brčko-Vlasenica-Neretva line) and on the littoral between the Cetina and the Bay of Kotor, medieval Croats spoke the old western štokavian dialect, which some consider an outgrowth of čakavian.

Medieval Serbs spoke two dialects, old eastern štokavian and Torlak (or Prizren-Timok), which were a part of the eastern South Slavic group. The former was spoken in the present-day Vojvodina, easternmost Bosnia along the Drina River, much of eastern Hercegovina, the whole of Montenegro, most areas of Serbia (west of the Donji Milanovac-Kruševac line), and among the Serbian speakers in Metohia and western Kosovo (west of the Priština-Djakovica line). The Torlak dialect was spoken in the rest of present-day Serbia proper and Kosovo, from the elbow of the Danube north of Negotin, and in parts of northern Macedonia.

From the twelfth century, however, the two štokavian dialects started coalescing and at the same time increasingly separated themselves from the other dialects of their respective groups. Significant distinctions between the čakavian-kajkavian dialects, on the one hand, and the štokavian on the other, date from that period. The convergence of western and eastern štokavian dialects proceeded unevenly. In old Hercegovina it was completed by the beginning of the fifteenth century. The new dialect (the so-called neoštokavian) then expanded, partly as a result of migrations prompted by the Ottoman conquest. The area of the čakavian and kajkavian dialects was thus considerably reduced. In the east, the Torlak dialect also lost ground.

The distribution of Croatian and Serbian dialects after the period of migrations (about 1700) demonstrates the expansion and variegation of štokavian (see map 1-2), four of whose fringe subdialects (Slavonian, East Bosnian, Zeta, Kosovo-Resava) were bypassed by the process of neoštokavian innovations, thereby retaining the elements of old štokavian dialects. Moreover, the postmigratory štokavian subdialects are divided into three basic divisions (ijekavian, ikavian, ekavian), depending on the reflexes of Church Slavonic ѣ (*jat*ь), for example, Sr*ije*m, Sr*i*m, Sr*e*m, in the name of old Roman Sirmium. Of the štokavian subdialects, the East Hercegovinian (spoken by the Serbs, Bosnian Muslims, and Croats of southern Dalmatia and parts of eastern Hercegovina), East Bosnian (Serbs, Bosnian Muslims), and Zeta dialects (Montenegrins) are ijekavian, the Western (Croats and Bosnian Muslims) and Slavonian (Croats) are ikavian, the latter with exceptions, and the Šumadija-Vojvodina and Kosovo-Resava, spoken by the Serbs, are ekavian.

1-2. Serbian and Croatian dialects

In addition, the ekavian reflex is present in some čakavian dialects (Croats), in kajkavian (Croats) and Prizren-Timok or Torlak (Serbs), and in Slovenian and Bulgarian-Macedonian.

If the passage of peoples, lands, national and regional names, and idioms in the terrae incognitae of the western Balkans was not as regular as the changes of the moon, it was as constant. The numbers—and therefore the influence—of each national group were dependent on its historical fortunes. This sobering realization regularly prompted idle conjectures on unrequited wrongs. Using Porphyrogenitus's information, Ivan Frano Jukić (1818–1857), a Bosnian Franciscan and one of the Illyrianist awakeners, contended that the Croats should be ten times as numerous as the Serbs, but concluded that the "number of Illyrians who call themselves Serbs is probably greater."[14]

The first census taken in the new state of Yugoslavia in 1921, though it reveals a good deal about the official ideology, is not particularly helpful as a statistical guide to the size of each national community in the second decade of the twentieth century.[15] For one thing, nationality was not a census rubric. The religion and the maternal language of the population are therefore our only guides to nationality. But here also, official attitudes got in the way of clarity. As far as the Slavic population was concerned, there were only three linguistic possibilities: (1) "Serbian or Croatian," (2) "Slovenian," (3) "other Slavic." The second rubric is quite clear and, based on it, it may be concluded that there were 1,024,761 Slovenes in Yugoslavia, 39,606 of them outside Slovenia proper, that is, outside Yugoslavia's portions of Austria's former provinces of Carniola, Styria, and Carinthia, as well as outside the Prekomurje region, which was taken from Hungary.

The third rubric is less clear. It refers of course to the Slovaks (mainly in Bačka and the Banat), the Ukrainians (Ruthenes) in Bačka and Bosnia, the Czechs around Daruvar (Slavonia), and the handful of Poles and Russians. Except for the last group, made up mainly of postrevolutionary émigrés, the "other Slavic" speakers were the remnants of various Habsburg offices or colonizing efforts. "Other Slavic" did not, however, include the large Macedonian or Bulgar population of southeastern Yugoslavia. The official position was that they were Serbs. As a result, excluding a portion of the population in northern Macedonia who may have felt themselves to be Serbs, the census Serbianized perhaps as many as 585,000 people. It is indicative of the period in the development of the Macedonian question that the census takers made no distinction between the population of Macedonia and the Bulgars in the districts of Bosilegrad, Caribrod, and in the other salients

14. S. D—ć Pravoljub [Ivan Frano Jukić], "Potomci hàrvatah i sèrbaljah u ilirskih dèržavah," *Danica ilirska*, vol. 8 (1842), no. 29, p. 116.

15. Direkcija Državne statistike u Beogradu, *Prethodni rezultati popisa stanovništva u Kraljevini Srba, Hrvata i Slovenaca 31. januara 1921. godine* (Sarajevo, 1924).

along the Bulgarian border (in the counties of Negotin, Krajina, and Za-ječar), which were turned over to Yugoslavia by the provisions of the Treaty of Neuilly (1919). A still greater difficulty is that the "Serbian or Croatian" language category does not help in establishing the size of the two na-tionalities, nor that of the Bosnian Muslim and Montenegrin communities within the same category. The misleading linguistic information must there-fore be augmented with the data on the size of religious communities.

The Orthodox church is one of the keys to the Serb census. Its members were widely diffused (see map 1-3) and cannot all automatically be counted as Serbs. But if one excludes the approximate number of Macedonians, or Bulgars, (585,000) and the other non-Serb Orthodox groups, notably the Romanians, Vlachs, and Cincars (229,398), and applies linguistic criteria in the other cases, the Serb community emerges as approximately 4,665,851 strong and divided into five basic groups: (1) Serbians of the pre-1912 Kingdom of Serbia (2,259,746); (2) the Serbs of Vojvodina (401,386), Croatia-Slavonia (658,242), Dalmatia (105,460), and Bosnia-Hercegovina (827,829); (3) Montenegrins of the pre-1912 Kingdom of Montenegro (168,392), only a small fraction of whom considered themselves dis-tinctively Montenegrin, rather than Serb; (4) the Serbs of the Sandžak of Novi Pazar (98,868), Metohia (15,213), and Kosovo (78,506); and (5) the fraction of the Macedonian population that may have considered itself Serb (52,209).[16]

It is much easier to appraise Yugoslavia's Muslim community (see map 1-4). This community numbered 1,337,687 strong, and nearly half of them (588,247) lived in Bosnia-Hercegovina. The Bosnian Muslim diaspora in pre-1912 Serbia (11,981) and in the former Habsburg territories (5,497), and the Slavic Muslims of Montenegro (13,370), the Sandžak of Novi Pazar (90,302), Metohia (955), and Kosovo (17,298) should be added to this number to yield 727,650 persons, the approximate numerical strength of the Bosnian Muslim community.[17]

16. In the absence of any information on the subject in the census, it is assumed here that the entire population of the districts of Bosilegrad and Caribrod and half the population of the countries of Negotin, Krajina, and Zaječar was Bulgar. For Macedonia, it is assumed that the Serbian national propaganda gained the allegiance of at least a fifth of the "Serbian or Croatian" speakers in the districts of Tetovo, Skopje, and Kumanovo, and of the county of Ovče Polje in the district of Bregalnica, all in the northern reaches of Vardar Macedonia.

17. Though there is a contingent of Muslim gypsies, it was assumed that the Islamic population of Yugoslavia consisted of four groups: Bosnian Muslims, Muslim Albanians, Turks, and Slavic Macedonian Muslims. To determine the number of each group in the areas where they lived together (the Sandžak, Metohia, Kosovo, Macedonia), it was necessary to proceed in a somewhat indirect fashion: (1) Though there is a small Croat Catholic contingent in Kosovo (Janjevo near Priština), it was assumed that all Catholics in the border areas around Albania and in Macedonia were Albanians. Their number was subtracted from that of all Albanian speakers to yield the number of Muslim Albanians. (2) The sum of all "Serbian or Croatian" and Albanian speakers was subtracted from the sum of all Muslims, Catholics, and Orthodox to yield the number of the Turks. (3) The combined total of the Turks and Muslim Albanians was subtracted from the number of all Muslims to yield the Bosnian Muslim contingent in the Sandžak, Metohia, and Kosovo, and the Muslim Macedonian contingent (27,357) in Vardar Macedonia.

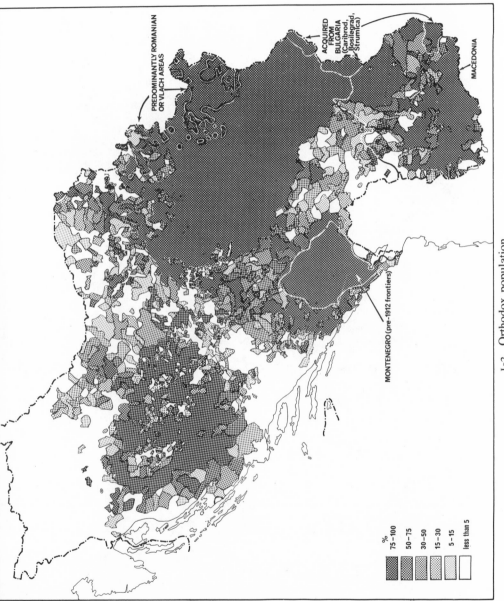

I-3. Orthodox population

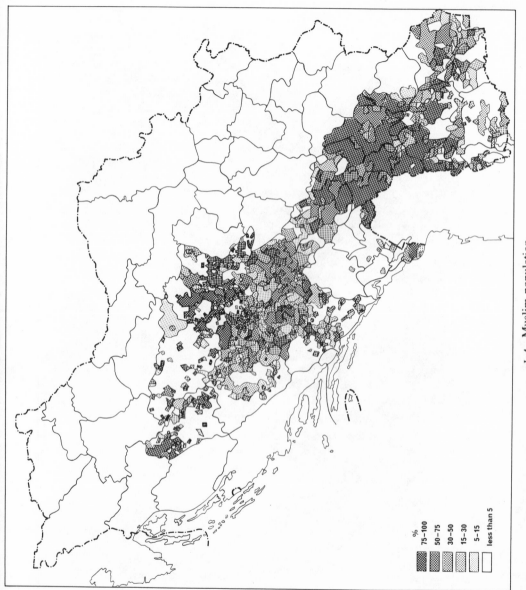

%
75–100
50–75
30–50
15–30
5–15
less than 5

I-4. Muslim population

The conclusion drawn from contradictory evidence on the size of Serb, Bosnian Muslim, and Macedonian or Bulgar communities permits us to make the final deduction: the remainder of 2,967,825 "Serbian or Croatian" speakers approximates the number of Croats. But that conclusion must still be checked against the data for the membership in the Catholic church, whose adherents in Yugoslavia numbered 4,735,154 persons in 1921 (see map 1-5) and to which most Croats belonged. One must also take into account the large German (513,472) and Hungarian (472,409) minorities, which were predominantly, but not exclusively, Catholic. The matter is complicated, but by subtracting the total number of Yugoslavia's Germans and Hungarians (985,881) from the total number of Catholics and Protestants (4,952,001) one obtains a pool of non-German and non-Hungarian adherents of Western churches; subtracting from that figure the number of Slovak Lutherans (54,000) gives us the number of Yugoslavia's predominantly Catholic Croats, Slovenes (1,024,761), and Italians (12,825). Further subtracting the last two groups as well as the small Catholic Albanian community (25,543) yields the Croat Catholic contingent of 2,848,991, a number that is fairly close to the original Croat approximation. To this number one should add the Greek Catholics of Croatia-Slavonia, or at least the 7,560-strong contingent from Croatia proper, who were clearly Croat. (This community produced among others, the great Croat historian Tadija Smičiklas.) Significantly, though the Greek Catholics (Uniates) were a part of the Catholic community, the census takers counted them separately. Map 1-5 combines the two counts. The end result of Croat numerical strength would therefore appear to be 2,856,551, which will be taken as final.

Map 1-5 portrays this national diversity of Yugoslavia's Catholic community with fair accuracy. Clearly non-Croat Catholic areas are to be found in Slovenia and among the Albanian Catholics along the Albanian frontier. The Catholics of eastern Slavonia and Bačka included many Germans and Hungarians, but there were substantial Croat communities there also—in Bačka and Baranja, alone, as many as 125,857. These were the so-called Šokci, the indigenous Slavic population, and the Bunjevci, who are descended from the seventeenth-century migrants from Dalmatia and Hercegovina, probably of Vlach origin. Before 1918, the Bunjevci were subject to extensive Magyarization, which continued among their fellows in Hungary.

The maps of Yugoslavia's religious communities (1-3, 1-4, and 1-5) also reveal the geopolitical features of the country's national question. The most noticeable oddity is the Ottoman-induced Serb Orthodox island in the middle of old Croat lands, encompassing portions of northern Dalmatia, Croatia proper (Lika, Kordun, Banija), northwestern Bosnia, and, less compactly, western Slavonia (the counties of Požega and Virovitica). Clutching the island from the southeast and the northeast are the two compact Croat Catholic claws in western Hercegovina and central Bosnia. The compact Muslim

53

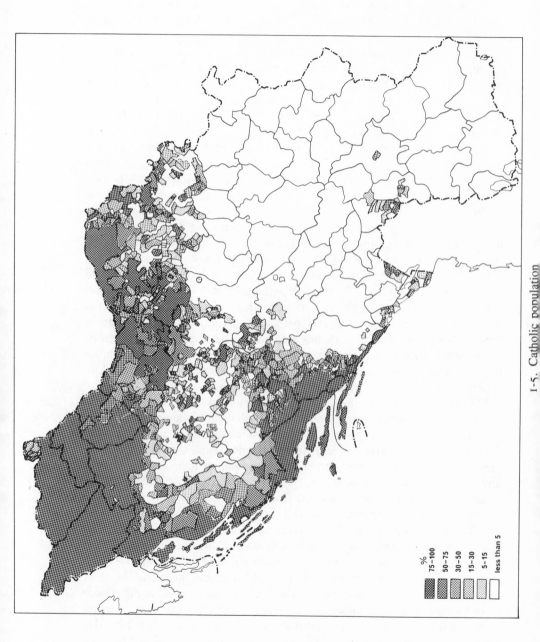

%

75-100
50-75
30-50
15-30
5-15
less than 5

I-5. Catholic population

communities of eastern Bosnia separate the island from Serbia. And within the island there is a solid Muslim lagoon around Cazin and Bihać, sometimes referred to as Turkish Croatia. In the southeast, the ethnologically uniform Serb island of Montenegro and eastern Hercegovina is separated from Serbia proper by a Bosnian Muslim channel in the Sandžak, which connects with the predominantly Muslim Albanians of Kosovo and western Macedonia and with the Turks farther east. The dense and suffocating frustration inherent in the complicated picture is self-evident.

The 1921 census provides somewhat less equivocal information about Yugoslavia's minorities. Language is the principal indicator for the size of the German minority (see map 1-6). The Germans (513,472) had significant contingents in Slavonia, Bačka and Baranja, the Banat, and parts of Slovenia (notably Kočevje and Maribor). These were the descendants of German colonists, whom the Habsburgs imported from southern Germany (chiefly from Swabia) in the eighteenth century and settled in the recently liberated and depopulated Danubian basin. Their area of settlement was to a large extent identical to that of the 472,409-strong Hungarian minority (see map 1-7), except that the Hungarians predominated in northern Bačka and had their smaller colonies in Slovenian Prekomurje. The Hungarians, too, were largely eighteenth-century settlers, though a considerable portion of urban Hungarians were Magyarized Slavs. The Ashkenazic Jews of northern Yugoslavia were on the whole of German or Hungarian culture, though this pattern was increasingly changing in Croat and Serb favor. The somewhat smaller Sephardic community was autochthonous since the Ottoman conquest and largely integrated in the urban society of former Ottoman possessions and Dalmatia. Its members usually spoke Ladino (Judeo-Spanish) as their first language. The two communities together numbered 64,159 people.

The other non-Slavic minorities included 12,825 Italians, mainly Italianized Croats of Dalmatia and the Croatian littoral, and 229,398 Romanians, Vlachs, and Cincars of the Banat, eastern Serbia, and Macedonia. There were 441,740 Albanians in Kosovo, Metohia, western Macedonia, and southeastern Montenegro (see map 1-6), but their symbiosis with the Turks in the urban centers of these provinces presents a difficult task for those who would determine the exact Turkish contingent (see map 1-7). There is no doubt that a sizable portion of the urban, upper-class population in these areas consisted of Turkized Albanians. The situation is somewhat clearer in eastern Macedonia, where the Turks lived in compact colonies after the Ottoman conquest. The application of several postulates will yield the approximate strength of Yugoslavia's Turkish community in 1921, which numbered some 168,404 people.[18]

Table 1-1 sums up the reconstruction of Yugoslavia's national structure

18. The process is described in note 23.

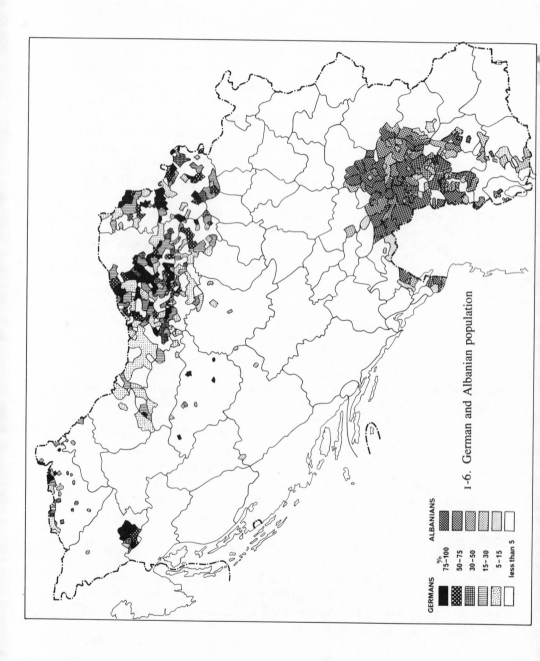

I-6. German and Albanian population

GERMANS

% 75–100
50–75
30–50
15–30
5–15
less than 5

ALBANIANS

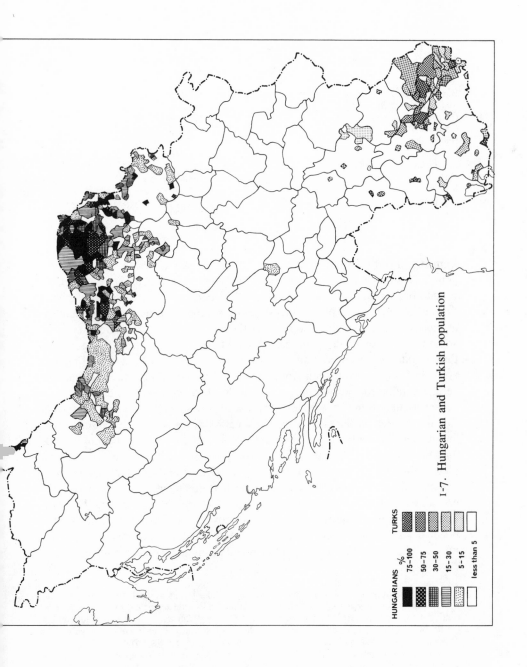

HUNGARIANS %
75-100
50-75
30-50
15-30
5-15
less than 5

TURKS

Table 1-1. Yugoslavia's national structure, 1918

	Number	Percent
Serbs	4,665,851	38.83
Croats	2,856,551	23.77
Slovenes	1,024,761	8.53
Bosnian Muslims	727,650	6.05
Macedonians or Bulgars	585,558	4.87
Other Slavic	174,466	1.45
Germans	513,472	4.27
Hungarians	472,409	3.93
Albanians	441,740	3.68
Romanians, Vlachs, and Cincars	229,398	1.91
Turks	168,404	1.40
Jews	64,159	0.53
Italians	12,825	0.11
Others	80,079	0.67
Total	12,017,323	100.00

immediately after the establishment of the kingdom. These findings agree generally with similar reconstructions based on various censuses conducted a decade before and a decade after the 1921 census.[19] Still, they are greatly flawed. Besides the arbitrary classifications introduced by the census takers, as mentioned earlier, there were other flaws, some a result of circumstances, some not. For one thing, the census could not be taken in the littoral areas that were under partial Italian occupation; the figures for the affected regions are therefore only approximations based on previous censuses. This almost certainly reduced the number of Croats.[20] Moreover, there are grounds for accepting the often repeated charges that the census takers deliberately falsified the figures on the size of minority nationalities, notably the Hungarians and Albanians. Perhaps most important of all, reconstructions cannot provide answers to unasked questions of a subjective nature. There were, for example, Orthodox Croats (Petar Preradović, Dimitrije Demeter, and August Harambašić, to mention only three important nineteenth-century Croat writers, all came from Orthodox families) and Catholic Serbs (among the urban intellectuals of southern Dalmatia). Moreover, the Bosnian Muslims were not really nationally conscious. Muslim intellectuals were increasingly taking sides between the Croats and Serbs and promoted their allegiances among

19. Vladimir Stipetić deduced an alternate version of Yugoslavia's national structure in 1910 and 1931, assuming present-day frontiers. If accurate, his statistics would augment the Croat and Slovene contingents through inclusion of those Croats and Slovenes who lived under Italian rule during the interwar period. See Vladimir Stipetić, "Jedno stoljeće u brojčanom razvoju stanovništva na današnjem području Jugoslavije," *Forum*, vol. 12 (1973), no. 12, pp. 885–915.

20. For another view on the numerical growth of the Croats in their historical provinces and in diaspora, a study which is, however, predicated on the assumption that all Bosnian Muslims were Croats, see Mladen Lorković, *Narod i zemlja Hrvata* (Zagreb, 1939).

the Muslim masses. Nonetheless, despite all these difficulties, Yugoslavia's national structure reveals one important reality: no national or religious group had an absolute majority. To ignore this fact and to govern as if such a majority existed could only bring misfortune.

Fates, Mentalities, Invisible Frontiers

> Ovaka je krvava Krajina
> s krvi ručak, a s krvi večera,
> svak krvave žvače zalogaje,
> nikad b'jela danka za odmorka.

> The bloody Frontier is this-like
> with dinner blood, with supper blood,
> everybody chews bloody mouthfuls,
> never one white day for repose.

>   Muslim epic song from Hercegovina

The most elementary characteristic of the Balkan lands is that they are, as circumstances dictated, an area in which three great Mediterranean religious traditions, Roman Catholicism, Eastern Orthodoxy, and Sunnite Islam, met head on. But even before these confessional—and therefore also cultural—frontiers were set, the Balkans were a frontier zone. During the Roman period, Latin was spoken from the Danube to the line set by Dyrrachium (Durrës in Albania), Scupi (Skopje in Macedonia), and Serdica (Sofia in Bulgaria), and then straight east to the Black Sea. Greek prevailed south of that line. When Theodosius divided the empire at the end of the fourth century, the east-west frontier in the main followed the course of the Drina River, the present border of Serbia and Bosnia.

Genuine frontiers between distinct civilizations speak with the voice of menace. In order to assert itself, the periphery often argues for an identity that is more integrated than the identity of a metropolis. To an extent this is what happened among the South Slavs. Their historical communities learned how to relent ("the hand that cannot be cut off, must be kissed"), but they also knew how to carry advantage to the extreme.[1]

Adherence to the three principal religious communities was of decided importance for the cultural and political content of nationality. These allegiances were deep-rooted, and should not be underestimated. Though the South Slavs often appeared innocent of theology and indifferent to religious

1. Vuk Stefanović Karadžić, *Srpske narodne poslovice*, 3d ed. (Belgrade, 1900), p. 174.

obligations, their faith was usually strong and resistant to change. A passage in the famous *Gorski vijenac* (The Mountain Wreath) of Petar II Petrović-Njegoš (1812–1851), the prince-bishop of Montenegro, illustrates this attitude.[2] Vojvoda Batrić, one of the Montenegrin chiefs, urges the Turks (actually Muslim Montenegrins) to return to the ancestral faith:

> No lomite munar i džamiju,
> pa badnjake srpske nalagajte
> i šarajte uskrsova jaja,
> časne dvoje postah da postite;
> za ostalo kako vam je drago.

> So tear down minarets and mosques,
> also kindle the Serb yule logs
> and paint our Easter eggs,
> the two fasts observe honestly;
> as for the rest, do as you will.

And though Batrić's conception of Christianity may be rudimentary, he is willing to kill for it:

> Ne šćeste li poslušat Batrića,
> kunem vi se vjerom Obilića
> i oružjem, mojijem uzdanjem,
> u krv će nam vjere zaplivati,
> biće bolja koja ne potone!
> Ne složi se Bajram sa Božićem!

> Should you not listen to Batrić,
> I swear to you by Obilić's faith
> and by my arms, my trusty weapons,
> our faiths will be immersed in blood,
> the better one will not sink!
> Bairam cannot make peace with Christmas!

The Christianization of the South Slavs was a complicated process, and it is still not fully understood. Suffice it to say that the distinctive influence of Christian East and West were prominent among the South Slavs soon after their settlement. In some cases these influences were direct and lasting. The ancestors of the Slovenes, for example, were evangelized in the eighth century by the Latin rite missionaries from Salzburg, and from then on the Slovenes were by and large undeflected from the Catholic religious and Central European cultural orbit. Similarly, the Bulgars unswervingly be-

2. Petar II Petrović-Njegoš, *Gorski vijenac* (Belgrade, 1947), pp. 82–83.

longed to the Christian East from the ninth century and established their first autocephalous patriarchate on the Byzantine model in the year 918.

The Croat and Serb cases were somewhat less straightforward. In Byzantine Dalmatia and its hinterland, the Croats (and the Slavs of the Adriatic Sclavinias) established an early contact with the local Christian churches, which although Latin in rite belonged to the Constantinopolitan jurisdiction. But in the domain of the Croat kings, the Christianization of the Croats was largely a result of Aquileian missionary activity and was therefore accomplished under Frankish political and Latin liturgical auspices.

Matters were complicated when Saints Cyril and Methodius, two Greek brothers from Salonika, undertook to apply the Slavic idioms from the hinterland of their native city to the codification of a liturgical language, which was to further the evangelization of all Slavic peoples. The so-called Old Church Slavonic, written originally in the Glagolitic script invented by the Salonikan brothers, gave rise to the late ninth-century missionary venture in Central Europe (Great Moravia). As Byzantine Greeks, Cyril and Methodius were more tolerant than Rome in accepting "barbarian" tongues in divine liturgy. But their mission nevertheless received the support of Pope John VIII (872–882), who was inclined to benefit the Holy See by promoting the direct influence of Rome over the Slavic churches of Central Europe and the Balkans at the expense of both Byzantium and the Carolingians. This policy floundered under the subsequent pontificates, as the popes went along with the German clerical campaign to regain Moravia for the Latin rite. The disciples of Cyril and Methodius were expelled from Central Europe and soon reverted to the Balkans, where they found hospitable shelter in the two areas where papal influence was not entrenched.

Bulgaria was one of the areas, and from there the revitalized Cyrillo-Methodian tradition spread its rays to the Serbs, some of the Croats, and the Eastern Slavs in new Cyrillic script, which was probably devised in Macedonia. The other Balkan asylum was Byzantine Dalmatia, where the Latin prelates, much like their ecclesiastical superiors in Constantinople, were not inured to the so-called trilingual heresy, that is, the belief that worship could be offered only in Hebrew, Greek, and Latin. The incoming Slavic clergy ministered to a largely unpriested Croat flock and therefore performed a decided service for the bishops.

From this base, Slavic liturgy and literary activity (in Glagolitic script) spread to the nearby lands of the Croat kings. Church Slavonic was thus in use by a sizable Croat contingent, and eventually the Holy See, which exercised jurisdiction over Croatia (and after the beginning of the ninth century, also over Byzantine Dalmatia), was persuaded to tolerate the Church Slavonic liturgy, justifying it in part on the basis of a spurious tale that the Glagolitic script was invented by Saint Jerome, one of the most venerated Western fathers and a native of Dalmatia. For a long time the

Croats were culturally divided. Some belonged to the churches of strict Latin tradition; others, mainly in the northeastern Adriatic area, used Glagolitic script and Church Slavonic in liturgy; still others, in Bosnia and central Dalmatia, used a distinctive Cyrillic recension (*bosančica,* Bosnian script), though not for liturgical purposes (unless, of course, they belonged to the Church of Bosnia). Except for the Bosnian heretics, however, they all belonged to the Catholic tradition. The Croats of the Glagolitic zone were vastly proud of the unique status of their liturgical language in the Catholic church. In the words of an eighteenth-century Glagolitic codex, Saint Jerome "elevated his Slavic language in which or with which, but in no other language except Latin, the Catholic church allows the divine service."[3] Though this claim applied only to the Western rite of the Catholic church, it did reflect a significant achievement, one that is in no way diminished by the repeated challenge that the Slavic liturgy had to meet in the Croat lands.

The relative insecurity of the Church Slavonic liturgy in Croatia, as opposed to its absolute hegemony in the Orthodox liturgies of Bulgaria, Serbia, and Russia, led to an unexpected result. Precisely because they were insecure, the Croat Glagolitic churchmen were not obliged by a higher authority to maintain the received integrity of the Church Slavonic language. They accordingly continued to enrich it with the elements of Croatian vernacular. During the great age of Glagolism in the fourteenth century, the vernacular (written in Glagolitic letters) became the dominant idiom in epigraphy, diplomatic and statutory documents, and most other nonliturgical texts. This practice prepared the ground for the flowering of Croat vernacular literature in Dalmatia and Dubrovnik. Hence, from the end of the Middle Ages onward, the Croats joined their literary expression to the prevailing Western genres. Their culture, especially in its intellectual and political aspects, ultimately developed within the West European (Catholic Mediterranean and Central European) zone, yet at the same time they never completely severed themselves from the traditions of the Slavic East. Though Catholic (and therefore separated from Orthodox Slavdom), the Croats consistently resisted the Latin universalism of the Roman church and were thus hardly typical representatives of the trends in Catholic Slavic countries.

Matters were completely different in Serbia and Bulgaria. In the Eastern Orthodox zone the position of Church Slavonic was infinitely more secure, and the undisputed dominance of the Church Slavonic prevented the emancipation of popular languages until the eighteenth century in Russia and the nineteenth century in Serbia and Bulgaria. These countries, especially after the Ottoman conquest, remained isolated from the cultural trends of Western Europe. But in Serbia's case, at least, the inclusion into the Eastern Orthodox

---

3. Cited in Eduard Hercigonja, "Društveni i gospodarski okviri hrvatskog glagoljaštva od 12. do polovine 16. stoljeća," *Croatica,* vol. 2 (1971), no. 2, p. 12.

zone was not necessarily preordained. Stefan Nemanja's state maintained the distinct ecclesiastical traditions of Orthodox Raška and Catholic Doclea (Duklja, later Zeta), which Nemanja conquered in the years before 1186. Nemanja himself received the "Latin baptism," and his son Vukan, who ruled Zeta, was a devout Catholic. The decisive turn in Serbia's orientation toward Orthodoxy was therefore more a result of great thirteenth-century upheavals in Balkan power relations (and of a fateful breach between Rome and Constantinople) than a consequence of a premeditated state policy. Nevertheless, Orthodoxy did have an influential spokesman in the house of Nemanja. This was the prince's youngest son, Rastko, who by his monastic name of Sava became the central figure of Serbian history.

From his earliest youth, when he followed a Greek monk to Mount Athos, Saint Sava deported himself as a partisan of Orthodoxy. In short, he followed the traditions of Raška, though his bent was not an imminent danger to the Catholic status of Zeta. But after the Crusaders' conquest and pillage of Constantinople in 1204, the two churches could hardly maintain peaceful relations. Unlike the earlier schisms (of the Photian and Cerularian periods), which did not greatly affect mass passions, the establishment of the Latin (and Catholic) Empire in Constantinople engendered a deep mutual hatred, which the Greeks, as the humiliated party, abidingly nursed for the Western Church.

The abasement of Orthodoxy could not be ignored even in peripheral Serbia, which in addition had the ill luck of having the ecclesiastical frontiers running straight through its territory. More important still, the temporary displacement of Byzantium and the establishment of an exiled empire in Nicaea presented an opportunity for the Serbian dynasty. During this period, Stefan Prvovjenčani obtained his royal crown from the pope (1217), and Saint Sava received permission from the Nicaean emperor and patriarch to establish an autocephalous Serbian Orthodox archbishopric (1219), with himself as its first head. Neither of these events would have been possible had not Byzantium, or rather its remnants, found itself in such an enfeebled condition.

Saint Sava was certainly instrumental in providing Serbia with a lasting Orthodox orientation. This is obvious from the sites he chose for some of his suffragan bishoprics. Many of the bishoprics were established in previously solid Catholic territory—his aim clearly being to bring about a uniconfessional (Orthodox) state. But even in his time, the relations between the churches in the western Balkans were not necessarily inimical. Sava was himself instrumental in gaining his brother's crown from Rome and in the opinion of a noted historian "was not fond of dogmatizing and did not pay much attention to that side of church education."[4] Indeed, though the Catho-

---

4. Vladimir Ćorović, *Istorija Jugoslavije* (Belgrade, 1933), p. 109.

lic religion was slowly disappearing in all possessions of the Serbian state, the Catholic archbishops of Bar, who from the sixteenth century sported the title of Primates of Serbia, noted the presence of the Catholic faithful among some of the Montenegrin tribes as late as the 1640s. It is nevertheless characteristic that the same historian who spoke of Saint Sava's religious tolerance felt it necessary to stress that the founder of the Serbian church independence "worked systematically to shape Orthodoxy into a synthetic part of Serbian state culture."[5]

Western scholars have frequently (and often unfairly) drawn attention to the fact that the Eastern churches were coextensive with the state. But though the examples of Caesaropapism were common enough in Byzantium and among its Slavic emulators, it is much more germane to note that the supremacy of civil power over the church shaped the character of Serbian Orthodoxy far less than the dyarchy of Serbian patriarchs and Ottoman sultans. For, paradoxically, the Serbian church quickly surmounted the setback of Ottoman conquest and then proceeded to thrive as the sole privileged Serbian institution within the Ottoman Muslim state. In 1557, in response to the urgings of Grand Vezir Mehmet Paşa Sokullu (Sokolović, who was himself a Serb *acemi oğlan,* or foreign youth, taken by the Turks in his childhood, Islamicized, and trained for the Janissary service), the Porte authorized the autocephalous Serbian patriarchate, centered in Peć (Metohia).

The Patriarchate of Peć embraced an enormous area from Slovakia in the north to the Adriatic littoral (from Senj to the mouth of the Drin) in the south. Ottoman-held Serbia, Montenegro, Hungary, Croatia, Slavonia, Dalmatia, and Bosnia-Hercegovina all lay within its frontiers. Its jurisdiction also extended over a wedge-shaped portion of western Bulgaria, as well as over the last non-Ottoman remnants of Croatia. The first patriarch was Makarije Sokolović, who was either a brother or a nephew of the grand vezir. Makarije was succeeded by the paşa's three other relatives.

The establishment of the Patriarchate of Peć was in itself an epic-making event. Even more important, however, were the powers that the Porte added to the new institution. As part of their overall policy toward the conquered Christian peoples, the Ottomans transferred almost all civil authority of the former Serbian state to the patriarchs of Peć. This was an aspect of the so-called *millet* system, whereby the non-Muslim subjects of the Porte were provided with an autonomous self-government under their respective religious leaders, the term conveying both nationality and religion in the Ottoman scheme of things. The non-Muslim *millets* (Orthodox, Jewish, Armenian) were subject to their own native regulations and not to the *Şeriat*

5. Vladimir Ćorović, "Sava Sveti," *Narodna enciklopedija srpsko-hrvatsko-slovenačka,* 1929, vol. 4, p. 41.

(Islamic law). Their dealings with the Ottoman state were conducted through their respective community leaders. As ethnarchs of the Serbs, the patriarchs of Peć thus had not only all the prerogatives of their spiritual station but also the authority that belonged to medieval Serbian kings. In transactions with the Porte, they were the sole representatives of the Orthodox faithful under their jurisdiction, and these were by no means all Serbs. The Patriarchate also acquired a significant amount of judicial power within the Orthodox community, and it was largely due to the influence of the church that consciousness of Serbian state and national traditions not only survived but was even extended to communities where they had never before existed. In short, the Ottoman overlordship had the paradoxical effect of investing the Serbs with a great instrument of national expansion.

In the seventeenth century, in the general decline of institutional order in the Ottoman state, the fortunes of the Serbian church deteriorated, and in 1690, after the Patriarchate proved disloyal to the Ottomans during the course of the Vienna War (1683–1699), the first migration of Serbs to southern Hungary took place. Two successive patriarchs of Peć led the migratory waves. The emigrants fully expected that in Hungary they would be confirmed in the same status that they enjoyed under the Turks, and in this they were not entirely disappointed. Though the *millet* system could not be reproduced in the Habsburg lands, the court granted a series of special privileges to the Serbian church, so that it was reconstituted as a metropolitanate centered on Karlovci in the Slavonian Military Frontier. As a result, the Orthodox metropolitans of Karlovci exercised a degree of spiritual and secular authority that was inconceivable among the Catholic prelates.

The status of *patrimonium domus Austriacae* also shielded the Serbs from the Hungarian and Croat counties, whose noble assemblies wished to reduce the migrants to the status of dependent peasants. When the Turks abolished the Patriarchate of Peć in 1766, the center of Serb spiritual life had already long shifted to the communities of the newly settled Serbs in the lands north of the Sava and the Danube. By that time, the Habsburg Serbs had lost many of their Byzantine-Slavic characteristics and were increasingly adjusting themselves to the cultural climate of Central Europe. Their cultural and literary revival and the growing importance of the bourgeoisie in their communal affairs transformed not only the Serb Danubian diaspora but in due course started affecting the vegetating, patriarchal, and largely leaderless Serbian peasant world under the declining eighteenth-century Ottoman state.

The *millet* system, which the Serbs, in a fashion, transplanted to the Habsburg Monarchy, was a great instrument for the spread of Serb national identity in the western Balkans. Of the Orthodox Balkan peoples, only the Serbs escaped the Greek spiritual tutelage during the Ottoman period—the autocephalous Archbishopric of Ohrid being also a largely Greek institution. And just as the Phanariot Greeks utilized the Ecumenical Patriarchate of

Constantinople as an agency for the Hellenization of Orthodox Bulgars, Vlachs, Romanians, and Albanians, so also the Patriarchate of Peć—and later the Metropolitanate of Karlovci—Serbianized the parts of the same Balkan Orthodox peoples. Moreover, since the Turks frequently obstructed the work of the Catholic clergy in the western Balkans, and since they occasionally permitted the Orthodox tax collectors to gather the Catholic tribute on top of the amount already accumulated, significant numbers of Catholic Croats also passed into the Serbian church and through it acquired new national identity. The process of steady equation between Orthodoxy and Serbdom was completed after the Serbian uprisings and the establishment of an autonomous Serbian principality (1830), events which prompted the growth of modern Serb national ideology.

Among the Bosnian Muslims, the *millet* system engendered a special communal feeling. But unlike the effect of religious autonomy on the self-governing Greek and Serb Orthodox, adherence to the Muslim *millet* conveyed a strong quantity of Islamic universalism. Though conscious of their distinct (Bosnian) status, Bosnian Muslims also subscribed to the Ottoman imperial ideology, which included the veneration of the sultan ("tsar-caliph, the Saint's [Muhammad's] generation").[6] Because of the universalist element in Islam, the religious experience of Bosnian Muslims was similar to that of Catholic Croats, who also belonged to a religious body of universalist aspiration.

The national component of universalist religions (Catholicism and Islam) was not an exact equivalent of the national-religious symbiosis of the Serbian Orthodox tradition. The difference was not simply that the universalist confessions were "catholical" and the Orthodox "local": national traditions were certainly present in the Catholic culture in the Croat lands or in the Islamic culture in Bosnia and elsewhere. A better way of looking at the difference is to note that neither Catholicism nor Islam had the implicit functions for the shaping of Croat (national) or Bosnian (regional or national) sentiment. Far more than among the other South Slavs, religious affiliation among the Serbs helped to shape national identity. Wherever they exercised jurisdiction, Serbian church organizations promoted Serb nationhood. Even more interesting, in the modern secular era, non-Orthodox individuals who came to espouse Serb national ideology often converted to Orthodoxy. Catholicism certainly had no power to turn a German from Kočevje into a Slovene nor an Italianate Fiumano into a Croat. As for the Bosnian Muslims, their identity stems directly from religious affiliation, and that is why the promoters of Croat and Serb national ideologies within this community tradi-

6. Muhamed Hadžijahić, "Političke posljedice islamizacije," in *Islam i Muslimani u Bosni i Hercegovini* (Sarajevo, 1977), p. 100.

tionally have affirmed the universalism of Islam, thereby undermining the claims of separate Muslim national identity.[7]

A word of caution is necessary, however. Social and intellectual relations that are, loosely expressed, secular, certainly to a considerable extent originate from religious traditions. But even if they emanate from a single religious community, they need not always accomplish uniform results. Jovan Cvijić, the foremost Serbian anthropologist, years ago observed that the Serbs and other Orthodox in the zones of altered Byzantine culture (that is, in the major Serbian cities, along the Belgrade-Istanbul and Belgrade-Salonika roads, and, highly concentrated, in Thrace, Macedonia, and Greece) were bigoted, superficially devout, and mercilessly greedy. Among them, Cvijić wrote, "The feeling of duty, responsibility, and solidarity was on the whole poorly developed. . . . Orthodox faith in the areas of Byzantine civilization is different in spirit and sense from the Orthodoxy of Saint Sava in the patriarchal [Serb] regions."[8] Cvijić's fine discernment in this case suggests that he was probably one-sided when he singled out the dissonant combination of Oriental *yavaşlık* (slothfulness, indolence), a kind of probity, and an occasional outburst of cruelty as the salient features of Islamic influence among the Balkan peoples.[9] Similarly, one should be cautious about interpretations that exaggerate the role of the church as the sinew of the Orthodox state. Though many of his observations were very shrewd, Ivo Pilar clearly overstated the ability of Orthodoxy to fashion a single-minded political community:

> Face to face with his God, as well as in the secular matters, the Catholic always stands as an individual who cares little about his surroundings. Among the Orthodox, however, even the divine service is so ordered as to elicit the feeling of solidarity and of belonging to a powerful mass with one's coreligionists.
>
> And that is why there is also an ability among the Orthodox to assert themselves as part of a mass. Even their divine service lends itself to the aims of power.[10]

The relationship between the Serbian church and the Nemanjić state can, however, be compared to the sensitive relationship between, to use Pilar's image, the soul and body. When the body succumbed to the Turks, the soul kept its memory alive. The Serbian church canonized the royal Nemanjić lineage (except for Stefan Dušan) and also several of the despots. Their

---

7. Muhamed Hadžijahić, *Od tradicije do identiteta: Geneza nacionalnog pitanja bosanskih Muslimana* (Sarajevo, 1974), pp. 73–76.

8. Jovan Cvijić, *Balkansko poluostrvo i južnoslovenske zemlje: Osnovi antropogeografije,* 2d ed., trans., Borivoje Drobnjaković (Belgrade, 1966), p. 118.

9. Ibid., pp. 119, 121.

10. L. v. Südland [Ivo Pilar], *Die südslawische Frage und der Weltkrieg* (Vienna, 1918), p. 271.

names were recited in the holy liturgy day in and day out for centuries, reminding even the most humble worshipers that the holy kings of Serbian blood and language once reigned over them—and, it could be inferred, might do so again. There is good reason to think that the epic poetry of the Serbs, the more popular preserver of the Nemanjić state tradition in some of its cycles, developed under the influence of church sources, preserved especially by the nationally minded monks.

Except for the ecumenical patriarchate and—much later—the Bulgarian Exarchate (founded in 1870), the Serbian church, in all its parts, was the only Balkan church organization capable of stamping its national movement with its own imprint. And inasmuch as the Serbian church was a carrier of state tradition, after the establishment of Serbian state independence, no Serbian secular authority and its representatives, even when entirely irreligious, could regard Orthodoxy as an illegitimate force. On the contrary, they furthered its influence, recognizing its assimilationist potential. Anticlericalism was not a force among the Serbs. Though they certainly ridiculed the clergy, as in Stevan Sremac's satire *Pop-Ćira i pop-Spira* (Pope Ćira and pope Spira, 1898), the Serbs did it with a modicum of malice, as if teasing a member of the family.

In the Catholic zone of the western Balkans, chiefly among the Croats, the church was not nearly so national. Not only was it not in the spirit of the Roman church to identify itself with a specific state or people, but in the Croat case, the traditions of the medieval state were uninterrupted and were maintained in separate Croat estate institutions, notably the Sabor headed by the Ban. It is wholly unhistorical to project Croatia's nineteenth-century status, when it was no more than a ward of Hungary, into the distant past under the Árpád, Anjou, and other royal lineages of the pre-Habsburg period, whose members ruled over both Hungary and Croatia. To be sure, after the Venetian and Ottoman conquests, the Sabor had authority over a miniscule territory, to which its members sorrowfully referred as the "remnants of remnants of the once great and renowned Kingdom of Croatia" (*reliquiae reliquiarum olim magni et inclyti regni Croatiae*). Matters were not improved under the Habsburgs and the establishment of the Military Frontier. As the Turks—and later the Venetians—were obliged to vacate various Croat crownlands, Vienna only exceptionally entrusted their governance to the Sabor. Nonetheless, the first serious limitations on the sovereign power of the Sabor occurred only in the eighteenth century, when Maria Theresia first created the Croatian Royal Council (Consilium regium, 1767), thereby establishing a body that in many ways usurped the administrative prerogatives of the Sabor. She then abolished it (1779), turning its affairs over to the Hungarian Regency Council (Consilium locumtenentiale). Though the latter action was unconstitutional, the Croat nobility itself sanctioned it in 1790, opting for a common government with Hungary as the best guarantee for joint defense against the sort of centralization that Joseph II imposed in 1780–1790.

Once conceded, the old prerogatives were almost impossible to restore. This was certainly one of the main motifs of Croat parliamentary life, as Sabor after Sabor sought to marshal old documents and privileges against Habsburg and Hungarian usurpations. Legalistic and obstructionist politics, the mentality of struggle for the violated rights (*pravdaštvo*), thereby became a part of Croat political culture. Miroslav Krleža (1893–1981), the greatest Croat writer of the interwar period, described it in the following way:

> The political lottery of the Crotian Sabor was played . . . with conceptions which in their semblance to state-right chess had an occult meaning of their own. Unless one was a chess player and inured to the rules of this parlor game, it would not be possible to fathom such terms as autonomy, independence, agreement, octroi, dualism, address, the discourse of homage, the supreme rescript, fragments, real or personal union, annexed lands, federal states, state union, *Társországok* (Hungarian, associate states), *Staatsgemeinschaft* [state community]. . . .[11]

It is characteristic of the South Slavs that the civilizations that separated them were not always territorially constituted. Folk costumes could incorporate elements of Levantine and Occidental urban dress; a Glagolitic mass could be heard in one church and the Orthodox liturgy of a slightly different Church Slavonic recension in another. Still farther to the east, oddly, one could attend a Latin mass in a rural church and hear the muezzin's call from a nearby minaret. The *meclis* of Bosnian notables in the last years of the Ottoman period resembled the county assemblies of Croatia-Slavonia, while, at the same time, the Orthodox prelates sat in the Croatian Sabor among the other temporal and spiritual lords. But though the differences of historical and philosophical allegiances did not promote accord, it should also be remembered that the degree of intolerance, which was not always marked, coexisted with the acceptance of variety, which was held to be perfectly natural and, indeed, unalterable. In 1672 a group of Hercegovinian Muslims argued that there were seventy-two religions in the world and that they were all good.[12]

---

11. Miroslav Krleža, "Prije trideset godina (1917–1947)," in *Davni dani*, vols. 11–12 of *Sabrana djela* (Zagreb, 1956), pp. 370–371.

12. Karlo Jurišić, *Katolička crkva na biokovsko-neretvanskom području u doba turske vladavine* (Zagreb, 1972), p. 190.

National Ideologies

> The South Slavs are a people of ideas; religious, state, and other ideas
> played and today still play a role in their history.
>
> Vladimir Dvorniković, 1939

During the "springtime of peoples" in 1848–1849, when most Habsburg
Slavs recoiled at assimilationist Magyar nationalism and supported the Monarchy as the lesser evil, their motivations were frequently misunderstood.
Friedrich Engels, who wholeheartedly supported the Magyarizing program
of the Hungarian insurgents, derided their South Slavic opponents as quixotic
fantasts: "The age of Panslavism [understood here in the broadest of senses,
as Slavic integration]," wrote Engels, "was in the eighth and ninth centuries, when the South Slavs still ruled the whole of Hungary and Austria and
threatened Byzantium."[1]

Engels's appraisal of Slavic prospects in the Balkans is fairly typical of a
significant section of European opinion. There were, it was thought, only
two courses open to the South Slavs. Either they could lose their identity and
fall in with the Magyars and Germans, or, what Engels thought unlikely,
they could seek to build their own special hybrid nationality. The nurturing
of separate national identities, within their traditional bounds, was rarely
considered. Indeed, despite all the South Slavic differences, foreign pressure
often compelled the South Slavs to view one another as a possible recourse,
or, more exactly, as possible material for national hybridization, out of
which could come a vibrant power, rather along the lines that Engels ruled
out as impossible after the ninth century. But though the ideas of hybridization were suggested especially by linguistic similarities, a keen sense of
belonging to the Slavic world, and a certain communality of historical experience, the content of these ideas and their interaction reflected a pattern of
reasoning that shaped the character of nineteenth-century South Slavic national ideologies.

Among the Croats, the search for Slavic integrations was very old. Krleža
attributed it to a feeling of hopelessness in the face of overwhelming obstacles standing in the way of Croat unity: "The Croat flesh instinctively felt
too weak in its isolation to tackle the fateful problems of liquidating the
Turkish occupation, bringing down imperial Vienna, and removing the Venetian tyranny. Hence the rise of the idea of integration, true-born of an
illusion . . . the idea of linguistic unity in spite of church schism, and
dreams of ethnic continuity from Karlovac to Moscow and from Salonika to
Prague and Kraków."[2]

1. Karl Marx and Friedrich Engels, *Werke,* vol. 6 (Berlin, 1961), p. 172.
2. Miroslav Krleža, "O patru dominikancu Jurju Križaniću," in *Eseji III,* vol. 20 of *Sabrana djela* (Zagreb, 1963), pp. 65–66.

The initiator of the idea of Slavic reciprocity among the Croats was Vinko Pribojević, a Dominican theologian from Hvar, whose oration on the origin and occurrences of the Slavs, delivered before a gathering of Hvar's nobility in 1525, glorified the Slavic peoples out of all proportion to what his audience knew or expected. In accordance with the humanist practice, Pribojević blended scriptural testimony with ancient myth to derive the Slavs from Noah's grandson Thyras, who sired the Thracians, who in turn begot the Illyrians, who were, according to Pribojević, the forefathers of all the Slavs. That meant that all the ancient heroes of Thrace, Macedonia, and Illyricum were actually Slavs. Alexander and his generals, Aristotle, scores of Caesars, and Saint Jerome were Slavs. And bellicose Mars was himself born among them.

Reversing the direction of Slavic settlement, Pribojević had Czech, Lech, and Rus, three Dalmatian patrician brothers, flee their homeland and rule over the three mighty Slavic peoples that came to bear their names, "so that from Czech, in their own language, they are called Czechs, whom we call Bohemians, from Lech they are called Lechians, who are now Poles, and from Rus they are called Russians, who are also called Muscovites."[3] From these in turn rose mighty kings, such as Pribojević's contemporary Sigismund I of Poland, whose sword repeatedly brought low the Tatars and Turks. It followed that a people as mighty as the Slavs, who humbled the arrogant Persians, overpowered the rude Germans, prostrated the overbearing Gauls, and weakened the lofty Romans, could match all those who oppressed the Croats of Pribojević's generation.[4]

Where Pribojević pinned his hopes on the Poles, one of his most original successors expected the deliverance from the rising Russian autocracy. This anticipation was the great dream of Juraj Križanić (1617–1683), Croat patrician and priest, who sacrificed his security and liberty to the cause of church unification and Slavic reciprocity. To Križanić, all Slavs were a single people and spoke a single language. But, in Križanić's rash—though sincere— overstatement, all except the Russians had lost their "state and power and language and wit."[5] In 1651 Križanić, against the wishes of his religious superiors, went to Russia to rouse the Russians to the responsibility they owed to their Slavic kinsmen. By 1659 he had gained the confidence of Tsar Aleksei Mikhailovich, who employed him in Russia's foreign department. But in 1661, though still in the tsar's service, Križanić was exiled to Siberia, where he spent the next fifteen years writing political treatises on his national conception. The most famous was the manuscript collection called *Razgo-*

3. Vinko Pribojević, *De origine successibusque Slavorum*, 2d ed. (Zagreb, 1951), p. 67.
4. Ibid., pp. 79–80.
5. Juraj Križanić, *Politika ili razgovori o vladalaštvu*, trans. Mate Malinar (Zagreb, 1947), p. 342.

wori ob wladatelystwu (Conversations about Statecraft, 1661–1667), popularly known as *Politics*. In this work, written in Križanić's curious mixture of several Slavic tongues, Križanić called upon Aleksei Mikhailovich to liberate the "Slavs beyond the Danube," that is, the Bulgars, Serbs, and Croats: "If thou, o tsar, cannot help them in this difficult period to liberate themselves completely and to establish and put in order the states that they once had, you can at least correct and nurture the Slavic tongue in books and thereby open the eyes of these men to suitable and wise volumes, so that they can learn to honor their own dignity and to apply themselves to their liberation."[6]

Križanić has frequently been misrepresented as a promoter of Russian expansionism or of South Slavic political unification. All he really proposed was that the Slavs should rely on one another, since they in essence constituted one people and spoke a single language.[7] But though far less radical than some imagine, Križanić's thought can indeed be regarded as characteristic of Croat national conceptions. His emphasis on the need of furthering a common ("corrected") Slavic linguistic media became the favored Croat means toward national integration. Still, just as Križanić envisioned the restoration of old South Slavic states (Bulgaria, Serbia, Croatia), he presumably favored the maintenance of separate Bulgar, Serb, and Croat identities within their overall—and perhaps overriding—Slavic framework. This also remained a constant in Croat national ideologies.

It has already been noted that the strong emphasis on Slavic reciprocity was a result of Croat debility in the face of various forms of foreign domination, which affected the majority of Croat lands. But the idea of reciprocity remained a cardinal national conception among the Croats for yet another reason. The parceling of Croat lands strengthened various Croat regional identities, often to the detriment of a wider Croat feeling. The increasing use of the general Slavic name or of the Illyrian appellation, which in the Renaissance convention of restoring ancient names denoted the South Slavs—a tendency especially notable among the Dalmatian and Ragusan writers of the Baroque period—was part of a disposition to balance the regional affiliations against a common framework, which was perhaps more acceptable at the time when Croatia denoted the region around Zagreb. But as in Joakim Stulli's dictionary, the general terms had a specific weight; Stulli defined the term *illirico* as "Slavic or Croat."[8] As a result, room was always open for the substitution of the common Slavic or Illyrian appellation with the strictly

6. Ibid.
7. On this question see Jaroslav Šidak, "Početi političke misli u Hrvata—J. Križanić i P. Ritter Vitezović," *Naše teme*, vol. 16 (1972), nos. 7–8, p. 1125.
8. Gioacchino [Joakim] Stulli, *Vocabolario italiano-illirico-latino*, pt. 3, tome I (Dubrovnik, 1810), p. 731. In the same rubric (p. 732) Stulli also included the following definiton: "Fatto di costumi, o di lingua illirica,—pohârvatjen [lit. Croatianized], qui illyriorum linguam didicit, vel eorum mores induit."

Croat one. In short, the strong tradition of Slavic reciprocity could sire forms of Pan-Croatianism.

Pavao Ritter Vitezović (1652–1713), a nobleman from Senj, was the first Croat national ideologist to extend the Croat name to all the Slavs, and not just those in the Balkans. Vitezović chose to reconcile Porphyrogenitus's trustworthy account of the Slavic settlement with the legend of Czech, Lech, and Rus. Drawing on several seventeenth-century Croat sources (Mavro Orbin, Juraj Ráttkay), who identified the brothers as Croats, Vitezović apparently concluded that all the Slavs were descended from Croats and that antiquity belonged to the Croat name.

Vitezović's conclusion, though essentially a historical interpretation, was to some extent suggested by the struggle between Venice and the Habsburgs for a share of Croat lands vacated by the Ottomans at the end of the Vienna War (1699). In order to demonstrate that Venice had no right to Dalmatia, Vitezović wrote a memorandum delineating "the frontiers of whole Croatia" (*limites totius Croatiae*). His work, published under the title *Croatia rediviva* (Zagreb, 1700), was a "fiery protest against the Peace of Carlowitz, which . . . mercilessly and unjustifiably deprived Croatia of her ancient territories."[9] It fully justified Vitezović's purpose, which was to breathe life into his own version of Great Croatia, a territory worthy of Habsburg imperial ambition.

Starting from his newly acquired belief that the Croat name embraced all the Slavs or Illyrians, Vitezović divided the Slavic world into two parts: Northern Croatia (*Croatia Septemtrionalis*) north of the Danube (and—since this region included Hungary—presumably also north of the Drava), and Southern Croatia (*Croatia Meridionalis*) on the Balkan peninsula. Southern Croatia was further subdivided into White Croatia (*Croatia Alba*, that is, everything west of the Shkodër-Drina-Sava line, including the Slovene settlement) and Red Croatia (*Croatia Rubea*, that is, Serbia, Macedonia, Bulgaria, and Thrace).[10]

Vitezović's Pan-Croatianism was thus both a historical construct and a political program, and *Croatia rediviva* not only a protest against the centuries-old fragmentation of the Croat lands (and of the whole South Slavic territory) but also a polemic against Venetian territorial pretensions and a legitimist entreaty for Habsburg support. Vitezović's arguments were almost exclusively historical. Though he helped develop the descent theory on the derivation of all Slavic peoples from the Croat tribe, he paid almost no attention to the cultural, linguistic, and religious attributes of nationhood. It

9. Ferdo Šišić, "Hrvatska historiografija od XVI do XX stoljeća," *Jugoslovenski istoriski časopis*, vol. 1 (1935), nos. 1–4, p. 44.
10. Pavao Ritter Vitezović, *Croatia rediviva; regnante Leopoldo Magno Caesare* (Zagreb, 1700), p. 32.

was far more important to him that this or that part of his revived Croatia was Croatian by virtue of historical appropriation. (For example, the Adriatic region was Croatian because "Krešimir [Peter Krešimir IV] the king of the Croats appropriated the Adriatic Sea under his jurisdiction" (*Cresimirus Croatorū Rex Adriaticum Mare suae appropriabat jurisdictioni*).[11]

The legitimist way of arguing was, in a sense, imposed upon the Croats. The Habsburg court, the Venetians of Vitezović's times, and later the Hungarian legal theorists, all advanced historical arguments in favor of diminshing Croatia's territorial integrity or its ancient municipal autonomy (*jura municipalia*). As a result, beginning with Vitezović's generation, Croat national apologetics were lopsidedly historicist. The Croats never felt safe enough with strictly national—lingustic and cultural—arguments in favor of their autonomy and statehood. They clearly believed that the rusty weapons of historical and state right were most effective in the struggle against Habsburg and Hungarian centralism.

The emphasis on historical and state rights had significant consequences for the Croat attitude on the national standing of Croatia's minorities. Since the *jura municipalia* were indivisible, all the inhabitants of Croatia-Slavonia were "political" Croats. This did not mean that the Croat political thinkers assumed that Croatia was a homogenous whole. Like Vitezović, who recognized the differences of frontiers, names, emblems, and customs within his Great Croatia, they simply believed that these distinctions were not as important as the common Slavic (in Vitezović's terms, Croat) nationhood of Croatia's population.[12]

The apotheosis of Croat appellation might easily have led to integralist definitions of nationhood, but until the 1850s, the emphasis on Slavic reciprocity kept Croat national thought from lapsing into exclusivism. Vitezović, in fact, influenced the national movements of the Serbs and Bulgars. His *Stemmatographia, sive Armorum Illyricorum delineatio, descriptio et restitutio* (Vienna, 1701), a heraldic manual containing all the "Illyrian" (that is, Slavic) coats of arms, was adapted, translated, and expanded by Hristofor Žefarovič under the direction of Arsenije IV Jovanović-Šakabenta, the Patriarch of Peć, who lived in Habsburg exile.[13] Žefarovič's version had an incalculable effect on the growth of modern nationalism and was also felt among the Bulgars and Romanians.

It is useful to contrast the two *Stemmatographias* for clues to the similarities and differences between the early Croat and Serb national ideologies. Žefarovič's volume had a pronounced Orthodox tenor. It included portraits of twenty-nine saints, mainly Serbian kings, queens, and bishops, notably

11. Ibid., p. 13.
12. Ibid., p. 32.
13. *Stemmatografia: Izobraženïe oružïj Illÿričeskihъ* (Vienna, 1741).

the last Nemanjićes. Seven of these images represented the saints of Bulgarian tradition, and two were the favorites of Orthodox Albanians. But despite the diversity of origin (the Albanian Ioannъ Vladimirъ or Shën Gjin was actually Vladimir, the Catholic king of Doclea), reflecting the multinational flock of the refugee Serbian prelates, the collection clearly conveyed the notion that adherence to Orthodoxy made for Serb nationhood. This impression was strengthened through the depictions of Arsenije IV, the officiating head of the Serbian church, who was counterposed to the wholly secular images of Tsar Stefan Dušan. The aim was to suggest that Arsenije was the heir of Serbian kings and, as is noted in the volume's introductory dedication, the "patriarch of whole Illyricum by hereditary right."[14]

Quite apart from the religious significance of Žefarović's version of the *Stemmatographia,* a matter almost imperceptible in Vitezović's original, the contrast between the two manuals shows that the gravitational center of early Serb national concepts had little in common with the position of its Croat equivalent. The Croat national thinkers embraced the wider Slavic world in an attempt to foster the integrations of heteropolar Croat lands. Unlike the Serbs, who had their common church organization, the sole institutional instruments of Croat national integration were the Sabor and the office of the Ban, both visible expressions of Croatia's historical and state right. But precisely because the authority of these institutions was itself increasingly diminished and in any case encompassed only a small portion of the Croat lands, the Croats also relied on self-reflective ideas, thereby giving ground to a diapason of national ideologies. By contrast, the Serbs, however scattered, were far more uniform in their self-consciousness. The Serbian church had a powerful assimilationist history, which did not need any new secular ideas to assist in the steady Serbianizing of its Orthodox congregation. Moreover, though the church's identification with the medieval Serbian state and its most distinguished royal personages represented an embryonic form of the theory of historical right, the Serb diaspora in the Habsburg lands had scant hope of obtaining a territorial autonomy based on historicist claims. Where Vienna acceded to Serb demands for a modicum of self-rule, it was governed by momentary political calculations, as in the establishment of Serbian Vojvodina in 1849–1860.

The best way to illustrate the differences between the Croat and Serb national ideologies is to examine the classic phases of national revivals among the two peoples. The Croat Revival, beginning in the late eighteenth century, in large part emanated from resistance to awakened Magyar nationalism. Stirred by the Germanizing policies of Joseph II, the Magyar nobility wasted no time after his demise in 1790 in introducing Hungarian as the replacement for Latin, previously the official language of Hungary. The

14. Ibid., f. 11.

threat of Magyarization implicit in this change provoked the opposition of the Croat nobility. But though the Croats expressed their objections by restating their claims to ancient municipal autonomy within the common Hungarian constitution, their spokesmen were aware that the vibrant Magyar national idea could best be countered only by an alternate national program. The construction of such a program, which moreover included a linguistic alternative to Hungarian, was the task performed by the Illyrianist movement of the 1830s and 1840s. Dominated from its start by the energetic figure of Ljudevit Gaj (1809–1872), the Illyrianist phase of the Croat Revival brought the centuries-old attempts at Croat integration to a level that had eluded the earlier generations.

The Illyrianist awakeners knew that the Hungarians would ignore a movement of a few counties that composed Croatia-Slavonia. Their national idea therefore could not be, strictly speaking, Croatian, because that could be misunderstood as an expression of narrow Croatian regionalism—of the kajkavian dialect area around Zagreb, which was generally regarded as Croatia proper in the early nineteenth century. The Illyrianist leaders were of course aware that the Croat appellation coexisted with regional names far beyond the Zagreb area. Moreover, Gaj, in particular, knew that Vitezović extended the Croat name to all the South Slavs; following Vitezović's example, Gaj early on counted the Slovenes among the "Croats of the old [Croat medieval] kingdom."[15] Nevertheless, the awakeners preferred a more neutral name, which could override all the regional differences, so characteristic of the contemporary Croat situation. Being firmly persuaded that the ancient Illyrians gave rise to all the South Slavs, they settled on the Illyrian appellation, which already had wide currency as a synonym for Croats and frequently for all the South Slavs. The Illyrianists, according to one of their leaders, used this neutral name "only to show that the Croat and Slavonian tribe is not so insignificant . . . and that the Croats and Slavonians are only a part of the great Illyrian people, just as in turn the Illyrian people are a part of the great Slavic people."[16]

The linguistic part of the Illyrianist program presupposed a common language, which would in turn become the first stone in the construction of a single national culture and consciousness for all the South Slavs. But here again the exacting linguistic situation of the South Slavs made the choice of a standard language far from obvious. The search for a linguistic standard among the Slovenes was already fairly well advanced. Among the Serbs and

15. Ljudevit Gaj, "Horvatov sloga i sjedinjenje," in Franjo Fancev, ed., "Dokumenti za naše podrijetlo hrvatskoga preporoda (1790–1832)," *Gradja za povijest književnosti hrvatske*, vol. 12 (1933), p. 319.
16. The author of these words was Bogoslav Sulek (1816–1895), a very gifted linguist and publicist. Cited in Jaroslav Šidak, "Stranački odnosi u Hrvatskoj prije 1848.," in *Studije iz hrvatske povijesti XIX stoljeća* (Zagreb, 1973), p. 141.

Bulgars the principal issue was still the replacement of the outworn Church Slavonic literary medium with the respective vernaculars. In neither case was the choice of a vernacular dialect seemingly as complicated a matter as among the Croats, who were divided among three fairly divergent dialectal zones, each with an established literary tradition. In the northwest, around Zagreb, from the Drava to south of the Kupa, the Croats used the kajkavian dialect, which was structurally close to the neighboring Slovene idioms. Istria, parts of the Croatian and Dalmatian littoral, and most of the Adriatic islands were areas of čakavian predominance. The štokavian, also spoken by the overwhelming majority of Serbs, was used everywhere else.

Despite the intricate nature of the Croatian linguistic situation, generations of Croat writers practiced what amounted to a modicum of dialectal convergence. Moreover, they often consciously favored programs that could effect a single Croat literary standard. Seventeenth- and early eighteenth-century linguistic developments simplified the drive for the standardization of Croatian. The čakavian dialect, the idiom of the oldest Croat literary activity, was already in complete decline and was hardly present in literature. The vast štokavian zone, representative of most Croatian speakers, was consolidated and its literary prestige augmented with the works of Ragusan Baroque poets and various popular writers from Dalmatia, Bosnia, and Slavonia, notably the Franciscan bards, foremost among them being Andrija Kačić Miošić (1704–1760). In the northwest, however, kajkavian Croats succeeded in standardizing their own dialect. Their writers compiled a representative body of literature, which indeed in some genres was superior to comparable štokavian works.[17]

Despite its considerable prestige, however, kajkavian literature could not provide the basis for Croat linguistic standardization. The very limited extent of the kajkavian territory and the openness of this dialect to other linguistic influences indicated its ultimate deference to štokavian. It was in this area that Gaj and the Illyrianists, most of them native kajkavian speakers, performed their most lasting service. The Illyrianist intellectual elite was at the head of Croat national consolidation and conceivably could have opted for the unlikely kajkavian solution to the South Slav language question. Instead, just as in the matter of the most suitable national name, the awakeners practiced self-denial. They were convinced, in the words of Count Janko Drašković (1770–1856), the senior Illyrianist statesman, that kajkavian Croats must turn to a "fuller" (*puniji*) dialect, which could presumably be acceptable to all the other South Slavs and in which "everything that heart

17. For the most up-to-date exposition of the main phases in the development of the Croat language question see Dalibor Brozović, "Hrvatski jezik, njegovo mjesto unutar južnoslavenskih i drugih slavenskih jezika, njegove povijesne mijene kao jezika hrvatske književnosti," in *Hrvatska književnost u evropskom kontekstu*, ed. Aleksandar Flaker and Krunoslav Pranjić (Zagreb, 1978), pp. 34–66. Cf. Zlatko Vince, *Putovima hrvatskoga književnog jezika* (Zagreb, 1978).

and mind demand [could] be expressed."[18] The dialect in question was štokavian, and the Illyrianist authors believed that the cultural unity not only of the Croats, but of all South Slavs, sould be achieved on the štokavian basis. They therefore adopted it in a slightly modified form as their literary idiom, abandoning most of the rich literary traditions of their native kajkavian region.

To be sure, the kajkavian reading public was psychologically prepared to accept a single literary language based on štokavian well before 1836, when Gaj gave up the kajkavian dialect in his publications. The proštokavian sentiment, connected especially with the immense literary prestige of Dubrovnik's Baroque poets, notably Ivan Gundulić, steadily gained ground in eighteenth-century Zagreb. Nevertheless, the self-denying step of kajkavian Croats was in many ways a unique gesture in the history of nineteenth-century national movements and was possible only in the context of tolerant Illyrianist ideology, which was so preoccupied with the conciliatory give and take.

The linguistic policy of the Illyrianists is the key to their national ideology. Gaj practiced the politics of concession, whereby all Croats and South Slavs would give up something in order to achieve one literary language and one cultural (Illyrian) identity. The kajkavian Croats, for example, gave up their dialect, but the modified štokavian of the Illyrianists was infused with elements of kajkavian literary heritage. To this end Gaj explicitly rejected the forcible imposition of any single dialect on all South Slavs, but he also rejected the notion of forging a literary language from all the existing dialects. In a similar way Gaj was opposed to the imposition of any exclusive national name—either Slovene, Croat, Serb, or Bulgar—on all South Slavs, but at the same time repeatedly stressed that the Illyrian appellation was no more than a neutral South Slavic surname, which could not root out the "genetic" Serb, Croat, Slovene, and Bulgar names.[19] Nonetheless, the Illyrianist solutions were so heavily dependent upon Croat national and cultural traditions that they failed to attract the other South Slavs—who of course had no particular interest in Croat literary monuments, notably the heritage of Dubrovnik, nor in the defense of Croatia's municipal autonomy—

18. Janko Drašković, "Disertacija iliti razgovor," in Fancev, "Dokumenti," p. 297.
19. Dragutin Rakovac (1813–1854), the most sober and practical promoter of Illyrianism, put it this way in his "Small Catechism for Grown Men," the movement's most significant ideological statement, published in Zagreb in 1842: "The Croat, Serb, and Slovene names would *caeteris paribus* have the greatest right as the common appellation for our language and literature. These three names are genetic in southwestern Slavia, as the names of the three main branches of the southwestern Slavic people. But we know that a brother does not tolerate a brother's overlordship, and experience teaches us that a Croat will never accept a Serb or Slovene name, a Serb will never accept a Croat or Slovene name, and neither will a Slovene accept a Croat or Serb name." Cited in Jaroslav Šidak, "Prilog razvoju jugoslavenske ideje do I. svjestkog rata," in *Studije iz hrvatske povijesti*, p. 49, n. 15.

matters which preoccupied the Illyrianist National Party in its regional confines. For numerous reasons the Illyrianists could not forsake the centuries of Croat literature nor ignore the pressing political concerns of their home region, and as a result, in spite of the breadth of their intentions, they only succeeded in unifying practically all the articulate Croat strata of Croatia-Slavonia, Dalmatia, Bosnia-Hercegovina, and elsewhere behind the Illyrian nomenclature and Gaj's linguistic and orthographic standard. Had an integral Croat national ideology prevailed in their ranks, the Illyrianists would have recognized this achievement as their preeminent contribution. Instead, the very accomplishment seemed to dampen the reformers' self-confidence. Most distressing of all was the growing anti-Illyrianist polemic on the part of various Serb spokesmen, who were themselves shaping an alternative and vastly different national ideology.

Though a few Serbs, notably a group gathered around a Novi Sad journal *Bačka Vila* (The Dryad of Bačka), were eager supporters of Illyrianism, the majority of Serb intellectuals were hostile to the movement. Their antagonism had many sources. Some Serb writers, especially those who were favorably inclined to the maintenance of Church Slavonic forms in Serbian, were highly critical of Gaj's modified štokavian, which they thought consciously avoided "anything akin to Church Slavonic."[20] Most Serbs also had no use for Gaj's reformed Latin script, considering it an obstacle to the introduction of Cyrillic, which they recommended to the Croats as the only truly Slavic and national alphabet. Most of all, Serbs felt that the Zagreb reformers were attempting to denationalize the Serbs under the guise of the neutral Illyrian name and, indeed, that Illyrianism was fundamentally calculated to stop the expansion of Serb national consciousness to its rightful limits. Teodor Pavlović (1804–1854), the most vociferous Serb opponent of Illyrianism, put it this way: "We feel that we can never accept the terms Illyrian, Illyrian language, Illyrian people, where it concerns the historical appellation, language, and nationality of those people of our lineage who live in Hungary, Serbia, Bosnia, Montenegro, Hercegovina, Slavonia, and Croatia. Why, these people are by descent, name, and language all true Serbs, who call themselves Bosnians, Montenegrins, Slavonians, Dalmatians, and so on, by their home regions."[21] If Pavlović had had only the Orthodox in mind, his observation would have been in keeping with the old Serb national ideology, which equated Serb nationality with Orthodox religion. But his statement made no mention of religion, giving primacy to language. Moreover, he also added the following: "It is truly remarkable that our Serb brethren of Roman dispensation, who live in Bosnia, Slavonia,

---

20. On this subject see Ilija Mamuzić, "Ilirizam i Srbi," *Rad JAZU*, 1933, no. 247, esp. pp. 68–88.

21. Teodor Pavlović, editorial note in "Domaći ili narodni istočnicy drevne slavenske istorie," *Novyj serbskij lětopisъ*, vol. 11 (1837), no. 41, p. 29.

Dalmatia, Croatia, Bačka, Srem [Srijem], and the other parts of Hungary, do not wish to call themselves Serbs, though they speak the Serbian language.''[22] This was indeed something new and represented a significant change in Serb national ideology.

The decisive force behind the new linguistic definition of Serbdom was Vuk Stefanović Karadžić (1787–1864), the famous Serbian language reformer, who had devoted much of his adult life to the campaign designed to replace the artificial Slavo-Serbian literary activity, favored by the conservative Serb Orthodox hierarchy and the thin bourgeois stratum of the civil Danubian belt (northern Serbia, Srijem, southern Hungary), with the robust štokavian dialect of the Serb masses. Karadžić himself stemmed from the humblest Serbian peasant stock. Unlike many of his detractors, he had spent his youth in thrall of Ottoman misrule, and he received his early schooling during the turmoil of the Serbian Revolution. Karadžić knew from his own experience that the foundations of autonomous Serbian principality had been laid by the bobtail peasant host, which had quickly learned the rudiments of statecraft from the Serb intelligentsia of the nearby Habsburg regions. But though their vision of nationhood may have been blurred, the insurgents' success lifted Serb national pride more effectively than scores of learned treatises. The church was no longer the only Serb national institution. Moreover, the ecclesiastical influence was increasingly overshadowed by an upstart peasant state, raised in armed revolt.

Karadžić tapped this source of energy to countrify the Serbian culture, but he challenged his conservative opponents in a still more fundamental way. In a reversal of all traditional standards, he broadened the definition of Serbdom to include all those who spoke the štokavian dialect, regardless of religion. As early as 1814, for example, he held that one of štokavian subdialects was characteristic of ''Roman Catholic Serbs.''[23] The Serb nation, therefore, was not exclusively Orthodox. As long as they spoke štokavian, common to Croats and Serbs, which in Karadžić's system belonged to the Serbs alone, Catholics and Muslims had to be Serbs. Karadžić, in short, brought forth a modern Serb national ideology, the purpose of which was to assimilate the vast majority of Catholic Croats and all Bosnian Muslims, whose dialects were akin to the štokavian subdialects spoken by Serbs.

Karadžić's ''linguistic'' Serbianism was not based on any new theory of his own but followed the erroneous teachings of the earliest Slavistic scholars, beginning with the German historian August L. von Schlözer (1735–1809). Schlözer distinguished between Croatian (that is, kajkavian), Bosnian, Dalmatian, and Illyrian dialects: though the last dialect was clearly

22. Ibid., pp. 29–30.
23. Vuk Stefanović Karadžić, *Pismenica serbskoga iezika, po govoru prostoga naroda* (Vienna, 1814), p. 105.

štokavian, Schlözer called it *"Illyrisch oder Serbisch."* Czech, Slovak, and Slovene pioneers of Slavic studies, among them Josef Dobrovský, Jernej Kopitar, Jan Kollár, Pavel Josef Šafařík, and Franc Miklošič, continued this error. In addition, the philologists usually expropriated Croat kajkavian dialect for the Slovenes or considered it Croat only by virtue of popular belief. This meant that since čakavian alone was recognized as a genuine Croat dialect by the first specialists in Slavic linguistics, Croat national territory was reduced to the area of the čakavian dialect, that is, to Istria, bits of the eastern Adriatic littoral, and most of the offshore islands. In his *Slowanský národopis* (1842) Šafařík, for example, maintained that there were only 801,000 Croats, all Catholics who lived only in the Habsburg Monarchy; by contrast, there were 1,151,000 Slovenes and 5,294,000 Serbs (including 2,880,000 Orthodox, 1,864,000 Catholics, and 550,000 Muslims).[24]

The unique Croat dialectal situation, that is the use of three distinct dialects (štokavian, kajkavian, and čakavian—in that order and with štokavian preponderance in the creation of the Croatian koinè), could not be reconciled with the romantic belief that language was the most profound expression of national spirit. Obviously, one nation could not have three spirits, nor could one dialect be shared by two nationalities. It followed, therefore, that regardless of what their actual national consciousness might be, all štokavian-speaking people were Serbs. Karadžić merely popularized this notion and lent it his own and the other authorities' scholarly prestige. Though a few Croat voices were raised against this bookish theory, which entirely discounted historical, cultural, social, and emotional phenomena, Illyrianists attached little importance to the whole issue. They preferred to think that a common Illyrian culture would make such farfetched theories beside the point—an attitude which probably encouraged Karadžić to think that the Croats could indeed be assimilated.

Once proposed, an idea may make inroads ever so much more easily if it gains powerful backing. The idea of Serb "linguistic" nationhood concerned not only the intellectual circles whence it originated but also the statesmen in autonomous Serbia. Ever since the early days of the Serbian Revolution there were numerous attempts to establish the idea that the twelve *nahiyes* of liberated Serbia were only a nucleus of the emerging Greater Serbia. Most of these plans were the handiwork of Habsburg Serbs, who usually tried to involve Russia as the protector of Serbian expansion. But some of the plans, and almost certainly the first plan calling for a Russian-sponsored "new Slavo-Serb state," which was secretly proposed to the Russians by Stefan Stratimirović, the Metropolitan of Karlovci, probably had the tacit support of Karadjordje Petrović, the leader of the first Serbian uprising in 1804.

Despite the traditions of Empress Catherine's "Greek Project," the

24. Pavel Josef Šafařík, *Slovanský národopis* (Prague, 1955), pp. 146–147.

beleaguered St. Petersburg diplomats rejected or ignored the plans for Serbian expansion under the aegis of Russia, schemes that were impossible during the age of Bonaparte. For example, they did not seriously consider the petition (*Chelobitnaia*) for the creation of a Serbo-Bulgarian state, which was advanced in October 1804 by Jovan Jovanović, the Serb bishop of Novi Sad. Jovanović's state also included the Danubian principalities (Wallachia and Moldavia), Bosnia, and all the other Ottoman holdings in the Balkans. His petition much resembled an even more complicated plan thought up by Sofronije Jugović-Marković, a Habsburg Serb in Russian service, who called for a Serbian protectorate (akin to Georgia's status in Imperial Russia) that also would have embraced all the Habsburg South Slavic possessions as far west as Istria within the social order modeled on Russia's service state. Both plans envisioned a monarchy headed by Grand Duke Konstantin Pavlovich, whom Jovanović wanted to crown as the "Serbian and Bulgarian Tsar Konstantin Nemanich," after the medieval Serbian Nemanjić dynasty.[25]

All these schemes were clearly collateral branches of the earlier Serb national ideology, posited on the equivalence of Orthodoxy and Serbdom, and heavily dependent on Orthodox reciprocity under Russian patronage. Where the envisioned Great Serbia embraced Croat and Bulgarian lands, it did so as the state appointed to gather all the Orthodox South Slavs, wherever they might live. But even the modern "linguistic" definition of Serbdom had a sort of a forerunner in a scheme of Sava Tekelija, a learned Serb jurist and nobleman from Hungary, who approached the French legation in Vienna in 1803 (before the beginning of the Serbian Revolution) with a plea that Napoleon help fashion the South Slavic areas conquered by the French into an "Illyrian" state, which would then aid the liberation of Ottoman Serbs. And in 1805, Tekelija sent a memorandum to Franz I warning him that the House of Habsburg must aspire to become the head of all the Germans and should abandon the South Slavs to Serbia, sell Dalmatia and the Bay of Kotor to the emerging Serbian state, and help it to acquire Bosnia, Albania, and Bulgaria. The influence of the Russians in the Balkans would thereby be stopped.[26]

In the 1840s, especially after 1842 when the Constitutionalist party succeeded in dethroning the Obrenović dynasty, which had dominated Serbia since 1815, and brought Karadjordje's son Aleksandar to the Serbian princely throne, Serbian leaders themselves started considering plans for Serbian expansion. Ilija Garašanin (1812–1874), Serbia's minister of the

25. On Stratimirović's memorandum to the Russians and other similar proposals see Slavko Gavrilović, *Vojvodina i Srbija u vreme Prvog ustanka* (Novi Sad, 1974), pp. 20–24. See also I. S. Dostian, "Plany osnovaniia slaviano-serbskogo gosudarstva s pomoshch'iu Rossii v nachale XIX v.," *Slaviane i Rossiia,* ed. Iu. V. Bromlei et al. (Moscow, 1972), pp. 98–107.

26. Dušan J. Popović, "Sava Tekelija prema Provom srpskom ustanku," *Zbornik Matice srpske: Serija društvenih nauka,* 1954, no. 7, pp. 122–123.

interior and the leading personality of the Constitutionalist regime, became the pivotal figure in these considerations, and it has fairly been said that he "laid the foundations of the Great Serbian policy of [South Slav] unification, [which remained axiomatic among] the conservative political circles and individuals in Serbia . . . until 1941."[27]

Like many of his contemporaries, Garašanin believed that Serbia's national mission was to complete the liberating task initiated by the Serbian Revolution. The frontiers of new Serbia had to be extended to all areas where the Serbs lived, and these frontiers, after Karadžić, were linguistic; hence the responsibility of "liberation and unification" of all Serbs into a single Great Serbian state gradually became the master principle of Serbian policy. Garašanin codified this idea in a secret document called Načertanije (Outline, 1844), which was suggested to him by František A. Zach (1807–1892), a Moravian enthusiast of Slavic reciprocity, who entered the service of Prince Adam Czartoryski's Polish émigré organization.

From his base in Belgrade, Zach hoped to steer Serbia clear of Russian influence and to persuade its statesmen to build Serbia into a standard-bearer of a powerful South Slavic state, which would act as a barrier to Habsburg and Russian influence in the Balkans and aid the Polish independence movement. To this end he composed a memorandum on Serbia's domestic and foreign policy, which he thrust upon Garašanin. Zach's note proposed—and Garašanin's version affirmed—that the new Serbia should be seen as the continuer of Stefan Dušan's medieval realm and that it should resume the old Nemanjić task of building a "Serbo-Slavic empire," which had been interrupted by the Turks in the fourteenth century.[28] But whereas Zach envisioned this new empire as a product of the steady expansion of Serbian state idea among the South Slavs, a process that he held inevitable because no other South Slavic people except the Serbs could undertake to lead the South Slavs into a unified state, Garašanin adapted Zach's document to bring reasons for Serbia's embracing "all the Serb peoples that encircle it."[29]

The Načertanije was prepared at a time when most notables of autonomous Serbia were still mistrustful of outsiders, even when they happened to be Serbs from the Habsburg Monarchy. One of the purposes of Serbia's new national plan was to break, as Zach said, the Chinese wall by which Serbia had cut itself off from its neighbors. But though Garašanin clearly accepted the new conception of Serbian linguistic nationhood, thereby rejecting the

27. Vasa Čubrilović, Istorija političke misli u Srbiji XIX veka (Belgrade, 1958), p. 176.

28. Zach's "Plan" and Garašanin's Načertanije were printed side by side for the first time by Dragoslav Stranjaković in 1939. All citations from the two documents are taken from Stranjaković's version. See Dragoslav Stranjaković, "Kako je postalo Garašaninovo 'Načertanije,'" Spomenik SKA, vol. 91, (1939), pp. 77–78. For the most complete critical appraisal of the literature on Načertanije see Nikša Stančić, "Problem 'Načertanija' Ilije Garašanina u našoj historiografiji," Historijski zbornik, vols. 21–22 (1968–1696), pp. 179–196.

29. Stranjaković, "Kako je postalo," p. 75.

positions of Orthodox traditionalists, he was not accepting the Illyrianist idea of South Slavic reciprocity, which Zach also championed. Whereas Zach wanted a Great Serbia in harmony with the larger Slavic world, Garašanin's inclinations were strictly Serbian. Therefore he diverged from the overcareful adherence to the language of Zach's memorandum only in instances where Serbia's supremacy was diminished, even to a small degree. Where Zach often wrote of the "South Slavic state" or of the "South Slavs," Garašanin regularly turned these phrases to "Serbian state" and just plain "Serbs."[30] More important, Garašanin excluded Zach's two long sections on the need for Serbia's cooperation with the Croat Illyrianist movement and with the Czechs, the latter on the grounds of practicality.

Zach was convinced—and Garašanin concurred—that the Ottomans inevitably would be deprived of their Balkan possessions. The problem of Ottoman succession could be solved only in two ways: either the Habsburgs and Russia would expand at Turkey's expense, dividing the Balkans between themselves to the chagrin of Britain and France, or a new power, Serbia, would supplant the Turkish losses on the peninsula. Serbia's expansion was bound to incur Russian and especially Habsburg enmity. But though the growth of the Serbian state presented a mortal danger to Austria, which was faced with the estrangement of the allegiances that her South Slavic subjects had been paying her, Garašanin felt that Serbia need not exacerbate relations with Vienna. Though the outputs of the propaganda and intelligence agency he built to foster Serb national sentiment among the non-Orthodox "linguistic" Serbs were in the Habsburg South Slavic possessions, Garašanin ruled out expansion at Habsburg expense. He left this thrust in abeyance, again for reasons of practicality, and fixed Serbia's ambition upon Ottoman patrimony, notably Bosnia-Hercegovina, in which he saw only the Serb populace.

Both Zach and Garašanin feared the possible independence of other South Slavic areas, especially Bosnia. The Bosnians had to be convinced that, should they object to a state union under Serbia's aegis, "it would follow that the Serbs would be split up into small provincial principalities under separate dynasts, who would without fail surrender themselves to foreign influence, because they would rival and envy each other."[31] Only the hereditary Serbian dynasty could unite the Serbs (South Slavs), a premise which in due course also spelled peril to the dynastic and self-governed Montenegro. The aim of the ideology expressed in the *Načertanije* was to assimilate and expand. The existence of South Slavic interests apart from those of the Serbs (more correctly of the Serbian state), were simply discountable.

The growth of Serb "linguistic" nationalism, with the unmistakable ear-

30. Ibid., pp. 75, 77, 79, 87, etc.
31. Ibid., p. 87.

marks of an integral national ideology, disturbed the Croat Illyrianists less than their resultant inability to attract the Serbs to Illyrian nationhood and unitary culture. Their disappointment was compounded by the return of absolutism and harsh Germanization that followed the defeat of the 1848 revolutionary wave, and it became more and more difficult to believe in a federated Monarchy, in which the South Slavs, under Croat leadership, would enjoy extended autonomy. The time had perhaps come to assert one's own interests in plain Croat colors.

The cudgels of controversy were picked up by Ante Starčević (1823–1896), Karadžić's first public opponent among the Croats. A sardonic ex-seminarian, who later earned a philosophy degree in Pest, Starčević hailed from the rustic backwaters of multiconfessional Lika and was himself a progeny of a mixed marriage, his mother having been an Orthodox before wedlock. Though crusty and unapproachable, he was the sort of natural captain whose asceticism and singleness of purpose swayed men's hearts and whose unyielding personality in time became a political symbol. An ideologue and writer more than a politician, Starčević lived in continence, as alone as a lightning conductor that disarms the hostile clouds. The Old Man (*Stari*) and the "Father of his Country" to his political offspring, he always attracted either intense admiration or intense hatred.

Starčević's efforts on behalf of Croat national radicalism were completed by Eugen Kvaternik (1825–1871), a sensitive wanderer steeped in Croat historicist theory, who crisscrossed Europe trying to find diplomatic sponsors for Croat liberty. Jointly, Starčević and Kvaternik produced an integral Croat national ideology that negated Illyrianism in almost every respect. Unlike the old Illyrianists, who in 1848 and before counted on the Habsburgs to aid them against the Hungarians, Starčević and Kvaternik had good reason to fear Habsburg policies. They viewed Franzjosephine centralism as an illegal encroachment upon the Croat historical rights, which the Habsburg rulers were bound by oath to uphold. In one of his famous satirical pieces, Starčević expressed his feelings for Austria: "In the name of our three-hundred-and-forty-year history within Austria, I tell you: Austria is always one and the same; she never changed, nor is she changing. . . . Despotisms do not improve, they are instead reduced to ruins."[32]

The ideology of Starčević and Kvaternik rested on their affirmation of state right that by supposition belonged to the Croat "political people" as far

32. Ante Starčević, *Misli i pogledi*, comp. Blaž Jurišić (Zagreb, 1971), p. 244. A bibliography of the important literature on Starčević and Kvaternik and selected excerpts from their writings are included in the most recent editions of their selected works. See Ante Starčević, *Politički spisi*, comp. Tomislav Ladan (Zagreb, 1971); Eugen Kvaternik, *Politički spisi*, comp. Ljerka Kuntić (Zagreb, 1971). For a biography of Starčević see Josip Horvat, *Ante Starčević: Kulturno-povjesna slika* (Zagreb, 1940). For two important recent contributions on the history of Starčević's movement see Mirjana Gross, *Povijest pravaške ideologije* (Zagreb, 1973), and V. I. Freidzon, *Bor'ba khorvatskogo naroda za natsional'nuiu svobodu* (Moscow, 1970).

Ante Starčević (in the pose of Diogenes, from the title page of one of his satirical journals)

back as their migration to the Adriatic basin. The conquest of the new homeland in the sixth and seventh centuries, the "primary acquisition," established the eternal and natural Croat right to the ownership of the land. To be sure, the idea of a political people was already outmoded in much of Europe. The *populus* of medieval Croatia was the nobility, and its nation-hood extended as far as the state frontiers. Starčević and Kvaternik believed that beginning in the eighteenth century, when the exclusive noble responsi-bility to defend the homeland was transferred to the popularly based standing armies, the nobility had lost all its exclusive rights in favor of the people. Thus the lower classes became the political people, a concept that still carried a great deal of weight in the legitimist Habsburg Monarchy. But, as had been true in medieval times, there could be only one political people in a given state, and the Croats, as the bearers of the indivisible Croat state right, were the sole political people on the territory of Starčević's Great Croatia.

As originally envisioned by Kvaternik, who based his notion on an in-terpretation of Porphyrogenitus, Croatia extended from the Alps to the Drina,

Vuk Stefanović Karadžić

from Albania to the Danube. Starčević pushed this line farther to the east, as far as the Timok on the border of Serbia and Bulgaria, recognizing only two South Slavic nations, the Croats and the Bulgars.[33] On this territory the Croats had organized their state, which had lasted through the ages, and on this territory there could be none but the Croat "political people." The Slovenes were "Highland Croats," or the "Croats of Noricum," after the ancient Roman province. As for the Serbs, the term could be applied only to an "unclean race" of various origins, dating to ancient times, which was bound together only by its servile nature; Aristotle had noticed this makeshift people in Thrace.[34] The name derived from the Latin *servus* (servant) and was resurrected by Russian and Orthodox propaganda to divide the Croats by religion at the time of Peter the Great's first efforts to penetrate the Balkans. Starčević's negation of the Serbs went as far as the claim that the "ruling

33. Gross, *Povijest pravaške ideologije*, p. 138.
34. Starčević, *Misli i pogledi*, p. 112.

family of Doclea was the most ancient and most illustrious Croat family—the Nemanjić family.''[35]

So far as Starčević and Kvaternik were concerned, there could be no Slovene or Serb peoples in Croatia because their existence could only be expressed in the right to a separate political territory. Despite the early loss of its national dynasty and the slow diminution of its territory, Croatia was indivisible. The rise of the Árpád and other Hungarian kings—and later of the Habsburgs—to the Croat throne was a result of free election and was not accomplished by conquest. Therefore, the Habsburgs broke their contract with the Croat people every time they failed to restore the original Croat lands to their Croatian kingdom—not only the Military Frontier, Dalmatia, and Istria, but also Styria, Carniola, Carinthia, and, after the Austro-Hungarian occupation of Bosnia-Hercegovina in 1878, of that province as well. The only ties that bound Croatia to Hungary and Austria were strictly personal; these lands had the same ruler as Croatia. Moreover, the Croat "political people" had the right to depose treacherous monarchs. Though the two leaders of what came to be called Stranka prava (Party of [Croat State] Right) never concealed their aspiration toward full national independence, the extreme consequence of their train of thought, the dethronement of the Habsburgs, amounted to treason against the dynasty, a matter that they wisely preferred to gloss over.

Starčević wished to believe that all the South Slavs except the Bulgars would eventually be Croatianized on the basis of his ideology. He regarded the manifestations of Serb national sentiment as unfortunate successes of anti-Croat propaganda, inspired by Vienna and St. Petersburg. But he could not scorn the Serb masses, because these were after all simply wayward Croats. Moreover, the Party of Right attracted a fair number of Orthodox followers in Croatia, who regarded themselves as Croats. And it was for the benefit of all "Orthodox Croats" that Kvaternik wished to establish an autocephalous Croatian Orthodox church.[36] Indeed, Kvaternik's faith in the Croat patriotism of Orthodox Military Frontiersmen was such that, when in 1871 he decided that the time had come to start an armed uprising against the Habsburgs, he chose to begin it in Rakovica, in the predominantly Orthodox area of Lika. This desperate gamble, to which Starčević was not privy, ended in defeat and Kvaternik's premature loss of life.

For all that, there was enough detestation of "political Serbs" in Starčević's ideology to raise questions about his belief that the Serbs were really Croats. Starčević no doubt shared the sentiments of Petar Krešimir Kačić, his fictional follower in Ksaver Šandor Djalski's novel *U noći*: "The oddest

35. Cited in Gross, *Povijest pravaške ideologije*, p. 161.
36. Ibid., p. 161.

thing was that he did not feel himself to be the same as what he thought the Serbs were, so that deep down, in a rather half-conscious way, he was aware of a certain difference between himself and the 'Vlachs' [Serbs].''[37] The circle of Starčević's integralist reasoning was not quite perfect.

By the last decades of the nineteenth century the Party of Right had become the standard-bearer of Croat opposition to the 1867 *Ausgleich* and the subsequent Croato-Hungarian *Nagodba* (Agreement) of 1868. Starčević's ideology helped arouse Croat national sentiment far outside its hothouse in Croatia-Slavonia. Starčević's influence was especially great among students and young intellectuals, and the first generations of Croat political leaders in Dalmatia, Istria, and Bosnia-Hercegovina were formed largely in his mold. Nevertheless, a large segment of Croat intelligentsia never abandoned Illyrianism, and it underwent a sort of a modified revival in the 1860s under the different—South Slavic, or Yugoslav—name.

The principal proponents of *jugoslovjenstvo* (Yugoslavism) were Bishop Josip Juraj Strossmayer (1815–1905) of Djakovo and his close collaborator Canon Franjo Rački (1828–1894), a leading historian and the first head of the Yugoslav Academy, which Strossmayer, a great philanthropist, helped establish in 1866. Strossmayer and Rački, like most of their followers, represented everything that was best in the Croat liberal intelligentsia. Their efforts were preeminently cultural, rather academic in character, but these men were practical minded as well and quite aware that the Croats had little wherewithal to resist the Austro-Hungarian denationalizing efforts and must therefore rely on their Slavic kinsmen in the Balkans and elsewhere. The essence of Strossmayer's program, a somewhat more updated Illyrianism, was the spiritual unification of the South Slavs, founded upon a common culture and literary language. In order to assure the success of this effort, Strossmayer encouraged and financed various cultural institutions, which were designed to bring the Croats out of their provincial isolation and expose them to the modern European cultural trends, and, in addition, to encourage the building of a genuinely South Slavic national culture.

The Yugoslav Academy, the Croatian University at Zagreb, and the Zagreb philological circle were the linchpins of Strossmayer's program. They were to foster the unification of South Slavic languages (on the Illyrianist model) and to establish Zagreb as the center of common South Slavic arts, humanistic and scientific research, and educational institutions. Besides these principal endowments, Strossmayer lent his financial support to myriad publications, schools, exhibits, and edifices from Slovenia to Bulgaria. His immense wealth, derived from the revenues of his diocesan landholdings in

---

37. Djalski, *U noći* (In the night; 1866), vol. 52 of *Pet stoljeća hrvatske književnosti*, ed. Veljko Gortan and Vladimir Vratović (Zagreb, 1962), p. 109.

Slavonia, was at the service of nearly every good South Slavic cause. In time, however, he developed an aversion for the esoteric strangers who came to pump him.

Though a Catholic bishop, Strossmayer was incapable of bigotry. He continually reassured the Holy See that national sentiment was not necessarily inimical to the church. He fostered a revival of interest in Church Slavonic. His great dream was to reconcile Rome and the Eastern churches and bring an end to the religious schism that was so harmful to the Slavic peoples. To prevent further cleavages between the churches, he, among a small minority of prelates, opposed the dogma of papal infallibility at the First Vatican Council.[38]

Strossmayer and Rački—unlike Starčević—for the most part operated within the Habsburg framework. They wished to unify the Habsburg South Slavs in a federalized Habsburg Monarchy that would be truly Slavic (hence the hostility that their program encountered in the ranks of the Party of Right). At the same time, however, they were not trying to encourage Habsburg expansion into the Balkans: they supported the anti-Ottoman movements in Bosnia-Hercegovina and Bulgaria because they believed that the liberation of Ottoman Slavs ultimately strengthened the Croat hand in Austro-Hungarian politics, not because they wished to bring these lands under Habsburg aegis. Moreover, their ultimate goal—about which they were understandably furtive—was a federal South Slavic state, built on the ruins of Habsburg Monarchy and embracing Serbia and Montenegro.[39]

The political instrument of the Yugoslavist program was the National Party, and it was used both for dynastic loyalism and for subterranean plotting. In 1867, for example, the National party reached an agreement with the Serbian government for a common action aimed at a step-by-step construction of an "allied state." This goal proved illusory. The Serbian policy under the Obrenovićes, who were restored in 1858, was hardly different from that pursued by the preceding Constitutionalist regime. Moreover, Garašanin became Serbia's prime minister during the second year of Prince Mihailo's reign (1860–1868), and his efforts to prepare ground for an anti-Ottoman uprising in Bosnia and for the province's unification with Serbia cast the followers of Strossmayer in the role of auxiliaries, not partners.

The principal reason the ideology of Yugoslavism could not please the adherents of the Serbian state idea was that Strossmayer and Rački, like Starčević and Kvaternik, stuck fast to the doctrine of a Croat "political nation." Though they continued the Illyrianist tradition of seeking to unite

38. For the list of important sources on Strossmayer and Rački and a handy compilation of their most important political writings see Josip J. Strossmayer and Franjo Rački, *Politički spisi*, comp. Vladimir Košćak (Zagreb, 1971).

39. Šidak, "Prilog razvoju," p. 55.

the South Slavs behind a common name, in this case the Yugoslav appellation, they were nevertheless far more ready than the Illyrianists to accent the supposed historical right of the Croat state to most of the western Balkans. Rački believed that the "Croat people [had] a legal and permanent right of ownership to the whole space [west of the line extending] from the Bojana [an Adriatic affluent that formed the southern border between Montenegro, later Yugoslavia, and Albania after 1912] to the Drina and the Danube."[40] On this territory there were no Serb of Slovene "political people," that is, no organic group that could express any but Croatian statehood. But unlike the Party of Right, which completely denied the existence of the Serbs and Slovenes, the proponents of Yugoslavism—like the Illyrianists before them—recognized the Serb or Slovene "genetic nationhood." The Serbs and Slovenes did have their cultural and emotional peculiarities, but, inasmuch as they formed one political nation with the Croats, their task was to sustain Croat political nationhood as the "form of national development" best suited "in the struggle against Magyar supremacy and German centralization."[41] On the other hand, "Serbian political nationhood" existed in the Serbian principality, and one could accept its expansion within its proper perimeters. The ultimate South Slavic union would be based on full equality of nationhood, overcoming the questions of territorial proprietorship, which remained a visible expression of the differences between the Croat and Serb national ideologies.

The 1867 *Ausgleich* divided the Habsburg Monarchy into two halves, with Croatia-Slavonia in the Hungarian half. This relationship was formalized in the 1868 Croato-Hungarian *Nagodba,* in which Croat statehood was reduced to a bare minimum. To be sure, under its provisions, Croat political nationhood and its symbols were officially recognized, and the Sabor retained control over the internal affairs of Croatia-Slavonia, but all concerns that are the prerequisities of genuine statehood, such as external affairs, finances, defense, and trade, were subject to the joint parliament in Pest, in which the Magyars predominated. Moreover, the Croatian Ban was appointed by the prime minister of Hungary, and the port of Rijeka (Fiume) remained under the direct control of Pest. Dalmatia and Istria were within the Austrian half of the Dual Monarchy, and were thus administratively separate from Croatia-Slavonia.[42]

The dualist system was a blow to the federalist aspirations of the National Party and a great provocation to the followers of Starčević. Inasmuch as the moderate majority of the National party accepted the *Nagodba,* the Croat

40. Cited in Gross, *Povijest pravaške ideologije,* p. 45.
41. From an 1863 polemical article in the populist *Pozor* (Notice), cited in ibid., p. 105.
42. For an analysis of the implications of the *Nagodba* in Croat political and national life see Jaroslav Šidak et al., *Povijest hrvatskog naroda g. 1860–1914* (Zagreb, 1968), pp. 38–43.

opposition became visibly weakened. Still, the Magyarophile elements in the Croat political life, who maintained their influence by means of various manipulations, were not able to exercise full control over the developments in Zagreb until 1883, when Budapest appointed Count Károly Khuen-Héderváry (1849–1918) as the new Ban of Croatia-Slavonia. The twenty-year absolutist regime (1883–1903) of this Magyar great landowner constituted an attempt to uphold the dualist system by repressive methods. In addition to the hectoring of political opposition, Khuen-Héderváry sought to perpetuate the dualist division of the Croat lands. He was a determined foe of the unification of Dalmatia with Croatia-Slavonia and a promulgator of a separate Slavonian regional consciousness. Needless to say, he ruled out any Croatian interest in Bosnia-Hercegovina, which the Monarchy occupied in 1878, following the decisions of the Congress of Berlin.

The base of Khuen-Héderváry's regime was the bureaucracy, a handful of Croat and other entrepreneurs whose undertakings he subsidized, and the Serb political party in Croatia-Slavonia (organized in 1881), which was an example of the deteriorating Croat-Serb relations. Croatia's Serb minority was distressed by the establishment of secular elementary schools, undertaken by the regime of the National party in 1874. The old Orthodox grammar schools were hotbeds of Serb nationalism, and their stagnation under the new system occasioned a campaign for religious-educational autonomy. Nor were the Orthodox churchmen, who took their cues from the Metropolitanate of Karlovci, brought round by the amendments that permitted continued religious instruction in secularized schools, the equation of Croatian and Serbian languages, and the teaching of the Cyrillic script. Lurking in the background of this struggle was the sharpening polarization between Croat and Serb state ideas, which reached its culmination in the anti-Ottoman uprising of 1875 in Bosnia-Hercegovina.

The Croat public, with the exception of Starčević's followers, who blithely idealized the Ottoman regime in order to bring out the defects of the Habsburg system, supported the insurgents, but many Croats recoiled at Serbia's growing influence in the insurrectionary movement, especially after the rebels proclaimed their unification with Serbia. For its part, the Serb opinion was agitated by Russian efforts on behalf of a Greater Bulgaria and alarmed by the Austro-Hungarian occupation of Bosnia-Hercegovina. The approving comments of a few Croat politicians, who hoped that Vienna would eventually restore Bosnia to Croatia, did not improve matters. Nor did the international recognition of Serbian and Montenegrin independence at the Congress of Berlin come at small cost. Official Serbia became Vienna's stalking horse in the Balkans, if not for the duration of the Obrenović rule, until 1903, then certainly up to the abdication of Milan Obrenović in 1889. Contrary to the ingrained dogmas of Serb national ideology and the instincts of her revolutionaries, Serbia made up for her seemingly permanent losses in

Bosnia by turning toward the southeast—and the growing conflict with Bulgaria over Macedonia. Under the circumstances, Serb politicians in Croatia-Slavonia and Dalmatia declined to cooperate with the Croat opposition.

Khuen-Héderváry chose to exploit Serb apprehension in order to attract their party to his fold. After the final phasing out of the Military Frontier in 1881 and the entrance of its representatives into the Sabor, which increased the political importance of Croatia's Serb minority, Khuen-Héderváry, taking on the role of peacemaker, demanded that "sober administrators carry out his intention of bringing about a politically united Serbo-Croat people of two faiths, who still belonged to two cultures, into national-cultural unity."[43] In the hands of Khuen-Héderváry and his Magyarophile "mamelukes," this old Illyrianist dream turned into an additional incitement against Croat individuality at the very moment when Starčević's followers were starting to moderate their total negation of the Serbs.

Russia's role in the Great Eastern Crisis of the 1870s suggested to the Party of Right that Russia might be depended on to support Croatian independence. Overnight the despotic eastern bugbear and inspirer of bogus Serbianism became the liberator. The "Cossack hoof" on the Viennese pavement would mark the day of reckoning. This drastic revision of Starčević's view of Russia obviously compelled a reinterpretation of his position on the Serbs. This was not a concession to official Serbian policy, which was bound to Austria-Hungary by the 1881 secret convention that guaranteed Milan Obrenović's throne and Serbia's southeasternward expansion in exchange for Serbian docility in regard to Bosnia-Hercegovina. (As a result, Milan was emboldened to proclaim Serbia a kingdom in 1882.) Rather, the Starčevićists were impressed with the gains of the anti-Habsburg Serbian opposition, led by the newly formed Narodna radikalna stranka (NRS, National Radical Party), which resembled them in many respects.[44]

Starčević hoped that the politically organized Serbs of Croatia-Slavonia and Dalmatia would follow the example of Serbian Radicals (and their equivalents in southern Hungary) by developing an anti-Austrian opposition of their own that could work along with his movement and aid Russia's supposed "shot on the Vistula," aimed at bringing the Habsburgs down. If Croatia's Serbs could bring themselves to that sort of cooperation, the matter of their preferred name would be a mere trifle. The leaders of the Party of Right made it plain that national affiliation should indeed be based on "scientific" facts, but conceded that the choice of appellation often depended on subjective inclinations. If segments of Croatia's population wished to call themselves Serbs—or for that matter Hottentots—it ultimately made no difference so long as they acted within the framework of the Croat "political

43. Martin Polić, *Ban Dragutin grof Khuen-Hederváry i njegovo doba* (Zagreb, 1901), p. 77.
44. Gross, *Povijest pravaške ideologije*, pp. 215–217.

nation.'' To be sure, Starčević still denigrated the Serbs to the rank of a sect, classing them in 1883 alongside Croatia's religious minorities (Lutherans, Calvinists, Jews).[45] But his willingness to indulge the misappropriation of the Serb name by a group of "Croats" prefigured a possible move away from his Great Croatian ideology in the direction of Yugoslav unitarism.

Such a transformation did not happen in Starčević's lifetime. The hopes vested in the Russians and Serbian Radicals proved misplaced, as each party avoided clashes with Vienna. And in Croatia-Slavonia, Khuen-Héderváry's policies hardened the estrangement between the Croats and Serbs. Nevertheless, the stability of the dualist system was showing strains by the end of the 1880s. Vienna and Budapest were increasingly uneasy in their partnership, and each party viewed the *Ausgleich* as more favorable to the rival side. The renewal of clashes between Budapest and Vienna inevitably brought the followers of Strossmayer and Starčević closer together. Within the Party of Right, in which Starčević, old and in ill health, was no longer exercising active leadership, these developments lent themselves to the conviction that it was possible to reach an agreement with Vienna for a satisfactory solution of the Croat national question. A rapprochement with Vienna presupposed the revision of the core of Starčević's ideology within its unmitigated loathing of Austria and plain proindependence orientation. The person principally responsible for standing Starčević's original program on its head was his newly found associate Josip Frank (1844–1911). But accommodation to Vienna was not Frank's idea alone. It was becoming increasingly accepted in the ranks of the Party of Right, as the party desperately turned to practical politics after years of Khuen-Héderváry's misrule.

Among Starčević's "apostles," Frank was the most improbable. He was a Jewish convert to Catholicism from Osijek, who never quite mastered Croatian, and was too successful as a lawyer and financial wizard, one would have thought, to be interested in a party suspected of treasonable activities. But interested he was, and he slowly edged Starčević's old guard into the background. And as a master of intrigue, he mesmerized a fair number of old oppositionists, including Starčević himself, who never quite noticed that the ferocity of Frank's patriotic verbiage neatly obscured his dynastic loyalism. Instead of maintaining Starčević's refusal to consider any common affairs with Austria, Frank and his followers, the Frankists (*frankovci*), believed that Croatia's fortune could be realized only within the imperial framework, and that it was therefore in Vienna's interest to establish a Croat unit within the Monarchy, embracing all of the Habsburg South Slavic possessions and with all the prerogatives that the Hungarians enjoyed under dualism. The Frankists sought to convince the Viennese camarilla that a tentative rearrangement of the Monarchy would bring about a satisfied Croatia, which

45. Ibid., pp. 217–219, 331–332.

would in turn become a bulwark against Hungarian pretentiousness and Serbian irredentism. To this end, Frank discarded Starčević's policy of viewing Budapest as an oppressor of secondary importance. Moreover, he abandoned the old tactical avoidance of aggravating Croat-Serb relations and incited a wave of emotional anti-Serbianism, which charged the Serb minority in Croatia-Slavonia with high treason on account of their consistent identification with Serbia.

As the crisis of dualism entered its acute phase, the Croat lands found themselves at the intersection of two competitive imperialisms. The route of the Drang nach Osten ran eastward across Croatia-Slavonia at the time when Berlin was garnering the exponents of this policy among sections of the Austrian ruling classes. From the north, Hungary's drive toward the Adriatic harbors led Budapest to intensify its domination over the Croats. Wherever he could—and against the letter of the *Nagodba*—Khuen-Héderváry was introducing Hungarian language and symbols, deepening national tensions at the very time when the Party of Right was undergoing internal travails. The student youth, hitherto the core of Starčević's movement, began recognizing the limitations of traditional opposition and questioning the validity of Croat state right. The Croat-Serb conflict was also increasingly viewed as an obstacle to effective defenses against the Austro-Hungarian crosscut. While Frank and his followers were staking Croat frustrations upon sterile anti-Magyar and anti-Serb hazards, the principle of natural right of nationality and the renewed emphasis on Yugoslavism was slowly gaining ground among the youth, including the unwavering Starčevićists.

Franz Joseph's visit to Zagreb in 1895 provoked an outpouring of protest against the Magyarizing regime of Khuen-Héderváry. A group of student demonstrators even burned the Hungarian flag almost under the eyes of the visiting monarch. The protesters, who included Frank's two sons and some of the forthcoming literary talents (Vladimir Vidrić and Osman Nuri Hadžić), were tried, imprisoned briefly, and expelled from Zagreb's institutions of higher learning.[46] The actual leader of the group was Stjepan Radić (1871–1928), a young law student from Trebarjevo Desno, a humble village on the Sava slightly downstream from Zagreb, who was already famous for his private war against "tyrant Héderváry."

Although he was repeatedly imprisoned and maltreated for his protests against the "hussar Ban," this nearsighted prophet of the peasant masses crisscrossed the Croat and Slovene lands—often on foot. He was frequently thrown off trains by irate Magyar ticket porters, who insisted on the monopoly of Hungarian in communications on the "common" rail lines. He visited "Golden Prague" and even Kiev, the "Mother of Russian Cities," whose solemn titles rang joyously in his Slavophonic ears. But though Radić's

46. Josip Horvat, *Politička povijest Hrvatske* (Zagreb, 1936), pp. 307–314.

romantic belief in the power of persuasion often prompted ridicule ("I am going by foot to visit the sultan," one important modernist critic spoofed Radić's style, "to win him over to our cause"),[47] his failure to convince the old oppositionists that they must broaden their political base to the nine-tenths of Croatia's population who lived in rural poverty did not imperil his message of "realistic" politics, which won a significant following among his generation of dissident students.

The sources of Radić's inspiration were partly his own practical experience and partly Czech political theory, which he acquired—along with a Czech wife—as a result of intermittent studies in Prague. He persuaded most of his fellow flag-burners to continue their education in the liberal Czech capital. Their presence there coincided with the intensification of Czech national struggle against Vienna, and like Radić before them, the Croat newcomers soon became deeply influenced by the Western-oriented ideas of Tomáš Garrigue Masaryk, the father of Czechoslovak independence, who introduced into the Czech national movement the concept of realistic politics, with its emphasis on practical "small deeds" and work among the lower classes. Masaryk was a determined foe of Bohemian state right traditions and political parties that based their struggle on "historiomanic romanticism." His choice of basing the Czech—and, by extension, every other—national struggle on the natural right of every nation to freedom and self-determination was an eye-opener to youths accustomed to the politics of state right.

After their return to Croatia-Slavonia by the end of the 1890s, these Croat Masarykists, who were usually referred to as *napredna omladina* (Progressive Youth), emerged as an independent oppositional movement that participated actively in the regrouping of Croat parties. The Party of Right had already split in 1895 into two separate branches, Frank's wing, officially called the Čista stranka prava (Pure Party of Right), and the group gathered around the newspaper *Hrvatska domovina* (Croatian Homeland). The latter group, which unlike Frank's party increasingly favored cooperation with the Serbs, fused with Strossmayer's followers in 1903 and fostered South Slavic unity. The Progressive Youth simply encouraged the latter tendency, deemphasizing the old preoccupation with state right. In Dalmatia and Istria, where the Progressivists had no base, their ideas were echoed within the local Starčevićist organizations, which, perhaps because they were not in the Monarchy's Hungarian half and were, moreover, only lately begun, depended far less on the dogma of Croat "political nationhood."

The principal leaders of Dalmatia's liberal Starčevićism were Ante Trumbić (1864–1938), a prim young barrister from Split, and Frano Supilo (1870–1917), a boisterous plebeian journalist from Dubrovnik, whose public

47. Antun Gustav Matoš, *Sabrana djela*, ed. Vida Flaker and Nedjeljko Mihanović, vol. 13 (Zagreb, 1973), p. 45.

personalities in each case belied local stereotypes. Both were convinced that the Croats could no longer survive within the Habsburg Monarchy and that their future could only be assured within a South Slavic state, which would include Serbia and Montenegro. They were determined to bring about common action with the Serbs and to this end insisted on the equality of the two nations. Supilo did not entirely renounce all state right traditions, but it was clear from his statements that he attached far greater importance to the natural right of peoples in the shaping of their national future. Like the Progressive Youth of Croatia-Slavonia, Trumbić and Supilo were instrumental in weaning the opposition away from Starčević's classic postulates on the Croat "political people."

The crisis of dualism reached its culmination in 1903, when the Hungarian Independence Party struck at the common Austro-Hungarian army, the base of Austrian supremacy. Hungarian demands for a separate military were part of a wholesale program of reforms, calling for exact parity with Austria in all areas of public life. The bitterness of the clash between Budapest and Vienna cleared the way for a great revival of South Slavic political activity. In the spring of 1903, popular demonstrations against Khuen-Héderváry's regime contributed to the removal of this universally hated Ban. The system that he had fashioned during his twenty-year rule was not, however, substantially changed, although Khuen-Héderváry's heirs were obliged to moderate his tactics. As a result of these developments, the Serbs were increasingly impressed with the vitality of the Croat opposition. Moreover, in May—in an unrelated but decisive turn—King Aleksandar Obrenović of Serbia was assassinated in a military coup d'état. The conspirators who masterminded the plot brought the Karadjordjević dynasty to the Serbian throne in the person of Petar I Karadjordjević (1844–1921), whose regime rejected the Austrophile foreign policy of the Obrenovićes.[48]

All these changes, as well as the weakness that Russia manifested in the war with Japan and in the revolutionary wave of 1905, contributed to the feeling that Croats and Serbs must depend on each other. This "New Course," formulated into a set of principles by Supilo, was based on the belief that the "German expansion to the east is the greatest danger to all the small peoples in the southeast of Europe. Therefore, all the endangered peoples had to reach an agreement, organize themselves, and start offering resistance. The agreement between these peoples was possible on a just basis."[49] In practice, the policy of the New Course implied a consistent opposition to the Great Austrian circle of Archduke Franz Ferdinand, the heir to the Austro-Hungarian throne, who utilized Frank to promote a form of

48. For details on the background of the coup d'état and the first five years of King Petar's reign see Wayne S. Vucinich, *Serbia between East and West* (Stanford, 1954).
49. Milan Marjanović, *Savremena Hrvatska* (Belgrade, 1913), p. 326.

bogus patriotism, whereby the Croats would feel like Austrians who spoke Croatian. Moreover, the New Course was explicitly antidualist in its advocacy of the unification of Croatia-Slavonia and Dalmatia, to which the Serb parties in the two provinces extended their agreement. Implicit in this concession was the mutual recognition of Croat and Serb equality.[50]

The public resolutions that delineated these principles contributed to the rise of the Hrvatsko-srpska koalicija (HSK, Croato-Serb Coalition), in which Supilo's leadership initially carried the greatest weight. The Coalition was an alliance of Croatia's Serb parties, the fused Strossmayerites and anti-Frank Starčevićists, and an independent group of Progressive Youth. A similar form of Croat-Serb cooperation was reached in Dalmatia, also in 1905. During the following year, after Vienna settled on a compromise with the Hungarian Independentists that allowed them a share of power, the HSK won a great majority of the Sabor elections and became the ruling party in Croatia-Slavonia. The official status of the HSK underwent a great many ups and downs during the remaining years of the Habsburg Monarchy, especially after Supilo's departure in 1910 but continued to be an important factor in South Slavic cooperation, surviving all Great Austrian attempts to link its leaders with Serbia.[51]

However expedient in their dealings with the Austro-Hungarian authorities, and this trafficking was occasionally plainly servile, the HSK's leaders upheld a form of Yugoslavism that was revived during this period under the label of "Croat-Serb national oneness" (*narodno jedinstvo*). This variously interpreted formula, which was largely the handiwork of Progressive Youth, became the most influential idea in prewar Croat politics, preparing the ground for the solution of the Croat question "outside the framework" of the Dual Monarchy. As the influence of Serbia grew after 1903, the status of Croatia was increasingly becoming an aspect of the overall South Slavic question, that is, the problem of splitting off the Habsburg South Slavic possessions and uniting them with Serbia and Montenegro.

The somewhat vague premises of *narodno jedinstvo*, the propositions that the Croats and Serbs were—or were becoming—one people (the "Serbcroat" people) with two names, that with the Slovenes they jointly formed—or should form—one people with three names (three "tribes" of the united "Yugoslav people"), may suggest the emergence of unitarist Yugoslavism within the HSK, that is, the ideology that abolished Croatia's state right tradition in order to justify the natural right of the "Yugoslav nation" to establish a uninational Yugoslav state. This was not quite the case. With the possible exception of some Progressivists, the Croat portion of the HSK used

50. For the origins of the New Course see Rene Lovrenčić, *Geneza politike "novog kursa"* (Zagreb, 1972).

51. For details on the HSK's political practice during its first administration see Mirjana Gross, *Vladavina Hrvatsko-srpske koalicije, 1906–1907* (Belgrade, 1960).

98

these ideas to affirm the political cooperation of the South Slavs after decades of Croat-Serb hostilities. The Croat HSK leaders had not entirely given up on the Croat state right. Neither they nor their Serb partners contemplated the hybridization of the South Slavs.[52] On the other hand, the idea of *narodno jedinstvo* carried the seeds of integralist and unitarist Yugoslavism. Its acceptance by some of the Monarchy's Serbs was influenced by the hope that this concept would above all advance the hour of Serb unification. In addition, official Serbia's endorsement of Croat-Serb cooperation after 1903 mollified some of the most emphatic Serb skeptics. Spurred by the new forces among their younger generation, best represented by Svetozar Pribićević (1875–1936), who was indeed committed to a variant of unitarism, and by the increase of pro-Russian sympathies in Serbia, the Monarchy's Serb politicians actively participated in the HSK. In short, the HSK on the whole remained within the traditions of Croat Yugoslavism. But though not necessarily the party of monistic or unitarist Yugoslavism, the HSK was susceptive to this tendency after Supilo's departure, when Pribićević and his group, ever attuned to the wishes of Belgrade, inherited the HSK leadership.

The doctrine of *narodno jedinstvo* prompted several reactions. The Frankists, who were increasingly infiltrated by Catholic clericalist elements friendly to Franz Ferdinand's vision of a Catholic Great Austria, considered all cooperation with "political Serbs" a betrayal of Croat state right and accordingly loathed it. But the accommodation of the Pure Party to the demands of the Great Austrian Circle had already prompted dissent within Frank's movement. One group, known as Starčevićeva stranka prava (SSP, Starčević's Party of Right) split off in 1908 in order to return to the founder's principles; its leaders did not go back as far as Starčević's renunciation of all ties with the Monarchy, but they made all such cooperation conditional on Habsburg support of Croat interests. As for the Serbs, the SSP acknowledged the existence of a religio-national Serb community in Croatia, that is, in the Habsburg South Slavic possessions, but it denounced all plans for their political incorporation within Serbia. Croatia's Serbs were therefore inseparable from the Croats in questions of state right. They were still "political Croats." The sentiments of the SSP were best expressed in the slogan, "Neither with Austria nor against it, neither with Hungary nor against it, neither with Serbia nor against it, but only for Croatia."[53]

The split within Frank's movement coincided with the unrelated emergence of Mlada Hrvatska (Young Croatia), a Frankist youth group, whose growing independence was, however, very much an aspect of the Pure Party's decline. Following the Monarchy's clash with Serbia over the annexation of Bosnia-Hercegovina in 1908, Frank gambled away his political

52. Gross, *Povijest pravaške ideologije*, p. 388.
53. Cited in ibid., p. 404.

credit with many Croats in a campaign of calumnies against Serbian subversion. As his party sank under contumely of exposure, it fell into the waiting arms of Catholic clericalists, who merged their organization with Frank's in 1910. The Young Croatians were firmly persuaded that Serb treason was a threat, and not just to the Monarchy, that their maintenance of Croat "political nationhood" was not compatible with Catholic clericalism, and that the triconfessional Croat people could be united only by means of religious tolerance.[54]

The Young Croatians agreed with Antun Gustav Matoš (1873–1914), their mentor and the leading modernist writer-critic, that "Serbianism will always find political proselytes and separatists among us, especially among the Orthodox . . . for as long as [Croat] culture is anational, un-Croat, as Yugoslav as [Strossmayer's] Academy, for as long as our popular education . . . is in the claws of anti-Croat, Magyarophile powerholders, the archfoes of Croat name and history, or under the control of the Jesuits, the sworn enemies of all healthy national enlightenment."[55] But though they longed for a rebirth of liberal Starčevićism, some of the most ardent adherents of Mlada Hrvatska set off in an unsuspected direction. Their despair at the prospect of beating back the clericalist usurpation of Starčević's inheritance made them question the wisdom of continuing to negate the Serbs, who had evolved into the most determed obstacle in the path of the Drang nach Osten. Augustin Ujević (1891–1955) and Krešimir Kovačić (1889–1960), the latter a son of Ante Kovačić, the best Starčevićist novelist, were among the leading Young Croatians who concluded that there existed a logical inconsistency between the traditional Starčevićist belief that all the Serbs were really Croats and the growing recognition of all Party of Right splinters that some Serbs, even in Croatia, if their convictions were sincere, constituted a separate nationality. But if Starčević was right in his belief that the whole population from the Alps to the Timok belonged to one people, then the only dispute between Starčević and the ideologists of Serbian expansionism was over the question of national appellation. In one stroke, the differences between the Croat and Serb national ideologies were papered over. Starčević, Karadžić, and all the others, were really the adherents of *narodno jedinstvo* in its unitarist reincarnation. As Kovačić put it, "The greatest harm that has befallen the Croats and Serbs is that we are too much a name and too little a nation."[56]

The distinctive thing about the transformation of some Young Croatians into the ideologues of Yugoslavist unitarism was that, in taking that step,

54. Mirjana Gross, "Nacionalne ideje studentske omladine u Hrvatskoj uoči I svjetskog rata," *Historijski zbornik*, vols. 21–22 (1968–1969), p. 91.
55. Antun Gustav Matoš, "Mi i oni," *Sabrana djela*, vol. 14 (Zagreb, 1973), pp. 88–89.
56. Cited in Gross, "Nacionalne ideje," p. 103.

they abandoned the tradition of Croat state right almost as an afterthought. There were no longer any serious obstacles to the identity of conviction between these young activists and the other contingents of what was increasingly called the *nacionalistička omladina* (Nationalist Youth).[57] Along with the former Young Croatians, this patchwork included the student movements that grew out of Croatia's Progressive Youth and Social Democracy, the Slovene Popular-Radical Youth, and various Serb organizations, including the predominantly Serb Mlada Bosna (Young Bosnia). Since none of these groups possessed a firm theory, the "unitarist Yugoslav idea among the youth . . . operated within the framework of a certain psychology, of irrationalism, and preoccupation with ethical norms."[58] But as the significance and insurrectionary activity of the young nationalists increased, a need was felt for a rounded expression of their views. This need was met by Milan Marjanović (1879–1955) in his articles on the "people that is in the process of becoming," published in Rijeka in 1913.

Marjanović belonged to the generation of the older Progressive Youth, and it is therefore highly indicative that his elucidation of unitarist ideology in fact constituted a polemic not only against the Croat (and even Serb) state right traditions, but against the whole idea of national and state continuity among the Serbs and Croats. According to Marjanović, the Turks entirely destroyed all South Slavic "tribal-state" formations and created a single "Yugoslav national mass." At the beginning of the nineteenth century there were no Serbs or Croats, only a "mass of people that *no longer* had states or political life, a mass which was *not yet* anything akin to a people either in whole or in parts."[59] Proceeding from these false premises, Marjanović concluded that the "Serbocroat" territory (he did not discuss the Slovenes or Bulgars) could be divided between seven "regional groups: (1) the Old Serbian group [presumably Macedonia and Kosovo]; (2) the Hercegovinian group (with Montenegro and a part of southern Dalmatia); (3) the Bosnian group (with a portion of central Dalmatia); (4) the Serbian group; (5) the Slavonian group (with the portion of the Bosnian Sava region, Srem [Srijem], Mačva, Bačka, and the Banat; (6) the Upper Croatian region (old Civil Croatia); and (7) the Lika region with the Croatian Littoral."[60]

Marjanović's effort is expressive of the dilemmas faced by all Yugoslavist unitarists in his time and thereafter. Since their predispositions obliged them

---

57. In addition to the cited article by Mirjana Gross, which is of overriding importance, useful information on the Nationalist Youth, including the Mlada Bosna, can be found in Vice Zaninović, "Mlada Hrvatska uoči I. svjetskog rata," *Historijski zbornik*, vols. 11–12 (1958–1959), pp. 65–104; Vladimir Dedijer, *Sarajevo 1914* (Belgrade, 1966); Predrag Palavestra, *Književnost Mlade Bosne* (Sarajevo, 1965).

58. Gross, "Nacionalne ideje," p. 132.

59. Milan Marjanović, *Narod koji nastaje: Zašto nastaje i kako se formira jedinstveni srpsko-hrvatski narod* (Rijeka, 1913), p. 24.

60. Ibid., p. 25.

to view the obvious differences between the Serbs and Croats as nonorganic, that is, nonnational, the unitarists blamed these differences on the effects of history and hence could not help viewing them as accidental—and therefore reversible. The crucial element of unitarist mentality was the belief that separate linguistic and literary media, state traditions, confessional allegiances, and so on, could be fused into a new quality. Though Karadžić and Starčević used language and state right as their respective criteria for determining the composition of Serb and Croat national communities, they never thought that a higher purpose could mitigate the relevancy of these distinguishing national characteristics. The unitarists thought otherwise. They wished to fire the crucible of the uninational Yugoslav blend by denying the importance of historical influences in the life of the South Slavs. Temporary political needs, geopolitics, and external pressure were sufficient to overcome the Serbo-Croat differences. In that sense, the unitarists represented a genuine antihistorical faction. Their voluntarism was ill digested.

There was, however, one seducement that circumscribed the appeal of unitarist ideology. In their impatience with the lack of a sufficiently ardent response to their revolutionary appeals in Croatia, the Croat unitarists were increasingly viewing the "Croat part of the Serbcroat people" as somehow inferior to the "Serb part," an idea that had long a following in the Great Serbian circles. It was increasingly agreed that owing to their exposure to the "decaying West," an old Slavophile byword of Orthodox superiority, the Croats were less national and dynamic than the Serbs:

> The Croat wants to live. The Serb is ready to die. . . . The Croat, as an intellectual, wants to know, perceive, understand, and criticize more and more, and is as a result more contemplative, forgives more, reacts less, is more of a skeptic, almost a cynic, rather than a fanatic. He feels himself superior even when he has fallen low, because intellectualism leads to relativism and inactivity. And perhaps he is such a great moralist precisely because he has so little moral strength. The Serb is not a moralist, but he has strong morality, the morality of activism and of reacting . . . the morality of atonement and revenge. His aim is not to *understand* everything, but to *be able* to do more. Croatdom represents statics, Serbdom dynamics. Croatdom is the potential and Serbdom the kinetic energy of our people, Croatdom is reflection, Serbdom is action.[61]

In terms of an ideology that worshiped pure national dynamism, the Croats were clearly in no position to lead the struggle for the creation of the unitarist Yugoslav nation and state. And since the dross of foreign culture, which in some unitarist appraisals included the Catholic religion and legalist scruples, could not but detract from the purity of unitarist melt, it became important to

61. Ibid., pp. 55–56.

promote the advantages of Serb culture and tradition, an approach that led straight into Serbianization by another name.

As the unitarists promoted Serb superiority, Belgrade became the mecca of young Croat artists and visionaries. Ivan Meštrović (1883–1962) established his brilliant reputation as the major Croat sculptor with figures taken from Serbian history and folk epic. He was lauded by the unitarists as the "Prophet of Yugoslavism" and the leading practitioner of the much-propagated "racial art," and his sculptures of Prince Marko and of the fallen heroes associated with the loss of Serbian statehood at the Battle of Kosovo (1389), the central event in the Ottoman conquest of the Nemanjić state, were displayed at the Serbian Pavilion of the International Exhibition in Rome (1911). Ivo Vojnović (1857–1929), the leading Croat dramatist, based his disputed play *Smrt majke Jugovića* (The Death of the Jugovićes' Mother, 1907) on one of the most beautiful folk poems from the Kosovo cycle. And after the Balkan wars, which pitched Serbophilia to unprecedented euphoric heights among the unitarist Croats, Serbia's reconquest of Kosovo from the Turks inspired Vojnović to write his *Lazarevo vaskresenje* (The Resurrection of Lazar, 1912). Lazar Hrebeljanović, the martyred Serbian prince of the Kosovo epopee, was raised with the other fallen Kosovo heroes in the new life of Serbocentric Yugoslavism.

The infusion of Serbophilia and belief in Serb superiority influenced the drift away from pure unitarism in the ranks of the Nationalist Youth. Sections of this disparate movement in addition became more and more conservative, glorifying the army and the monarchy among the other Serbian institutions. Some unitarists were increasingly turning from revolutionary activism into heralds of Serbian military intervention in the Habsburg Balkans. Hence, Yugoslavia would rise as Serbia expanded, a product of piedmontization:

> A mi ovamo, sa plavog Jadrana,
> gdje goli krš cvate, umjesto ruža,
> Slavjanstvo hoćemo, sve od Japana
> do pošljednje hridi kod Palagruža!
>
> Hoćemo slogu, snagu i ponos,—
> mi djeca sunca, mora i vjetra,—
> i čekamo vjerno,—jer doći mora!—
> našega Kralja, našega Petra!

> And we here, from the blue Adriatic,
> where the bare karst blooms, instead of roses,
> we want Slavdom, from the distance of Japan
> to our last reef near Palagruža!

> We want unity, power, and pride—
> we the children of sun, of sea, and of wind—
> and we faithfully await—for He must come!—
> our King, our Petar![62]

Small wonder that the Serb unitarists had no incentive to abandon forms of expansive Serb assimilationism that still thrived among them. They simply could not match the growing Serbophilia of Croat unitarism with a corresponding Croatophilia of their own. By unitarist logic, that would have meant a cultivation of a less distinguished and diluted national alloy that had to be purified. The abandonment of the Croat state right traditions on the part of Croat unitarists permitted the positive appraisal of Serbian expansionism, which was increasingly viewed as sound and necessary.

It is important to stress that the growth of Serbophile unitarism did not affect all sections of Croat and Slovene political life, even among the youth. After the Second Balkan War (1913), which pitted Bulgaria against the other Balkan states, the irreconcilibility of many of the separate South Slavic interests became increasingly clear. Nevertheless, the abandonment of Croat state right on the part of many youths represented an obstacle to the growth of equitable relations between the Serbs and the Croats. In this respect, the case of Stjepan Radić is particularly instructive. Though Radić was instrumental in the shaping of Progressive Youth, unlike his erstwhile confederates he did not join the HSK or evolve into unitarism. Convinced that the future belonged to the Croat peasantry, the politically unrepresented stratum of the overwhelming majority of Croats, Radić organized his Hrvatska pučka seljačka stranka (HPSS, Croat People's Peasant Party) in 1904.

Radić's views on national ideology are important: he was simultaneously a consistent partisan of Croat state right and of South Slavic *narodno jedinstvo,* but he was also convinced that the perpetuation of the Habsburg Monarchy, in a democratized and federalized version, represented a solid guarantee for the progress of the small Central European peoples increasingly threatened by Germany's Drang nach Osten. He therefore became an advocate of a belated Austro-Slavic formula that called for the establishment of the Czech, Galician, Hungarian, Alpine, and Croat federal states, united in the person of a monarch from the Habsburg family.

According to Radić's proposal, the Kingdom of Croatia would be a federal unit in which the Monarchy's Croats, Serbs, and Slovenes would organize their own affairs on the basis of their *narodno jedinstvo.* As for the non-Habsburg Serbs and Bulgars, he suggested that they work for the creation of a separate Yugoslav or Balkan federation. Radić was therefore not a partisan

---

62. Quoted in Niko Bartulović, *Na prelomu* (Belgrade, 1929), p. 67. Palagruža (Pelagosa) is a group of Adriatic islands that is closer to the Italian shore (Monte Gargano) than to Dalmatia.

of a Yugoslav state that would include all the South Slavs. He believed that the establishment of such a state would weaken, perhaps even destroy, the Habsburg Monarchy. In short, his Yugoslavism ended on the borders of Austria-Hungary. Radić tenaciously held on to his Austro-Slavism during the Monarchy's agony and to some extent even after the establishment of Yugoslavia in 1918. Because of his Austro-Slavism and adherence to his updated version of Starčević's theory of Croat state right, Radić's abandonment of *narodno jedinstvo,* after 1918, was relatively painless, and as we shall see, it permitted him to synthesize the previous Croat national ideologies in a new mass-based movement that completed the shaping of modern Croat nationhood during the interwar period.[63]

The comparison of Serb and Croat national ideologies suggests that the Serb national idea went through two distinct stages. Early on, when Orthodoxy and Serbdom were synonymous in Serb national thought, the Serb national concepts were understandably static. Moreover, where the Croat preoccupations with the reciprocity of the Slavic world occasionally led to Croatocentric ideologies (Vitezović), the solidly Serbocentric condition of Serb national concepts was impregnable to the intrusion of Slavophilic ideas. The Serbs felt a communality with the Orthodox Slavs, the Russians in particular, but the enthusiasm for things Slavic never overwhelmed them, as often happened among the Croats and some other Slavic peoples (Slovenes, Czechs).

In the second stage of Serb national ideology, the religious definition of Serbdom was significantly weakened. Nevertheless, the new secular ideas of Serb nationhood were not predominantly—nor even significantly—historical. Instead, the Serb national movement increasingly based itself on the natural right of nationality, defined largely in linguistic terms. This emphasis undermined the state right tradition of Croat national ideology but did not at the same time weaken the emerging Serbian statehood, achieved in the Serbian Revolution, beginning in 1804. Implicit in this emphasis was the idea that the Serbian state should ultimately coincide with the limits of Serbian settlement, regardless of the local historical tradition. In that sense

---

63. On the circumstances of Radić's valediction to Austro-Slavism see Vladko Maček, *In the Struggle for Freedom,* trans. Elizabeth and Stjepan Gazi (University Park, Pa., 1957), p. 69. Maček's claims were challenged by Jere Jareb in *Pola stoljeća hrvatske politike: Povodom Mačekove autobiografije* (Buenos Aires, 1960), pp. 19–20. See also: Vladimir Košćak, "Mladost Stjepana Radića," *Hrvatski znanstveni zbornik,* vol. 1 (1971), no. 2, pp. 123–164; Milan Marjanović, *Stjepan Radić* (Belgrade, 1937); Ante Hikec, *Radić: Portrait historijske ličnosti* (Zagreb, 1926); Robert G. Livingstone, "Stjepan Radić and the Croatian Peasant Party, 1904–1929" (Ph.D. dissertation, Harvard University, 1959); Stjepan Gaži, "Stjepan Radić: His Life and Political Activities (1871–1928)," *Journal of Croatian Studies,* vols. 14–15 (1973–1974), pp. 13–73; V. I. Freidzon, "Sotsial'no-politicheskie vzgliady Antuna i Stepana Radichei v 1900-kh godakh i vozniknovedenie khorvatskoi krest'ianskoi partii (1904–1905)," *Uchenye zapiski Instituta slavianovedeniia,* vol. 20 (1960), pp. 275–305.

the new secularism of Serb national ideology maintained much of the old Orthodox reserve in the face of all-Slavic infatuations and was just as assimilationist as at the time of the Partriarchate of Peć.

Croat national thought, on the other hand, always aimed at making an integral whole of separate South Slavic nationalities. For the love of Slavic integration the Croats have often, in Krleža's words, "renounced their own concrete subject in favor of an abstract totality."[64] But though these fanciful attempts usually ended in disappointment, Krleža is not quite correct in stating that "reaction against this moonstruck architecture always set in: after 1848, Starčević: after 1918, Radić."[65] Krleža assumed that the inward turns in Croat national ideologies were explicitly anti-integrationist. But this was not entirely correct. True, Starčević said, "Under the Illyrian name, the Croats as always worked more for the others than for themselves. They passed in silence over much that should not have gone unsaid. The Croats did this in the name of love and fraternal unity. But since it has come to pass that each looks after his own spoon, be certain that the Croats will also not eat with a common spoon."[66] But though Starčević's spoon was definitely Croat, his porridge was made by stirring all the South Slavs except the Bulgars.

Moreover, Starčević was an integrationist in yet another sense. Though he identified nations with states and therefore denied the multinational character of his Great Croatia, he was nevertheless conscious of its composite nature. His Croats were a historical—indeed a moral—community, not a community of blood. The borders of Croatia were set by right of the primary acquisition, not by migrations of a linguistic community. As a result, even the inward-looking Croat ideologies included elements of Slavic reciprocity. The opposite applied in Karadžić's ideology. Karadžić was not trying to prove that all the South Slavs were Serbs, only those who spoke štokavian. Since the čakavians were not Serbs, he had no interest in assimilating them.

Integrative tendencies in Croat national ideologies were always in tension with the idea of Croat state right. If the tradition of state right was entirely lacking in a Croat-based ideology, the tendency was no longer Croat, as happened in the case of Yugoslavist unitarism. On the other hand, the tension between religiously and linguistically based Serb national ideologies was not stirred up over the question of assimilation. Though the idea of anything but Orthodox Serbs was inconceivable to the old Serb hierarchs, both tendencies were assimilationist and in that sense increasingly complemented each other.

The idea of Serb linguistic nationhood, for example, encouraged the spread of Orthodoxy in heterodox štokavian communities. Though Garašanin

---

64. Krleža, "O Jurju Križaniću," p. 67.
65. Ibid.
66. Cited in Vince, *Putovima*, p. 286.

envisioned religious freedom for all Bosnian Christians after Serbia's ac-quisition of Bosnia-Hercegovina, in his *Načertanije* he allowed for only a limited guarantee of toleration and then only "perhaps in time to a few Muhammadans."[67] The words of Stojan Protić (1857–1923), a leading NRS politician, were even more revealing on what was in store for the Bosnian Muslims at the end of First World War. "As soon as our army crosses the Drina, it will give the Turks [that is, Bosnian Muslims] twenty-four—per-haps even forty-eight—hours to return to the faith of their forefathers [which, in Protić's view, was Orthodoxy] and then slay those who refuse, as we did in Serbia in past."[68]

Where the Serbs shared the Orthodox religion with their Slavic neighbors, with the rise of Bulgarian nationalism and then of the Macedonian autono-mist movement, confessional unity became an insufficient means toward Serbianization. It was therefore complemented with linguistic theories, which were also the favorite Bulgar weapon. Karadžić had already held that the Macedonians of Kičevo, Debar, Gostivar, and Tetovo "spoke Serbian, which approached Bulgarian a bit," and a Belgrade newspaper reported as early as 1852 that "pure Serbian" was spoken in Skopje and its environs and, moreover, in the dialect of Srijem, that is, in the ekavian subdialect of štokavian, spoken in Vojvodina and Serbia proper.[69] These hopeful mis-claimers could only be "proved" by intricate pseudomethodology, leading to theories about how "Macedonian speech is covered with rust and mud. . . . This . . . rusty sediment is the characteristic Macedonian Vola-pük, accumulated under foreign influence," which, once washed away, revealed the pure Serbian core.[70] For all that, Serbian propaganda blamed the Bulgarian priests ("cassocked conquerors") for the importation of "Bul-garism" to Macedonia. Moreover, a Serbian version of historical right was applied so as to establish Macedonia's Serbian character.

Both the Serb and Croat national ideologies were very much characterized by their different attitudes toward religion. The Serbs, because of the patriot-ic traditions of Serbian Orthodoxy, naturally looked upon their church as a national institution. Even when they were totally irreligious, many of their intellectuals propagated Orthodoxy, much to the irritation of those who wished to establish pure linguistic Serbianism. One "Catholic-Serb" histo-rian from Dubrovnik denounced this practice as unspeakable insincerity:

67. Stranjaković, "Garašaninovo 'Načertanije,'" p. 87.

68. Ivan Meštrović, *Uspomene na političke ljude i dogadjaje* (Buenos Aires, 1961), p. 73.

69. Ljubiša Doklestik, *Srpsko-makedonskite odnosi vo XIX-ot vek do 1897 godina* (Skopje, 1973), p. 76. Serbian Slavicist Stojan Novaković admitted that the adoption of ekavian in Serbia, after 1878, was in part motivated by the possibilities of expansion into Macedonia. See Stjepan Ivšić, "Etimologija i fonetika u našem pravopisu," *Hrvatski jezik*, vol. 1 (1938), no. 1, pp. 12–13.

70. Steva J. Radosavljević-Bdin, *Istorija bugarizma na Balkanskom poluostrvu: Narodnost i jezik Makedonaca* (Belgrade, 1890), p. 124.

Our Orthodox Serb intelligentsia has no faith. It is terrible to say so, but it is true. There is not the slightest doubt that the Orthodox intelligentsia is much more unbelieving than its Catholic equivalents. But [even if this were not the case] did you ever hear of a Catholic *layman* mixing religion and nationhood and speaking of Catholicism as if it were a political slogan? But this is our [Serb] wound! . . . To believe in nothing, to ridicule one's own [Orthodox] priests, to attend church only because [political] interests so dictate, and at the same time to elevate Orthodoxy over Croatdom—indeed over Serbdom itself—turning it into a beacon of schism and discord—this is . . . wretched![71]

The ideologists of Croat nationhood, almost to the last practicing Catholics, resisted the equation of Catholicism and Croatdom. Kvaternik's Catholic mysticism still gains him the epithet of religious fanatic, but he nevertheless found it natural to believe that "Orthodox Croats" were the "purest Croat type," because, unlike the Catholics, they were not corrupted by Latin and German influences.[72] In similar fashion, Starčević was one of the first Christian thinkers anywhere to express admiration for Islam, describing the Bosnian Muslim elite as Croat by nationality and as the "oldest and purest nobility in Europe."[73]

Under the circumstances, the attempts to link Croat nationality with Catholicism were extremely rare, though they occurred intermittently in the second half of the nineteenth century, especially in Dalmatia (Mihovil Pavlinović, Ivo Prodan). Only after 1900, in Bosnia-Hercegovina, did the Croat-Catholic equation gain a great spur in the activities of Josip Stadler (1843–1918), the Archbishop of Vrhbosna (Sarajevo), who denied the primacy of national over religious sentiment and sought to build Croat nationhood on a firm Catholic basis. His dream of converting Bosnian Muslims merely succeeded in driving a fair number of them away from Croat organizations. Stadler's views became the hallmark of Catholic clericalism among the Croats, but this tendency should not be viewed as a form of inward-looking Croat nationalism. On the contrary, Catholic clericalists wished to integrate Croats and Slovenes, creating a Catholic South Slavic nation.

The distinctions drawn between the assimilationist character of Serb national ideologies and the integrative nature of Croat national thought raise an important historiographic question: What precisely is the meaning of Yugoslavism? There is a tendency, especially in Serbian historiography, but not there alone, to view any attempt at South Slavic conglomeration as Yugoslavism. And since the ideology of Karadžić and the policy of the Serbian state did take an expansive direction, their Yugoslavist character is

71. L. G. Dubrovčanin [Lujo Vojnović], *Srpsko-hrvacko pitanje u Dalmaciji: Nekoliko iskrenijeh riječi narodu* (Split, 1888), p. 13.

72. Gross, *Povijest pravaške ideologije*, p. 161.

73. Starčević, *Misli i pogledi*, p. 90. Cf. Gross, *Povijest pravaške ideologije*, p. 33.

frequently assumed. A more critical school of thought tries to distinguish between Serbian state policy and the federalist aspirations of the radical Serb intelligentsia. The Ujedinjena omladina srpska (United Serb Youth), one of the most radical of the Monarchy's Serb societies, formed in Novi Sad in 1866, is often presented as a genuine Yugoslavist group. But its program did not transcend the calls for a unification of all the Serbs in a restored Serbian state, and some of its units were explicitly irredentist, for example, the club Prvenac, which, according to one of its reports from 1868, spread Serb national propaganda throughout the "Serb littoral, from Budva [in the Kotor area] to Zadar."[74]

The case of Svetozar Marković (1846–1875) is somewhat different. The founder of Serbian socialism, from which evolved both the Radical movement and the Social Democratic party, was indeed the most consistent critic of Serbian state expanionism, the concept for which he was the first to use the Great Serbian label. But though Marković opposed Serbia's conservative, dynastic, and bureaucratic circles, whose only thought was to "ape Cavour and Bismarck" by expanding Serbia's rule to neighboring lands, he never doubted that Bosnia-Hercegovina, Montenegro, and some of Serbia's other neighbors properly belonged to the Serbian state "by blood and language." The difference was that he preferred a federal and revolutionary Serbia:

The idea of Serb unity is the most revolutionary idea that exists on the Balkan peninsula, from Istanbul to Vienna. The idea already contains within it the need of destroying Turkey and Austria, the end of Serbia and Montenegro as *independent principalities* and the revolution in the whole political make-up of the Serb people. A new Serbian state will rise from portions of these two empires and two Serbian principalities—that is the meaning of Serb unification.[75]

Federated Serbia should then seek to build a still larger federation with Bulgaria, then perhaps with the other Balkan peoples, and ultimately with "our neighbors across the Sava and the Danube." This enlarged federation would "not be founded on the principle of nationality, but on personal liberty of those who joined this community. In that way, everybody's nationality would nevertheless be guaranteed, because [civil freedoms] give right to each nationality to constitute itself as an independent group in the alliance."[76] Marković, however, never reconciled the principle of—essen-

74. Cited in Nikša Stančić, "Hrvatska nacionalna i državna misao Mihovila Pavlinovića," *Encyclopaedia moderna*, vol. 6 (1971), no. 16, p. 78. On the program of the United Serb Youth see Čubrilović, *Istorija političke misli*, pp. 240–249.

75. Cited in Jovan Skerlić, *Svetozar Marković: Njegov život, rad i ideje* (Belgrade, 1910), p. 203.

76. Ibid., p. 204. For a detailed analysis of Marković's critique of Great Serbianism and his advocacy of the Balkan federation see Čubrilović, *Istorija političke misli*, pp. 300–308.

tially linguistic—nationality, which applied in the construction of his Serbian federation, and the absence of this principle in the larger Balkan federal state. Was the autonomy of the Serbs territorial and of the others—virtual? Jovan Skerlić (1877–1914), a Serbian literary critic and political thinker, who in many ways continued the trend of Marković's thought, meant to give a backhanded compliment to the latter-day Radicals when he wrote in 1910 that Marković's federalist program was the "program of the old Radical party, which in that area is perhaps even today closest to its old traditions."[77] The truth was, however, that the Radicals "always kept hatching up something or other about the Balkan federation, which the Bulgars were expected to join, but their work in Macedonia kept widening the wedge between them and the Bulgars."[78]

It has been fairly said that "all bourgeois political parties of Serbia [that is, all parties except the miniscule Social Democrats] had a Pan-Serbian or a Great Serbian program after 1903—that being to work, within the limits of the possible, to achieve the liberation and unification of all Serbdom."[79] The Radicals, who split in 1901 over tactics toward the constitutional machinations of the last Obrenović king, were of one mind in this regard. True, the Old Radicals of Nikola Pašić (1845–1926) and Stojan Protić, the mainstream of the NRS, maintained the elements of Marković's Balkan federalism, whereas the Young or Independent Radicals added the call for the "fostering of the spirit of Yugoslav community" to their 1905 program, in which they spoke of Serbia as the "Piedmont of Serbdom." But though this section was, in the words of Dragoslav Janković, "the only place in the programs of all political parties of Serbia until 1914 in which the 'Yugoslav community,' in fact the Yugoslav name itself, was explicitly mentioned," it did not detract from the Independents' Great Serbian orientation.[80]

The governing Radicals of Nikola Pašić began contemplating common action with the Monarchy's South Slavs only after Serbia's heady victories in the Balkan wars, but even then their intentions did not go much beyond the idea of Serbia's expansion. Much the same can be said of various nationalist organizations, particularly the Black Hand, a secret officers' group responsible for the bloody overthrow of the Obrenovićes in 1903. According to paragraph 7 of its constitution, the faction's program of "unifying Serbdom" actually meant that the "Serb provinces" of Bosnia-Hercegovina, Montenegro, Croatia, Slavonia and Srijem, Vojvodina, and the Littoral (that is, Dalmatia), should be joined to Serbia.[81]

77. Skerlić, *Svetozar Marković*, p. 205.
78. Slobodan Jovanović, *Vlada Aleksandra Obrenovića*, vol. 1 (Belgrade, 1934), p. 163.
79. Dragoslav Janković, "Niška deklaracija (Nastajanje programa jugoslovenskog ujedinjenja u Srbiji 1914. godine)," *Istorija XX veka: zbornik radova*, vol. 10 (1969), p. 9.
80. Ibid.
81. Ibid., p. 17.

The implications of *narodno jedinstvo* were perceptibly different among the Serbs and Croats. Autun Gustav Matoš put it this way: "It is an undeniable fact that among the Serbs the idea of [South Slavic] national concord is an incentive to 'Serbing-it-up,' whereas among the Croats this notion . . . weakens the Croat idea."[82] This was quite evident in the Serb contingents of Nationalist Youth. While Meštrović and the other Croat unitarists glorified Serb traditions, Dimitrije Mitrinović (1888–1953), one of the leading ideologists of Young Bosnia, saw Meštrović's work as the expression of Serb "racial history," and declared that he "never before felt more deeply, beautifully, and powerfully a Serb as in front of Meštrović's divine work."[83] Mitrinović wanted to "nationalize" the Croats, who were in part "our denationalized contingent," and to "correct" their language.[84] His utopian vision of Great Yugoslavia was a powerful indication of how the idea of Yugoslavism could be grafted unto Serbian expansionism: "Yugoslavia will be the new and great Balkans, modern and socialist Balkans; and Serbia and Serbdom will be the creating form, the Father entelechy, the spirit of these Balkans. Bulgaria, Croatia, Slovenia, and perhaps Albania will be the body, the palisade, the Mother, the substance of these Balkans."[85]

The belief that Yugoslavism meant the respect for the statehood and independence of each South Slavic nation, including the acceptance of minority status where one group was numerically inferior, was not as prevalent among the Serbs as among the Croats. It could not have been otherwise. The national ideologies of the two peoples were completely different, and moreover the Serbs had an independent national state with a history of expansion and assimilationism. "During the first ten years [after the war], a military dictatorship must be established [in the former Habsburg South Slavic possessions]," Boža Marković, a former editor of Belgrade's unitarist weekly *Slovenski jug* (Slavic South), said to Meštrović in early 1917. When asked why, Marković responded, "So that the Croats would be assimilated and acculturated to state life. You Croats do not know the meaning of the word state, hey-ho, little brother."[86]

It remains to connect the Serb and Croat national ideologies with those of the Bulgars and Slovenes. The growth of the Bulgarian state after 1878 precluded Serbia's southeastward expansion. Bulgar national ideology was fairly similar in structure to its Serb equivalent and used similar means for its expansion—linguistic nationhood, the tradition of medieval Bulgarian states,

82. Matoš, "Mi i oni," p. 87.
83. Dimitrije Mitrinović, "Ivan Meštrović," in Palavestra, *Književnost Mlade Bosne*, vol. 2, pp. 188, 197.
84. Mitrinović, "Izložba Hrvatskog umjetničkog društva 'Medulić' u Zagrebu" and "Niz napomena," in ibid., pp. 164, 36.
85. Cited in Predrag Palavestra, *Dogma i utopija Dimitrija Mitrinovića* (Belgrade, 1977), p. 82.
86. Meštrović, *Uspomene*, p. 71.

and the Exarchate, that is, the autocephalous Bulgarian Orthodox church organization, permitted by the Porte in 1870. Moreover, in Macedonia, which was under the Turks until 1912, the Bulgar national propaganda promoted the autonomy of Macedonia. Stojan Novaković, Serbian historian-philologist, politician, and diplomat, who was instrumental in developing Serbian strategies in Macedonia, believed that Serbian propaganda had little chance of uprooting the deeply embedded Bulgar sentiment in that region through direct confrontation. As a result, after 1866, he counseled that the Serbs finance the so-called Macedonists, who preached Macedonian national and linguistic separateness from Bulgaria.[87] This action had little immediate success, and the Serbs soon returned to the propagation of Macedonia's Serb character. The competition over Macedonia by the Balkan states was mitigated by the end of the century through the emergence of Macedonian revolutionary movement, which scored great successes in uniting the Macedonians of all national persuasions in the struggle against the Turks.

The Slovene situation was not as uniform and in some ways resembled what happened among the Croats and the Serbs.[88] Like the Croats, the Slovenes had a strong tradition of Slavic reciprocity but had absolutely no state tradition. This is one reason the Croat national ideologists from Vitezović to Starčević (and even Supilo) regularly tried to incorporate the Slovenes within the tradition of Croat state right. But if they had no state tradition, the Slovenes had a history of cultivating their separate linguistic medium. Primož Trubar (1508–1586), a leading Carniolan Protestant reformer, was the pioneer in this area. Though he wanted to spread the reformers' ideas throughout the Balkans, hoping to convert even the Turks, Trubar separated the Slovenian idiom from the čakavian-based dialect, which was used by his Croat Protestant associates, and thereby laid the foundations of Slovenian literature and unitary linguistic standard. As a result, the Slovene national ideology in some ways resembled Serb linguistic nationalism. The Slovenes could only struggle for the natural right of national liberty based on their linguistic individuality. Unlike the Croats, they had few historicist ambitions. Also, since religion did not separate them from their immediate neighbors, who were, like the Slovenes, all Catholics, no particular attention was attached to confessional affiliation as a mark of national uniqueness.

During the Illyrianist period, the Croat awakeners tried to bring the Slo-

---

87. Klime Džambazovski, "Stojan Novaković i makedonizam," *Istoriski časopis,* vols. 14–15 (1963), p. 141.

88. On the growth of Slovene nationhood see Fran Zwitter, "Narodnost in politika pri Slovencih," *Zgodovinski časopis,* vol. 1 (1947), nos. 1–4, pp. 31–69; Zwitter, "Slovenski politični preporod XIX stoletja v okviru evropske nacionalne problematike," ibid., vol. 18 (1964), pp. 75–153; Bogo Grafenauer, *Zgodovina slovenskega naroda,* vol. 5 (Ljubljana, 1962); Ivan Prijatelj, *Slovenska kulturnopolitična in slovstvena zgodovina: 1848–1895,* 5 vols. (Ljubljana, 1955–1966); Zwitter (in collaboration with Jaroslav Šidak and Vaso Bogdanov), *Les problemes nationaux dans la monarchie des Habsbourg* [sic] (Belgrade, 1960).

venes to their štokavian-based linguistic standard and even succeeded in some isolated, though spectacular, cases (Stanko Vraz). Nonetheless, their Slovene adherents were mainly intellectuals from peripheral Slovene areas, who were alarmed at the steady progress of Germanization among their countrymen and therefore sought unity with the other South Slavs. The bulk of the Slovene intelligentsia, however, followed a separate course, initiated during the Napoleonic occupation by the circle of Valentin Vodnik and brought to a culmination in the powerful poetic voice of France Prešeren (1800–1849), the great romantic poet whose opus confirmed the separate Slovene linguistic standard.

Separate linguistic traditions were at the root of Slovene nationalism. Moreover, the erroneous teaching of the early Slavicists that all the kajka-vians were Slovenes, which was accepted by Jernej Kopitar, the notable Slovene linguist and Karadžić's mentor, gave confidence to the Slovenes and strengthened them in the conviction that the natural right of their linguistic nationality would in the long run overpower the traditions of Slovene histor-ical provinces, which were maintained by the Habsburgs to the permanent division of the Slovene people. As a result, beginning with 1848 most of the Slovene national programs were directed at gaining the unification of the Slovene lands within a separate Habsburg unit. Where individual Slovene leaders deviated from this direction (as happened with Janez Bleiweiss after 1859), the response was usually in the direction of seeking allies among the other South Slavs on behalf of Slovenia's unification.

A marked novelty in Slovene political life of the 1880s and thereafter was the rise of the Catholic political movement, initiated by Anton Mahnič (1850–1920), and the subsequent division between the clericalists and their liberal opponents. In this bitter conflict (the Carniolan struggle), the Catholic People's Party, headed by Janez Krek (1865–1917), Ivan Šušteršič (1863–1925), and Anton Korošec (1872–1940), among others, applied its superb organizational machinery to the economic, educational, and social regeneration of the Slovene peasants, workers, and petit bourgeois, gaining the adherence of the vast majority of Slovenes. During the pontificate of Pius X (1903–1914), who improved the Holy See's relations with Italy and Aus-tria-Hungary, the Catholic parties of Central Europe were increasingly losing their reformist edge and becoming a pillar of Habsburg order. It was during this period that the Slovene clericalist party, known since 1905 as the Slo-venska ljudska stranka (SLS, Slovene People's Party), became the ruling party in Carniola (1908) and, under Šušteršič ("the uncrowned Duke of Carniola"), was turned into the linchpin of Franz Ferdinand's Great Austrian circle for the penetration of Croatia-Slavonia.

Šušteršič's overtures to the pro-Habsburg Croats began during the 1908 Bosnian crisis. Under the banner of trialism he organized a bloc with the Frankists and Croat clericalists, and, in October 1912, on the very eve of the

Josip Frank

Ivan Lorković

Frano Supilo

Ante Trumbić

Anton Korošec

Stojan Protić

Balkan wars, promulgated the so-called Vienna Resolution, which recognized the Frankist version of the Croat state right and on its basis concluded that the Slovenes and Croats were one people. The resolution called on Vienna to "carry out its obligations to the people," by establishing a separate Croat-Slovene entity out of the Habsburg South Slavic possessions.[89] Šušteršič stuck to his Austro-Yugoslavism (which included hostility for "political Serbs") until the demise of Austria-Hungary. In the meanwhile, the Slovene unitarists, who had the sympathies of some anticlerical liberals, followed the lead of similar organizations in Croatia. And during the war, Šušteršič's Austrophile orientation was increasingly challenged in the ranks of his own party, as Krek and Korošec started arguing for closer action with the Croats and Serbs, perhaps outside the discredited Austro-Hungarian framework.

The Unification

In the aftermath of the Sarajevo assassination, South Slavic politics were thrown into a state of flux. The changing international situation opened new avenues for the solution of the South Slavic national question. The search for a solution, however, was characterized by often divergent political programs. The disparity in wartime strategies of the various Serb, Croat, and Slovene political tendencies perpetuated the features intrinsic in the national ideologies of the three peoples, but it was also dictated by considerations of expediency.

Though many people felt that the outcome of the unleashed world conflict was by no means certain, most political plans were based on the assumption that the Monarchy would survive the holocaust of war, preferably in a reconstructed version, and possibly without all of its possessions. But those who advocated the unification of the South Slavs outside the Monarchy's framework were not without influence, and as time passed, divergent approaches came to be represented by three separate, but increasingly cooperating, groups: the exiled Serbian government, the organization of the Monarchy's South Slavic émigrés in the Entente countries, and the political leaders of the South Slavs who remained in Austria-Hungary. Together with the workings of continental diplomacy, the changing fortunes on the European battlefields, and the disposition of the war-weary populace, the relative influence of the three South Slavic nuclei—not always homogeneous themselves—determined not only the path to Yugoslavia's unification but also the characteristic features of the emerging new state.

89. Gross, *Povijest pravaške ideologije*, pp. 376–377, 398–399.

Serbia and Montenegro successfully repulsed the initial Austro-Hungarian offensive in the summer and fall of 1914. In October 1915, however, the bravery of the Serbian and Montenegrin armies was not sufficient to resist the combined offensive of the Central Powers, recently joined by Bulgaria. After massive losses, the Serbian army, with King Petar, Regent Aleksandar (1888–1934), Petar's younger son and Serbia's de facto head of state after the transferral of "Old King's" powers in June 1914, the government of Nikola Pašić, and most of Serbia's influential figures, succeeded in crossing the snowbound Albanian highlands, harassed in their retreat by the hostile populace. The survivors of the Albanian crucible were sent to Salonika, from which the Allies commanded their part of the relatively stable Balkan front. The Serbian government temporarily made its headquarters on the Greek island of Corfu. Like Serbia, Montenegro was also occupied, and its government found refuge in France.

Though defensive considerations understandably dominated Serbia's initial war aims, the government of Serbia understood from the very beginning of the hostilities that the outcome of conflict would bring vast changes in Serbia's position in the Balkans. Serbia could either become a colony of the enlarged Habsburg Monarchy (rather like Bosnia-Hercegovina), or it could realize its ambitions at the expense of Austria-Hungary. As early as September 4, 1914, well before the reversals of 1915, the Serbian government informed its allies that, should victory be achieved, it expected "to create out of Serbia a powerful southwestern Slavic state; all the Serbs, all the Croats, and all the Slovenes would enter its composition."[1] The official Serbian version of South Slavic unification, as advocated by the men gathered round Regent Aleksandar and Prime Minister Pašić, the leader of the governing NRS, was, of course, burdened by visions of Serbian expansionism. "Liberation" and "unification" of the Serbs, Croats, and Slovenes meant essentially Serb unification, which, as a secondary aim ("great solution"), did not exclude a wider program of "incorporating the Croats and Slovenes within a Great Serbia, should a favorable opportunity present itself after the war."[2]

Pašić made a definite distinction between the Serbian claims to the territories inhabited by the Serbs, defined linguistically, and his government's demands for purely Croat and Slovene territories—that is, between the irrevocable claims of Serbia's "little solution," and the secondary claims, which were advanced as the most convenient way of getting at the first. Though he repeatedly asserted Serbia's intention of subjoining all of the Habsburg South Slavs, the Allies never had any doubts about what Pašić considered essential and what he was prepared to bargain away.

1. Cited in Dragoslav Janković, "Niška deklaracija," *Istorija XX veka: zbornik radova*, vol. 10 (1969), p. 97.
2. Ante Smith Pavelić, *Dr. Ante Trumbić: Problemi hrvatsko-srpskih odnosa* (Munich, 1959), pp. 34–35.

Pašić's main fear was that the Allies might decide to give their support to an independent Croatia, embracing all, or at least most, of the Habsburg South Slavic possessions. (The idea of such backing, prompted largely for religious reasons, was in fact raised in French and Italian diplomatic circles in September 1914.)[3] Pašić was determined that any plans for Croatia must be frustrated, and to this end he assigned Jovan M. Jovanović-Pižon (1869–1939), his assistant in the ministry of foreign affairs, the task of organizing a commissioned group of university professors to prepare a treatise on Serbia's war aims. The main idea was to show that Austria-Hungary should not retain its South Slavic possessions after the war; but also, since Jovanović was "convinced that the Croats would seek an independent state," the treatise was supposed to demonstrate that, separated from Vienna and Budapest, the Monarchy's South Slavs could only be incorporated within Serbia: "It must be shown that each of these provinces could under no circumstances be an independent state. . . . Some of them wanted a Yugoslav state, well [pointing at Serbia], here it is."[4] Pašić himself responded to rumors about Allied sympathies for a Catholic Great Croatia by stressing that Serbian views must be publicized: "We must begin to work in a Great Serbian direction and bring forth our opinions."[5] And if the Allies insisted on a Croat state, it had to be denied not only Bosnia-Hercegovina and Dalmatia, but also Srijem, Slavonia, and even Lika.[6]

The real challenge to Pašić was to satisfy those Croat political leaders who wanted South Slavic unification—not Croatian independence—but on the basis of national equality, with Serbia as a partner. Pašić hoped he could transform the idea of *narodno jedinstvo* in a way that would ensure Serbian supremacy, and he elicited several deductive studies along this line by some of the eminent Serbian scholars (among them Stanoje Stanojević, Stojan Novaković, Jovan Cvijić, Ljubomir Stojanović, and Aleksandar Belić). A Serbian memorandum of June 1915, for example, written by Stojanović and Belić for the benefit of the Russian foreign ministry, proceeded from the premise that the Serbs and Croats were one people by virtue of Serb colonization and (štokavian) linguistic assimilation of the Croat lands. Pure Croats lived only north of the Kupa (kajkavian dialect area) and in Istria and some north Adriatic islands (čakavian dialect area); the Croat national question was therefore an essential part of the Serb question, and this mutual connection had spurred Yugoslavist thought among the Croats.[7] Small wonder that Pašić believed that the Croats and Slovenes (the latter were always introduced as an

3. Dragovan Šepić, *Italija, Saveznici i jugoslavensko pitanje, 1914–1918* (Zagreb, 1970), pp. 22–23.

4. Cited in Janković, "Niška deklaracija," p. 96.

5. Ibid., p. 77.

6. Šepić, *Italija*, pp. 93, 100.

7. Ibid., pp. 102–103.

afterthought in his calculations), or for that matter the Serbs of Austria-Hungary, could play only a passive role in the struggle for unification. The leadership in this process was the exclusive prerogative of Serbia, which had earned this right by its sacrifices, central position in Serb national life, national independence, statehood, and loyalty to the cause of its allies, primarily Russia. The unification of the South Slavs could therefore be accomplished only by piedmontization.

Pašić's views were soon being countered by the group of anti-Habsburg Croat and Slovene politicians, notably Supilo and Trumbić, who had taken refuge in Allied or neutral countries when war broke out. This group, known as the Jugoslavenski odbor (JO, Yugoslav Committee), with Trumbić as president, wanted to cooperate with the Serbian government, but not as Pašić imagined, simply as a Serbian propaganda agency. Despite its limited resources, collected mainly from the Croat (notably Dalmatian) emigrants in the Americas, the committee sought to influence the Allied leaders and public opinion to support the South Slavic unification. Its hushed, but firm, opposition to the Serbian government's conception of Serbia's expansion circumscribed the options at Pašić's disposal.[8]

Trumbić and Supilo were in no sense separatists. They held that the Serbs, Croats, and Slovenes were one people, but unlike Pašić, they made no distinctions between the three Yugoslav "tribes." They believed that the principles of national right and self-determination, and not simply Serbia's wartime performance, entitled the South Slavs to a state of their own, which would have to be worked out by an agreement between the JO and the Serbian government. The assumption of equality, or as the Serbs said, the attempts of the JO "to equate itself with Serbia," created problems at the outset—indeed, even before the committee was consolidated. Pašić's proposal, transmitted to Trumbić and Supilo by Pašić's Serb allies within the émigré group, was that they should work together to build a "unitary Yugoslav, eventually Serbo-Croat, state" in which the Croats could be given "concessions that do not spoil the unity of the state and do not aggravate the final crystallizing of a single nation."[9] Croatia could be mentioned in the state name and the future Yugoslav king could also be invested with the Croat crown.

But Trumbić and Supilo were not interested in concessions. It was all right for Serbia to take the leading role in Yugoslav unification in the South Slavic lands outside the Habsburg Monarchy, but inside the Monarchy the leading

8. The JO was conceived at a meeting between the Croat and Bosnian Serb political émigrés in Florence on November 22, 1914. It was constituted in Paris on April 30, 1915; London was chosen as its headquarters. For a history of the JO see Milada Paulová, *Jugoslavenski odbor* (Zagreb, 1925); and Vaso Bogdanov, Ferdo Čulinović, and Marko Kostrenčić, eds., *Jugoslavenski odbor u Londonu* (Zagreb, 1966).

9. Šepić, *Italija*, p. 26.

role belonged to Croatia. Therefore the unification could not be accomplished by Serbian military expansion. The Serbian leaders were inured to a certain style of unification. But Croatia was not like the four districts in the south (Niš, Pirot, Toplica, Vranje), which Serbia incorporated in 1878, nor like Vardar Macedonia, Kosovo, and the Sandžak, which were subjoined in 1912–1913. The Serbs, Trumbić suspected, "understood this matter of unity and unification in a completely one-sided, exclusivistic way, so that by their criteria, this would be no liberation at all for the Western, Croat, part of our people, but rather a new conquest"; Supilo, too, expressed fears that "Serb-Orthodox exclusivism will spoil everything."[10] Supilo therefore started insisting that Croatia be guaranteed certain prerogatives in the new state. So as to make sure that the Serb appellation would not be imposed on the others, he declared his preference for Yugoslavia as the common state name and hinted that Zagreb might be the best site for the future common capital. He also made it a point to insist that Serbia show its good intentions by example: let it create Yugoslav volunteer units, staffed by South Slavic deserters from the Austro-Hungarian army, the POWs captured by the Russians, and the volunteers from the overseas diaspora, and let it introduce a JO committeeman to its cabinet, as a minister without portfolio. In short, Trumbić and Supilo fought for a new state entity, whereas Pašić envisaged only the expansion of Serbia's institutions to new territories.

From the outset the JO was impeded not only by Pašić's attempts to limit its diplomatic activity but also by the attitude of the Entente governments, whose war aims did not yet include the breakup of Austria-Hungary. Though the JO found valuable friends in a circle of influential British intellectuals (R. W. Seton-Watson, Henry Wickham Steed, Arthur Evans), who were keenly interested in the émigrés' work on the process of Yugoslav unification, most of their contacts saw the South Slavic question as a nuisance that should be treated as convenience suited, in whatever way did the most to shorten the war. The terms for Italy's accession to the Allied side were the gravest case in point: the secret Treaty of London which the Entente powers concluded with Italy on April 26, 1915, promised Italy extensive territories, including Görz (Gorica), a portion of Carniola, Trieste, Istria, and northern Dalmatia with most of the offshore islands in exchange for a declaration of war on Austria-Hungary.[11] Word of the provisions of this treaty, which handed over hundreds of thousands of Croats and Slovenes to Italy, was sufficient to temper the JO's criticism of Serbia, since it was now apparent that the unity of the Croats and Slovenes more than ever depended on Serbia's successes.

Pašić's government was not pleased with the provisions of the Treaty of

10. Cited in Janković, "Niška deklaracija," p. 83.
11. For details on the Treaty of London consult Milan Marjanović, *Londonski ugovor iz godine 1915: Prilog povijesti borbe za Jadran 1914–1917* (Zagreb, 1960).

London, especially since it was not even consulted, but it was positively dismayed by the Allied offers of May 1915 to assign portions of Serbian Macedonia to the Bulgarians, as part of the last-ditch effort to woo Bulgaria away from alliance with the Central Powers. The Allies then offered Serbia compensation in the form of control over Bosnia-Hercegovina, Slavonia, Bačka, portions of Dalmatia unaffected by the Treaty of London, and parts of northern Albania. Though Pašić kept the JO entirely in the dark about these negotiations, word leaked out, and the JO was once more on guard. Supilo, for one, was convinced that Croatia was being divided between Italy and Serbia, with the truncated remainder left as bait for Hungary, should its leaders break with Vienna and join the Allies. For Supilo and the non-Serb members of the JO, the Yugoslav state made sense only if it included all the South Slavic lands. The unjust cessation of the Croat lands to Serbia had a meaning only if the Serbian government made a determined effort to rid Serbia of its "Orthodox exclusivism" and helped transform the country into a genuine Yugoslav state. Under those circumstances, Croat lands outside the Serbian union would gravitate toward Belgrade and remain strongly irredentist. But if Serbia proved unwilling to endure this "transformation," then the "duty of all Croats should be to work to unite with Croatia all Yugoslav areas [of the Monarchy] in which the majority of the population so expressed itself by its genuine and free will."[12]

Supilo's challenge to Pašić went beyond the thinking of most of the JO. Trumbić and the majority did not doubt Supilo's analysis, but they still thought the struggle against Great Serbianism could commence only after all the Croat and Slovene lands were safe from Italian and Hungarian encroachments, and they were therefore prepared to go a long way in order to prevent an open break with the Serbian government. Supilo, who believed that all disputed matters must be freely aired and resolved, urged the Croat members of the JO to break with Serbia, abandon the JO, and create a Croat committee, which would argue for an independent Croatia with the Allies.[13] He hoped at least to put pressure on Pašić by reaching an understanding with Italy, the power least pleased with the prospect of united Yugoslavia. "I am going to Rome," he said to Seton-Watson in March 1916, "to save Croatia."[14]

Increasingly, however, Supilo was prepared to accept an independent statehood for Croatia as an alternative to its unequal status within projected Yugoslavia, for he was convinced that only an equitable confederation of the South Slavic peoples could prevent the rise of hegemonistic tendencies

12. Supilo's memorandum to Sir Edward Grey, Sept. 30, 1915, Paulová, *Jugoslavenski odbor*, pp. 203–204.

13. Šepić, *Italija*, p. 162.

14. Hugh Seton-Watson et al., eds. *R. W. Seton-Watson and the Yugoslavs: Correspondence 1906–1941*, vol. I (London, 1976), p. 261.

among any of them. He had been forced to confront the concept of *narodno jedinstvo* from experiences gained firsthand in practical political encounters. His ultimate break with Yugoslav integralism foreshadowed the disillusionment of an entire generation of unitarist Croat intelligentsia.[15] This pattern would be repeated over and over again in the cases of individuals whose role in the popularization of Yugoslavism was incomparably less meritorious than Supilo's. When the JO rejected his approach, he withdrew from it on June 5, 1916, and for a year more—until his death in 1917—continued his lonely struggle for the ideal of a "national and political community in which there would be no conquerors and no conquered."[16]

The JO's relations with the Serbian government did not improve with Supilo's departure from the committee. Suspicions over Pašić's intentions were increasingly stirred up by his refusal to permit the introduction of the Yugoslav appellation for the volunteer units under Serbian command gathered from among the South Slavic POWs in Russia and planned among the emigrants in the Americas. The JO had great hopes for these special Yugoslav units, which would visibly demonstrate the eagerness of Habsburg South Slavs to fight for the unification with Serbia, but Pašić viewed this effort as an attempt by the JO to obtain its own armed force (a "Croat army"), which would be used to liberate Croatia and therefore deprive Serbia of this distinction.

Instead of the Yugoslav force, Pašić wanted volunteers to serve under strictly Serbian appellation. Since the fall of 1915, his diplomats in Russia, aided by the JO's representatives, had been assembling large contingents of South Slavic POWs and organizing them in Odessa as the Serbian Volunteer Corps under the command of Serbian officers, specially dispatched from Corfu. Since these units had from the start a taint of Serbian exclusivism, only a very small number of the rank-and-file Croat and Slovene POWs— whose numbers greatly exceeded those of the captured Serbs—joined the corps. By mid-March 1916, there were only 85 Croat and Slovene soldiers among the total of 5,365 volunteers. The same was not true of the officer corps; indeed, there was a predominance of Croats and Slovenes among the additional 181 officers gathered in Odessa, showing a greater readiness to cooperate with the Serbs among the higher orders.[17] This imbalance was

15. For an analysis of this phenomenon see Vladimir Košćak, "Formiranje hrvatske nacije i slavenska ideja," *Kritika*, 1971, no. 17, pp. 277–279.

16. For evaluations of Frano Supilo's political activities before 1914 and in emigration see Josip Horvat, *Supilo: Život jednog hrvatskog političara* (Zagreb, 1938); Horvat, *Frano Supilo* (Belgrade, 1961); Dragovan Šepić, *Supilo diplomat: Rad Frana Supila u emigraciji, 1914–1917 godina* (Zagreb, 1961).

17. Paulová, *Jugoslavenski odbor*, p. 192. For a detailed account of the Serbian Volunteer Corps in Russia see Ilija Jovanović, Stevan Rajković, and Veljko Ribar, *Jugoslovenski dobrovoljački korpus u Rusiji: Prilog istoriji dobrovoljačkog pokreta (1914–1918)* (Belgrade, 1954). Figures on the numerical standing of different nationalities in the corps are given on pages 135 and 184.

adjusted somewhat by the end of the war, but the Serbs continued greatly to outnumber the other South Slavs in the volunteer corps, which totaled some 42,000 men at its peak in early 1917.

Mistrust of the Serbs was not the only deterrent to joining the volunteer corps. There were also threats of reprisals against the Croats and Slovenes by the Austro-Hungarians and fear of the terrible conditions in Odessa. The latter included the attitude of the Serbian officers toward the corps. Colonel Stevan Hadžić, who took command of the corps in April 1916, and his staff of twelve other Serbians were quite in agreement with Pašić and others that the volunteers were merely another branch of the Serbian army. The Pašić government made it clear that Hadžić's task was to fashion "firm, disciplined units, inspired with Serbian ideas."[18] Any discussion about the name of the corps, as well as any political activity or participation in decision-making by the volunteers, was strictly forbidden.

The situation was not helped by the Serbian officers' bad judgment in punishing dissident volunteers. According to Franko Potočnjak, a JO emissary who was summoned to Odessa to reassure the volunteers, "matters had gone so far there that [the officers] threatened those who espoused 'Yugoslavism' with the death penalty."[19] Some volunteers withdrew in protest, and after the disastrous Dobrudža campaign against the Bulgarians in August-September 1916, the volunteers' baptism of fire, disturbances erupted in the garrison. After the rebellion, 44 percent of the volunteers either deserted or withdrew.[20] Some men in Captain Milorad Majstorović's auxiliary battalion in Odessa were killed outright, and their bodies were thrown into the Black Sea.[21]

The February Revolution in Russia, according to the report of one volunteer captain, "shook the foundations of the corps, because the moral-disciplinary means of 'fear of fetters' was lost."[22] Some entire detachments refused to obey orders; others disrupted assemblies; some fled. In the midst of a general breakdown of order within the country, the corps members, led by the former POW officers, were asserting their longstanding opposition to the policies of the Serbian authorities. The POW officers wanted a "Yugoslav Corps," which would not be strictly military but would be used also to promote ideas of Yugoslav unity and communality. When the Pašić cabinet in April 1917 granted only token concessions in the form of soldiers' councils and adoption of the name Volunteer Corps of the Serbs, Croats, and

18. Jovanović et al., *Jugoslovenski dobrovoljački korpus*, pp. 19–20.
19. Franko Potočnjak, *Iz emigracije IV: U Rusiji* (Zagreb, 1926), p. 7.
20. Paulová, *Jugoslavenski odbor*, p. 254.
21. Nikola Grulović, *Jugosloveni u ratu i Oktobarskoj revoluciji* (Belgrade, 1962), p. 84.
22. From the report by Adam Gašparović, a volunteer captain in Odessa, dated Sept. 1, 1917 (O.S.), in Nikola Popović, comp., *Jugoslovenski dobrovoljci u Rusiji, 1914–1918: Zbornik dokumenata* (Belgrade, 1977), p. 316.

Slovenes (but not Yugoslav Corps), some 149 officers and 12,741 soldiers left the corps and joined Russian units. This massive withdrawal represented 60.76 percent of all Croat officers and 77.43 percent of all Croat volunteer privates, and 56.76 percent of Slovene officers and 82.84 percent of Slovene soldiers; only one-third of Serb soldiers and practically no officers left the corps.[23]

Like Supilo, the dissident Croat and Slovene officers were disenchanted unitarists. Though they denounced the goals of fighting for a Great Serbia, a Great Croatia, a Great Slovenia as criminal utopias which must be overcome by the alternative of a tolerant and federative Yugoslavia, they refused to render their nationality subordinate to the Serbs under the guise of Yugoslavism.[24] Sublieutenant Gustav Barabaš, a Croat from the Zagreb area and later a Red commander in the Russian civil war, thought that the offer of Serbian citizenship to the volunteers was an unsatisfactory substitute for genuine equality. Barabaš foresaw "something that is horrible for us all, but is not to be excluded, namely that a time might come when our [Croat] people would rise up against the hegemony of the Serb people, and I, as a Serbian officer, reservist, and a subject would be obliged to lift my hand against my own people."[25] There is evidence that the dissidents believed that they had the backing of the JO.[26]

One of the effects of the February Revolution was to weaken Pašić's position at the very time when Austria-Hungary was hinting at a separate peace with the Entente powers. Deprived of his former strong diplomatic support from Petrograd, Pašić was forced to resolve his conflicts with the JO, and on July 20, 1917, at Corfu, an agreement was signed between the Serbian government and the JO.[27] This agreement, known as the Corfu Declaration, proclaimed the determination of Serbs, Croats, and Slovenes to form a united and independent state that would be a "constitutional, democratic, and parliamentary monarchy headed by the Karadjordjević dynasty."[28] The task of writing the constitution was assigned to the future Constituent Assembly, whose members had to accept it in its entirety, by a "numerically qualified majority," that is, by more than a simple majority of 50 percent plus one. The constitution also had to be sanctioned by the Serbian king. Significantly, the declaration made no mention of any histor-

---

23. The figures are based on information from the report of Captain Gašparović, ibid., pp. 311–312, 315–316.

24. Ibid., p. 260.

25. Pero Damjanović et al., eds., *Uchastie iugoslavianskikh trudiashchikhsia v Oktiabr'skoi revoliutsii i grazhdanskoi voine v SSSR: Sbornik dokumentov i materialov* (Moscow, 1976), p. 32.

26. Popović, *Jugoslovenski dobrovoljci*, pp. 272–273.

27. For details on the Corfu Declaration see Dragoslav Janković, *Jugoslovensko pitanje i krfska deklaracija 1917 godine* (Belgrade, 1967).

28. Ferdo Šišić, comp., *Dokumenti o postanku Kraljevine Srba, Hrvata i Slovenaca, 1914.–1919.* (Zagreb, 1920), p. 98.

ical territories. Its reference (in Article 13) to the "counties and other administrative units" was later interpreted as a "break with the historicism of historical right and the legitimism of provinces."[29]

On the whole, the Corfu Declaration was a compromise between the positions of the JO and the Pašić government. It recognized the equality of the three "tribal" names, the three flags and religions, and the two alphabets. At the same time, however, though these provisions were rightly hailed as "our Magna Carta," the declaration also fatally prejudiced the future form of the Yugoslav state by implicitly denying the prerogatives of the Constituent Assembly for or against the monarchy, a specific dynasty, and state name (Serbian delegates were opposed to the Yugoslav appellation, considering it a Western contrivance aimed against the Serb name). During the proceedings, the JO delegates generally took an antifederalist stand, but Trumbić spoke in favor of limiting the powers of the future central parliament to foreign and military affairs, customs, currency and credit, management of state lands, postal service, and transportation, leaving the internal affairs, education, judiciary, and most economic matters outside its competence.

Trumbić later claimed that, at Corfu, he was "decidedly against centralism, espoused by Mr. Nikola Pašić."[30] But though the declaration included no provisions on the internal form of government, federalism was in effect proscribed by Pašić's attitude toward the question of "qualified majority." Trumbić asked that the parliamentary majority in favor of the future constitution be "qualified tribally"—that is, by the individual show of support by each of the separate majorities of Serb, Croat, and Slovene deputies in the constituent assembly—so that the Croats and Slovenes could not be outvoted by a Serb majority. Pašić saw this as no more than federalism and rejected it outright. In his opinion, the option of federalism would inevitably lead to the redrawing of historical frontiers by the new "tribal" (in effect, linguistic) yardstick, and he wanted the Croat federalists to understand that their domain would be the environs of Zagreb and the Adriatic islands, most of them already claimed by Italy. Pašić was in favor of fairly extensive local autonomy, but the administrative units could not be historical entities. And so such historical institutions as the Croatian Sabor found no place in the Corfu Declaration, and the JO, preoccupied with Italian menace, chose not to press such matters. Hence, though the declaration envisioned no institutional protection of national rights, its egalitarian emphasis made it a welcome part of the autonomist political arsenal in the subsequent clashes against Pašić and other centralists.

29. Bogumil Vošnjak, *U borbi za ujedinjenu narodnu državu: Utisci i opažanja iz doba svetskog rata i stvaranja naše države* (Ljubljana, 1928), p. 265.

30. Ante Trumbić, "O federaciji u vezi sa Krfskom Deklaracijom," *Samouprava*, Aug. 4, 1925, p. 1.

The Corfu Declaration referred to the Austro-Hungarian rule over the South Slavs in the past tense. The method of procedure open to the South Slavic politicians in the Monarchy, which was still capable of muzzling all disloyal opposition, was understandably different. The most active Croat, Serb, and Slovene leaders—many of whom expressed sympathies and even maintained secret ties with the JO—placed themselves at the head of the movement for the restructuring of the Monarchy. In Croatia-Slavonia the oppositional Frankists on the floor of the Sabor accused the dominant HSK, in which Pribićević's Serb wing held the leading position, of moral responsibility for the assassination of the Archduke at Sarajevo, and called the assassination a Serb plot against the trialist solution of the Croat question, which Franz Ferdinand had allegedly supported. The general anti-Serb hysteria that prevailed at the beginning of the war forced the HSK, particularly the Pribićević group, to draw even closer to Budapest, which for its own reasons protected the HSK against the excesses of pro-Habsburg Frankists. In return, the HSK faithfully upheld the Hungarian supremacy, which the Sabor opposition sought to undermine by taking advantage of the wartime upheavals.

Besides the Frankists, the Oppositional parties included the more consistent Starčevićists of the SSP, and Radić's HPSS.[31] The anti-HSK alliance was frequently represented as the united Croat front of the most nationally conscious urban and village strata. In truth, the opposition was mainly united over its vision of the trialist reorganization of the Monarchy, the idea that was also supported by the Slovene clericalists. Therefore, unlike the JO émigrés, the three Croat opposition parties for the time being genuinely supported the Austro-Hungarian war effort.

After the death of Franz Joseph (November 21, 1916), political sentiment among the Monarchy's South Slavic politicians increasingly centered on demands for a completely autonomous status based on the national principle and the Croat state right. These demands were pointedly expressed in the May Declaration, a manifesto of the South Slavic club in the Vienna Reichsrat and promulgated on May 30, 1917. The signers of this document, among whom were the three principal leaders of Slovene clericalists (Korošec, Krek, Šušteršič), departed from the old Croat-Slovene—essentially Great Austrian—trialism by calling for the unification of "all the lands in the Monarchy, inhabited by the Slovenes, Croats, and Serbs."[32] In effect, the Serbs were recognized as a political people in Croatia. Wartime exasperations, losses, shortages, fear of Italy, and the propaganda of the JO had done their work. Less than a week later the SSP followed suit, supporting the May

31. On the relations and programs of the parties in the wartime Sabor see Bogdan Krizman, "Stranke u Hrvatskom saboru za vrijeme I svjetskog rata," *Zgodovinski časopis*, vols. 19–20 (1965–1966), pp. 375–390.
32. Šišić, *Dokumenti*, p. 94.

Declaration on the floor of the Sabor in a statement that also mentioned "political" Serbs. Under Ante Pavelić (1869–1938), its new leader, the SSP was evolving into a federalist force, willing to entertain unification with Serbia.[33] Like most of the Croat politicians, Pavelić finally understood that Vienna was not going to grant them concessions even at the time of its greatest peril. Thus Pavelić, unlike Pribićević, whose hands were tied by the Hungarian liaison and whose HSK refused to take a stand on the May Declaration, had no reason to shrink from a version of *narodno jedinstvo* that increasingly transcended the Monarchy's frontiers.

During the fall of 1917 the Entente powers and the United States, which had recently joined the war, were still calculating on the preservation of the Dual Monarchy. The tendency to seek a separate peace with Austria-Hungary and thus to detach Vienna from its German ally was strengthened after the Bolshevik seizure of power in Russia. In his famous Fourteen Points speech of January 18, 1918, President Woodrow Wilson promised autonomy, but not independence, to the peoples of Austria-Hungary; three days earlier Prime Minister David Lloyd George had stated that the dissolution of the Monarchy was not a war aim of the Allies. Pašić, too hastily as it turned out, and in contravention of the Corfu Declaration, instructed his envoy in Washington to see if the Americans could be persuaded to support the voiding of Austria-Hungary's annexation of Bosnia-Hercegovina, which would secure at least these lands for Serbia should the Monarchy be preserved. He wanted these inquiries to be kept secret from the JO: "Our brothers stand by the demand of 'all or nothing.' They do not work as one would expect from a good father, who, if he cannot liberate all of his children, liberates as many as he can; and for the rest he awaits the next opportunity."[34]

The Italians, however, stung by the rout of their armies by the Austro-Hungarians at Caporetto in October 1917, were particularly resistant to any Allied moves toward a compromise, and after the signing of the Treaty of Brest Litovsk on March 3, 1918, arrangements with the Monarchy were finally abandoned. The Allies were now becoming justifiably fearful that the enfeebled Monarchy could not deal with the impact of the October Revolution in the Austro-Hungarian lands, which were by now torn by social unrest, strikes, desertions, and nationalist movements, including the telltale mutiny of the Austro-Hungarian sailors in the Bay of Kotor in February 1918.[35]

33. Except for his name, Pavelić had absolutely nothing in common with the better-known Ustaša leader.

34. Dragoslav Janković and Bogdan Krizman, eds., *Gradja o stvaranju jugoslovenske države (1.I–20.XII 1918)*, vol. 1 (Belgrade, 1964), p. 45.

35. On the revolutionary stirrings in the South Slavic lands inspired by the October Revolution and particularly on the naval rebellion in the Bay of Kotor see Ferdo Čulinović, *Odjeci Oktobra u jugoslavenskim krajevima* (Zagreb, 1957); Čulinović, *1918 na Jadranu* (Zagreb, 1951); Bernard Stulli, *Revolucionarni pokreti mornara 1918* (Zagreb, 1968).

Hence, in June 1918, the Allies consented to the creation of the Polish and Czechoslovak states.

Revolutionary movements in the South Slavic lands of Austria-Hungary were increasingly troubling the domestic authorities. By the end of the war, along with military mutinies, there was widespread desertion from the military forces; in the forests, the so-called *zeleni kader* (green cadre) guerrilla bands, made up of military deserters, were growing steadily, and the peasants were increasingly becoming radicalized.[36] All these forces contributed to the movement for a national concentration of the political forces who saw the necessity of asserting their authority in the face of general dissolution. After coalescing within regional representative bodies, first in Dalmatia (Split, July 2, 1918), then on the Croatian Littoral and Istria (Sušak, July 14), the South Slavic political parties of the Monarchy's Austrian half, at Ljubljana on August 16, established a National Council (Narodni svet), for the purpose of the "uniting of the Yugoslav people within an independent state."[37] The younger, pro-Yugoslav, generation of Slovene clericalists, led by Korošec, was the chief force behind the Ljubljana council. Steps in the same direction were taken in Croatia-Slavonia, largely thanks to the initiative of the SSP.

The military situation was rapidly turning against the Monarchy. On September 14, 1918, Austria-Hungary offered an armistice to its adversaries. Less than a week later, Serbian and French troops, aided by British and Greek units, crushed the resistance of the Central Powers on the Salonika front. Bulgaria capitulated, while in the west the Italians took the offensive on the Piave River. Serbian units were simultaneously making rapid advances toward their principal goal—Belgrade. In the end, on October 5 and 6, in Zagreb, the delegates of the Croat, Serb, and Slovene parties, which favored an independent South Slavic state, formed their supreme political-representative body, the National Council of the Slovenes, Croats, and Serbs (Narodno vijeće SHS). The HSK joined it almost immediately, at last abandoning its cooperation with Budapest. Korošec became the president of the National Council; Pribićević and Pavelić were made vice-presidents; and Radić became the head of its agrarian section.

On October 16, Emperor Karl promulgated his belated plan for the federalization of Austria-Hungary, but his proposal did not envisage any changes in the integrity of the Hungarian crownlands. The emperor's address attended the paralysis of state authority. The fronts broke, soldiers headed homeward, the police stopped functioning. The passing of the Monarchy seemed to some

---

36. On the distinctions between desertion and the organized activity of the *zeleni kader* see Bogumil Hrabak, "Dezerterstvo i zeleni kadar u jugoslovenskim zemljama u prvom svetskom ratu," *Zbornik Historijskog instituta Slavonije i Baranje*, vol. 16 (1979), pp. 1–131.

37. Janković and Krizman, *Gradja*, vol. 1, p. 254.

anticlimactic: "Austria . . . disappeared so silently from our little town, that none of our much respected and dear fellow townsmen even noticed that Austria was in fact no longer among us."[38] But there were attendant troubles in great measure. On October 29, for example, in Zagreb, mobs broke into jails and military stockades, freed the prisoners, and proceeded to loot.[39] On the same day, the Croatian Sabor unanimously accepted the proposal of Pribićević, Pavelić, and their colleagues, declaring "Dalmatia, Croatia, Slavonia, with Rijeka, a completely independent state." The Sabor also decided that the united Croat state had immediately entered into the new sovereign State of the Slovenes, Croats, and Serbs, "constituted on the territory of South Slavs, which hitherto belonged to [Austria-Hungary]." Though the state was limited to these contestable frontiers, it was clear that it was incomplete. Pribićević, who proposed the motion, did not mention Serbia, but he noted that the new united state would extend "from the Soča [Isonzo] up to Salonika."[40] Hence, when the Sabor, in its penultimate action, went on to accept Pavelić's proposal to transfer its powers to the National Council in Zagreb, it also accepted a provisional state-building solution, leading to the unification with Belgrade. On October 31, the National Council declared that the State of the Slovenes, Croats, and Serbs "was ready to enter into a common state with Serbia and Montenegro."[41]

Since the Croatian Sabor did not meet for well over a generation after October 29, its demise should offer clues about the end of a Croat political era. Provided one upheld legalism and Croat political tradition, none of the acts of state, such as the dissolution of all ties with Hungary and Austria, the nullification of the *Nagodba,* the joining of the State of the Slovenes, Croats, and Serbs, and the transfer of the supreme power to the National Council, could have been effected without the Sabor. Yet, though all these acts followed from the theory of Croat state right, this cornerstone of Croat legitimism was never mentioned in the deliberations of October 29, not even by the Frankists, who proclaimed the dissolution of their party during the proceedings. The talk was only of the "modern principle of nationality," national self-determination, and *narodno jedinstvo*: though the appearance of state right was duly attended, the substance was cast out. The Croat political elite, middle classes, and most intellectuals were by this time committed to Yugoslavist unitarism. From that point of view, the Sabor and the traditions of statehood were a relic. The real power was vested in the National Council,

38. Miroslav Krleža, "Pijana novembarska noć 1918," in *Davni dani,* vols. 11–12 of *Sabrana djela* (Zagreb, 1956), p. 497.

39. Arhiv Hrvatske, Rukopisna ostavština Dr. Djure Šurmina RO-3, Box 5: Report of Dr. Lav Mazzura.

40. Janković and Krizman, *Gradja,* vol. 2, pp. 406–407, 430.

41. Ibid. For the best summary of these deliberations see Bogdan Krizman, *Raspad Austro-Ugarske i stvaranje jugoslavenske države* (Zagreb, 1977), pp. 67–89.

an institution of pan-Yugoslav progressionism, to which the regional national councils of Ljubljana, Split, Sarajevo, and Subotica were nominally subjected and to which they sent their representatives. These ad hoc political bodies empowered the National Council in Zagreb with the supreme authority in the same way as the Sabor did, making them the Sabor's functional equals.

The concessions of the National Council could have been understandable had this body been intended as in any sense permanent. Instead, most of the National Council's leaders viewed their role as strictly transitional. And even when they tried to assert their authority, as in the building of the national guard, their power proved most haphazard and not always a match for the ravages of jacqueries and riots by bands of deserters. The Italians showed their disdain for the authority of the National Council by sinking as enemy targets two council-commanded ships of war in the harbor of Pula, an action in which hundreds of sailors lost their lives. Both ships were former Austro-Hungarian naval vessels, including the prized former flagship *Viribus Unitis*. And after the Allied armistice with Austria-Hungary, on November 3, the Italian forces started occupying all territories in the Julian region, Istria, and Dalmatia that had been promised to Italy by the Treaty of London.

The most critical problem, however, especially in northern Croatia, was the widespread popular belief that the collapse of the Monarchy meant complete liberty, that is, a world free of bureaucrats, landlords, extortionist merchants, and usurers, and a redistribution of goods and land. The leaders of the National Council of course had no intention of satisfying these expectations, and they had to rely on the existing administration to keep things in hand until unification was complete. And so the peasant grievances worsened and, with the council and its local agencies powerless to mount preventive measures, a period of intense disturbances ensued.

Throughout late October, all of November, and the greater portion of December 1918, northern Croatia was in the grip of general turmoil. During this period of "great rebellions and terrible days," stores were looted; landed estates and estate manors plundered and often burned; furniture, clothes, and farm animals were removed; and the forbidden solitude of estate forests was disturbed by the peasants and armed bands of *zeleni kader,* who could finally completely satisfy their yearning for game and firewood.[42] Disorder was rampant. As one leader of a Slavonian local council reported to Zagreb, he was powerless to do anything: "He cannot introduce a court martial, because he would have to hang the whole locality."[43]

42. Josip I. Vidmar, comp., "Prilozi gradji za povijest 1917.–1918. s osobitim obzirom na razvoj radničkog pokreta i odjeke Oktobarske revolucije kod nas," *Arhivski vjesnik*, vol. I (1958), no. I, pp. 107, 154–155.
43. Arhiv Hrvatske, Narodno vijeće SHS, Središnja kancelarija NV SHS, Box 7: Group B, no. [b.b.]–1918–[267], Okučani, Nov. 4.

It was obvious from the disturbances that the peasants believed that the National Council "prosecuted only the poor people and not the rich oppressors,"[44] and also, which was more important, that the Croat masses did not share the unitarist ideals of middle-class intellectuals. A commander of the national guard in Valpovo (Slavonia) complained bitterly that the local intelligentsia failed to explain the new trends to the ordinary people: "The people have no idea about what is actually at hand. . . . Only because of the intelligentsia's sluggishness are the people still incapable of understanding that His Majesty Petar Karadjordjević must be their king. Instead, the people vent their true opinions in conversations, saying that they would prefer [emperor] Karl to [Petar]."[45] In a similar vein, a council member from Daruvar (Slavonia) noted that his town, the "focus of provincial intelligentsia," must be safeguarded, because it was the "only bastion of our new state in the chaos of Daruvar district."[46] In Nova Gradiška (Slavonia), the peasants looted Serb stores and in Brinje (Lika), the Serbs, members of the HSK, had their stores burned.[47] In Bosnia-Hercegovina, the disorders were largely communal, as the Serbs burned the properties of Muslim feudatories. The Serb peasants "were rebelling, killing *ağas* and *subaşis* [estate supervisors], burning *çardaks* [manors], and creating uproar."[48] And Muslim bands from Cazin fell upon Serb villages in neighboring Croatia.[49]

Many upper-class conservatives in the National Council, absolving themselves of any responsibility in the matter, blamed the disorders on peasants, who "were not sufficiently intelligent to understand the great task at hand" and some proposed the remedy of "iron discipline . . . as a prelude to liberty."[50] The truth was that the National Council was incapable of changing the dispositions of Croat peasants. Its influence hardly extended outside the towns. Moreover, the Serbs and unitaristic nationalists undermined its authority. In Kutina (Slavonia), they burned Croatian flags and cheered Great Yugoslavia.[51] In Srijem, the Serb-dominated local councils urged the quick establishment of a "monarchist, united, and centralist" state and predicted that should Zagreb demonstrate "tribal separatism, the deputies of the national council in Srijem, as representatives of the people, [will] declare

---

44. Ibid., Narodno vijeće SHS, Sekcija za organizaciju i agitaciju, Box 12: Group B, no. 393–1918–[f. 791], Slavonski Brod, without date.

45. Ibid., Box 14: Group B, no. 684–1918–[160], Valpovo, Dec. 9.

46. Ibid., Box 15: Group C, no. [b.b.]–[22], Daruvar, without date.

47. Ibid., Box 12: no. [b.b.]–[621], Nova Gradiška, Oct. 28; Odjel za unutrašnje poslove Zemaljske vlade, Box 1: Kotarska oblast u Brinju, no. 8560, Brinje, Nov. 22.

48. Ibid., Narodno vijeće SHS, Središnja kancelarija NV SHS, Box 7: Group B, no. [b.b.]–1918–[308], Banja Luka, Nov. 4.

49. Ibid., no. [b.b.[–1918–[362], Vrgin Most and Glina, Nov. 5.

50. Ibid., Sekcija za organizaciju i agitaciju, Box 10: Group B, no. 197/18, f. 187, Bela, Nov. 15.

51. Ibid., Box 12: Kutina, Oct. 29.

themselves for direct unification with the Kingdom of Serbia."[52] In Bosnia the politician who headed Sarajevo's national council, Atanasije Šola, a Serb, refused to accept the military officers who were sent from Zagreb to organize the Bosnian national guard and invited the Serbian army to come instead.[53] Elsewhere in Bosnia the Serb councils disclaimed all allegiance to the National Council. In Bihać they proclaimed a unilateral unification with Serbia and "subjected themselves only to the authority of His Majesty King Petar I Karadjordjević and his constitutional government."[54] And in Prijedor, they declared that the "provincial governments can act only in the name of [the king] and of the Serbian royal government inasmuch as it transfers its powers to them."[55] Unilateral unifications were also carried out in Banja Luka and, in Dalmatia, in Kotor.

These sentiments did not break out all at once and certainly intensified as disorders mounted, becoming increasingly shrill by the end of November 1918, adding another insurmountable obstacle to the National Council's other failures. Isolated, ignored by the Allies, its men on the coast repressed by the Italians, the National Council was increasingly driven to seek Serbian intervention: "The people are in revolt. Total disorganization prevails. Only the army, moreover only the Serbian army, can restore order. The people are burning and destroying. I do not know how we shall feed Dalmatia and Bosnia. The mob is now pillaging the merchants, since all the landed estates have already been destroyed. Private fortunes are destroyed. The Serbian army is the only salvation."[56] The reporter, a national council official in Slatina (Slavonia), relied on released Serbian POWs against the looting peasants. In Karlovac, also, the Serbs were considered more reliable than the local national guard.[57] And in Osijek, local authorities invited the Serbian army on their own initiative.

As early as November 5, the National Council sent a delegation to the Serbian supreme command, pleading for the entrance of Serbian army to Croatia-Slavonia. To be sure, as the Serbian military delegate in Zagreb noted in a message to his command, sent on November 18, the "representatives of the Croat people would not agree to the bringing of very large detachments [*jače snage*] of our [Serbian] army, because they would see in that a military occupation of their country,"[58] but the scruples on this issue

52. Ibid., Središnja kancelarija Narodnog vijeća SHS, Box 7: Group B, no. [b.b.]–1918–[824], Indjija, Nov. 20; no. [b.b.[–1918–[897], Sr. Karlovci, Nov. 26.

53. Krizman, *Raspad Austro-Ugarske*, pp. 146–148.

54. Arhiv Hrvatske, Narodno vijeće SHS, Sekcija za organizaciju i agitaciju, Box 9: Group A, no. 447–1918–[178], Bihać, Nov. 29.

55. Ibid., Prijedor, Nov. 29.

56. Ibid., Središnja kancelarija Norodnog vijeća SHS, Box 7: Group B, no. [b.b.]–1918–[197], Slatina, Nov. 2.

57. Ibid., no. [b.b.]–1918–[263–264], Otočac, Nov. 3.

58. Bogdan Krizman, ed., "Izvještaj D. T. Simovića, delegata Srpske vrhovne komande kod vlade Narodnog vijeća SHS g. 1918," *Historijski zbornik*, vol. 8 (1955), nos. 1–4, p. 127.

and on the nature of projected unification were increasingly set aside. Though the Croat members of the National Council kept deliberating on the form of the Yugoslav state, openly expressing "their fear about the future more powerful position of the Serbs and the possibility that the Croats may lose their individuality,"[59] preparations for the unification with Serbia and Montenegro were in fact hastened. This all the more so, since the HSK, especially its Serb wing, headed by Pribićević, was gaining in influence in the National Council's central committee, and this party was "from the very beginning [of independence] for the unconditional and all the more rapid unification with Serbia."[60]

Though the Allies failed to recognize the State of the Slovenes, Croats, and Serbs, they—Italy excepted—favored its unification with Serbia, but a coolness in the relations between Pašić and the JO, which had prevailed since the summer of 1918, complicated the process. The conflict started over Trumbić's demand that the Allies acknowledge the JO as the legitimate representative of the Monarchy's South Slavs, much along the lines of the recognition already extended to the exiled Czechoslovak National Council. This Pašić categorically opposed: "Serbia has the same position among our allies as Italy, which, in the unification of its brothers, represents its country-men from Austria. . . . It is therefore plain that it is not necessary to ask from the Allies to act toward us as they did toward the Czecho-Slovaks and Poles, because those two peoples do not have their own free state, which could represent their Piedmonts."[61] Obviously, equal recognition of the Serbian government and the JO would jeopardize Pašić's goal of unification along Great Serbian lines: "Serbia wants to liberate and unite the Yugoslavs and does not want to drown in the sea of some kind of Yugoslavia. Serbia does not want to drown in Yugoslavia, but to have Yugoslavia drown in her."[62]

At this point, however, Pašić was faced with formidable opposition: Steed and Seton-Watson, the British friends of Yugoslav unification, openly attacked him, and their opinions found interested ears in the Foreign Office.[63] Trumbić, usually fond of compromises, this time quite freely denounced Pašić to the British government:

> The position in which Mr. Pašić wishes to maintain the Yugoslavs from Austria-Hungary is that of submission and humiliation, because that people would only be an object of liberation, and not the subject of right and liberty. The

59. Ibid., p. 126.
60. Krizman, *Raspad Austro-Ugarske*, p. 201.
61. Janković and Krizman, *Gradja*, vol. 1, p. 244.
62. Pašić to Jovan M. Jovanović-Pižon in London, Oct. 5, 1918. Cited in Šepić, *Italija*, p. 358.
63. R. W. Seton-Watson, "Serbia's Choice," in Seton-Watson, *Correspondence*, vol. 1, pp. 385–391.

stand of Mr. Pašić is anti-liberal, anti-democratic, and contrary to the principle of nationality. Moreover, his stand is inspired by the spirit of conquest and annexation of our regions by the Serbian state. . . . "The right to liberate our brothers," the creation of a Yugoslavia that would lie "under the aegis of Serbia," would mean that the Serbs would receive a position similar to the primacy of Prussia. . . . The Yugoslavs outside Serbia want national unification, but no province will submit to the hegemony of another province. Every tendency that goes after hegemony will undermine internal harmony of a homogeneous race and will imperil the establishment of a state that is in the interest of future civilization and peace in Central Europe.[64]

Moreover, there were repercussions to the execution of the Serbian officers found guilty by the Serbian military tribunal in Salonika (June 1917) of being members of the Black Hand organization. The Independent Radicals and Progressive leaders withdrew from Pašić's cabinet and started a campaign for the revision of this rigged trial.[65] Though the anti-Radical opposition in no sense objected to Pašić's idea of unification, its leaders were willing to use the JO's clash with Pašić for their own ends.[66] They negotiated with Pašić for a new coalition cabinet and at the same time encouraged Trumbić. Trumbić, cheered still more by the developments of October 29 in Zagreb, the National Council's mandate to the JO to represent it abroad, and the friendly messages from British and French leaders, hoped momentarily that Pašić could be undone.

Since some time in October, Korošec, the head of the National Council, had been in Geneva trying to ascertain the international position of the Yugoslav cause. Pašić who apparently was advised that the National Council was closer to his ideas than to those of the JO, decided to accept the proposal of the Serbian opposition and join in a quadripartite meeting, at which his government, the opposition, Korošec, and the JO could come to terms about

64. Janković and Krizman, *Gradja*, vol. 1, p. 334.
65. Colonel Dragutin Dimitrijević-Apis (1877–1917), the reputed mastermind of the assassination of Archduke Franz Ferdinand in 1914 and head of the Unification or Death, a secret society of Great Serbian nationalist officers, better known as the Black Hand, was executed in Salonika in June 1917, together with several of his close associates. The Serbian government charged him with the conspiracy to assassinate Regent Aleksandar. In fact, Apis was a victim of an artfully contrived plan that could have assured a separate peace between Serbia and Austria-Hungary. No negotiations with Austria were possible as long as those responsible for the Sarajevo assassination were at large, and Pašić and Aleksandar, who feared Apis's power in the army and his links with the South Slavic nationalist circles outside Serbia, rigged the trial. On this affair see Milan Živanović, *Solunski proces* (Belgrade, 1955).
66. Dragoslav Janković, the most distinguished authority on Serbia's wartime policy, rightly points out that the Serbian opposition was the JO's "least reliable ally." The same oppositionists who seconded Trumbić's resistance to Pašić only a half year earlier assured Regent Aleksandar that the Serbians were capable of carrying out the "great task of free-minded and modern administration over our several times larger Serb-Croat-Slovene kingdom." Cited in Dragoslav Janković, "Ženevska konferencija o stvaranju jugoslovenske zajednice 1918. godine," *Istorija XX veka: zbornik radova*, vol. 5 (1963), p. 238.

the course of unification. The meeting convened in Geneva on November 6 through 9. Pašić, realizing that he stood alone, finally abandoned his position that only Serbia represented all the South Slavs and agreed to recognize the "National Council in Zagreb as the legitimate government of the Serbs, Croats, and Slovenes, who live on the territory of the [former] Austro-Hungarian Monarchy."[67] The recognition paved the way for fruitful discussions on the establishment of a common government. Despite Pašić's mumbled warnings, Trumbić was successful in obtaining the support of all other parties for a proposal calling for a twelve-member common ministry (with jurisdictions over foreign and military affairs, navy, maritime affairs, constituent assembly, transportation, reconstruction, relief, and common finances) to which the Serbian government and the National Council would delegate six members each, none of them party leaders.

The old institutions, the Serbian government and the National Council, were to remain until the first Constituent Assembly convened, but as equal partners: "The ministers delegated by the Kingdom of Serbia will take their oath according to the Serbian constitution to their ruler, and the ministers delegated by the National Council in Zagreb will take their oath to the National Council . . . before its president, Dr. Korošec."[68] Pašić reluctantly consented to this formula, and on November 9 a united state of the Serbs, Croats, and Slovenes was agreed upon, and Montenegro was also invited to join. The common ministry was partially filled, and the entire matter seemed closed until the Constituent Assembly.

Pašić's acceptance of the Geneva conference was only a tactic, however. Not only were the conclusions entirely alien to the whole thread of Pašić's policy, but he himself expected to head any common ministry and maintain conduct of foreign affairs. Instead, he was stung by the reminders of his interlocutors, including his own Serb compatriots, that, in his own words, "former Austria-Hungary [had] 8,000,000 South Slavs and Serbia 4,000,000, therefore twice as many; would it not therefore be right that a foreign minister in a common ministry be a Croat or a Slovene, instead of having a Serb as both the premier and minister of foreign affairs?" Though he protested that even these results were better than an impasse, he hinted, in a letter to Stojan Protić, deputy prime minister in charge of the Serbian cabinet at Corfu, that "in any case the regent can entirely and without limitations use his right and seek other crown advisers."[69] Protić took the hint and, on November 11, resigned from the cabinet on behalf of his Radical colleagues, who found that the Geneva ministry was a "travesty" and an

67. Janković and Krizman, *Gradja,* vol. 2, p. 514. The phrasing was typically ambiguous. It committed Pašić to the government, not to the State of the Slovenes, Croats, and Serbs.
68. Ibid., pp. 523–525.
69. Pašić to Stojan Protić in Corfu, Nov. 9, 1918, ibid., pp. 528–529.

"expression of mistrust in Serbia."[70] He urged Pašić to do the same. The Radical cabinet could not accept the limiting of Serbia's sovereignty at its prewar frontiers.

Stojan Protić believed that Serbia could no longer maintain the view that its government "internationally represented all of our people until the conclusion of peace," but in repudiating the Geneva conference he envisaged another solution that amounted to the same outdated position: he played the Pribićević card, assured that "we have reasons to believe that there are people in Zagreb who do not think like Trumbić, who is a conservative with the ideology of Starčević."[71] The best course was an agreement with the pliable forces in Zagreb and Sarajevo. Accordingly, only seven days after its beginning, the Serbian government crisis was resolved with the installation of a coalition cabinet, headed by Pašić, which included the members of the parties that opposed him in Geneva. Having committed the JO and the National Council to speedy unification, Pašić had to change the confederalist slant of the Geneva agreement. Trumbić and Korošec could only offer idle protests, moreover at great distance from their political base.

The Serbian government rightly placed its trust in Pribićević. He was increasingly the power arbiter in Zagreb and all along maintained covert ties with Belgrade. It was in response to one of his messages, urging that a common government immediately supplant the "separate" ones, that Momčilo Ninčić, one of the leading Radicals, hinted a campaign of Serb pressure on the National Council: "It seems to me," Ninčić wrote, "that the majority of Croats in Croatia will accept the idea of an inseparable and indivisible state of the Serbs, Croats, and Slovenes under the Karadjordjević dynasty only if it is tangibly proved to them that unless they quickly and sincerely accept that idea, all the Serbs will go over to Serbia without hesitation."[72] Soon thereafter, the Serbian military representative in Zagreb informed his command that Pašić's concessions in Geneva were too extensive and that the representatives of the National Council opposed them: "The majority in the National Council wishes to solve the question of annexation to Serbia and Montenegro without regard to the work and opinion of the JO and Mr. Korošec. Only the members of Starčević's party [SSP], who espouse the idea of autonomy for individual regions, wish to postpone this question until the return of the JO [to the homeland]."[73]

The SSP was not the only obstacle in Pribićević's way. Stjepan Radić emerged as a far more formidable opponent. Though Radić accepted the dissolution of Austria-Hungary, he became convinced that his peasant fol-

70. Ibid., p. 553.
71. Ibid., p. 554.
72. Ninčić to Pribićević, Nov. 16, 1918, ibid., p. 591.
73. Ibid., p. 636.

lowers were not receptive to the prospect of unification with Serbia, particularly not under the aegis of Serbian dynasty, and that the republican form of government was the common political denominator in the calls of the more articulate peasant rebels in northern Croatia.[74] Though the peasants may have thought, as one county administrator believed, that a republic simply meant "no military obligation, no taxes or other burdens," the actions of some segments in the spontaneous peasant movement during the transitional period were certainly political in nature.[75] There were repeated demands for the socialization of land and factories, for the end of price limits, elections of a constituent assembly on the basis of universal suffrage, and the establishment of an "American-style" republic, and there were even three completely autonomous peasant republics proclaimed for a brief time.[76] Radić took the pulse of the peasant demands and started espousing the cause of preserving Croat statehood within a republican polity.

Though Radić could hardly reverse the drive for a speedy unification pursued by the National Council's majority, he did propose a confederate state headed by three regents (the Serbian king, the Croatian Ban, and the president of the Slovene National Council); they were to name the only three ministers (for foreign affairs, food distribution, and defense), who would be responsible to the council of delegates sent by all the regional parliaments representing the members of the confederation: Slovenia, Croatia-Slavonia, Serbia-Montenegro, Bosnia-Hercegovina, Dalmatia, and Vojvodina, each with its own government.[77] The Central Committee rejected this proposal as an example of "extreme separatism,"[78] and during an all-night session on November 24, 1918, decided on immediate unification with Serbia and Montenegro. It elected a delegation of twenty-eight members who were to "execute without delay" the organization of the newly united state in agreement with the Serbian government and all the Serbian and Montenegrin parties.

---

74. On Radić's wartime policies see Bogdan Krizman, "Stjepan Radić i Hrvatska pučka seljačka stranka u prvom svjetskom ratu," *Časopis za suvremenu povijest*, vol. 2 (1970), no. 2, pp. 99–166. For a brief summary of the evolution of Radić-Pribićević relations see Hrvoje Matković, "Stjepan Radić i Svetozar Pribićević u jugoslavenskoj politici od ujedinjenja do šestojanuarske diktature," *Jugoslovenski istorijski časopis*, 1969, no. 4, pp. 148–153. For a detailed analysis of Pribićević's role during this period see the same author's *Svetozar Pribićević i Samostalna demokratska stranka do šestojanuarske diktature* (Zagreb, 1972), pp. 15–29.

75. Arhiv Instituta za historiju radničkog pokreta Hrvatske (AIHRPH), 1921/Sig. VI/C, Box I: Predstojništvo kr. kotarske oblasti, no. 82 prs. 1921, Donja Stubica, March 14, 1921.

76. Vidmar, "Prilozi gradji za povijest," pp. 116–117, 140. Three autonomous peasant republics were established in the course of peasant disturbances of November 1918: the Petrijevci Republic (near Valpovo), the Donji Miholjac Republic, and the Feričanci Republic (near Našice), all in Slavonia. Ibid., pp. 123, 148, 150. Quasi-Communist ministates were set up in Novo Mesto (Slovenia) and Banova Jaruga (Croatia). See Pero Morača, Milinko Djurović, and Dragan Marković, eds., *Četrdeset godina: Zbornik sećanja aktivista jugoslovenskog revolucionarnog radničkog pokreta*, vol. I (Belgrade, 1960), pp. 16–17, 18–21.

77. Šišić, *Dokumenti*, p. 271.

78. Janković and Krizman, *Gradja*, vol. 2, p. 641.

The National Council instructed its delegation to conduct the negotiations on the basis of special instructions, which included four key points. (1) The final organization of the state (constitution, state form, that is, monarchy or a republic, and so on) could be established only by the Constituent Assembly, which had yet to be elected. (2) Provisional legislative authority would be vested in the State Council, which would include representatives of Zagreb's National Council, the JO, and the Serbian and Montenegrin assemblies. (3) Until the decision of the Constituent Assembly, the governing power would be vested in the person of Regent Aleksandar, who would not be responsible to the State Council. He would appoint a ministry, which would have the approval of the State Council. (4) The ministerial cabinet would attend to joint businesses, while all the other matters would be vested in the regional governments, which would be responsible to the regional assemblies.[79] The National Council's directives were a compromise between federalism and centralism and were principally inspired by the provisions of the Corfu Declaration.

Independently of the action of Zagreb's National Council, the Serbian government was seeking to promote unilateral unifications with Serbia in Vojvodina, Bosnia-Hercegovina, and Montenegro. In Novi Sad on November 25 a special regional assembly proclaimed the unification of Entente-occupied parts of the Banat, Bačka, and Baranja with Serbia; similar action was contemplated in Bosnia-Hercegovina. On November 26, in Montenegro, occupied by the Serbian troops since mid-November, the "Great National Assembly of the Serb people in Montenegro," specially assembled for the occasion, proclaimed the dethronement of the Petrović dynasty and Montenegro's unification with Serbia.

Stjepan Radić was one of the twenty-eight notables elected to serve as members of the National Council's delegation, which was about to depart for Belgrade. He was the only member of the central committee to vote against the unification proposal. Before the vote he delivered his famous speech, the often cited "final warning" against the National Council's reckless leap into uncertainty ("like drunken geese into a fog"), which was in his opinion being taken against the will of the overwhelming majority of the Croat people.[80] His struggle against the unification thus began even before the Yugoslav state was formally inaugurated.

The National Council's delegation arrived in Belgrade on November 30. Because Pašić and most of the other Serbian leaders were still abroad, it fell

79. Šišić, *Dokumenti*, pp. 275–276.

80. Stjepan Radić, *Politički spisi*, comp. Zvonimir Kulundžić (Zagreb, 1971), pp. 323–335. It should be stressed that Radić recorded this speech "from memory" two years later. A heavily censored version of his remarks appeared in the HPSS newspaper *Dom* (Home) on March 25, and 31, 1920, and in a special pamphlet *Gospodska politika bez naroda i proti narodu: Govor predsjednika hrvatske seljačke stranke nar. zast. Stjepana Radića na noćnoj sudbonosnoj sjednici Narodnog Vieća dne 24 studena 1918* (Zagreb, 1920).

to Regent Aleksandar to play the key role in the negotiations with the Zagreb delegation, and he took the opportunity, with Pribićević's help, to speed matters up and reach a unification agreement without Pašić. Despite a certain opposition from Pavelić, Pribićević managed to persuade the delegates that details could be settled later and that they need not insist on full implementation of their directives for the conduct of the negotiations; as Pavelić recalled events, Pribićević thought that the delegation's address to the regent should "only be an outpouring of loyalty."[81] The compromise unification address, read by Pavelić in the presence of Aleksandar on December 1, 1918, was in fact little more than a generalized statement; it mentioned a few wishes and suggestions but said nothing about conditions or safeguards. It was understood that the regent's hands were unbound. In replying to this meek address, Aleksandar proclaimed the unification of Serbia with the lands represented by the National Council into a single unitary Kingdom of the Serbs, Croats, and Slovenes.[82] The Yugoslav state was thus established.

The superior power of Serbian government led to a unification that did not meet even the basic desires of those who wanted a federal state organization. It did not establish any guarantees against the dominance of Belgrade, whose armies were already occupying former Habsburg South Slavic possessions and Montenegro, realizing the age-old dream of Serb unification. Given the role of the Serbian state in the construction of Yugoslavia and the actual if not formal continuation of Serbian state institutions after the unification, the Serbs could adjust to the new circumstances without a feeling of loss, without being deprived of their sense of national individuality.

For the other nationalities, the unification was not so simple. Croats and Slovenes, barely a month after the end of their long-standing association with the Habsburg Monarchy, were now bound in a unitary state with Serbia and Montenegro. The decision to unite with Serbia was made for them by circumstances and by a class of political men who did not know how to establish or wield political power. None of the South Slavic nationalities, including the Serbs, had had an opportunity to express desires or preferences by means of a popular referendum; among the Croats, if not others, a democratic test of popular sentiment would probably have shown a reservoir of opposition to the unification. Among the Slovenes, who were in danger of partition between Italy and Austria, opposition was tempered by external menaces. In any case, once the characteristics of the new state were firmly established, various forms of homegrown opposition asserted themselves in all non-Serb areas, even among the educated and propertied classes (notably on the Italian-threatened eastern Adriatic littoral), which were considered strongly unitarist in 1918.

81. Ante Pavelić, "G. Dr. A. Pavelić o izjavi g. Sv. Pribićevića," *Novosti*, Nov. 28, 1926, p. 13.
82. Šišić, *Dokumenti,* pp. 280–283.

Svetozar Pribićević

Stjepan Radić

Nikola Pašić   Regent Aleksandar

Among the Croats particularly, the unitarist idea represented one step toward the solution of a considerable problem of regionalism. It also stood as an ever-present danger to the full affirmation of Croat statehood, especially since unitarism was very attractive to the articulate urban strata. But unitarism, based as it was on the idea of Slavic reciprocity, could only be maintained when it was truly reciprocal. When the national question emerged in the new Yugoslav state, chiefly as a result of the dominant position of the Serbian ruling classes, unitarist ideology lost most of its impact, and the individual South Slavic nations moved toward a final consolidation. Once the individuality of these nationalities was finally accepted, first of all by themselves, a discussion on their respective rights could commence.

PART II

Great Serbia and Great Yugoslavia

Institutions

> Pored Drima, blizu Vezirova Mosta,
> Videh Starog Kralja, svetiteljska lika.
>   .   .   .   .   .
> A, daleko, napred, dodje prizor novi:
> Kao da, odjednom, Kralja oblak ovi—
> Spustio se s neba, njegov prolaz čeka.
> Sve je izgledalo k'o vizija neka.
> Pa se, namah, razbi taj oblak, k'o para.
> Ja poznah, u Kralju, lik Kosovskog Cara.

> Along the Drin, not far from the Vezir's Bridge,
> I saw the saintly figure of the Old King.
>   .   .   .   .   .
> And far away, ahead, a new display set in:
> As if a cloud suddenly engulfed the King—
> Dropping from the sky, in front of his passage.
> The whole apparition seemed like as dream.
> And then, all at once, the cloud and mist lifted.
> I saw in the King—the Kosovo tsar.
>   Vladimir Stanimirović

Of all the many differences between the political culture of Serbia and of the lands united to it in 1918, those in the area of state institutions were most evident. Nineteenth-century Serbian politics had of course been dominated by the "mutual extermination of two mortally discordant dynasties," the Obrenovićes and Kardjordjevićes, whose methods of struggle engendered the bitter conviction, even among Westernized statesmen, that "force amounts to everything in public life and that there are moments when one must choose between killing or being killed."[1] Not only were political altercations in

---

1. Slobodan Jovanović, *Vlada Aleksandra Obrenovića*, vol. 2 (Belgrade, 1935), p. 421.

Austria-Hungary far tamer, but, what is of equal importance, no institutional tokens of statehood, not even the Croatian Sabor, could express the national ideologies of the Monarchy's South Slavs as completely as the manifestations of their Serb counterpart in the monarchic, military, and ecclesiastical institutions of independent Serbia. The unrestrained extension of Serbian state institutions to the "new territories" in 1918 accented the difference. Even if steps had been taken to change the composition of Serbian monarchy, legislature, judiciary, and army in a pan-Yugoslav direction, much time would had been needed to arrive at a new quality. Since changes of that sort were never really attempted, Serbia's institutions were able to exercise their traditional role in a vastly different state.

The institution of the monarchy was interconnected with the most decisive events in the modern history of Serbia. The forms of headship produced by the insurrections of 1804 and 1815 were necessarily princely. Karadjordje and Miloš Obrenović developed in the Ottoman frame of society and emulated its institutions. Miloš, Serbia's "little sultan," treated the state as if it were his personal *damızlık* (Turkish for grazing land). But despite these Oriental effluvia, the founders of modern Serbian dynasties also saw themselves as the continuers and restorers of the Nemanjić throne. Karadjordje included the double-headed white eagle of the Nemanjićes on his personal signet.

Princely power was restricted after 1842, during the rule of the Constitutionalist party, though never firmly enough to eliminate its falling back into despotism. After the Obrenovićes were restored to power in 1858, they often brought the monarchy into disrepute with their intensely personal regimes. The prestige of the crown was restored by Petar Karadjordjević, who genuinely believed in parliamentary power. Humble, self-deprecating, the popular *Čika Pera* (Uncle Pete) was less avuncular than hard-tested. He spent most of his life in exile in Switzerland, France, and Montenegro, following the overthrow of his father, Prince Aleksandar, in 1858, when Petar was a boy of fourteen. He graduated from Saint-Cyr, fought in the Foreign Legion in the Franco-Prussian War, and earned the Legion of Honor at Viller-Sexel (January 9, 1871). During the Bosnian insurrection of 1875–1876, under the pseudonym Petar Mrkonjić, he led a number of Serb guerrilla actions against the Turks and local Muslims. Upon the overthrow of the Obrenovićes in 1903 and the summons to assume the Serbian throne, Petar was already ripe to rule.[2]

Serbian royalist propagandists liked to say that the new king was the head of a dynasty in peasant boots. They stressed his acquaintance with the exiled Bakunin and the liberal convictions that were evident from his early transla-

2. For a biography of Petar I see Milenko M. Vukićević, *Kralj Petar od rodjenja do smrti* (Belgrade, 1922).

tion of Mill's *On Liberty*. But though Petar undoubtedly harbored democratic sentiments and preferred simplicity, avoding the luxurious Western tastes of his doomed predecessor, his populist image was also the stuff of dynastic legend, inseparable from the redemptive themes of Serbian history. His bronze crown, cast from a piece of Karadjordje's first cannon, linked him to the legacy of the 1804 insurrection, and his army's victories in the Balkan wars assured him the prize of avenger, making up for the loss of Serbian statehood at Kosovo. In 1915–1916, in the disaster of retreat before the armies of the Central Powers, Petar was seen at the "new Lazar," the prince of the Kosovo defeat and a saintly martyr for liberty. "The old man," said his elder son, Prince Djordje, "got it into his head to die and become a saint, like Lazar at Kosovo. He put on the soldiers' cap, took up a rifle, and joined the men in the trenches."[3]

Hapless Djordje, who renounced his claim to the throne in 1909 in favor of his younger brother Aleksandar, apparently believed that his beloved father's mildness could at least in part be attributed to ripe old age: "Our democracy will end up exactly as our aristocracy," he said to his uncle Prince Arsen in 1916, during Regent Aleksandar's visit to Paris. "If somebody has a different opinion, a pistol to his forehead. Hell, we are bullies. That Uncle Pete is the way he is, that's another matter. But I would like to see him were he young and not afraid of the costs. He is as much a democrat as Pašić is a Gladstone."[4] But as Djordje's private quarrel with Aleksandar deepened into near fratrophobia, he was convinced that Aleksandar was the main danger to constitutional monarchy: "Aleksandar did not like any comparisons between his ideas and those of our father. Such comparisons always ended fatally for Aleksandar."[5]

The regent—and after Petar's death in August 1921, king—was a proud, withdrawn man, who hardly ever lived up to the rash reputation of his house. But though he kept a tight grip over his turbulent emotions, he was not forgiving. He brooded over real or imagined injuries, lulling the offenders into a false sense of security, and ultimately exacted his revenge.[6] In due course, his influence became apparent in the ranks of the major Serbian

---

3. Ivan Meštrović, *Uspomene na političke ljude i dogadjaje* (Buenos Aires, 1961), p. 84.
4. Ibid., p. 94.
5. Djordje Karadjordjević, *Istina o mome životu* (Belgrade, 1969), p. 380.
6. No scholarly biography of Aleksandar Karadjordjević is yet available. The following works are either hagiographic or totally negative: Stephen Graham, *Alexander of Yugoslavia: The Story of the King Who Was Murdered at Marseilles* (New Haven, 1939); Stjepan F. Vukojević, *Aleksandar I: Tvorac države i ujedinitelj* (Belgrade, 1937); J.-N. Faure-Biguet, *Le roi Alexandre Ier de Yougoslavie* (Paris, 1936); Svetozar Pribićević, *Diktatura kralja Aleksandra*, ed. Sava N. Kosanović, trans. Andra Milosavljević (Belgrade, 1952). Pribićević's volume was first published in emigration in Paris (1933) and records a personal view of the unitarist politician's break with the king. Pribićević understandably obscured his role in encouraging Aleksandar's autocratic tendencies at the time when he was the king's friend and ally.

parties. In his attempts to impose himself as the dominant political element in all parties, Aleksandar did not hesitate to undermine the influence of the otherwise unconstrained party leaders by building up his own factions, some-times by awarding subtle—or not so subtle—favors that only he was in a position to bestow. Pašić, who aspired to dominate the youthful regent, felt Aleksandar's initially gloved hand within his own Radical party, but the regent's initiatives bypassed no major party that was in the least capable of coming to power. In this way, Aleksandar became instrumental in precipitat-ing cabinet crises and imposing political leaders more favorable to his auto-cratic designs.

It soon became evident that the regent and his personal retinue were an extraparliamentary force to be reckoned with. One of their opponents, the leader of Serbia's tiny Republican party, noted in 1922 that in Yugoslavia the king "both reigns and governs":

> The defense ministry is entirely removed from the government and belongs only to the crown. The minister of defense is not a responsible member of the government, but is some sort of royal plenipotentiary. . . . But this is not all. The ministry of foreign affairs has also been removed from the authority and control of the government. It has been established that during the [war] the monarch communicated with our envoys abroad without the agreement, nay without the knowledge, of the government.[7]

Strongmen of Aleksandar's stripe, nihilistic monarchs or generals in charge of "nonpartisan blocs in cooperation with the government," were a regional phenomenon in the unstable and half-made societies of interwar Eastern Europe.[8] In that sense, Aleksandar was not unique. The distinct feature of his reach for complete power, which he finally realized after the royal coup d'état of January 6, 1929, was that it was played out in Yugoslavia's multinational society, where the regent's initiatives on behalf of greater central power, vested in his own hands, strengthened the impres-sion that he had not risen above his dynasty's purely Serbian affiliations. In March 1920, according to a Croat official who suffered Aleksandar's wrath by taking a moderate course against Stjepan Radić, already the leader of Croat opposition, the regent "spoke rather sharply, to the effect that order must be brought and no concession made at any price. 'Either his [Radić's] head or mine, while I am at the responsible post'—he said."[9]

Aleksandar was fully aware that the most outspoken detractors of his dynasty were some of the leaders of Yugoslavia's non-Serb national move-

7. Jaša M. Prodanović, "Kralj i vlada i upravlja," *Republika*, Sept. 14, 1922, p. 1.

8. On this subject see Milorad Ekmečić, *Osnove gradjanske diktature u Evropi izmedju dva svjetska rata*, 2d rev. ed. (Sarajevo, 1967), pp. 12–13.

9. Cited in Hrvoje Matković, "Odnos Aleksandra Karadjordjevića prema političkom djelovanju Matka Laginje," *Časopis za suvremenu povijest*, vol. 6 (1974), no. 3, p. 43.

ments, particularly those in Radić's peasant and republican bloc. Radić never suggested that Serbia should dethrone its dynasty, but he did assert that, although the monarchical order might well be the appropriate system of supreme state authority in Serbia, it was no longer fitting in Croatia. This was sufficient to make the defense of monarchy the touchstone of Yugoslavist unitarism. "Let us remember," commented the editorial writer in the main Radical daily, "that Mr. Radić is against monarchy, because the Serbs and Croats, according to him, are two peoples. As a result, his wish for two separate states could easily be accomplished—by way of a republic."[10] The doctrine of *narodno jedinstvo* was therefore confirmed in the institution of the monarchy, because only those who distinguished between the Serbs and Croats could find fault in the reign of a Serbian dynasty over Croatia. Moreover, the monarchical system also assured Serbian supremacy. It was the visible symbol of Serbia's state continuity. The construction of a modern Serbian monarchy was a "reality and a fact," which was a "consequence of [Serbia's] general historical development." When this state of things is "clearly noted and underlined . . . the whole republican system falls like a house of cards."[11]

The indispensable monarchy had to be defended by force of arms. František Zach's suggestion of 1844 that the "whole [Serbian] state should be given a military character" came into its own during the Karadjordjević restoration.[12] The Serbian performance in the Balkan wars established the army's solid reputation, and the dazzling blaze of victory in the early battles of the Great War (Cer, Kolubara) and the subsequent triumphs, at Kajmak-čalan in September 1916 and at Dobro Polje in September 1918, overawed all friends of Serbia and intimidated its enemies. Politicians of skeptical temper, even those Radicals who recalled how the army hectored them under the Obrenovićes, had to admit that the armed forces successfully completed their historical mission and had a no-less-hallowed task after the unification of guarding "our national state, which had to wait twenty centuries for its establishment."[13]

Unhappily, the Serbian army, though battle-tested, disciplined, and certainly loyal in comparison with the manpower available to the National Council in Zagreb, was increasingly prone to corruption and arbitrariness. The Spartan simplicity of its legendary marshals, men like Stepa Stepanović and Živojin Mišić, was becoming a rarity in the officer corps. The rank and file, many of whom had been on the march since the beginning of the Balkan wars in 1912, were tired and weary. The wars had cost the army some

10. R., "Monarhija!" *Samouprava*, Feb. 22, 1921, p. 1.

11. Ibid.

12. Dragoslav Stranjaković, "Kako je postalo Garašaninovo 'Načertanije,' " *Spomenik SKA*, vol. 91, p. 101.

13. R. [Momčilo Ivanić], "Naš vojni budžet," *Radikal*, Oct. 28, 1921, p. 1.

370,000 men—almost half of all those who fought in Serbian uniform. The remaining military commanders, whose very survival was taken by some romantics as evidence of unnatural selection, could not resist the lucrative political advantage to be gained through the manipulation of the army's genuine merits. The Monarchy's South Slavs were gradually worn down by the constant reminders that their liberty was purchased by a sea of Serbian blood. The honorifics lavished upon the Triumphatrix of the Salonika front increased in direct proportion to the sullying of the army's previously untarnished reputation. None contributed more to this moral ruin than the so-called White Hand, a secret proregent officers' society, which "slowly warped into a camarilla."[14]

The White Hand had its origins in the military conspiracy which overthrew the Obrenovićes in 1903. The dominant faction among the conspiratorial group consisted of officers who sought to carve out a privileged position for themselves, reminding King Petar that it was they who brought him to the throne. This group, better known as the Black Hand, formally constituted itself as a secret organization in 1911, under the name Unification or Death, for the purpose of waging a revolutionary struggle on behalf of Serbian unification. The extent of the Black Hand's part in the Sarajevo assassination is still contested. But it is certain that the Black Hand's methods of struggle were far more prejudicial to Serbia's internal stability than to the country's external enemies. To combat the Black Hand, Regent Aleksandar, sometime around 1914, began cultivating the other faction of the old conspiratorial group of officers. This group, in 1917, or even as early as 1914, became the White Hand, the aim of which was to organize the dynastic loyalists and "thereby continue the struggle against the internal enemy."[15] After the rigged trial of the Black Hand leaders and the purge of their adherents in 1917, the White Hand became all powerful in the Serbian armed forces, and its determination to stamp out "internal enemies" hypertrophied after the unification.

Stojan Protić noted in 1921 that he was not aware that the White Hand officers formed an organization. The society was, it seems, more like an informal cabal, but the informal structure did not lessen its effectiveness. Though Protić may have been confident that any efficient government could easily check the White Hand's "unneccessary eagerness and errors," other observers viewed the group as a cancerous growth for which the "Parliament and the government meant nothing":

14. Stojan M. Protić, "Crna i Bela Ruka?" ibid., Dec. 25, 1921, p. 1. For the history of the White Hand see Branislav Gligorijević, "Uloga vojnih krugova u 'rešavanju' političke krize u Jugoslaviji 1924. godine," *Vojnoistorijski glasnik,* vol. 23 (1972), no. 1, pp. 161–169.
15. D. Dj. O. [Dragutin Dj. Okanović], "Postoji li 'Bela Ruka'?" *Smotra,* April 8, 1924, p. 2.

They provoke crises and influence their course and solutions. . . . They tear decrees, promote, and pension [officers]. *They have special telephones at their disposal,* and, by admission of one of their members, they have *their own police and detectives.* They organize violent attacks, hold secret meetings, denounce and imprison whomever they please. In order to be closer to each other, they change posts and establish separate commands. They influence censorship, shape the course of investigations, and, day by day, continue undermining what little is left of our legal system, debasing the country to the level of an ordinary colony.[16]

The all-powerful "they," also charged with wholesale pecuniary corruption and the taking of kickbacks from military provisionment, were most feared because of the regent's favor and their apparent readiness to foster the establishment of his personal regime.[17] Colonel Petar Živković (1879–1947), later general, commander of the royal guard, and premier during the early stages of Aleksandar's dictatorship (1929–1932), the "first among the court's favorites and Aleksandar's most influential adviser,"[18] was among the White Hand leaders who encouraged the regent's autocratic tendencies and strengthened him in the belief that military force was the best cure for the country's national question. The greatness of the army, according to one White Hand officer, was that in "critical moments it assumed the political role and in that way, facing great events, it prepared the country and itself for great deeds."[19] In the "newly liberated" territories that meant that the Serbian army was cast in the unpopular role of gendarme; even worse, its commanders viewed themselves as practicing preventive political warfare against any non-Serb national movement. The result was a series of unfortunate skirmishes, which lost the army whatever goodwill it may have had initially among the Croats and Bosnian Muslims.

Among the peasants, especially, the army already had a bad name, because it had been used to disarm the population of former Austro-Hungarian provinces at the close of the war and then to safeguard landlord properties and suppress republican, socialist, and anti-Serb agitation. The Serbian army personnel had certainly not won any friends by acting, as they often did, as if they were patrolling enemy territory. One army edict actually used the word "enemy." This edict, of April 28, 1919, establishing the jurisdiction of military courts over a wide-ranging set of civil cases, as authorized by Serbian military code, declared that "the inhabitants of enemy districts,

---

16. Dragomir D. Ikonić, "Belorukaško krdo . . . ," *Republika,* Jan. 21, 1922, p. 1.
17. Dragomir D. Ikonić, "Na putu propadanja," ibid., June 8, 1922, p. 2; "Bela i Crna Ruka," ibid., Nov. 24, 1920, p. 2.
18. Karadjordjević, *Istina,* p. 423.
19. D. Dj. O. [Dragutin Dj. Okanović], "Vojskina politika," *Smotra,* March 21, 1924, p. 1.

occupied by the army, are subject to the jurisdiction of military courts.''[20] This was a blatant misappropriation of authority, quite contrary to the realities that led to the unification, and engendered great discomfiture, especially since the army applied brutal, coercive, and, as one historian dubbed them, Miloš-style punishments, frequently even without the formality of a military court-martial. The most infamous of these was the practice of meting out corporal punishment by blows with clubs or truncheons.[21]

The last was especially appalling to the Croats. Since 1869, when the Croatian Sabor abolished all corporal punishment, thus ending a form of retribution that had existed as part of old urbarial relations, the Croat peasants had not experienced physical penalties. Now, after half a century, the unification—though the contents of Serbian military laws were never publicized—had brought corporal punishment back. Beatings administered by clubs became so much an accepted thing that in some military districts local commanders even promulgated their own codes for the use of corporal punishment. One particularly outrageous example was the Penal Ordinance instituted by Lieutenant-Colonel Petar Teslić, a Serb from Croatia, who commanded the Zagreb Infantry Regiment. Among the numerous provisions of the Ordinance, twenty-five blows were to be inflicted on soldiers or civilians found guilty of affronts to the king or because they espoused republicanism. The same prescription was reserved for military deserters, with the proviso that all the relatives of the deserters would be jailed as hostages until the deserters returned. Plunder was to be punished "by firing squad, and moreover immediately on the spot." Concealment of venereal disease and "where it was obtained" brought on ten blows. The last of Teslić's "laws" was an example of their originator's unerring touch: "He who beats mildly will have the same number of sharp blows measured to himself."[22]

In Slovenia, which was never thought of as a distinct part of Great Serbia, military authorities were far more restrained. But in northern Croatia and Bosnia, and to a lesser extent in Dalmatia, military assaults and beatings became a daily staple. Innkeepers and waitresses were taken to the barracks and beaten for objecting to the use of the term Great Serbia as a substitute for Yugoslavia. Respected burgers were assaulted and had their guns confiscated in their private preserves by military interlopers. Boats were confiscated for military purposes without explanation or subsequent satisfaction. There were cases of wholesale pillage of private property. And in one instance a Zagreb city policeman who shot a soldier in self-defense during a tavern brawl was

20. Cited in Milan Rojc, "Prilike u Hrvatskoj," *Nova Evropa*, vol. 2 (1921), no. 2, p. 57.

21. Dragoslav Janković, "Društveni i politički odnosi u Kraljevstvu Srba, Hrvata i Slovenaca uoči stvaranja Socijalističke radničke partije Jugoslavije (komunista): 1.XII.1918–20.IV.1919," *Istorija XX veka: zbornik radova*, vol. 1 (1959), p. 93. The reference is to Prince Miloš Obrenović's "Turkish" depotism.

22. Cited in Ferdo Čulinović, *Jugoslavija izmedju dva rata*, vol. 1 (Zagreb, 1961), pp. 178–180.

himself set upon by a military unit in full battle array.[23] Stjepan Radić related the following incident that took place in Topusko (Banija) in January 1921, involving a group of gendarmes who were being used to police the rural areas:

> Sixteen gendarmes came to the village on orders from an officer and proceeded from house to house, stripping all occupants naked. Then they placed bayonets on one side and Pašić's picture on the other, forcing [the peasants] to kiss Pašić's picture and repeat, "The bayonet is your Mother of God and Pašić's picture is your God the Father." The people were silent and nobody submitted to the gunbutt. So they say over there. We shall not even go to church with those who do such things.[24]

The army's abuses in Bosnia were made worse by the unchecked activities of paramilitary groups, notably the exvolunteers from Russia and the veterans of guerrilla formations who operated in the forefront of the Serbian army (Chetniks). These men, 25,000 at most, were promised land after victory, the prospect that led some 70,000 persons to seek the status of volunteer veterans after the unification. In Bosnia-Hercegovina, Kosovo, and Macedonia, where much of the land belonged to Muslim feudatories, the likelihood that the predominantly Serb volunteers would benefit from the agrarian reform of Muslim estates introduced a communal note in the volunteer question. Moreover, many exvolunteers were squaring accounts with the Muslim population, whether Bosnian Muslims, Albanians, or Turks, who, out of loyalty to Turkey or hatred of Serbia, or both, had favored the cause of Berlin and Vienna in the Great War. In addition, in Bosnia-Hercegovina, Muslims predominated in the ill-famed auxiliary militia (*Schutzkorps*), which was used by the Austrian military authorities to intimidate the Serb population, and whose members were responsible for hundreds of Serb casualties inflicted in search-and-destroy missions, dominated by lynch courts. The activities of the *Schutzkorps* in part were undertaken as retaliations for the misdeeds of Serbian Chetniks, who were fairly active in attacking the Muslims of eastern Bosnia in the fall of 1914. After 1918, however, nearly all Muslims became fair game for the volunteers. In the opinion of the chief Muslim political journal, the volunteers formed a "separate social class, which can be compared only to that of the hated Roman praetorians."[25] In Rogatica they appropriated livestock belonging to the Muslims, but in eastern Hercegovina (Bileća, Gacko), where the worst excesses took place, Muslims were systematically assaulted. In one planned massacre in June

23. Rojc, "Prilike u Hrvatskoj," pp. 61–62.

24. Arhiv Instituta za historiju radničkog pokreta Hrvatske (AIHRPH), 1924/Sig. VI/C, Box 2: Predstojništvo kr. kotarske oblasti, no. 393 prs. 1924, Djakovo, Oct. 12, 1924.

25. "Iskrena riječ dobrovoljcima," *Pravda*, July 17, 1920, pp. 2–3.

1920, the gendarmerie apparently aided Serb vigilantes.[26] In Sandžak, the Muslims rose in resistance to abuses, and some of those arrested were held in jail for two years before trial.[27]

Some high military authorities did attempt to restrain beatings and other abuses. And certainly not all the blame should fall on the Serbians. Stojan Protić blamed Pribićević's followers—Serbs of Croatia. There were also Croat officers, former members of the Austro-Hungarian army or of the Serbian volunteer corps, who had a hand in the army's repressive actions after they were introduced to the Serbian military apparatus. Still, attempts at reversing the "truncheon system" were halfhearted at best. Not only was the Serbian army used even in purely civilian police matters, such as searches and arrests, but, once the Serbian military laws were extended statewide, the Serbian army's customary prerogatives, which had no tradition in the former Austro-Hungarian territories, necessarily provoked intense resistance.[28] The extensive jurisdiction of military courts and the incarceration of relatives of military deserters as hostages were prevalent practices.[29]

Immediately after the unification, the Serbian army command proceeded to fashion the new national army on the former Austro-Hungarian territory. Six infantry regiments were authorized. These were built on a nucleus of officers and soldiers who had lately been under the command of the National Council. The Serbian army staff appointed three regimental commanders; the National Council appointed the rest, as well as all the other officers. Though the beginning of the new force seemed sensible, the former Austro-Hungarian officers soon found themselves not only in subordinate, but in cast-off positions. They were accepted as a temporary evil, and discrimination followed them from the moment they applied to join the new army.

Only former Austro-Hungarian and Montengrin officers had to apply to join Yugoslavia's army. Serbian officers simply changed the coat-of-arms on their caps, though even the change of name was sometimes considered a concession. The seal of the Royal Serbian City Command was affixed to military documents in Osijek well into 1919. In fact, except for seals and appellation, no outward sign distinguished the new Yugoslav army from its Serbian predecessor. The uniforms, ranks, and regulations were all Serbian, as were the principal military and civilian medals, the Order of White Eagle, the Order of Saint Sava, and Karadjordje's Star. Drawing on figures and symbols of strictly Serb national tradition, these decorations dated from the pre-1914 period, the first two from the reign of King Milan Obrenović.[30] In

26. "Dobrovoljačka nasilja u Rogatici," ibid., June 6, 1920, p. 1; "Bilećki slučaj," ibid., Aug. 7, 1920, p. 1.
27. "Prilike u Sandžaku," *Demokratija*, Jan. 26, 1921, p. 2.
28. Janković, "Društveni i politički odnosi," pp. 92–94.
29. Rudolf Horvat, *Hrvatska na mučilištu* (Zagreb, 1942), pp. 82–83.
30. Desanka Nikolić, *Naša odlikovanja do 1941* (Belgrade, 1971), pp. 47–50, 56–58, 81–83.

the navy, where Serbia had no tradition or experience, the authorities had no choice but to accept 117 former Austro-Hungarian officers in 1919, among them two rear-admirals, Dragutin Prica and Metod Koch; the latter, a Slovene, was the chief of the naval department until 1920. Without them, the Yugoslav navy could not have functioned. But here also the former Austro-Hungarian officers were made to feel second-best.[31]

In the new army one of the chief grievances was the question of rank. In the Austro-Hungarian army, officers waited as much as twenty years to be promoted to the rank of major; in the old Serbian army, officers customarily became majors after eleven years of active service, and after twenty-one years most were already colonels. Since ranks were retained in the new Yugoslav army, officers accepted from the Austro-Hungarian army, all of them with at least twelve years of elementary and secondary education, found themselves inferior in rank to much younger Serbian officers, often totally unschooled peasant lads who had been rapidly promoted during the long war period since 1912. The governments of Romania and Italy took such differences into account in the integration of their conationals, former Austro-Hungarian officers, within their respective armies. Yugoslavia, quite the contrary, made an effort to show how unwelcome the Austro-Hungarian officers were by reducing their pay and sending them to posts far from their native areas, most often in Macedonia, Kosovo, or Serbia.[32] For all that, extensive discrimination was not their chief complaint. Croat officers, especially, were most offended by direct attacks on their national pride. Since patriotism and loyalty, above all, meant devotion to Serbian state traditions, non-Serb officers were frequently found at fault. For example, as in most state services, the equality of Latin and Cyrillic scripts was almost entirely ignored in the armed forces. As a result, the use of Latin script was often taken as evidence of "antistate sentiment." Faced with such standards, many non-Serb officers resigned their commissions. One captain, punished for his refusal to use Cyrillic, protested to a Croat politician in these words:

> We, officers, are upbraided by the "patriots," who claim that we are Frankists, Austrians—that we are unreliable. I ask myself, can I, can any man with a morsel of honor, remain in this kind of army? My service as an active officer in the former A-H army should not imply that I am a traitor—though this was said to us at the end of 1918 and the beginning of 1919—or a thief. But the treatment

31. Jovan Vasiljević, "Stvaranje ratne mornarice Kraljevine Jugoslavije (oktobar 1918–septembar 1923)," *Istorija XX veka: zbornik radova*, vol. 11 (1970), pp. 167–172, 192–193.

32. Arhiv Hrvatske, Rukopisna ostavština Dr. Djure Šurmina, Box 3: Fogl. 38 (1920), "Zašto bježe iz vojske?" This report, prepared for a Croat autonomist leader, was designed to show why the non-Serb officers were leaving the Yugoslav army. The author, probably himself an officer, admitted that his conclusions were defective in the case of lower ranks (lieutenants and lieutenant-captains). Their promotions in the Serbian army were somewhat slower than in the former Austro-Hungarian armed forces.

that we are receiving from our superiors and among many of our people is tantamount to the desert of [traitors and thieves]. . . . I am a Croat, body and soul, and I shall not allow myself to be Serbianized. And when I am ordered, moreover under physical duress, to use Cyrillic, it is plain to me where this is leading. I shall not be deprived of my nationality.[33]

Often, however, resignations were refused, and in some cases the petitioners were imprisoned.[34] In time, Croat officers constituted an insignificant minority, 1,000 out of the total of 10,000 officers in 1938.[35] Of the 191 staff officers on the eve of the Second World War, only 31 were Croats and 22 Slovenes; the rest were Serbs.[36]

National inequality in the armed forces was reflected in frequent desertions and occasional mutinies by non-Serb, especially Croat, soldiers. There were scattered rebellions in the Croat regiments in Osijek (December 18, 1918) and Našice (January 21 to 22, 1919), both in troubled Slavonia. Certainly the most serious mutiny took place in Varaždin (Croatia) on July 22, 1919. The rebels were leftist republicans and under the influence of Béla Kun's Hungarian Council Republic.[37] The Croat recruits objected not only to forms of Serbian supremacy in the army but also to wretched living conditions, dangerous missions against Albanian insurgents, unhygienic surroundings that bred typhoid fever, and unspeakable rations.[38]

The disproportionate concentration of Serbs was also a prominent feature of the gendarmerie, a branch of the military service that carried out police responsibilities but was distinct from the local police. The gendarmerie was actually an extension of the prewar Serbian gendarmerie. Svetozar Pribićević, Yugoslavia's new minister of the interior, in one of his first official

33. Ibid., Fogl. 36/1, Captain Marko Škuljević to Djuro Šurmin, Zaprešić (Croatia), May 8, 1920.

34. Ibid., Box 5, anonymous Croat officer to Vladimir Lunaček, editor of the Zagreb daily *Obzor*, July 31, 1919.

35. On this and other matters relating to national inequality in Yugoslavia's army, with particular reference to the Croats, see Rudolf Bićanić, *Ekonomska podloga hrvatskog pitanja*, 2d ed. (Zagreb, 1938), pp. 120–125. There are, however, no published official statistics on the national makeup of Yugoslavia's officier corps immediately after the war or, for that matter, for the whole interwar period. Progovernment authors, such as Bogdan Prica, conceded that the "higher officer corps of the continental army was made up almost entirely of the Serbians and the naval officer corps almost entirely of the Prečani [that is, people from the former Austro-Hungarian Monarchy, though not necessarily non-Serbs]." Prica also claimed ("even without concrete facts") that the national makeup of officers schooled after 1918 was "truly ideally just from the tribal point of view" (Bogdan Prica, *Hrvatsko pitanje i brojke* [Belgrade, 1937], p. 42).

36. Djordje Dimitrijević, *Generalštabni oficiri Kraljevine Jugoslavije* (London, 1974), cited by Zoran Raketić, "Jedan prilog za istoriju Vojske pre 1941.," *Naša reč*, vol. 28 (1976), p. 9.

37. For more details on this incident see Josip I. Vidmar, comp., "Prilozi gradji za povijest radničkog pokreta i KP 1919. god.," *Arhivski vjesnik*, vol. 2 (1959), no. 2, pp. 160–172, 179–180, 190–194, 196–197.

38. Arhiv Hrvatske, Rukopisna ostavština Dr. Djure Šurmina, Box 3: Fogl. 34, anonymous Croat soldier to the Zagreb newspaper *Hrvat*, Niš (Serbia), Jan. 9, 1920.

acts in February 1919, recognized the Serb gendarmerie on a statewide basis and raised its personnel to 12,000 men.[39] The civil administrators were supposed to rely on the gendarmes in matters of law enforcement, but since this higly centralized corps was completely under the military's thumb, efforts by the local authorities to moderate the gendarmes' often arbitrary actions soon became considerably frustrated. Moreover, the corps was purged of large numbers of gendarmes who were inherited from the Austro-Hungarian gendarmerie.[40] The national composition of the gendarmerie and its highly politicized character contributed to the lack of sensitivity, which its members repeatedly demonstrated in operations involving non-Serb national movements.

The immediate conjunction of the crown and the military, rooted in Serbian political tradition and expressing Serbian national ideology, presented a great obstacle to equitable relations in Yugoslavia. The institutions of supreme power and armed compulsion remained strictly Serbian and closed to the influence of non-Serb political leaders. Moreover, through groups like the White Hand, representing persons closely associated with the regent, the combined force of the monarchy and the army threatened to undermine the parliamentary order, propped by the same monarcho-centralist parties, notably the Radicals and Democrats, which permitted the almost unlimited sway of Aleksandar and his camarilla.

The Radicals

> During the horrible war, many a Serb suffered and not a few paid with their heads only because they were Radicals. . . . There was no pardon for the Radicals. Why? . . . The Radicals do not bend with every breeze. The frontline walls of the Serbian Kingdom, of United Serbia, of Great Serbia may firmly lean on their backbones. That is why there was no pardon for the Radicals.
>
> *Zastava,* organ of the NRS, 1920

39. The establishment of the gendarmerie corps was regulated by an official act signed on February 25, 1919, by Pribićević and General Mihailo Rašić, minister of the army and the navy. The extent of the gendarmerie's operational initiative may be inferred from Article 49 of this act, which specified that "in subduing disturbances, the gendarmerie's superior receives only the assignment from the authorities, while he arranges the means of its execution on his own and is responsible for this [execution]." "Uredba o formaciji, opremi, nadležnostima, dužnostima i nastavi žandarmerije," *Službene novine,* March 11, 1919, pp. 3–5.

40. Arhiv Hrvatske, Rukopisna ostavština Dr. Djure Šurmina, Box 3: Fogl. 41, "Popis vrhu nekih dalmatinskih bez mirovine otpuštenih oružnika." This is a partial list of sixty-nine Dalmatian gendarmes who were retired without pension by July 1922.

Among the architects of modern Serbia there were none more deserving than the men of the Radical Party (NRS). The Radicals transformed Serbia, strengthened its parliamentary and representative institutions, and, in the words of their self-congratulating editorials, "destroyed the Obrenovićes and created democratic Serbia out of peasant boots." The party was also credited with "avenging [the battle of] Kosovo, resurrecting Serbia, and uniting the Serbs."[1] No Serbian faction bore the title Grand Old Party with greater justice or with more abuse.

The Radical party was a party of contradictions. It was founded in 1880, after the way for it was paved by Svetozar Marković, the apostle of Serbian socialism, and Adam Bogosavljević (1844–1880), possibly the only Serbian peasant with three years of university education behind him. These forerunners of the NRS were students of the Russian populists. Marković, who studied in Petersburg, was inspired by Chernyshevskii; later, in Zurich, he also discovered Marx. And Bogosavljević's return to the plow was almost certainly prompted by the populist glorification of the peasantry as the chief revolutionary force, which the educated were to serve and enlighten.[2]

Svetozar Marković was the great furtherer of Russian utilitarianism and materialism. He scorned the old romanticist generation of early Serbian liberals, whom he accused of making compromises with the autocratic regimes, being lukewarm toward swift political reform, and failing to grasp the economic basis of Serbia's social problems. His realist school glorified the scientific method and technological innovations, whereas the humanistic pursuits were considered important only as a means to social progress. Maintaining the utilitarian spirit, the intellectuals of the Radical party—mostly the products of German postivist education—were in the practical professions. Three of the four most prominent early Radical leaders (Pašić, Pera Todorović, Lazar Paču) studied at Zurich, as Marković had, and pursued engineering, pedagogy, and medicine. The fourth, Stojan Protić, the "first journalist of the Radical party and its principal doctrinist," studied history and philology at Belgrade.[3] Unlike the "Parisians" of the other, more Westernized, Serbian parties, the Radical leaders followed their forerunners into dungeons.[4] None died in chains like Bogosavljević, but most of them served time. Pašić and Todorović were sentenced to death in 1883 and Protić to

---

1. M. Dj., "Je li lako biti radikalac?," *Zastava*, Nov. 13, 1920, p. 1.
2. Rastislav V. Petrović, *Adam Bogosavljević* (Belgrade, 1972), pp. 24–25.
3. Slobodan Jovanović, *Vlada Aleksandra Obrenovića*, vol. 2 (Belgrade, 1935), p. 150.
4. Slobodan Jovanović, the keenest student of nineteenth-century Serbia, has observed that the students schooled in German Europe "received just as good education as those schooled in France, but the latter were more imbued with the western spirit. Our young people felt the West intimately and deeply only in Paris and transformed themselves from Balkanites into Europeans. The Radical intelligentsia, among whom there were almost no Parisians, represented in comparison with the intelligentsia of the [other Serbian parties] the same level of education, but not the same level of westernism." Ibid., vol. 1, p. 176.

twenty years in heavy chains in 1899. The sentences were eventually commuted, and these old conspirators held high office under the same Obrenović regimes that prosecuted them. But the NRS did not become fully legitimated as the main political force of Serbia until after the 1903 coup d'état. After the unification, during Yugoslavia's parliamentary period (1918–1929), the Radicals, former students of Russian nihilists, were out of office for exactly 312 days. The party of agrarian populism became the chief pillar of the Serbian establishment and was increasingly seen as the main practitioner of graft, pecuniary corruption, and political favoritism.

To be sure, the Radical party at the outset clearly disassociated itself from Marković's agrarian socialism. Collective ownership of land on the model of Russian *mir* was not a program likely to appeal to the peasants of Serbia, most of whom were small or middling proprietors. The natural enemies of the Serbian peasants were not the traditional exploiting classes of the countryside, which had been dispossessed in the Serbian Revolution, but rather the new class of urban creditors and tax collectors, personified in a bureaucratic officialdom that had little relationship to the familiar paternalistic rule of Prince Miloš's time. The Radicals very shrewdly recognized that the peasants felt increasingly alienated from the state, and they assured them that if the state rested on different institutional foundations, the bureaucracy would have no leeway. As long as the government used the police to interfere with the elections, the Radicals said, the representative agencies, from the local ones to the national assembly, would not reflect the will of the people. It was therefore necessary to curb arbitrary princely power, create a system of governmental responsibility to the sovereign national assembly, and bring the real representatives of the people to legislative authority—in a word, to establish a system of popular self-administration (*samouprava*).[5] Pera Todorović had had the word emblazoned in white letters on the red flag that he paraded through Kragujevac in 1876, and it was just as firmly superimposed upon the fading red hues of the Radical party's socialist heritage.

The secret of the Radicals' success in the 1880s had not lain simply in their class peasant program; it had been also the result of superb organization and conspiratorial guildsmanship, guided by an intense sense of party spirit. Todorović later noted that early Radicalism was not far from being a powerful religious sect—the Radicals organized the peasants by means of local offshoots, or filials, enlisting the country people of the most distant provinces in a way that recalled the spirit of evangelical excitement.[6] The novel idea had great appeal; and to some extent the Radicals supplanted the assimilationist role of the Serbian church under new increasingly secular circumstances and stimulated a Serb consciousness in newly acquired southeastern

5. Jovanović, *Vlada Milana Obrenovića*, vol. 3 (Belgrade, 1934), pp. 9–13.
6. Ibid., p. 7.

Serbia, where it formerly had not existed. The NRS and other Serb parties did much the same thing after 1918 in Bosnia-Hercegovina, the Sandžak, Kosovo, and Macedonia. Wherever the non-Serb locals "tied themselves with this or that Serb political party, they soon felt themselves Serbs once again [?] by means of [participation in] that party."[7]

Despite their peasant base and conspiratorial past, however, increasingly the NRS, even under the Obrenovićes, was radical in name only. It evolved into a conservative party of large proprietors and rich merchants, run by businesslike politicians like Nikola Pašić. With the advent of the Karadjordjevićes, the Radicals also became a dynastic party, though their service to the crown never exceeded the benefits they derived from the dexterous handling of the monarchic institution. Similarly, they relied on the army but kept the officers' corps at arm's length, slowly undoing the Black Hand, until its fall in 1917. Above all, they were the party of Serbian nationalism, combining into a complex whole all of its traditional elements. Earlier Bazarovs cultivated forms of peasant piety, albeit in an unconcerned Serbian way, but were far more deliberate in advancing and protecting the institutional church. (At Corfu in 1917, Pašić insisted that the king of Yugoslavia be Orthodox by constituitonal restriction.)[8] Linguistic Serbianism was also assumed among the Radical intelligentsia. Pašić's encounters with the JO and the Allied diplomats during the Great War testify to the ideal of Great Serbia that prevailed in the Radical ranks.

The Radicals were fairly unostentatious in their national allegiances, in part because these were obvious. A glance at their electoral performance in 1920 (see map 2-1) shows that they were an almost exclusively Serb party.[9] Their base was pre-1913 Serbia, and they did even better in Vojvodina and Srijem, where their showing represented the traditional strength of the kindred Serb Radical Party of Hungary, Croatia, and Slavonia, which merged with the Serbian Radicals after the unification. They did fairly well among the Serb population of northwestern Bosnia, eastern Hercegovina, and the Bay of Kotor, but not well at all among the Serbs of Croatia-Slavonia, Montenegro, and Macedonia. In the Priština and Prizren districts of eastern Kosovo, the Radicals also took in the local Muslim alliance (Cemiyet), whose members voted for the NRS in exchange for Radical support of Muslim candidates in the rest of Kosovo, Metohia, and the eastern Sandžak. Aside from this arrangement, the Radicals attracted only isolated non-Serb

7. Kosta St. Pavlović, *Vojislav Marinković i njegovo doba (1876–1935)*, vol. 1 (London, 1955), p. 55.

8. Bogumil Vošnjak, *U borbi za ujedinjenu narodnu državu: Utisci i opažanja iz doba svetskog rata i stvaranja naše države.* (Ljubljana, 1928), pp. 233–234.

9. Maps 2-1, 2-2, 2-3, 3-1, 3-4, 4-1, 4-2, and 4-3 show the electoral strength of various political parties in the elections for the Constituent Assembly, November 28, 1920. The elections and their implications are discussed in Part IV. Italian-occupied areas of northern Dalmatia are not included.

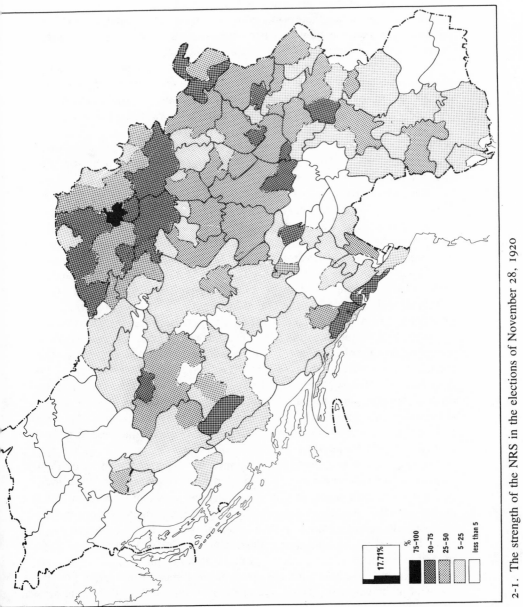

	%
■	75–100
▨	50–75
▦	25–50
░	5–25
□	less than 5

17.71%

2-1. The strength of the NRS in the elections of November 28, 1920

votes, largely among the landholders, who counted on Radical goodwill in political jockeying over agrarian reform.

The Radicals, unlike their principal rivals, devoted little attention to ideology, perhaps because they had been accustomed since 1903 to having a major say in Serbian state policy. Stojan Protić, the party's vice-president, noted during the 1920 electoral campaign that Yugoslavia's party leaders carefully avoided any serious discussion about the most elementary questions of state organization, "pulling words out of each other's mouths, as it were, by forceps."[10] Coming from garrulous Protić, who was always alert to ideas and fond of polemics, this was undoubtedly a criticism of his colleagues in the NRS leadership, especially Pašić, the party's president, whose personal traits marked the Radicals of the 1918 generation far more than any consistency of program.

It has been fairly said that "Protić speaks and Pašić keeps silent for the Radical Party." Habitual silence was indeed Pašić's chief characteristic. His advanced age (Pašić was seventy-three years old at the time of unification) and patriarchal white beard that reached to his midriff gave him the appearance of a sage. Taciturnity increased this impression. Where others fulminated, Pašić, the legendary Baja, as the Serbian masses affectionately called him, whispered even in his infrequent parliamentary speeches. The stinginess with words of this architectural engineer from eastern Serbia, who never practiced his craft, had distinct advantages. Because he seldom spoke, it was easy for his interlocutors to assume that he was a man of great wisdom, a conclusion that often meant that they assumed he agreed with them. But though it was generally believed that "Baja knows what he is doing," quite frequently, Pašić was merely sliding by. His talents were few. He was not a creative thinker, much less a tolerable ideologist, writer, speaker, or even a demagogue. His grammar was atrocious, and his paltry knowledge of history and literature was the butt of many jokes. Most important, though he exploited events, he was not a man of vision.

Not everyone interpreted Pašić's silence as unabashed assurance. Pera Todorović, who roomed with him in the party's early years, described him as a bungler and procrastinator who was terrified of reaching decisions and always waddled behind events. In 1899, when ex-King Milan decided to implicate the leading Radicals in an attempt on his life (the Ivanjdan—or Saint John's day—assassination), Pašić alone capitulated before the court-martial. Though he denied personal guilt, he admitted that he had contributed to the plot by failing to curb the antidynastic forces in his party. For his cooperation he was sentenced to five years and granted immediate amnesty. Other Radical leaders, including Protić, were given far stiffer terms and went straight to jail. Pašić undoubtedly thought that he was saving the leadership

10. Stojan Protić, "Jedna država-jedan surerenitet!" *Samouprava*, Oct. 9, 1920, p. 1.

for better times, but public opinion condemned his action as cowardly opportunism: "He became the most unpopular politician in the whole country and experienced the greatest measure of public contempt that a politician can possibly experience."[11]

Pašić soon regained the lost ground, but he never quite lived down the reputation of master intriguer. Prince Djordje, who blamed Pašić for most of his own travails, regarded him as a patient, calculating plotter who "knew how to be silent and wait for his moment" and always wanted to be first, ahead even of the royal house.[12] Seton-Watson loathed him and warned that after the unification the "Beard" was "simply playing his old dilatory game of Balkan party intrigue."[13] Cultivated Westernized intellectuals attributed to him all the disreputable qualities of the Balkan past, including moral insensitivity, an "Oriental," provincial, and narrowly Serbian mentality, intolerance of genuine talent, cronyism, and a stubborn refusal to step aside in favor of new blood.[14] He was a peril to his party's nobler figures, whose virtues were precisely the qualities he could least abide. Protić, whom he ultimately pushed aside, "suffered from a certain spiritual stateliness, very dangerous in a circle where temper and tone were set by Nikola Pašić."[15]

For all that, the Serbian masses worshiped Pašić. His wiliness was recognized as the welcome trait of a survivor who, like the people, withstood all odds. In the villages they believed that Pašić brought good luck. He was regarded with an almost superstitious wonder as a sly patriarch who knew the score. The sophisticates were perplexed by his mesmeric influence on ordinary people, but not a few of them also fell for his charms. Even Supilo, one of Pašić's bitterest opponents, found it difficult to resist him. At the end of one of his last meetings with Supilo in August 1917, in London, Pašić patiently listened to Supilo's upbraidings and then (as Supilo wrote to a friend), "that old man with a long apostolic beard sealed our long and serious conversation by getting up, his eyes red with tears. He then grasped my head with his strong hands and pressed innumerable kisses on my forehead, whispering 'this forehead, this forehead,' thanking me for the struggle which I conducted 'in the fronde' against him."[16]

11. Jovanović, *Vlada Aleksandra Obrenovića*, vol. 2, p. 452.

12. Djordje Karadjordjević, *Istina o mome životu* (Belgrade, 1969), pp. 192, 417. Prince Djordje believed that Pašić poisoned him with alkaloids in November 1922 to prevent his appearance before the Crown Council, which had been convened to consider Djordje's charges about the violations of his dynastic rights by his brother, King Aleksandar. Ibid., pp. 399–401.

13. Hugh Seton-Watson et al., eds., *R. W. Seton-Watson and the Yugoslavs: Correspondence 1906–1941*, vol. 2 (London, 1976), p. 13.

14. Typical examples of Pašićophobic views by liberal intellectuals can be found in Ć. [Milan Ćurćin], "Naš Gledston, i naš Gandi," *Nova Evropa*, vol. 12 (1925), no. 2, pp. 52–57; and Simplex, "Ličnost Nikole Pašića," ibid., vol. 13 (1926), no. 12, pp. 410–416.

15. Vladimir Dvorniković, *Karakterologija Jugoslovena* (Belgrade, 1939), p. 885.

16. Bogdan Radica, ed., "Supilova pisma Ferrerovima," *Hrvatska revija*, vol. 7 (1957), no. 4, pp. 400–401.

If Pašić and the NRS were, as many thought, identical, then the key to the Radicals' national ideology must be sought in Pašić's practice. Here there were no ambiguities. Pašić subscribed to the policy that was laid out in the NRS's program of January 1880, the first party program in Serbian history: "As the goal of our state organization," wrote the Radical deputies headed by Pašić, "we favor, internally, popular well-being and freedom, and, externally, state independence, liberation, and unification of the other parts of Serbdom."[17] For Pašić, it was only natural that in the new Yugoslav state "Serbia must dominate [*rukovoditi*, literally, lead by the hand] in political affairs, just as she led in military affairs."[18]

The NRS's guiding principle of Serbian hegemony was evident in Pašić's dealings with the JO and the National Council but was disguised in the NRS's public statements. The Radicals' most authoritative proclamation, the conclusions of the party's conference of October 1920, offered no systematic position on the national question. The delegates simply cited the larger part of the Corfu Declaration, carefully avoiding references to the "trinominal people" and omitting the phrase from Article 1 in which the Serbs, Croats, and Slovenes were said to be "also known by the name of South Slavs or Yugoslavs."[19] Clearly, the NRS wished, as much as possible, to avoid open identification with Yugoslavist unitarism. But since the policy of Serbian hegemony presupposed a centralist state organization, the Radicals had to accept elements of unitarism, the theoretical underpinning of centralism— hence the apparent muddle in Radical positions, which led one scholar to note in bewilderment that the history of the NRS's relations with the Croat parties "was stormy and, in many of its aspects, almost indecipherable."[20]

The Radicals were actually of two minds on the question of nationality. They were torn between the reality of South Slavic national differences and the illusion about the beginning of a new era in Serb assimilation. Jaša Tomić (1856–1922), the leader of the Radicals in Vojvodina, whose failing health prevented him from taking a more active part in NRS politics, was perfectly straightforward in stating to Croat politicians that "we are not one" in nationality.[21] Protić, too, believed that the South Slavs developed separately in three state centers and with three state traditions—those of Belgrade, Zagreb, and, interestingly, not Ljubljana but rather Cetinje.[22] He thought it

17. Cited in Živan Mitrović, *Srpske političke stranke* (Belgrade, 1939), p. 72.

18. Pašić to Stojan Protić in Corfu, Nov. 18, 1918. Dragoslav Janković and Bogdan Krizman, eds., *Gradja o stvaranju jugoslovenske države*, vol. 2 (Belgrade, 1964), p. 566.

19. "Zaključci Radikalne zemaljske konferencije o programu," *Samouprava*, Oct. 6, 1920, pp. 1–2.

20. Djordje D. Stanković, "Neuspeh Stojana Protića u okupljanju političkih snaga radi rešavanja hrvatskog pitanja 1921. godine," *Istorijski glasnik*, 1971, no. 1, p. 31.

21. Arhiv Hrvatske, Rukopisna ostavština Dr. Djure Šurmina, Box 5: I–7. Političke bilješke 1906–1936, Notebook 6, Jaša Tomić to Vjekoslav Spinčić, Belgrade, May 17, 1919.

22. Stojan Protić, "Iz tri centra!" *Radikal*, Oct. 16, 1921, p. 1.

unrealistic to ignore these differences and, moreover, attached great importance to national ideologies. He was skeptical about claims of those unitarists who blamed all reversals in the relations between the Serbs and Croats on Serbian misrule: "The discontent of Croats in [Croatia-Slavonia] also has other elements, which are far more important and which must not be overlooked. The whole ideology of Croat intelligentsia has its part in [this discontent], together with the well-known idealization of Croatian history, to which Strossmayer, Starčević, and Frank contributed so much."[23] Pašić, though noncommital publicly on this subject, spoke of the Serb people (*narod*), not tribe (*pleme*), in private letters and needed no instruction on the difference between the Serbs and their "weaker, that is, less numerous brothers"—the Croats and Slovenes.[24]

In drawing a line between the Serbs and the other South Slavs, the NRS took a step in the direction of Croat and Slovene autonomists and, opening itself to the taunts of separatism, joined the combat against radical unitarists. On the other hand, there was also the absorptive warrant to increase the Serb nation. In this, assimilationist, aspect of its activity, the NRS was the most consistent upholder of the principal elements in the sweep of Serbian nationalism. The Radicals assumed the identity of Orthodoxy and Serbianism in the western Balkans. It was impossible to be both Croat and Orthodox. Therefore, even Josip Runjanin (1821–1878), the composer of the Croatian national anthem, was a pure Serb.[25] Karadžić's linguistic Serbianism was also taken for granted. Even the least supremacist Radicals, such as Protić and Momčilo Ivanić (1886–1940), who cooperated with the Croat autonomists, had no doubt about the strictly Serbian nature of štokavian dialect. A reconstruction of their views points to a belief that the Croat appellation always excluded the speakers of štokavian. And once the kajkavian Croats adopted the štokavian dialect, or, in Protić's and Ivanić's terms, once the "Croats accepted the Serbian language as their literary expression," they became Serbs: "Is it not a fact that once a whole language is adopted, moreover adopted voluntarily, and what is more, adopted by the Croats single-mindedly, is it not a fact, then, that this action expresses a purely instinctive will? And is not that will . . . entirely equal to the Serb national will, even if it be called—Croatian?"[26]

The Croats simply did not exist. There was only the Croat name, a tattered label on a Serb bottle. The Croat masses sang folk songs that glorified Prince Marko and the heroes of the Kosovo battle. Nobody sang about the Croat

23. Stojan Protić, "Ustav i većina," *Tribuna*, May 4, 1921, p. 1.
24. Nikola Pašić, "Ili centralizam ili plemenska federacija," *Hrvat*, May 5, 1926, p. 2. This is a transcript of Pašić's letter to Milenko Vesnić, a Radical leader and then Yugoslavia's prime minister, written in Paris on June 8, 1920.
25. "J. Runjanin-pravoslavni Hrvat," *Radikal*, Dec. 13, 1921, p. 1.
26. Momčilo Ivanić, "Jedan narod?" *Samouprava*, Jan. 19, 1921, p. 1.

kings. Nor were there any songs about the equally great "Serb" rulers of medieval Bosnia. The national tradition accepted only the rulers of the Serbian state from the time of the Nemanjićes and thereafter, and then only under the Serb name. The Slovenes existed because there was the Slovenian language, but it should not be encouraged, since its separation from "Serbian" was strictly a result of Austrian manipulation. The further differentiation of Slovenian could lead to an unwelcome bilingual situation, as in Belgium.[27] Clearly, the opposite was desired, that is, the steady confluence of Slovenian into "Serbian" and with it the accompanying national transformation.

The NRS leaders invoked the arguments of religion and language less frequently than the argument of the confirmative experience of the Serbian state, whose role in the spread of Serb national consciousness they revered as the ultimate point of national legitimation. Unlike the Yugoslavist unitarists, such as Marjanović, who resisted the very idea of state continuity in order to diminish the impact of historical influences among the South Slavs, the Radicals worshiped the Serbian state as the moving force of Serb history. It could not have been otherwise. To a generation that took credit for "avenging Kosovo" and self-consciously viewed itself as the restorer of the Nemanjić empire, the centuries of Ottoman rule were no more than a distant and very brief hiatus. There was only the uninterrupted growth of Serbian state, which produced Serbs with mechanical industry wherever it expanded.

The Serbs came into being—that is, the Serb name, the idea of Serbdom, and Serb national consciousness—after a certain primary tribe, called Serb, separated itself from the other tribes by virtue of its number, power, and the intelligence of its elders and leaders, and succeeded in excelling [among the other tribes], and distinguishing and uplifting itself. And so the Serb name spread in all directions, the more the original Serb tribe succeeded in drawing the other neighboring, less powerful, and less important tribes into its [political] community.[28]

Since the continuity of the Serbian state was assured in Yugoslavia, there was no reason to suspect that the centuries-old process of assimilation could not continue. But the Serbs had to keep hold of their identity and shun the Yugoslav label, which was another invention of Serb-hating Austria. Indeed, the Yugoslavist unitarists of all backgrounds and Croat autonomists like Trumbić and Pavelić preferred the all-embracing Yugoslav name, the former in order to suppress all components of "separatism," the latter because they

27. Stojan Protić, *Oko Ustava: Kritika i polemika* (Belgrade, 1921), pp. 8–9. Pašić also thought that the Slovenes would, on account of their "bad dialect," accustom themselves to Serbian. See Dragoslav Janković, "Niška deklaracija," *Istorija XX veka: zbornik radova*, vol. 10 (1969), p. 14.
28. R. [Momčilo Ivanić?], "Na domaku novoga doba," *Samouprava*, Dec. 22, 1920, p. 1.

saw the Yugoslav appellation as the guarantee of national equality. The Radicals made it plain that they would not follow Croat tomfoolery in acting "like Peter toward Christ" in Caiphas's courtyard, by denying their proud nationality. The vitriolic NRS attacks on the term "Yugoslavia" were strikingly reminiscent of Teodor Pavlović's polemics against the Illyrian name some ninety years before. As in Pavlović's time, Croat undertakings on behalf of a common national name for all the South Slavs were seen as an attempt to bring Serbdom down. "Free Kingdom of Serbia and the Serb name were a real bogey for Vienna and German policy, and so, Yugoslav water was poured into strong Serbian wine." But, "should the Serbs today get the cockeyed idea of giving up their national name, they would first of all have to burn the whole Vuk [Karadžić], which means, they would have to tear out of themselves their very heart."[29] Pretending to stand apart from such Serb extremists as Djordje Čokorilo, the initiator of the ultranationalist Serb National Organization in Bosnia-Hercegovina, who wanted the new state to be called the Great Serbia of the Kingdom of Serbs, Croats, and Slovenes, the Radicals pursued a subtler, and surer, way of assuring Serbian predominance.[30]

Stojan Protić, who stood head and shoulders above most Serbian leaders in his knowledge of Croatian history, countered Croat importunings on behalf of Yugoslav appellation with a claim that "Ante Starčević, who undoubtedly had more and stronger national feeling than Strossmayer, was opposed to the artificial Yugoslav name." The Croats clamored for "Yugoslavia and the Yugoslav [name] . . . out of fear [that the Serb name], being stronger and better known, would push aside or overshadow [the Croat appellation]."[31] Protić's reasoning was uncomfortably close to the truth, but his conclusion was pure Radicalism. Let the Serbs, Croats, and Slovenes each use their own national appellation, but not in perpetuity: each name would survive for as long as it showed signs of vitality. In short, he was inviting the Croats and Slovenes to an ordeal of endurance, the outcome of which seemed to him certain.

The Yugoslavist unitarists favored the centralist state organization in order to forge a common Yugoslav nationality. The Radicals, unlike the Croat and Slovene autonomists, had no fear that centralism would succeed in accomplishing the unitarist aim. If centralism provided no guarantees for the maintenance of separate South Slavic national—or, in unitarist parlance, "tribal"—individualities, so much the better for the Serbs. The continuity of the Serbian state was assured in the Kingdom of the Serbs, Croats, and Slovenes. Therefore, where the unitarists believed that centralism would bring about a

29. Momčilo Ivanić, "Jugoslavija!" ibid., Feb. 20, 1921, p. 1.
30. "Oko državnog imena," ibid., May 6, 1921, p. 1.
31. Protić, *Oko Ustava*, pp. 7–8.

hybrid South Slavic nationality, the Radicals were confident that the result would in fact be the Serbianization of Yugoslavia's non-Serb nationalities, though they wisely preferred to obscure their view of the state's assimilative partiality. The same Radicals who sang paeans to the absorptive power of the Serbian state easily changed step to profess that the state was, after all, neutral in the contest for the predominance of a single national individuality. Though the rules of this contest were purely imperialistic ("imperialism of [one national] individuality" would prevail), the weapons of struggle could not be physical. National differences could be safeguarded only by "moral and spiritual power," which meant that the Croats and Slovenes did not have to fear the state but only their own inherent inferiority. The fear of Croats and Slovenes for their national individuality in a centralist state only demonstrated that their "individuality [was] very superficial and that at the same time they express[ed] silent suspicion about the strength of their moral and spiritual power": "Why not leave [the superiority] of moral and spiritual forces to a free contest? Let the superior ones win. Their victory would mean progress and would not be a defeat for any tribe of our people. The *capitis deminutio* of individual tribes in our new community would condition the higher order of our people's affirmation and individuality, that is, their progress and national security."[32]

The use of an ancient Roman legal term for the lessening of citizens' legal rights, which, in the most extreme cases, conveyed the loss of life, was a telltale sign that the Radicals did not see themselves as competitors in an innocuous contest. There could be no equilibrium of influence among the South Slavic nationalities. And since one group had to prevail, the Radicals, in their self-created role of guardian of Serb national unity, were not about to give up their advantages for the sake of pleasing the Croats and Slovenes. To be sure, individual Radicals made various attempts at glossing over the implications of the NRS's theory of Serb natural selection, but these efforts were . not particularly convincing. For example, Ljuba Jovanović (1865–1928), a leading Radical politician and a respected historian, advanced his own inconsistent unitarist theory of *narodno jedinstvo* to demonstrate that there were in fact no differences among the Serbs, Croats, and Slovenes. Their forefathers in the Transcarpathian protohomeland belonged to a single group. They were not differentiated upon their arrival in the Balkans, owing mainly to incessant migrations that prevented regional solidity. Their language was identical: the various dialects were not distinguishing marks of separate national formations, since, in a major departure from Karadžić's teaching, there were "hundreds of štokavian Croats." Their religions, too, were not nationally constituted. There were Orthodox Croats and Catholic Serbs. And since religion was the determining aspect of "na-

32. Ž., "Federalizam i plemenske posebnosti," *Samouprava*, Feb. 6, 1921, p. 1.

tional mentality," the South Slavs were single in that area as well. Nor were there any separate "political mentalities" among them.[33]

Even so, after dismissing all the main criteria for South Slavic national differentiation, Jovanović was obliged to admit that differences did exist. In an odd inversion of his argument, he in effect said that, from the point of view of idealized South Slavic integrity, the consequences of historical and confessional differences might not have been real but were certainly apparent. It could not have been otherwise. Jovanović was not willing to accept the logic of his argument—that is, that the Serbs, Croats, and Slovenes did not exist as separate national individualities—because to accept that premise would constitute a denigration of his Serbianism. Like most Radicals, though in this case by his own peculiar method, he wanted to establish that the loss of national individuality ought not, after all, be a bitter pill for the non-Serb South Slavs.

The argument comes down to the typical Radical paradox of denying the effects of historical consciousness in the abstract, while simultaneously holding high the banner of historically conditioned Serb national consciousness. This contradiction was nowhere more apparent than in the debate over the upholding of historical provinces. The anticentralist opposition (Slovene clericalists, Croat autonomists, Bosnian Muslims, and so on) wanted to preserve the pre-1918 frontiers between the South Slavic provinces against the resistance of Radical leaders. To the mind of men like Pašić and Ljuba Jovanović, Yugoslavia's historical provinces were artificial, heterogeneous, and, therefore, alterable.[34] This was of course true of Serbia no less than of any other province, but it should not lead to the conclusion that the Radicals were opposed to all historical boundaries. They simply did not want to allow the diminution of Serbia's historical frontiers to the level of any other provincial line. It was inconceivable "that a state, as was, for example, Serbia, should be turned into a mere province." Serbia's historical statehood had to continue in Yugoslavia but not on equal footing with the other, "previously incomplete, state-right formations."[35] From the NRS's point of view, the insistence on the unalterable status of old frontiers amounted to the legalization of pre-1918 barriers against Serbian expansion.

The Radicals also objected to the supposed danger of federalism, inherent, in their opinion, in the maintenance of historical provinces. Most of the old provinces had had their own legislative bodies. If the provinces continued within their traditional frontiers, the former legislatures could easily be restored at some future date. That would engender the fragmentation of central legislative power, a bias that was at the heart of federalism. But it would be

33. Ljuba Jovanović, "Naše ustavno pitanje," *Srpska riječ*, Jan. 3, 1922, p. 1; Jan. 4, 1922, pp. 1–2; Jan. 5, 1922, pp. 2–3.
34. Nikola Pašić, "Radikalima i radikalnim organizacijama," *Samouprava*, Sept. 9, 1921, p. 1..
35. "Ko parcelira državu," ibid., June 5, 1921, p. 1.

wrong to think, as is often claimed, that the NRS was antifederalist in principle. On the contrary, its opposition to federalism was strictly conditional. The Radicals ruled out any concession to the federal structure based on historical provinces. But though they preferred full centralism, they were not opposed to a different federal arrangement, based on "tribal" units. In other words, the NRS was prepared to accept the redrawing of Yugoslavia's internal frontiers and the establishment of Serb, Corat, and Slovene federal units. However, as the NRS leaders repeatedly and pointedly reminded their Croat counterparts, under such an arrangement the most the Croats could expect was kajkavian and čakavian dialect areas. Pašić warned that a "Serb, no matter where he lived, wishes to unite with Serbia, without asking about its internal organization."[36] Lazar Marković (1882–1955), the NRS's legal theorist, predicted the "slashing and hewing on both sides" of religious-linguistic frontiers.[37] And even Stojan Protić observed that the South Slavs were "so divided by tribe and religion that a division on a federal basis could in no way be accomplished without an outbreak of strong and sharp conflict among us."[38]

The Radical party, in effect, was confronting the Croats (the Slovenes not being involved in these territorial disputes) with the alternative of centralist domination or amputation. The county of Lika-Krbava, for example, might well have been the historic heart of old Croatia, but almost 53 percent of its people were Orthodox and almost all the rest štokavian-speaking, both good Serb arguments for its belonging to the Serbian federal unit. The same logic did not, however, obtain in Kosovo, where the Serbs constituted only 23.28 percent of the population. There, the Radicals did not propose to accommodate the Albanian majority (61.95 percent) with a federal unit of their own, nor to let them join Albania. In areas like Kosovo, the Radicals were great defenders of historical right, arguing for Serbian proprietorship on the basis of historical precedence and outright conquest. In short, should federalism be considered in Yugoslavia, the Serbs were never to be brought to the position of a minority. Districts with Serb majorities (for examplke, Lika-Krbava) within the historical provinces with non-Serb majorities (in this case, Croatia-Slavonia) had to be plucked from the larger historical whole in order to safeguard the local Serbs from the possibility of majority rule by the non-Serbs. On the other hand, the presence of overwhelming non-Serb majorities in "historical" Serb regions meant that the whole area had to be integrated within larger Serbia, transforming a local majority into a minority within the larger Serbian unit. The strident refusal to accept the majority rule exercised by the non-Serbs over any Serb enclave was based in part on the conviction

36. Pašić, "Ili centralizam ili plemenska federacija," p. 2.
37. Lazar Marković, "Protiv federalizma," *Samouprava*, Oct. 21, 1920, p. 1.
38. Stojan Protić, "Jedna država—jedan suverenitet!" ibid., Oct. 19, 1921, p. 1.

that federalism was the first step on the road to full independence. And the Serbs refused to sanction any move that would have returned them to a position of a minority in a non-Serb state. In Pašić's words: "To divide our Serb people among large provinces endowed with legislative power is tantamount, in my opinion, to creating the basis for a future separation. To divide our people among several provinces, only to ease the establishment of Croatia and Slovenia, I believe does an injustice to our people, which mortgaged everything so that the Serbs might be united."[39]

For all that, the Radicals tried to steer what they considered to be the middle course between pure centralism of the unitarists and the autonomist or federalist programs, proposed by the non-Serb parties. True to their tradition of fighting for self-administration on the local level, a policy that worked admirably in uninational Serbia of the simpler pre-1912 years, the NRS advocated "political centralization and administrative decentralization."[40] That way, Serbian predominance could be assured, while the Croats and Slovenes could protect their separate cultures. It only remained to establish the criteria for arriving at the self-governing districts, as well as the nature of their prerogatives. It was in this area that the Radicals came to odds between Pašić's majority and the minority led by Protić and Ivanić, both sides expressing their views in separate constitutional proposals.

Pašić's dominant wing of the NRS called for the division of the state into thirty-five districts with between two hundred thousand and six hundred thousand (later changed to eight hundred thousand) inhabitants in each. The seemingly arbitrary nature of this division, which was supposedly aimed against historical frontiers, was in fact modified by deals with two autonomist parties. But in the area of self-administrative prerogatives, Pašić's proposal offered little self-administration. All the local agencies of power (districts, circuits, counties, communes) were subjected to central authorities (king, national assembly, government) and had only limited and strictly delegated authority. Protić, on the other hand, proposed delegated legislative power to the districts, though under the supervision of centrally appointed governors and with the limitation that no local laws could contradict central legislation. Furthermore, he offered an entirely different scheme for the establishment of districts, or as he called them, provinces, which was in many ways a compromise with the proponents of historical frontiers.

Protić envisioned nine provinces: (1) pre-1912 Serbia, (2) Old Serbia (Sandžak, Kosovo, Metohia) with Macedonia, (3) Croatia-Slavonia with Medjimurje, Istria, and Rijeka, the last two regions already in grave danger of falling to Italy, (4) Bosnia, (5) Montenegro with Hercegovina, the Bay of Kotor, and its littoral, (6) Dalmatia, (7) Srijem, Bačka, and Baranja, (8) the

39. Pašić, "Ili centralizam ili plemenska federacija," p. 2.
40. [Krsta Miletić?], "Za jedinstvo, a protiv hegemonije," *Samouprava,* Dec. 22, 1920, p. 1.

Banat, and (9) Slovenia. As Ivanić put it, Protić's proposal was distinguished from Pašić's by the "far greater attention it paid to [regional] feelings . . . and by the considerable concern it attached to our previous national historical life."[41] Nonetheless, the changes Protić proposed in the makeup of old provinces (the separation of Srijem from Croatia-Slavonia, of Hercegovina from Bosnia, of the Bay of Kotor from Dalmatia) all favored the concentration of Serbs. The Serb share of Bačka's population was only 20.87 percent, but, with Srijem, it would rise to 29.63 percent in the new unit. The Serbs constituted 43.87 percent of the population of Bosnia-Hercegovina; if Bosnia stood alone, the share would be somewhat larger (45.53 percent). The Croat Catholic plurality in Hercegovina (42.94 percent) would be significantly reduced if Hercegovina were turned to Montenegro, and so on.

Protić understood that Serb interests could best be protected by a modicum of concessions to the non-Serbs, especially to the Croats. "I would be very naïve," wrote Protić, "if I thought that the Croats would accept my proposal with open arms . . . but every serious political man will have no doubt that the Croats, though perhaps not completely satisfied at once, will nevertheless be a lot happier with the constitution based on my proposal than with the one offered by . . . Mr. Pašić.[42] Unlike Pašić, he was afraid that unremediable centralism would only succeed in provoking a storm of resistance that might endanger all Serbian gains: "Nature recognizes only unity in diversity. Those nations and states, which paid sufficiently serious attention to this basic rule, became great, glorious, and lasting. Vast tsarist Russia disappeared, but the unitary—and at the same time self-administered, parliamentary, and diverse—British empire not only did not disappear in the last war, but [became] even greater."[43] Where Pašić proposed to govern in the autocratic Russian manner, Protić preferred the more enduring and subtler British style. This enabled him to transfer responsibility for the excesses of centralization from his own governing Radicals to Pribićević's Yugoslavist unitarists, a gambit which in turn allowed for the partnerships between Protić's Radicals and the various autonomist factions in Yugoslavia's early cabinets. For it was only ostensibly ironical that the party that favored diminished national individualities to the non-Serbs seemed eminently preferable to unitarist leveling. Protić therefore had to endure the barrage of charges of trafficking with separatism, though in fact the differences between his views and those of Pašić were largely tactical. Lazar Marković, who like many Radicals feared a party split, pointed out that Protić's critics frequently mistook the less important aspects of his proposals for the heart of the matter.[44] Moreover, Pašić, too, knew how to deflect reactions against the

41. Momčilo Ivanić, "Protivrečnosti u Ustavnom Pitanju," ibid., Feb. 3, 1921, p. 1.
42. Stojan Protić, "Neko se vara, zaista!" *Tribuna*, April 26, 1921, p. 1.
43. Stojan Protić, "Naše nevolje," *Radikal*, Oct. 15, 1921, p. 1.
44. Lazar Marković, *Jugoslovenska država i Hrvatsko pitanje (1914–1929)* (Belgrade, 1935), p. 133.

harshness of early centralizing measures, from which the Radicals certainly benefited, by shifting all the blame to provocative Pribićević.

In one area, however, Protić and Pašić differed profoundly. Unlike Pašić, Protić was convinced that autocratically imposed centralism in the end also endangered Serbian liberties. The measures designed to stem the resistance of non-Serb nationalities—stricter police control over the press, procedures that opened doors to the manipulation of elections, refusals to limit the categories of civil servants who could simultaneously hold parliamentary seats, and the encouragement of widening jurisdiction for military courts— all strengthened Protić in his belief that Yugoslavia was on the road to having "perhaps the worst constitution in Europe among the states which existed before the war [!] and which have had a constitution."[45] Protić, in short, differed from the Radicals loyal to Pašić in his concern that the harm to Serbia's democratic institutions outweighed the possible benefits of central- ism. He became convinced that the preservation of the democratic system was well worth an agreement with the Croats, who would in any case be guaranteed no more than a modicum of autonomy. He was among the few Radical dissidents who opposed the decision of Pašić's majority in putting together the coalition with Pribićević's unitarists who assured the adoption of the 1921 centralist constitution. Hence, in the summer and fall of 1921, Protić attempted to bring the Croats to his point of view, determined to avert the steady drift toward dictatorship. He feared the consequence of NRS's partnership with Pribićević's Democrats, a party which in Protić's opinion was "neither democratic nor freedom loving, but which instead had entirely erroneous and wrongheaded ideas about public order, state administration, and civil liberties."[46]

The Democrats

> The Irish Home Rule Bill, passed by the commons during Asquith's cabi- net, remained thwarted and unrealized on the eve of the war as a result of the opposition of Ulstermen led by Carson, who were covertly aided and abetted by English Unionists, both civilian and military.
>
> Stojan Protić, 1921

As is often the case with onetime revolutionaries, the Radical leaders were worldly-wise and pragmatic. Since they no longer believed that the world could be made perfect, they were extremely tolerant of their own imperfec-

45. "S. Protić i Ustav," *Epoha*, April 18, 1921, p. 3.
46. Stojan Protić and Momčilo Ivanić, "Proglas g. Stojana Protića," *Balkan*, Sept. 14, 1921, p. 1.

tions and also willing from time to time to tolerate the imperfections of others. The same cannot be said of the men who formed the Demokratska stranka (DS, Democratic Party), inebriated as they were with the consuming belief in the superiority of unitarist Yugoslavism. The Democrats sustained a vision of a consistently centralized state, and, like most idealists, they were aggressive and very dangerous to their opponents. The degree of dedication varied somewhat, of course, but it can be fairly said that the party's main characteristics were epitomized in the person of Svetozar Pribićević.

There were not one, but four, Pribićevićes. Besides Svetozar, the leader of the clan, who briefly taught mathematics after graduating from the University of Zagreb, there were Valerijan (1870–1941), an Orthodox hieromonach and ultimately bishop; Milan (1875–1936), an Austro-Hungarian officer who defected to Serbia and became a colonel in the Serbian army; and Adam (1880–1957), a jurist and journalist, who, with Milan, became the prophet of return to the virtues of rural life. It was said that they all missed their professions. Svetozar should have been a soldier, Valerijan a politician (a pursuit in which this worldly archimandrite nevertheless dabbled), Milan a professor, and Adam a monk.[1] The Pribićevićes were not a particularly prominent Serb lineage in the former Croatian Military Frontier, but their father, a schoolteacher from the village of Glavičani in Banija, had them all educated, an advantage uncommon for the time and place. They went on to become the natural leaders of the Serbs of Croatia-Slavonia, with Svetozar as the most influential Serb politician in Croatia-Slavonia during the first three decades of the twentieth century.[2]

Svetozar Pribićević's life was a sort of witches' prayer, dispensing curses or blessings depending on whether it was read backward or forward. The man whom the Croats saw as the evil genius of 1918 unification and the chief force behind centralism, who destroyed Croat statehood in partnership with Pašić's Radicals, brought the crowns of Croatia, Dalmatia, and Slavonia to the House of Karadjordjević, and used strong-arm methods in the persecution of Radić's movement, later changed his direction one-hundred-eighty degrees. After the Radicals sacrificed him in 1925 in order to bring about a short-lived coalition with Radić, Pribićević went into opposition, vowing that his group would no longer be misused by the Radicals as "chained bulldogs, who are unleashed to bark when it is needed."[3] His revulsion at the Radicals and their narrow Serbian policies brought him into partnership with

---

1. Dragoljub Jovanović, *Ljudi, ljudi . . . (Medaljoni 56 umrlih savremenika)*, vol. 1 (Belgrade, 1973), p. 396.

2. On the course of Pribićević's political career see Hrvoje Matković, *Svetozar Pribićević i Samostalna demokratska stranka do šestojanuarske diktature* (Zagreb, 1972); Ljubo Boban, *Svetozar Pribićević u opoziciji 1929–1936* (Zagreb, 1973); Vaso Bogdanov, 'Hrvatska i srpska prošlost u interpretaciji S. Pribićevića," in *Likovi i pokreti* (Zagreb, 1957), pp. 223–231.

3. Cited in Matković, *Svetozar Pribićević*, p. 188.

Radić and ultimately—after the assassination of Radić in 1928 and the subsequent imposition of the royal dictatorship—into an open clash with Belgrade and the king. The man who used to irritate the Croats with unending reminders of Serbia's sacrifices in blood and treasure at the altar of unification became overnight an immoderate Belgrade-baiter who scornfully requested that the Serbians submit the final bill for their blood, which they had turned into a resalable commodity. Confined in 1929 to the village of Brus in southern Serbia, Pribićević subsequently emigrated, and, in 1933 in Paris, he brought out his famous volume *La dictature du roi Alexandre,* in which he denounced the king as a squalid tyrant, who preferred to "amputate" Croatia rather than permit federalism. Pribićević died a lonely émigré's death, in 1936 in Prague, crowned with a chaplet of martyrdom. One of the wreaths on his bier was consigned by the Central Committee of Yugoslavia's Communist Party, which he had helped to ban in 1921. "He ended up better than he started and died better than he deserved."[4]

It has been said that Pribićević represented the "unadulterated mentality of a county pristaf from the Military Frontier."[5] Indeed, his political evolution cannot be understood without reference to his constituency, Croatia's claustrophobic Orthodox minority, whose religious separation from the Catholic majority in the Croat heartlands had been heightened since the turn of the eighteenth century by the espousal of Serb national consciousness. So long as the Croat national leaders refused to acknowledge a separate Serb "political nation" in Croatia, and so long as the Serbs rejected the status of "political Croats," the security of Croatia's Serbs could be guaranteed only in two ways: either by cooperation with the external forces that could benefit from the reversals in the onward march of Croat nationalism, or by a concerted effort to downplay the clash between Croat and Serb national ideologies by recourse to unitarist Yugoslavism. From the time of his earliest political engagement, in 1897, Pribićević, for his Serb followers, combined elements of these two rather different avenues. On the one hand he espoused the national identity of Croats and Serbs, covering this unitarist formula with a patina of Serb national symbols, and, on the other, he sought the patronage of Budapest and Belgrade by way of the HSK, and also by more covert means, ultimately imposing a Serbian military solution to the unification of the South Slavs.

In Pribićević the logic of a mathematics instructor was combined with the insensitivity of a gendarme from Banija (the traditional recruiting ground of the imperial constabulary). It was almost as if Pribićević had set out to enrage the Croats. He taunted the autonomists by admitting that he was the one who "forced the pace of liquidating the sovereignty of the National Council,"

4. Jovanović, *Ljudi, ljudi,* vol. 1, p. 397.
5. Miroslav Krleža, *Davni dani,* vols. 11–12 of *Sabrana djela* (Zagreb, 1956), p. 203.

having rejected the decisions of the Geneva conference: "In a forceful telegram to the Serbian government I stood up against that act, declared that I did not recognize it, and added that the National Council would go to Belgrade to carry out a complete unification."[6] On other occasions he allowed that his acceptance of the National Council's special instructions for negotiating the unification with Serbia was only a tactic to assuage the SSP, which was prepared to hold up the delegation's departure for Belgrade without these assurances; the Serbian representatives did not want to hear anything about conditions.[7] Moreover, the exchange of notes with the regent at the time of unification was no international compact, but only a "technical form" and a "manifestation for the foreign world."[8] One did not enter into agreements with a sovereign of one's own blood. When these arguments proved less than compelling, Pribićević's lieutenants explained that the unification was a revolutionary act, which would be legally sanctioned by the Constituent Assembly.[9]

Until the elections of November 1920, Svetozar Pribićević's reputation in Belgrade was to a large extent based on his supposed authority in Croat matters. Except for a few skeptics in the Radical ranks, most Serbian politicians assumed that Pribićević represented the Croat opinion, which was generally regarded as prounitarist. Pribićević's obvious lack of concern for Croat national sensitivities and the ingrained legalistic standpoint of Croat tradition might indicate that he, also, labored under a delusion about the strength of his unitarist program among the Croat masses. Indeed, this may have been true in the case of Dalmatia, which the HSK's press considered Pribićević's solid and unchallengeable territory, but Pribićević himself certainly had an unclouded perception of his standing among the Croats of Croatia-Slavonia. Two of the leading Croat Progressivists, Ivan Lorković and Djuro Šurmin, defected from the HSK as early as June 1918; eventually, their disagreement with Pribićević widened to embrace the demands for basing South Slavic unification on institutionalized equality. The departure of these men left Pribićević with only a few prominent Croats, mostly lawyers, some moderately popular in their electoral or home districts (Hinko Krizman in Varaždin and Ivan Ribar in Djakovo), others less so (Edo Lukinić, Tomislav Tomljenović, Ivan Paleček), and a few influential journalists (Većeslav Wilder, Juraj Demetrović, Budislav Grgur Andjelinović). Pribićević was keenly aware of the problem: "We have a very difficult position in the Croat part of our people, so that it almost appears that these friends are entirely isolated on the Croat side. We must cull and gather them

6. "Ministar Pribićević o položaju pred izbore," *Jug*, Nov. 10, 1920, p. 1.
7. Svetozar Pribićević, "Konstituanta i Narodno Veće," *Demokratija*, Feb. 1, 1921, p. 1.
8. "Govor Svetozara Pribičevića," *Riječ Srba-Hrvata-Slovenaca*, Feb. 19, 1919, p. 1; "Govor min. Svetozara Pribićevića," *Jug*, Nov. 12, 1919, p. 4.
9. Juraj Demetrović, "Monarhija i centralizacija," *Demokratija*, Feb. 1, 1921, p. 1.

so that we all may find ourselves in a great company, because unity lifts the will and energy."[10] But he was still determined to force unitarist centralism on the Croats and expected compliance to follow in due course.

Pribićević's strategy was to work around Croatia-Slavonia, bringing the pressure of all other parts of Yugoslavia to bear on this fortress of "separatism." Immediately after the unification he set out to establish one all-Yugoslav party, which would be zealously attached to the cause of monarchical order, unitary statehood, centralism, and social progress. This aim was shared by more than a dozen other unitarist parties and groups from the former Austro-Hungarian territories and among the South Slavic émigrés in Western Europe, a disposition which the Serbian parties did not oppose, and on Pribićević's initiative, the leaders of the HSK and most of the other unitarist organizations from the former Austro-Hungarian lands convened a political conference in Sarajevo on February 15 and 16, 1919. Besides the HSK, the most important group present at the Sarajevo meeting was the party of Slovene anticlerical liberals. This group had been formed in 1918 out of the merger of the Carniolan Progressive Party and the Styrian People's Party and had become Pribićević's chief partner among the non-Serbs; some of its leaders (Gregor Žerjav, Albert Kramer) were among Pribićević's closest collaborators.

The assembled unitarists decided to disband their organizations and form a new political party, the DS, which would subsequently include parties from Serbia and Montenegro. Though the association with the NRS was not originally excluded, events and outside influences, significant among which were the regent's attempts to weaken the Radicals and prevent the forming of any powerful parties that could curtail his autocratic designs, determined the incipient DS's merger not with the NRS, but with its Serbian opponents. This was effected in April 1919, when the parliamentary club of Pribićević's group fused with those of the Independent Radical Party and with the majority of deputies in the clubs of Serbia's Progressive and National (Liberal) parties.[11]

The Democrats, joined also by most leading Montenegrin proponents of the union with Serbia, were still something of a patchwork, their disparate factions being plainly discernible well after the party's statutes were finally approved in 1921. Significantly, though Pribićević remained the chief party spokesman, the presidency itself went to Ljubomir (Ljuba) Davidović (1863–1940), the leader of the Independent Radicals, who would be better able to make the DS competitive in Serbia, where the Radicals were entrenched. Hence, the old Serbian political rivalries, which had little relevan-

10. "Govor Svetozara Pribićevića," *Riječ Srba-Hrvata-Slovenaca*, Feb. 21, 1919, p. 3.

11. For the best appraisal of the DS's origins see Branislav Gligorijević, *Demokratska stranka i politički odnosi u Kraljevini Srba, Hrvata i Slovenaca* (Belgrade, 1970), pp. 15–81.

cy outside Serbia, became extended statewide as the Democrats and Radicals fought for the control of what was in effect a Serb electorate, though it must be said that the ideological implications of this clash were more pronounced among the Serbs of the former Habsburg lands.

The NRS leaders were not perturbed by Pribićević's attempts to conjoin the unitarist forces of the former Habsburg territories, especially since he originally assured them that, according to his plan, the DS would not function in Serbia, where it would "mainly lean on the Radical Party."[12] His fusion with the NRS's traditional opponents, however, made him the Radicals' chief rival. In truth, neither Pribićević nor the Radicals could afford a merger. Pribićević's espousal of unitarism as well as his personal prestige would have lost all credence among the non-Serbs if he had joined forces with the party that was rightly suspected of being the chief bearer of Great Serbian ideology. For their part, the Radicals had every reason to protect the integral tradition of their party. Just as they wished to protect the integrality of Serbia, they were themselves unprepared to become yet another scrap in Pribićević's quilt. They therefore proposed to absorb Pribićević's followers. Pribićević naturally offered resistance; but his arrangement with the Serbian opposition, though in some ways less charged than a possible merger with the NRS, opened its own set of problems, particularly in regard to the fixed inclinations of Davidović's Independent Radicals.

Stojan Protić has claimed that the merger of Pribićević's and Davidović's parties was logical, since their pasts were remarkably similar. By this he meant, among other things, that both groups aimed at imposing their control on the NRS by means of coalition cabinets in which the Radicals would be obliged to share power.[13] Indeed, both parties radiated an aura of moral superiority over the NRS, and their leaders evidently believed that without them the NRS would flounder in corruption and separatism. Unlike the Old Radicals, both parties aspired to political consistency and both were the refuge of those socialists who believed that the goals of economic democracy could be advanced by means more practical than those favored by revolutionary ideologues. But while the HSK mixed unadulterated royalism and unitarism, the Independent Radicals were a great deal more deliberative on these subjects. One of their founders, Ljubomir Stojanović, broke with the regent over the treatment of Colonel Apis at the Salonika court-martial and went on to found the Serbian Republican Party together with three other notable Independentist leaders (Jovan Žujović, Jaša Prodanović, Milovan Lazarević). In fact, the Independent Radicals had strong ties with the Black Hand, but though this was also true of Milan Pribićević, his loyalties to the increasingly antimonarchist conspirators were attenuated after the unification. Davidović, on the other hand, initially had difficulties in holding on to

12. Stojan Protić, "Evo razjašnjenja!" *Radikal*, Dec. 9, 1921, p. 1.
13. Stojan Protić, "Demokratska stranka," ibid., Nov. 19, 1921, p. 1.

two of his closest younger collaborators, Milan Grol and Kosta Kumanudi, who were tempted by the lure of republicanism.

Avuncular Davidović, popularly known as Uncle Ljuba, or Ljuba the Ant (Ljuba Mrav) because of his small stature and his qualities of diligence and patience, was the very opposite of temperamental Pribićević. Whereas Pribićević was feared, Davidović was genuinely admired, though his mildness, honesty, and goodness, all remarkably uncharacteristic of the ordinary Yugoslav politician, were occasional objects of good-humored jest. Davidović, having been one of the regent's tutors, had an intimate knowledge of Aleksandar's bilious temperament and himself tried moving him to show clemency to Apis ("Not to blood, majesty!"). He was devoted to the monarchy but had no illusions about the regent ("Ever since Salonika I was alert to where that young man was shooting") and therefore never had the occasion to experience the intense disenchantment of those, who, like Pribićević, worshiped Aleksandar uncritically.[14] Moreover, as a Serbian his instincts were not unitaristic. He adopted Pribićević's terminology of *narodno jedinstvo* but was inclined to be tolerant of non-Serb demands and agreeable to negotiation.

Just as some of Pribićević's followers increasingly leaned toward Davidović, there were men among the former Independent Radicals, notably Milorad Drašković (1873–1921), who saw things Pribićević's way and did not hesitate to back him with calls for repressive measures against "state enemies." As long as there was no evidence of Pribićević's actual strength, the voices of moderation within the DS went unheeded, but the parliamentary elections of November 1920 demonstrated the weakness of the Democratic party (see map 2-2). The DS, though formally a winner with the highest percentage of votes (19.88 percent), did very badly for a party that considered itself above Yugoslavia's national divisions. Only 41.48 percent of its votes came from the former Austro-Hungarian territories, and almost two-fifths of that was in areas of Serb concentration in Croatia proper. In other words, even in the regions where Pribićević's influence was strongest, the DS ran far above its statewide average only among Pribićević's most immediate constituency, the Serbs of Croatia.

In the other parts of the former Monarchy, the DS ran close to its national average only in Vojvodina (19.45 percent); it was still far behind the NRS, which captured most of Vojvodina's Serb votes. The Democrats' performance was even worse in Slavonia (14.53), Dalmatia (10.38), and Slovenia (7.76), and remarkably poor in Bosnia-Hercegovina (5.59), where the Radicals and Agrarians deprived the DS of almost the entire Serb constituency. In the purely Croat areas, with the exception of the district of Sušak, whose voters were certainly affected by the festering dispute with Italy over adjoin-

14. Jovanović, *Ljudi, ljudi*, vol. 2, pp. 23–31.

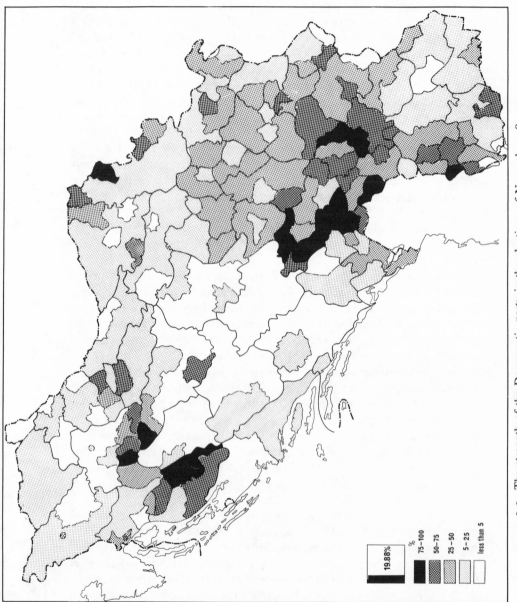

	%
19.88%	
■	75–100
▨	50–75
▨	25–50
░	5–25
□	less than 5

2-2. The strength of the Democratic party in the elections of November 28, 1920

ing Rijeka, the DS's showing was negligible. The DS got a third of Sušak's votes (33.71 percent), and the town of Bakar, which lay geographically within this district but was counted separately, became the only Croat city that gave the DS a clear majority (51.08 percent). But though the DS generally ran better in urban centers than in the surrounding countryside—receiving, for example, 17.43 percent of the vote in Zagreb and only 0.66 percent in the rest of Zagreb's district (*kotar*)—there were very few Croat towns that gave it more than a quarter of their votes, notably, besides Bakar, its neighbor Senj (28.17) and, in Dalmatia, Sinj (35.86), the latter a quirk that can be attributed to the exceptional prestige of Mirko Tripalo, a local landowner and one of Dalmatia's leading Democrats.[15] Even in Split, the supposed capital of unitarist Yugoslavism, the DS got only 17.24 percent, showing that Dalmatia's unitarist reputation, even with the fears engendered by Italian imperialism, was vastly exaggerated. In Slovenia, the DS's base in the old anticlerical movement was evident from its respectable performance in the main urban centers: Ljubljana, 36.33 percent, a plurality; Maribor, 16.90; Novo Mesto, 33.62; Celje, 35.59; and a spectacular 65.94 percent in Kranj. Elsewhere in Slovenia the Democrats did badly.

The 1920 electoral vote showed clearly that the Democrats' strength depended not on Pribićević's constituency but on the votes garnered in Serbia proper and the adjoining southeastern provinces. The majorities achieved in Kosovo (53.65 percent), Metohia (62.99), and the Sandžak (69.11) were particularly impressive, though they seem less so when translated into fractions of eligible votes (29.71, 33.34, and 46.64 percent, respectively). The DS also did fairly well in western Macedonia and in pre-1912 Montenegro, in the latter case augmented by the nominally independent list of Novica Šaulić, which won 82.48 percent in the district of Piva, but whose showing is not registered on the map. In short, in the absence of minority nationalist parties, the voters of Yugoslavia's turbulent southeast preferred the Democrats over the Great Serbian Radicals, though it must be admitted that in some of these areas, notably in Macedonia, the DS was seen as no less Great Serbian than the NRS. Davidović had himself been one of the organizers, in May 1904, of the first Serbian guerrilla actions in Macedonia. Nonetheless, since the elections negated the DS's unitarist claims, showing it as essentially a Serb party, moreover a party of the less influential sections of the Serb bourgeoisie, Davidović was strenghened in his conviction that the Democrats, like the NRS, simultaneously had to become more Serbian and more conciliatory to the non-Serbs. This precipitated a split in the DS ranks, leading to Pribićević's defection in March 1924.

Croatia's Serbs, and most, though not all, of the Croat unitarists, followed Pribićević out of the DS, leaving it with an almost wholly Serbian base. In

15. Stojan Protić, "Izborne karakteristike i kuriozumi!" *Samouprava*, Dec. 3, 1920, p. 1.

addition, Davidović's opening to the Croat opposition and Radić, which precipitated the split with Pribićević, was drastically usurped by the NRS in 1925. The DS was left with the proclaimed goal of revising the centralist constitution, which it dared not advance in the period of relative political harmony that existed after 1925. By 1928, when acute parliamentary clashes took a violent turn, the Democrats for the first time openly identified with the defense of Serbian hegemonism. They were in fact filling the political vacuum created by the disintegration of the NRS, which, after Pašić's death, had split into numerous factions and was increasingly becoming the plaything of the king. Hence, by the twilight of Yugoslavia's parliamentary period, the DS, while never abandoning centralism, was by default simultaneously becoming a defender of Serbian supremacy.

All these developments were in the future. The DS of the immediate postwar period still spoke with the voice of Svetozar Pribićević, the most articulate member of its leadership, who attached great importance to the development of and strict adherence to party ideology. As early as 1897, Pribićević had advanced what he called the "guiding idea" of Serbo-Croat unity—the notion that the "Serbs and Croats were parts of a single people, from which fact flowed the basic principle of *narodno jedinstvo* between Serbs and Croats." Though he realized that this notion "was not generally held," he attributed the lapse to the low level of unitarist consciousness.[16] Though Pribićević held that a unitary Yugoslav nation already objectively existed, he at the same time maintained that it had to be propagated by careful missionary work of enlightened Yugoslavist intelligentsia. Meanwhile, as Pribićević consistently maintained, there could be no negotiations, agreements, or forced congruities between the Serbs and Croats. Because they were one, the only acceptable relationship between them was oneness.[17] In this way, from the beginning of his public life, Pribićević used a unitarist proposition to establish a principle that could in turn lay the foundations for the accuracy of the original proposition. At the same time, however, he only grudgingly admitted to the discussion of furthering unitarist nationhood, fearing to detract from its declared substance. The circle of Pribićević's logic was rather angular.

In the aftermath of the unification Pribićević reasserted his theory that there could be no agreements between Serbs and Croats, widening it also to the Slovenes. But though his enemies made biting jest of Pribićević's outlandish notion—Protić having observed that "every high schooler knows that the ancient Greeks, who were also a single people, living in their small states, agreed and fought between themselves, without reaching a higher state of

---

16. Cited in Sava N. Kosanović's introduction to Svetozar Pribićević's *Diktatura kralja Aleksandra*, trans. Andra Milosavljević (Belgrade, 1952), pp. ix–x.

17. See Pribićević's speech of July 9, 1918, to the Croatian Sabor in Većeslav Wilder, *Dva smjera u hrvatskoj politici* (Zagreb, 1918), pp. 60–61.

unity in the course of antiquity," something that was obviously beyond the grasp of the "former instructor at the Pakrac normal school,"[18]—the notion was a necessary link in unitarist theory. In Pribićević's own words, "agreements and haggling can exist between Czechs and Germans, between peoples who have different interests and wish to bring them into harmony, but among members of the same people, among the Serbs, Croats, and Slovenes, such things cannot and should not exist, because the disposition toward agreements and bargains shows that they are not one people."[19] By extension, the same applied to all federal arrangements. Except for Germany, and there only because of selfish interests of a myriad of petty dynasts, there had never been an instance of a single people forming a federal union. "Switzerland is a federal state, but, as you know, the Swiss are not a single nation, as they embrace Frenchmen, Italians, and Germans."[20] But though the artificiality of this ostrich theory lay in an attempt to overcome Yugoslavia's national question by establishing an obstacle between its perception and its existence, Pribićević himself did not abide by its rules. Instead, he set out to undo all the institutional resources of Serb, Croat, and Slovene national individuality.

From the beginning of his work for the establishment of the DS, Pribićević wanted the party to be one that would above all express the determination "to do away with all regional governments, all autonomies, all historical provinces."[21] Moreover, like Pašić's Radicals, he believed that the administrative division of the country had to be undertaken in such a way that "a district, a province, or a department—however they might be called—might include portions of Serbia, Bosnia, and Croatia; another parts of Bosnia, Slavonia, and Dalmatia; and so on, depending on economic needs, but in any case to speed up the tempo of our national unification."[22] The point was to abolish all references to historical frontiers and with them the traditions of national statehood. In Croatia, for example, the office of the Ban had to be reduced to the level of an ordinary appointment by the ministry of the interior, or, better still, abolished together. Pribićević's objection was not that the title was of medieval origin—much the same could be said of the royal title—but that it was strictly Croatian: "The King unites us, the Ban divides us."[23]

Pribićević's Democrats could not form a mental representation of mon-

18. Stojan Protić, "Njegova teorija!" *Radikal*, Oct. 23, 1921, p. 1. Protić was nearly incapable of writing titles that did not end with an exclamation mark!
19. "Govor Min. prosvjete g. Svet. Pribićevića na Kongresu jugosl. profesora u Zagrebu," *Narodna riječ*, Oct. 5, 1921, p. 2.
20. "Govor Svetozara Pribićevića u Karlovcu na povratku iz Like 26.-X. 1920.," *Karlovac*, Oct. 19, 1920, p. 3.
21. "Za Jugoslavensku demokratsku stranku. Izjave ministra Svetozara Pribićevića," *Riječ Srba-Hrvata-Slovenaca*, Jan. 28, 1919, p. 1.
22. "Govor Svetozara Pribičevića," ibid., Feb. 20, 1919, p. 1.
23. Milan Pribićević, "O banu i autonomijama," ibid., Aug. 21, 1920, p. 4.

archy in Croat eyes, where it was widely considered a strictly Serbian institution. They were, in fact, irritated by the objections of those Croats who reminded Pribićević of his HSK days, when he defended Croatian autonomy against the Hungarians. The Democrats could not understand how "separatist" Croats managed to consign the Hungarians and Serbs to the same category. Keeping the Croatian Sabor made sense because the Hungarians were an alien foe; but the Serbs were the same as Croats. The Serbian army in Croatia was in its own house, not on foreign territory. Worrying about the preservation of one's national traditions and institutions was a sign of backwardness. And since inequality was impossible, the insistence on its manifestations was bad faith: "Brother Croats sit in the assembly in Belgrade. Uncle Pete is their king just as surely as he is to the Serbs, Aleksandar is their regent, and there are Croats among the ministers in Belgrade, just like the Serbs."[24]

Pribićević and his followers could not counter the strength of historically based national identities among the South Slavs without a historical interpretation of their own. But as the leaders of a truly antihistoricist faction, they proved most deficient in this area. Certain variants of unitarist ideology, which emanated from the DS, posited a unitarist millennium. Ljudevit, the early ninth-century prince of Pannonian Croatia, was seen as the ruler of the "first Yugoslav state of the Croats, Serbs, and Slovenes, which progressed splendidly, until domestic discord and quarrels among the Croats themselves destroyed it."[25] But this golden age could not have been shattered by deliberate discord alone. That would have been contrary to the unitarist dogma, which held that the common consciousness of South Slavs compelled them to cohere unto themselves inseparably. Though discord was also evidence of kinship, since "one always wrangles first of all with members of one's own household, with those who are closest," inwardly considered acts were not really at work in South Slavic differentiation. Rather, the South Slavs were separated either by largely casual turns of their own making ("In antiquity, many centuries ago, the Croats and Serbs lived under one roof as brothers, and then they migrated, the Croats to the West, the Serbs to the East. The Croats accepted Catholic religion, the Serbs—Orthodoxy") or by outright foreign intervention.[26] The most extreme formulation of the latter view can be found in Milan Pribićević: "All our provinces were the handiwork of our enemies, the Swabians and Magyars. Not our work."[27] The obvious im-

24. "Šta treba da traže crkvene opštine," *Srpsko kolo,* June 10, 1920, p. 2.
25. Milivoj B. Janković [pseud. of Milivoj Blažeković], *Hrvatski seljak u novoj državi: Razgovori za seljački puk* (Zagreb, 1919), p. 5.
26. Ibid., pp. 13–14, 16.
27. Milan Pribićević, "Pisma bratu rataru: Pripazimo na one što hoće autonomije," *Srpsko kolo,* June 10, 1920, p. 1.

plication was that the consciousness, too, of separate Serb, Croat, and Slovene nationhood was the work of foreign enemies.

The notion that "separatist" sentiment resulted from foreign subversion fitted well with Svetozar Pribićević's view that the Croat and other national movements were in the pay of the Habsburg pretender, Italy, and other revisionist neighbors; but this view was ultimately untenably, representing simply a fanciful craving for the overturning of historical record. Pribićević said as much in his second speech at the founding of the DS in Sarajevo, when he incongrously praised one of the fiercest "alien foes," the Ottoman Turks, for crushing the germs of Bosnian national individuality in the bud:

> In the difficult days of our distant past, the destruction of the old Bosnian state's sovereignty was in fact a great good fortune for the people; had sovereign Bosnia and Hercegovina remained, it is quite possible that our people would now have a fourth name [in addition to the Serb, Croat, and Slovene]. With the fall of old feudal and sovereign Bosnian state, a carrier of another separate sovereignty among our people, which could have created an additional national appellation in [our] state, was also destroyed. In addition, you should know that we were faced with the danger of Montenegro's separate sovereignty creating another national identity among our people. Today we must destroy all those sovereignties.[28]

It turned out that foreign rule was welcome after all, but only where it upset South Slavic differentiation, which must have been started by the logic of internal state-building. As might be expected, Pribićević swerved from admitting the possibility of any such internal causation, nor did he express regret that no single foreign power had succeeded in subjugating all the South Slavs. But he was distressed that his friends and he were powerless to turn the unified Yugoslav territory into a tabula rasa.[29]

In a way, the tragedy of the unitarists was that they were unable to rub out the long and complicated history of the South Slavs and start afresh with a clean tablet on which they could inscribe a new, simpler, and less discordant and frustrating chronicle. Try as they might, the goal of a "unified or, as is more pleasantly put, simple state" kept eluding them.[30] They themselves were partly to blame, because their own motives were inconsistent. The craving for simplicity was not just an abstract principle but to a considerable extent reflected the interests of Pribićević's constituency among the Serbs of Croatia, whose centralism was above all a means to the final uprooting of Croat state tradition.

28. "Sa sarajevske skupštine," *Riječ Srba-Hrvata-Slovenaca*, Feb. 24, 1919, pp. 3–4. Pribićević did not anticipate the recognition of Bosnian Muslim and Montenegrin nationhood in post-1945 Yugoslavia.
29. "Govor min. Svetozara Pribičevića," *Jug*, Oct. 8, 1919, p. 4.
30. "Govor Svetozara Pribićevića," *Riječ Srba-Hrvata-Slovenaca*, Feb. 19, 1919, p. 1.

Svetozar Pribićević feared "tribal" autonomies, because he was certain that their champions counted on the fact that "every autonomy contains an element of dynamism that goes after final independence of individual parts.[31] Since most Serbian political leaders were centralists and hoped to realize their predominance without carving out a separate Serb unit within Yugoslavia, they were not a direct danger to Pribićević's ideal order. Similarly, the Slovenes were, in Pribićević's words, "too realistic" to be interested in a Great Slovenia.[32] The Croats, however, retained a vast reserve of proindependence sentiment. From the standpoint of the Serb minority in Croatia, that was a lasting source of danger. And since it was taken for granted that the autonomies would lead to independent states, the DS opposed them, "because they concealed the continuation of Serb-Croat struggle."[33] Yugoslavist unitarism was seen as the surest solution to the Serb problem in Croatia, since it was certain to destroy Croat national consciousness, though not necessarily its Serb equivalent.

The mobilizing tactic of Pribićević and the DS in the struggle against Croat nationalism was to convince the Croats that they would never be allowed to unite all the Croat lands within an autonomous Croatia. A united banate of Croatia-Slavonia-Dalmatia would rightly provoke Serbian annexation of Bosnia-Hercegovina and Vojvodina. "On the one side, on the basis of rights earned with blood, there would emerge a legitimate Great Serbia, led in the [central] parliament and government by men from within her frontiers, and on the other, Little Croatia, whose sons would not have the right to influence the course and affairs of the whole state on account of their insignificant autonomous prerogatives. The Croats would find themselves in the position of stepsons, exactly as they were in the Hungarian parliament and government."[34] Clearly, even if autonomy were granted to Croatia, no Serbian institutions, distinct from the existing central representative and executive agencies, were necessary. Moreover, it was not even certain that the Croats could count on all parts of Croatia-Slavonia and Dalmatia. It was taken for granted that the "Dalmatians and the inhabitants of the Croatian littoral [did] not want to go with the destitute Zagreb area, with the impoverished counties of Zagreb and Bjelovar-Križevci, which barely managed to survive; instead, they wanted to join strong Serbia. The same [was] true of Srijem, Bačka, and the Banat."[35] Though the disagreements among Croats and the comparative state of collective riches in the cited areas were nowhere close to this representation, the Croats were told that an autonomous Croatia could be certain

---

31. "Govor min. Svetozara Pribičevića," *Jug*, Oct. 7, 1919, p. 4.
32. "Kongres Demokratske Stranke: Govor g. Svetozara Pribićevića o unutrašnjoj politici," *Demokratija*, Nov. 6, 1921, p. 2.
33. Pribićević, "Pisma bratu rataru," p. 1.
34. H., "Nova situacija u Hrvatskoj," *Jedinstvo*, March 4, 1920, p. 1.
35. Janković, *Hrvatski seljak*, p. 19.

of including only the counties of Virovitica, Požega, Varaždin, Zagreb, Bjelovar-Križevci, Modruš-Rijeka, and Lika-Krbava—in the last two cases without their coastal areas. It would be a small, poor, and landlocked country, easy prey for the Italians and the Hungarians. But oddly, quite unlike Pašić's solution, it could well include the heavily Serb areas of Lika, Kordun, and Banija.

Where the Croats were confronted with the threat of smallness, the Serbs were warned of greatness. Great Serbia, however expansive, was nonetheless smaller than a Great Yugoslavia. In answer to Pribićević's rhetorical question, raised in 1920 among the pro-Radical Serbs of Bačka, Great Serbia was equivalent to organizing the "Serb parts of our country into one state and cutting out those parts of the [Yugoslav] state where there were no Serbs, for example, cutting off the littoral, where the Croats were in the majority, though there were many Serbs there, too. That way, more than a half of our state would [remain outside Serbia]. Who is for that? Did we fight the war for that? Was Serbia overrun and subjugated so that these chunks might now be cut? Does Serbia need only Vojvodina? Does it not also need the sea?"[36] Though greater than the allowable Great Croatia, Great Serbia, too, would be an incomplete entity, in fact a Little Serbia. Like Pašić, the Serbs of Croatia refused the status of minority for any Serb group, above all themselves. But unlike Pašić, most of their leaders were realistic enough to know that Great Serbia could not extend to twenty-five miles southeast of Zagreb: "We live mixed with our Croat brothers from Zemun [Srijem] and Montenegro to Varaždin and Gorski Kotar [the hinterland of Rijeka]. How can we separate outselves from them within a Great Serbia? Those who teach us thusly, direct us to something that can never be, and even if it could, it would only lead to a Serbo-Croat massacre."[37]

Contrary to these warnings, the Serbs of Croatia were quite susceptible to Great Serbian propaganda. According to the editors of Milan Pribićević's *Srpsko kolo* (Serb Circle), a DS semiweekly for the Serb peasants in Croatia, "before the liberation we wrote much more about Serbdom, Serbia, King Petar, Cyrillic script, and the flag, because it was then necessary to create the opinion for the destruction of Austria. . . . Now the Swabian is toppled."[38] Having prepared the ground for the boundless exaltation of everything Serbian, the DS leaders were faced with the guileless resistance of their constituents to anything that smacked of lèse Serbianism. "What do we need [local] self-administration for, Milan" they said to the younger Pribićević in Lika and Kordun in 1919. "Just send one Serbian to each district and let him rule

36. "Ministar Pribićević u Srbobranu," *Jedinstvo,* Nov. 17, 1920, p. 1.
37. Milan Pribićević, "Poruka za izbore! Braći ratarima i dobrovoljcima i svoj narodnoj gospodi na svoj Krajini, u Baniji, na Kordunu i Lici, a na čelu njihovim svima 'Seljačkim Većima,'" electoral supplement to *Srpsko kolo,* Nov. 14, 1920, p. 2.
38. "Na pitanja o 'Seljačkoj snazi,'" *Srpsko kolo,* July 3, 1920, p. 2.

over us.'' And when Milan responded that not all Serbians were angels, they disbelievingly burst into roars of laughter.[39] Nevertheless, Milan Pribićević himself exploited this sentiment, reminding his Serb voters that those who stayed away from the ballot box "betrayed Uncle Pete and the Kingdom, helped Radić's republic, and drove a knife into their own Serb hearts."[40] The same feeling was expressed in Svetozar's famous slogan, "Dok je Like nema republike!'' (For as long as there is Lika, there will be no republic!)

The political career of the Pribićević brothers was devoted to the emancipation of Croatia's Serbs. They wanted to assure that community's equality with the Croats by destroying Croat nationhood. At the same time, within the larger Serb world they wanted to establish the parity between Croatia's Serbs and Serbia proper by a policy that was more monarchist and militarist than that of the Radicals. Though no fair-minded person could possibly object to the goals of equality and parity, the tactics they chose were in both cases detrimental to the best interests of Croatia's Serb community. Moreover, the Serbs of Croatia could take one of the two tactics in hand, but not both, because it was impossible to undermine Croat national consciousness by promoting Serbian institutions. When Svetozar Pribićević advanced his party as the surest "support of the throne and dynasty," when he misrepresented Protić's extenuated autonomism as an attempt to deny the command of the army to the king, or when Milan swaggered that the Democrats were "King Petar's men" and that "Regent Aleksandar kept Svetozar knee to knee," they were in fact unwittingly helping to stiffen the Croat resistance to unitarism.[41] Their regional flavor was most evident when they argued for an autonomous "Una region," in effect the conjoining of Lika, Kordun, and Banija with Bosnia's predominantly Serb northwest, bringing together the Serbs from both sides of the old Ottoman frontier on the Una River.[42] Their hopes in this direction were thwarted by the deal between the Radicals and Bosnian Muslims, which prevented any tampering with Bosnia's frontiers. Nevertheless, the district of Krajina (literally, the frontier), which emerged in 1922, was an attempt at Serb concentration in Croatia. Protić described it as embracing the "counties of Lika-Krbava, Modruš-Rijeka (minus one district), and a fairly large portion of . . . Zagreb county, inhabited mainly by Serbs." He added, with a touch of dry humor, that this was done "to satisfy that Croatian [*Hrvaćanin*] of ours, who measures all relations and affairs of our kingdom with the yardstick of Banija, Kordun, and Lika."[43]

39. Milan Pribićević, "Pisma Seljačkim Većima. Kralj i Srbija," ibid., Jan. 4, 1923, p. 49.
40. Pribićević, "Poruka za izbore!" p. 1.
41. "Govor g. Svetozara Pribićevića," *Jedinstvo,* March 4, 1920, p. 1; "Ministar Pribićević u Srobranu"; Pribićević, "Poruka za izbore," pp. 1–2.
42. Milan Pribićević, "Pisma bratu rataru. Pripazimo na one što hoće autonomije," *Srpsko kolo,* June 17, 1920, p. 1.
43. Stojan Protić, "Oblasti i državno uredjenje," *Radikal,* Nov. 23, 1921, p. 1.

Milan Pribićević was perfectly straightforward when he denied Croat accusations that he encouraged the "secession of Serb Lika and Banija from Croatia and their unification with Serbia."[44] His way of putting it seemed to imply a challenge to the historical integrity of Croatia; still, though he and the other Pribićevićes, unlike the Radicals, did not want to turn the question of Serb status in Croatia into one of Serbia's immediate concerns, he and his brothers sincerely believed that by promoting Serbian institutions they were strengthening the position of the Serbs in Croatia. Indeed, they saw the unification of all state services in terms of extending the existing Serbian agencies.[45] Instead of equality of opportunity, they obtained various privileges and sinecures from the central institutions for their constituents, obliging the Serbs of Croatia to defend the status quo against the Croat opposition. Svetozar Pribićević's struggle agains "tribal" quotas in administration was not an attempt to secure the precedence of ability, but rather a rearguard action against the equal distribution of government positions. He certainly did not win any Croat adherents by his sophistic claims that the "Croats were one people with the Serbs, requiring no special protection, enjoying the same rights as the Serbs, hence there [was] no Croat question in relation to the Serbs."[46] Nor was the Croat public unmindful of the fact that elements within the DS believed that Serbianization was the surest road to genuine Yugoslavism. These were all stumbling blocks to the consistency of the DS's ideology and to the party's affirmation among the non-Serbs.

Svetozar Pribićević's proposed solution for these problems was the "creation of a great people," directed on the road of national integration by the unitary Yugoslav state.[47] If the past historical processes could not be undone, they could be redirected. All the DS factions agreed on this point, Milan Grol having noted Ramsay Muir's dictum that "every nation had to prove its right to existence by a show of unshakable will."[48] By rule, the Democrats were voluntarists, regarding will as the fundamental principle in the shaping of nations. As Pribićević saw it, the opposition to unitarism ought not prevent the formation of a "great national personality, a great people of twelve million, and soon, God willing, fifty million people."[49] The indomitable triumph of the will would wipe away all obstacles to this "new great people," whose emergence would assure Yugoslavia's "rank

44. Pribićević, "O banu i autonomijama," p. 4.

45. This is evident from Svetozar Pribićević's approach to the unification of Yugoslavia's legal codes: "During the past two years [1918–1920], we had a regional system [of laws]. Vojvodina had its own laws, Croatia had Hungarian laws, Dalmatia Austrian laws, Montenegro the laws of King Nikola. Only Serbia and Macedonia had Serbian laws." It is not clear how the laws of King Nikola were less native than the laws of King Petar ("Ministar Pribićević u Srbobranu," p. 1).

46. Svetozar Pribićević, "Državno-pravni monstrumi," *Demokratija*, April 4, 1920, p. 1.

47. "Ministar Pribićević o situaciji," ibid., July 21, 1921, p. 1.

48. Milan Grol, "Savremeni nacionalizam," *Jugoslovenska demokratska liga*, 1919, no. 1, p. 11.

49. "Kongres Demokratske Stranke," p. 2.

among the great powers in ten to fifteen years."⁵⁰ The only prerequisite was that unitarism become planned state policy.

The extravagant etatism of Democrats was an aspect of their belief that a "people can be a single entity only if it has a single national soul, a single national consciousness, and a single will." But this ideal unity could only be accomplished by the state. The schools had to teach unitarism, the laws had to reflect it, and so on. In each case "to whatever area you direct your attention, you will see what great tasks the state has in constructing a single national soul." As a result, the centralizing measures promoted by the DS were not a caprice, but actions that proclaimed premeditated policy.⁵¹ Above all, the state could never be entrusted to autonomist forces, since this could only delay the forging of a Yugoslav nation and its assimilation; calls for the maintenance of provincial autonomies were contrary to state interest and reflected the regrettable "conceptions of pessimism."⁵²

The credulous worship of the state was seen as a specifically Serbian virtue, reflecting an established native state tradition. The Serbians loved their state "no less so when they [did] not agree with it, and even when they growled at it."⁵³ In Pribićević's view, Milorad Drašković, Pribićević's chief ally among Davidović's Democrats and Yugoslavia's minister of the interior during the stormy period from August 1920 to July 1921, who was assassinated by a group of Communist youths, was the best example of a patriot who "boundlessly loved the state. He was terribly pained by attacks on the state," recalled Pribićević, "and often told me that he would not tolerate such phrases as 'this accursed state' or 'this precipice.' The state should not be referred to in that way, because it is our mother, our holiness." Indeed, the DS considered it its duty to defend the state with all available means:

> This great—and if I may be allowed to say—state man, saw clearly that in this age of great convulsions and worldwide troubles, when the old order is bursting and breaking under the weight of new rising state formations, the methods of Nazarean tolerance and stereotyped formulas about liberty, thought up by pre-war idealists, are no longer applicable. He loved and respected liberty, but was deeply convinced that full, real, and lasting liberty could be granted only by an organized and universally respected state.⁵⁴

Pribićević admired Drašković's willingness to wield the sword of repression over the two hostile camps of "Bolshevik revolutionists" and "national separatists," failing to perceive the full vengeance exacted by this policy. To be sure, since the resistance to unitarism was an outgrowth of formed national ideologies, their strength would not have been lessened by a more

---

50. "Govor min. Svetozara Pribićevića," *Jug*, Nov. 7, 1919, p. 4.
51. "Govor Svetozara Pribićevića," *Riječ Srba-Hrvata-Slovenaca*, Feb. 20, 1919, p. 1.
52. "Jugoslavenska demokratska stranka i jugoslavenska demokratska liga," ibid., Feb. 19, 1919, p. 2.
53. "Kongres Demokratske Stranke," p. 2.
54. Svetozar Pribićević, "Milorad Drašković i zaštita države," *Život*, July 17, 1924, p. 1.

enlightened policy. Nonetheless, the readiness to apply harsh repressive measures against national dissidents and Communists, so characteristic of the DS, certainly contributed to the resolve of non-Serb national movements. Still, the grim abandon with which Pribićević sallied forth against "separatists" cannot be understood apart from his belief that the state was preordained to triumph, since states historically shaped individual national communities. As the most influential Democrat and important cabinet minister, he pursued a deliberate policy of polarization, envisioning a struggle to the end between "two opposing camps, the camp of action and the camp of reaction."[55] His private war against Radić's party was to be fought to the point of extermination. "Everything among us that is stunted, weak, indecisive, and unclear will die out in the struggle for survival." There would be "one people, one state, one party," and, presumably, one leader.[56]

A certain predilection for totalitarian forms and methods was indeed evident in the DS. Pribićević saw his organization as the most devoted patriotic force, to which all friends of the state should belong. Since there was little or no political legitimacy outside the DS, no quarter was to be given to its enemies. This attitude encouraged the growth of client organizations, devoted to special tasks in mobilization or intimidation. For example, the peasant councils of Milan Pribićević gathered some 15,000 Serb peasants in Banija, Kordun, Slavonia, and parts of Bosnia and Dalmatia, aimed against the influence of Radić's peasant movement. Far more menacing were the openly terrorist unitarist organizations, such as the Orjuna (acronym for the Organization of Yugoslav Nationalists), founded at Split in March 1921, whose members used physical violence against political opponents and openly preached the abolition of parliamentarianism, prevention of social revolution, dictatorship of Yugoslavist nationalists—perhaps under royal patronage, corporativist legislature, and the need "to knock out of the heads of our masses the idea that they still have a right to decide whether this state should or should not exist."[57] The similarities between the Orjuna and

---

55. "Govor Svetozara Pribićevića u Karlovcu," *Karlovac,* Nov. 26, 1920, p. 3.

56. "Jedan narod—jedna država—jedna stranka," *Riječ Srba-Hrvata-Slovenaca,* Feb. 19, 1919, p. 1.

57. Cited in Branislav Gligorijević, "Organizacija jugoslovenskih nacionalista (Orjuna)," *Istorija XX veka: zbornik radova,* vol. 5 (1963), p. 344. Consult the same article for the best analysis of the Orjuna's origins, methods, program, and ties to the DS. The Orjuna was not the only paramilitary "patriotic" organization with ties to the DS. Democrats had influence in various veterans' organizations, notably among the former volunteers in the Serbian army and guerrillas (Chetniks) who fought behind the enemy lines in Bosnia-Hercegovina, Serbia, and Macedonia. In response to the DS's prestige among these groups, the Radicals tried to create their own paramilitary factions, notably the Srnao (acronym for Serb National Youth). The Communists and Croat national parties countered the terror of unitarist and Great Serbian groups with their own paramilitary organizations, the Communist PAČ in Slovenia and the nationalist Hanao (acronym for Croat National Youth). For more information on this phenomenon see Nusret Šehić, *Četništvo u Bosni i Hercegovini (1918–1941)* (Sarajevo, 1971); Branislav Gligorijević, "Srpska nacionalna omladina (Srnao)," *Istorijski glasnik,* 1964, nos. 2–3, pp. 3–38; Gligorijević, "Demokratska i Radikalna stranka prema revolucionarnim pokretima u Jugoslaviji 1919–1921," ibid., 1969, no. 2, pp. 95–106.

Italian fascist *squadristi* are obvious. And Pribićević was exactly the sort of "Yugoslav Mussolini," whom these extremists imagined mounted on a white horse. But for all of his horror of Soviet Russia, Pribićević and his followers had a weakness for the "universal centralism" of Lenin's state. Moreover, they often described the DS as a modern, progressive, and social party, and criticized the "tribal" parties, such as Radić's HPSS, as "non-class" formations, as if the DS were a party of the revolutionary classes.[58]

It has been observed that agreement and coexistence between the Serbs and Croats were impossible without democracy.[59] The Democrats believed that democracy was possible without agreements, and if it could not be had without recognition of Serb, Croat, and Slovene individualities, so much the worse for democracy. Some of their leaders persisted in believing that the conglomeration of South Slavs was within reach and was only prevented by "those chains that are always imposed on new movements of humanity by the masses, which never run after changes."[60] As a result, the differences between the Democrats and Radicals never seemed that fundamental to the anticentralist forces. Both parties used the slogan *narodno jedinstvo,* but only because this principle justified centralism. To the Radicals, centralism was a guarantee of Serbian predominance; to the Democrats it was an expression of their belief that the South Slavs constituted one nation. In addition, central-ism "suited Pribićević's group because of their fears that the question of the role of Serbs in Croatia might be raised in a federal or confederal state community."[61] Moreover, the NRS and the DS were ruling parties; they possessed power, which under the prevailing conditions was nine-tenths of the law. Hence, in the political terminology of many anticentralists, Yugoslavist unitarism was assumed to be a convenient disguise, deceptively flaunted by Serbian hegemonists and their supporters. This conviction was strengthened by the fact that both the NRS and the DS were monarchist parties, vying for the patronage of the court, an eminently Serbian institution openly committed to centralism.

Pribićević's devotion to the Serbs of Croatia was the stage trap in the Democratic drama. The impossible dream of turning a minority into a major-ity, which was at the heart of his faction's operations, became the tragedy of his life; by the time Pribićević understood that his constituency was least protected when it did Belgrade's bidding against the Croat majority among which it lived, the Serbs of Croatia were already at bitter odds with their

58. Demetrović, "Monarhija i centralizacija," p. 1; "Ministar Pribićević u Srbobranu" p. 1; "Govor Svetozara Pribićevića u Karlovcu," *Karlovac,* Nov. 26, 1920, p. 3; "Govor min. Svetozara Pribičevića," *Jug,* Nov. 12, 1919, p. 4.

59. Mita Dimitrijević, *Mi i Hrvati: Hrvatsko pitanje (1914–1939); Sporazum sa Hrvatima* (Belgrade, 1939), p. 14.

60. Većeslav Vilder [Wilder], *Bika za rogove* (London, 1957), p. 128.

61. Branislav Gligorijević, "Razlike i dodirne tačke u gledištu na nacionalno pitanje izmedju Radikalne i Demokratske stranke 1919–1929.," *Jugoslovenski istorijski časopis,* 1969, no. 4, p. 155.

Croat neighbors: "After the war," he wrote, "Belgrade power holders always called upon the Serbs of Croatia for help when it was feignedly necessary to defend imperiled state unity or to fight against 'Croat separatism." But as soon as official Belgrade felt that it could profit from some sort of compromise with the Croats, it would sacrifice the Serbs of Croatia without hesitation and with merry heart, making them a red rag to the Croat eyes."62

Unitarist Pribićević was fond of denouncing the Croat penchant for political behavior that was reminiscent of the policy "conducted by the Irishmen in [Britain]."63 But unlike the casting in Protić's analogy, Pribićević's Ulstermen became the whipping boys for the policies of Pašić's Unionists. They were as much victims as villains.

The Democratic Centralists

The great ambition of Svetozar Pribićević was to unite all the "democratic elements," that is the unitarist and centralist forces, within the DS. "I ask you, gentlemen," he entreated at one rally, "does the forming of small groups, especially of nonparty groups, make any sense?"—though he knew full well that the Radicals accused him of creating splinter factions for the sake of undermining the NRS.1 Still, there was an array of parties and affinity groups, some not at all insignificant, to the left of the DS, that formed a kind of an ideological kinship with the Democrats and in some cases shared the same line of descent as the main DS factions. They may be called the democratic centralists with only a touch of irony, because they were less authoritarian than the DS, shared its centralism, and on the whole its unitarism. The foremost among these groups was the Savez zemljoradnika (SZ, Alliance of Agrarian Workers), sometimes called simply the Agrarian party or Serbian Agrarians, though the SZ was quite literally an alliance that included Slovene and Croat peasant groups.2

The Agrarians were a fairly important political group. The party ranked fifth in numbers among Yugoslavia's parties, and thanks to the boycotting of the Constituent Assembly by Radić's deputies, their parliamentary club of thirty-nine members was the fourth largest. A survey of their electoral performance (see map 2-3) points to a fair showing in Serbia and Slovenia, and a

62. Pribićević, *Diktatura*, p. 206.
63. "Kongres Demokratske Stranke," p. 2.
1. "Govor Svetozara Pribićevića u Karlovcu," *Karlovac*, Nov. 1920, p. 3.
2. For the most concise presentation of the SZ's origins, early years, and ideology, see Milan Gaković, "Osnivanje Saveza zemljoradnika i njegov program (1919–1921)," *Godišnjak Društva istoričara BiH*, vols. 21–27 (1976), pp. 199–218.

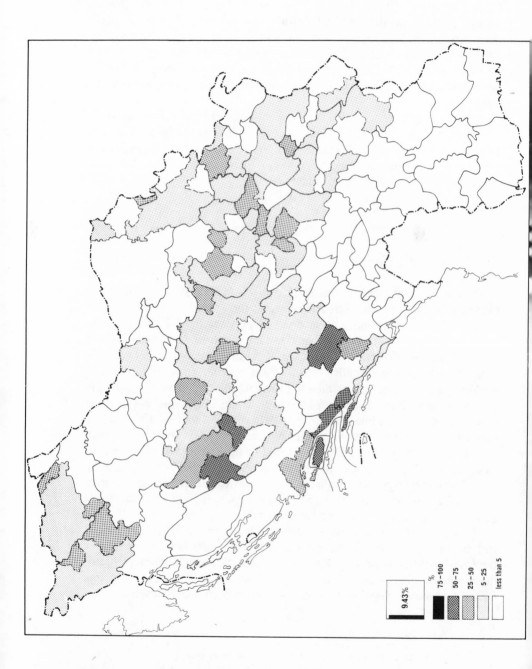

9.43%

%
75–100
50–75
25–50
5–25
less than 5

rather strong showing in northwestern Bosnia, eastern Hercegovina, and central Dalmatia. In the elections of 1920, they did not put up any electoral lists in Bačka, Baranja, Montenegro, the Sandžak, Metohia, Kosovo, Macedonia, or for that matter in the three principal cities (Belgrade, Zagreb, Ljubljana), an odd district in Serbia, and two counties of Croatia-Slavonia, where they were in general no match for Stjepan Radić's HPSS among the Croat peasants and the DS among the Serbs. The Agrarians were, in short, a predominantly Serb party; about three-quarters of their votes came from Serb voters, and of that, slightly over half from Bosnia-Hercegovina. Their following among the Croats was strictly regional (central Dalmatia) and could have in part reflected the absence of Radić's electoral lists outside Croatia-Slavonia during the campaign of 1920. As for Slovenia, the Agrarians were the second largest party there, getting a quarter of Slovene votes, though it must be stressed that this was no reflection on the policy of the SZ as a whole, since its Slovene branch functioned quite independently.

The Agrarians united several related traditions. Their Serbian contingent grew out of the peasant cooperative movement, which was founded and led by Mihailo Avramović (1864–1945), long an advocate of the peasantry's organization within a separate class party. Unlike Radić's HPSS, with which they had no ties, Avramović's followers did not see the peasants as the unalienated nation but rather as an unrepresented class. Whereas Radić believed that he was expressing the needs of eternal peasantry, the salt of the Croat earth, Avramović was organizing "agrarian workers" (*zemljoradnici, zemljodelci*), a term that obliterated the differences with factory labor. The overtones of agrarian socialism in the SZ's program were derived in part from the Russian revolutionary tradition and in part from corporativism, the latter expressed in the demand for a parliament of estates, rather along the lines of Stambolijski's agrarian populist program in Bulgaria, in which the peasant estate would have the proportional edge.

Most of these ideas were shared by the SZ's contingents from Croatia-Slavonia, Dalmatia, and Bosnia-Hercegovina. The most important of these groups was the Bosnian Savez težaka (Alliance of Husbandmen), which had roots in the political faction of Petar Kočić (1877–1916), a noted writer, who led the most uncompromising anti-Austrian Serb nationalists in Bosnia-Hercegovina with ties to the Mlada Bosna, and was a strong partisan of radical agrarian reform. Two other groups, the Slovene Agrarians, the Samostojna kmetijska stranka (Independent Peasant Party), among whom Ivan Pucelj (1877–1945) and Bogumil Vošnjak (1882–1959) had a decisive say in the early 1920s, favored a far more flexile course, less tied to class struggle, which boiled down to peasant self-help, education, and organizational independence from both the political left and right.[3]

3. Albin Prepeluh, *Kmetski pokret med Slovenci po Prvi svetovni vojni* (Ljubljana, 1928), pp. 7–21.

The SZ's ties with the Democrats were frequently explicit. In Bosnia-Hercegovina, for example, the Agrarians were originally an independent pressure group, which tried to influence the political parties, notably the DS, to bring about a radical agrarian reform, aimed largely against the Muslim landowners. It was only after the Democrats, in May 1920, moderated their stand on this issue, thereby making themselves eligible to join the coalition cabinet with the NRS, that the Bosnian Agrarians became organized as a political party. Even so, Vasilj Grdjić, one of the Bosnian Democratic bosses, ran on both the DS and SZ electoral lists in November 1920, and the Democrats continued to count on the Agrarians for the passage of the centralist constitution.[4] In a similar vein, though the SZ had not put up any electoral lists in Montenegro, its subsequent base in that province came from the ranks of Montenegro's prounification faction, which was closely tied to the DS.[5] In Slovenia, the Agrarians shared the anticlerical bias of the Slovene liberals, and liberals who did not join the DS usually found their way into the Agrarian ranks. And in Serbia, where the SZ's political independence was most enviously guarded, making the Agrarians anything but enthusiastic exponents of Independent Radicals (Democrats), the SZ was quite explicitly anti-Radical, leading to Protić's charge that the "peasant party was born and developed with the participation, and perhaps even the initiative, of the DS, with the aim of weakening the NRS still further."[6] A number of left-leaning Democrats joined the SZ, most notably, in 1927, Milan Pribićević.

The most obvious link between the Agrarians and the DS was the similarity of their views on the question of nationality. As a class party, the Agrarians devoted most of their attention to immediate peasant concerns, but their attitudes toward full national unification, internal cohesion of the "trinominal people," the monarchy, and the defense of the state were almost identical to those of the DS. Indeed, the Croat Agrarians in Dalmatia were accused of "leading the Croat peasants into the service of Serbian tribal supremacy."[7] Though the Agrarians were not as explicitly centralist as the DS, putting greater stress on local self-administration, they were generally in favor of breaking up historical provinces, the exception being the Slovene Agrarians, who preferred a type of autonomy for Slovenia that "would not harm state unity."[8] And just as Davidović's Democrats retained elements of Great Serbianism from the old Independent Radical days, the Agrarian intellectuals of pure Radical pedigree, such as Jovan M. Jovanović-Pižon and

4. "Razgovor sa g. Sv. Pribićevićem. O situaciji posle izbora," *Epoha*, Dec. 6, 1920, p. 2.

5. Dimitrije-Dimo Vujović, "Gradjanske političke stranke u Crnoj Gori u periodu formiranja KPJ," *Istorijski zapisi* vol. 22 (1969), nos. 2–3, p. 211.

6. Stojan Protić, "Izborne karakteristike i kuriozumi!" *Samouprava*, Dec. 3, 1920, p. 1.

7. Quoted in Hrvoje Matković, "Djelovanje i sukobi gradjanskih političkih stranaka u Šibeniku izmedju dva svjetska rata," *Radovi Instituta za hrvatsku povijest*, vol. 2 (1972), p. 267.

8. Miroslav Stiplovšek, "Slovenske politične stranke in njihovi kmečki programi 1918–1920," *Jugoslovenski istorijski časopis*, 1973, nos. 3–4, p. 197.

Milan Gavrilović, who became the real leaders of the SZ, were awkward in their new unitaristic garb. In fairness to Jovanović, as unlikely an Agrarian as could stem from one of Belgrade's "old families," it must be noted that Pašić dismissed him from the post of envoy to London in 1919, precisely because the tormented *Joca Pigeon* proved too dovish toward the JO and its British supporters.[9] "His was first of all Serb patriotism, but that was soon lifted to the Yugoslav level, which was never the case with his senior Pašić or his junior Gavrilović."[10]

As it turned out, the unity of the SZ was tested very early. In March 1921, Pucelj's Slovene Agrarians broke with the SZ mainstream and joined Pašić's cabinet, helping the passage of the centralist constitutional proposal, which was supported by the NRS and the DS. This seemingly incongruous action, the support of strict centralism by the least centralist wing of the SZ, was nothing more than political horse trading to assure the passage of the 1921 constitution. Along with various economic concessions, Pucelj was rewarded with the ministry of agriculture and water supply and Vošnjak got the ambassadorial post in Prague. Contrary to Pribićević's predictions, the bulk of the SZ, almost entirely Serb in nationality after the Slovene defection, voted against the centralist constitution—but not so much because they disliked centralism as because they disapproved of the government's increasingly conservative tenor. After the banning of the Communist party, the SZ stepped into the left. It still had its share of conservatives, indeed king's men, but its own left wing was a permanent thorn in the side of all administrations and the foremost recruiting ground of young Marxists.

Where the Agrarians neglected the national question because of their class position and Serb base, the Republicans neglected it because they viewed all internal developments through the prism of monarchophobia. The Republikanska demokratska stranka (Republican Democratic Party) was inspired by Aleksandar's bloody handling of the Apis affair at Salonika. The new party started by an influential segment of Independent Radical leadership, such men as Ljubomir Stojanović, Jovan Žujović, Milovan Lazarević, and Jaša Prodanović, the first two among Serbia's leading intellectuals, had as its sole aim the propagation of the abolition of the monarchy, which they thought ought to be discarded forever as an institution that properly belonged to the infancy of the human race and which was unworthy of enlightened modern democracy. Despite its strictly Serbian leadership, the Republican party got little support in Serbia proper, except in Lazarević's native district of Kolubara (Lazarevac), where it got a fourth of the total vote. Its strongest base, like that of the Communists (though the Republicans were far from

9. Hugh Seton-Watson et al., eds., *R. W. Seton-Watson and the Yugoslavs: Correspondence 1906–1941*, vol. 2 (London, 1976), p. 33.
10. Dragoljub Jovanović, *Ljudi, ljudi . . . (Medaljoni 56 umrlih savremenika)*, vol. 1 (Belgrade, 1973), p. 275.

being revolutionaries), was in Montenegro and southeastern Macedonia. In some districts in those areas (Cetinje, Rijeka Crnojevića, Kolašin, Kočane), where the voters did not go for the Communists, they went for the Republicans. The lack of any lists at all, aside from Dalmatia, in the former Austro-Hungarian territories cut into the average, however, leaving the Republicans with only 1.13 percent of all votes and three deputies, two of them from Montenegro.

The tenet of *narodno jedinstvo,* which was beyond dispute for most Republicans, constituted the link with the DS. Indeed, though Montenegrin Republicans questioned various key aspects of state policy, they in fact belonged to the left wing of Montenegro's prounification camp, which was in no sense partial to Montenegro's independence. Moreover, Jovan Djonović, the leading Montenegrin Republican, published several articles in *Narodna riječ* (People's Word), Montenegro's pro-DS newspaper, in which he argued, among other matters, that since Montenegro had been subjoined to Serbia, the laws and constitution of Serbia should have been extended to Montenegro immediately after the unification.[11] But though the Democrats counted on the unitarist forces among the Republicans, there were a number of divergencies among the two parties, which undid their lingering affinities.

For one thing, the Republicans preferred the peaceful road to the "amalgamation" of the South Slávs. Though they agreed with Pribićević that the South Slavs were in the process of national consolidation, being one people but not one nation, they did not believe that this process should be hastened by the use of force. Djonović, for example, observed that the Americans were bringing forth a "great nation" by "assimilating developed nationalities according to strictly cultural means."[12] He resented the imputations of disloyalty that the Democrats and Radicals frequently brought in, and he grouped his party among those on Yugoslavia's republican left, alongside Radić's HPSS, Pribićević's chief aversion. Most important, the Republicans were really committed to the abolition of the monarchy. Their republicanism was not simply a matter of form, a compliance with the party's tradition, as was the case with the Social Democrats. Republicanism brought them together and was their chief issue. And since they rejected the monarchy, as the source of Yugoslavia's every trouble, they were much more willing to overlook Radić's "tribalism" than the monarchism of the DS.

The Republicans were alert to the Serbian nature of Yugoslavia's monarchy, something that the Democrats simply refused to acknowledge. Indeed, they were far more consistent in their unitarism than the DS, seeing the monarchy as the obstacle not only to the forging of a single Yugoslav nation, but to the survival of tbe state itself:

11. Vujović, "Gradjanske stranke," pp. 210–211.
12. Jovan Djonović, *Govori Jovana Djonovića, narodnog poslanika* (Belgrade, 1921), p. 15.

[The monarchy] is precisely the element that divides us, which will slow down the formation of the [Yugoslav] nation and the consolidation of the state. Those who call themselves state builders [allusion to the Democrats] and still opt for the monarchy are committing a verbal violation. . . . we cannot maintain the state unless we build the nation, and we cannot build the nation with monarchy. As long as the monarchy exists, one part of our people will be afraid of the other; there will be endless squabbles about our differences and ceaseless calls for the grouping of our people's separate parts. Only the Republican party can be the true and genuine state-building party, because all the parts of our people can join together without fear only in a republic.[13]

The Republicans were convinced that "Paris, with its centralist tendencies, carried over as an inheritance from the fallen monarchy, played a fatal role [in continental history] and ruined the establishment of a united Europe, founded on the liberties of citizens."[14] Their ideal was English Home Rule and the decentralized republic of the Girondists, whose undoing by the Mountain on the eve of the Terror preserved the centralism of the Bourbons in revolutionary garb. Unlike the DS and contrary to the logic of Yugoslavist unitarism, the Republicans did not permit their belief in *narodno jedinstvo* to become the underpinning of centralism. They were decentralistic unitarists and, by extension, implied that the process of South Slavic "amalgamation" was irreversible, despite their own warnings that this was impossible under the Karadjordjevićes. An irreversible process could not be harmed by decentralization, but democracy could be harmed by centralism.

To be sure, although the Republicans voted against the centralist constitution, they did not necessarily favor the maintenance of historical provinces.[15] Their federalism, formally adopted in 1924, was therefore inconsistent. Moreover, having failed to elect a single deputy after 1921, their diminishing and increasingly Serb base was becoming reconciled to a type of Serb republicanism. As their unitarism evaporated, some of their leaders, such as Dragiša Vasić, went on to advocate a Serb unit within Yugoslavia. Indeed, with the notable exception of Prodanović, the party's last leader during the interwar period, most active Republicans joined the Great Serbian Chetniks of Draža Mihailović during the Second World War.

The Republican evolution is indicative of the course followed by the Social Democrats, with the difference that the Republicans were not Marxists and therefore did not link their unitarism to a developed historicist scheme, whereby class confrontation fueled the progression of socioeconomic formations. According to this indiscriminate idea, the defense of South Slavic

13. Ibid., pp. 15–16.
14. Evan., "Osnovno pitanje," *Republika*, Nov. 24, 1920, p. 1.
15. For more on the Republican program see Jaša Prodanović, "Republikanska demokratska stranka," *Narodna enciklopedija srpsko-hrvatsko-slovenačka*, 1928, vol. 3, pp. 894–896.

national individualities was no more than an expression of moribund medieval particularism, waged by the "tribal and confessional separatists" against the forces of progress. The Serbs, Croats, and Slovenes were one nation, spoke one language, and constituted one economic-geographical whole, and it was practically impossible and utopian to try to divide them by "tribe." Though all the Social Democratic groups expressed variants of these ideas, their attitude toward the national question was actually quite a complicated one, reflecting the histories of, depending on the count, six or more Social Democratic organizations that operated on the territory of Yugoslavia before 1914.[16] The most important of these old parties were the Social Democratic parties of Croatia-Slavonia and Slovenia, essentially reformist parties in the Austro-Marxist tradition, which were mostly concerned with trade union problems and had almost no intellectual leadership, and the parties of Serbia and Bosnia-Hercegovina, both more doctrinaire, with the Serbian party, especially, largely dominated by intellectuals and preoccupied with the purity of doctrine and class independence of the socialist movement.But whereas the parties of Croatia-Slavonia and Slovenia broke away from the Austro-Marxist strictures against reducing the national question to the struggle for "cultural-national autonomy," and eventually came to espouse unitarist Yugoslavism, the Serbian socialists steadfastly shunned preoccupations with nationality as activities that properly belonged to the sphere of purely bourgeois concerns.

After the war, the Social Democracy in Serbia and Bosnia-Hercegovina practically ceased to exist. The Serbian and Bosnian Social Democratic organizations helped found the Communist party and joined it in a body. There were no Social Democratic electoral lists in Serbia in 1920, and the "Social Democratic list" of Bosnia-Hercegovina, which polled a mere 0.84 percent of the vote in the province (against the Communists' 5.46 percent), represented a labor-based Serb nationalist group gathered round the journal *Zvono* (Bell). In Croatia-Slavonia, Vojvodina, and Slovenia, however, the socialists split over the stand toward the Bolshevik experiment and the emerging Communist movement. Croatia's veteran socialist leader Vitomir

16. On the history of Yugoslavia's Social Democracy after the unification, with special reference to the various parties' previous stands on the national question, see especially Toma Milenković, "Socijalreformistički pravac u radničkom pokretu jugoslovenskih zemalja (od sredine 1917. do 2. avgusta 1921)," *Istraživanja Instituta za izučavanje istorije Vojvodine*, vol. 2 (1973), pp. 195–287; Milenković, *Socijalistička partija Jugoslavije* (Belgrade, 1974), pp. 658–686; Vlado Strugar, *Socijalna demokratija o nacionalnom pitanju jugoslovenskih naroda* (Belgrade, 1956); Strugar, *Socijaldemokratija o stvaranju Jugoslavije* (Belgrade, 1965); Mirjana Gross, "Socijalna demokracija prema nacionalnom pitanju u Hrvatskoj 1890–1902.," *Historijski zbornik*, vol. 9 (1956), no. 1–4, pp. 1–27; Fedora Bikar, "Nacionalna politika hrvatske socijalne demokracije od 1902. do 1905.," in Vasa Čubrilović, ed., *Jugoslovenski narodi pred prvi svetski rat* (Belgrade, 1967), pp. 29–115; Bikar, "Razvoj odnosa izmedju hrvatske i srpske socijalne demokracije i pokušaji usklađivanja njihovih koncepcija o nacionalnom pitanju od 1909. do. 1914.," *Putovi revolucije*, vol. 3 (1965), no. 5, pp. 165–192.

Korać (1877–1941), a Serb from Srijem, best represented the attitudes of old guard Social Democrats, who constituted the socialists' dominant right wing. He believed that the unification of Yugoslavia amounted to a bourgeois national revolution that secured the climate in which socialism could be achieved through peaceful electoral means. The role of Social Democrats was to contribute to the stability of new order through cooperation with progressive bourgeois parties, such as the Democrats, thereby prodding the liberal bourgeoisie onto the road toward social reform. Most important, he wished to create a clear demarcation line between the Social Democrats and Communists by carrying out the unification of all anti-Bolshevik socialist factions.

Korać's Social Democratic Party of Croatia-Slavonia had been part of the original HSK and had remained in the coalition in 1905 and 1906. It had a strong base among the Serb field laborers of Korać's native Srijem, harbored an intense animosity against Croat nationalism, and subscribed to a version of unitarist Yugoslavism that was almost indistinguishable from Pribićević's in both manner and inducement. It welcomed the dissolution of Austria-Hungary and participated in the local councils as well as in Zagreb's National Council, where Korać and two of his closest associates held seats in the Council's central committee, one of them, Vilim Bukšeg, in the capacity of commissioner for social welfare.

Korać became the minister for social policy in Yugoslavia's first cabinet and held this post, except for a brief interval, until February 1920. His close alliance with Pribićević, which the Democratic leader lauded as the lasting coalition of the "rational left," brought some immediate improvements in social legislation, but also provoked a split in the ranks of Croatia's Social Democracy. The party's left wing was indignant over Korać's "ministerialism" and took the majority of trade unionists over to the Communists. At the elections of 1920, Korać polled only 7,611 votes in Croatia-Slavonia, close to half of them from the Serb districts of eastern Slavonia and Srijem and the rest from the provincial industrial towns like Sisak. Neither Korać nor any of his associates was elected to the Constituent Assembly, though the three Serb Social Democratic deputies, elected in western Bačka and Baranja, expressed his position. The Communists bettered Korać's showing in Croatia-Slavonia by almost four times, but their percentage was still unimpressive (7.13 percent). Both parties were hurt by their unitarist and centralist stands, which eased Radić's mastery of Croat electorate.

The Social Democrats did much better in Slovenia, where the majority faction of Anton Kristan duplicated Korać's participation in the regional and central governments; Kristan himself became the minister of forests and mines in Davidović's cabinet of 1919–1920. But though a substantial minority of Slovene socialists opposed ministerialism, neither side pressed for a split nor heeded Korać's calls for the unification of Yugoslavia's Social

Democrats. Moreover, the Slovene socialists avoided committing themselves on the question of Bolshevism, expressing sympathies for Lenin while pursuing their own quite different policies. Nor did they join Korać's conference of April 2 and 3, 1920, which brought about a Social Democratic Party of Yugoslavia, by uniting the reformists of Croatia-Slavonia, Vojvodina, and Bosnia-Hercegovina.

When the pro-Bolshevik faction finally emerged in the ranks of Slovene socialists, in 1920, it succeeded in taking along only a minority of Slovenia's socialist base. In the elections of 1920 the Social Democrats showed that they were a significant force in Slovene politics, winning 18.67 percent of the vote, against 10.29 percent for the Communists. The socialists were the strongest party in the industrial cities of Celje and Maribor, and throughout Styria they ran only slightly behind the leading Slovene clericalists. To some extent their strength was due to their moderate unitarism, or, more correctly, to the care they exercised in disguising the unitarist convictions of socialist leaders, the convictions that ran counter to the autonomist preferences of Slovene voters. Still, unlike Korać, the Slovene socialists toyed with the idea of autonomism. Seven of the ten Social Democratic deputies in the Constituent Assembly were Slovenes, and they were apparently ready to include a provision for a limited Slovene autonomy in the socialist constitutional proposal. The idea was discarded in order to obviate a dangerous precedent.[17]

At the Second Congress of the Communist party, held in Vukovar from June 20 to 24, 1920, a minority group, reacting to the harsh repressive measures that the government had taken against the Communists in hopes of stopping the growing strike movement, proposed a more moderate stance for the party—more cooperation with the government, a milder revolutionary tone and a greater distance from the Comintern. The leaders of this minority, whom the Communist left consigned to the morass of "centrism," that is, disloyal fence sitting between the Communists and Social Democrats, were the stubborn independents of old Serbian and Bosnian Social Democracy, including Živko Topalović (1886–1972), Dragiša Lapčević, and the brothers Jovo and Sreten Jakšić. In November 1920 this group issued a Manifesto of the Opposition, signed by 115 party members, which attacked the whole of Bolshevik policy and its manifestations in Yugoslavia. They were all promptly expelled from the Communist party.[18] But though the "centrist" leaders promised an evenhanded struggle against both the Communists and reformist Social Democrats, along the lines of the so-called Two-and-a-Half International, their weakness and mutual losses incurred in competition with Korać's party obliged them to join in the project of unification with Korać and the Slovene socialists. Preliminary steps in that direction were taken in

17. Milenković, *Socijalistička partija Jugoslavije*, p. 662.
18. "Odluke plenarne sjednice C.V.K.P.J.," *Oslobodjenje*, Dec. 24, 1920, p. 4.

August 1921, and in December the Socialist Party of Yugoslavia was announced. The resistance to this solution, which still existed in various centrist quarters, was mitigated by the opportunities open to the anti-Communist left by the government's ban of the Communists, formally completed in August 1921.

In the debate over the centralist constitutional proposal, Yugoslavia's Social Democrats were "closer to the government than to the opposition."[19] The Radicals and Democrats adopted many socialist proposals, expecting the socialists to support the centralist draft. This did not happen, but not because the Social Democrats opposed centralism. Rather, though they admired the centralist constitution as the "realization of Yugoslav national unification," they did not wish to identify themselves too closely with the ruling parties at that particular moment. Nor did the ostensible republicanism of the socialists present any difficulties for them. Korać was famous for his "holding out of Norwegian monarchy over Portuguese republic," and the *Zvono* group in Bosnia thought it pointless to debate this issue. Indeed, the derisive term "Social Patriots," which the Communists enlisted in the struggle against the Social Democrats, fitted the policies of Yugoslavia's socialists to the letter. Nevertheless, it must be recognized that theirs was a unitarist form of "Social Patriotism," founded on the premise that any opposition to the amalgamation of Yugoslavia's constituent nationalities amounted to clericalist and petite bourgeois reaction. Though they bowed to the slogan of national self-determination, they did not recognize it in the case of "Yugoslav tribes" and mocked the very idea as an example of Leninist "Turkestanism," after the Soviet federal unit in Central Asia.

The steady electoral defeats and growing isolation of the Social Democrats forced some of their leaders to reexamine the party's stand on the national question. Jovo Jakšić, one of the Bosnian centrists, clearly perceived that the socialists' clamor against separatism made them a left-wing appendage of the DS. And since it was evident that a number of "Yugoslav tribes" considered themselves separate nations, Jakšić thought the socialists had a duty to stay abreast of the popular demands for autonomy and not side with those who wished to override these demands by antidemocratic means. But though some other former centrists, for example Topalović, agreed that the majority of Yugoslavs had in fact turned against Yugoslavist unitarism, Jakšić's voice was ignored in socialist councils.[20] To men like Korać, who reduced the national question in Yugoslavia to its Croat component, time was working against the "tribal separatists." Contrary to their expectations, however, the nationality conflict was continually expanding. The effect within the socialist movement was that, as the Communists, who had begun by sharing the

19. Milenković, *Socijalistička partija Jugoslavije,* p. 662.
20. Ibid., pp. 672–679.

socialists' unitarist ideology, moved away from unitarism and, to the extent possible under the conditions of illegality, widened their base among the non-Serbs, the socialists like Korać stepped along with Pribićević, retaining, except in Slovenia, an almost exclusively Serb base. Some of the Social Democratic groups, such as the Bosnian Zvono, had indeed long since lapsed into a brand of Serb chauvinism. The *zvonaši* incited the police to expel the Communist "foreigners" from Bosnia, a term that embraced not only an odd German or Czech worker but Slovenes and even Bosnian Croats.[21] Thus, ironically, the increasingly Bolshevized Communist party began to develop a far more democratic nationality program than the parties of the so-called democratic left.

No appraisal of democratic centralists would be complete without a reference to the group of nonparty intelligentsia, which tried to reconcile its unitarist ideals with political and regional pluralism. Academics, writers and artists, men from the professions, especially jurists, representative of the trends in the intellectual circles of Zagreb, Belgrade, and a few other principal centers, notably on Yugoslavia's cosmopolitan western rim circling from Novi Sad to Split, repeatedly organized themselves into special leagues, aimed, in the words of one of their manifestos, at "establishing a golden mean, that is, a state organization, which, disposing with the results of all united forces, at the same time gives full sway to free local initiatives."[22]

The first elaborate plans for a harmonious union were drafted by exiled South Slavic intellectuals during the last phases of the Great War. Working as a representative of the JO to the colonies of Dalmatian Croats in remote Chile, Milan Marjanović, an associate of the prewar Nationalist Youth, envisioned a Yugoslav state that, in his opinion, reconciled the historical and psychological differences among the South Slavs with their economic needs. He proposed the establishment of an autonomous Slovenia (with Trieste), Croatia-Slavonia (with Medjimurje, Baranja, and northwestern Bosnia, but without Srijem and the thin Adriatic littoral from Rijeka to Starigrad), Serbia (in the pre-1912 frontiers), Old Serbia and Macedonia (that is, Kosovo and Vardar Macedonia), Montenegro (with the Sandžak, Metohia, and portions of eastern Hercegovina), Bosnia-Hercegovina (without its two Adriatic salients and the territories ceded to Croatia-Slavonia and Montenergro), Vojvodina (Srijem, Bačka, and the Banat), and the Littoral (that is, Istria, the Croatian littoral, Dalmatia, and the Montenegrin littoral from Spič to Shkodër). Marjanović was certain that Yugoslavia could develop as a con-

21. Toma Milenković, "Socijalšovinistička grupacija u Bosni i Hercegovini—Zvonaši (1919–1921. godine)," *Istorija XX veka: zbornik radova*, vol. 7 (1965), p. 427.

22. [Milan Grol], "Naši zadaci i naš delokrug rada," *Jugoslovenska demokratska liga*, 1919, no. 1, p. vii.

federal or centralist state. He preferred autonomism, though he did not distinguish it from federalism.[23]

The trend represented by Marjanović's scheme, which was an expression of the kind of thinking that prevailed in the JO's intellectual circle, received its organized expression in the Jugoslovenska demokratska liga (JDL, Yugoslav Democratic League), founded in Paris in November 1918. The JDL was a product of the JO's cooperation with the Serbian opposition, notably the Independent Radicals, sealed at the Geneva conference. Though the League was misrepresented by its NRS critics as an instrument of a possible coup d'état aimed against Pašić and perhaps even the dynasty, it was true that some of its prominent Serbian members, who were almost to the man associated with the Independent Radicals, leaned toward republicanism (Milan Čemerikić, Milan Grol, Kosta Kumanudi, Boža Marković, Jovan Žujović), while still others, for example the JDL's president Jovan Cvijić (1865–1927), harbored animosities toward the Karadjordjević dynasty.[24] The JDL's Croat members included some distinguished leaders of the JO (Ante Trumbić, Ivan Meštrović) and representatives of domestic autonomist opposition to Pribićević (Ivan Lorković). But its chief shortcoming in the eyes of unyielding unitarists was that, though guided by Yugoslavist ideology, it was opposed to centralism as a means to South Slavic hybridization. In the words of Boža Marković, "our common aim, amalgamation, will be accomplished least of all by centralism."[25]

Serbian members of the League were by no means completely free of supremacist aspirations. (Urbane Boža Marković's lapse into a defense of military dictatorship for Croatia has already been noted.) But warts and all, they sensed the need to relegate many important state activities to Yugoslavia's projected autonomous units, though they ruled out the "tribal" principle in the establishment of these units. The JDL as a whole believed that a common parliament should deliberate on foreign, defense, financial, monetary, and transportation policy and that there should be a single cabinet and civil code. All other concerns "would be left to individual regions, so that the latter might develop according to their separate needs."[26] The affairs that should be subjected to regional control, according to Marković, included regional administration and security, local transportation, judicial and penal institutions, agriculture and forestry, education, religious affairs, health, and

23. Milan Marjanović, *Obnova: Zbornik za inicijativu i diskusiju poratnih problema* (Valparaiso, Chile, 1918), pp. 32–35, appendix map 12.

24. Marković, *Jugoslovenska država i Hrvatsko pitanje (1914–1929)* (Belgrade, 1935), pp. 78–82; Ivan Meštrović, *Uspomene na političke ljude i dogadjaje* (Buenos Aires, 1961), p. 116.

25. Božidar [Boža] Marković, "Unutrašnje uredjenje Jugoslavije," *Jugoslovenska demokratska liga,* 1919, no. 1, p. 8.

26. "Privremena pravila Jugoslovenske demokratske lige," ibid., p. i.

local finances.[27] Even these modest concessions to autonomism aroused Pribićević's ire.[28] His press conceded that though the League and the DS shared the same ideology (unitarism), the "League advocated a regional autonomist standpoint . . . while the Yugoslavs in the fatherland seek a centralistically ruled and a decentralistically administered state."[29]

Under Pribićević's barrage the League started changing its position. In March 1919, in Paris, its members accepted a draft program "with a widened section on the rights and competencies of central authorities."[30] After their return from emigration, whereupon the League effectively ceased functioning, most of the Serbian members joined the DS, though some, like Cvijić, having "completely immersed [themselves] in socialism," denounced the system that allowed loyal intellectuals "to be cheated and deceived by all those who govern, not excluding the highest state factor [the regent]." Cvijić placed his faith in the "new generation," which was, in his opinion, "completely Yugoslavist and unitary."[31] Cvijić's disenchantment was shared by other democratic unitarists, most of them independent of party affiliations, who continued the traditions of the League in their attempts to combine the unitarist ideal with greater decentralization. The intellectuals of this "left wing of the DS," who increasingly gathered round Milan Ćurčin's journal *Nova Evropa* (New Europe) and the Zagreb newspaper *Slobodna tribuna* (Free Tribune) were closest to Davidović's Democrats.[32] Their unitarist ideology kept them in the proximity of such consistent unitarists as Pribićević, whose policies they increasingly rejected, and prevented them from drawing closer to "separatist" popular leaders like Radić. If the beginnings of a unitary Yugoslav culture could somehow have caught on in all segments of Yugoslavia's population, their ideal would have been unsnared.

Racial Messianism in Culture

The formation of the Yugoslav state is the greatest accomplishment that our people have hitherto performed. Men of art and literature started contributing to its realization a long time ago; let others judge how much. Now it is

27. Marković, "Unutrašnje uredjenje," p. 6.
28. "Za Jugoslavensku demokratsku stranku," *Riječ Srba-Hrvata-Slovenaca*, Jan. 28, 1919, p. 1.
29. "Jugoslavenska demokratska stranka i jugoslavenska demokratska liga," ibid., Feb. 19, 1919, p. 2.
30. Branislav Gligorijević, *Demokratska stranka i politički odnosi u Kraljevini Srba, Hrvata i Slovenaca* (Belgrade, 1970), pp. 62–67.
31. Jovan Cvijić, "Današnja naša situacija," *Novosti*, April 11, 1920, p. 1.
32. Gligorijević, *Demokratska stranka*, pp. 260–261.

the turn of scientists. Artists should provide the sally of creative energy. Thinkers should construct. We must start constructing at once. We must construct our new common life and our Yugoslav culture with words that will come from our soul and have the resonance of our lungs. In that way we shall best serve ourselves and humanity. . . . There will be no pasture-lands or hunting preserves on tomorrow's earth, and above all there will be no cemeteries. Everything will be turned into plowlands and vineyards, because the army of tomorrow wants neither the hungry, the almsmen, nor alms. There will be no commissaries in that army. Everyone will have to bring his own bread and wine to the common table. There will be no room at the table for those who do not bring their own. So let us plow and sow so that our harvest, too, will be gathered on time.

Ivan Meštrović, 1918

Bez gospodara dvori. Niko ih ne mete
Na prijestoljima podvornici puše cigarete

Palaces without masters. Nobody sweeps them.
On the thrones janitors smoke cigarettes.

Antun Branko Šimić, 1921–1924

Unitarist apothecaries prized no sedative over unitary Yugoslav culture, the herb of healing virtue for all of Yugoslavia's ills. The proof of a unitary nation was in the unitary culture. But, as Antun Branko Šimić (1898–1925), a young Croat poet and critic, noted soon after the unification, "if it is said of a certain art that it is an expression of the soul of a certain nation, then one must already have the firm grasp of that nation's distinctive marks. On the other hand, those characteristics can be learned only from their expression. A circle is closed."[1] In truth, there was no unitary Yugoslav culture. There was a need for an assertion of Yugoslavist individuality and an exultation of that spurious individuality to the level of national faith. Then, too, there was a hopeless quest that commenced around 1904 with Ivan Meštrović's first sketches for a monument dedicated to the epic Serbian defeat at the hand of the Ottomans in the Battle of Kosovo in 1389.

Ivan Meštrović was the first modern Croat artist who attracted international attention and, moreover, by monumental sculptures distinctly native in subject matter. His life story had all the elements of extravagant fancy, taking the shepherd boy from the slopes of Svilaja Mountain, in the wretchedly poor hinterland of central Dalmatia, to the Viennese Academy and membership in the Secession group. And just as his masterful early figurines reflected the world of South Slavic folk imagination, his first academic products sought to interpret the popular cult of defeated Kosovo

---

1. Antun Branko Šimić, "Meštrovićevo kiparstvo," *Obzor*, Oct. 16, 1920, p. 1.

heroes on a monumental scale, in which symbolic gestures expressed the sacrifices and sufferings of the South Slavs and turned their historic disadvantage into a source of retributive wrath.

Meštrović's great scheme, embodying all that he felt about his "religion of extreme sacrifice," was the Kosovo Temple. This sanctuary, never built, was Meštrović's dream, and he labored on the designs from 1904 on. The temple took the form of a Latin cross, with an octagonal crossing under a dome "bigger than Saint Peter's" and cubical towers surmounted by octagonal cupolas at the end of each of the three short arms. The lower arm or nave had two rows of caryatids holding the entablature of the temple's "mysterious corridor." A five-tiered "tower of ages," symbolizing "five centuries of slavery," rose over the corridor, closer to the central octagon than to the entrance pavilion; each tier was a steadily decreasing cube mounted by figures of "martyrs' spirits," their arms extending toward the heavens, and at the very top was to be a torch of eternal fire, a "people's prayer."[2]

Meštrović's powerful sculptures, fleshy widows mourning the loss of their menfolk in the battle, blind *guslars,* chanters of heroic songs, and Kosovo heroes, attracted wide attention and were much imitated, inspiring a peculiar quest for the national style, moreover a unitary Yugoslavist style, pursued by the principal artists of the Croat Secession. The high point of this movement was the exhibit of the Medulić Society in November-December 1910, in Zagreb. Under the motto "in spite of unheroic times," the exhibition followed the theme of Prince Marko, the legendary hero of Serbian folk epic. In Meštrović's words, "proud Marko . . . is the fighter for justice and humanity, the defender of the oppressed. . . . He does not tolerate foreign misdeeds and humiliations and prefers to die rather than submit to injustice. This Marko is our Yugoslav people with its gigantic heroic and noble heart."[3]

Following Meštrović's portrayal of muscular Marko, covered only with a redoubtable moustache and handsome locks, astride his piebald steed Šarac, several other Croat artists (Mirko Rački, Tomislav Krizman, Ljubo Babić, Tomo Rosandić) illustrated Marko's heroic exploits in terms of Meštrović's iconography. At the International Exhibition in Rome (1911), celebrating the fiftieth anniversary of Rome's status as the capital of united Italy, these and other Croat artists exhibited their works in the Serbian Pavilion, built at Meštrović's instigation, as a way of allowing his group to show independently of the Austrian and Hungarian displays. The charged political atmosphere of the event, heightened by the great artistic success of "Serbian" art, was underscored by the fact that fourteen of the twenty-three exhibiting artists at the Serbian Pavilion were Croats (181 works) and four were Serbs from Austria-Hungary (22 works); only five, with 33 works, were Serbs from

2. This description is based on the photographs and explanations in Milan Marjanović, *Genij Jugoslovenstva Ivan Meštrović i njegov hram* (New York, 1915[?]), pp. 19, 22, 24.

3. Ivan Meštrović, "Poruka Jugoslovenima Amerike," *Jadran,* Dec. 2, 1916, p. 34.

Serbia. The exhibit was also stamped by the unusual predominance of sculpture—123 pieces, 93 of them massive works by Meštrović.[4] Considering that a good number of the exhibits had no ideological message at all and could easily had belonged to any European national culture, it is not an exaggeration to say that the "Yugoslav national expression" was in fact a trend in the Croat artistic colony and was, moreover, largely the matter of Meštrović's monumental plastics.

Meštrović's success at the Rome Exhibition established him as the "Prophet of Yugoslavism." It was understood, of course, that the aesthetic side of the Roman manifestation, as enviable as it was, took second place to its ideological importance, "because, in its essence, the national principle in art triumphed in Rome, presenting to the Croats and Serbs, through the medium of Meštrović's synthetic spirit, the genius of our art, which is as unitary as the national spirit [of the Croats and Serbs] is one and the same."[5] Meštrović, a "born Dalmatian Croat, entered into the spirit of the Kosovo epopee so deeply that even the easternmost Serb could not have done better, making him a greater Serb than most Serbs."[6] Meštrović's heroes, unlike Michelangelo's Moses, could not hold their fury. They instilled the will for struggle and revenge and were a source of undying national energy. Meštrović, the lapidary poet of the "Yugoslav race," was seen as the Messiah of Yugoslavist unitarism, pointing the way to national salvation.

The results of the Great War had a sobering effect on unitarist artists, creating a climate for the reevaluation of Meštrović's "national expression." Although the Kosovo Temple designs were still much acclaimed, clearer vision showed that the great sculptor's style was more personal than national. There was little that was national about his design for the Kosovo Temple, which remained unbuilt even after the unification, since the authorities were loathe to subsidize a vision of the national epic that was a touch too libidinous for common taste. The temple was a fine example of Art Nouveau's vision of the monumental in architecture, down to its decorative details, but neither the design nor its various finished figures were particularly South Slavic. Much the same could be said of the art of Meštrović's colleagues, for example the paintings of Joza Kljaković, who emulated the expressively curvaceous draftmanship of the Secession in a far more obvious way than Meštrović ever did. Kljaković's splendidly illustrated postwar edition of Ivan Mažuranić's Illyrianist epic *Smrt Smail-age Čengića* (The Death of Smail-aga Čengić, 1846) is the case in point. True, the Smail-aga and his two companions wear gold-embroidered costumes of Bosnian Muslim dignitaries, and the aga's deputy Bauk is playing a *gusle,* but the streaming fire in the hearth and the nude androgynous figure on whom Smail-aga rests, sym-

4. M., "Rimska izložba i hrvatski umjetnici," *Jug,* vol. I (1911), no. 4, pp. 104–105.
5. M. M., "Triumf smjelosti i karaktera," ibid., no. 5, p. 133.
6. Mirko Deanović, "Naša umjetnost u Rimu," ibid., p. 136.

bolizing the aǧa's tyrannical excesses, are pure Secession and could have been made by any number of artists from the Wiener Werkstätte.[7]

The representatives of the postwar generation of writers, activists of the emerging expressionist generation, were among the first to challenge the search for a unitary Yugoslav culture. Antun Branko Šimić was the best representative of the new radical critics, totally dedicated to a personalist art, which was at the same time critical of existing verities and social relations. Šimić was openly hostile to the "so-called culture of our country" and denounced all quests for any sort of style, not excluding the national style, as sheer absurdity: "The best style needn't mean anything at all. We shall, if necessary, express ourselves in such a way that nobody will be able to find a trace of any sort of grammar, syntax, or even the famous style. If necessary, we shall shriek inarticulate sounds, like animals."[8] Small wonder that his search for an expression of internal spiritual life led him to conclude that the "deeper we enter the souls of individual peoples, the more the differences disappear."[9] And since the expressionists viewed art as internal spiritual activity, national culture was of secondary importance. "The [prewar] Nationalist Youth saw our national expression in [poet Vladimir] Nazor and Meštrović," Šimić wrote: "One of these nationalists, writing about Nazor in 1914 . . . [called him] the 'poet of those of us, who are the men of tomorrow.' I understood almost nothing of his twaddle, only that Nazor was somehow sent to us directly by God as a prophet and that we shall begin to return our debt to civilization, through [Nazor] and Meštrović, by '*Slavicizing and Yugoslavicizing Europe.*' Some day, those who know and dare, will for once explain the psychology of our antebellum Nationalist Youth."[10]

Šimić was not the only critic of "Yugoslavist culture." He was joined by a number of Croat liberal intellectuals. Vladimir Lunaček, the principal writer on cultural themes for the Zagreb autonomist daily *Obzor* (Horizon), saw Meštrović as the creator not so much of a "Yugoslav style," which was impossible, but of a *völkisch* (populist) art akin to that of Franz Metzner in Germany.[11] Also, the former members of the Nationalist Youth were joining the critics of their earlier preoccupations. Many, such as Miroslav Krleža, August Cesarec, Steven Galogaža, turned to radical socialism, finding a ready outlet for their relentless attacks against monarchist and bourgeois Yugoslavism within the yet unbolshevized Communist movement. Others, such as Augustin Ujević, passed through a brief phase in which they called for the building of unitary culture, only to reject the "rottenness of bourgeois

7. Ivan Mažuranić, *Smrt Smail-age Čengijića*, illus. Joza Kljaković (Zagreb, 1922), p. 33.
8. Antun Branko Šimić, "Juriš," *Juriš*, vol. 1 (1919), no. 1, pp. 4–5.
9. Šimić, "Meštrovićevo kiparstvo," p. 1.
10. Antun Branko Šimić, "Nazorova lirika," *Vedrina*, vol. 1 (1923), nos. 3–4, pp. 79–80.
11. Vladimir Lunaček, "Dvije izložbe. Marin Studin i R. Krusnjak," *Obzor*, March 8, 1919, p. 2.

society and the lie of the entire present situation,'' and then turned to pure aestheticism.[12] They recognized that ''Yugoslavism received a sort of official seal, becoming above all a matter of personal advantage.''[13] Ujević wanted no part of that. Faithful to the heretical course, he proclaimed himself an Irishman, in protest against the society in which Rade Pašić, the politician's profligate son, was the hero of Yugoslav unification.[14] Most important, the chief architects of ''Yugoslavist culture,'' Meštrović and his imitators, struck out in new directions. Meštrović entered a new and vibrant religious phase, his greatest period, finding solace for his spiritual dilemmas, his ''mysticism without God,'' in New Testament themes. Some of his companions from the old Medulić Society, such as Ljubo Babić, imbued their religious paintings with the spirit of social protest. Babić's Christ was the ''defender of the proletariat and the leader of the great oppressed mass.''[15] Finally, with but a few exceptions (Ivo Andrić, Niko Bartulović), most of the Croat writers and artists associated with the prewar Nationalist Youth protested against national inequality by discarding their unitarism and—in the misleading phrase of the day—''returned to the ranks of the Croat people.''[16] Meštrović himself experienced many unpleasantries over his increasingly lukewarm attitude toward official policies.[17]

Inasmuch as the prewar Yugoslavist unitarism was a predominantly Croat intellectual phenomenon, the depletion of its ranks among the leading Croat *kulturnjaks* represented an incalculable blow to any notions of constructing a new unitary culture. This does not mean that attempts were not made to keep up the idea, especially among the intellectuals close to the DS, but to the great regret of the unitarists, though they invoked the work of prewar Meštrović, contrasting him to the cosmopolitanism of ''Krleža's generation,'' they could not count on any significant contemporary creators.[18] Left-wing cultural journals frequently ridiculed the ''pestering wares'' of cultural unitarists. Writing about Kosta Strajnić, one of these ideologists, a leftist critic noted:

12. Augustin Ujević, "Lepota mladosti," *Demokratija,* March 11, 1920, p. 2.

13. Milan Bogdanović, "O srpskoj književnosti izmedju dva rata," *Rad JAZU,* 1954, no. 301, p. 29.

14. Mirko Žeželj, *Veliki Tin: Životopis* (Zagreb, 1976), p. 223. Ujević's unrestrained criticism of Yugoslavia's social order may have been the main reason for his expulsion from Belgrade, in 1925, on charges of vagrancy. See Ante Stamać, *Ujević* (Zagreb, 1971), pp. 68–69.

15. Vladimir Lunaček, "Rad naših umjetnika. Iz naših umjetničkih ateliera," *Obzor,* Sept. 12, 1920, p. 1.

16. "Narod i umjetnici," *Hrvatska riječ,* Oct. 4, 1924, p. 1. Cf. Bogdan Radica, "Naše likovne vrijednosti," ibid., pp. 3–4.

17. For examples of these annoyances see Meštrović, *Uspomene na političke ljude i dogadjaje* (Buenos Aires, 1961), pp. 160–170.

18. Marin Pavlinović, "Kulturni pokret djaka i Krležina generacija," *Vrelo,* vol. 1 (1920), nos. 3–4, pp. 27–29. Cf. Vladislav Kušan, "Moderna skulptura u Hrvata: Geneza i prvi tokovi razvoja," *Forum,* vol. 19 (1980), nos. 1–2, p. 302.

For years Mr. Strajnić has made a pest of himself with his folk ornaments, fabrics, costumes, embroidery, monasteries in Old Serbia and Macedonia, etc., and the time has come for us to tell him that he is sitting right on the top of our heads. This is because all of Mr. Kosta Strajnić's theories are so dismal and dilettantish that all of his stories about "Yugoslav artistic culture" amount to no more than dust for the eyes. He never probed so deeply as to render an account of the creative spirit that brought about his patterns, ornaments, and fabrics. (It is as if Mr. Kosta Strajnić lived in a museum spirit jar. He keeps talking of "modern monstrosities" that are destroying our [oh! ugh! ah!]— Baroque and Renaissance . . .) In other words, Mr. Strajnić . . . remains a partisan of external forms and seeks to have them imitated. When will Mr. Strajnić understand that an artist can be born, for example, in Pirot, without knowing a thing about the Pirot kilims.[19]

For all that, the expressionist generation produced some aberrant forms of cultural unitarism. The Zenith Group of Ljubomir Micić, a minor Serb writer from Croatia, was rather similar to Futurism in external appearances, but its aim was to spark the war of civilizations in which the South Slavs would form the Slavic vanguard against Latinity and the West in general. Micić's half-baked ideas were misrepresentations of some of Dostoevsky's themes and were applied to proclaim the South Slavs as "pioneers and shareholders in the construction of the Universal Man's new culture, which is brought forth by the EASTERNER, the Man from the Urals, the Caucasus, and the Balkans, born in the cradle called RUSSIA."[20] Indeed, the cultural nihilists among the remnants of Nationalist Youth reveled in the supposed barbarism of the unspoiled "Yugoslav race." The proximity of these notions to the fascist idea of Italy as a proletarian nation is self-evident. But even in its tamer forms, in terms of pure Slavophilic messianism, these variants of unitarism were essentially nihilistic. Where some of the nihilistic unitarists praised the creative chaos of Yugoslavia's cultural scene, others started expounding obscurantist mysticism. Among the Serbs especially, the idea of "Yugoslavist culture" was seen as a redeeming alternative to the "Faustian rationalism" of Western Europe, but in the hands of Orthodox philosophers like Nikolaj Velimirović and Justin Popović it became the vehicle for the assertion of Orthodox superiority. This form of unitarism was narrowly Serbian, Orthodox, and, inasmuch as it was proselytizing and assimilatory, only conditionally Yugoslavist.[21]

It must be said that the idea of unitary Yugoslav culture made the smallest headway among the South Slavic intellectuals in spite of considerable ideo-

19. Vigil., "Kosta Strajnić i nacionalna umetnost," *Vedrina,* vol. 1 (1923), no. 1, p. 27.

20. Ljubomir Micić, "Delo Zenitizma," *Zenit,* vol. 1 (1921), no. 8, p. 2.

21. Dragan M. Jeremić, "O filozofiji kod Srba," *Savremenik,* vol. 13 (1967), no. 12, pp. 491–500. Cf. Andrija B. Stojković, *Razvitak filosofije u Srba 1804–1944* (Belgrade, 1972), pp. 392–412.

logical dispositions in its favor. Because the inclination toward *narodno jedinstvo* was still strong in the ranks of the intelligentsia, notably among the Croats, no significant mental reservations toward cultural unitarism emerged in the immediate postwar period. The nature of the only avenues available for the realization of cultural unitarism, directed by the political establishment and official art overseers, was what repelled most unitarist intellectuals—and ultimately created the climate favorable to the separate Serb, Croat, and Slovene cultural integrations. No distinct ideological barriers were mounted against cultural unitarism until the mid-1920s, however, and in the immediate postwar period unitary Yugoslavism did have a limited success in one special area where the intelligentsia felt itself in command, the area of linguistic practice.

It was noted earlier that the Serbian and Croatian literary standards were founded on the štokavian dialect, spoken by almost all Serbs and the vast majority of Croats. Whereas the Serb choice was clear-cut, the Croats in theory could also have chosen either their čakavian or kajkavian dialects, which they did not share with any other South Slavic people, for their literary standard. But guided by the evolving proštokavian trend that could not ultimately bypass the kajkavian northwest around Zagreb, the geographical center of the Croat Revival, the Illyrianist generation opted for štokavian. Moreover, though most Illyrianist awakeners, as natives of the Zagreb area, were themselves speakers of the kajkavian dialect, they recognized that their idea of uniting all the South Slavs within one linguistic medium depended on the adoption of štokavian. But though their choice was strengthened by the knowledge that the štokavian was dominant among Serbs, the Illyrianists did not adopt the linguistic standard practiced by the circle of Vuk Karadžić, which they regarded as too narrowly Serbian. Instead of Karadžić's robust neoštokavian, which from the beginning of the seventeenth century was the Croat regional literary idiom of Dalmatia and Slavonia (Andrija Kačić Miošić, Matija Antun Relković), they preferred a modified version of the štokavian dialect enriched by elements of čakavian and kajkavian, which figured in the rich Croat literary tradition.[22]

The traditions of Illyrianism prevailed among the Croats until the 1890s, when the school of Croat followers of Karadžić (Tomo Maretić, Franjo Iveković, Ivan Broz), aided by the Zagreb administration of Khuen-Héderváry, succeeded in promulgating the wholesale adoption of Karadžić's orthographic norms. But though their success gave rise to the myth that the Croats accepted something called "Vuk's language" (indeed, Serbian, which the consistent partisans of štokavian Serbianism saw as accepted in

---

22. On this subject see Ivo Banac, "Main Trends in the Croat Language Question," in Riccardo Picchio and Harvey Goldblatt, eds., *Aspects of the Slavic Language Question*, vol. 1, *Church Slavonic—South Slavic—West Slavic* (New Haven, 1984), pp. 189–259.

kajkavian Croatia since the time of the Illyrianists), Maretić and his group attained their desired end only where their activities coalesced with the neoštokavian trend that triumphed among the nonkajkavian Croats well before the Illyrian movement. The Croat followers of Karadžić could hardly revise the whole Croat literary heritage by excluding its lexical and morphological wealth, and since living practice moderated those of Karadžić's orthographic solutions that were alien to Croat neoštokavian idioms, the success of Maretić, Iveković, and Broz was more formal than real.

Paradoxically, though the Croat followers of Karadžić, as cultural unitarists, above all wished to establish full linguistic unity with the Serbs, they met their most significant reversals in that area. Quite unexpectedly, the three reflexes of Church Slavonic ѣ (*jatъ*) (ijekavian, ikavian, ekavian), present in the štokavian subdialects, became the new source of division. Despite the fact that ijekavian was least represented among the Croats, the Illyrianist awakeners settled on this subdialect because it was the idiom of Dubrovnik's great literary tradition, its influx into the other Croat regional literatures being evident since the early eighteenth-century writings of Bosnian Franciscans, and because Karadžić chose the ijekavian speech of eastern Hercegovina (the "southern dialect") as the basis for his Serbian linguistic reform. Moreover, ijekavian was predominant among the Orthodox or Serb population of Croatia. Had they chosen the Croat ikavian subdialect (the "western dialect") the Illyrianists might have risked a nationality-based linguistic division.[23] But though it seemed that the Serbs and Croats would ultimately share not only the common štokavian dialect but also its ijekavian subdialect as their literary standard, things did not work out that way. At approximately the same time as the Croats started using a variant of Karadžić's orthography, Belgrade and Novi Sad departed from Karadžić's standard in favor of Šumadija-Vojvodina ekavian (the "eastern dialect"). The Serbs of these politically and intellectually dominant areas understandably preferred their own influential idiom as the basis for literary activity centered on Belgrade. But, as Stojan Novaković readily admitted, ekavian permitted expansion into Macedonia, a major Serbian preoccupation after Austro-Hungarian troops closed the doors to Bosnia-Hercegovina in 1878.[24]

One unanticipated result of the turn-of-century linguistic fluctuations was an integration of Croat and Serb linguistic forms in Croatia-Slavonia, Dalmatia, and Bosnia-Hercegovina. Serbia and Vojvodina simultaneously carried out their own standardization, whereas Montenegrin ijekavian stood midway between these two linguistic-literary complexes. Thus, while the Croats definitely united under one linguistic and scriptory standard (neo-

23. Pavle Ivić, *Srpski narod i njegov jezik* (Belgrade, 1971), pp. 186–187.
24. Stjepan Ivšić, "Etimologija i fonetika u našem pravopisu," *Hrvatski jezik*, vol. 1 (1938), no. 1, pp. 12–13.

štokavian ijekavian written in thirty Roman letters), the Serbs maintained two subdialects of standard neoštokavian, ekavian in Serbia and Vojvodina and ijekavian everywhere else, written in Karadžić's reformed Cyrillic. Though these new ramparts between the Croatian and Serbian linguistic practice represented a natural continuation of long-standing trends, they were a challenge for linguistic unitarists, convinced as they were that the want of a single Serbo-Croatian linguistic standard cast a pall over the dogma of *narodno jedinstvo*. Moreover, though most unitarists were determined not to allow any distinctions between Serbian and Croatian, some allowances were made for Slovenian. Increasingly, however, consistent linguistic unitarists sought to obliterate the autonomy of Slovenian, arguing that it was absurd for one people to have two languages. After Yugoslavia's constitutional committee accepted the separate status of Slovenian, Momčilo Ivanić protested that "no special philological knowledge is necessary . . . to hit upon the simple idea that it is impossible for one and the same people to have—two languages."[25]

The new search for a single Serbo-Croatian linguistic standard began in 1913 when Jovan Skerlić, the leading Serbian literary critic, proposed a solution whereby the Serbs would give up the Cyrillic script in exchange for the Croat acceptance of the "eastern dialect." Almost all Serb writers, whether from the ijekavian or ekavian areas, who were queried by the Belgrade journal *Srpski književni glasnik* (Serbian Literary Messenger) in 1914 on Skerlić's proposal, supported this idea. So did some unitarist Croats (Josip Smodlaka, Milan Marjanović, Vladimir Čerina) and Slovenes (Fran Ilešić, Ivan Hribar, Niko Županić), though a number of leading Croats rejected it (Frano Supilo, Ivo Vojnović).[26] A separate survey conducted by the Slovene journal *Veda* (Science) in 1913, which failed to attract the cooperation of leading Slovene writers, nevertheless established that the Slovenes were reluctant to abandon their language for the sake of unity, though a number of Croats expected them to do so, some for ostensibly unitarist reasons (Frano Supilo) and others because they hoped to see Slovenian integrated within the Croatian literary standard, an old aspiration of the Party of Right.[27]

Although the realization of Skerlić's plan was cut off by the war, in the ranks of the Nationalist Youth the plan was followed voluntarily and became the badge of cultural unitarism. As soon as circumstances permitted, during the last—relatively liberal—year of Austria-Hungary, the quest was revived, and it reached a crescendo immediately after the unification, leading many to

25. Momčilo Ivanić, "Slovenački jezik!" *Samouprava*, March 16, 1921, p. 1.
26. "Anketa o južnom ili istočnom narečju," *Srpski književni glasnik*, vol. 32 (1914), no. 2, pp. 112–115; no. 3, pp. 217–228; no. 4, pp. 285–293; no. 5, pp. 375–389; no. 6, pp. 438–447; no. 7, pp. 526–528.
27. Niko Bartulović, "Kulturno jedinstvo i Slovenci," *Književni jug*, vol. 1 (1918), no. 7, pp. 257–258.

suspect that South Slavic linguistic unity was within reach. The commonest argument in favor of Skerlić's plan was the impracticality of several linguistic standards. Yugoslavia was too small a country for the free reign of linguistic pluralism. Progress and national unification necessitated a single linguistic standard. Why should there be simultaneous Serbian and Croatian translations of Dostoevsky's *The Idiot,* when the second translator could find a more constructive use of his precious time by translating another novel by the Russian master?[28] Some Croat proponents of the "eastern dialect" tried to deflect the charge that the introduction of ekavian would deflower the Croat linguistic standard and expose it to Serbianization by arguing that the Croat kajkavians, who were also ekavians, had their own "Croat reasons" for favoring the innovation.[29] Another argument, favored by the Croat expressionists like Antun Branko Šimić, who were not so much interested in promoting unitarism as in fighting the established practices, was that the defense of ijekavian among the Croats and the consistent Serb followers of Karadžić amounted to sterile conservatism: "The philological defense of the ijekavian dialect is always unimportant and often provokes hilarity. Tradition, they say. Oh, when shall we throw that word, which always causes obstacles, out of our souls!"[30] Yet it was precisely out of respect for the national tradition that many Serbs, who were otherwise strong supporters of ekavian, hesitated to abandon the Cyrillic script. Hinting at Habsburg attempts to ban the use of Serb Cyrillic after the Sarajevo assassination, Vladimir Ćorović noted that the "Cyrillic script thereby became our fellow sufferer . . . and a graphic symbol of [the Serb] struggle for self-preservation and of [Serb] consciousness and endurance. And, as a result, for as long as [the Serb] national existence is endangered, the Cyrillic script will remain one of the emblems that cannot be abandoned, a banner under which we must endure."[31]

After the establishment of Yugoslavia a great number of leading Croat authors (notably Augustin Ujević, Ulderiko Donadini, Miroslav Krleža, A. B. Šimić, Gustav Krklec) followed the Skerlić formula. Indeed, to the chagrin of antiunitarist Croats and Slovenes, Serbian ekavian was pushed through as Yugoslavia's official language, most often in Cyrillic garb. Nor could it have been otherwise. There was nothing neutral in the acceptance of ekavian, which was frequently the code word for the wholesale adoption of Serb linguistic practices, including the Serb lexical wealth. In short, Belgrade's political centralism had a parallel linguistic direction, which amounted to the infiltration of Serbian terms and forms throughout

28. Anton Loboda, "Za kulturno zedinjenje Jugoslovanov," ibid., nos. 8–9, p. 299.
29. Zvonko Milković, "Za ekavštinu," ibid., pp. 349–350.
30. Antun Branko Šimić, "E," *Glas Slovenaca, Hrvata i Srba,* March 3, 1918, p. 2.
31. Vladimir Ćorović, "Za književno jedinstvo: Pitanje narečja i pisma," *Književni jug,* vol. I (1918), nos. 3–4, p. 100.

Yugoslavia by means of the military, civil administration, and schools. But where the Yugoslavist unitarists of the DS were hard pressed to explain what sacrifices the Serbs had made at the altar of linguistic unity, Serbian nationalists of the NRS never even bothered to consider any linguistic concessions on the Serbs' part.

For a man like Momčilo Ivanić, who was otherwise relatively considerate of Croat autonomist aspirations, the question of linguistic unity was the question of Serbianization. Ivanić earnestly believed that under Gaj the Croats "accepted the Serbian literary language." The Slovenes should do the same, and "that way, the Serbian language would become the language of our whole people, and a linguistic form of *narodno jedinstvo* would be realized in exactly the same way as was the feat of our national liberation and unification."[32] Other Radicals, such as Milenko Vesnić, went further and insisted on Cyrillic as the common South Slavic script. "Those Slavic tribes that use Cyrillic," reasoned Vesnić, "were more successful in safeguarding their ethnic characteristics, whereas the Roman script is foreign."[33] So, presumably, was the literature written in Roman script, which explains the undisguised hostility toward biscriptualism on the part of Serbian supremacists. When a group of Hercegovinians presented Regent Aleksandar with a sword bearing a dedication in both the Cyrillic and Roman scripts, a Radical journal protested, noting that "there is no place for Roman script on a sword presented in the name of Serb Hercegovina to the prince regent. . . . In Hercegovina . . . after the fall of Austria, the Slavic Cyrillic, at last, must also feel like a victor."[34]

Though Skerlić's formula was widely used among the intellectuals, in light of the growing Serbianization of Yugoslavia's linguistic practice, Slovene and Croat intellectuals began to have second thoughts about linguistic unitarism. Almost all the Slovenes rejected any tampering with their language, which, as the "most intuitive age-old experience of the popular masses, cannot be changed casually like a shirt on Sunday."[35] Among the Croats by the end of the 1920s, most of the writers and journals that had been using the Skerlić formula were beginning to abandon it. But oddly, the struggle for Croat linguistic autonomy took a peculiar turn. As inconsistent as it may appear in light of earlier developments, Maretić's school became Croatianized during the 1920s. After three decades of usage, combined with the regulatory power of literary creators and consumers, the Croat public accepted the innovations of Karadžić's Croat followers and viewed their work as peculiarly native. In the same fashion, ijekavian, which was steadily

32. Momčilo Ivanić, "Jedinstvo jezika," *Samouprava*, March 18, 1921, p. 1.
33. Milenko Vesnić, "Za našu ćirilicu," *Balkan*, April 4, 1920, p. 3.
34. "'Kraljeviću Nasljedniku vjerna Hercegovina'. Latinica na Regentovoj sablji," ibid., Sept. 1, 1920, p. 1.
35. Ivan Mazovec, "'Slovenački jezik,'" *Slovenec*, April 1, 1921, p. 1.

endangered by the centralist preference for ekavian, demonstrated its general acceptance as the Croat national idiom on the part of the Belgrade administrations and the Croats themselves—this despite Karadžić's espousal of ijekavian and the trace of his linguistic concepts in post-1892 Croat ijekavian recension. For all his countenance of Croat-Serb linguistic unity, in 1921 Maretić himself could not forbear the dismissal of proposals for the acceptance of ekavian in Croatia as idealistic and impractical. Thus the Croat struggle against linguistic centralism was fought not under the banner of old Illyrianist linguistic standard but in defense of Broz's phonetic orthography and Maretić's grammar, both based on Karadžić's linguistic credo. Where the most stubborn among Croat unitarists struggled on with ekavian, often with comical results, the majority of Croats rejected linguistic Serbianization.[36] With the growing consciousness that the Serbs, Croats, and Slovenes constituted separate nationalities, linguistic unitarism was deprived of its ideological foundations. The Croats confirmed their own linguistic standard, which owed a great deal to Karadžić's Croat followers. Two experiments in linguistic unitarism parted ways.

Centralization

Although the proponents of Yugoslavia's unification had presumed that the establishment of the Yugoslav state, freed from external tutelage, would remove the nationality conflict from the political agenda, events proved otherwise. Owing to the systematic fostering of centralizing measures, the primary result of both the Great Serbian and unitarist conceptions of Yugoslavia's state organization, and the resistance that those measures provoked among the non-Serb nationalities, the national question became the most important problem of Yugoslavia's internal relations. The essence of Yugoslavia's national question was the conflict between the protagonists of several antagonistic national ideologies, which expressed themselves in the struggle over the organization of the new state. Whereas the proponents of unitarism sought to obliterate all historically derived differences between the Serbs, Croats, and Slovenes by means of a strictly centralized state, the majority of Serbian political parties used centralism to further Serbian pre-

36. The awkwardness of unitarist Croats in their use of ekavian stemmed from the fact that not every *je* syllable was a reflex of *jatь*. Such unitarist enthusiasts as Mijo Radošević, a Croat socialist who became a sort of unitarist fascist, often committed the folly of changing every *je* into *e*, thereby coining such nonwords as *oduševlenje*, instead of *oduševljenje* (enthusiasm), which is the same in ijekavian and ekavian. See Mijo Radošević, *Osnovi savremene Jugoslavije: Nova Politika* (Zagreb, 1935), p. 514.

dominance. This meant that the partisans of a unitarist and a Great Serbian version of Yugoslavia were counterposed to the representatives of the non-Serb national movements, who either demanded a federated (or confederated) state structure or sought guarantees for their national aspirations outside the framework of Yugoslavia.[1]

From the outset, Serbia had the upper hand. The delegation sent by the National Council to Belgrade did not negotiate with the Serbian government strictly in accordance with the directives, which had allowed for several alternative forms of state organization; instead, Pavelić's address to Regent Aleksandar, in which the term "unitary state" was repeatedly emphasized, left little doubt that the delegation considered that form of state as incontrovertible. References to the regent's "reigning power" also gave a veneer of conclusiveness to the continuing debate between the monarchists and the republicans. In addition, the delegation agreed to the formation of a unitary, though parliamentary, government, responsible to a unitary legislature, which had yet to be formed. They also agreed that the existing autonomous administrative organs would continue their work under the control of the new government—though the simultaneous responsibility of these organs to the autonomous legislatures was also reaffirmed.

On December 3, 1918, the leadership of the National Council promulgated the unification act and the consequent end of its own supreme sovereign authority in the former Austro-Hungarian territories. The statement of the National Council specified that the administrative function of this body would cease to exist upon the establishment of the new joint cabinet in Belgrade. Protests from sections of Croat opinion were voiced even before this formal notice could be imparted. On December 2, the Frankists, revived by the mass disenchantment, began disseminating a proclamation that condemned the undemocratic nature of state unification. On December 5, popular discontent erupted. Soldiers of the still active Croat units of the former Austro-Hungarian army, the Fifty-third Infantry Regiment and the Twenty-fifth Home Guard Infantry Regiment stationed in Zagreb, marched to Jelačić Square in the center of the city, protesting the unification. They confronted the militia and regular units loyal to the National Council, which were awaiting the demonstrators. According to official accounts, the pitched battle

1. On the interwar history of Yugoslavia, with special reference to the national question, in addition to the already cited works of Ferdo Čulinović and Rudolf Horvat, the following works can be used with profit: Franjo Tudjman, "Uvod u historiju socijalističke Jugoslavije," *Forum,* vol. 2 (1963), no. 2, pp. 292–352; no. 3, pp. 530–564; no. 4, pp. 702–741; Sergije Dimitrijević et al., eds., *Iz istorije Jugoslavije 1918–1945: Zbornik predavanja* (Belgrade, 1958); Julijana Vrčinac, *Naša najnovija istorija: Pregled (1919–1945)* (Belgrade, 1967); Wayne S. Vucinich, "Interwar Yugoslavia," in *Contemporary Yugoslavia: Twenty Years of Socialist Experiment,* ed. Wayne S. Vucinich (Berkeley, 1969); L. B. Valev, G. M. Slavin, and I. I. Udal'tsov, eds., *Istoriia Iugoslavii,* vol. 2 (Moscow, 1963); Momchilo M. Dzhurich, *Obrazovanie mnogonatsional'nogo gosudarstva Iugoslavii (1918–1921 gg.)* (Moscow, 1970).

claimed the lives of thirteen combatants, and an additional seventeen persons were wounded. The overwhelming majority of victims were from the ranks of demonstrating soldiers.[2]

This incident, which envenomed political sentiments in its own right, ushered in a series of official acts aimed at the gradual obliteration of administrative autonomy in Croatia and elsewhere through the extension of Serbian laws and institutions to all areas of the new state. Privately, most Serbian politicians, notably the Radicals, did not consider Yugoslavia a new state at all but merely an expansion of Serbian state territory. Serbia's sovereignty was not ending but rather was being aggrandized within a Greater Serbia. This view was still muffled, but the first centralizing measures were not in marked variance with the concept. Thus, even though Regent Aleksandar consented to the demand of the National Council that the existing regional authorities would continue performing their administrative tasks until the impending constitutional assembly made the final decision on the nature of state organization, in reality only the Serbian government remained sovereign in the interregnum between December 1 and the naming of Yugoslavia's first cabinet on December 20. This situation continued all but in name until the proclamation of the 1921 Constitution, while the exercise of governmental authority on the part of the National Council and its nominally legally subject equivalents in Ljubljana, Split, Sarajevo, and Novi Sad, was becoming increasingly dependent on the Serbian military authorities, and after December 20, on the joint cabinet in Belgrade. In this way, also, universal expectations of national equality were seriously compromised.

On December 10, shortly after the demonstration of the Croat troops, the National Council announced the reorganization of the military hitherto under its command. Former Croat units of the Austro-Hungarian army were disbanded, while the Serbian military mission, headed by Milan Pribićević, proceeded to fashion new regiments in agreement with the military section of the National Council.[3] This was but a prelude to more systematic centralizing measures in which Regent Aleksandar and Svetozar Pribićević played particularly prominent roles. On December 15 an agreed list of members of Yugoslavia's first cabinet was submitted to Aleksandar for approval. This was the result of a negotiated compromise between the representatives of the National Council and the various Serbian parties. Of the twenty allotted portfolios, nine were assigned to ministers from Serbia, six to those from Croatia, two each to the representatives of Slovenia and Bosnia-Hercegovina, and one to a minister from Montenegro. In national terms, thirteen ministers were Serbs, four were Croats, two were Slovenes, and one was a

2. Josip Horvat, *Politička povijest Hrvatske 1918–1929* (Zagreb, 1938), pp. 165–169.
3. Ferdo Šišić, comp., *Dokumenti o postanku Kraljevine Srba, Hrvata i Slovenaca, 1914.–1919.* (Zagreb, 1920), p. 285.

Bosnian Muslim.[4] This unequal distribution of cabinet responsibilities established a precedent that held throughout the interwar period.[5] Presented with such a list, which predictably did not include representatives of the HPSS, Regent Aleksandar brought on the new state's first government crisis by refusing to sanction the appointment of Pašić as prime minister. The premiership was then offered to Stojan Protić, who Aleksandar considered less apt to counter his political designs. Significantly, Aleksandar's confirmation of the Protić cabinet on December 20 was made part of the same official act that accepted the resignation of the previous Serbian cabinet.[6] Trumbić, however, became minister of foreign affairs, while Pribićević acquired the weighty ministry of the interior, with the proviso that Marko Trifković (1864–1930), an NRS dissident and minister of justice, would de facto be responsible for internal affairs on the territory of the preunification Serbia.

The first steps of the new government confirmed the forebodings of the anticentralist forces. Pribićević's cabinet position enabled him to become an unlimited arbiter in administrative and political matters, and he energetically made the most of it to carry out strict centralizing measures. One of his first actions was to demand the resignations of regional governments. This act was motivated by customary principles of parliamentary responsibility, although the interim legislature was not yet summoned. On January 7, 1919, after the resignations had been submitted, Aleksandar, on Pribićević's advice and without consulting the regional legislative bodies, confirmed some of the

---

4. *Službene novine,* Jan. 12, 1919, p. 1.

5. Rudolf Bićanić, a noted Croat economist and an aide to Vladko Maček, Radić's successor at the head of the Croat Peasant Party, arrived at the following table showing the national composition of Yugoslavia's cabinets between 1918 and 1938. Bićanić defined Croats of national parties as members of anticentralist, strictly Croat political groups; Croats by descent were unitarist Croats. Big ministries were premiership, foreign affairs, interior, army, finances, justice, and education; economic ministries were trade, transportation, forests and minerals, agriculture, construction, social policy, national health, posts and telegraph; small ministries were without portfolio, religion, agrarian reform, standardization of laws, nutrition, physical education. See Bićanić, *Ekonomska podloga hrvatskog pitanja,* 2d ed. (Zagreb, 1938), pp. 63–67.

Ministers	Ministries			
	Total	Big	Economic	Small
Serbians	399	208	133	58
Serbs from outside Serbia	53	23	19	11
Croats of national parties	26	2	19	5
Croats by descent	111	14	56	41
Slovenes	49	5	58	6
Bosnian Muslims	18	0	14	4
Total	656	252	299	125

6. *Službene novine,* Jan. 12, 1919, p. 1.

previous heads of regional administrations and rejected others.[7] Similarly, most of the regional administrative branches (commissions) were abolished, in some regions altogether (Vojvodina), while in Croatia-Slavonia, out of eleven previous commissions, only the *ressorts* for interior, judiciary, and worship were continued.

The new government also saw fit to compel constitutional solutions that would prevail until the decisions of the Constituent Assembly. Attempts were made to lift out certain sections of the old Serbian constitution and extend them, in part at least, to the whole territory of Yugoslavia. Although these attempts were not completely successful, many sections of the Serbian constitution dealing with, among other matters, citizens' rights, as well as numerous Serbian laws, were extended statewide, with or without reference to the source of their inspiration.[8] In this way, too, the prerogatives of the forthcoming Constituent Assembly were prepossessed.

Serious conflict arose on the question of ratification of the unification act. On December 29, 1918, the Serbian National Assembly formally upheld the decision to ratify. The Croats were insistent that the Croatian Sabor should similarly ratify Croatia's entrance into the new state, but Protić's cabinet acting on Pribićević's advice, sought to circumvent the Sabor, fearful of the complications that might arise if the Croat deputies who opposed the unification could openly air their views, and perhaps obstruct the ratification. Although the refusal to sanction the convening of the Sabor could have provided some limited immediate advantage for the centralist forces, in the long run this tactic rebounded with a vengeance, since the Croat opposition (and particularly Radić's HPSS) could henceforth challenge the legality of the unification. But where Protić would have preferred to restore the prerogatives of the regional assemblies in the extremely attenuated way, he was confronted by Pribićević's intransignece. The minister of the interior went so far as to declare that as long as he was alive there would be no Croatian Sabor.[9]

Pribićević's determination to devalue Croat institutions was again demonstrated on the occasion of Aleksandar's appointment of Pribićević's protégé,

7. Ibid., Feb. 3, 1919, p. 1.

8. On February 20, 1919, the cabinet signed a decision that extended statewide Serbia's 1915 Law about the Treatment of the Property of the Subjects of States in War with Serbia. Ibid., Feb. 27, 1919, p. 1. On February 25, 1919, the cabinet decided that chapters 9 and 10 of Serbia's Criminal (Penal) Code should be extended statewide. Ibid., April 10, 1919, p. 1. On August 19, 1919, at the suggestion of the minister of the army and the navy, the regent decided to extend statewide the military laws of Serbia, including the Law about the Organization of the Army; the Law about the Military Provisioning; the Military Penal Code; the Law about the Organization of Military Courts; the Law about the Procedure of Military Courts in Criminal Cases; the Law about the Military-Disciplinary Court; and the Law about the Marriages of Officers, Noncommissioned Officers, Corporals, and Privates, with all the attending additions and provisions based on the listed laws. Ibid., Sept. 9, 1919, p. 1.

9. Horvat, *Politička povijest*, p. 202.

Ivan Paleček, as the new Croatian Ban, as if such a decision were within the regent's legal capacity.[10] This nomination, inspired by Pribićević, ran counter to the wishes of the SSP, which would have preferred to see its leader Pavelić in the post. Paleček's immediate declaration to the effect that he would perform his duties in accordance with the directives from the Protić cabinet, since in his view the Zagreb authorities were no longer autonomous, merely compounded the resentment aroused by his appointment. Thus, the office of the Ban was seriously debilitated. Matters were improved slightly during Protić's second cabinet (February to May 1920) owing to the appointment of Matko Laginja (1852–1930), a Croat autonomist, as the new Ban. Laginja succeeded in righting another violation of the old Croatian constitution: during his tenure the authorities released Stjepan Radić and several other political prisoners, who, though old Sabor deputies, had languished in jail from March 1919 after being arrested and held without trial at Pribićević's express order.

The role of the military and the gendarmerie in the process of centralization has been discussed earlier. But though the policies of these agencies had a dramatic effect on popular feelings outside Serbia, ordinary citizens had relatively few contacts with military officers and gendarmes. Matters stood otherwise in regard to the civil administration. Since the activities of the state bureaucracy concerned everyone, the state's reputation was dependent on its performance. Even before 1918 the prestige of the civil servants left much to be desired in all parts of the future Yugoslav state. The peasants in particular traditionally viewed the bureaucrats as unrelenting foes, who enforced unpopular legislation to the economic detriment of the countryside and seemed to enjoy humiliating the downtrodden and the humble.[11] This is not the place for a detailed examination of the accuracy of such popularly held opinions; nor is it possible to evaluate the comparative standing of the various civil services before 1918, including a prevalent view that the Austro-Hungarian bureaucracy, for all its shortcomings, was composed of trained and competent administrators, who operated in an efficient and disciplined manner, within a structure of a state that upheld rigorous legality. It can be concluded, however, that whatever expectations the populace nurtured in regard to improvement in the civil service after unification did not materialize.

There were many reasons for this blighted hope. In Yugoslavia, in marked contrast to the official policy in some other successor states, notably Czechoslovakia and Poland, the old Austro-Hungarian bureaucratic apparatus was thoroughly destroyed. The reputedly harsh practices and association with an alien regime were taken as sufficient grounds for dismissal not only of

---

10. *Službene novine*, Feb. 3, 1919, p. 1. The appointment was made on January 7, 1919.

11. For an excellent analysis of relations between peasants and bureaucrats see Jozo Tomasevich, *Peasants, Politics, and Economic Change in Yugoslavia* (Stanford, 1955), p. 250.

German and Hungarian employees but also of Croats, Slovenes, and even Habsburg Serbs. In their place the centralized state apparatus appointed large numbers of Serbians, who, to make matters worse, often had few or no qualifications for the tasks they were expected to undertake.[12] In large part, the concentration of Serbians in the bureaucracy was a result of the patronage dispensed by the Serbian political parties, and as these parties became entrenched, the bureaucracy grew larger and larger and rife with corruption.[13] By the 1930s, the state bureaucracy numbered some 350,000 individuals, or roughly every ninth citizen. Under this burden, efficiency declined, state expenditures had to be limited, and, inevitably, the taxpayers suffered.

Ideological criteria in public service appointments were most evident in public instruction. Pribićević, as minister of education from 1920 to 1922, carried out a wholesale purge of schoolteachers who were judged not sufficiently unitaristic: at the end of the 1921–1922 school year he transferred or pensioned off some 600 teachers in Croatia-Slavonia alone.[14] Like Franjo Šekretar, in the short story by Jakša Kušan, many teachers were "sent down" for years of "rustication" in the provinces of Yugoslavia's southeastern rim, where they yearned for a post in the "most neglected, most distant, blackest, and smallest village in Croatia . . . moreover where there [were] no politics."[15] Pribićević would have had them become heralds of unitarism, bending the historical record for the sake of "correct development of citizens' consciousness and solidarity: . . . My aid and that of the other educational factors, indeed of all conscious citizens, is to work by all powers and means to improve the unfavorable situation in our national instruction."[16]

The process of centralization affected other institutions as well. Serbian politicians placed great importance on the exaltation of the Orthodox church, which, though not officially the state religion, was quite established, Pašić

12. For a study of bureaucratic advancement in postunification Yugoslavia see Bogomir A. Raïkovitch, *L'avancement et le traitement des fonctionnaires publics du Royaume des Serbes, Croates et Slovènes* (Paris, 1929[?]). There are no comprehensive studies on the national makeup of Yugoslavia's civil service, diplomatic corps, and the judiciary in the 1920s. Writing on the developments of the 1930s, however, progovernment authors usually concede the minimal Croat presence in the foreign service (in 1934, of Yugoslavia's 18 ambassadors, 15 were Serbs, 3 Croats, and none Slovenes; of the 127 embassy counsellors and secretaries, 106 were Serbs, 18 Croats, and 3 Slovenes), central ministries (there, the Croats constituted only 16.21 percent of university-trained officials in 1935), and notarial service. On the other hand, fair Croat participation was citied in education (though this often reflected the greater number of schools in the Croat lands) and judiciary (28.48 percent of all judges in 1934). See Bogdan Prica, *Hrvatsko pitanje i brojke* (Belgrade, 1937), pp. 38–43.

13. For a highly personal and dramatic study of corruption in interwar Yugoslavia see Zvonimir Kulundžić, *Politika i korupcija u kraljevskoj Jugoslaviji* (Zagreb, 1968).

14. Stojan Protić, "Proganjanje učitelja u Hrvatskoj," *Radikal*, Sept. 28, 1922, p. 1.

15. Jakša Kušan, "Suhi Ponor," *Forum*, vol. 17 (1978), nos. 1–2, p. 111.

16. Svetozar Pribićević, "Nacionalna zadaća škole: Inicijativa ministra prosvjete: geografsko istoriska predavanja u školama o ujedinjenju," *Riječ Srba-Hrvata-Slovenaca*, May 2, 1921, p. 2.

having insisted as early as the Corfu conference of 1917 that the monarchs of future Yugoslavia be Orthodox.[17] But since the Serbs before 1918 belonged to five autocephalous Orthodox churches—the Metropolitanate of the Kingdom of Serbia, the Metropolitanate of the Kingdom of Montenegro, the Metropolitanate of Karlovci (Hungary, Croatia-Slavonia), the Metropolitanate of Bukovina-Dalmatia (in the Austrian half of the Dual Monarchy), and the Ecumenical Patriarchate of Constantinople (Bosnia-Hercegovina, Sandžak, Metohia, Kosovo, Macedonia)—Serbian political leaders pressed for the speedy subordination of the churches outside Serbia to the Metropolitanate of Serbia.[18] But soon they expressed the preference for the unification of Yugoslavia's Orthodox churches within the new organization, which would be superior in dignity to the hierarchical status of the prewar Orthodox church organizations—the Serbian Patriarchate of the Orthodox church of the Kingdom of the Serbs, Croats, and Slovenes, as the successor of the Patriarchate of Peć.

Though Yugoslavia's Orthodox churches had specific ecclesiastical traditions, the government, riding the wave of Serb nationalism, did not encounter serious obstacles in steering the local churchmen into union. And where the canonical releases were necessary, as in the cases of the metropolitan of Bukovina-Dalmatia, now in Romania, and the ecumenical patriarch in Istanbul, the government was prepared to purchase these releases. On September 19, 1919, Davidović's cabinet approved the payment of 800,000 francs, Serbia's old debt to the Ecumenical patriarchate, "in addition to 200,000 francs in expenses" in order to complete the separation of "our Church from the Patriarchate of Constantinople."[19]

The unification of Yugoslavia's Orthodox churches was solemnly proclaimed in September 1920, and the Holy Archihieratic Synod of the united church then elected Dimitrije Pavlović, hitherto the metropolitan of Serbia, as the first patriarch of renewed Serbian patriarchate, with its see in Belgrade. In fact, the state quickly intervened in this procedure and promulgated a special patriarchal electoral code, whereby the election was carried out by a special electoral chamber that included, ex officio, a fair number of high state officials, though it stood to reason that, even under the prevailing circumstances, these office holders would not always be Orthodox.

The new election of Patriarch Dimitrije showed the extent of state control over the Orthodox church, something that could not be accomplished to the

17. Bogumil Vošnjak, *U borbi za ujedinjenu narodnu državu* (Ljubljana, 1928), p. 233.

18. Dr. Milan Pećanac, adviser to the commander of Serbian troops in Bosnia-Hercegovina, appraised Protić on December 11, 1919, of the request by his superior for Belgrade's instructions on how the Orthodox eparchies of Bosnia-Hercegovina "should be subjoined to the autocephalous church of the Kingdom of Serbia." Dragoslav Janković and Bogdan Krizman, eds., *Gradja o stvaranju jugoslovenske države*, vol. 2 (Belgrade, 1964), p. 713.

19. Bogumil Hrabak, ed., "Zapisnici sednica Davidovićeve dve vlade od avgusta 1919. do februara 1920.," *Arhivski vjesnik*, vol. 13 (1970), no. 13, p. 26.

same degree over the Catholic church or the Islamic community. Indeed, according to the Decree on the Establishment of the Ministry of Cults (July 31, 1919), the minister of cults had supreme executive power over the Orthodox church in Serbia and Montenegro, thereby maintaining the confessional policy of prewar Serbia. Moreover, despite the official separation of church and state (1929), the king and the government of Yugoslavia continued to intervene in church finances, educational institutions, appointments of bishops, and patriarchal election.[20] The unification of Yugoslavia's Islamic communities was carried out in similar fashion, but the powerful Bosnian Muslim community refused to transfer the seat of the *reis ul-ulema*, the highest Muslim religious official in Yugoslavia, to Belgrade. Sarajevo thereby became the center of Yugoslav Islam.

The establishment of a united economic system was no less sensitive. Portions of Yugoslavia were utterly ravaged in the war. Serbia, which had lost some 30,000 men in the Balkan wars, suffered 275,000 additional combat casualties (or 40 percent of its army) in the First World War, while Montenegro lost 25,000 men. Various epidemics and other casualties claimed the lives of an additional 800,000 civilians in Serbia. Not only did these losses amount to almost a quarter of Serbia's inhabitants, but its postwar population included some 114,000 invalids and over half a million orphans. The loss of life in the former Austro-Hungarian portions of Yugoslavia was only a trifle less dramatic. According to one approximation, these regions lost some 757,000 people, 150,000 of whom were combat casualties.[21]

Economic problems were aggravated by dislocations caused by wartime destruction and speculation in the purveyance of food and materiel. Though the Belgrade government was uncharacteristically slow in attempting to cope with the autarkic tendencies in the economies of Yugoslavia's constituent regions, the most economically pressing and politically sensitive problem of unified currency could not be postponed.[22] At the point of unification, the territory of the new state was saturated with no less than four distinct currencies: Serbian dinars (circulation 340,600,000 on December 31, 1918), Montenegrin perpers, Bulgarian leva (circulation about 50 million), and, most important, the Austro-Hungarian crowns (circulation 5,323,000,000 in January 1919, of that 4,900,000,000 outside Serbia and Montenegro).[23] The overriding necessity of creating a new, autonomous state currency opened up endless possibilities for political manipulation, since it was not a matter of

20. Djoko Slijepčević, *Istorija Srpske pravoslavne crkve*, vol. 2, *Od početka XIX veka do kraja Drugog svetskog rata* (Munich, 1966), pp. 610–622.

21. The figures are from Tomasevich, *Peasants, Politics*, pp. 225, 223. See also Délégation du Royaume des Serbes, Croates et Slovènes à la Conférence de la Paix, *Rapport sur les Dommages de Guerre causés à la Serbie et au Monténégro présenté à la Commission des Réparations des Dommages* (1919), p. 15.

22. For more details on the currency question see Jozo Tomašević, *Novac i kredit* (Zagreb, 1938), pp. 152–159.

23. Ibid., p. 153.

indifference how the circulating currencies would be converted. Therefore, the currency question produced the first direct clash between Serbia and the former Austro-Hungarian provinces in the realm of financial policy, with the status of the Austro-Hungarian crowns as the focus of contention.

The relatively large number of crowns in circulation can be explained in terms of the substantial wartime exports of agrarian products from the Monarchy's South Slav territories. But since crowns were also circulating in the other successor states, it was necessary to distinguish the "Yugoslav" crowns from all the rest and so put an end to the surreptitious "import" of crowns from the neighboring countries, particularly from Austria, which was still issuing them. This was effected on January 31, 1919, by a primitive method of stamping the circulating crowns. In fact, since the imprints could easily be forged, the import of the contraband currency did not cease. It was then decided to further distinguish the circulating crowns by fastening them with special stamps. All told, by November 5, 1919, over five and a half million crowns were thus "retreaded" but this time with a difference, since the government unilaterally decided to withdraw 20 percent of all crowns brought in for validation. This decision was defended as a deflationary measure, but since the government did not withdraw the seized crowns and instead used them to cover its debts, the inflationary currents were in fact increased.[24] The government's action can be evaluated only as an aspect of a calculated political strategy, whose aim was to stabilize the dinar at the expense of the crown. In the first phase of this process, the immediate result was the expropriation of 20 percent of private savings from former Austro-Hungarian territories, which—contrary to the government's hue and cry—did not affect the speculators but did affect the relatively unsophisticated savers, most notably the peasants.

Even if it was necessary to take into account the special interests of devastated Serbia, the rate of exchange between the dinar and the crown was quite unjustifiable. The government was clearly intent on decreasing the value of the crown in order to prepare ground for the final conversion rate, which would be favorable to the dinar. Accordingly, the politically motivated Belgrade stock exchange registered the steady decline of the crown, while the Ministry of Finance used such estimates to sanction the crown's lower rate of exchange, in turn enhancing the value of the dinar.[25] In addi-

---

24. Bićanić, *Ekonomska podloga*, pp. 41–42. In Kočevje (Slovenia), Communist-led miners revolted against the government's seizure of a fifth of the crowns brought for special stamping. The army had to be used to suppress them.

25. For more details see Tomašević, *Novac i kredit*, pp. 156–157. The rate of exchange between dinars and crowns was:

Nov. 1918 to March 18, 1919: 100 dinars = 200 crowns
March 19, 1919 to June 4, 1919: 100 dinars = 250 crowns
June 5, 1919 to Nov. 12, 1919: 100 dinars = 300 crowns
Nov. 13, 1919 to Dec. 31, 1919: 100 dinars = 350 crowns
Jan. 1, 1920 to the exchange of crowns: 100 dinars = 400 crowns

tion, the government's determination to prevent the parity conversion of the two currencies was implemented by initiatives that directly precipitated the crown's inflationary decline. Besides the already mentioned floating of the withdrawn crowns, the government also continued to circulate some three-hundred million "damaged" crowns, which were nominally replaced by an equivalent sum obtained from the Austrian bank of issue.

The final rate of exchange, carried out between February and June 1920, sanctioned the issuing of one dinar for four crowns. This step in effect depleted the savings of the population in the former Austro-Hungarian areas and changed the economic relations between these areas and Serbia, whose purchasing power was considerably strengthened. This, however, was only the beginning. The privileged status of Serbia and the narrow national considerations that guided its political leaders in fashioning the economic policy were reflected in practically every branch of economic life in which the state had its hand. This necessarily fanned the national conflicts.

One of the most important of the economic issues was the inequitable distribution of taxation, since the levying system directly affected Yugoslavia's entire population and had a significant impact on the attitudes of ordinary citizens, particularly the peasants. As in many other branches of public life, taxation practices that existed in Yugoslavia's component parts before the unification were markedly diverse. Not only did differences exist between the levying systems in Serbia and Austria-Hungary, but also the South Slavic areas of the latter state were subject to different taxation regulations. The practical difficulties in unifying these systems were compounded by a disorderly and, in large part, corrupt, administration. Nevertheless, administrative abuses were only one aspect of the problem, for the central government in fact encouraged the perpetuation of different standards of taxation. Income taxes, for example, were paid only in Vojvodina, Croatia, and Slovenia.[26] Land taxes on a hectare of land of equal quality were twice as high in Vojvodina and Croatia as in Serbia. Table 2-1, derived by the Novi Sad Chamber of Commerce in 1928, graphically illustrates the prevailing practices. These statistics were based on information obtained from the Ministry of Finances, which fact has led some observers to suspect that the real situation was in fact worse.[27] A conclusive statement on this subject is not yet—and may never be—possible. Nevertheless, it does not alter the fact that severe inequalities in the taxation system favored Serbia and were unfair not

26. The following, a modified version of Bićanić's table (*Ekonomska podloga*, p. 49), illustrates discrepancies in land taxation, showing taxes in dinars, by land surface:

	3 hectares	5 hectares	10 hectares
Vojvodina and Croatia	209	341	674
Serbia	103	172	344

27. Ibid., pp. 50–51.

Table 2-1. Yugoslavia's land taxation, 1919–1928

Province	Indirect taxes in millions of dinars	Percentage of total taxes	Dinar amount of tax per inhabitant	For every 100 dinars paid in Serbia, amounts paid in other regions
Slovenia	1,411	13.9	1,336	240
Croatia-Slavonia	2,123	20.9	915	160
Dalmatia	296	2.9	454	80
Bosnia-Hercegovina	1,312	12.9	634	110
Vojvodina	2,550	25.2	1,864	330
Serbia and Montenegro	2,420	23.9	559	100
Total or average	10,112	100.0[a]	777	

Source: Bićanić, *Ekonomska podloga.*
a. Rounded figure.

only to the Croats and the Slovenes but also to the Serbs outside Serbia proper. The taxation systems were finally unified in 1928 as a result of a political campaign initiated by Radić's party in alliance with the Serb minority of Croatia-Slavonia.

The policy of centralization was the logical consequence of the political advantage taken in the new state by the Serbian national and unitary Yugoslavist ideologies, which, though not complementary, promoted similar policies. Whereas the men of the Radical party wished to turn Yugoslavia into an extension of the old Serbian state, abolishing all non-Serb national identities, their Democratic opponents sought to impose an integral Yugoslav identity under essentially Serbian symbols. In both cases these were the programs of the educated classes, representing most of what was good and everything that was bad about South Slavic intelligentsia, whose members were impatient to change Yugoslav reality and were not too particular about the means.

Yugoslavia's intellectuals were not distinguished by a high level of democratic spirit. They were intolerant, often irascible, largely ignorant of history, narrowly rationalistic, and unduly impressed with the superiority of Western Europe. They looked upon themselves as engineers who would pull a passive backward country into modernity, if need be by force. Instead of recognizing that the separate South Slavic peoples were long formed and could not now be integrated, they tried to bring about a Great Serbia or a Great Yugoslavia, some out of sheer idealism, some for more pragmatic reasons. Their attempts to accomplish the impossible were doomed to failure and only succeeded in provoking resistance of such intensity, notably among the Croats, that it could be stemmed only at the expense of parliamentary democracy. Instead of creating a powerful modern state, the intellectual makers of Yugoslavia paved the way for instability, dictatorship, and foreign intervention.

PART III

The Hard Opposition

The Party of Radić

> Gentlemen, your mouths are full of words like *"narodno jedinstvo,* one unitary state, one kingdom under the Karadjordjević dynasty." And you think that it is enough to say that we Croats, Serbs, and Slovenes are one people because we speak one language and that on account of this we must also have a unitary centralist state, moreover a kingdom, and that only such a linguistic and state unity can make us happy. . . . Gentlemen, you evidently do not care a whit that our peasant in general, and especially our Croat peasant, does not wish to hear one more thing about kings or emperors, nor about a state which you are imposing on him by force. . . . You think that you can frighten the people [with the Italian menace] and that in this way you will win the people to your politics. Maybe you will win the Slovenes, I do not know. Maybe you will also win the Serbs. But I am certain that you will never win the Croats . . . because the whole Croat peasant people are equally against your centralism as against militarism, equally for a republic as for a popular agreement with the Serbs. And should you want to impose your centralism by force, this will happen. We Croats shall say openly and clearly: If the Serbs really want to have such a centralist state and government, may God bless them with it, but we Croats do not want any state organization except a confederated federal republic.
>
> Stjepan Radić to the Central Committee
> of Zagreb's National Council, 1918

There was never anybody quite like him in Croat history. A romantic, and yet a pragmatist, Stjepan Radić illuminated the Croat skies like the luminous flash of a meteor. His age was the decade of 1918–1928. It began with his Cassandrian speech before the Central Committee of the National Council at Zagreb on November 24, 1918, in which he warned a disbelieving middle-class audience of ills to come. It ended with his lying near death on the floor of Yugoslavia's National Assembly on June 20, 1928, his body riddled with bullets fired from the rostrum by a Radical deputy, who was shooting at more than Radić and his closest associates.

Before 1918, few people took Stjepan Radić seriously. He was a deputy in the Sabor, but he spoke for a class that was effectively disenfranchised. Only in 1920, after the new state introduced universal manhood suffrage and after his own republican agitation won him new followers, did Radić's hold over the Croat masses become obvious (see map 3-1). He swept the Croat rural districts with overwhelming majorities. But where Sv. Ivan Zelina, Stubica, and Velika Gorica gave him over 90 percent of their votes, bourgeois and proletarian Zagreb gave him only 6.77 percent. For all that, his party gained the biggest bloc of Croat ballots, making the HPSS Yugoslavia's third largest party (230,590 votes) with the fourth largest group of deputies (fifty). In 1923, when he reached outside Croatia-Slavonia to tap the Croat votes in the other provinces, his party did even better, gaining 473,733 votes and seventy deputies. Through the agency of Radić's party the Croat national ideology came to grip the most remote villages, wherever the Croats lived. Radić's movement completed the process of Croat national consolidation, bringing to an end the century that began with the Illyrianist awakeners. Though the effects of his influence were obscured by the dictatorships that followed his assassination, nonetheless, even those regimes, and certainly every movement that sought the support of the Croat masses, had to pay obeisance to the memory of Stjepan Radić.[1]

He was called a demagogue, yet his speeches were delivered in almost a whisper. He filled his newspapers with his own articles and wrote five sociological and political monographs, yet he was so shortsighted that he had to hold the printed sheet inches from his eyes to read. He was born in a village, enjoyed singing folksongs accompanied by a tamburitza, and gloried in arcadian feasts in vinedressers' huts, where the slightly sour white wines of northern Croatia flowed with magnificent fowl, yet he had a laureat from Paris. He was profoundly devout, yet he opened his rallies with the invocation "Praise be to Jesus and Mary, down with the priests!" He believed in the superiority of native soil, showering often undeserved praise on everything that was Croat and Slavic, yet he frequently—and always without results—expressed an almost childlike faith in Western culture and fairness. His enemies called him a separatist, yet he wrote whole letters in Serbian Cyrillic to his Czech wife, obliging her to learn the scriptory medium of the Serbs. Croat purists considered him an unstable ally, an "aviator" apt to go in zigzags, yet he once said to a cellmate in one of the Khuen-Héderváry jails

1. For works on the HPSS's ideology see Rudolf Herceg, *Die Ideologie der kroatischen Bauernbewegung*, intro. Stjepan Radić (Zagreb, 1923); Ivo Šarinić, *Ideologija hrvatskog seljačkog pokreta* (Zagreb, 1935); [Ante Bonifačić], "Les idées du mouvement paysan croate: Antoine et Étienne Radić," *Le monde slave*, vol. 15 (1938), no. 1, pp. 342–369. On the history of the Radić brothers' peasant movement and the HPSS see Rudolf Herceg, *Seljački pokret u Hrvatskoj* (Zagreb, 1923); Ljubica Vuković-Todorović, *Hrvatski seljački pokret braće Radića* (Belgrade, 1940); Petar Preradović, *Die Kroaten und ihre Bauernbewegung* (Vienna, 1940).

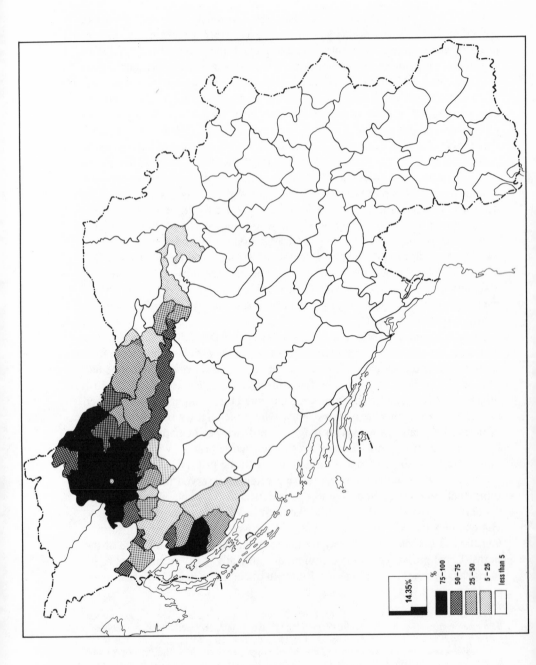

14.35%

%
75−100
50−75
25−50
5−25
less than 5

that he "only wished that as many Croats as possible would come to love him, as he had come to love the whole Croat people."[2]

Radić's reputation among the Croat masses was found on his dogged opposition to the form of unification that was concluded without the consent of the Croat electorate. The two main elements of his agitation were a refusal to recognize the unification act and the demand for a Croat constituent assembly that would bring about a Croat peasant republic. Radić had a keen, almost intuitive, appreciation of the peasant mentality, which made it possible for him to express his ideas in slogans that not only got to the heart of the party's position but at the same time had for the peasants very special and appealing connotations. The use of slogans was one of a number of features that made the HPSS unique as a party in the postunification period.

One characteristic aspect of the role of the HPSS was summarized in Radić's often-repeated and unquestionably sincere claim: he "neither leads, nor represents, but only faithfully and loyally *interprets* [Radić's emphasis]" the Croat peasantry (even though practical political encounters might occasionally compel him to initiate actions that were far from the wishes of his peasant constituency).[3] Radić was also unquestionably sincere in his belief that genuine national consciousness had become the sole property of the rural population (as the result of his "apostolic" work, the tireless industriousness of the Croat peasantry, and its numerical predominance)—and therefore that the HPSS was not just another political party but a mass *movement*. As Radić said in 1918, with its enormous potential base, the movement "is today what Starčević's party was yesterday, that is, the first and the main representative of the Croat people."[4]

A party is usually thought of as being a higher form of organization than a movement. In HPSS terminology the terms were reversed. The word *party* was never actually removed from the HPSS's repeatedly altered nomenclature, but Radić made it clear that parties could only represent *classes,* whereas peoples were represented by *movements.* A movement, it seemed, had the potential of attracting all the Croat people—not just peasants—in a way that no mere political party could ever do. The strategy was indeed successful. Within several years after the unification, the majority of the Croats, at least in Croatia-Slavonia, swelled Radić's oppositional ranks.

One risk of such a wide base was, as Radić knew, that the base would run ahead of the party leadership. In a letter written from prison on February 4, 1920, Radić noted, "Our *old* supporters, who are inspired by a thoroughly Christian spirit of gentleness and forgiveness, will at most pray to God for me, and will send Prib[ićević] to the devil; but the ardent younger supporters,

2. Stjepan Radić, *Uzničke uspomene*, 3d ed. (Zagreb, 1971), p. 53.
3. Stjepan Radić, *Korespondencija Stjepana Radića,* comp. Bogdan Krizman, vol. 2 (Zagreb, 1973), p. 510.
4. Stjepan Radić, *Politički spisi*, comp. Zvonimir Kulundžić (Zagreb, 1971), p. 339.

who were in the war, and perhaps even in Russian captivity and who understood the peasant party as a *social militant* party, these are capable of starting and carrying out a conspiracy."[5] Because the HPSS, as part of its plan to develop a mass movement, encouraged direct participation in the party's decisions, the possibility of violent action was very real. But the risk was evidently worthwhile. Rudolf Herceg (1887–1951), a leading HPSS theorist, made that very clear:

> In cases of parties, supporters choose their leaders, representatives, deputies, to work *for them and instead of them.* If the supporters are not satisfied with the leadership, they then *leave* the given party and enter some other party. *In cases of movements it is the opposite.* There (among movements, which always go after one specific aim, after some elevated thought) the supporters *shake off* the leaders—even the [parliamentary] deputies—*if these do not carry out the business exactly in the way, as they have assumed it.*
>
> Something else follows from that: In parties all the work is done by the leaders, notables, *and in cases of movements all suporters participate in the work.* He who does nothing for the aim—for the idea—of his movement, who does not act, who does not move—such a person does not belong in a movement.[6]

As a populist movement, committed to upholding the doctrine of the people's collective wisdom, the HPSS allowed for the broadest initiative on the local level. The ideas generated in this way were not ignored in the leadership's councils; but since there was no clear organizational structure to transmit ideas between the leadership and the base, the movement tended to be very amorphous. Radić's authority had to serve in place of a firm party apparatus, and the HPSS relied to a great extend on Radić's charismatic leadership. The popular use of the terms *radićevci* and "the party of Radić," though following a tradition of Croat politics—as in "Starčević's party" of the last decades of the nineteenth century—was quite justified. The significant point is that, although the HPSS tried to foster local, autonomous, organizations, it never quite developed an efficient mechanism that could weld them into a coherent force and make the movement a truly formidable foe of the central government. If the government's agencies felt frustration, it was more at the sheer size of the movement, rather than its political astuteness. The government might pale in the face of the passive resistance of the Croat masses, but the resistance was far more often the people's own than the outcome of the conscious initiatives of the HPSS. It is true that representatives of the authorities often attributed peasant rebelliousness to planned HPSS conspiracy, but that really only shows how little the government

5. Radić, *Korespondencija*, vol. 2, p. 515.
6. Rudolf Herceg, "Zašto je HRSS pokret, a ne samo stranka?" *Slobodni dom*, July 13, 1921, pp. 2–3.

appreciated the extent of the opposition. Local resistance often concurred with the party's sentiment, but the resistance did not necessarily manifest itself with the leadership's knowledge. Nor, on the other hand, did the leadership always succeed in effecting its decisions, particularly its more or less steady desire to avoid militant clashes with the authorities.

Problems of (Con)Federalist Politics

Federalist (or confederalist) conceptions of Yugoslavia's state organization, the latter reducing joint affairs among the federal units to a bare minimum, would by the end of the 1920s become the shared principle of several political groups. In the immediate postunification period, federalism was almost exclusively associated with the HPSS. In order to challenge the centralists, Radić had to abandon the dogma of *narodno jedinstvo* and recognize the Croat, Serb, and Slovene national individualities. The parties that uncritically upheld the principle of *narodno jedinstvo,* while at the same time calling for regional autonomy, quite rightly were open to accusations from the centralists of following an inconsistent course.

Were consistency on the issue of *narodno jedinstvo* the essential component necessary for mounting a successful campaign against centralism, Radić's positions would be misconstrued in one important respect; that is, it would be impossible to explain how this prominent partisan of *narodno jedinstvo* of the pre-1918 period, who, furthermore, remained committed to a variant of Pan-Slavism even after the creation of Yugoslavia, assumed the role of the principal proponent of Croat national individuality and, consequently, of a Croat state, whether it be independent or a self-governed unit of Yugoslavia. At his trial in 1920, Radić said in his defense speech, "All the Slavs generally, and the South Slavs especially, are one and a united people, both by their speech and by their present foundation."[1] Though this statement could be taken to mean that his position on *narodno jedinstvo* was essentially the same as that of Pribićević, Radić, later in the same speech, clarified this seeming inconsistency by noting that he was himself "a personification of *narodno jedinstvo.*" Radić was objecting not to *narodno jedinstvo* as an equivalent of a desirable principle of Slavic reciprocity but to the notion that only the existing Yugoslav state, with its monarchical and centralist organization embodied the idea of *narodno jedinstvo:* "The state attorney [prosecutor] . . . thinks that *narodno jedinstvo* is [to be found] only

---

1. "Osamsatni govor obtuženoga narod. zastup. Stjepana Radića," *Slobodni dom,* July 28, 1920, p. 2.

in the present centralist monarchy. But that is completely wrong; . . . this indictment cannot be maintained, since it is based on this wrongheaded understanding of *narodno jedinstvo*."[2] Radić also maintained that there was no discrepancy between advocacy of *narodno jedinstvo* and his efforts to organize the Croats alone:

> Is it culpable that I am gathering only the Croats in Yugoslavia? . . . Croats are by themselves a people in a historical, cultural, and political sense, and [they] entered into Yugoslavia so that they might preserve their Croatdom. Millenary Croat territory, undisputable Croat territory, etc. . . . prove that it is not at all true that I have spoken everywhere and unceasingly about the "Croat part of the [Yugoslav] people," but [instead] that I speak of Croat political and territorial individuality. . . . Had the state attorney studied this entire matter, he could not have accused me of considering the Croats, the Croat people, as some "tribe," as if we were in Albania or perhaps even somewhere in the Middle Ages.[3]

Radić was divesting the principle of *narodno jedinstvo* of all attributes that made it an easy foundation of centralism. This left *narodno jedinstvo* a flaccid principle, recast to fit Radić's belief that elements of mutuality such as linguistic links and shared popular culture were far stronger among the Slavs than among other branches of the European family of nations. Such links were not necessarily sufficient for state building by themselves, however, and therefore national reciprocity of the Slavs was counterposed to their political uniqueness and to their exclusive state traditions, on which were based the claims of their separate nationhood: the Croats were a separate nation because of their distinct state tradition and state right. In other words, the theory of "tribal" relations between various branches of South Slavdom was totally unacceptable.

This conception of Croat state right was no more than a variation on Starčević's national ideology, which Radić had upheld from the start of his political career. Eventually, and rather painfully, Radić's equally long-standing espousal of *narodno jedinstvo* gave way.[4] Indeed, by 1920, despite Radić's interpretation of *narodno jedinstvo*, it was more apparent than ever that insistence on Croat political—and, therefore, national—uniqueness could not but constitute a departure from Yugoslavist unitarism. There is no reason to think that Radić's public statements, particularly in the courtroom,

---

2. "Osamsatni govor obtuženoga narod. zastup. Stjepana Radića," ibid., Nov. 17, 1920, p. 4.
3. Ibid., p. 3.
4. According to one view, "The party [HPSS] accepted the Croat state-building program, which was formulated [by Starčević's party] in 1894. Though [the HPSS] accepted the ideational fiction of *narodno jedinstvo* of Croats and Serbs, [it] never became a state-building party in the Yugoslav sense. Because of this, after 1918, it easily shook off the fiction of *narodno jedinstvo*." Jere Jareb, *Pola stoljeća hrvatske politike: Povodom Mačekove autobiografije* (Buenos Aires, 1960), p. 19.

were at variance with his private sentiments.[5] Nevertheless, even if it was true that Radić did not completely abrogate his allegiance to the concept of *narodno jedinstvo* (in an attenuated meaning that was uniquely his own), he increasingly avoided all references to this principle.

The crux of Radić's new interpretation of *narodno jedinstvo* seemed to be his feeling that the idea no longer applied. He expressed his misgivings in a prison letter dated May 14, 1919: "All of our gentlemen are now where we—the peasant party—were 15 years ago. *Then* it was necessary unconditionally to defend the national principle [*narodnost*], therefore [to defend] concord, oneness [*jedinstvo*] with the Serbs, because over us and around us there was a *foreign* brute force; now that *foreign* force no longer exists" (*Korespondencija*, p. 141). At this same time, commenting on R. W. Seton-Watson's study *Racial Problems in Hungary* (1908), which he had just been reading, Radić remarked in a letter (May 17, 1919), "My soul aches when I see that these bashi-bazouks are doing to us *to a hair* the same thing that the Hungarians were doing to the Slovaks; only our predicament is that we are 'brothers,' we are 'one,' so that you cannot complain against this" (p. 144).

Rather than complaining, Radić preferred to offer an alternative to the practical effects of this principle, as it was then applied. "*Now* it is necessary to defend justice [*pravica*] (democracy, peasantry) against *domestic force and injustice*" (p. 141). He rejected his daughter's suggestion that he write something against national unity with the Serbs:

That which you, Milica, think that I should write . . . about the Serbs etc.— that is superfluous. Before the dissolution of the [Austro-Hungarian] Monarchy and the military collapse of Germany it was necessary to swallow all of that [probably a reference to byproducts of common action with the Serbs] and to be patient, or rather, apostolically fervent; today NEW facts are here, not only the beatings, but the old Serbian military, bureaucratically corrupt and conspiratorial system, which was shameful before the war, and is now catatrophic. It is not a question of whether we Croats want to go with *Serbia,* or rather under Serbia, but whether we want to go with the new spirit of pacifism, i.e., with *practical humanism,* with the new order of PRACTICAL democracy ("socialism") and practical, scientific, trade union administration (not bureaucratic *clichés*). [p. 271]

Assuming that Milica Radić's suggestion was an expression of a broader HPSS sentiment, one can guess that Radić's emphasis on the practicality of his alternatives to an open disavowal of *narodno jedinstvo* was his response

5. In his private correspondence, Radić occasionally reiterated his espousal of *narodno jedinstvo* but in interpretations that completely devalued the original meaning of the term. For a typical example of his intimate thoughts on this matter see Stjepan Radić, *Korespondencija Stjepana Radića,* comp. Bogdan Krizman, vol. 2 (Zagreb, 1973), p. 509. (The following four quotations are from this work.)

to an implied—or spoken—criticism along such lines. In fact, Radić's firm refusal to recognize the unification constituted the most significant challenge to the implications of *narodno jedinstvo*. Radić could accept the idea of the South Slavs' national mutuality, but unlike the Yugoslavist unitarists, he did not agree that national kinship imposed the necessity of political unification: his insistence on Croatia's right to determine its own political future could have been raised without direct references to the concept of *narodno jedinstvo*. Nonetheless, Radić must have understood that, though this concept was already debilitated as a result of centralization, it would certainly have succumbed had the Croats actually succeeded in gaining a state of their own.

The alliance of *narodno jedinstvo* presupposed two parties, but the extent of the enthusiasm had a lot to do with who was on top. In 1904, commenting on Radić's use of the *narodno jedinstvo* formula to explain the HPSS's attitude toward the Serbs of Croatia, Svetozar Pribićević noted that the anthropological, philological, cultural, and historical reciprocity of the Serbs and Croats was beside the point. What mattered was whether the "Croats aim to take into account the separate Serb demands, based on the consciousness of the Serb people about its separate national personality and on the love of the Serb people for its own national name." The idea of *narodno jedinstvo*, he said, "may mean all and nothing. It may mean that the peasant party unconditionally accepts all the Serb demands. But it may also mean . . . that the peasant party rejects the Serb demands with finality, in order that the dualism in the relations between the Serbs and Croats would not grow stronger at the expense of popular oneness."[6]

After the unification, the roles were reversed. In the immediate postwar years, Radić's goal was always the establishment of "our Croat republic without any regard to the Serbs [and] the Slovenes," but in the pressure of circumstances, and feeling that Belgrade's rule was bound to be temporary, he did consider—perhaps not wholly seriously—numerous other alternatives. Possibly Croatia could become a French protectorate, or be made part of a Danubian federation (with Austria and Hungary). And in the event that these possibilities failed, he thought of utilizing adjoining territories under Entente occupation—Rijeka, Bačka, and even Sopron (Hungary)—as bases for his political work.[7] Radić lived in hopes that the European powers would compel the Belgrade authorities to withdraw from Croatia, or that "in the worst case, the Entente would *in its own interests* also impose these three conditions [for the recognition of Yugoslavia]: constituent assembly, autonomy for Croatia, political liberty" (p. 182). Certainly in Radić's calculations, the least attractive alternative to Croatia's independence was a perpetuation of Yugoslavia.

6. О. [cipher of Svetozar Pribićević], "Hrvatska pučka seljačka stranka," *Novi Srbobran*, Dec. 28, 1904, p. 1.

7. Radić, *Korespondencija*, vol. 2, pp. 129, 165, 137, 149, 182, 152, 283, 202, 231, 240. (Page numbers in this and the following paragraph refer to this work.)

It was not that Radić was opposed to any South Slavic state. He was, for example, in favor of plebiscites in Croatia, Slovenia, and Bosnia-Hercegovina, which might have resulted in an establishment of a "federal peasant republic of Yugoslavia" (p. 455). But this would be, as he wrote on January 14, 1920, a republic with its nucleus in Croatia: "the Entente cannot *now* solve our Croat question *by itself,* only because it is connected with the entire South Slavic question of the former Monarchy. If these South Slavs would *gather around Croatia,* or rather as many as so gather, they neither would nor could obstruct the dominance of Croat spirit in such a Yugoslavia" (p. 473). Radić had foreseen trouble. Writing to his wife on May 28, 1919, he noted that she was "quite right . . . Austria [the Danubian federation] will be restored. Only, I am afraid that the whole of Yugoslavia, that is, Serbia, too, will enter it" (p. 159). After the unification, Radić's main reason for opposing the new Yugoslav state was his instinctive dislike for Serbia's behavior, and he believed that he was speaking for the Croat people when he showed his opposition: "Dr. *Laginja* is naive with that [statement] of his, that we do not want Germans [*Švabe*] and Hungarians. Today this is not an issue; rather, [now] we [also] do not want [to go] *with* Serbia, and especially not *under* [Serbia]—and that we really do not *want,* i.e., the [Croat] *people themselves* do not wish that" (p. 491). Radić's condemnation of Serbian officialdom was so severe that one can well have questions about the precise nature of the federalism usually ascribed to Radić's program.[8] Radić's private correspondence and public espousal of a Croat republic would seem to belie a supposed commitment to a federated Yugoslavia, that is, a Yugoslavia in which Serbia also would participate.

Radić's growing lack of faith that the Allies would intervene on behalf of the Croats had had a great deal to do with his original, if reluctant, interest in federalism. During the summer of 1919, as the Peace Conference met in Paris, Radić feared that nothing at all would be done about the Croat question.[9] By August he was wondering whether regional autonomies (which he then equated with Yugoslavia's federalization) would actually be imposed by the Radicals. In Radić's opinion, this was not sufficient (pp. 280–281). But as the question of federalization started being publicly debated, and as Radić perceived this debate to be a byproduct of the Entente's pressure, he began discovering numerous unsuspected advantages to a federal polity. He was, in

8. According to Čulinović, "Under conditions of struggle against the Belgrade [centralists, the HPSS] primarily stressed the significance of state right questions, and especially demanded a reorganization of old Yugoslavia into a *composite* state; for all that, combinations with federalism and confederalism, and the reverse, were made from time to time." Ferdo Čulinović, *Jugoslavija izmedju dva rata,* vol. 1, (Zagreb, 1961), p. 289. Čulinović's opinion is fairly representative of how the HPSS's positions on Yugoslavia's state organization are portrayed in that country's post-1945 historiography; that is, those elements of Radić's thought that diverged from federalism or confederalism are usually downplayed.

9. Radić, *Korespondencija,* vol. 2, p. 164. (Page numbers in this and the following two paragraphs refer to this work.)

any event, no longer indignant at any suggestion of Croatia's federal relations with Serbia.

Radić did not change his opinions on the desirability of Croatia's independence, but he did come round to the position that a federated Yugoslavia would be but a step away from secession, and without blood being shed (p. 285). By December 17, 1919, he was drawing what seemed to him an encouraging parallel: "to us (*and to the people*) the main thing is a republic and federalism, because republic = self-determination, and federalism = Norway toward Sweden and at an opportune moment Norway away from Sweden (1907)'' (p. 431).

Radić's correspondence suggests that his original support of federalism was only a political gesture, undertaken to secure his release from prison. In a letter written to his wife on February 2, 1920, he says:

> We [himself and the other HPSS prisoners] have agreed that my imprisonment is a purely *political* matter, and that it has to be "solved" in a purely political way. *Because of that* I made a statement that I am for "*narodno jedinstvo in regard to foreign countries* [*prema vani*] (which is true), for a *common* [*zajednička*] state *toward* foreign countries, (which is also true, but "*so vremenem',*" after some time), for fraternity with *all* Slavs (therefore also with the Bulgars), and for an intellectual West European orientation. [p. 509]

In fact, Radić became a resolved federalist only after the results of the Constituent Assembly forced him to abandon any further illusions about the willingness of foreign powers to effect Croatia's independence, and after the NRS and Aleksandar launched several trial balloons about a possible "amputation" of troublesome northwest Croatia, which would have mutilated Croat national territory.[10] Meanwhile, Radić's party concentrated on spreading its influence only among the Croats, since, as one of Radić's lieutenants put it, the "people throughout the whole homeland are ours, it is but necessary to awaken them, because they are still unconscious."[11] The success of

10. For an elaborate explanation of Radić's mature federalism see his interview with S. M. Bralović, a correspondent of the London *Daily News* and the New York *Tribune* (July 26, 1922), ibid., pp. 560–564. Certain NRS circles and their allies in the camarilla repeatedly threatened to create a Great Serbia by "amputating" northwestern Croatia and Slovenia and letting these areas fend for themselves. A concrete amputation proposal was voiced in a 1923 pamphlet, following the centralist reversals in parliamentary elections. The author of this anonymous work proposed to incorporate most of Slovenia, parts of Croatia proper, and all of Bosnia-Hercegovina and Dalmatia into such a Serbian state. For more details on this subject see Čulinović, *Jugoslavija*, vol. 1, pp. 412–413.

11. Radić, *Korespondencija*, vol. 2, p. 548. Radić's reaction to an HPSS electoral list for the directorate of a Zagreb economic society shows that his party's organizational efforts were consciously directed only toward the Croats: "I am glad that not one Serb was on our list. We Croats will have to be even more reserved toward them than they are toward us—until Serb peasantry becomes conscious—because the Serb bourgeois are super jackasses (in comparison with ours)." Ibid., p. 221.

this awakening policy became apparent at the 1923 parliamentary elections, when the gains of the HRSS (previously the HPSS) in Dalmatia and Bosnia-Hercegovina clearly demonstrated that Radić's movement was no longer confined to its original base in Croatia-Slavonia. The hegemony of the HPSS over the Croat national movement was complete. For the first time in modern history an overwhelming majority of Croats was politically united behind one national leadership. In spite of all the vicissitudes that confronted the Croats in the period before the Second World War, this situation would not change.

For a Croat Peasant Republic

The systematic expression of the peasantry's republican aspirations was one of Stjepan Radić's great achievements. His own observations led him to the conclusion that the war had served to alienate the rural population from the last vestiges of their supposed monarchist enchantment, so that it was now no more monarchist than any other class. In a statement published on the eve of unification, Radić described what hardships the Croat peasantry had recently undergone: "Throughout the entire four years of the war our peasant was not only a state serf (and really a genuine state slave), but he was worse than a beast of burden to the sundry official and unofficial gentlemen. All the insults and all the humiliations, all the fines and the violence from the most horrible Turkish days—all that seemed to have returned and settled on [the peasantry]."[1] But the burdens of military service, forced labor, and animal and produce requisitions—all of which he described in detail—would be left behind in the peasant republic of the future. Anyone who could have seen the assembled peasants at the recently convened meeting of the HPSS's main assembly "would have been convinced that this war created a completely new opinion and conviction in our peasant people; the opinion that the root of all evil and in particular of this war are the kings [*vladari*] and the conviction that the entire government and administration must be changed in their foundations according to peasant need and peasant right" (p. 337).

On December 31, 1918, Radić published a statement in which he described some of the essentials of the republican polity he wanted established. Though he always claimed that a republican order was equivalent to the social organization of the traditional Croat *zadruga* (extended family), the republican model he proposed bore a great similarity to Western parliamentary systems. They were, he acknowledged, notable for their opposition to

---

1. Stjepan Radić, *Politički spisi,* comp. Zvonimir Kulundžić (Zagreb, 1971), p. 336. (Page numbers in this and the following paragraph refer to this work.)

militarism, their commitment to human rights, and their use of the federal principle (Switzerland, United States), in addition to their safeguarding of the democratic process of popular representation; Radić emphasized that the "Peasant party teaches that we Croats want a republic on the American model" (pp. 342, 344).

Radić's republican conception, however, was not simply a call for the implementation of popular sovereignty. It had an unmistakable national coloration and was therefore intended to be an alternative to the (by then) established position of the Serbian dynasty. The struggles of the American colonists and the French revolutionaries, which resulted in the dethronement of George III and Louis XVI, thus had double significance—not only as examples of successful republics but also because they came about as a result of revolutions against monarchs "of the same blood and language" as their respective rebellious subjects (pp. 344, 345). Though the monarchists consistently lauded the new Serb dynasty as "national" and even "peasant," Radić was suggesting that simply because the king and regent were not obviously foreign, as were the Habsburgs, they did not necessarily merit the loyalty of the Croats.

Numerous passages in Radić's private correspondence indicate that his republicanism was primarily an expression of his defense of Croat sovereignty, but it was a point on which Radić seemed to vacillate—depending on the political situation. "Republ[ic]. = self-determination," he wrote in November 1919; five months earlier he had noted, "our republ[ican]. cause (= nothing with Belgrade) advances *almost day by day*."[2] It was this vacillation between self-determination within Yugoslavia and "nothing with Belgrade" that constituted the essence of the HPSS's dilemma. In the immediate postwar period, while hopes were still high that the Allies, and particularly the United States, would intervene against the excesses of the Belgrade administration, Radić's struggle for a Croat republic was increasingly voiced in the form of a demand for a Croat constituent assembly.

Anticipating that the Belgrade government would soon summon its own version of a constituent assembly, in which the Croats would probably get nowhere with their demands, Radić wanted to prepare for such an eventuality by convening a purely Croat representative body. Only a Croat constituent assembly, following its own course of national self-determination, could arrive at a constitutional document founded on the principles advocated by the HPSS. And if the document were not drawn up immediately, future attempts to right the solutions imposed from Belgrade could only assume an unwanted revolutionary character.[3]

2. Stjepan Radić, *Korespondencija Stjepana Radića*, comp. Bogdan Krizman, vol. 2 (Zagreb, 1973), pp. 431, 237.
3. Radić, *Politički spisi*, p. 345.

In order to raise his demands publicly, Radić convened an extraordinary assembly of the HPSS. Sessions of this gathering, attended by 5,856 HPSS activists, took place in Zagreb on February 3, 1919. The assembly amounted to an open challenge to the government. In his remarks Radić condemned the arbitrary and violent actions of the new authorities, stressing the need for democratic reforms, and without equivocation called for a Croat republic and a Croat constituent assembly, "because we see that our Croatian homeland, which you defended with your lives, is being destroyed." But though he refused to recognize the legitimacy of the unification, Radić demanded a "federal republic of the Serbs, Croats, Slovenes and Bulgars." In an even more explicit speech, Rudolf Horvat (1873–1947) referred to the South Slavic federation as a demand to be raised only if Croatia's full independence could not be effected.[4]

The rest of the speeches proceeded in similar vein to the unanimous approval of the delegates. Finally, Stjepan Uroić, a peasant from Repušnica who became a leader of the 1920 revolt against cattle branding, read a resolution (subsequently edited and expanded by Radić) in which he called for a South Slavic republic that would be united toward the outside world but internally would be constituted on a federal model akin to that of the United States. The resolution, which Radić hoped to send to the Paris Peace Conference, also included demands for the withdrawal of the Italian troops from the eastern Adriatic littoral and the withdrawal of the Serbian units from the Croat lands. A protest against the unification was coupled with demands for free elections and a Croat constituent assembly. In line with Radić's abhorrence of violence, Uroić appealed to the people to remain calm and shun revolutionary actions.[5]

Uroić's resolution was the consummate expression of the HPSS's program in the immediate postunification period, and it was adopted unanimously. Although it was by no means as explicit in its language as some of Radić's private pronouncements, it was sufficiently lucid for the Belgrade government to interpret it as a seditious document. The battle between Pribićević and the HPSS thus entered a new phase. After Radić refused, on February 24, 1919, to send two representatives to the preliminary parliament in Belgrade, the authorities, invoking a wartime Franzjosephine ordinance, banned the HPSS organ *Slobodni dom* (Free Home).[6] Since the Sabor resolution of October 29, 1918, had ended all ties with the Monarchy, the ordinance was presumably no longer valid, but legal remedies were not forthcoming. The government followed up the attack by refusing to permit the

4. Source for references in paragraph, Rudolf Horvat, *Hrvatska na mučilištu* (Zagreb, 1942), pp. 65, 66.

5. Krizman, intro. to Radić, *Korespondencija*, vol. 2, pp. 58–59.

6. "Hrvatska seljačka stranka u godini bezzakonja, nasilja i progona," *Slobodni dom*, March 13, 1920, p. 3.

convening of an HPSS public assembly scheduled for February 8, 1919. Peasants "in thousands" succeeded in breaching the police barricades that were thrown up on the outskirts of Zagreb to prevent attendance at the assembly, and Radić led them to the Mirogoj cemetery where they paid homage to his recently deceased brother Antun Radić (1868–1919), the HPSS's cofounder and early theoretician. On this occasion the police were thwarted in their attempt to arrest Radić, but he was now an object of attention.

On the same day, the HPSS leadership initiated its campaign to collect signatures on a petition to be sent to the Paris Peace Conference. The wording of the petition summarized the party's fundamental demands:

TO THE PEACE CONGRESS IN PARIS

To American President Wilson

All of us here undersigned or marked Croat citizens over 18 years of age declare on the basis of the internationally recognized right of national self-determination that we are in our hearts and minds for a neutral Croat peasant republic, and therefore we demand the convening of a special Croat constituent assembly for the thousand-year-old Croat people, [and] furthermore unconditionally, before the peace congress in Paris makes the final decision about the fate of the Croat people. We authorize the Main Committee [*glavni odbor*] of the HPSS and the HPSS's president Stjepan Radić to bring this demand of ours before the peace congress in Paris.[7]

The gathering of signatures for this petition proceeded immediately and became the focus of the HPSS's agitational work. Within six weeks of its drafting, 115,167 signatures had been collected.[8] Although the action continued, Radić was not fated to witness its culmination. On March 9, his bookstore in Zagreb was attacked by a mob of unitarist students, who caused considerable damage. Chased away by groups of laborers, the students sought Ban Paleček's intervention and Radić's arrest.[9]

Radić's arrest occurred two weeks later, on March 25, 1919. Despite his immunity, which would ordinarily have protected him as a member of the Croatian Sabor, he was imprisoned and held without trial—in "police custody"—for 339 days. Numerous other HPSS leaders were also imprisoned, and public meetings of the HPSS were prohibited.[10] Members of the party's main committee, Vladko Maček (1879–1964) and Ljudevit Kežman, were held for nine months, Ivan Pernar for three months, and the party's vice-

7. Josipa Paver, comp., *Zbornik gradje za povijest radničkog pokreta i KPJ 1919–1920: Dvor, Glina, Ivanić-Grad, Kostajnica, Kutina, Novska, Petrinja, Sisak* (Sisak, 1970), p. 54.

8. Krizman, intro. to Radić, *Korespondencija*, vol. 2, p. 61.

9. "Hrvatska seljačka stranka u godini bezzakonja," p. 3.

10. Josip I. Vidmar, comp., "Prilozi gradji za historiju radničkog pokreta i KPJ 1919. god.," *Arhivski vjesnik*, vol. 2, no. 2, p. 55.

president, Josip Predavec (1883–1933), was jailed for two months.[11] Nor was that all: Radić's wife Marija and his two daughters, Milica and Mira, were confined for seventeen days in September 1919, and Vilma Radić, the widow of Antun Radić, committed suicide, in protest, it was thought, against the persecutions of the party of her late husband.[12]

In prison, Radić continued to be optimistic about the success of his initiatives. His messages to the Peace Conference were smuggled from the Zagreb Court Jail (Hotel Republic, as he called it), as was his regular correspondence with his family, and he thus remained in full control of the party's limited public activities. One of the first results of the installation of Protić's second cabinet was the freeing of Stjepan Radić (February 27, 1920) and the lifting of the restrictions on the HPSS press and public meetings, but Radić's freedom was brief. On March 22, he was arrested again, this time on the direct orders of Franko Potočnjak, the vice-Ban and the Regent's confident in Croatia's regional administration, for antimonarchical statements uttered at the HPSS's public assembly in Galdovo on March 21. These statements were interpreted as criminal offenses, and in July, despite a brilliant defense, a criminal court found him guilty and sentenced him to thirty months in jail.[13] Radić was obliged to serve only a few months of this sentence, thanks to the amnesty declared on the following November 28, the day of the nationwide elections for the Constituent Assembly. The HPSS's simultaneous electoral victory in Croatia-Slavonia vindicated Radić's previous work in the Croat countryside and made him a recognized leader of the Croat national movement on the eve of the crucial political round over Yugoslavia's first constitution.

Throughout his career Radić was an opponent of violence as a method of political struggle. Though the "Croat Gandhi" never failed to point out that the numerical weakness of the Croats, coupled with the military strength of Belgrade regimes, inevitably relegated all revolutionary attempts to failure, Radić's pacifism was a considered political principle embracing more than the obvious tactical considerations. For example, on August 3, 1919, anticipating an early release from jail, he wrote, "We shall at once renew the [newspaper] *Dom* . . . and begin a monthly *Svjetski mir* [World Peace], and will also rename the party (at the first Main Assembly), the Croat Pacifist Peasant Party."[14] But though Radić's pacifism rendered him a most unlikely

11. "Hrvatska seljačka stranka u godini bezzakonja," p. 3.

12. Radić (*Korespondencija*, vol. 2, pp. 229, 237) considered his sister-in-law to be an "innocent victim of militarism," and noted that her tragic end "gained us the sympathies of *all* Zagreb."

13. A transcript of Radić's eight-hour-long defense speech was printed in *Slobodni dom*, July 21 through Nov. 17, 1920, under the title "Osamsatni govor obtuženoga narod. zastup. Stjepana Radića pred zagrebačkim sudben. stolom dne 9. srpnja 1920."

14. Radić, *Korespondencija*, vol. 2, p. 272. Radić's pacifism was not only a reaction to the horrors of the late war and a conscious antidote to the signs of revolutionary psychosis around him but also an attempt to strengthen the opposition to the militarism of the Belgrade government—in his opinion, the most salient feature of the regime and the source of all of its abuses.

choice for an insurrectionary catalyst, the role that the authorities repeatedly ascribed to him, the more down-to-earth instincts of his followers were indeed a plausible reason for his confinements. Conscious of this fact, Radić noted that "Pribićević and 'they' in Belgrade consider us . . . really as hostages, *personal political guarantees* first of all against an uprising, and secondly against an exceptionally sharp reaction to all of their violence and illegalities (against assassinations and the like)."[15] And though it is also true that Radić and his closest associates regularly coupled their denunciations of the existing order with appeals for calm, the authorities had every reason to suspect that the aroused populace could not be allayed by exhortations, regardless of their source.[16] In the absence of any official willingness to modify the centralist course, other means were necessary to curb the rising disaffection.

Official estimates of the effects of Radić's republicanism in the Croat countryside had assumed alarming proportions in the spring of 1919. A county prefect in Petrinja noted that the "administrative communes of Gora, Hrastovica, Mošćenica, and Slunja are infected with republicanism, mainly because of the reading of the peasant party's [HPSS's] newspapers and the propaganda of Radić's followers."[17] Another prefect in Jastrebarsko noted that "it seems it is mainly at the fairs in Zagreb—where the local peasants go in great numbers—that they become infected with that idea [republicanism]."[18] Some county prefects took their troubles in stride. From Sv. Ivan Zelina came the following report, typical of many: "So far there are no apparent signs that some kind of republican or anti-Serb propaganda is being

---

15. Ibid., p. 403.
16. One can cite numerous examples of appeals for calm. In a speech delivered in Kutina on March 23, 1919, Predavec noted that "everybody is obliged to respect the present laws, until the Croat constituent assembly creates new [regulations]." Paver, *Zbornik gradje*, p. 55. Radić, writing from jail on May 18, 1919, commented that the interminable vicissitudes of a prolonged peaceful struggle against centralism "are better than revol[ution] and blood." Radić, *Korespondencija*, vol. 2, p. 146. But there were some HPSS leaders who, mindful of the widespread restlessness in the party's base, stressed what they personally considered to be the conditional nature of the HPSS's pacifism. During the gathering at the tomb of Antun Radić on March 8, 1919, Dragutin Hrvoj told the crowd that it should "always remain sober and peaceful as in a church . . . but that it should not yield even by a hair, and furthermore should fight force with force in case there are scoundrels and bullies who would try forcefully to frustrate or to falsify through fraud the expressions of popular will at the [approaching] elections for a constituent assembly." "Hrvatska seljačka stranka u godini bezzakonja," p. 3. Of the HPSS leaders, Ivan Pernar was by far the most belligerent. In preparing a case against him in 1924, Zagreb police found in its files numerous reports on his pugnacious behavior. For example, on April 1, 1919, during a demonstration at Zagreb's Jelačić Square, Pernar shouted at a proregime acquaintance who was present, "There will be nothing of your Great Yugoslavia; we shall tear it apart even if you have to shoot us all." Arhiv Instituta za historiju radničkog pokreta Hrvatske (AIHRPH), 1924/Sig. VI.C, Box 2: Predsjednički ured Kr. Redarstvenog Redateljstva, no. 8668 prs. 1924, Zagreb, Nov. 28, 1924.
17. Ibid., 1919/Sig. XXI, Box 4: Predstojništvo kr. kotarske oblasti, no. 15 res., Petrinja, April 18, 1919.
18. Ibid., Predstojništvo kr. kotarske oblasti, no. 14 Res., Jastrebarsko, April 19, 1919.

conducted, while on the other hand it must be admitted that there exists in all layers of the population—except among the negligible intelligentsia in Sv. Ivan Zelina—an indisposition against [*sic*] the new order, and particularly against some imaginary hegemony from the Serb side.—That, however, is a phenomenon, which, as the undersigned happens to know, is notable in all the counties with the Croat population.''[19]

Like many others, this prefect seemed to feel that little could be done in the face of the widespread national disaffection, a precondition for the rapid spread of Radić's republicanism. Many reports took note of the almost exclusively Croat aspect of Radić's movement and its unpopularity among the local Serbs. A report from Petrinja, for example, pointed out that ''because of Radić's well-known agitation, republicanism . . . is deeply rooted—except among the Orthodox populace, to the extent that no measures help against it.''[20] In Pisarovina, ''There have not been any republican agitators of late, probably because all the peasants, except the Orthodox, are disposed toward republicanism anyway.''[21]

It was clear that the HPSS's national coloration, which accounts for the magnitude of its base, presented a much more serious threat to the existing order than did the republican attitudes of the openly revolutionary groups, such as the left socialists, who evolved toward communism. In the district of Sisak, one report said, ''there is no special socialist movement; there exists, however, the movement and agitation stemming from the peasant party [HPSS] with the cooperation of the worst elements.''[22] Similarly, in Zagreb, the county prefect reported that ''the socialist party has a substantial number of supporters in this county. . . . It has not been noted, however, that these [socialists] would start a greater action against Serbdom and against the monarchy, although it is known that they are republicans in principle. A greater action for a republic was started by the followers of the peasant party.''[23] Even by April 1920, by which time the nascent Communists had succeeded in developing a mass movement of their own, Zagreb's district prefect claimed that ''In my opinion, the agitation of Radić's Peasant party is more dangerous than the Communist movement, since [the HPSS] has a completely political and antistate character.''[24]

Apart from the jailings of the HPSS leaders and the ban on the party's public assemblies, the authorities seemed unable to devise any effective countermeasures to the growing republican movement in Croatia. It was

19. Ibid., Predstojništvo kr. kotarske oblasti, no. 14 Res., Sv. Ivan Zelina, April 25, 1919.
20. Paver, *Zbornik gradje*, p. 60.
21. AIHRPH, 1919/Sig. XXI, Box 4: Predstojničtvo kr. kotarske oblasti, no. 53 praes, Pisarovina, April 26, 1919.
22. Ibid., Predstojničtvo kr. kotarske oblasti, no. 68 Prs., Sisak, April 16, 1919.
23. Ibid., Kr. kotarska oblast, no. 81. pr./1919, Zagreb, April 22, 1919.
24. Paver, *Zbornik gradje*, p. 135.

obvious that "the stern measures for the arrest of the agitators, [as well as] . . . preventive imprisonment [*koluzivni zatvor*] and strict prosecution," were not sufficient for the maintenance of order.[25] Furthermore, as Pribićević himself noted in a telegram to Ban Paleček, the domestic army in Croatia was completely untrustworthy.[26] Proposed agrarian reforms interested the peasantry far less than the promises of Radić's movement, and the arrest of Radić and HPSS agitation to force the government to free him only worked up enthusiasm for the cause.

For the most part, the actions undertaken by the Croat peasantry against the existing order during 1919 and 1920 seemed to be expressions of personal displeasure with the state and the monarchy, and the agitation was on the whole ranking but not violent. On December 10, 1919, Radić noted with delight that "*Before the Zagreb District Court alone* there are 400 '*active*' cases for offenses against 'Majesty' (Petar and Aleks[andar])!"[27] Some peasants sent threatening letters to the sundry opponents of the HPSS, and a few went so far as to shoot off guns during demonstrations and physically attack government officials.[28] There were also some instances of offenses against private property, poaching and the like, which authorities blamed on Radić's influence. Thus, the county prefect in Samobor reported on April 15, 1919, that "In connection with the imagined liberty, which would be enshrined in that republic [propagated by Radić], and in view of the forthcoming agrarian reform, peasants have repeatedly started encroaching on other people's property, especially int he forests, which they have proclaimed their own."[29]

The real force of the peasant movement was its size, and the HPSS thought it could use its power of numbers by organizing actions that would, it hoped, directly threaten the stability of the state and, at the same time, broaden the base of the Croat opposition by involving many thousands of people in direct

25. Ibid., p. 64.
26. Vidmar, "Prilozi gradji," p. 62.
27. Radić, *Korespondencija*, vol. 2, p. 423. Radić would probably not have been so enthusiastic about the coarser expressions of peasant displeasure with the ruling dynasty. One example of the latter was a demonstration in Varaždinske Toplice on March 4, 1919, organized as a mock funeral of the monarchy. According to an unnerved district prefect's report, the participants "buried the [coffin representing the] dynasty outside the church near the road in the most unworthy manner, [and some] untied their pants . . . as if to p——s on [the buried dynasty]." Vidmar, "Prilozi gradji," p. 50.
28. Ibid., pp. 45–46. Paver, *Zbornik gradje*, pp. 56–57. On December 27, 1920, a group of peasants from the environs of Glina, with shouts of "Long live the Republic, long live Radić, down with Serbia, . . . captured the customs guard Marko Pavušek who was on vacation, took his repeat pistol with eight . . . bullets [and his] knife, took his military hat from his head and threw it on the ground, proceeded to pound on it with their feet; they later beat the same [official], without causing visible bruises, after which he fled and [one of the peasants] shot after him with the captured repeat pistol, with the aim of killing him." AIHRPH, 1921/Sig. VI C, Box 1: IV žandarm. Brigada, no. 826, Stankovac, Dec. 28, 1920.
29. Ibid., 1919/Sig. XX, Box 4: Predstojničtvo kr. kotarske oblasti, no. 41 Pr., Samobor, April 15, 1919.

political confrontations. One of the most ambitious actions of this sort was a food boycott of the cities, plotted by the local HPSS organizations in the spring of 1919, with the aim of forcing the authorities to release Radić.

Beginning with the first days of April, leaflets calling upon peasants to deny food to the cities while Radić was imprisoned were spread throughout northwestern Croatia, particularly in Radić's native Posavina.[30] Rallies were held in different localities, indicating a promising start of the action.[31] In the long run, however, the boycott seems to have failed. The reaction of the authorities was swift and effective. Although Pribićević was angered by the (apparently inaccurate) reports that the strike action was in some cases encouraged by the local officials, there were no actual grounds for such apprehensions. Pribićević's order for an "energetic action of the authorities" against the hostile agitators was strictly upheld (pp. 71–72). Mass arrests of the boycott's organizers occurred in many localities, considerably weakening the direction of the movement (pp. 79–80, 84, 85). Not all areas observed the boycott by any means. Where the peasants set up barricades to prevent the flow of goods to the cities, such as in the vicinity of Sisak, their aim was wholly realized. Even there, however, the blockage could not be permanent, because the military very shortly dispersed the peasant guards and arrested the ringleaders (p. 67).

The failure of the 1919 boycott of the cities, though it exposed the HPSS's weakness in organizing direct confrontations with the authorities, did not lessen Radić's resolve to try more elaborate boycotts in the future.[32] Nor did

30. Following is the full text of the strike proclamation leaflet issued by the Peasant Committee for the Carrying out of the Boycott (from Paver, *Zbornik gradje*, p. 61): "To the Croat peasant people: The president of the HPSS and the leader of the Croat peasantry, Stjepan Radić, is imprisoned against the clear letter of the law because he fearlessly defends the Croat and peasant rights and because he is even more fearlessly fighting for a Croat peasant republic. For the same reasons, the only Croat peasant newspaper, *Dom*, was banned. Countless peasant deputations have gone before H. E. the Ban in regard to this matter, in order to assure respect of the law, but without results. Therefore, we have no other recourse except to reply to this trampling of human and political liberty through the corresponding stronger means, and to say to the ruling gentlemen: While you trample our rights and liberty, you will not eat our bread. Therefore, we immediately declare A GENERAL PEASANT STRIKE, that is, we conclude that from this day until the day of the release of President Stjepan Radić, and until the first issue of *Dom* is published, the peasants will not and should not: 1) bring any food or provisions (milk, etc.) to any city; 2) bring any cattle or swine, fodder, or wood, to any fair; 3) sell at their own homes anything that is necessary for the provisioning of the cities to any merchants or middlemen. We know that this will hurt the urban poor, but we have no other choice. To the [urban] poor we recommend: Help us in our struggle for human rights and we shall help you in acquiring a life suitable for human beings. This strike must be carried out by the entire peasant people; he who betrays will be a traitor of his own interests and that of his children. [He will be] a betrayer of the Croat peasant republic and of our peasant rights. The peasant people will know a fitting way to judge such traitors. Therefore, let a special peasant committee be organized in every village; [a committee] which would do everything to facilitate the complete success of this peasant strike, so that we may show that a peasant also is no longer anybody's servant or slave, but a sole master of his home and of our Croat homeland."

31. Paver, *Zbornik gradje*, p. 67. (Page numbers in the rest of this paragraph refer to this work.)
32. Radić, *Korespondencija*, vol. 2, p. 430.

it diminish the HPSS's ability to inspire more obvious forms of passive resistance, which were still its principal strength. Since the HPSS openly stood for the nonrecognition of the new state, passive resistance necessarily implied noncooperation with the state organs, first of all with the tax-collecting agencies and the military.[33] It was in this area that the Croat peasant movement caused most damage to the authorities.

Charges that the HPSS was preventing the orderly payment of taxes in Croatia were more numerous than the documented cases of tax evasion.[34] In part, this was a result of the great disorder in the state's levying system during the first years after the unification. Draft evasion was another matter. The precise extent of draft evasion is unknown, but it was great, and the HPSS, led by the jailed Radić, had a direct hand in the antidraft agitation.[35] Radić's leaflet (or petition), written in prison on July 8, 1919, during a period of intense agitation against recruitment, outlined the reasons for his party's view that the new state was illegitimate, and why, therefore, the party supporters were refusing to serve in the army. The petition was addressed to the government of France, and appealed directly for its help in the final paragraph:

> We, the undersigned Croat citizens, most firmly protest against the fact that Serbia's military laws were extended to the territory of the state of Croatia by a mere ministerial order and that, contrary to law, Croat citizens are being drafted into the Serbian army. We, therefore, seek the protection of the French Republic for our lives, for our families and property, which are threatened by the Serbian military command, which behaves in Croatia as in a conquered country; in fact, worse, since according to international law, recruitment is not at all permitted even in a conquered country.[36]

Several groups of antidraft agitators had already, in June 1919, been captured by authorities in Croatia, and early in July there were demonstrations around Kratečko. Inaccurate reports which contained allegations that the demonstrators at Kratečko were armed upset authorities far in excess of the actual importance of the affair, but there was no doubting the extent of the apprehension, and Radić's leaflet—even rumors of its existence—tended to increase the alarm.[37]

One specific result of the agitation was a wave of desertions by soldiers

---

33. In Radić's own words, "I hold that it is today most practical—in the real meaning of that word—not to recognize this brute violence." Ibid., p. 240.

34. For a typical example of these charges, see Paver, *Zbornik gradje*, p. 88.

35. Radić used a stronger term. In a prison letter to his wife (June 17, 1919), he wrote, "It is likely that you also hear that the resistance to the draft, militarism, and monarchy is general." Radić, *Korespondencija*, vol. 2, p. 193.

36. Ibid., p. 231. Radić made a French translation of the document, which was sent to the Paris Peace Conference, but which did not reach its destination.

37. Paver, *Zbornik gradje*, pp. 82–83, 86, 88–89.

already serving their military duty. The desertions were in such numbers that the military commanders in Belgrade began systematically collecting documentation on deserters, who were subsequently captured and interrogated.[38] This documentation shows that the deserters were principally influenced by their villagers and other acquaintances, who were generally supporters of the HPSS. Although there were several cases of desertion allegedly inspired by HPSS deputies, "Radić's agitators," and Radić himself, most of the captured deserters attributed their prolonged absences from their units to informal influences, such as the village sentiment, "unknown civilians," and other deserters.[39] Only one deserter claimed that he failed to return to his unit because of peasant pressures, and very few cited fear of the Albanian border, where the Yugoslavs fought pitched battles with the troops of Sulejman Bej Delvina's Tirana government.[40] The most common reason for flight from the barracks was the conviction that the political situation was only temporary and "that military recruits should not go to the army in Serbia, because a *preokret* [literally, "turnabout," that is, revolution] will take place and each will serve in his own country." More specifically, the Croat countryside was apparently convinced that "Radić will establish a Croat republic . . . and besides, soon all the Croats will free themselves, because a Croat Republic will be founded" (pp. 3, 8). This expectation was particularly strong before the elections for the Constituent Assembly in the fall of 1920 (pp. 5, 6).

Combined with the republican aspirations present in the Croat peasant stirrings of 1918, Radić's anticentralist national program became a common

38. The results of this fact-finding were used in preparing evidence against Radić in 1924, under the supervision of Yugoslavia's chairman of the military court system, Brigadier General Vladimir S. Jovanović. Although the latter's purpose warrants extreme caution in the evaluation of the interpretive statements found in the report submitted by its compiler to the Ministry of the Army and the Navy, there exists no apparent reason to doubt the truth of the evidence itself. For the report see AIHRPH, ZB-S-11/56: Ministarstvo Vojske i Mornarice, Sudsko odelenje, no. 57, April 20, 1924. The report exists in two identical versions, in Cyrillic and Roman scripts. The latter version, twenty pages in length, is used here. Jovanović's report listed sixty-four cases of desertion, covering the period between 1919 and 1924. He noted that these were "only a few cases . . . from a mass of exactly the same cases." Here, we are concerned only with those instances of desertion that occurred before July 1921.

39. Ibid., pp. 1, 7, 2, 4, 10. The deputies in question were Franjo Malčić and Ante Adžija, both elected to the Constituent Assembly in 1920 on the HPSS list. A deserter captured in April 1921 claimed that "at a meeting in Koprivnica Radić personally said that it is not necessary to serve in the army" (p. 4). Another deserter confessed that "he personally went to Stjepan Radić [probably in March 1920] to buy [the newspaper] *Dom* and on that occasion Radić personally said that he did not guarantee that any soldier who is going to Albania [where the Yugoslav units were engaged] would return to his home alive. On that occasion, several military deserters were with Radić, and he [Radić] explained to them that the army no longer exists and that they are not obliged to serve in it" (p. 11).

40. Deserter Franjo Pleško, from the environs of Bjelovar, claimed that during his vacation in the fall of 1920 "all kinds of agitation for the Constituent Assembly was going on and various antistate elements came, trying to persuade us; they threatened us with death if we were to return to our commands, so that, as the rest from my district, I also remained at home." Ibid., p. 5. The possible exaggeration in Pleško's statement should be viewed in terms of the circumstances in which he made it. (Page numbers that follow refer to the same work.)

property of a mass movement that spread under the auspices of the HPSS in the postunification period. Continued demonstrations against the monarchy, demands for a Croat republic, attempts at food boycotts, as well as the highly successful campaign against recruitment, undermined the stability of the new state and provided the counterweight to the crisis created by the unilateral introduction of centralism. This situation could not be disentangled without significant concessions to the Croat national demands. In the absence of the official willingness to make such concessions, Radić's clear and often reiterated pleas for nonviolence were bound to be overlooked. A highly politicized peasant movement, which recognized Radić as its undisputed leader, could not be kept at a feverish level of opposition for a prolonged period of time. Any official initiative that affected the Croat peasantry could be perceived as an intolerable attack and could provoke a chain of stirrings, whose political content necessarily had to be identical to Radić's republican, anticentralist and antiunitarist program. In September 1920 the stirrings came to a head in the resistance to the government's policy of draft-animal registration. The events that occurred during one stormy week in September are extremely important for understanding Radić's movement. They also demonstrate that the national question had ramifications in matters that would ordinarily have been purely economic, and that during this period solutions to social problems in Croatia regularly assumed national colorations, with a republic as their strategic object.

The 1920 Croat Peasant Revolt against Draft-Animal Registration

The rural violence that erupted in September 1920 was of a quite different sort from the violence that occurred in the Croat countryside in 1918–1919. The immediate cause of the 1920 rebellion—for rebellion it was—was economic, but the uneasiness had existed since Radić's second arrest in March 1920, and the general tenor of the rebellion assumed distinctly political tones.[1] It was not by accident that the revolt took place in the wider environs

---

1. The terms "rebellion," "revolt" and "uprising," which are used interchangeably for the September 1920 events in northwest Croatia, are not random. All the elements of a rebellion were present: armed clashes, the creation (however short-lived) of rebel units, planned attacks on government contingents, attempts to disrupt state communications, and even the rudiments of political leadership and organization. All this leads to an inescapable conclusion that the 1920 "disturbances" were qualitatively different from the 1918–1919 turmoil. Although no systematic studies have yet been made on the events of 1920, historians have consistently referred to them as a rebellion. There does not seem to be any evidence that could challenge such a characterization.

of Zagreb, including Radić's native Posavina, where the HPSS had already put down deep roots (see map 3-2).

As noted earlier, in 1919 the new Yugoslav Ministry of Defense had extended Serbia's military laws statewide. One provision of these statutes was the obligatory draft-animal registration, since horses and oxen were still used for the towing of weapons and supplies both for the purposes of maneuvers and in actual warfare. Croat peasants were used to this procedure from Austro-Hungarian times. In Serbia, however, inventory also included the branding of animals, to distinguish between those that were fit and those that were unfit for army use. Branding was a novelty in Croatia, and the peasants' misunderstanding of the procedure and its purposes and effects was so great that trouble began as soon as the military started its work in mid-August 1920. The Croat peasants, remembering the recent requisitioning of their animals by the Austro-Hungarian authorities, were angered by the army's demand for a certain number of harnessed horses from each county, which were ostensibly to serve during the forthcoming two-month military maneuvers, although the peasants were quite aware that warfare still continued in northern Albania. Not being used to branding, they feared that the procedure would harm the animals, perhaps permanently, and they were certain also that the potential sale value of the rejected animals, which were branded with o (zero), would be seriously diminished. The requisitioning authorities either shrugged off these real or imagined fears, or, some believed, took a perverse delight in not bothering to explain the purpose of their measures and to elaborate on the compensation procedures that were taken into account in the law. "When the peasants asked the military commissioners who would reimburse them for the livestock, these would answer them by pointing a finger toward the heavens."[2]

Resentment fed rumors and rumors fed resistance. By August 27, the communal officials in Gora, some fifty kilometers south of Zagreb, had knowledge of the peasant resolve to impede the registration in the villages of Strašnik and Marinbrod; conspiratorial meetings were commonplace, although the authorities did not always scent them in time.[3] On August 31 a leaflet calling on the peasants to resist the cattle branding surfaced in Taborište, Hrastovica commune, a few kilometers to the east of Gora. After invoking "the Most Holy Name of Jesus," the leaflet promised the aid of *zeleni kader,* which would make away with all the gendarmes (p. 283). On September 1, the authorities in Kostajnica disclosed that the peasants in three villages on the lower Sava (Bobovac, Žreme, and Sunja) known as "infected" by Radić's ideas were expecting revolution (p. 290). These were but

---

2. L. and M., "Seljačka buna u Hrvatskoj," *Nova Evropa,* vol. 1 (1920), no. 2, p. 73.

3. Josipa Paver, comp., *Zbornik gradje za povijest radničkog pokreta i KPJ 1919–1920* (Sisak, 1970), pp. 282–283, 376. (Page numbers that follow refer to the same work.)

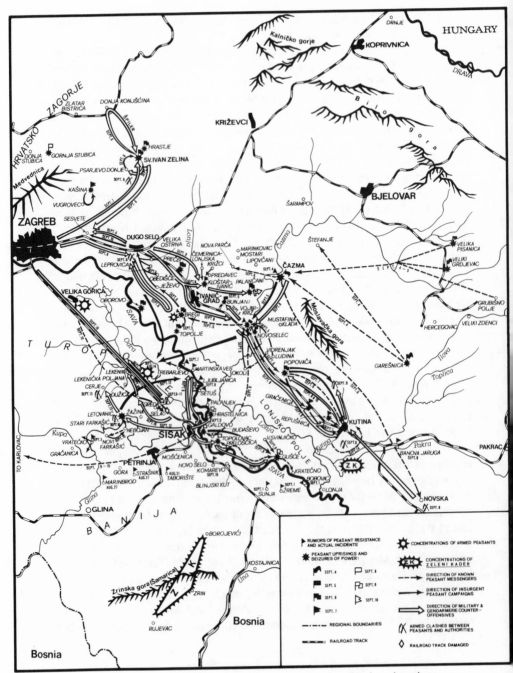

3-2. The 1920 Croat peasant revolt against draft-animal registration

rumblings before a tempest, which in no time lashed into fury in several areas.

The next incident occurred some fifty kilometers to the northwest, when a group of peasants from Ivanje Selo went to Veliki Grdjevac, southeast of Bjelovar, to protest the registration, and met explanations of provision for compensation for the requisitioned livestock with blows; they disarmed several gendarmes, and the rest fled. News of this incident, which occurred around September 2, spread quickly through the entire countryside, and peasants from Grubišno Polje, in the east, to Dugo Selo, a district seat near Zagreb, began planning similar confrontations.[4] In Vratečko, in the Gora area, peasants hid their livestock, and one peasant attacked the gendarmes who were accompanying the military.[5] Although the regional authorities in Zagreb issued an order to all county officials on September 4 saying that the army had decided to stop the registration, this step apparently went unheeded in some localities, for two days later the order had to be reiterated in Sisak district (pp. 286 n. 3, 350–351). By then, however, the revolt was already general.

During the night of September 4–5, peasants took control of Čazma, a small town east of Zagreb. The next afternoon a gendarmerie patrol was attacked in the vicinity of Vojni Križ, a few kilometers distant, and a short time later the same patrol was disarmed after an exchange of fire by some fifty peasant youths at Bunjani. That evening a force of two thousand peasants successfully attacked the gendarmerie station in Vojni Križ, put the gendaremes in jail, and took control of the public offices. The rebels then proceeded to the Novoselec train station, and commandeered a train from Zagreb so they could spread the revolt to adjacent hamlets located along the railroad line. They also cut the telephone wires between Križ and Ivanić-Grad, and elsewhere. On the same day several gendarmes perished during the uprising in Garešnica (pp. 366, 304–305, 321, 288–290, 292).

Vojni Križ became a vital center of the revolt, and thanks to the commandeered train, uprisings in force began to take place all along the rail line in places as far apart as Dugo Selo and Novska, the southeasternmost point of the rebellion. On September 6 a somewhat ineffectual attempt by some one thousand peasants to disarm the gendarmerie station in Popovača, just southeast of Križ, was aided by peasant contingents from Križ that arrived around midday. Nine gendarmes and customs officials were fired upon, and by late afternoon they finally surrendered after running out of ammunition (pp. 291, 380). From Popovača the revolt spread toward Kutina, to the southeast, and on the east bank of the Sava the success at Križ inspired a similar success at Bregi, where two thousand rebels captured the village and confined the local

4. L. and M., "Seljačka buna," p. 73.
5. Paver, *Zbornik gradje*, p. 284. (Page numbers that follow also refer to this work.)

gendarmes (pp. 380, 303–304). The pattern was also duplicated in nearby Topolje (p. 375). From Bregi and the nearby villages, the insurgents marched to Dugo Selo, which was momentarily seized in the course of the day by a host of six hundred peasants, who disarmed ten gendarmes, killing one. After a brief skirmish, an incoming patrol succeeded in dispersing the insurgents, and that evening military units from Zagreb were dispatched to hold the town.[6]

On the fringes of the center, fires also flared. On the same fatal September 6, peasants from the villages around Sv. Ivan Zelina, north of Dugo Selo but not on the rail line, assembled in the early morning hours and descended on the townlet in hopes of freeing several of their fellows who had been arrested by the gendarmes for resisting the livestock registration. By nine o'clock they had captured the town and released the captives. One of the insurgents was killed by the retreating gendarmes, and in retaliation the insurgents forced the municipal headman, Špiler, whom they captured after his unsuccessful attempt to prompt aid from Donja Konjščina, to carry the fallen peasant's coffin to the churchyard, and then executed him.[7]

A military expedition suppressed the revolt in Zelina on September 7, but elsewhere in Prigorje it was only beginning.[8] In Kašina the peasants burned the communal records, murdered the notary, and tortured the local priest, whom they loathed for his part in the wartime food distribution, by forcing him to dance on broken glass and acacia thorns.[9] By this time authorities were noting that the revolt in Bregi and Dubrovčak was assuming a "serious character." Peasants were also massing around Kloštar-Ivanić, and they captured it in one day after a brief skirmish with the customs officials. In the southeast, the counties of Kutina and Čazma were still experiencing "revolution on the high level."[10]

The turning point came on September 8. A military mission from Dugo Selo captured Bregi, and at Novoselec and Križ units from Zagreb and Čazma engaged the rebels. After a serious clash, in which one soldier was killed, the "revolutionists" fled to the nearby forests (pp. 304–306). The Zagreb military contingents then proceeded to Kutina, while a gendarmerie column that had just defeated three hundred rebels in Novska approached Kutina from the opposite direction, the object being to cut off rebel units (led by units from Križ) that were grouping in Gračanica and Repušnica for an attack on Kutina. The combined military and gendarmerie reinforcements

6. Zvonimir Kulundžić, *Atentat na Stjepana Radića* (Zagreb, 1967), p. 158.
7. Bernard Stulli, " 'Idemo u bunu!'—'U Sv. Ivanu Zelini treba reda delati!' " *Kaj,* vol. 4 (1971), nos. 7–8, pp. 46–47.
8. Ibid., p. 47.
9. Franjo Šatović, "Seljačke bune," ibid., no. 6, p. 43.
10. Paver, *Zbornik gradje,* pp. 296, 293–294, 290. (Page numbers that follow also refer to this work.)

defeated the rebels soon after they entered Kutina, and with Križ and Kutina secured, the authorities henceforth had the initiative (pp. 296, 378–379, 297, 313).

The officials were still cautious, and the arrests of the "ringleaders" were postponed, in order to avoid provoking new resistance (pp. 352, 304). The revolt did gain some new ground on September 8 and 9; rebels seized a string of villages and townlets on the banks of the Sava downstream from Sisak, among them Prelošćica, Topolovac, and Galdovo, and the peasants destroyed sections of the Zagreb-Sisak railroad line near Lekenik, but these successes were short-lived. In the southern confines of Sisak, some two to three thousand peasants succeeded in seizing Gušće, but Topolovac had to be given up, and in the vicinity of Dugo Selo the army regained Kloštar-Ivanić. From Kutina, the gendarmes of the Fourth Zagreb Brigade were advancing against the rebels toward Popovača, meeting sporadic resistance. The insurgents were also active in the wooded areas around Križ, where the peasants attempted to recapture the Novoselec railroad station (pp. 353–354, 322, 337–338, 388, 325, 299).

The rebellion in Gušće was crushed on September 10, a day that witnessed several of the most dramatic incidents of the rebellion. In Letovanić, a village on the Kupa River, west of Sisak, peasant attempts to capture the gendarmerie station were frustrated by an exceptionally strong resistance. The defenders were eventually forced to retreat, but not before they killed four insurgents in a gun battle that lasted four hours. More importantly, a host of insurgents, numbering from one-hundred-fifty to a thousand depending on the source, some armed with machine guns, attacked workers and soldiers who were repairing the rail track near Lekenik. The battle lasted for most of the day, and resulted in the death of one gendarme and the wounding of several soldiers (pp. 309, 315, 346–347, 361–362). Peasant casualties are not known.

The insurgents' ability to harass this vital transportation point proved rather durable. The forested areas around Lekenik, which were largely uninhabited, apparently became the refuge of the most determined fighters. The authorities noted that "It seems that the rebels fled from the other areas where the army came and have congregated in these large forests, and have called on the military deserters from the commune of Sela, who joined them in destroying the rail track and in attacking the army" (p. 315). Attacks on the military contingents sent to defend the Lekenik rail junction continued on the eleventh and the twelfth. As late as September 14, when the rebellion was completely defeated elsewhere, the express train from Belgrade was halted for an hour until the army succeeded in putting the insurgents to rout (p. 328).

Letovanić fell on September 12. Scattered fighting continued in Cerje, but to no avail (pp. 330, 332, 347). The rebels no longer had the initiative, but their previous successes could not be underestimated. As late as September 20, the county administration in Kutina informed the regional officials in Zagreb that the army must remain in that locality, for fear that its withdrawal might revive the rebellion (p. 363). There followed mass arrests of real or suspected rebels, unimaginable without likely military excesses. Beatings of the peasants were commonplace. Military units that advanced on Letovanić on September 12 thought nothing of holding all males as hostages (pp. 395–396). In Lekenička Poljana the army actually plundered the villagers, and in Novoselci a gendarme killed a seventy-nine-year-old peasant who did not hear the official order to squat.[11]

According to the official statistics, between September 4 and 24, fifteen casualties were counted on the peasant side (the actual figure may well have been higher), while the authorities lost three soldiers, two gendarmes, three civil servants, and two customs officials.[12] The disturbing impression of these losses was concomitant with the authorities' dismay at the strength of the peasant movement, and the authorities were suitably cautious about the future. The regional administration in Zagreb, for example, pleaded for cooperation in a September 10 dispatch to the editorial offices of the metropolitan newspapers: "The previous refraining from reporting the news to the press was based on the hope that the movement would be stifled in a day or two, and that the details could then be presented to the public. But the course of events now makes it urgent for the authorities to appeal for the keenest cooperation of the patriotic press, with the special request that it complies by eschewing political recriminations and partisan bickering, and bear in mind the sole good of the people and the state."[13]

Recriminations could hardly be avoided. In the government, though some officials fully recognized that it was the draft-animal registration that had been the cause of the first resistance, which developed into open rebellion, others—out of shortsightedness or bigotry—found it advisable to insist on the external inspiration of the stirrings.[14] There was little doubt in the government, however, about the rebellion's real motives. In his report to Milorad Drašković, the minister of the interior, Ban Laginja listed numerous economic and political grievances, including the newly regulated currency rate of exchange, forcible recruitment (which did not exempt the war veterans), the holding of hostages from the families of the deserters, reneging on the promises to allow unregulated tobacco planting and legalized distilling,

11. Ibid., p. 394; Šatović, "Seljačke bune," p. 43.
12. Paver, *Zbornik gradje,* p. 386.
13. Ibid., pp. 307–308.
14. For example, Sublieutenant Tadejević, of the gendarmerie unit that captured Kutina, noted that "according to all signs, the cattle branding was definitely not the cause of the rebellion . . . [which was instead a result] of the well-organized movement on the part of Hungarians and Italians, while the branding was but the occasion for the movement to commence." Ibid., p. 326.

and so on.[15] Quite clearly, no conspiratorial group could have moved the peasants to risky confrontations had there not been genuine grievances, but the revolt nonetheless was seen to have highly politicized connotations.

Numerous official reports, regardless of their tone or objectivity, stressed the political element. For example, the district administrators in Čazma noted in a dispatch to Zagreb that the rebellion "at its origin had an economic [quality], and later assumed a clear Bolshevik-political character and made its aim the overthrow [of] the state and the establishment of a Croat peasant republic."[16] In fact, organized Communists took no part in the uprising. The participation of the returnees from Russia—who were to a degree influenced by Leninism—was indeed noticeable, nor could it have been avoided, considering the numerousness of this group; but even some officials made it clear that, as one notary put it, "The Communists, who also exist in [the Križ] commune, behaved fairly passively during all of this" (p. 294). Nor could the authorities blame the Frankists, although one of thier electoral leaflets hailing Ivica Frank, the late Frank's émigré heir, surfaced in Kutina in the course of the disturbances (pp. 326–327).

Only a group that was already active in the Croat countryside could give direction to the peasant movement. That group was, of course, the HPSS. Evidence of its participation in the uprising is abundant. The key insurgents usually belonged to Radić's party, as was the case of two peasant leaders, Filip Lakuš (1888–1958) and Stjepan Uroić (1884?–?), whose paramount part in the rebellion and personal stamp clearly emerge from the sources, particularly in Lakuš's case.[17] Lakuš, the peasant leader in Križ and a member of the HPSS executive committee, consistently dominated the events around Križ and made every effort to spread the rebellion.[18] It was Lakuš who "agitated for a republic, which would have to be proclaimed, and said that Zagreb must be attacked, the government there overthrown and . . . a republican [government] established."[19] Uroić, a peasant from Repušnica,

15. Ibid., pp. 370–372. Cf. Kulundžić, *Atentat,* pp. 156–159.

16. Paver, *Zbornik gradje,* p. 366. (Page numbers that follow also refer to this work.)

17. The sources permit such a deduction on the basis of the limited data on the leaders' political affiliation. The authorities, for example, noted that Ivan Mrazovac, Djuro Kurjak-Fratrić, and Nikola Kelčec, the respective leaders of the HPSS organizations in Odra, Greda, and Prelošćica, assumed key roles in the uprising. Ibid., p. 365. Nikola Srdović, a member of the HPSS executive committee, led the rebellion in Bregi and steered the attack on Dugo Selo on September 6. Kulundžić, *Atentat,* p. 158. Certainly no other party actively participated in the rebellion.

18. For more information on this remarkable peasant tribune, a former prisoner-of-war in Russia, later a deputy of Radić's party, and throughout the tireless propagator of Radić's ideas, see Matija Kovačić, *Od Radića do Pavelića* (Munich, 1970), pp. 41–43. Lakuš's attempts to disseminate "rebellious" literature in Križ encouraged the authorities to close his illicit bookstore. AIHRPH, 1924/ Sig. VI/C, Box 2: IV Žandarmerijska brigada, no. 242, Jan. 31, 1924; ibid., kr. kotarska oblast, no. 16 prs., Čazma, Feb. 14, 1924. During the Second World War, Lakuš was one of the large group of Radić's followers who joined the Communist-led partisan movement. See his obituary, "Umro Filip Lakuš," *Slobodni dom,* Aug. 7, 1958, p. 3.

19. Paver, *Zbornik gradje,* p. 367.

similarly took the lead in the peasant raid on Kutina, and was captured there. In a gendarmerie report it was noted that "among the rebels caught during the battle one finds the well-known rebel [*bundžija*] Stjepan Uroić, who organized this movement throughout this area. Special attention should be devoted to this man during the inquiry, because the latter was closely tied with Stjepan Radić."[20]

The guiding hand of the HPSS was evident not only in the composition of the rebel leadership but, even more, in the initiatives of the insurgents. Again and again the authorities reported on the mass slogan that Radić—who was still imprisoned in the Zagreb court jail—must be freed.[21] Several reports testified that the reason the peasants destroyed the railroad track near Lekenik was because of the popular belief "that the Serbs will take Radić to Belgrade," via this principal rail line.[22] The HPSS had good reason to feel certain that the Belgrade administration was preparing to conduct its prize prisoner to the capital, and the local party leaders certainly engaged themselves in interfering with at least the most obvious means of transport.[23]

The decidedly republican tenor of the rebellion was another indication of HPSS influence. Lakuš repeatedly insisted on the establishment of a republic, with Radić at its head.[24] That the rebellion was in fact aimed against all manifestations of the existing order is apparent not only in the burning of pictures of King Petar and Regent Aleksandar and the attacks on the gendarmes, but also in the numerous attempts that were made to set up insurgent administrations.[25] In Križ, the civil servants were sent packing and their

---

20. Ibid., pp. 378–379, 325.
21. For an example see ibid., p. 296.
22. Ibid., p. 333; cf. p. 324.
23. Ibid., p. 333.
24. Ibid., p. 368. According to Kovačić (*Od Radića,* p. 42), Lakuš and another HPSS leader, Mijo Stuparić, actually proclaimed a "Croat peasant republic" in Križ and Ludina. "The maturity they both demonstrated can be seen from the proclamation [that was posted] on the communal building. [In it] the secession of Croatia from Serbia was proclaimed. . . . In order to prevent any chaos during the revolution, the proclamation, which they both signed, provided for capital punishment for each violation against private property." Kovačić's claims could not be corroborated by the sources. If the proclamation that Kovačić refers to ever existed (as was seemingly a tradition in Kovačić's politically active family), Kovačić's copy has apparently not survived. Kovačić's claim that Lakuš had every intention of leading peasants to take Sisak (ibid., p. 43), stands on firmer ground; cf. Paver, *Zbornik gradje,* p. 368. It appears that Lakuš hoped to capture not only Sisak but eventually Zagreb. His plan was frustrated by the government's ability to counter the peasant gains relatively speedily. As a result, the peasants were demoralized and moreover uncertain whether the HPSS leadership approved their action. According to Kovačić (*Od Radića,* p. 43), at a rally in Palanjek after the fall of Križ, "Lakuš spoke militantly, but he made a psychological blunder, because he described the course of the struggle in Vojni Križ and how the peasants had to writhdraw owing to the lack of ammunition. This made a bad impression on some thousand gathered [peasants]. Some distinguished village notables proposed that the attack on Sisak be postponed until it could be seen whether the movement were general or not, and how the party [HPSS] related to it. The attack on Sisak was thus abandoned."
25. Kulundžić, *Atentat,* p. 157. According to a gendarmerie report, in Gušće "[the rebels] took a picture of Wilson out [of a public office] in order to destroy it, thinking that it was a picture of His

offices closed, and the peasant "national guard" patrolled the key points in the areas.[26] In addition to the almost obligatory militias, the rebel organs of power sometimes included "people's courts," and other institutions, which were almost regularly staffed by individuals from the local leadership of the HPSS.[27] Indeed, it was so commonplace for the insurgents to install their own administration in place of the old that this most appropriate indice of the rebellion's relatively high level of organization was contrasted to the singular situation in Gušće. According to an obviously bewildered official, in this locality "after the disarming of the gendarmerie station they [the rebels] threw out the communal officials, but they did not install other [officials]." Even this solitary aberration proved not to be true, for a later report says that in this village "[the mob] elected a 24-person 'National Council,' which removed the communal officials and undertook the takeover of the office and the treasury, and appointed its officials."[28]

Here and there, some naïve attempts were made to preserve "legality" within the framework of usurpation—perhaps inspired by the pacifist and parliamentarian traditions of the HPSS. In Topolovac, the rebels actually sent the report on their takeover from the established authorities to the county administration in Sisak.[29] But the essence of the matter was still the seizure of power, and the local organizations of the HPSS committed their ideas,

---

Majesty King Petar, but others who recognized that it was Wilson prevented this.'' Paver, *Zbornik gradje*, p. 338. Despite the apparent hostility to the royal house, overt anti-Serb sentiment was rarely displayed and then mainly in Hrvatsko Zagorje, where slogans against the "Vlachs" (derogatory term for Serbs) were raised. Even there, the targets were not necessarily true Serbs; for example, in an attack on several proregime Croat merchants, the peasants screamed against "Serb proselytes" (*posrbice*). As one victim wrote to the Office of the Prime Minister in Belgrade, "I, Juraj Žukina, as a native of Gornja Stubica, who conducted a sizable business in Gornja Stubica, was thoroughly victimized by plunder and arson on September 8, 1920, mainly because they proclaimed me a 'Serb proselyte'! . . . On my premises I had, as a loyal adherent of the unification and of the Kingdom of the Serbs, Croats, and Slovenes, a picture of His Majesty the King, which they of course tore and pierced to thousands of pieces, as they would have done to me, had I not fled!'' AIHRPH 1923/ Sig. V [Box II]: Preuzvišeni gospodine Kraljevski Namesniće! (Gornja Stubica, June 28, 1923). Of course Žukina could only profit by exaggerating the implications of the incident, since the purpose of his letter was to secure reparations from the government, but it is true nevertheless, that "One of the principal distinctions of these September peasant disorders was their *tribal* [i.e., national, I.B.] quality—only the Croat peasant rebelled." L. and M., "Seljačka buna," p. 74. It would therefore seem that Lakuš was exaggerating when he claimed in 1945 that during the rebellion "All of us here were organized in the Croat Republican [*sic*] Peasant Party, and our Serb brothers, who live here, fought together with us." Filip Lakuš, "Narod je slobodan i suveren samo u republici," *Slobodni dom*, Sept. 11, 1945, p. 5. In 1920, it was most unlikely to expect antidynastic sentiments or revolutionism from the Serb peasants in Croatia. A gendarme who was captured by the rebels in Križ later told the investigators that after he was tied and laid on a bed, "Filip Lakuš came to me and told me that none of us who took the oath to King Petar were needed in the new state [i.e., in the peasant republic], and that we were traitors, and therefore they [the peasants] did not trust us." Paver, *Zbornik gradje*, p. 368.

26. Paver, *Zbornik gradje*, p. 321.
27. Ibid., p. 359; L. and M., "Seljačka buna," p. 75.
28. *Paver, Zbornik gradje*, pp. 315, 342.
29. Ibid., p. 314.

leadership cadre, and technical resources (such as the party's equestrian communications network) to this cause. The only rebel message that survives amply summarizes the rebellion's principal strategic and tactical concerns:

A CALL TO [THE VILLAGE OF] JELENSKA

Headman [!] such is the command of the entire people of Croatia that you at once go to Popovača and disarm the gendarmes and confiscate all the arms you find as we also have so done in Čazma in Petrička in Križ and send the message on to Kutina, and they further, you must not harm anybody, but at once cut the rail track and the telephone wires, if you do not do that there will immediately be fire and every evil among you.

With the respects of the entire people of
liberated Croatia
Čazma, Križ, Petrička   at once[30]

Clearly the HPSS leaders encouraged the rebellion, but this does not necessarily mean that they planned it, though many officials thought so. Since Radić's imprisonment did not keep him from developing channels of communication with the members of his family, and through them with the other HPSS leaders and base—primarily by way of Radić's Slavic Bookstore (his private shop cum party club in the heart of Zagreb, regularly visited by throngs of peasants who turned up in the city), he could well have directed the whole affair. There is no specific evidence, however, that the actions of several HPSS leaders, who had connections with some of the rebels, were actually the results of Radić's initiatives.

Marija Radić, Radić's wife and political aide, was suspected by the authorities of transmitting Radić's orders to the rebels. She was observed in Galdovo on September 15 in the company of Ivan Kovačić, Radić's cousin, who played a large part in the uprising in Palanjek later that same day.[31] Ivan Kovačić's son, the journalist Matija Kovačić, said in his memoirs that on Lakuš's insistence his father went to ascertain the attitude of unnamed party leaders to the rebellion, and was told "to let the revolutionary wave widen."[32] A police informant reported overhearing Lakuš on September 8 say that the HPSS's vice-president, Josip Predavec, had criticized him for not instigating an uprising in Križ after learning that Čazma was up in arms. Authorities were also convinced of the nefarious purposes of the illegal meetings held by Vinko Lovreković, Radić's close associate, during a visit he made to Čazma, Križ, and Ivanić-Grad, before the uprising.[33]

30. Ibid., p. 381.
31. Ibid., pp. 332, 348.
32. Kovačić, *Od Radića*, p. 43.
33. Paver, *Zbornik gradje*, pp. 368, 333, 329. Predavec, the youngest member of the Sabor at the time of his election in 1912, was one of Radić's closest associates and was vice-president of the party until he was assassinated in 1933. Lovreković was the first peasant deputy in the Croatian Sabor. Elected on the HPSS ticket in 1908, he was repeatedly reelected to the Sabor and later to the National

The leadership of the HPSS was apprehensive about Radić's prolonged incarceration, and it is possible that it would have welcomed and even arranged a demonstration of popular discontent. But the 1920 cattle-branding rebellion was far more than a demonstration, and Radić and the other HPSS leaders, while welcoming the uprising's political trend and the havoc it wreaked in the ranks of the centralists, were probably not prepared to let the rebellion get out of hand. Certainly the buildup toward violence was contrary to Radić's pacifistic inclinations and statements. In a letter to a cousin, written before the beginning of the rebellion, Radić's daughter Milica noted the widespread disaffection in Croatia and added that "only God knows whether this discontent will lead to other consequences. Of course, in keeping with his spirit and education, father does not wish that, but he is completely helpless in jail, and even were he out, who knows whether he would have succeeded in restraining the people."[34] According to Lakuš, speaking many years later, Radić insisted on the maintenance of his rules against violence. Lakuš said at a 1945 rally in Križ, "we wanted to widen this republican revolution of ours even wider, but twenty-five years ago the HPSS was not everywhere so well organized as here. Stjepan Radić therefore halted the struggle. When I started to seek ties with the other districts, a voice came from Stjepan Radić, that this rebellion of ours must be halted."[35]

The HPSS leadership never entertained revolutionary violence as a serious or feasible strategic course. The party was also never quite given the opportunity to show whether it would or would not use revolution as a necessary tactical weapon, because even at its darkest moments its leaders were not sufficiently convinced that they had no other choice but this last resort. In the section of his remembrances devoted to the 1920 revolt, Radić's successor, Vladko Maček, is noncommittal; he only says that after the maltreatment of the peasants following the rebellion he "feared a second, more serious insurrection."[36] Similarly, in 1924, Pavle Radić, Radić's nephew and closest political associate, found an occasion to exult publicly that "there never was rebellion or confrontation from our [HRSS] side."[37]

Still, the fact remains that the leadership did not repudiate peasant rebelliousness when it occurred spontaneously. In 1920, the HPSS leaders even encouraged it, and after the rebellion was put down such noted insurgents as Lakuš and Uroić received the backing of the HPSS as candidates for

Assembly, until his break with Radić in the mid-1920s. For more details on the early careers of these HPSS notables see Stjepan Radić, *Devet seljačkih zastupnika izabranih prvi put po proširenom izbornom pravu u banskoj Hrvatskoj: Pogled na politički njihov rad* (Zagreb, 1912), pp. 25–34.

34. Stjepan Radić, *Korespondencija Stjepana Radića*, comp. Bogdan Krizman, vol. 2 (Zagreb, 1973), p. 545.

35. Lakuš, "Narod je slobodan," p. 5.

36. Vladko Maček, *In the Struggle for Freedom*, trans. Elizabeth and Stjepan Gazi (University Park, Pa., 1957), p. 89.

37. AIHRPH, 1924/Sig. VI/C, Box 2: Predstojništvo kr. kotarske oblasti, no. 315/Prs., Velika Gorica, Oct. 20, 1924.

the Constituent Assembly.[38] In picking these men for the party's parliamentary club, the HPSS leaders were acting with no more premeditation than the peasant masses when they rebelled against the military abuses. Nevertheless, with the ground prepared by the HPSS, the party's organizational capabilities could not but be asserted even under conditions of spontaneity. In this way the HPSS influenced the course of peasant rebelliousness, which in turn served as a militant leverage on Radić and the other party leaders.

Croat Mnemonists

> Those who are privy to a genetic cognition of history are acquainted with national memory. The history of ancestors fills the subconscious awareness of each individual. The sum of individual subconsciousnesses is the consciousness of the collective unit—of the nation. Historicism in politics is not the play of individuals, but the imperative of national *mnémē*—of national memory.
>
> Milan Šufflay, 1921

> As a nation, within the framework of the 1918 unification, the Croats have lost all the attributes of their statehood. These attributes, to be sure, were falsely decorative, but nevertheless, in spite of centuries, they were preserved as relics and symbols of a certain liberty, which, though a negation of every democratic liberty, was not entirely devoid of political reality: the crown as the mark of sovereignty, banners, arms, army, autonomy . . . From any current Croat conservative aspect, it cannot be proved to the Croats that in Austria they did not live in the Kingdom of Croatia, and that they are today not a satrapy, ruled by the most anonymous chiefs of cabinet.
>
> Miroslav Krleža, 1933

The Frankists were a party of historical hubris. They were insolent enough to think of themselves as the only true Croats, which, in their terms, meant that they were uncompromised by any type of Yugoslavism or Serbophilia. As a result, divine Nemesis punished them forever to serve all outsiders—including the Serbians. It is commonly thought that the Frankists were nothing but a bunch of Habsburg chameleons, whose exclusive Croat nationalism was no more than a red herring, diverting attention from their cacodoxy. But though they had their share of scoundrels, they also had their saints. Their manner was so inimical to Hungarian supremacy that it attracted a lot of young rebels, who evidently paid little attention to Frank's insistence on an

38. Paver, *Zbornik gradje*, p. 410.

alliance with the Habsburg dynasty—a move that most Frankists regarded as an unwelcome but necessary tactic. Antun Gustav Matoš, the reigning prince of Croat bohemia, confessed that he regarded Frank as "one of those unbreakable Hebrews who gave prophets to Judea and the best liberals and democratic revolutionaries to Europe. I thought him our Gambetta and Disraeli, our first realistic politician . . . our only patriot who played political chess with his head and not with his heart, unlike the rest of us sentimental and soft Croats."[1] Indeed, Frank's cadets were not just crass informers ready to denounce every anti-Habsburg Serb or unitarist Croat to the authorities. The ranks of the Frankists also included such people as Vladimir Ćopić, a son of an Orthodox sexton from Senj, who became a leading Communist, Comintern instructor, and—before Stalin dispatched him—the commander of the Fifteenth International Brigade in Spain.[2]

The Party of Pure Right floundered after 1908 and was close to extinction at the time of Frank's death in 1911. The war gave the Frankists a new lease on life. They sounded the alarums of Serb regicide and offered themselves both to the court in Vienna and to the Hungarian leaders as the surest barrier to treason in Croatia-Slavonia. As late as June 1918, when every simpleton could see that the collapse of Austria-Hungary was imminent, the Frankist leaders secretly were urging that the HSK-dominated "Great Serb" Sabor be disbanded in favor of martial rule. "Only in such way can there be an end to the circumstances that have much worsened at this time and that could, at the moment propitious to the Great Serbs, lead to the grievous acts of sabotage on the Monarchy's southeast."[3] But, like the loyal snow-white crow that rushed to Apollo to inform him of Coronis's infidelity, the Frankists were turned black for their failure to do more. Their tragedy was the conviction that "working for the salvation of the Monarchy, they were *rebus sic stantibus* at the same time working for the salvation of Croatdom."[4]

The fury of the Frankists fell from them unawares as Austria left them in the lurch. On October 29, 1918, moments after the Croatian Sabor annulled all ties with Austria-Hungary and proclaimed the State of the Slovenes, Croats, and Serbs, the head of the Frankist parliamentary club informed the Sabor that the abolition of the *Nagodba,* the break with Hungary, and the unification of all the Croat lands into one state constituted the fulfillment of his party's program. As a result, he added, "the club of the [Pure] Party of Right in the Sabor will propose to the party's council . . . that the Party of

1. Antun Gustav Matoš, "Zašto odoh?," *Sabrana djela,* ed. Vida Flaker and Nedjeljko Mihanović, vol. 14 (Zagreb, 1973), p. 49.

2. Ivan Očak, *Vojnik revolucije: Život i rad Vladimira Ćopića* (Zagreb, 1980), pp. 25–26.

3. See the memorandum of Aleksandar Horvat and Ivica Frank in Većeslav Wilder, *Dva smjera u hrvatskoj politici* (Zagreb, 1918), pp. 83–84.

4. Dragutin pl. Hrvoj, "Proti izkrivljavanju historijske istine: Uspomene na saborske sjednice od 29. listopada 1918.," in Ante Pavelić, *Putem hrvatskog državnog prava: Članci, govori, izjave, 1918–1929* (Madrid, 1977), p. 23.

Right be dissolved. New age demands new programs and new party formations."[5]

The Frankists could only hide their heads. As vocal exponents of "hereditary Croat loyalty to the House of Habsburg" and the most persistent anti-Serbs, they had to expect blackballing and Pribićević's retribution. The victorious "grand traitors" threatened them with lynch courts and vowed to set them swinging from the lamp poles. Many Frankists, notably former Habsburg officers, preferred exile to insecurity and possibly violence. Some opted for Austrian citizenship, thereby swelling the ranks of Yugoslavia's first political emigration. Soon, however, the Frankists showed yet another fresh spurt of life. They issued an antiunification manifesto on December 2, 1918, charging that the Croat people and their legal representatives were not consulted on the unification with Serbia under the Karadjordjević dynasty. Instead of the imposed solution reached at Belgrade, the Frankists espoused the "unification of all Croat lands within a republican state in an alliance with the free, independent, and sovereign states of Slovenes, Croats, and Serbs," thereby displaying their newly devised republicanism as if it were the most ordinary doctrinal innovation for seasoned monarchists. Moreover, there was no longer any reference to the dissolution of the Frankist party. The Pure Party of Right aimed to help the Croats in finding the "right path toward their happiness, salvation, and progress, for which [the party] worked up to now and will continue to work in the future."[6]

Two days after the manifesto appeared, Grga Andjelinović, the Zagreb chief of police and a close associate of Pribićević, banned the Frankist daily *Hrvatska* (Croatia). Authorities also suspected the Frankists of having instigated the soldiers' protests that occurred on December 5 and immediately arrested many of their leaders, though without charge. The Frankists were exposed to new harassment after they protested the exclusion of their party from the interim parliament in Belgrade (February 27, 1919) and then promulgated the new party program (March 1, 1919), which called for a legal struggle on behalf of an independent Croat state.[7] Immediately after the issuing of these documents (the former was sent to the Paris Peace Conference), two Frankist leaders, Vladimir Prebeg and Josip Pazman, were arrested on Pribićević's orders, with the approval of the Belgrade cabinet.

The persecution of the Frankists was not exceptionally severe by the standards of the time, but it did much to maintain their nationalistic reputation in their preserves of urban northwestern Croatia. The Frankists sounded their new official name of Hrvatska stranka prava (HSP, Croat Party of Right) with a proud aspirate, though it did not gain them a tremendous

5. Dragoslav Janković and Bogdan Krizman, eds., *Gradja o stvaranju jugoslovenske države*, vol. 2 (Belgrade, 1964), p. 411.
6. Cited in Rudolf Horvat, *Hrvatska na mučilištu* (Zagreb, 1942), pp. 50–51.
7. Ibid., pp. 71–76, 68–69.

following. They won only 10,880 votes in the 1920 parliamentary elections, with two-thirds of that number coming from the counties of Zagreb and Modruš-Rijeka; the city of Zagreb alone contributed 30.52 percent of their total vote. They received only 21.23 percent of the total vote in Zagreb, however. Their best showing was in the small towns of nationally mixed Kordun and Banija (Slunj, 73.13 percent; Ogulin, 29.62 percent; Kostajnica, 26.46 percent; Dvor, 23.79 percent) and in the hinterland of Zagreb (Križevci, 35.21 percent; Zlatar, 32.29 percent). Their only district plurality was in the district of Slunj, which they took with 40.9 percent. (Perhaps appropriately, they polled 60.72 percent in Cetingrad, a township in Slunj located below the ruins of the Cetin castle, where the Croat estates elected Ferdinand the Habsburg as their king on New Year's day of 1527.)

Nonetheless, though their showing was far from spectacular, the Frankists undeniably appealed to a significant section of Croat intelligentsia and petite bourgeoisie. The executive leadership of the party in the summer of 1918 consisted of four lawyers, two priests (both also professors), an academic economist, and a self-made industrialist. The petit bourgeois character of the party is evident from the breakdown (in percentages) of the HSP's electoral candidates in 1920: lawyers, 33.77; other professionals, 10.39; priests, 10.39; craftsmen, 12.99; merchants, 2.6; landowners, 5.19; peasants, 24.68. For this reason the policy of the HSP was frequently called the "policy of Vlaška Ulica (Vlach Street)," an ironic reference to the historical (if in this case highly inappropriate) name of a petit bourgeois neighborhood of row houses and small shops, east of the main square in Zagreb. But when baited, the Frankists took the bait. "It is an eternal shame that in 1918 the Croat policy was conducted by the National Council and not by the Vlaška Ulica, [because in the latter instance] Croatia would today be free."[8]

It was, indeed, this very attraction they held for many in the intelligentsia and middling urban strata that made the Frankists something of a force to be reckoned with. The HSP very shrewdly did not attempt to compete with the HPSS in the countryside. Though peasants constituted nearly one-fourth of the HSP candidates in 1920, the HSP knew its political limitations. Radić, though he dismissed Josip Frank in 1908 as nothing but a "cunning and shameless Jewish fixer,"[9] united with the Frankists in the wartime Holy Alliance against the HSK, broke with them in April 1918, united with them again in 1921 within the Croat Bloc against centralism, and finally, in 1922, expelled them from it. So far as the Frankists were concerned, Radić was not "agile enough to chase the Serbs out of Croatia."[10] Only the Frankists could

---

8. Ante Pavelić, "Politika Vlaške ulice," in Pavelić, *Putem hrvatskog državnog prava*, p. 391.

9. Stjepan Radić, *Korespondencija Stjepana Radića*, comp. Bogdan Krizman, vol. 1 (Zagreb, 1972), p. 61.

10. Arhiv Hrvatske, Rukopisna ostavština Dr. Milana Šufflaya, Box 2: Kr. državno odvjetništvo u Zagrebu: Optužnica I.8248/1920., p. 69.

measure up to the task, but since they could hardly hope to accomplish it by relying on their own strength, they looked to the Frankist émigrés, who in turn hoped to lure powerful foreign patrons by misrepresenting themselves as a detachment of Radić's movement.

The history of the Frankist emigration is complex and must of necessity be reconstructed from sources that are often hostile. The anti-Yugoslav Croat émigrés who left for Italy, Austria, and Hungary in 1918–1919 included several important Frankists, among them Ivica Frank and Vladimir Sachs, both members of the Pure Party's executive. (Ivica, the surviving son of Josip Frank, was a Sabor deputy. He died in 1939.) These émigrés joined various exofficers and noncommissioned officers, notably Lieutenant Colonel Stjepan Duić, and a handful of former civilians, mainly police officials; among the latter Emanuel (Manko) Gagliardi, one of the most deceitful adventurers in the police service of the old regime, deserves special mention. This motley group convened in Graz in May 1919 and founded the Hrvatski komite (Croat Comité), a revolutionary organization dedicated to Croatia's secession from Yugoslavia.[11] The Comité removed to Vienna, and then, in March 1920, after Miklós Horthy's counterrevolutionary government was fully established throughout Hungary, installed itself in Budapest. With Hungarian support, the Comité started organizing the Croat Legion, a volunteer force that had been announced in November 1919. Recruitment by one device or another was among the displaced Austro-Hungarian prisoners of war of Croat nationality who were returning from Russia via Hungary or were stranded there during the chaos of Béla Kun's revolutionary regime.[12]

The Legion's headquarters were first in Kőszeg (Vas County) and later in Zalaegerszeg (Zala County), both conveniently close to the Yugoslav and Austrian frontiers. Leaflets and proclamations were smuggled into Yugoslavia with the aim of attracting additional volunteers. It is not clear how many men gathered under arms in Zalaegerszeg. Though the Comité's literature boasted of 300,000 volunteers, some of the Frankist leaders privately confessed to no more than eighty or ninety.[13] One young man, who was prosecuted by the Zagreb district attorney for his alleged ties with the Comité, testified in court that "there were six battalions in Zalaegerszeg and that each battalion had 800–900 men." He believed that the Legion's arms, including six batteries, each with four cannon, came from Italy, and that many of those legionnaires who came directly from Yugoslavia were recruited under false pretenses.[14]

---

11. In Gagliardi's version, the Comité was founded somewhat earlier in Vienna. Gagliardi claims that the initiative was his and that at the time Frank had not yet emigrated from Croatia. Manko Gagliardi, *Istina o hrvatskom emigrantskom revolucionarnom komiteu 1919–21: Odgovor na napadaje Stjepana Radića* (n.p., 1922), p. 6.

12. Arhiv Hrvatske, Rukopisna ostavština Dr. Milana Šufflaya, Box 2: Optužnica, pp. 18–21. For more on the Croat Comité see Josip Horvat, *Hrvatski panoptikum* (Zagreb, 1965), pp. 195–210.

13. Arhiv Hrvatske, Rukopisna ostavština Dr. Milana Šufflaya, Box 2: Optužnica, p. 69.

14. Ibid., p. 28.

The Croat Legion was commanded first by Major Gojkomir Glogovac and later by Captain Josip Metzger, one of the stars of the perplexing "Diamantstein Affair," uncovered by the Zagreb police in July 1919. Alfred Diamantstein, an emissary of Béla Kun, was sent to Zagreb to serve as a liaison with the local Communists, notably Vladimir Ćopić, himself a former Frankist. Diamantstein and Ćopić were in touch with Metzger, then on active duty in the Thirty-fifth Infantry Regiment in Zagreb, who directed an extensive network of military conspirators ready to begin a mutiny against the established order. The plot was uncovered after its principals succeeded in fomenting a good deal of trouble. Diamantstein then betrayed the group's secrets under torture and agreed to testify against Ćopić, Metzger, and the rest. Though acquitted by the court, Metzger fled to Hungary and joined the Croat Comité, vowing his speedy "return to Zagreb, where he would fry Serbs in boiling oil."[15]

Metzger's willingness to allow himself to be used by both Kun and Horthy may have been, as some believed, an indication of an abnormal personality, but in serving two such contrary masters Metzger differed from the rest of the Comité men only in degree. From the beginning, the Comité was split into two factions. Ivica Frank pretended to a formal authorization from Stjepan Radić and advocated a Croat republic, which would be either independent or "would enter into an alliance with some foreign state."[16] In addition, Frank and Gagliardi maintained ties with Gabriele D'Annunzio, the madcap Italian poet-condottiere, whose private army was at that moment illegally occupying Rijeka and whose antics the Italian government coolly ignored.[17] According to Gagliardi, the Italian government also financed the Comité. Duić, too, pretended to have Radić's sanction, but his orientation was quite different from that of Frank. Duić was a consistent legitimist and entered into covert ties with ex-Emperor Karl, who received Duić in Switzerland and financed some of his efforts. Emboldened by this backing, Duić naturally hearkened to the old Frankist trialistic scheme, though his ideal of a Danubian confederation under the Habsburgs envisioned a territory very unlike that of the defunct Monarchy. Duić, for example, spoke of a "confederation of the South Slavs in which all their historical traits would remain intact and which alone would determine the most important state affairs as common to all."[18] This was also the vision of Baron Stjepan Sarkotić, the former Austro-Hungarian commanding officer in Bosnia-Hercegovina and the leading figure of the Frankist emigration by the end of the 1920s, who kept his own ties with Prangins, Karl's refuge on Lake Geneva. Duić's ally Sachs first served D'Annunzio and then added to him yet another master, ex-King Nikola

15. Ibid., p. 96. For the most complete summary of the Diamantstein Affair see Očak, *Vojnik revolucije*, pp. 84–97.

16. Arhiv Hrvatske, Rukopisna ostavština Dr. Milana Šufflaya, Box 2: Optužnica, p. 19.

17. Gagliardi, *Istina o hrvatskom komiteu*, pp. 22–27.

18. Arhiv Hrvatske, Rukopisna ostavština Dr. Milana Šufflaya, Box 2: Optužnica, p. 95.

Petrović of Montenegro, in whose honor he changed his family name to Petrović, after adopting hypothetical Montenegrin citizenship.[19] Metzger was the most direct: "He lived in Vizvár, very close to the [Yugoslav] frontier . . . [and] distributed leaflets throughout Medjimurje, in which he urged the people not to let themselves be bludgeoned by the Serbs and [told them] that they would be better off under Hungary or Austria."[20] Gagliardi was the most original. He returned to Zagreb in 1922 and with Pribićević's subvention published an exposé of the émigré organization.

The Frankists always had a knack for attracting formidable individualists. One of the most imaginative and whimsical of their company, medievalist Milan Šufflay (1879–1931), expressed their Janus face, with one countenance displaying deep conviction, the other all harebrained scheming and abjection. Šufflay was arrested toward the end of 1920 for his alleged ties with the Croat Comité. He admitted writing a letter to Captain Ferenc Horvát, the head of Hungarian espionage in Budapest, but seemed to regard the whole affair as a trifling joke. His predicament was provoked, he thought, by his hostility to Yugoslavism. "Those who are acquainted with history know that the Yugoslav idea is not sufficiently dynamic. This idea is young and fragmentary. It is as nothing in comparison with the mighty Serb national consciousness, steeled in a century-long struggle for liberation. . . . And in Croatia itself, the Yugoslav idea is but a fragile, thin crust, under which boils the Croat national volcano. Only a small spur was needed to trigger off an eruption. And this has happened. The ballot boxes of Croatia-Slavonia [in November 1920] poured out Croatian history, the faith of the fathers, Western culture, classical belief in justice, carried on by the inherited cells of the hundreds of thousands of ethical Croat peasants."[21] Šufflay expressed the basic historicist conviction of Frank's party: the Croats were a formed historical community with an unalterable collective psyche. Their national biology could not be melted down in a superordinated amalgam, and certainly not by fiat.

As the party of historical memory, the Frankists naturally recognized not only the Croat individuality but also that of Croatia's South Slavic neighbors. The 1919 program of the HSP called for an independent Great Croatia made up of "all Croat lands (Croatia, Slavonia, Dalmatia with its islands, Rijeka with its whole district, Medjimurje, Prekomurje, Bosnia, Hercegovina, and Istria with its islands)." Moreover, should the "Slovene brothers, of their own free will, decide to join the Croat state, the Party of Right would support [this effort] with enthusiasm." The program also envisioned a loose alliance with Serbia, Montenegro, and Bulgaria.[22] And in a further departure from

19. Ibid., p. 96.
20. Ibid., p. 138.
21. "Veleizdajnički proces proti pravašima god. 1921.," *Hrvatska sloboda*, Jan. 28, 1925, p. 2.
22. "Program Hrvatske stranke prava (HSP) godine 1919.," in Pavelić, *Putem hrvatskog državnog prava*, pp. 71–72.

Frankist tradition, these partners of Croatia were chosen on the basis of "Slavic reciprocity," though it is perhaps more useful to note that each of these lands was recognized as having a distinct state tradition. In the Croat case, that tradition was expressed in the call for the restoration of "Tomislav's state," after the ruler of the united tenth-century Croat kingdom, which, however, would be a republic, though directed by the traditional Sabor and Ban. The respect for the bygone traditions of Croat nobles was a curious but important feature of this petit bourgeois party that was "both bourgeois, and peasant, and working-class," and no one in the party exemplified it better than Dr. Milan pl. Šufflay de Othrussewecz, the gentleman historian, who was a master at summoning the spirits of old.

The spirit of gentry traditionalism enabled the Frankists to believe that they alone defended Croat statehood: "The Habsburgs and Austria and Hungary could have vanished beyond saving, but that should not have been allowed to happen to Zvonimir's [Croatian] kingdom. No acts and no remedies would have been too late to bring about its resurrection. Only the *men* were lacking! The Croat intelligentsia, poisoned with Yugoslavism, betrayed their people and covered themselves with eternal shame. They had the occasion and the means to resurrect Zvonimir's kingdom, but they chose not to do so. This is a fact, a historical fact, and all else is only idle, empty, and meaningless sifting and whitewash."[23]

But the Frankist Janus had another face. The old mnemonists so despaired of effecting any changes in the position of Croatia and became so despondent over the poor prospects of popular revolution under Radić's leadership that their unquestionable dedication to Croat independence assumed unnatural and self-destructive forms. Šufflay, for example, was pleased at the chance of making Croatia an "international object" and hoped that the "foreign components would correspond to the Croat fighting line."[24] The ties of the Croat Comité were already revealed. Moreover, some of the exiles' combinations would have produced anything but the resurrection of Tomislav's Croatia. One such agreement, concluded with D'Annunzio's representatives in Venice (July 5, 1920), called for an independent and neutral Republic of Croatia that would include only the old Habsburg Croatia-Slavonia, without some salients around Rijeka. The agreement proposed an "autonomous" Republic of Dalmatia (without the islands of Rab, Palagruža, and Vis, and the Bay of Kotor, which were to be turned over to Italy and independent Montenegro, respectively). Truncated Dalmatia could join Croatia upon a referendum, but, in any case, the cities of Zadar, Šibenik, Split, Trogir, and Dubrovnik would remain *perpetuamente autonome*.[25] A slightly different

23. Spoken by Karlo Bošnjak, a member of the Frankist leadership, and cited in "Predsjednici Hrvatske stranke prava iza smrti Otca Domovine Dra Ante Starčevića," ibid., pp. 549–550.
24. Arhiv Hrvatske, Rukopisna ostavština Dr. Milana Šufflaya, Box 2: Optužnica, p. 4.
25. Giovanni Giurati, *Con D'Annunzio e Millo in difesa dell' Adriatico* (Florence, 1954), pp. 223–226.

version of this plan was outlined in what was perhaps a related agreement; in addition it envisioned the independent republics of Bosnia-Hercegovina and Vojvodina (with Srijem). Under the plan, Hungary was to receive Medji-murje and a "piece of Bačka," and Vojvodina was to be placed under the sovereignty of Bavaria, because "most of [Vojvodina's] population was German."[26]

In 1926 Miroslav Krleža assessed the balance of the Croat struggle against the Belgrade regimes as a replay of an ancient motif, which a papal legate, writing in Buda in 1526, the year when the Croat estates started pursuing the Habsburg candidate for the Croatian throne, called *trovarsi altro Signore* (searching for a new master). In Krleža's sardonic view, "Croatdom is searching for somebody to submit to, somebody to sign a political agreement with, so that it can rebel against that political agreement for another four hundred years. . . . If it is indeed true that history is the instructress of life, then it is likely that the Croats will succeed in breaking their so-called Agreement of 1918 some time around A.D. 2228 and will then sign a new political agreement with some new, as yet unknown Signore, against which they will fight until A.D. 3228."[27]

The Frankists fitted this exaggerated moral allegory all too well. They preferred almost every alternative to the "Serb Moloch" and to what they saw as the moderation of "false prophets" (Radić). But they had no real strategy of their own and for the most part only played at revolution. Šufflay "liked semihumorous situations" and signed his letter to Captain Horvát in invisible ink (in fact, lemon juice) with a "ligature of letters *S* and *F*, that is, of Sinn Fein." He foresaw no resistance from Pašić should the Croat deputies proclaim independence, but, "in case our estimate is wrong, there remains, after the legal break, the struggle according to the Irish method."[28] Ivica Frank and Gagliardi contemplated a general cataclysm, whereby Yugoslavia would be attacked by émigré armies of Croats, Montenegrins, and Macedonians, as well as by Bavarians, Albanians, Bulgars, Hungarians, Styrian peasant legions (the *Bauernkommando* of Dr. Brodman), and, presumably, Italy.[29] To this effect they signed an agreement with D'Annunzio's representatives, preparing a "mouvement offensif général pour occuper tout le territoire serbe," which was to commence in August 1920.[30] These were idle fancies. In 1925, the HSP in effect executed a turnabout. It entered into negotiations with Pašić, whereby the Frankists would join the Radical party as its autonomous Croat section. In connection with the millennium of

---

26. Arhiv Hrvatske, Rukopisna ostavština Dr. Milana Šufflaya, Box 2: Optužnica, pp. 60–62.
27. Miroslav Krleža, "Nekoliko riječi o malogradjanskom historizmu uopće," in *Deset krvavih godina*, vols. 14-15 of *Sabrana djela* (Zagreb, 1957), pp. 102–103.
28. Arhiv Hrvatske, Rukopisna ostavština Dr. Milana Šufflaya, Box 2: Optužnica, p. 4.
29. Ibid., p. 60.
30. Giurati, *Con D'Annunzio*, pp. 221–222.

Tomislav's kingdom (1925), the plan also called for the crowning of Aleksandar in Zagreb as the legitimate Croat king. According to an editorial in an HSP organ, all the Croat parties except HSP betrayed Croatia. The only way to prevent total debacle was to reach an agreement with the most Serbian of parties.[31] *La altrissima Signora.*

The abortive negotiations between the HSP and Radicals were inauspicious. The principal go-between was Manko Gagliardi, who was drawing on his old Frankist ties. The chief negotiator on the Frankist side was Ante Pavelić (1889–1959), a rising Zagreb lawyer and politician.[32] Nothing came of these talks, though in 1926 Šufflay, on his own, tried to establish a party of Croat Radicals, whose aim was "organically to harmonize" the differences in the "national memories" of Serbs and Croats. By the time of Radić's assassination in 1928, Pavelić had already established his links with Mussolini's government. He emigrated to Italy after the beginning of Aleksandar's personal dictatorship in 1929 and, exploiting the bitterness that the Yugoslav dictatorship provoked in Croatia, founded the *Ustaša* (Insurgent) movement, dedicated to wresting Croatia from under Belgrade's sway. These were the dark years of police terror and Ustaša counterterror. Gentle Šufflay was among the first victims. He fell on a pavement in Zagreb in February 1931, his head cracked like an almond shell with an iron rod wielded by a police agent. Somewhat later, in October 1934, King Aleksandar was assassinated in Marseilles by a Macedonian revolutionist leased to the Ustaša organization. In April 1941, following the Italo-German occupation of Yugoslavia, Slavko Kvaternik, Ivica Frank's brother-in-law, proclaimed the establishment of the Independent State of Croatia. Soon thereafter, Ante Pavelić assumed the title of Poglavnik (chief) of this newly founded Axis ally. Ivica Frank did not live to see this day. He died in Budapest in 1939, a lonely and forgotten exile, still annoyed at Pavelić for involving Eugen Dido Kvaternik, Frank's nephew, in the Marseilles assassination. Would Frank have been surprised to learn that, as far as Dalmatia was concerned, the territorial delineations that his pepole reached with D'Annunzio in 1920 were more favorable to the Croats than those reached between Italy and Pavelić in 1941? Among the least mourned victims of Pavelić's dictatorship was Manko Gagliardi, executed by a firing squad in 1942.

The history of the Frankist party is a history of defeat. With Pavelić, whose aim was to show that the Croats need not show the other cheek, it turned into moral defeat. During the 1920s, the Frankists remained in the backwaters of the Croat national movement, ready to exploit Radić's

---

31. Hrvoje Matković, "Veze izmedju frankovaca i radikala od 1922–1925," *Historijski zbornik*, vol. 15 (1962),pp. 41–59. See also Zvonimir Kulundžić, "O vezama frankovaca i radikala i od god. 1918. do 1941.," ibid., vol. 17 (1964), pp. 311–317.
32. On Pavelić see Bogdan Krizman, *Ante Pavelić i ustaše* (Zagreb, 1978).

eventual compromises with the Belgrade authorities, and in turn exploited by the Radicals whenever it suited the latter to pressure Radić. Despite the importance of the Croat national question, the Frankists proved in the end to be far less a threat to the centralists than to the moral standing of the Croat national movement.

Montenegrin Greens

Braćo moja i junaci,
Dan stravični sjutra sviće;
Ovi Božić Crna Gora
S krvlju brackom proslaviće.

My brothers and brave heroes,
A dreadful day will shine tomorn;
This Christmas will Montenegro
Celebrate with fraternal blood.

From a 1919 Montenegrin ditty

The national movements in Yugoslavia's southern borderlands shared many characteristics with the Frankists, but they were more serious, popular, and effective. This was especially the case with Montenegro, which, just like Croatia, possessed a powerful state tradition. Unlike the Croats, however, the Montenegrins also had a strong tradition of not just belonging to, but indeed leading the Serb people, something that mitigated their feeling of separateness.

Montenegro's prestige in the Serb world was not by dint of wealth. It is said that on the eve of a certain battle Prince Nikola Petrović-Njegoš (1841–1921) told his warriors, "Montenegrins, what we have to defend can be measured with three fingers." They responded in unison, "We shall defend as always."[1] In 1921 Montenegro numbered only slightly less than 200,000 people, living on some 3,733 square miles, or 54 per square mile, the lowest population density in Yugoslavia. But this stone wilderness, whose forests, meadows, and wildlife had been ravaged almost to nothing over the centuries by hungry highland clans and their herds, could not sustain even that number. The only agriculture possible was limited to a few lowland karst fields, where a bit of wheat and maize grew alongside collards, chard, and potatoes. Grapes and orchards worthy of the name could be found only in the *nahiye* of Crmnica and in Metohia, the latter having been won by Mon-

---

1. Djordje Karadjordjević, *Istina o mome životu* (Belgrade, 1969), p. 25.

tenegro in 1912. There was no industry, few crafts, and little trade. Towns were small and new. Of the ten principal market towns, five (Pljevlja, Plav, Gusinje, Djakovica, Peć) became Montenegrin only in 1912 and had predominantly Muslim population. Four others (Nikšić, Bar, Ulcinj, Podgorica) had fallen to Montenegro in 1878, and their predominantly Muslim population was only gradually losing ground to the Montenegrins. Only one town, Cetinje, Montenegro's capital—Little Zion—which grew around the monastery of its Orthodox metropolitans, could boast of a modest urban tradition that was genuinely Montenegrin; yet, Cetinje's first secular dwelling was an inn for travelers built in 1847.

Before the beginning of the nineteenth century Montenegro was no more than a community of embattled tribes presided over by the metropolitans of Cetinje, who generally belonged to the Petrović branch of the Herkalović clan in the tribe of Njeguši. Montengrin territory consisted of four small districts (Turkish *nahiyes*), the most important of which was the *nahiye* of Katuni with its nine tribes (Cetinje, Njeguši, Ćeklići, Bjelice, Cuce, Čevo, Pješivci, Zagarač, Komani). This Montenegro proper, or Old Montenegro, had been de facto independent of the Turks since the Peace of Požarevac (Passarowitz, 1718), though elements of self-rule existed in this and the adjoining Ottoman areas of eastern Hercegovina and the Brda (Highlands) since the early days of Turkish rule. For one thing, the people of these lands were treated as unsubjected *filuricis,* that is, as free Vlachs, who once a year paid only their Vlach Ducat of *filuri* (Turkish for florin), a fixed tax upon every hearth, which did not increase with the wealth or size of a household and, moreover, exempted the taxpayer from the usual poll tax and other levies paid by the Christian subjects of the Porte.[2]

Though the privileges visited upon the highland herdsmen were meant to stem the discontent in these poor, but strategically vital, pivots on the Venetian frontier, the consequences drawn from them were far from the expected. Not only did the *filuricis* fail to conform to the ethos of loyal dependents, but they increasingly accepted the remissions of regular Ottoman taxes as no more than their right. And when the local Ottoman feudatories, at the end of the sixteenth century, attempted to cut back some of these Montenegrin privileges, they provoked a struggle for "liberty that was not given to others" and in time a complete rejection of Ottoman power.

As time went on, the unremitting struggle of the Montenegrin and highland tribes against any Ottoman design intended to curtail the privileges of the mountaineers was strengthened by the growth of native institutions of self-defense. To some extent, the Turkish policy of light taxation contributed to the institutional bonds of unity: that policy had a retardant effect on social differentiation and kept the tribe the strongest institution of Montenegrin

---

2. Branislav Djurdjev, "Filuridžije," *Enciklopedija Jugoslavije* (Zagreb, 1958), vol. 3, p. 339.

resistance. The tribe in Montenegro did not necessarily imply consanguineous ties. Though the rudiments of tribal organization existed at least as early as the fifteenth century, perhaps even earlier, the Montenegrin and highland tribes did not assume their final contours until the eighteenth century (see map 3-3). So strong was this code of tribal solidarity, based on social ownership and internal hierarchy of valor, that the Montenegrins were able to hold their own against the Turks in centuries of mutual ravage. The territorial and customary affirmation of the tribes in turn strengthened conciliar power. Every adult male was obliged to participate in the deliberations of his tribal council, as well as in the common council (Zbor), the supreme administrative body of the land. To be a Montenegrin was to be a councillor; when the tribal chieftains, acting on the authority of the Zbor, decided in 1749 to introduce the men of the Ridjani tribe into their midst, it was noted that the newcomers were accepted "into the Zbor of Montenegro and were thereafter Montenegrins forever."[3]

The institutions of tribal order, however, were offset by the lawless majesty of Montenegrin blood feuds, which greatly limited the effectiveness of the common stand against the Turks. The Zbor had neither the desire nor the real power to regulate intertribal relations; only an institution of spiritual compulsion had authority in this matter. Temporal title thereby became the fitting adjunct of churchly ministry. The ablest of the Petrovićes fulfilled this mission in two ways. First, they constantly nudged the tribes toward a construction of a supratribal polity, the state, and, for their own part, themselves assumed an increasingly larger role as political intermediary. Second, they fashioned the ideology of Montenegrin merit which simultaneously exalted the elements of Montenegrin self-rule (unique among the Orthodox South Slavs long before Montenegro became a real state) and underscored Montenegro's ties with the Serbian church and people. Metropolitan Danilo, for example, who officiated in 1700–1735, insisted on the extermination of Montenegrins who still adhered to Islam, thereby superseding the old tribal code of protecting all members of a tribal fraternity by a superior national concern. Stories of Danilo's carnage, said to have commenced on Christmas Eve in 1709, survived in folk memory (if not in documents) and were later (1847) apotheosized in "The Mountain Wreath," the epic poem by Metropolitan Petar II (popularly Njegoš), who viewed it as a milestone of Montenegro's struggle for independence, marking the decisive break with the Turks. But Danilo himself also had a wider claim. As can be gathered from one of his self-chosen appellations—the commander (*vojevodič*) of Serbian land—Danilo's ambition was expansive, with Montenegro forming the center of Serb power.

3. Gligor Stanojević, "Crna Gora početkom XVII vijeka," in *Od početka XVI do kraja XVIII vijeka*, vol. 3, pt. 1, of *Istorija Crne Gore*, ed. Milinko Djurović et al. (Titograd, 1975), p. 93.

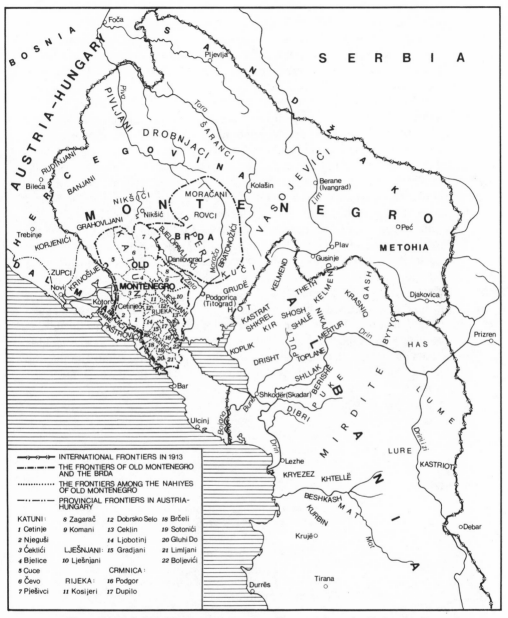

KATUNI:
1 Cetinje
2 Njeguši
3 Ćeklići
4 Bjelice
5 Cuce
6 Čevo
7 Pješivci

8 Zagarač
9 Komani

LJEŠNJANI:
10 Lješnjani

RIJEKA:
11 Kosijeri

12 Dobrsko Selo
13 Ceklin
14 Ljobotinj
15 Gradjani

CRMNICA:
16 Podgor
17 Dupilo

18 Brčeli
19 Sotonići
20 Gluhi Do
21 Limljani
22 Boljevići

Legend:
- INTERNATIONAL FRONTIERS IN 1913
- THE FRONTIERS OF OLD MONTENEGRO AND THE BRDA
- THE FRONTIERS AMONG THE NAHIYES OF OLD MONTENEGRO
- PROVINCIAL FRONTIERS IN AUSTRIA-HUNGARY

3-3. The tribes of Old Montenegro, eastern Hercegovina, the Brda, the Bay of Kotor, and northern Albania

273

There were in fact two Montenegrin traditions, reflecting the area's divided history and rigid Manichean mores, about the proper place of Montenegro among its neighbors. The native—intensely Montenegrin—tradition, which maintained the separate heritage of Doclea/Zeta, permitted the Montenegrins to suffuse themselves in the genial warmth of self-being. Vasilije Petrović, for example, who officiated between 1750 and 1766 as coadjutor to Metropolitan Sava, tried to convince Maria Theresia that "since the time of Alexander the Great [Montenegro] has been a pure virgin, a separate Republic . . . [over which] rules her metropolitan."[4] The tradition of Montenegrin self-centeredness did not, however, prevent reciprocity with the Serbians, though on the basis of a veritable worship of Montenegro. On the contrary, the Serb tradition percolated down to the consciousness of most ordinary herdsmen by a system of mnemonic devices by which the church continually admonished the Montenegrins to remember the glories of the Nemanjić state. Time and again, Montenegrin rulers took the lead in attempting to restore the medieval Serbian empire. From 1807, when Metropolitan Petar I (Saint Petar, ruled 1782–1830) tried to persuade General Budberg, the Russian foreign minister, to create a new Slavo-Serbian empire by joining the Bay of Kotor, Dubrovnik, Dalmatia, and Hercegovina to Montenegro and some of its highland neighbors, the Petrović dynasty constantly harped on the theme.[5] Njegoš admired Karadjordje above the other heroes of early nineteenth-century warfare because the "hero of Topola" restored to life the leonine hearts of a people unaccustomed to chivalry, thereby "breathing life into the soul of the Serbs."[6] And Prince Nikola prepared for the reconquest of Kosovo by singing of Serbia's imperial castles that were lying in ruins beyond the hills of Montenegro:

> Onamo, 'namo, za brda ona,
> Gdje nebo plavi savija svod,
> Na srpska polja, na polja bojna,
> Onamo, braćo, spremajmo hod!
>
> . . . . .
>
> Onamo, 'namo, za brda ona,
> Milošev, kažu, prebiva grob! . . .
> Onamo! . . . Pokoj dobiću duši
> Kad Srbin više ne bude rob.
>
> Over there, o'er there, beyond those hills,
> Where the heavens bend the blue sky,

4. Stanojević, "Put mitropolita Vasilija Petrovića u Rusiju," ibid., p. 327.

5. For a version of this proposal, as transmitted by Simeon Ivković, a Montenegrin archimandrite, see S. A. Nikitin and Vaso Čubrilović, eds., *Pervoe serbskoe vosstanie 1804–1813 gg. i Rossiia: Kniga pervaia: 1804–1807* (Moscow, 1980), pp. 356–357.

6. Petar II Petrović-Njegoš, *Gorski vijenac* (Belgrade, 1947), p. 39.

Toward Serb fields, toward martial fields,
Over there, brothers, let's prepare to go!

. . . . .

Over there, o'er there, beyond those hills,
One can find, they say, Miloš's tomb! . . .
Over there! . . . My soul will receive its rest
When the Serb no longer will be a slave.[7]

It cannot be claimed that either Montenegrin tradition failed to contribute
its share toward the building of a strong Montenegrin state, least of all the
tradition of Montenegrin separateness. And though the Serb tradition contained the seeds of Montenegrin abasement, since Montenegro could not
realistically hope to unite all the Serbs around Cetinje, this was not obvious
during the country's expansive nineteenth and early twentieth centuries. But
as the new highland tribes fell under the increasingly stronger rulers of
Cetinje, first the Bjelopavlići, Piperi, Rovci, and Moračani under Petar I,
then the Bratonožići, Kuči, and Grahovljani under Prince Danilo (ruled
1851–1860), Montenegro expanded into territories where the tradition of
Montenegrin specialness and statehood did not obtain. With Prince Nikola,
Montenegro more than quadrupled its territory. By 1878, when the powers at
the Congress of Berlin finally recognized Montenegro as an independent
state, it bulged into Old Hercegovina to embrace the tribes of Banjani,
Nikšići, Šaranci, Drobnjaci, Pivljani, and a large number of Rudinjani. In
the east and south it expanded into the lands of the Vasojevići, the most
numerous highland tribe, and then along both shores of Lake Skadar, gaining, too, the coveted exit to the Adriatic on the littoral from Bar to the south
of Ulcinj. In the Balkan wars of 1912–1913 it conquered southern Sandžak,
Metohia, Plav, Gusinje, and more Skadar shoreline. For the first time, the
Montenegrins ruled not only over a large body of hostile Muslims, many of
them Albanians, but also over highland tribes with a tradition of strong ties to
Serbia. Karadjordje stemmed from one of the Vasojevići clans, Vuk Ka-
radžić from the Drobnjaci, Protopresbyter Mateja Nenadović, Pop-Luka
Lazarević, and Stanoje Glavaš from the Banjani, and Stojan Čupić from the
Pivljani, to mention only some of the leading figures from the age of Serbian
Revolution.

Princes Danilo and Nikola were also the first secularized rulers of Montenegro. This was the will of Njegoš, the last episcopal prince, who wanted
to deprive the Turks of the argument that Montenegro was just another
Ottoman province and its metropolitans only an ecclesiastical force to which
accrued the political loyalty of the tribesmen. With the help of Russia, which
recognized Danilo's title of "Prince and Ruler (Gospodar) of Montenegro

7. Nikola I Petrović-Njegoš, *Pjesme* (Cetinje, 1969), pp. 45–46.

and the Brda,'' the Petrovićes sought to obtain international recognition and internally pursued the course of centralization and absolute government. The Law Code of Prince Danilo (1855) established the supreme power of the prince, strengthened civil jurisprudence (as opposed to the old tribal common law), and generally abolished tribal self-rule. Conciliar power, which was eroding over the course of previous reigns, largely ceased to exist under Danilo's brutal blows. The "modernization" of Montenegro was completed under Prince Nikola, who presided over a society in the process of steady class differentiation. During Nikola's reign, as the tribes uniformly lost their social and clan integrity, the privileges of the tribal chieftains, who were increasingly reduced to the position of prince's agents in their home areas, and of the administrative-bureaucratic apparatus grew steadily. The prince, his kin, and his allies among the headmen profited from the introduction of the same market economy that denied most Montenegrins the solace of solidarity, though not necessarily the contentment of material progress.

Prince Nikola was himself a product of the contradictory new age. On the one hand, in the ancient patriarchal way, he was sufficiently acquainted with every notable Montenegrin to know each one's strengths and weaknesses. He dispensed his personal justice under an ancient elm tree in Cetinje and occasionally jotted down disagreeable comments, which betrayed familiarity and rough insight, about his supplicants. The state's Book of Petitions is full of Nikola's glosses: "And all that you have guzzled, you sot?!" (on a petitioner requesting relief); "Give him a passport as big as his highest position" (on a malcontent requesting exit papers).[8] Though addicted to medals, a modern weakness that he shared with most of his male subjects, he never gave up the Montenegrin national costume for a smart uniform. He genuinely believed in the old warrior code and until fairly advanced age personally led his men in battle. And although certainly not equal to Njegoš in poetic inspiration, Nikola, too, cultivated bardic leadership. He composed poems honoring each tribe, even the ones he persecuted—praise to the virtue of adversary being required by the nobility of conduct.

On the other hand, Nikola was the first Montenegrin ruler to have received a formal education, which, for a young man of his generation, meant foreign schooling (Trieste, Paris). Unlike most of his countrymen, he was worldly wise and a shrewd businessman, though always on the lookout for treasure and prestige. One notable itinerant painter, who was exasperated by the "old actor's" mercurial temperament, described Nikola as having an "agreeable and alluring little smile on his lips, so that even the devil from hell would be stuck fast to his glue."[9]

Nikola's great ambition was to be accepted in the courts of Europe. In this he succeeded to a degree inconceivable for a parvenu Balkan dynasty. But though the court of Cetinje was parodied in the operettas of the period (for

8. Vladimir Dvorniković, *Karakterologija Jugoslovena* (Belgrade, 1939), p. 890.
9. Vlaho Bukovac, *Moj život* (Belgrade, 1925), p. 127.

example, in Franz Lehár's *Die lustige Witwe,* 1905), Nikola managed to marry off most of his formidable array of offspring (seven daughters and three sons) to some of the most illustrious royal and princely houses. Two of his elder daughters, Milica and Stana (the ill-starred "Montenegrin sisters," who introduced Rasputin to Empress Alexandra), were married to two Romanov grand princes. His daughter Ana was married to a Battenberg, and Jelena to Victor Emmanuel III, the king of Italy. Although these alliances established Nikola as the "father-in-law of Europe," the marriage of his oldest daughter, Zorka, to Petar Karadjordjević in 1883, the first wedding that he arranged, was the most fateful of all.

By royal standards it was a penny wedding. Petar was a middle-aged émigré, only three years younger than Nikola, without much prospect of ever sitting on the throne of Serbia. Prince Milan Obrenović, who, with the backing of Vienna, had just proclaimed himself the king of Serbia (1882), was not pleased with Nikola's new position of an in-law to the Karadjordjević pretender. But Nikola had his own score sheet. He wanted to be seen as the "First Serb," the protector of a kindred dynasty that, unlike the Obrenovićes, rejected collusion with Austria-Hungary. He set up his new son-in-law with the stronghold and means for his operations, thereby garnering for himself and Montenegro the credit of Piedmont in Pan-Serbianism.

At this point, Nikola's reach for primacy in the Serb world, the acting out of Montenegro's Serb tradition, did not threaten, but, indeed, celebrated, the native tradition of Montenegrin self-centeredness. By way of example, three of Petar's surviving children, Prince Djordje and the future King Aleksandar among them, all of them born in Cetinje to a Montenegrin princess, were regarded as non-Montenegrins by their Petrović kin. As Djordje remembered, after one squabble over this matter, Prince Nikola took it upon himself to explain how things stood to his young grandchild. "Come—he said—I shall tell you about Serbs and Serbia. You will be proud that you are a Serb, just as if you were a true Montenegrin."[10] After 1903, however, the Montenegrin spirit could no longer animate the air of conscious superiority, or at least not to the same degree. Petar and his children, who had left Cetinje for good after Princess Zorka's untimely death in 1890, were no longer exiles but Serbia's new royal family, dedicated moreover to clear expansionist aims that boded no good for Montenegro's dynastic security or even its separate identity. It could no longer be assumed that a good Montenegrin was the best Serb, or even an acceptable Serb. In the words of Marko Daković (1880–1941), one of the leaders of Montenegro's Serbophile youth, "Montenegro became the stage of bloody conflicts, rebellions, protests, bombs, executions, chains, persecutions, of explicit collision between Serbdom and Montenegritude, between love of freedom and reaction."[11]

10. Karadjordjević, *Istina,* p. 50.
11. Marko Daković, "O padu Crnogorske Države i njene Dinastije," *Nova Evropa,* vol. 13 (1926), nos. 10–11, p. 319.

Montenegrin expatriates, who constituted almost half the country's population by the eve of First World War, especially the fair number of students who attended Serbian high schools and the University of Belgrade, had a great deal to do with the lessening of Montenegro's reputation and the spread of the sentiment that only a reactionary could be a loyal Montenegrin. They viewed Serbia for what is was, a rising democratic state that was superior to Montenegro in wealth, civilization, and technology, and took it as obvious that Montenegro ought to be more like Serbia, emulating Serbia's constitutional monarchy and parliamentary independence. It followed, too, that Montenegro had to take second place in the drive for Serb unification, which ought to be accomplished by Montenegro's accession to Serbia on Karadjordjević terms. Of course Nikola's position in Montenegro was entrenched, and the Club of Montenegrin University Youth in Belgrade, in which Daković and Jovan Djonović, the future Republican leader, pronounced the deciding word, began disseminating accusations that were calculated to injure the prince's reputation and prepare the ground for Montenegro's subjoining to Serbia. Openly or by oblique hints the youth movement accused Nikola of conducting a narrowly Montenegrin—as opposed to Pan-Serb—policy; it portrayed his interest as strictly dynastic and charged that his face-flattering of Serbia concealed the game of a backbiting dicer, indeed, of secret collusion with Serbia's chief enemy, Austria-Hungary. All these charges were taken up enthusiastically by the Belgrade press and nationalist organizations, and in various ways also by agencies of official Serbia.[12]

Prince Nikola seemed unable to meet the challenge. He toyed with reform, but only halfheartedly. Like Montenegro itself, he was caught in the evolving conflict between patriarchalism and modernity, between Montenegritude and Serbdom. In November 1905, exactly one day after the promulgation of the October Manifesto whereby Nicholas I proclaimed Russia's first constitution, Nikola announced a constitution for Montenegro. This concession, he readily admitted, "was not very generous, but was also not less than the conscious expectations [of Montenegrins]."[13] When a regular national assembly was convened in 1906, the proceedings were dominated by Nikola's domestic critics, who, influenced by his expatriate opponents, demanded that a "Serb policy be carried out in agreement with Serbia and in a direct and decisive manner."[14] The legislators even wanted the assembly to be officially called the Serb National Assembly of the Principality of Montenegro and wanted the capital to be moved to the interior, presumably to Nikšić, away from the prince's base in Cetinje and Old Montenegro.[15]

12. The framework for the discussion of this topic can be found in Danilo M. Radojević, "Problemi crnogorske historije oko prvoga svjetskog rata," *Kritika*, vol. 4 (1971), no. 16, pp. 65–87.

13. Cited in Nikola P. Škerović, *Crna Gora na osvitku XX vijeka* (Belgrade, 1964), p. 86.

14. Todor Božović and Jovan Djonović, *Crna Gora i napredni pokret* (Belgrade, 1911), p. 229.

15. Škerović, *Crna Gora*, p. 163.

Nikola's first reaction was to try and assimilate the opposition. The deputies critical of the regime, members of the Club of National Deputies, who formed the People's Party in early 1907 (popularly, the *klubaši*), were invited to form two successive cabinets (under Marko Radulović and Andrija Radović, November 1906 to April 1907). The expatriate student leaders, who were indicted for calumny and lese majesty, had the charges against them dropped by the Cetinje court in October 1906 at Nikola's behest. Their release spurred the rapid growth of opposition to the prince, and Nikola himself added fuel with his maudlin rebukes of real and imagined ingrates (he had the Karadjordjevićes in mind), which should have been left to solitary meditations. He harangued the student leaders with reminders that the "unification of Serbdom was his lifelong ideal" and that his "regime was no more than a patronal rule of a wiser 'brother, friend, father, superior, and voivode.'"[16]

Nikola soon realized that forbearance was not the best way to meet his opponents, but his efforts to stem the oppositional tide by repression were as unsuccessful and as badly handled as his attempts at cooptation. He deposed and hounded the *klubaši*, publicly denounced them in most vulgar terms, shut down their newspapers, promoted a new dynastic party called the True People's Party (popularly, the *pravaši*), and installed a loyalist premier (Lazar Tomanović). Moreover, in May and June 1908, an extraordinary court in Cetinje tried and sentenced a group of conspirators (many of their leaders like Daković and Djonović in absentia), who organized the smuggling of a supply of bombs to Cetinje with the aim of stirring up armed resistance to the regime. And in the fall of 1909 the high military tribunal in Kolašin handed down severe sentences (three executions were carried out) to a large group of conspirators who had planned an uprising among the tribes of Vasojevići, Bratonožići, and Kuči.[17]

All these measures had sufficient warrant. Serbian agents were clearly involved in both cases of conspiracy. Indeed, the bombs in the first case were procured from the Serbian arms factory in Kragujevac by a chain of plotters that involved military officers, members of the Black Hand. Yet the prosecution chose to demonstrate this in the worst possible way. Quite disreputable renegade Serbs, such as Austrian agent Djordje Nastić, testified at the Bombing Trial that Crown Prince Djordje of Serbia promised to finance the purchase of bombs that were to blow up his grandfather. In like manner, though members of the People's Party aided the conspirators (Nikola Mitrović, the principal figure in the Kolašin Affair was the author of the party's underground statute and the president of the party's covert central committee), Nikola used the trials as an opportunity to strike at the *klubaši* without

16. Jovan Djonović, *Ustavne i političke borbe u Crnoj Gori 1905–1910* (Belgrade, 1939), p. 97.

17. Detailed accounts of these trials can be found in Škerović, *Crna Gora*, pp. 269–428, 469–520. Among those sentenced to death in absentia at Kolašin was Puniša Račić, a fugitive high-schooler and Pašić's confidant, who assassinated Stjepan Radić and his colleagues in 1928.

exception. Andrija Radović (1872–1947), his former prime minister, as well as four other former ministers of the People's Party, were sentenced in the bombing trial—Radović to fifteen years—and in the course of the persecutions and trials of 1908–1909, Nikola managed to offend and estrange several important highland tribes, notably the Bjelopavlići (Radović's tribe) and Vasojevići. In the context of these damaging events, Nikola's decision to elevate Montenegro to the status of a kingdom and proclaim himself king (1910) appeared as self-serving and further evidence that his compass bearings were no longer reliable. The claims of his enemies and Serbian propaganda gained in trustworthiness: "Why should the Serbs have two kingdoms?"[18]

The ideology of Pan-Serbianism, to which King Nikola and most of his people subscribed to an eminent degree, left all the passes to Montenegro unguarded and open to Great Serbian penetration. In 1913, after the Turks were finally expelled from the Sandžak of Novi Pazar, Metohia, and Kosovo after the joint effort of two countries, Serbia and Montenegro expanded and, for the first time since their independence, established a common border of some two hundred kilometers in length. The tradition of Montenegrin priority in prowess had just been dealt some heavy blows as Montenegro lost more than half its army, of which a quarter (or approximately 7,500 men) was killed. Many Montenegrins demanded the immediate unification with Serbia and considered the "chaffering over frontiers between the two states as a purposeless, idle, and unpatriotic business."[19] Under the circumstances, the very existence of the Montenegrin state was seen as unnecessary. Tired and alone, shunned even by Russia, King Nikola resisted these demands only halfheartedly. He reprieved the offenders in the trials of 1908–1919, reconstructed his government, granted free elections at the end of 1913, which brought about a majority of the People's Party in the assembly, and in March 1914 initiated negotiations over a military, diplomatic, and financial union with Serbia.

The extreme pro-Serbian wing of the Montenegrin youth was not satisfied with the king's concessions, but their youthful enchantment with Serbia was shortly put to a test: after the Austro-Hungarian attack on Serbia in July 1914, King Nikola joined the war effort and appealed to his Montenegrins to follow in the footsteps of "two old Serb kings, so that we may suffer destruction and shed our blood for unity and golden liberty."[20] With government approval, Nikola, though he remained the commander-in-chief of the Montenegrin army, in August 1914 appointed General Boža Janković, the

18. Jovan Djonović, "Crna Gora u novoj Evropi," *Nova Evropa,* vol. 13 (1926), nos. 10–11, p. 303.
19. Škerović, *Crna Gora,* p. 586.
20. Ferdo Šišić, comp., *Dokumenti o postanku Kraljevine Srba, Hrvata i Slovenaca, 1914.– 1919.* (Zagreb, 1920), p. 7.

head of the Serbian military mission in Cetinje, as the chief of Montenegro's supreme staff, which, in addition to two Montenegrins, included another four Serbian officers.[21] The Montenegrin army was thereafter directed by Serbian officers, who themselves acted on orders from Pašić's cabinet. Thus it was soon evident that Serbian aims included subverting the authority of King Nikola and his government by making them appear disloyal in the eyes of Russia and other allies.

King Nikola did not help his cause by greedily attempting to extend Montenegro's territory into neighboring lands.[22] He had eyes on the whole of Hercegovina and the adjoining parts of southeastern Bosnia, the Adriatic littoral from the mouth of the Neretva to the mouth of Drin (with Dubrovnik and the Bay of Kotor), and most of northern Albania with Shkodër, which he especially coveted after the powers ordered his conquering army out of the city in 1913. But although Montenegrin officials affected astonishment at the suggestion that their plans for a Great Montenegro harmed the cause of Serbdom,[23] these plans, just as their almost identical antecedent which Metropolitan Petar I advanced in 1807, were a new attempt to assert precedence in Serb affairs. The Serbian government, quite as imperialistic, thwarted these ambitions by ordering the displacement of Montenegrin authorities from Goražde, Foča, and other towns of eastern Bosnia, which the Montenegrins occupied in 1914. Serbia was especially apprehensive that Italy, which was about to join the Allies, might aid Nikola's aspirations—hence its efforts to cajole the Allies with spurious proofs of Nikola's secret arrangements with Austria-Hungary and the systematic shortchanging of the Montenegrin army by its Serbian suppliers.[24]

21. On Montenegro's participation in the First World War see Velimir Terzić et al., eds., *Operacije crnogorske vojske u Prvom svetskom ratu* (Belgrade, 1954), and Novica Rakočević, *Crna Gora u Prvom svjetskom ratu* (Cetinje, 1969).

22. During the course of the war, there were three variants of King Nikola's territorial demands: first, by Grand Duchess Milica, Nikola's daughter and the consort of Grand Duke Nikolai Nikolaevich, to the tsar in April 1915; second, by King Nikola and his exiled government in Bordeaux to the Russian envoy in March 1916; third, by King Nikola in a memorandum to the Allied governments in September 1917. See Dragovan Šepić, *Italija, Saveznici i jugoslavensko pitanje, 1914–1918* (Zagreb, 1961), pp. 106, 178–179, 214, and map on p. 178.

23. Dimitrije-Dimo Vujović, *Ujedinjenje Crne Gore i Srbije* (Titograd, 1962), pp. 107–108.

24. Rumors of King Nikola's covert dealings with Vienna began with the bogus Secret Agreement of 1907 between Montenegro and Austria, which was composed in 1911 or 1912 by Radovan Perović (Tunguz-Nevesinjski), an expatriate writer hostile to the king, and then printed in Belgrade in 1912, through Vienna was listed as the place of publication. For a detailed analysis of this forgery and its role in the mounting campaign against King Nikola see Risto J. Dragićević, *"Tajni ugovor Crne Gore s Austrijom"* (Cetinje, 1968). Nikola's defenders have pointed out that, far from being disloyal to the Allies, the king and his government were themselves victims of disloyalty. According to these claims, Pašić expropriated Allied military aid to Montenegro, spending only 1.5 dinars per day for the materiel of every Montenegrin soldier, as opposed to 7 dinars per day for every Serbian fighting man, and also seized the remittances of Montenegrins in America to the Montenegrin Red Cross and diverted Russian arms that were intended for Montenegro. See P[etar] Plamenac, "Uzroci crnogorske kapitulacije," *Nova Evropa*, vol. 13 (1926), nos. 10–11, pp. 351–352.

In June 1915, after King Nikola, contrary to the wishes of General Janković, ordered the Montenegrin army to occupy Shkodër, Pašić sought Janković's resignation. But Colonel Petar Pešić, a Serbian officer who succeeded Janković as chief of the Montenegrin supreme staff, urged postponement of a confrontation with King Nikola, arguing that, "should our [Serbian] interests demand that Montenegro be brought into a hopeless situation, it would be better to use another pretext, and not the issue of Shkodër."[25] Pešić was particularly worried about the patriotic reaction of the Montenegrins, who were behind Nikola on this issue. But after the combined offensive of the Central Powers in the fall of 1915 broke the resistance of the Serbian army and forced its remnants into general withdrawal, restraint was no longer necessary. Though Nikola's forces loyally defended the line of Serbian retreat, Serbia had lost the war; the remnant of its army was not appreciably larger than the embattled Montenegrin forces, and Serbia's independence could only be restored in the event of an Allied victory, which was still not certain. It was therefore essential that Montenegro should not reap any benefits of precedence from these defeats. The Montenegrin state and dynasty had to be discredited by surrender and King Nikola propelled into exile without his army.

To accomplish this, Pešić concentrated Montenegrin forces in Hercegovina and the Sandžak, leaving Austro-Hungarian access from the Bay of Kotor, via the Lovćen massif, practically undefended. On December 28, 1915, claiming that the key outpost of Lovćen had already fallen to the enemy, Pešić succeeded in pressuring the reluctant King Nikola to sue for a brief ceasefire. The Austro-Hungarian side agreed, provided the Montenegrins laid down their arms and surrendered the Serbian forces in their country to the invaders. King Nikola demurred, claiming that the conditions were unacceptable. Three days later, again at the urging of Pešić and Pašić's cabinet, King Nikola finally sued for a separate peace. The Montenegrin soldiers, convinced that the king had betrayed them, started leaving their positions, and military chaos follows.[26] A decade later, General Pešić, who by that time had served as Yugoslavia's defense minister and chief-of-staff, defended himself against charges that he counseled Nikola to conclude peace with Vienna: "Did [my critics] stop to think of the situation that our whole people would havė had to face had not King Nikola sent that *dépêche* to Franz Joseph, and that in addition to the Serbian supreme command we also had the Montenegrin supreme staff at the Salonika front, and that upon the breach of that front and entrance to the Fatherland—besides King Petar there was also King Nikola?"[27]

In fact, King Nikola had expected nothing from Vienna. He left Cetinje in the middle of night on December 29. He rode with a small company, stop-

25. Cited in Terzić et al., *Operacije*, p. 23.
26. Plamenac, "Uzroci," pp. 360–366.
27. Petar Pešić, "Komandovanje u ratu," *Pravda: Dnevnik*, May 9, 1925, p. 2.

ping every few minutes to look back over the moonlit monuments of Montenegro's sacred history. In early January he left Montenegro for good and reached France via Shëngjin and Italy, establishing his government-in-exile first in Bordeaux and then Neuilly. In the meanwhile, Austro-Hungarian troops pushed toward Cetinje and Podgorica, entrapping the bulk of the Montenegrin army that was still in the Sandžak. All negotiations with Nikola's remaining ministers ceased, as Vienna imposed a special occupation regime on the defeated country. The rest of the war held only more reversals for Nikola's exiled government, which, thanks to the work of Serbian diplomats, was not favored by the Entente. Montenegro's peace initiatives, which Nikola no longer recognized, received the most negative interpretations.

In April 1916, Nikola engaged none other than Andrija Radović, his former prisoner, as his new prime minister. Radović proceeded to draw up a plan for the unification of Serbia and Montenegro, whereby Nikola would abdicate in favor of Regent Aleksandar, who would in turn be succeeded by Nikola's heir, Prince Danilo, and so on in alternate transmission of royal dignity. Nikola at first hesitated and then, with Italy's encouragement, put aside Radović's proposal. Radović, who in fact, coordinated his moves with Pašić, reiterated his plan and, upon Nikola's outright refusal, resigned. At this point Pašić started applying direct Serbian pressure on King Nikola. The Serbian leader influenced many notable Montenegrins against participation in Nikola's future cabinets and engaged Radović as head of the pro-Serbian Montenegrin Committee for National Unification, which was founded in Geneva in February 1917. Thereafter Pašić boycotted the exiled government of Montenegro, extending to Radović's committee the courtesy due Montenegro's legitimate representative. Nikola's position was further weakened by the overthrow of the Russian imperial government in February 1917. Though no Montenegrins were invited to participate in the conference that produced the Corfu Declaration, which in an offhand reference to Montenegro assumed its unification with Serbia, Radović's committee expressed its full agreement with the declaration, affirming the committee's conviction that "with this war Montenegro is ending its role as a separate Serb state."[28]

King Nikola was outmaneuvered. True, his ministers still in Montenegro tried, on their own authority, to obtain Austro-Hungarian support for a united Montenegro-Serbia, ruled by Nikola's son Mirko under Vienna's protection.[29] But try as Nikola did, he had little hope of countering Serbia. Pašić frustrated Nikola's attempts to mobilize the armed forces, made up of the few loyal Montenegrin units in exile as well as Montenegrin immigrants from

---

28. Šišić, *Dokumenti*, p. 100.
29. Novica Rakočević, "Politička aktivnost knjaza Mirka Petrovića u toku austrougarske okupacije Crne Gore," *Istorijski zapisi*, vol. 23 (1970), nos. 3–4, pp. 265–266.

North America. And Radović's committee, with Serbian aid, successfully recruited Montenegrin volunteers for the Serbian army, sometimes under provocative auspices. One unit, recruited in Canada, bore the name of Miloš Šaulić, an opposition leader who had allegedly been poisoned on Nikola's orders in 1904.[30] In October 1918, King Nikola came out for a "Yugoslav confederation, in which each [unit] will preserve its rights, religion, laws, and customs, and in which nobody will dare impose primacy."[31] This further stirred up the Serbian leaders. As one of them put it at the Geneva conference with the JO, "I would not hold [King Nikola's] past against him were he to hold by what is good today. But I have seen his last declaration, which is not ours, because he wants a confederation."[32] Nor did the JO avail the fading monarch. The exiled Croats and Slovenes feared upsetting Pašić on this issue and accepted his view that the question of Montenegro was an internal Serb matter.

For a time, Pašić's campaign against Montenegro caused no alarm among pro-Serbian Montenegrins, but the entrance of the Serbian army, made up in part of Montenegrin volunteers, into Montenegro in November 1918 brought a reaction. Before leaving for Montenegro, the commander of the Serbian troops was received by Regent Aleksandar who told him, "In your work in Montenegro do not be tenderhearted. King Nikola must be prevented from returning to Montenegro at all costs, even if we have to use extreme measures."[33] In fact, the Montenegrin irregulars and remnants of Nikola's army expressed friendship for the Serbians and fought alongside them against the retreating Austro-Hungarians. But though the Serbians showed great haste in demobilizing the Montenegrin troops, it was not immediately evident that they meant to do away with the Montenegrin state nor that King Nikola, who was denied access to his country by the French, would not be returning.

Nikola, meanwhile, was placing all his hope in his royal son-in-law in Rome, hoping to profit from Italy's occupation of Kotor and Bar and from Italian demands for a power condominium in Montenegro, from which Serbian troops would be excluded. Italian pressure and the possibility that the Allies might yet accept the exiled Nikola forced Pašić's hand. Serbian occupation officials and local partisans of Montenegro's unilateral unification with Serbia moved quickly to legalize Serbian rule over Montenegro and in the process displayed their intentions to the public gaze. Early in November 1918, men of Radović's committee carried out a campaign of sorts for the

30. Vujović, *Ujedinjenje*, p. 265.

31. Ibid., p. 176.

32. Vojislav Marinković, in discussion at Geneva Nov. 6, 1918, according to Trumbić's notes. Dragoslav Janković and Bogdan Krizman, eds., *Gradja o stvaranju jugoslovenske države*, vol. 2 (Belgrade, 1964), p. 501.

33. Cited in Vujović, *Ujedinjenje* p. 307.

election of deputies to the special Great National Assembly that was to decide on the future status of Montenegro. The election was public, indirect, proportioned to favor the partisans of unilateral unification with Serbia, and conducted under Serbian military scrutiny.[34] In Nikšić, for example, the votes were bought with the army's flour, and notices of the election were posted only after the voting was over.[35] And in Cetinje, the hotbed of opposition, the opponents of unilateral unification were jeered and withdrew from the polling place.[36] Their list of candidates was printed on green paper and the proponents of unilateral unification on white paper, leading to the later names of two Montenegrin camps, the *zelenaši* (Greens) and the *bjelaši* (Whites), which in a sense perpetuated the old divisions between the *pravaši* and the *klubaši*. For the moment, the Greens were overcome. The election of November 19 brought about a White majority for the Great National Assembly, which, on November 26, deposed King Nikola by a vote of 163 to 0, with three absent electors, and proclaimed the immediate unification of Montenegro and Serbia under the Karadjordjevićes.[37] The assembly set up a five-man executive national committee (three of whose members, Marko Daković among them, were sentenced in the Bombing Trial).

The Great National Assembly was held at Podgorica, away from Cetinje and the areas of greatest pro-Petrović sentiment in Old Montenegro. But in the *nahiye* of Katuni (especially in the tribes of Cetinje, Čevo, Bjelice, and Cuce), elsewhere in Old Montenegro, and even in the Brda (Moračani, Rovci, Piperi) and Montenegrin Hercegovina (Nikšići, Rudinjani), the decision of the assembly was understood as Serbia's annexation of Montenegro. But where the Green half of Montenegro nursed revenge against a burning shame, the Whites in the Brda (notably Bjelopavlići) and beyond (Vasojevići), and in Hercegovina (Drobnjaci, a part of Nikšići, and Grahovljani) celebrated effective Pan-Serbianism. Bipolar reactions represented historic divisions of Montenegro, though both orientations had adherents in every tribe. But whereas the Greens were mainly villagers, the Whites had practically all the townspeople, merchants, and craftsmen, most of the educated youth, and indeed, most of Montenegro's old administrative and military elite. Even the queen's brother, one of the five members of the executive national committee, belonged to their ranks, though not King Nikola's closest diehard supporters, such as Jovan Plamenac (1873–1944), a former minister of the interior, who personally supervised the prosecution in the Kolašin

34. For details on the electoral procedures see ibid., pp. 317–318.

35. Hoover Institution Archives, Charles W. Furlong Collection, Box 3: Outcard no. 283. Interview with Revolutionists in the Afternoon of Feb. 21st [1919] in the Mountains South of Nickich [*sic*].

36. Vujović, *Ujedinjenje* pp. 321–322.

37. Janković and Krizman, *Gradja*, vol. 2, 655–658.

Affair. In part by accident, in part by mnemonic power of Njegoš's "Mountain Wreath," the two halves of Montenegro clashed on Christmas Eve, just as in the days of Metropolitan Danilo.

At the very beginning of January 1919, Plamenac and other Green leaders stirred up the tribes to rebellion. By January 3 the Greens had besieged Cetinje and several other towns. Except at Cetinje, they were soon routed by the White militias and the Serbian army. At the capital, however, the numerically superior rebels held on against 887 defenders. The bloody battle began on January 6, Christmas Eve by the Julian calendar. Despite attempts at negotiations, fighting continued until Christmas morning. The rebels could not withstand the firepower of better-armed defenders, who also used artillery. With the lifting of the siege and the withdrawal of the Greens, who either surrendered or absconded to their tribal lands (or, like Plamenac, to the Italian zone of occupation), the rebellion collapsed. At Cetinje, sixteen Whites and Serbians fell in battle and sixty-three others were wounded.[38] Though the Greens had the support of the larger part of the people, they were not as organized and politically united as their opponents and apparently discounted the possibility of protracted insurgency, hoping instead to provoke Allied intervention by their armed demonstration. Moreover, they were irresolute, avoiding bloodshed wherever possible.[39] But instead of pressing their adversaries into a more reasonable stance, they merely provoked retribution, which grew into wholesale political terror.

Famine and turmoil followed in the wake of the Christmas rebellion. The Serbian authorities armed White youth detachments and set them upon Green villages, even when no collusion with the Green outlaws, or *komitas*, was apparent. The Whites, often aided by the gendarmes, did more looting and burning than pursuing. They stole livestock, destroyed beehives, burned houses, took hostages (often women and children), and sometimes executed prisoners without trial. They also committed many rapes and horrible atrocities, for example the flaying alive of two members of the Bulatović sept in the Rovci.[40] The Green *komitas* responded in kind. They burned and rustled, killed leading Whites, including members of the Great National Assembly, and attacked public buildings. Indeed, the situation in Montenegro from 1919 to the mid-1920s amounted to a state of war, as the insurgents commandeered trains, robbed banks, and fought pitched battles with the army and the Whites.[41] And though the Montenegrin Communists, themselves a detachment of Serbian-educated "youth," generally supported the Whites, there was even a Red form of Green insurgency, led by Dr. Vukašin Marković, an

38. Vujović, *Ujedinjenje*, pp. 362–364.
39. Ibid., pp. 367–369.
40. "Horrible Serbian Atrocities in Montenegro," *Montenegrin Press Bureau* (Rome), Sept. 19, 1920, pp. 2–3.
41. These actions are covered in some detail in Vujović, *Ujedinjenje*, pp. 469–520.

eccentric physician who joined the Bolsheviks in prerevolutionary Russia and returned to his native Piperi in 1921 to fight for a "free self-administration of Montenegro in a federation with Yugoslavia."[42]

In July 1919, the insurgents held a sort of congress in a mountain hideaway, the Ćeranića Gora, close to Nikšić. At this conclave, those who argued for a militant course prevailed, and, though there were probably never more than several thousand active outlaws at any one time, the authorities were aware that the new order was not popular. In January 1920, the army commander in Cetinje reported to Belgrade: "Today, in this district, the overwhelming majority of people, from children to old men, except for a third of the townspeople, are opposed to the [established] order."[43] In the absence of any national parties, electoral absenteeism in Montenegro was exceptionally high during the 1920 parliamentary elections. In two out of three electoral districts of Old Montenegro more than half of the eligible voters did not participate in the balloting. Of the tribes in the *nahiye* of Katuni, absenteeism was highest among the Cetinje tribe (50.38 percent), Ćeklići and Bjelice (48.18), and Cuce (45.64), which together were the most active base of Green insurgency. But though the police authorities were well aware that Montenegrin opposition stemmed from the initial "tampering with the sensitive cords of popular self-esteem, pride, and ambition," they only pointed to the mistakes that were made "in accepting the worst riffraff into the ranks of youth," called for weapons control and the resettlement of local officials, and urged "awakening the people's national consciousness."[44]

When informed about the Christmas rebellion at his headquarters in Neuilly, King Nikola expressed his confidence that Montenegro would "not be taken like a maiden without a dowry."[45] But despite the sharpness of popular opposition to the regime in Montenegro, the exiled monarch was hardly in a position to influence developments in his occupied kingdom. He had no international standing, the powers having decided that Montenegro's representation at the Paris Peace Conference would be settled once the situation in Montenegro had cleared up, nor did he have funds (he had even had to sell his diamond-encrusted baton of a Russian field marshal). True, Italy helped in transporting Montenegrin refugees, including the group Plamenac led out of the Christmas rebellion, who were shipped from Shëngjin in northern Albania to Gaeta and later moved to several other camps in Latium, Abruzzi, and Campania, where the Italians allowed and endowed the formation of

42. Dimitrije-Dimo Vujović, "Učešće dr Vukašina Markovića u oktobarskoj revoluciji i njeni odjeci u Crnoj Gori," *Prilozi za istoriju socijalizma*, vol. 5 (1968), pp. 490–514.

43. Cited in Vujović, *Ujedinjenje*, p. 504.

44. Gojko M. Žugić, "Javna bezbednost u Crnoj Gori," *Policija*, vol. 8 (1921), nos. 5–8, pp. 300–311.

45. Cited in Vujović, *Ujedinjenje*, p. 406.

Nikola's Montenegrin army.[46] The price of this assistance, however, was the almost total dependence upon Italy, a country that was not popular among the king's former subjects. The army in exile, which at its high point in August 1920 numbered 1,532 officers and men, was the chief resource of Italian intrigue that included the men of the Croat Comité, Albanians, and other enemies of Belgrade. Though some of these soldiers were sent on covert missions to Montenegro, the army in exile floundered after Italy settled its frontier disputes with Yugoslavia in the Treaty of Rapallo (November 1920) and agreed to liquidate the Montenegrin question, which meant the end of political and military support to the exiles.

Though Belgrade blamed King Nikola for most of its problems in Montenegro, the allegiance to the ex-king was not the principal source of the Green movement. Most Greens respected the king, but their first loyalty was to Montenegro's dignity. Most of them, in fact, were not opposed to a unification with Serbia, "but only befittingly," that is, on conditions of equality and the preservation of Montenegrin identity. Above all, the *zelenaši* were motivated by wounded patriotism. In a letter to the Serbian commander in Rijeka Crnojevića, the local head of the Green insurgents noted that "Montenegro, our Fatherland, had defended and safeguarded the torch of Serb freedom for six hundred years." Only the "Austro-Magyars" had succeeded in extinguishing that torch, and the Montenegrins awaited the day of liberation: "We greeted your [Serbian] arrival with great enthusiasm, thinking that you were coming as brothers to brothers, so that we should grasp each other's hand, kiss each other, and march embraced into our great Yugoslavia. . . . But you were insincere. You brought us Judas's silver pieces, to buy with them our dear Montenegro and turn her over as a dowry to the Karadjordjević king." As a result, the "whole Montenegrin people [*Crnogorski narod*], the people who honor their holy things, their traditions, their banner, and their sovereign rights," rose up in revolt.[47] The rights of the dynasty were not cited.

In their hierarchy of preferences, most of the insurgents probably preferred independent Montenegro, though not necessarily under Nikola's scepter. Failing this, like Nikola, they preferred a confederated South Slavic state, but not one ruled by the Serbian dynasty. A group of rebels who conferred with Major Charles W. Furlong, an American intelligence officer, explained it in the following way: "[The insurgents] said that if there is going to be a Jugo-Slavia they want a Republic, but if there must be a King, they want King Nicholas and not King Peter. They want a big Jugo-Slavia but no big Servia. They would rather have a big Montenegro than a big Servia. If they join Jugo-Slavia they want King Nicholas to be King of Montenegro and not

46. On the ups and downs of the Montengrin army in exile see ibid., pp. 416–438.
47. Cited in ibid., pp. 354–355.

to have King Peter king of Servia and Montenegro. They want to join independently and not lose their rights.''[48] But even the very existence of Montenegro could be sacrificed, should the course of settlement avoid impairing the dignity of Montenegrins. The demands of the insurgent committee to the Serbian troops and Whites at Cetinje included the following point: "We concur with the idea that Montenegro enter into a great Yugoslav state with the same rights as all the other provinces, without any internal political frontiers. The form of governance we leave to the legal decision of a *regularly elected assembly* of all Yugoslavs . . . to which we shall *heartily* submit.''[49]

King Nikola died on March 1, 1921, far away from Montenegro, in lush Antibes on the Côte d'Azur, thus depriving his phantom state of its sole dower—his presence and reputation. The last Petrović ruler realized one final wish. He did not die a street mendicant, as he feared, but "as befits men who had a history.''[50] Jovan Plamenac held on to an increasingly fragmented retinue, periodically stirring up tempests in the émigré teacup. Back home, the Green insurgency subsided, as the gendarmes smoked the outlaws, like badgers, out of their holes.[51] The land was worn out after more than a decade of almost incessant warfare. But if the outlawry stopped, the Montenegrin divisions were not filled. They were simply recognized as permanent fixtures of the Montenegrin landscape.

The Whites, though internally divided among various centralist parties, nevertheless retained their basic characteristic—Serbocentric opposition to any manifestation of Montenegrin separatism. In extreme cases, this led some of them to advocate the wholesale resettlement of Montenegrins in the interest of state unity.[52] Most often, however, the Whites were satisfied to note that their horizons transcended those of Montenegro, whose history they elevated inasmuch as it was complementary to the growth of Great Serbia. Accordingly, they pointedly contrasted Montenegro to "Šumadija," that is, to the central area of Serbia proper, in an attempt to extend the appellation of Serbia to Montenegro as well.[53]

The Greens, especially after those among them who were not compromised by insurgency entered electoral politics on a federalist (autonomist) platform (1923) and then established the Montenegrin Party (1925), in-

48. Hoover Institution Archives, Charles W. Furlong Collection, Box 3: Outcard no. 283. Interview with Revolutionists.
49. Cited in Vujović, *Ujedinjenje,* p. 360.
50. Nikola I Petrović-Njegoš, *Pisma* (Cetinje, 1969), p. 406.
51. The atmosphere of these pursuits is vividly reconstructed in a short story by Radovan Zogović, in which a group of insurgents is literally smoked out of a mountain cave. See his "Nerazdvojni," in Radovan Zogović, *Noć i pola vijeka* (Novi Sad, 1978), pp. 284–313.
52. This was advocated in Novica Šaulić, *Crna Gora* (Belgrade, 1924), pp. 35–36.
53. Nikola Škerović, "Crna Gora u Svetskom Ratu," *Nova Evropa,* vol. 13 (1926), nos. 10–11, p. 308.

creasingly shunned armed struggle and stressed that, though they were for a federal Yugoslavia, they remained true Serbs. Sekula Drljević (1884–1945), the party's leading theoretician, often stressed Montenegro's adherence to Serb nationhood and to the unity of Yugoslav state. At the same time, however, he argued that a single nation need not necessarily have a single state, leaving a back door open for the legitimation of Montenegrin statehood. In short, Green demands for a federal Yugoslavia did not imply that the country should be divided into three federal units, one each for the Serbs, Croats, and Slovenes, the only three South Slavic nationalities within Yugoslavia that the Montenegrin federalists recognized. Instead, they believed that the federalization of Yugoslavia could be accomplished within the framework of pre-1918 frontiers, which were historically determined, much like the nationalities themselves, but in a different pattern.[54] As a result, the legal form of Green struggle became no more than an annoyance to the centralist and Great Serbian forces. It was less than that after the amnesty of pro-Petrović émigrés in 1925 and the return of Jovan Plamenac, who, not all that incongruously, became an exponent of Pašić's NRS. Montenegritude and Serbdom settled on mutual permeation.

The path of the Green movement from armed resistance toward a form of regional autonomism was inevitable as long as the Montenegrins considered themselves Serbs. To be sure, some Montenegrin federalists tended toward a concept of separate Montenegrin nationhood. As early as 1921, Drljević stated that the mentalities of Serbians and Montenegrins were irreconcilable: "The visage of the former was speckled with [Ottoman] slavery; liberty gave the latter a new visage."[55] But it was not until the Axis occupation, which restored the frontier between Serbia and Montenegro, that he advanced the notion that the Montenegrins were not Serbs, indeed that they were not even Slavs: "Races are communities of blood, whereas peoples are creatures of history. With its language, the Montenegrin people belong to the Slavic linguistic community. By their blood, however, they belong [to the Dinaric peoples]. According to the contemporary science of European races, [Dinaric] peoples are the descendants of the Illyrians. . . . Hence not just the kinship, but the identity of certain cultural forms among the Dinaric peoples, all the way from Albanians to South Tyroleans, who are Germanized Illyrians."[56]

Drljević's racial theories belonged to the era of Hitler, but Green sprouts had burst into a theory of Montenegrin nationhood somewhat earlier under quite different auspices—within the Communist movement, which was exceptionally strong in Montenegro in part because of the tradition of Green insurgency. By the end of the interwar period the Communists concluded that

---

54. Dimitrije-Dimo Vujović, *Crnogorski federalisti, 1919–1929* (Titograd, 1981), pp. 203–210.
55. Cited in ibid., p. 78.
56. Sekula Drljević, *Balkanski sukobi 1905.–1941.* (Zagreb, 1944), p. 163.

the Montenegrins were indeed a separate nationality: "The old [Petrović] regime, owing to its expansionist pretensions, supported the legend that Montenegrins were Serbs, so that the forming of Montenegrins into a [separate] nation, in fact, started taking shape only when the Montenegrins experienced Serb violence and exploitation."[57] Commenting on this "legend," Milovan Djilas added the following note to the same text: "This was out of date way back, though not entirely out of date in the [popular] psyche, which is not essential."[58] But the bialate Psyche of the Montenegrins did not have butterfly wings.

The Kaçaks

> Albanians are the most chivalrous people in Europe.
>
> Antun Gustav Matoš, 1907

> And it is difficult, truly difficult, for a peaceful people like ours to have orderly relations with [the Albanians], a people who satisfied their needs in a way that was not known to any other European people. (Shouts: By pillage and theft!)
>
> Ljuba Davidović at the congress
> of the Democratic party, 1921

> Shtatë kraliat kanë thânë,
> se shqiptaret gjakun s'lâne.

> Seven kingdoms have said,
> that the Albanians do not forgive blood.
>
> From an Albanian folk song (Macedonia)

To the Serbs, Kosovo, Metohia, the environs of Shkodër, and the stretch of western Macedonia from the Šar Range to Lake Ohrid were sacred lands. Holy King Stefan Uroš III radiated tongues of flame against the would-be Turkish desecrators from his marble sarcophagus in the monastery of High Dečani. Holy Jelena, the widow of Stefan Uroš I, took the veil in the church of Saint Nicholas in Shkodër (Skadar on the Bojana), the capital of old Zeta. According to folk epic, Prince Marko awarded the empire to "young tsar" Uroš at the "white church" of Samodreža and slew brigand Musa Kesedžija

---

57. Moša Pijade, "Teze o nacionalnom pitanju," in Pero Damjanović et al., eds., *Peta zemaljska konferencija KPJ (19–23. oktobar 1940)* (Belgrade, 1980), p. 386.
58. Ibid., p. 386, n. ***.

(< Turk. *kesici* = cutter) in the Kačanik Gorge at the northeastern end of the Šar. Emperor Stefan Dušan was awaiting resurrection in the ruins of the Holy Archangels, down a slope of the Upper City of Prizren, which folk tradition referred to as Carigrad—Serbian Constantinople. And, of course, the Turks defeated the Serbs in the epic and thaumatogenisic battle that took place on the Field of Kosovo in 1389—an event that had no equal in the collective memory of the Serbs. Indeed, for over four centuries, with a hiatus of ninety-four years, Serb Zion was in Peć, the see of Serbian patriarchs, who in the early eighteenth century took the people and the tabernacle of witness to Habsburg exile. Small wonder, then, that when the Serbians and Montenegrins ended the Ottoman power over these areas in 1912–1913, they felt they were once again ascending to Jerusalem. When victorious King Petar visited Dečani in 1913, he lit the gigantic candle that was to be set burning only when the Battle of Kosovo was avenged.

The Serbs were so dazzled with the bright glow of recovered lands that they almost failed to notice that there were hardly any Serbs left in "Old Serbia." The overwhelming majority of the people were Albanians, a martial breed just like Musa Kesedžija, who, according to the Serb epic, "was begotten by a fierce Albanian woman, wrapped with bramble twigs, and nursed with oat starch." Moreover, though the Ottoman tradition included them among the seven Christian kingdoms that lost the Battle of Kosovo, in the course of Ottoman rule the Albanians had become thoroughly Islamized, except for a group of northern Catholic highland tribes and some Orthodox pockets in the south. As a stratum distinguished in Ottoman service (the dynasties of Köprülü [Qyprilli] grand vezirs and of the khedives of Egypt were of Albanian origin), the Albanian elite was awarded privilege by the Turks, and, as a result, was on guard against Slavic insurgency, a dread that increased after the flight of tens of thousands of Albanians from Kuršumlija (Toplica district) and Vranje, after the Serbian takeover in 1878. They retained no memory of alliances and blood ties between Albanian medieval princes (from the families of Dukagjin, Arianit, Muzaka, Mataranga, Gropa, Thopia, Kastriot, and many others) and the Serb and Bulgar dynasts, the Slavic *krajls*.[1] Instead they prayed with the Turks that the "seven kingdoms" should not be united. Albanian kingdom was a *mbretëri,* not a Slavic *krajli.*

In the course of 1877, Albanian notables, both Muslim and Christian, joined together to form the League of Prizren, which protested to the powers the further dissolution of the Ottoman empire while simultaneously working for Albanian cultural and administrative autonomy within the Turkish state.[2]

1. Milan Šufflay, *Srbi i Arbanasi (Njihova simbioza u srednjem vijeku)* (Belgrade, 1925), pp. 121–135.
2. On this large subject see Stavro Skendi, *The Albanian National Awakening, 1878–1912* (Princeton, N.J., 1967).

The League of Prizren and the attendant age of awakening (*rilindje* or renaissance) laid the foundations of the modern multiconfessional Albanian nation, in which, in the words of poet Pashko Vasa, "the religion of the Albanian is the Albanian cause."[3] But though the fear of territorial dismemberment made the Albanians hold fast with the Turks instead of demanding immediate independence, they were increasingly at odds with the Porte, especially after the Young Turk regime (1908) started threatening their cultural gains through a campaign of "Ottomanization," in effect, virulent Turcification. Still, they instinctively felt that the Slavic danger was the greater. Though King Nikola, for his own reasons, supported the Albanian uprising against the Turks in 1911, thereby precipitating the Balkan wars, no Ottoman contingent was as feared by the invading Serbians and Montenegrins in those encounters as the units of "wild Arnauts."

For Belgrade, more so than for Cetinje, the campaigns of 1912–1913 presented two contradictory problems. First, while Austria-Hungary was entrenched in Dalmatia, Serbia could realize its ambition for a seacoast only on the Albanian littoral, hence her designs on northern Albania precluded the establishment of any Albanian state. Second, in Kosovo, western Macedonia, and other portions of the northern Albanian settlement, Serbian expansionism was for the first time confronted with a compact, alien (predominantly Muslim) population that constituted overwhelming local majorities. Not all Albanians could be expected to flee from their native homesteads, as the Muslim urban classes of Serbia proper were obliged to do in several nineteenth-century migratory waves. As a result, Serbian propaganda simultaneously dehumanized Albanians, presenting them as utterly incapable of governing themselves and as the sort of element that ought to be exterminated, and elevated them to the standing that warranted their assimilation.

On the one hand, Albanians were savages. Dr. Vladan Djordjević, a noted Serbian statesman and public health specialist, showed no restraint in this line of defamation. Citing various foreign travelers and doctors of anthroposcopy, Djordjević had his Albanians skinny and short, possessed of gypsy and Phoenician features—indeed, reminding him of the "prehumans, who slept in the trees, to which they were fastened by their tails." Whereas other human beings had lost their simian tails in the course of evolution, it seemed that the Albanians had their tails well into the nineteenth century. They were modern Troglodytes, with bestial teeth, living *"in Blutschande."*[4] Over 70 percent of their menfolk died in blood feuds, many of which resulted from the fact that 50 percent of their brides proved not to be in a state of inviolate chastity, a breach of the marriage contract that had to be revenged. Though it was shameful to die in bed, the men who did not succumb to the hand of their

3. Koço Bihiku, *A History of Albanian Literature* (Tirana, 1980), p. 60.
4. Vladan Georgevitch (Djordjević), *Die Albanesen und die Grossmächte* (Leipzig, 1913), pp. 4, 94, 37, 113. (Page numbers in this paragraph refer to this work.)

fellows fell to the prevalent diseases of the land—typhus, influenza, and venereal afflictions. The Albanian ate only bread, maize porridge, and milk (pp. 40, 112, 205, 94, 96). He knew nothing of salt and mistook the travelers' sugar for snow: "And some would wish to claim that the people who do not know what salt is and who mistake sugar for snow seemingly know what a Fatherland is and that they would be ready to die for this exalted concept."[5] Djordjević was also convinced that the Albanians had no history, that their life element was anarchy, and that they changed religion lightheartedly, though religious fanaticism remained their most expressive characteristic (pp. 23, 93, 39, 40).

The otherwise moderate Stojan Protić saw the Albanians as "criminal interlopers," capable only of the sort of freedom that exists in the wild.[6] Another writer cited as evidence of turpitude the renowned Albanian customary law that protected the weak and laid down ironclad rules of warfare and hospitlity.[7] And Jaša Tomić, a leader of the Serb Radicals from Vojvodina, reported with disgust on the moschine scent that he caught in their empty harems: "In their soul the Arnauts were most surprised when individual European diplomats started doing their best to prove that the Arnauts cannot do without the sea; just as a goose in a walled courtyard would wonder, should somebody try to prove to her that she needs her wings."[8]

On the other hand, these European redskins were really lost Serbs. Since Serbian historiography denied that the ancestors of Kosovar Albanians were autochthonous to "Old Serbia," as some certainly were, it was necessary to explain their latter-day predominance in the area.[9] In addition to noting the

5. Ibid., p. 96.

6. Balcanicus [pseud. Stojan Protić], *Albanski problem i Srbija i Austro-Ugarska* (Belgrade, 1913), pp. 64, 30.

7. "The Code of Dukagjin [Albanian customary law], which shaped the legal consciousness of Albanians and greatly helped form their mentality, provided them with a malignant dispensation to view plunder, theft, robbery, and attack against one's neighbor as legally permitted; moreover, as matters that did not denigrate honor." Grigorije Božović, "Kačaci," *Policija*, vol. 7 (1920), nos. 13–14, p. 561.

8. Jaša Tomić, *Rat u Albaniji i pod Skadrom 1912. i 1913. godine* (Novi Sad, 1913), p. 33.

9. Albanian historians have asserted that Albanians were the majority in Kosovo even before the Ottoman conquest: "The documents of the period after the Ottoman occupation of Kosova, in 1455, and especially the land registers, provide many facts that show that these regions were inhabited by the Albanian population, while the Serbs, who came as colonialists, or as a ruling stratum during the period of Serbian occupation of these regions, constituted a minority, insignificant numerically but dominant from the political and social standpoints." Selami Pulaha, "The Scientific Truth about the Autochthony of the Albanians in Kosova," *New Albania*, 1982, no. 4, p. 20. In fact, the documents do not show any such thing. The Ottoman *defter* (register of landed property) of 1455 for the lands of the Serbian Branković princes (that is, most of present-day Kosovo with small bits of adjoining Sandžak and Serbia proper) record an overwhelming Slavic (Serb) majority. See Hamid Hadžibegić, Adem Handžić, and Ešref Kovačević, comps., *Oblast Brankovića: Opširni katastarski popis iz 1455. godine* (Sarajevo, 1972). Through Albanian researchers do have a point in maintaining that Slavic names do not necessarily convey Slavs, a "Todor" or a "Djuradj, son of Martin," could arguably be Albanian (or Serb), it is hard to believe that a "Radihna, son of Dabiživ" or a "Prijezda, son of Relja" has any Albanian ancestry. More to the point, wherever Albanians appeared in 1455, they

waves of documented Serb migrations, especially the mass flight after 1690, the chief explanation centered on Albanian assimilation. Though the logic of this reasoning contradicted charges of Albanian inferiority, it fitted the legend of Albanian atrociousness.

Accordingly, it was asserted that the early Muslim status of most Albanians facilitated their assimilation of subsequent Serb converts, who came trickling into Islam through Albanian violence. Dr. Jovan Hadži-Vasiljević drew general inferences about the spread of *arnautaši* (Albanianized Serbs) from a few cases of land grabbing and enserfment in rural Macedonia (Southern Serbia to him). For example, an Albanian outlaw, with a son, fell upon the village of Četirci (near Kumanovo), assumed the position of field guard, "seized and Mohammedanized Serb girls, grabbed Serb land, took livestock, killed Serbs, and so forth, until he gained a whole *çiftlik* [private estate] for himself and his son."[10] But it was never quite made clear why, in such a case, the nationality of a minority within the ruling religion prevailed in a hostile environment, nor why the Islamized Serbs became Albanians in Kosovo and other "southern regions," whereas in Montenegro and Serbia proper, for example, they retained their language though they called themselves Turks.

The Albanians had no nationhood and their nationalism was the product of Austrian and Italian intrigue, yet they assimilated Serbs. But since the greatest Albanian glory, the legendary Skenderbeg, was himself a "semi-Serb" ("O Skenderbeg, the name of Kosovar hero . . . thy whole life says that thou art of our kind"), it nevertheless made sense to contemplate the re-Serbianization of "denationalized brothers" in the newly acquired territories.[11] The opposition to the theories of historical right faded in the "southern regions," as Serbian leaders, in Krleža's sardonic words, contemplated driving the "herdful of Albanian renegades . . . that 'ravage-bearing' river, which was flowing down into the tame and civilized areas . . . back into its natural bed in the black and impenetrable mountains."[12]

The logic of this sort of chauvinistic harangue became evident in the Balkan wars. Serbian and Montenegrin units committed many massacres of Albanians in the course of hostilities. The indiscriminate slaughter in the Lume tribal area of northeastern Albania was reported in the Serbian socialist

---

were often, though probably not always, identified as such. For example, in the village of Šipitula, near Priština, there was a "Petko, Albanian" and a "Mihal, Albanian." Ibid., p. 67. In short, their nationality was not the rule in the area.

10. Jovan Hadži-Vasiljević, *Kumanovska oblast*, vol. 2 of *Južna stara Srbija: Istorijska, etnografska i politička istraživanja* (Belgrade, 1909), p. 186.

11. Vladimir Stanimirović, *Izgnanici: albanska odiseja, u tri dela, u stihu, sa prologom* (Belgrade, 1924), pp. 88–89; Jaša Tomić, *Rat na Kosovu i Staroj Srbiji 1912. godine* (Novi Sad, 1913), p. 158.

12. Miroslav Krleža, "O jedinim zastavama našega vremena," in *Deset krvavih godina i drugi politički eseji*, vols. 14–15 of *Sabrana djela*, (Zagreb, 1957), p. 413.

press and was later retold in the report of the Carnegie Endowment for International Peace, which summed up the rationale of Albanian horrors: "Houses and whole villages reduced to ashes, unarmed and innocent populations massacred *en masse,* incredible acts of violence, pillage and brutality of every kind—such were the means which were employed and are still being employed by the Serbo-Montenegrin soldiery, with a view to the entire transformation of the ethnic character of regions inhabited exclusively by Albanians."[13] Villagers, alerted to the intentions of invading armies "by tradition, instinct and experience," fled before the invaders, who set the abandoned cottages to flame (p. 151). In September 1913, Kosovar Albanians rose in rebellion, which was drowned in blood. As in Macedonia, extraordinary regulations were introduced by the Serbian authorities, whereby police assessment was sufficient proof of sedition, which was in turn punished by death (pp. 160–162). Once peace was restored, the first Serbian and Montenegrin settlers were sent to seize the new lands. Pašić himself bought 1,214 acres of land at the Gazimestan near Priština, where, according to popular belief, the fallen standard-bearers of the Ottoman and Serbian armies were buried after the Battle of Kosovo.[14] Small wonder that the indigenous Kosovar Serbs noticed a major turnabout: "We natives see that those [Muslims] who liked and helped us in Turkish times now show us far less good will. And vice versa."[15]

Only a small band of Serbian socialists, led by Dimitrije Tucović, spoke out against the anti-Albanian paroxysms. Tucović's critique of the "Serbian bourgeoisie's policy of conquest" was a ringing denunciation of what he considered a classic colonial war. An advocate of a Balkan socialist federation, Tucović was opposed to Albanian independence, but he directed his main blow against the "Serbian bourgeoisie, which has now, for the first time, removed the veil of the oppressed nation from the face of the Serb people."[16] Just as he abhorred the thought of seeing his homeland lost to the oppressors, he held up for reprobation the sham of racist stereotypes about Albanians, comparing these loathsome imputations to what foreigners often said about Serbians and Montenegrins:

> The deranged reactionary defense of the capitalist policy of conquest is evidence of how it has been forgotten that all cultured peoples have gone through a period of tribal social community and other primitive stages. But this fact

13. Carnegie Endowment for International Peace, *Report of the International Commission to Inquire into the Causes and Conduct of the Balkan Wars* (Washington, D.C., 1914), p. 151. (Page numbers that follow also refer to this work.)

14. Milovan Obradović, "Agrarni odnosi na Kosovu 1918–1941. godine," *Jugoslovenski istorijski časopis,* 1978, nos. 1–4, p. 443.

15. Grigorije Božović, "Braća Drage," *Savremeni pregled,* vol. 1 (1926), no. 1, p.1.

16. Dimitrije Tucović, *Srbija i Arbanija: Jedan prilog kritici zavojevačke politike srpske buržoazije* (Belgrade, 1914), p. 76.

should not be forgotten, especially by the representatives of the conquest-bound bourgeoisie of the Balkan peoples, who have not yet done away with the evident traces of their own previous tribal organization. Marko Miljanov [Popović (or Drekalović, 1833–1901), the great Montenegrin military commander and writer from the Kuči tribe], the best student of Montenegrins and Albanians, saw that the Montenegrin tribes were not far ahead of the Albanians, and stated: "Know you, that it is not all that hard to get along with the Albanians, as it seems to you, *since they are not far from you, or you from them.*"[17]

Tucović even claimed that Karadjordje himself was of Albanian descent, an assertion that was not entirely unfounded, considering the folk belief that the Vasojevići and the neighboring Albanian tribes of Hot and Krasniq had a common ancestor.[18] But most of all, Tucović feared that Serbian policy created such bad blood that peace and orderly conditions in relations with Albanians could hardly be expected in the near future.[19] Unlike so many West European socialists, who approved the "civilizing mission" of colonialism, Tucović was firmly convinced that the rebellion of most primitive tribes was always more humane than the practice of standing armies, the Serbian army included.[20]

Just as Tucović predicted, the effects of Serbian policy toward Albanians were proved all too injurious to the libertarian self-image of the Serbian government. Even the Austro-Hungarian occupation authorities in Kosovo (1916–1918), pursuing the policy of a government that the Serbs always considered as freedom-trampling, had allowed some 300 Albanian schools and encouraged the flying of Albanian colors.[21] To be sure, Vienna had its reasons for encouraging the already strong anti-Serbian sentiment among the Albanians, and it set up the Albanian volunteer units purposely to help reduce the number of Montenegrin and Serbian settlers, and the Serb minority in general.[22] Nevertheless, not a few Albanians fought against the Austro-Hungarian occupiers, though the return of the Serbian army in 1918 meant the end of all gains that had accrued to them under the two-headed eagle of the Habsburgs.

The Serbian occupation of Metohia in 1918, seized from Montenegro, and the second occupation of Kosovo and western Macedonia were as brutal as anything that had happened in 1912–1913. And just as in the course of

17. Ibid., p. 27.
18. Djoko Slijepčević, *Srpsko-arbanaški odnosi kroz vekove sa posebnim osvrtom na novije vreme* (Munich, 1974), pp. 69–70.
19. Tucović, *Srbija*, p. 3.
20. Ibid., p. 108.
21. Muhamet Pirraku, "Kulturno-prosvetni pokret Albanaca u Jugoslaviji (1919–1941)," *Jugoslovenski istorijski časopis*, 1978, nos. 1–4, pp. 357–358.
22. Miša Sretenović, "Zločini Ferad-beg Drage," *Reč*, April 11, 1925, p. 1.

Balkan wars, when Austria-Hungary restrained Pašić's appetite for more Albanian territory, this time also, a leading power, Italy, obstructed Belgrade's land grabs and thereby gained adherents for its own protectorate over Albania. The Serbian troops swooped down on Shkodër in October 1918 but were soon obliged to leave the city, which, under Allied, but mainly Italian, control, quickly became the center of anti-Serbian activities—a place where Albanians, the Montenegrin Greens, and Italians plotted against Serbian control over neighboring lands.[23] In action after action in 1918–1919, the Serbian army continued to suppress local Albanian uprisings and disarm the local population and, at the same time, penetrate deeply into the territory of post-1913 Albania. According to Albanian sources, in November 1918 the Serbian army ravaged the area of Podgor Metohijski (near Peć), massacring women and children and destroying 138 houses. The army massacred 700 Albanians in Rožaj (Sandžak) and 800 in the region of Djakovica, and in mid-February 1919 used cannon fire to destroy fifteen villages in the Rugovo Gorge, the main route between Metohia and Montenegro. Also in February, identical methods were used to suppress uprisings in the Plav and Gusinje districts, leading to a mass flight of Albanians, who, like their Dardanian ancestors, sought the high grounds of the Prokletije Range and thence, in many cases, fled south—to Shkodër.[24] In the late summer of 1920, despite the total lack of enthusiasm on the part of Yugoslav conscripts, many of them Croats, Yugoslavia waged a small war against Albania, penetrating the valley of the Drin in eastern Albania, on a wide front from Lume to Martanesh. The Albanians claimed losses of 738 civilians, total destruction of 6,603 houses, and loss of practically all properly.[25]

Under the circumstances, the lot of Albanians in Yugoslavia could not be propitious. State policy being either the assimilation or expulsion of Albanians, they became the most oppressed national group in Yugoslavia. "Our thesis was always," it was stated in a document of the Ministry of Foreign Affairs in 1929, "that there are no national minorities in our southern regions."[26] Indeed, the official census reports on Albanians probably halved their number (reducing it from approximately 800,000–1 million people to 441,740 in the preliminary report on the 1921 census and to 439,657 in the final report).[27]

Belgrade also dictated Albanian education. With the return of Serbian troops in 1918 all Albanian schools were shut down in the "southern re-

23. [Dimitrije-] Dimo Vujović, "Oslobodjenje Skadra 1918 godine i stanje na crnogorsko-albanskoj granici," *Istorijski zapisi,* vol. 13 (1960), no. 1, pp. 110, 121.

24. Hoover Institution Archives, Charles W. Furlong Collection, Box 3: Outcard no. 454. The Committee for the National Defense of Kossovo: Letter to David Lloyd George (no date, probably late winter or early spring 1919).

25. J. Swire, *Albania: The Rise of a Kingdom* (London, 1929), pp. 334–337.

26. Cited in Pirraku, "Kulturno-prosvetni pokret," p. 357, n. 6.

27. Ibid., p. 356 and pp. 356–357, n. 4.

gions." The authorities first tried to assimilate Albanian children and youth by allowing them only Serbian-language education, using Bosnian Muslim teachers of proved pro-Serbian orientation for the purpose. But when it appeared that the Serbian schools, far from Serbianizing Albanians, were providing them with the intellectual skills that could be used against the regime, Belgrade started discouraging public education for Albanians, permitting them only catechetical instruction, conducted by Muslim imams and Catholic priests. The authorities were convinced that these predominantly Muslim schools, *mektebs* (primary schools) and *medreses* (secondary schools), popularly known as "Turkish schools," would keep the Albanians behindhand and ignorant: "Should we leave everything as in the old days," one official wrote in 1921, "they will all remain backward, unenlightened, and stupid, nor will they know the state idiom [Serbian], which would help them to fight against us. It is in our interest that they remain at the present level of their culture for another twenty years, the time we need to carry out the necessary national assimilation in these areas."[28]

Again the calculation was wrong. Though in Kosovo and Metohia, for example, Albanians constituted only 2 percent of the high-school population in state schools, they turned the "Turkish schools," where instruction was ostensibly only in Koranic Arabic and Turkish, into formidable centers of underground national education and oppositional activity, stubbornly resistant despite frequent closings. In other words, even though the illiteracy rate among Albanians of Yugoslavia during the interwar period was a staggering 90 percent, there was no sure preventive measure against Albanian self-education. Indeed, the only state secondary school in which Albanian was employed in instruction, the Great Medrese of King Aleksandar in Skopje (opened in 1924, it was set up to train loyal Albanian imams and had a carefully screened enrollment) became a center of nationalist and even Communist activity. Illegal organizations, such as Agimi (Dawn) and Drita (Light), operated through legal youth clubs and sports organizations, disseminating books smuggled from Albania.[29]

Where Serb-directed education failed to "correct the national composition of Old Serbian areas," Serb colonization proved far more reliable.[30] Although Kosovo and Metohia, the provinces most affected by the Regulation for the Settlement of Southern Regions (September 9, 1920), were areas of extensive farming (although 55.8 percent of all peasant households had no plow), they were among the very few extremely fertile areas of the Balkan peninsula and were attractive to progressive farmers. By November 1940, the administration for agrarian reform (with offices in Peć, Uroševac, Kosovska Mitrovica, Prizren, and Skopje) had seized 154,287 acres of land

28. Cited in ibid., p. 360, n. 25.
29. Ibid., pp. 358–362.
30. Ramadan Marmullaku, *Albania and the Albanians* (London, 1975), p. 138.

in the "southern regions." Of those, 57,704 acres were given to predominantly Serb settlers (17,679 families), mainly from agriculturally poor Montenegro, Hercegovina, and Lika. In compensation, 30,582 local families of landowners, tenants, and former serfs received 35,659 acres. State schools, various agencies, the army, and the gendarmerie received 5,184 acres. The colonists moved into 15,943 new houses, of which 2,712 were built by the state and 207 with the help of the state.[31]

In all its aspects, the colonization of the "southern regions" worked against the native population. The state could take land from Albanian peasants and give it to the colonists in any areas earmarked for new settlements. Though the Albanian owners were supposed to be compensated in land of equal quality, in fact the land they got was usually of lesser quality, and though they could appeal the decisions of the agrarian reform authorities, they could never get back their original land, because the law guaranteed the colonists possession against any subsequent legal claims of former owners.[32] Moreover, when Albanians were unable to prove their rightful ownership of the land, a frequent situation in a traditional society where property was often held in common, they lost all claim to possession. The law also provided that land belonging to outlaws could be confiscated by the state: by 1939, 2,127 acres of "outlaw" land had been seized, much of it on very dubious grounds.[33] To make matters worse, the law was braced by the most notorious lot of carpetbagging chicaners in whole Yugoslavia. It was well known that "all the scum that existed in the bureaucratic cadre, who wanted to get rich quickly, went as administrators" to the Sandžak, Kosovo, and Macedonia.[34]

Though the NRS and the DS had agreed to a formula whereby the administration of the "southern regions" was to be carried out by nine Radicals for every seven Democrats, the NRS managed to retain a distinct advantage. Even Adam Pribićević, Svetozar's brother and himself a colonist in Kosovo, could not escape Radical terror and was several times set upon by bullies hired by the local NRS bosses. Pribićević mused over the fate of Albanian peasants if a minister's brother received the treatment he did. He noted that every attempt at reform in Kosovo ended in failure. For example, connected Albanians customarily paid thirty-six golden Turkish liras to corrupt communal authorities in order to avoid military service; those who tried to stop this practice were arrested, beaten, proclaimed outlaws, and even killed.[35] Small wonder that it hardly ever occurred to Albanians to entrust their case to the

31. Ali Hadri, "Kosovo i Metohija u Kraljevini Jugoslaviji," *Istorijski glasnik,* 1967, nos. 1–2, pp. 51–84.
32. Obradović, "Agrarni odnosi," p. 448.
33. Ibid., p. 452.
34. "Problem južne Srbije," *Pravda,* Aug. 27, 1921, p. 1.
35. Adam Pribićević, *Moj život* (Toronto, 1982), pp. 70–75.

authorities: "There is no *besa* [solemn word of honor] among the Vlachs [Serbs]."[36]

The agrarian policy in the "southern regions" also had the aim of forcing the Albanians to emigrate. Many hundreds of Albanians had fled to Albania proper or Turkey in 1913–1914, selling their lands very cheaply to the incoming Montenegrins. Between 1910 and 1920, according to some reports, Kosovo and Metohia lost 150,000 people, mostly as a result of emigration.[37] The trend continued throughout the interwar period. In the mid-1930s, following the negotiations with Turkey, which expressed willingness to accept 200,000 Albanian emigrants from Yugoslavia, Albanian landholdings in the counties of Djakovica and Šar Planina were restricted to 0.16 acre per every member of the household, unless the ownership could be documented. In the words of one official report, "This is below the minimum needed for survival. But that was precisely what we wanted; that is, to prevent them from living and thereby force them to emigrate. The convention on emigration [with Turkey] is initialed."[38] Similar restrictions impelling the option of emigration upon Albanians were planned for the other areas of Kosovo and Metohia.

A government bent on expelling Albanians was hardly one to permit legal functioning of their national parties. True, the Society for Preservation of Muslim Rights (Cemiyet—more on which in part 4) fought for the autonomy of Yugoslavia's Albanians and Turks. But this group was led by sections of Muslim landowning elite, whose members, frequently undecided about the national quality of Albanian grievances, were inclined to seek special arrangements with the Serbian parties. For the people, then, the main alternative to compliance and emigration was armed resistance. In Croatia, rebellions went against the grain of national leadership, and in Montenegro, insurgency affected only a part of the people; but in Kosovo and two other Albanian regions of Yugoslavia, armed resistance had almost universal support.

The government of Albania was in no position to aid the risings in arms among the Kosovars. Until November 1921, when the Conference of Ambassadors in Paris confirmed Albania's frontiers (rather along the lines of its 1913 limits), Albania was preoccupied with its struggle for international recognition, which Yugoslavia continued to undermine by its policy of intervention. Belgrade tried to influence Albanian developments by supporting the claims of its clients (Esat Pashë Toptani, for example) or by stirring up

36. *Zbornik dokumenata i podataka o Narodnooslobodilačkom ratu jugoslovenskih naroda*, tome 1, vol. 19, *Borbe na Kosovu 1941–1944* (Belgrade, 1969), p. 508.

37. Cited in Ali Hadri, "Nacionalno ugnjetavanje šiptarske narodnosti i stav i borba KPJ za nacionalna prava Šiptara za vreme stare Jugoslavije," *Gjurmime albanologjike*, 1965, no. 2, p. 148.

38. Cited in Pirraku, "Kulturno-prosvetni pokret," p. 366, n. 63.

Catholic tribalism in the north (Marka Gjoni's "Mirdite Republic").[39] But even after the withdrawal of Yugoslav troops from Albania in 1921, Belgrade continued to intervene in Albanian affairs, effectively preventing Albania from acting on behalf of its minority in Yugoslavia. In the words of Momčilo Ivanić, the problems between Yugoslavia and Albania would best be solved "should our borders be eliminated or allowed to become purely formal."[40]

In 1924, Yugoslavia charged the Wrangelite Russian troops in its service with the overthrow of the Albanian liberal government of Fan Noli. Briefly, the new president, Ahmet Bej Zogu, was no more than a creature of Belgrade, but he soon turned to Rome, and in 1928, with Italian encouragement, he crowned himself "King of the Albanians." But though he thereby claimed regal authority over all lands where Albanians lived, he was at the same time persecuting the democratic opposition to his despotic rule—opposition whose ranks included not a few irredentist leaders from Kosovo.

It can be fairly said that the activities of Kosovar exiles in Albania proper always nudged the Tirana authorities, nationalist or Zogist, toward however symbolic a policy of irredentism in Kosovo. At times, leading Kosovars participated in Albanian governments and parliamentary life. Avni Rustemi, who assassinated Esat Pashë Toptani in Paris (1920), later represented Kosovo in the Tirana parliament. Bajram Curri (from Djakovica), Hasan Bej Prishtina (or Šišković, from Vučitrn, whom the Serbs considered a national renegade), Zija Dibra, and Hoxha Kadriu were all ministers in the pre-Zogu governments, some of them in the strongly anti-Belgrade cabinets of Sulejman Bej Delvina (1920) and Pandeli Evangjeli (1921). Moreover, Bajram Curri, a renowned guerrilla leader, stirred up uprisings against Serbian rule in Rugovo and Drenica and was the commander of government-sponsored irregulars from the "Prefecture of Kosovo." As early as the fall of 1918, in Shkodër, some of these noted Kosovar leaders founded the Komiteti i Mbrojte Kombëtare e Kosovës (KK, Committee for the National Defense of Kosovo, popularly the Kosovo Committee), which, though lacking official status, smuggled arms into Kosovo and organized anti-Serbian resistance.[41] The KK also established ties with the Italians, Macedonian insurgents, and various Croat groups, notably Frankist émigrés.[42]

The principal goal of the Kosovo Committee was the encouragement of anti-Serbian insurgency. Considering the position of Albanians in Yugo-

---

39. On Yugoslavia's policy toward Albania see Desanka Todorović, *Jugoslavija i balkanske države, 1919–1923* (Belgrade, 1979), pp. 49–78, 121–145, 230–238.

40. Momčilo Ivanić, "Arbanasi i mi," *Radikal,* May 10, 1922, p. 1.

41. Stefanaq Pollo and Aleks Buda, eds., *Historia e popullit shqiptar,* vol. 2, 2d ed., rev. (Prishtina, 1969), p. 488.

42. Manko Gagliardi, *Istina o hrvatskom emigrantskom revolucionarnom komiteu 1919–21* (n.p., 1919), p. 28. According to Gagliardi, Ivica Frank selected Hasan Bej Prishtina for a central revolutionary committee that was to convene in D'Annunzio's Rijeka. Ibid., p. 30.

slavia, no special incitement was necessary. From the beginning of the second Serbian occupation, Albanians countered government attacks with guerrilla actions. Albanian partisans or *kaçaks* (< Turk. *kaçaklar* = outlaws, fugitives), in the words of a local DS politician, "were not plain criminal, political, or social brigands, as such, but a particular type of Albanian outlaw . . . who have become a revolting sickness, nowadays assuming a new, nationalist, and consequently antistate form, and thereby becoming our great problem."[43]

The kaçak raids were very dramatic during the first five postwar years, encompassing all regions of Albanian settlement, from Tuzi (Montenegro), where they cooperated with the Greens,[44] to Debar (Macedonia), where, according to the head of the Ohrid district, "The Arnauts have become a true grief and trial. We have neither army, nor sufficient gendarmes, so they have gone berserk." Indeed, the kaçak action was a direct result of military repression and Serbian efforts to disarm Albanians and install Serbian mayors and local officials. Kaçak bands in Macedonia started overthrowing Serbian offices, attacking courts and trains, and also rustling cattle; in late 1918, some 10,000 animals were stolen in the Debar area alone.[45] In the districts of Bitola and Ohrid, also in Macedonia, a certain Faik was evidently chosen to terrify itinerants, who "even in great company, could not feel secure in their lives, property, honor, and liberty."[46] Macedonian kaçaks, too, were the terror of Serbian schoolteachers.[47] But the greatest and most celebrated kaçak leader was Azem Bejta (1889–1924; sometimes called Galica after his home village), who kept his native Drenica, the central district of Kosovo, in permanent revolt during the early 1920s.

Azem Bejta and his wife Shota, an amazon shepherdess who hid her sex by assuming a male name (Qerim) and attire so as not to offend the patriarchal mores of her people, were the leaders of a powerful movement that in late 1918 alone commanded the allegiance of some 2,000 fighters and 100,000 other adherents. The Serbian authorities could not accuse Bejta of nestling close to the Austro-Hungarians during the war. In fact, he belonged to the anti-Habsburg resistance, and the Austrians executed his two brothers. In the last stages of the war he captured a whole Austrian garrison, gaining two medals from General Bachlet, the commander of advancing French troops. He cooperated with the Serbian irregulars of Kosta Pećanac, who

43. Božović, "Kačaci," p. 559.
44. Vujović, "Oslobodjenje Skadra," p. 115.
45. Cited from a report of October 31, 1918, in Bogumil Hrabak, "Reokupacija oblasti srpske i crnogorske države s arbanaškom većinom stanovništva u jesen 1918. godine i držanje Arbanasa prema uspostavljenoj vlasti," *Gjurmime albanologjike,* 1969, no. 2, pp. 268, 278, 267–269, 271.
46. Djusme-Pinga [pseud.], "Kačaci," *Razvitak,* Aug. 14, 1921, p. 1.
47. Radomir M. Petrović, "Na frontu smrti," *Učiteljska iskra,* vol. 1 (1922), nos. 5–6, pp. 57–58.

promised him, on King Petar's behalf, that after the war the Albanians would have their own schools and the right to fly the flag of Skenderbeg.[48] Instead, very soon after the Serbian advent, he was hunted as a fugitive.

On the advice of Bajram Curri and Hasan Bej Prishtina, Bejta urged Albanians not to pay the taxes and to refuse to serve in the army for as long as their rights were violated. According to Serbian sources, the response was tremendous: "The kaçaks were springing up like toadstools. Whenever somebody gets a court or administrative summons, he joins the kaçaks; and also when he is drafted, when he is a bit indisposed toward the county office, when somebody tells him that he is being watched."[49] And once among the kaçaks, Serbian officials thought, the Albanians started believing in autonomy, were "intoxicated with [the idea] of Great Albania," and thought that "if Karadjordje with his unarmed *rayas* could win a piece of land from a mighty empire, why could they not do the same, especially since they were well armed, compact, experienced, and likely to obtain aid from abroad."[50]

The authorities fought Bejta and other kaçaks with honey, then vinegar. The government of Ljuba Davidović gave the local authorities the right to suspend the death penalty and imprisonment in chains to the surrendering kaçaks.[51] Pašić's cabinet, more generous, offered an amnesty in early 1921 to those who surrendered during a month of grace.[52] That having failed, Milorad Drašković, the minister of the interior, established a special anti-kaçak command in Skopje, but "even after that, their numbers still grew from day to day."[53] Part of the explanation was that the struggle against the kaçaks was often no more than war against all Albanians. But in fact, the police and the administration suffered from other strategic weaknesses. According to an anonymous letter that a disgruntled Croat officer sent to a Zagreb newspaper editor, the chances of getting out alive from kaçak entrapments were less than the odds of surviving the Great War, because the fronts were not clear:

> . . . it could happen that I lose my life in these wild mountains in the struggle against the "Arnauts" and kaçaks—outlaws, and why? Because Svetozar's [Pribićević] enormous army (police) is not functioning, though every corner of the land is filled with them. Wherever one turns one sees only police scribes and gendarmes, who could maintain order if only they were responsible. . . . Instead

---

48. Nebil Duraku, "Grob 73 metra ispod zemlje," *VUS,* June 6, 1971, p. 35.
49. Božović, "Kačaci," p. 566.
50. Viktor D. Krstić, "Uzroci rdjave bezbednosti u Južnoj Srbiji i vladina 'Objava,'" *Policija,* vol. 8 (1921), nos. 5–8, p. 325; Božović, "Kačaci," p. 567.
51. Bogumil Hrabak, ed., "Zapisnici sednica Davidovićeve dve vlade od avgusta 1919. do februara 1920," *Arhivski vjesnik,* vol. 13, p. 58.
52. "Bezbednost u Južnoj Srbiji—Upućeno odmetnicima—kačacima," *Stara Srbija,* Feb. 13, 1921, p. 1.
53. "Borba s kačacima," *Epoha,* July 26, 1921, p. 1.

of disarming the people, [the police] are arming them. And why? Because each Arnaut has "golden liras," with which the police officials are getting rich. . . . For example, in one district here, the district commissioner gave the Arnauts 18,000 rifles; at least according to the ledgers. Do Mr. Davidović and the minister of the army know about this? . . . Does Mr. Davidović know that a day before yesterday [June 26, 1920] *one officer and nine gendarmes* were killed by the Arnauts, massacred, and buried in Mitrovica?[54]

As it turned out, Bejta's resistance, however popular, was halted not so much by government repression as by the self-contained policy of Ahmet Bej Zogu and Albanian conservatives. In 1922, Zogu, then Albania's minister of the interior and known as an opponent of the KK, started disarming the tribes of Albania's northern highlands and within the neutral frontier zone toward Yugoslavia, where, notably at Junik, the KK and Bejta had their bases. In March 1922, Bajram Curri, Hasan Bej Prishtina, and Elez Jusufi, an important kaçak leader, tried to overthrow the government in Tirana, but failed. Some months later, encouraged by Kemal Atatürk's victory in Asia Minor, Curri issued a special appeal to the Kosovars, in which he anticipated an extended (twenty kilometers wide) neutral zone between Albania and Yugoslavia, where "we shall be able to forge a sacred unity of Islam on Kemal Paşa's model."[55] In January 1923, soon after Zogu became the premier of Albania, Curri and Prishtina once again failed in overthrowing him—some 500 kaçaks from Kosovo notwithstanding.[56] Between the two aborted revolts, Zogu entered into a secret agreement with Belgrade, promising, among other things, to do away with Curri, Prishtina, the KK, and the kaçak bands.[57] Curri's third effort, in the wake of the Zogu-inspired assassination of Avni Rustemi, was part of the June Revolution of 1924, which brought the nationalist and progressive government of Fan Noli to power. Azem Bejta and his main force of a thousand kaçaks were betrayed to the Yugoslav gendarmes at the very end of disorders that marked the change in power. Bejta fell on July 15. On December 24, Zogu was back in power at the head of a Belgrade-sponsored regime. He quickly suppressed the Kosovo Committee, had Zija Dibra murdered "while attempting to escape," sent his troops to kill Bajram Curri, and scattered the other Kosovar leaders.[58] Nine years later, in 1933, his agents killed Hasan Bej Prishtina in Greece.

With the end of Azem Bejta, the victory of the Zogist counterrevolution, and the suppression of the KK, the kaçak rebellion came to a standstill. The KK became a part of Fan Noli's exiled Komiteti Nacional Revolucionar

54. Arhiv Hrvatske, Rukopisna ostavština Dr. Djure Šurmina, Box 3: Fogl. 34, anonymous Croat officer to the Zagreb newspaper *Hrvat*, Kosovska Mitrovica (?), June 28, 1920.
55. Cited in Todorović, *Jugoslavija i balkanske države*, p. 230.
56. Pollo and Buda, *Historia*, pp. 299–501, 503–504.
57. Todorović, *Jugoslavija i balkanske države*, p. 142.
58. Pollo and Buda, *Historia*, vol. 2, pp. 550–551.

(KONARE, National Revolutionary Committee), which, like Noli's over-thrown government, fought for the "vindication of [Albania's] ethnic fron-tiers."[59] Through KONARE, and also directly, the KK participated in the Balkan Federation, a Comintern agency for the communization of nationally disaffected nations of the Balkans, thereby continuing Curri's early contacts (1921) with Soviet officials.[60] But as the policy of defense of Yugoslavia became the official Communist line in the late 1930s, especially after the establishment of the Italian protectorate in Albania (1939), Communists no longer received even a modicum of support among the Kosovars.[61] It is a comment on Yugoslavia's policies that they experienced the Italian occupa-tion of 1941, which came in the guise of "Great Albania," as genuine national liberation.

Just as in October 1924, when Zija Dibra appealed to Stjepan Radić to help Albanians acquire what belonged to them, throughout the interwar period (and after 1945), the Albanians of Yugoslavia sought partnership with the country's other disaffected nationalities.[62] Precisely because Serbian power was at its weakest in the Albanian territories, the natural allies of Albanians, succumbing often to anti-Albanian racialism, feared challenging Belgrade in this sensitive area. Because the number of Albanians in Yugoslavia was large and growing, and because their own sense of nationhood was continually stimulated by the persistence and proximity of the Albanian state, ever different (Zogist, fascist, Marxist-Leninist) and ever sensitive to the unrea-son of its frontiers, the standing of the Albanian minority in Yugoslavia could not acquire the patina of permanence. A perceptive Serbian author noted in 1921 that the Albanians of Yugoslavia would accept and even love the state that made possible the free enjoyment of their ideals: "Some will say, 'Who is preventing them from enjoying the goods that we all have? Did not the state loyally receive them into its arms?' Yes, it did, but only formally and fictitiously. The practice is of a rather different kind. That is why they do not feel the same in this state as the rest of us. A constant feeling of fear and insecurity haunts them all."[63] A state that would lift the burden of Albanian national security would have to accept the ideal of Azem Bejta. Where his reputation followed the ups and downs of his countrymen in Yugoslavia, in Albania his exploits have even been adopted to choreographic notation. The ballet *Shota and Azem Galica* is not a ballet of divertissement.

59. Ibid., p. 561.

60. Nicholas C. Pano, *The People's Republic of Albania* (Baltimore, 1968), p. 27.

61. Hadri, "Nacionalno ugnjetavanje," pp. 160–165.

62. AIHRPH, 1925/Sig. VI/C, Box 3: Kabinet Ministra unutrašnjih dela, Pov. Kab. br. 1504, Belgrade, Dec. 18, 1924.

63. Milan Vukićević, "O uzrocima nemira u kosovskoj i podrimskoj Srbiji," *Novi život*, vol. 2 (1921–1922), no. 7, p. 163.

The Macédoine

[οἱ Σλαβοβουλγάροι, οἱ] ἀπογόν[οι] τοῦ ᾿Ιλλύρου, Κολλεδα, [καί]
τοῦ Σίλνι Στέφαν Νεεμάνοβηκ καί τῶν λοιπῶν.

[The Slavo-Bulgars], descendants of Illyrus, Koleda, the Mighty Stefan
[Dušan] Nemanjić and of others.

Dimitər Miladinov, 1852

Oko Strume i Vardara
divan cveta cvet,
a cvet taj je srpskog cara:
Car-Dušanov svet.
 Oko Strume i Vardara
 cveta cveće srpskog cara.

Round the Struma and the Vardar
a lovely flower blooms,
it is the flower of the Serbian tsar:
the holy blossom of Tsar Dušan.
 Round the Struma and the Vardar
 bloom the flowers of the Serbian tsar.

Stevan Kaćanski, 1885

Your tsars and kings ruled over our land with blood and infamy, and to this
extent, too, your title deed to the Macedonian land is bloody and infamous.

Kočo Racin, 1939

Macedonia had not yet been turned into the worms' kitchen for the short-
lived Balkan fellowship that marked the beginning of Ottoman decline, when
some domestic officer of French cookery christened a medley of fruits or
vegetables by the name of the most unhappy province of European Turkey.
By extension, this land "of stones and wild apples" (K. Misirkov) was no
more than the Macédoine of five nations, which, according to Sami Bej
Frashëri's account from the early 1890s, "in each case compactly inhabit[ed]
a definite area, though no place [was] populated by a single nationality."[1]
 If Macedonia was a Yugoslavia in miniature, it had an epic sadness all its
own. Its country people were noted for warmth and a meek sense of delight that
defied their circumstances. Among the poor shepherds and tobacco farmers,
more recently itinerant traders and migrating handymen, a great capacity for
uncomplaining suffering was mixed with muted sensuality, indeed with the

1. Bulgarian Academy of Sciences, *Makedonija: Sbornik ot dokumenti i materiali*, ed. Dimitər
Kosev et al. (Sofia, 1978), p. 410.

subdued glow that marked Kočo Racin's poetry: "If only I had a store in Struga so as to perch on its shutters; to see, only to see, and on a shutter to die."[2] Racin, a Communist more lyrical than any sensualist, was rephrasing a folk song that had a happier, though no less fleeting conclusion—the would-be storekeeper's quiet joy in watching a beauty pass by his emporium—but his version retold the refrain of an older sigh. More than three-quarters of a century before Racin, Konstantin Miladinov (1830–1862), one of the two brothers who began to awaken Macedonians, wrote from cold Moscow about his longing for the south. He prayed for eagle's wings to fly over Stamboul, Kukuš (Kilkis), Ohrid, and Struga: "There I shall play the pipe after sunset; the sun will set and I shall die."[3]

The story of Macedonia abounds in numerous broad parallels with the larger story of "southern regions." Belgrade coveted "Southern Serbia" (Macedonia) as much as it did the more accessible Old Serbia, and for many of the same historical reasons. Macedonians were themselves often uncertain about their allegiances and, rather like Montenegrins, did not initially deny any of their affiliations. The Macedonian awakener Dimitər Miladinov, whose early correspondence was in Greek, claimed Serbian Stefan Dušan among the ancestors of Slavo-Bulgars, and called their language strictly Bulgarian. The nineteenth-century arguments over Macedonia were often similar to those in Kosovo, at least in terms of pseudoscholarly propaganda and ultimate outcome. Serbian policies of Macedonia were similar to those practiced in Kosovo (prohibition of Bulgarian schools and language, agrarian reform at the expense of local population, Serb colonizing), and Macedonia also had a strong emigration, which, just like the Kosovar emigration, came to play a decisive role in a neighboring state—Bulgaria, which most Macedonians considered their matrix state. The policies of Sofia resembled those of the interwar Tirana governments, just as the tactics of Macedonian revolutionists resembled those of the Montenegrin Greens and Albanian kaçaks. In all three cases Italy played its anti-Belgrade hand, as did the Croat oppositionists. And finally, as in all instances of hard opposition, a flavor of condite communism could be detected in the Macédoine.

Just like Kosovo, Macedonia loomed large in the national memory of the Serbs. It was in Skopje, on the Orthodox Easter of 1346, that Stefan Dušan had himself crowned as "Christ God's well-believing tsar of Serbs and Greeks."[4] Prilep was the city of Prince Marko, the legendary hero of Serb

2. Kočo Racin, *Beli mugri i drugi tvorbi,* ed. Aleksandar Spasov (Skopje, 1974), p. 68.

3. Konstantin Miladinov, "Təga za jug," in Dimitər and Konstantin Miladinov, *Səčinenija* (Sofia, 1965), p. 123.

4. Before his crowning, Stefan Dušan raised the autocephalous Serbian archbishopric to the rank of a patriarchate and assembled the state council to Skopje to confirm his decisions. The crowning was also approved by the autocephalous Patriarchate of Bulgaria and Archbishopric of Ohrid, the latter in Greek hands. Dušan Blagojević, "Ideja i stvarnost Dušanovog carevanja," in Sima Ćirković, ed., *Od najstarijih vremena do maričke bitke (1371),* vol. 1 of *Istorija srpskog naroda* (Belgrade, 1981), pp. 527–528.

heroic epic. And in his memorial church of Saint Demetrius at Sušica (popularly Marko's monastery, near Skopje) fresco painters protrayed Marko in royal purple, holding the horn of a myrrh-anointed "New David."[5] But whereas in Kosovo the decisive Albanian presence and attachments dated after the collapse of medieval Serbia, in Macedonia the Serbian phase was relatively brief (a mere 113 years from Milutin's conquest of northern Macedonia in 1282 to the death of Prince Marko and Lord Konstantin Dragaš in 1395). Both the Greeks and the Bulgars could claim far deeper roots than the Serbs, pointing to Macedonia's place in Byzantine and medieval Bulgarian empires long before Serbian conquest (the Bulgar periods were roughly from Presian to Samuil's successors, 836–1018, and again in intervals during the Second Bulgarian empire, about 1197–1246, 1257–1277). Owing to this checkered history of state traditions, Macedonia's internal divisions were far more complicated than the bipolarity of Montenegrin national allegiances. Moreover, a precarious, but logical, tendency toward the overcoming of Greek, Bulgar, and Serb forms within a new, native, and syncretic blend was never far from the surface. The frescoes of Marko's monastery were marked in Serbian and Bulgarian recensions of Church Slavonic (the latter with the characteristic Ѫ (big *jus*), the thirty-seventh letter of paleo-Cyrillic), and in Greek. There were no frescoes of Serbian saints.[6]

Notwithstanding these ambiguities, there never was any serious doubt that the Slavic population of Macedonia belonged to the same linguistic, historical, and cultural zone as the Bulgarians. Moreover, the Bulgaro-Macedonian bipolarism ceases being an oddity when viewed in the context of Bulgarian history, which was noted for its continuous seesawing between southwest and northeast, between the Macedonian Ohrid of Saint Kliment and the northeastern Preslav of Saint Naum, two great centers of Cyrillo-Methodian literary activity in the ninth century. Since these early times, political troubles and foreign invasions had kept the Bulgar timber balanced up and down the bipolar corridor: the flight of the Preslav scholars to the west in the late tenth century; the rise of the School of Tərnovgrad in the northeast during the Second Empire (twelfth to fourteenth centuries); the custodial duty of the west during the Ottoman period (the monasteries of Rila, Zograf, and Hilandar, and the Catholic school centered on Čiprovec); the decisive role of the northeast in the nineteenth-century Bulgarian Awakening and the adoption of the Eastern Bulgarian dialect as the basis of Bulgarian literary language; Macedonia being excluded from the Bulgarian state by decision of powers at the Congress of Berlin (June–July 1878) some four months after its inclusion in the Great Bulgaria of the Treaty of San Stefano (March 3, 1878). But despite this alternate movement, no Serb observer before the late 1860s

5. Gordana Babić-Djordjević and Vojislav J. Djurić, "Polet umetnosti," in Jovanka Kalić, ed. *Doba borbi za očuvanje i obnovu države (1371–1537)*, vol. 2 of ibid. (Belgrade, 1982), p. 146.
6. Ibid., pp. 148–149.

really tried to cut a piece of timber for Serbia. Stjepan Verković, a Serbianized Croat and a former Franciscan friar who adopted Orthodoxy and entered the Serbian service in Ottoman Macedonia, entitled his collection of Macedonian folk songs (1860) *The Folk Songs of Macedonian Bulgars*, and noted in the introduction that the title was chosen because "should somebody today ask a Macedonian Slav, 'What are you?' he would immediately get the answer, 'I am a Bulgar and my language is Bulgarian.' "[7]

In the 1870s, as the result of several international developments, Serbia began at last to pay attention to its southern neighbor. The Bulgarians, though still stateless, had begun using their emporial power within the Ottoman state to persuade the Porte that an autocephalous Bulgarian church would be a useful counterweight to the expanding influence of cultural and political Hellenism that radiated from the Phanariot-dominated churches within the jurisdiction of the ecumenical patriarch of Constantinople. In 1870, Sultan Abdulaziz promulgated the Bulgarian Exarchate, which initially included only one Orthodox eparchy (metropolitan bishopric) in Macedonia (Veles; in the course of the same year the Macedonian eparchies of Bitola, Ohrid, and Skopje also accrued to the Exarchate) but included the eparchies of Niš and Pirot, which, though still under the Ottomans, were predominantly Serbian in population. Eight years later the Treaty of San Stefano, which Russia dictated to the Turks after the liberation of Bulgaria, established an enormous Bulgar state that contained not only the whole of Macedonia (except for Salonika and the Khalkidhiki peninsula) but also parts of east central Albania (with Korçë) and southeastern Serbia (Vranje, Pirot). Though the powers nullified this agreement at the Congress of Berlin, Serbia had reason to suspect that the revival of San Stefano would remain a lasting Bulgar goal. When the Congress of Berlin then decided to sanction the Austro-Hungarian occupation of Bosnia-Hercegovina, long a target of Serbian expansion, Serbia turned its eyes to the south, to Macedonia, hoping to realize its ambitions there. In the famous secret treaty with Milan Obrenović (1881), Vienna promised Serbia diplomatic support for this strategy.

Serbian aspirations soon gave rise to an elaborated system of theories about Serbia's right to Macedonia. The first theories along this line were utterly primitive, as in the works of Miloš Milojević, who talked about Serbian settlement of the Balkans in the pre-Roman period;[8] but gradually the claims became more sophisticated. Dr. Jovan Hadži-Vasiljević, an ethnographer from Vranje who crisscrossed Macedonia in the 1890s, part of the time as Serbian consular official, legitimated Serbian claims not so much by insisting on the purely Serb character of Macedonia as by providing argu-

7. Stefan I. Verković, ed., *Narodne pesme makedonski Bugara* (Belgrade, 1860), p. xiii.
8. Ljubiša Doklestiḱ, *Srpsko-makedonskite odnosi vo XIX-ot vek do 1897 godina* (Skopje, 1973), pp. 119–120.

310

ments against its Bulgar assignation. Writing about the Kumanovo area in 1909, he noted that the "population of this district never had any developed national consciousness. They do not know about any *Slavic* nationality, much less about Bulgar or *Macedonian* nationality. These appellations were unknown to them. The masses of people do not know them to this day. But the population knew and increasingly knows about its community with the Serbs, with Serbia. This *realization* effected a *feeling* that they were *one and the same* with the Serb people and Serbia, except that all of this is still at *the level of feeling.*"[9]

This approach, especially after the beginning of the twentieth century, marked the writings that were apologetic of Serbian interests in Macedonia, notably the works of Jovan Cvijić and Aleksandar Belić, two of Serbia's most distinguished scholars. In his studies of South Slavic ethnography, expounded since the turn of the century but synthesized during his wartime exile in France (1918), Cvijić devised a "Central Type," dissimilar at the same time to the "Dinaric Type" (the principal "Serb" ethnographic variant representative of the South Slavs south of the Isonzo-Krka-Sava-Danube line and west of the more or less straight line that could be drawn from the mouth of the Timok to the mouth of the Drin) and the "East Balkan Type" (representing the subdanubian Balkans from the influx of the Iskər into the Danube to the mouth of the Mesta on the Aegean Sea, that is, eastern Bulgaria, Dobrudža, and Thrace, excluding not just Macedonia but even the region of Sofia, Bulgaria's capital). The true Bulgars belonged only to the "East Balkan Type," especially to the ethnovariant of the Lower Danubian basin, between the Danube and the Balkan Mountains. They were a mixture of Slavs, three "Turanian" groups (Bulgars, Patzinaks-Cumans, and Ottoman Turks), ancient Thracians, and Vlachs, and, as such, were "different from the other South Slavs in their ethnic composition."[10] More important, their national character was decidedly un-Slavic. Bulgars were industrious and coarse. Their demeanor was grave, cheerless, and sullen and their life purely materialistic: "Where the western South Slavs are more or less cheerful at meanest work and in the worst circumstances, and where their magnanimity and even warmth of manner characterize their relationships, the Bulgars have none of that and consider such things as 'Serb business.' On the contrary, their cold egoism, their restless and constant thirst for profit and acquisition of material goods, niggardliness, and total absence of magnanimity are termed the 'Bulgar way' by the Serbs."[11]

The caricature of Bulgars permitted their clear differentiation from the

9. Jovan Hadži-Vasiljević, *Kumanovska oblast*, vol. 2 of *Južna stara Srbija: Istorijska, etnografska i politička istraživanja* (Belgrade, 1909), pp. 280–281.

10. Jovan Cvijić, *Balkansko poluostrvo i južnoslovenske zemlje: Osnovi antropogeografije*, 2d ed. (Belgrade, 1966), pp. 523–524.

11. Ibid., p. 531.

The Hard Opposition

"Central Type," within which Cvijić included Macedonians, western Bulgars (Šops), and Serbs of the Prizren-Timok (Torlak) dialects, a type that was eminently Slavic and therefore non-Bulgar. Dr. Tihomil Djordjević, a leading Serbian folklorist, strengthened Cvijić's descriptions by stressing the typically Slavic tribalism of Macedonians, divided as they were among modern ethnic groups (Brsjaci, Mrvaci, Šopovi/Šops, Polivaci, Babuni, Kečkari, Mijaci).[12] By constrast, Djordjević's Bulgars were a grim horde who respected only force: "The spirit of insatiable plunder that the Bulgars brought to the Balkan peninsula is maintained among their Slavicized descendents with the only difference that, where the Turanian Bulgars constituted an intrepid warrior horde, the Slavicized Bulgars do not appear greedy and insatiable for plunder, except in the case when the gain of plunder can be realized at the minimum of risks."[13] They were a people without imagination and therefore necessarily without art and culture. In Cvijić's words, it followed that in Macedonia, "which the Bulgars and Serbs ruled alternately, there are no monuments or monasteries save of Serbian or Byzantine provenance."[14]

Spiritual sluggishness neutralized the acquisitive character of the Bulgars in any free match with the Serbs. Aleksandar Belić, a leading Serbian linguist, tried to demonstrate that the similarities evident in the Torlak dialects of Serbian and the Macedonian dialects were due to Serbian colonization. Belić readily admitted that the ancient language of Slavic Macedonians, which Cyril and Methodius standardized in Old Church Slavonic, "rendered, together with the language of eastern Bulgaria, a single Bulgarian protolanguage," but he believed that the medieval Serbian acquisition of Macedonia and extensive Serbian colonization changed the linguistic map of the land: "The result of this colonization was the Serbianization of Macedonia. Had the Ottoman conquest never occurred, this process would have been completed. As it stands, it was only partly completed."[15]

It makes little difference that Belić exaggerated the Serbian elements in Macedonian dialects (the preponderance of sounds ć [k] and dj [ǵ] instead of št and žd, the change of the reflex ѣ into e, the change of ѫ to u, and so on, much of which is not typical of southern and eastern Macedonian idioms) and neglected the importance of Bulgarian structures (for example, the postpositive article).[16] Nor is it particularly important that Cvijić seriously claimed

12. T.-R. Georgevitch, *La Macédoine* (Paris, 1919), p. 23.
13. Ibid., pp. 21–22.
14. Cvijić, *Balkansko poluostrvo*, p. 537.
15. Aleksandar Belić, *Srbi i Bugari u balkanskom savezu i u medjusobnom ratu* (Belgrade, 1913), pp. 39, 40.
16. Ibid., pp. 39, 65–67. For a detailed discussion of Macedonian dialects and their characteristics see Božo Vidoeski, "Osnovni dijalektni grupi vo Makedonija," *Makedonski jazik*, vols. 11–12 (1960–1961), nos. 1–2, pp. 13–31.

312

that the Bulgar appellation in Macedonia conveyed not so much a nationality as lower social class: "The word 'Bulgar,' having lost its original ethnographic significance, became in Turkish times a synonym for population of any nationality that was enserfed, mean, and given to harsh agricultural life."[17] These were details, the purpose of which was not to show that Macedonia was Serbian but that it was not Bulgarian, that the "right of Serbs to [Macedonia] was no less real, no less justified, than the right of Bulgars."[18] In the opinion of one historian, Cvijić established that amorphous Macedonians will assimilate with the nationality of the state that gets hold of them, be it Serbian or Bulgarian.[19] It followed that where rights and prospects were matched, only force would decide.

After the Congress of Berlin and especially after the Serbo-Bulgarian war (1885) the extent of Serbia's aims in Macedonia were put on full display. The Society of Saint Sava was founded in Belgrade in 1886 with the stated purpose of fighting Exarchist "Bulgarism." The society's publications and educational institutions were powerful agencies of Serbian national propaganda; some 20,000 students from the "southern regions" passed through its schools in Belgrade in 1887–1912. Serbia plainly took advantage of the solemn imprecation that the eastern patriarchs in union with Constantinople invoked in 1872 against Bulgar ethnophiletism, that is, the precept of dividing the church within a single state along the national lines. As a result, the Exarchate was considered a schismatic church, permitting the elevation of rival bishops in the sees with Exarchal ordinaries. Since the patriarch of Constantinople and his Greek clergy viewed the Serbs as a lesser evil, some of the sees emptied by schism went to Serbian bishops (Skopje in 1897; Veles and Debar in 1910), the rest going to the Greeks. With the sees went the church schools, where instruction was offered in the national language of the patron church. And with education went the spread of national ideologies—hence the ominous divisions between the Exarchists and Patriarchists, the former Bulgarophile, the latter either Serbian or "Graecomane" in orientation. It was not uncommon for one family to have a member in each camp, for an individual to pass through several phases of religio-national orientation, for a village to switch sides at random, and, in an increasingly alarming change of venue to violent methods of redress, for these changes in loyalty to be coerced. Moreover, however enfeebled, the Turks still ruled Macedonia, and no solution was possible without armed challenges to their power.

The initial success of Serbian propaganda provoked Bulgar resistance.

17. Jovan Cvijić, *Govori i članci,* vol. 3 (Belgrade, 1923), p. 42.
18. Belić, *Srbi i Bugari,* p. 41.
19. Vasilj Popović, "Makedonsko pitanje," *Narodna enciklopedija srpsko-hrvatsko-slovenačka,* 1929, vol. 2, p. 751.

Macedonian students in Salonika and Sofia were determined to "make the liberation of Macedonia the order of the day, before Serbian propaganda succeed[ed] in growing powerful and pulverizing the people."[20] In January 1894 a group of these young men formed the Macedonian Revolutionary Organization, which, after intense agitation and propaganda that swelled its clandestine ranks, renamed itself the Bəlgarski makedono-odrinski revolju-cionni komiteti (BMORK, Bulgar Macedono-Adrianopolitan Revolutionary Committee) in 1896, and demanded "full political autonomy of Macedonia and the district of Adrianople [Ottoman Thrace]."[21] Meanwhile, in 1895, Macedonian émigrés in Sofia organized the Macedonian Committee, which, under its established name of Vərhovnija makedonski komitet (VMK, Supreme Macedonian Committee), started infiltrating its armed bands of *komitas* (literally, committeemen) into Macedonia, where they fought not only Turks but also terrorized Serbian and Greek clergy, teachers, and native adherents. The Macedonian movement thus acquired two wings, one (the *vərhovisti,* Supremists) external, rooted in Bulgaria, made up of followers of the Supreme Committee, and the other (the Internal Organization) working clandestinely under Turkish rule.

The differences between the two groups were not just tactical. Terrorist methods of the VMK, which the Internal Organization condemned, were an aspect of its strategic course that envisioned the liberation of Macedonia as the work not of Macedonians but of Bulgarian intervention, backed by Russia. The leaders of the VMK were Bulgarian officers, Macedonian-born or descended, who were close to Bulgarian Prince Ferdinand of Coburg (ruled 1887–1918) and the willing tools of his self-exalting adventures. Though they repeatedly urged a speedy uprising, they had little faith in the strength of the internal movement, nor were they sensitive to the danger of Macedonia's partition, a threat that caused the BMORK to fight for Macedonia's autonomy within the Turkish state in the first place, rather than for her incorporation within Bulgaria.

Since the term *autonomy* traced the Macedonian maze, it is essential to note its sense and reason. Its inspiration certainly belonged to the curious nineteenth-century Balkan practice whereby the powers maintained the fiction of Ottoman control over effectively independent states under the guise of autonomous status within the Ottoman state (Serbia, 1829–1878; Danubian principalities [Romania], 1829–1878; Bulgaria, 1878–1908). Autonomy, in other words, was as good as independence. Moreover, from the Macedonian perspective, the goal of independence by autonomy had another advantage. Goce Delčev (1872–1903) and the other leaders of the BMORK were aware of Serbian and Greek ambitions in Macedonia. More important, they were aware that neither Belgrade nor Athens could expect to obtain the whole of

20. Cited in Konstantin Pandev, *Nacionalno-osvoboditelnoto dviženie v Makedonija i Odrinsko 1878–1903* (Sofia, 1979), p. 68.
21. Bulgarian Academy of Sciences, *Makedonija,* p. 390.

Macedonia and, unlike Bulgaria, looked forward to and urged partition of the land. Autonomy, then, was the best prophylactic against partition—a prophylactic that would preserve the Bulgar character of Macedonia's Chrisian population despite the separation from Bulgaria proper. In the words of an editorial in *Pravo* (Right), a Sofia newspaper close to the BMORK, the idea of Macedonian autonomy (or separatism) was strictly political and did not imply a secession from Bulgar nationhood. Inasmuch as the ideal of San Stefano was unworkable, the autonomous idea was the only alternative to the partition of Macedonia by the Balkan states and the assimilation of its severed parts by Serbs, Greeks, and even Romanians (who claimed the areas of Vlach minority):

> The Bulgars of the principality [of Bulgaria]—if there be still some who dream of the Bulgaria of San Stefano, have no reason to object to the separatism of the Macedonian population. Irrespective of the harm that the dream of the Bulgaria of San Stefano might bring both now and in the future, irrespective of all the opportunities that political separatism can bring, there is one essential and important consequence of this doctrine, that is, the preservation of the Bulgar tribe—whole, undivided, and bound by their spiritual culture, though separated politically. Without this politically separatism, the spiritual integrity of the Bulgar tribe seems impossible. It is in the interest of the Bulgarian principality not only to support this idea but to continue to work for its realization.
>
> As far as the other small Balkan states of Romania, Serbia, and Greece are concerned, we think that, should their policy be free of egotistical incentives but instead based on the broad mission of Balkan confederation, and should they sincerely believe that the majority of the Macedonian population is of the same nationality as they, nothing would be more urgent for them than to support autonomy and political separatism.[22]

Goce Delčev, the tolerant, wise, and forgiving theoretician of the Internal Organization, himself a former Bulgarian military cadet, was so firmly committed to the idea of an autonomous Macedonia that (in 1902) he took the step of changing the statute and rules of the BMORK and, in a departure from its Bulgarocentric character, renamed it the Tajna makedono-odrinska revoljucionna organizacija (TMORO, Secret Macedono-Adrianopolitan Revolutionary Organization). The TMORO was to be an insurgent organization, open to all Macedonians regardless of nationality, who wished to participate in the movement for Macedonian autonomy. Delčev called for the "elimination of chauvinist propaganda and nationalist dissentions that divide and weaken the population of Macedonia and the Adrianople area in its struggle against the common [Ottoman] foe."[23] The TMORO guerrilla units (*četas*) started recruiting "Graecomanes," Vlachs, and others.

22. Ibid., pp. 424–425. The article appeared on June 7, 1902 (O.S.).
23. Cited in Mercia MacDermott, *Freedom or Death: The Life of Gotsé Delchev* (London, 1978), p. 307.

The Hard Opposition

Delčev's initiative was overtaken by the raids of the vərhovisti and the opposition of some of his own men. Moreover, the rivalry between the two revolutionary centers hastened the advance of premature insurrection. The vərhovisti provoked a bloody series of clashes in Gorna Džumaja in late October 1902. But the cost attending the ill-timed call to arms became apparent only with the uprisings of August 1903, which commenced in southwestern Macedonia (the *vilayet* of Bitola) and the region of Strandža (Thrace) on the feast days of Prophet Elijah (Ilinden, August 2, N.S.) and the Lord's Transfiguration (August 19, N.S.) respectively. Contrary to the expectations of the revolutionary leaders, the European powers failed to intervene on behalf of Christian insurgents. Both uprisings were drowned in blood, the Turkish soldiers and Albanian irregulars having burned some 150 villages round Bitola.

The failure of the Ilinden uprising effectively quelled the Macedonian insurrectionist organization for a long period, during which Bulgar initiatives in general gave way to the rise of Serbian and Greek insurgency. Beginning in the spring of 1904, Serbian guerrillas (Chetniks), started making raids into Macedonia. Unlike the Bulgar movement, which on the whole relied on native Macedonian peasantry with a smattering of educated men, mainly officers and students, these Serbian guerrillas were a motley lot that included simple adventurers from Serbia proper and the Serb communities of Austria-Hungary and Macedonians who were either itinerant workers domesticated in Serbia or men who had been for one reason or other expelled from Bulgar insurgent organizations. Of the five leading Serbian guerrilla chiefs, two were officers formerly in Bulgarian service (Djordje Skopljanče, native of Peć, and Cene Marković), one was a schoolteacher (Jovan Babunski), one had no profession (Petko Ilić), and one, Vasilije Trbić of Dalj (Slavonia), was a former monk who fled Mount Athos in 1902 after being charged with the murder of some Greek monks. (Trbić's career was crowned in 1924 when he was elected a deputy to the national assembly on the NRS ticket.) The Chetnik attacks on both Turks and Bulgars initiated a period of fearful Macedonian *bellum omnium in omnes,* which undid nearly every hope of autonomy.[24] The revived Internal Organization was increasingly under the

24. The scale of these battles in their early phase (1905–1906) can be gauged from Serbian sources which claim the loss of 101 guerrillas, 93 to the Turks, 8 to the Bulgar units. "Borba srpskih junaka—ustaša u Staroj Srbiji i Maćedoniji i izginuli junaci," *Vardar: Kalendar za redovnu godinu 1907* (Belgrade, 1906), pp. 78–82. According to Georgevitch, *La Macédoine,* pp. 248–269, Bulgar units killed 466 Serbs in Macedonia between 1881 and 1909. By my calculation, 89.53 percent of these people were killed in 1903–1908 alone, the worst year being 1904 (more than 120 killings). Since the principal aim of Serbian četas was the struggle against "Bulgarism," the clashes with the Turks were incidental to that higher aim, and there is indeed ample evidence that the četas collaborated with the Turks against the interal and external wings of the Macedonian revolutionary organization. See Gligor Todorovski, "Srpskata četnička organizacija i nejzinata aktivnost vo Makedonija," *Institut za nacionalna istorija: Glasnik,* vol. 12 (1968), no. 1, pp. 191–194.

influence of the VMK, though a left wing, associated with the Serres guerrilla group of Jane Sandanski, kept alive the autonomist tradition of Delčev,
who had fallen to a Turkish ambush in 1903.

Not unexpectedly, internecine guerrilla war was followed by partition.
Bulgaria's ambitions were ascendant after the proclamation of her independence in 1908, at which time Ferdinand assumed the grand title of tsar. Four
years later Sofia concluded alliances with Belgrade and Athens and the
Balkan states joined together to drive the Turk out of Europe. Though Sofia
and Belgrade agreed that Macedonia should be autonomous, Serbia recognized Bulgaria's claim to Macedonia south of a meandering line extending
from slightly north of Kriva Palanka to slightly north of the town of Ohrid.
The disposition of northern Macedonia (with Struga, Debar, Kičevo, Gostivar, Tetovo, Skopje, and Kumanovo) was to be arbitrated by the Russian
tsar. Bulgaria and Greece, however, agreed to no particular territorial arrangements. The decisive victory of the allies in the First Balkan War was
followed by a scramble over Macedonia, with Serbia and Greece allied
against Bulgaria, which, though isolated, slowly edged toward hostilities that
started in June 1913. The allies, joined by Romania and Turkey, quickly
defeated Bulgaria. Anything but autonomous, Macedonia was partitioned by
the Treaty of Bucharest (1913), whereby over half of the land went to Greece
(Aegean Macedonia) and most of the remainder to Serbia (Vardar Macedonia), leaving slightly more than one-tenth to Bulgaria (Pirin Macedonia).
Bulgaria also lost southern Dobrudža to Romania, but it was allowed to keep
a part of Thrace, providing access to the Aegean.

The immediate effect of the partition was the anti-Bulgar campaign in
areas under Serbian and Greek rule. The Serbians expelled Exarchist churchmen and teachers and closed Bulgar schools and churches (affecting the
standing of as many as 641 schools and 761 churches). Thousands of Macedonians left for Bulgaria, joining a still larger stream from devastated
Aegean Macedonia, where the Greeks burned Kukuš, the center of Bulgar
politics and culture, as well as much of Serres and Drama. Bulgarian (including the Macedonian dialects) was prohibited, and its surreptitious use, whenever detected, was ridiculed or punished.[25]

25. For a detailed report on Serbian expulsion of six Exarchist bishops, mistreatment of Bulgar
schoolteachers, and attempts to pressure Macedonians to renounce "Bulgarism" and take oaths of
Serb nationality, as well as on the atrocities of Greek *Boulgarophagoi* (Bulgar-eaters) in Aegean
Macedonia, see Carnegie Endowment, *Report of the International Commission to Inquire into the
Causes and Conduct of the Balkan Wars* (Washington, 1914), pp. 162–207. According to a Bulgar
source from the leadership of the interwar neosupremist Internal Organization, Serbian terror in
Macedonia in 1912–1915 claimed the lives of 1,854 people, while 285 "disappeared." In addition,
20 women were raped and 1,221 houses were burned. Ivan Mihajlov, *Spomeni*, vol. 2, *Osvoboditelna borba, 1919–1924 g.* (Brussels, 1965), pp. 383–524. My analysis of Mihajlov's list
yields the following results: among identified victims of Serbian terror, 554 of those killed were
Muslims, most of them Albanians. Since the casualties from the heavily Albanian Tetovo district

In 1915 the pendulum of intimidation swung back, as Bulgaria went to war on the side of Central Powers largely on account of Macedonia. Before that, under pressure from Russia, Serbia was obliged to consider territorial concessions to Bulgaria in order to win Sofia to the side of the Allies. That having failed, Serbia had reason to play up the Bulgarian "stab in the back" after the beginning of Mackensen's offensive in late 1915. Dislodged and in exile, the Serbian government, maintaining that the Macedonian question did not exist, demanded the restoration of pre-1914 borders, even though Macedonians in Serbian service were engaged by Serbian propagandists to declare their hope that the Corfu Declaration would be amended "by including within it the whole of Macedonia and all Macedonians."[26]

Wartime Bulgarian policies did, however, invite Serbian revanchism. Though the Bulgarian occupational administration in most of Vardar and in part of Aegean Macedonia (east of the Struma) was popular enough, except with the dislodged Serbian and Greek clergy and officials, the "Graecomane" and "Serbomane" Macedonians were doubtlessly persecuted; but their fate was nothing in comparison with the harsh regime that Bulgaria imposed in the parts of Kosovo and Serbia proper that were also within her occupational zone. The bloody suppression of a Serbian uprising in the Toplica basin (spring 1917) was entrusted to the same Supremist komitas, under the command of General Aleksandər Protogerov, who had made Surdulica, in southeastern Serbia, an infamous place of execution since December 1915.[27]

As in Kosovo, the restoration of Serbian rule in 1918, to which the Strumica district and several other Bulgarian frontier salients accrued in 1919 (Bulgaria also having lost all its Aegean coastline to Greece), marked the replay of the first occupation (1913–1915).[28] Once again, the Exarchist clergy and Bulgar teachers were expelled, all Bulgarian-language signs and

(482 in number) are not identified by name, it is likely that Muslim victims of Serbian terror numbered about half of the total. The most severe repression was in the Albanian areas of western Macedonia, followed by the eastern districts of Vardar Macedonia (from Kočani and Štip to the Bulgarian border), and the districts on the western bank of the Vardar from Prilep to Negotino. Serbians killed 23 Exarchist priests. In the district of Kičevo they crucified Hieromonach Teofan and 2 villagers. Ibid., p. 409.

26. Dragoslav Janković and Bogdan Krizman, eds., *Gradja o stvaranju jugoslovenske države*, vol. 1 (Belgrade, 1964), p. 238.

27. "General Protogerov u Toplici," *Politika*, July 10, 1928, p. 1.

28. For a synthetic presentation of political and socioeconomic developments in Vardar Macedonia in the 1918–1929 period see Mihailo Apostolski and Dančo Zografski, eds., *Istorija makedonskog naroda*, vol. 3, *Period izmedju dva svetska rata i narodna revolucija (1918–1945)* (Belgrade, 1970), pp. 9–55. On the wartime and immediate post-1918 period see Aleksandar Apostolov, "Vardarska Makedonija od Prvata svetska vojna do izborite za Konstituantata—28 noemvri 1920 godina," *Godišen zbornik na Filozofskiot fakultet na Univerzitetot vo Skopje: Istorisko-filološki oddel*, 1962, no. 13, pp. 27–90. See also Aleksandar Apostolov, "Revolucionarne prilike u Makedoniji u godinama 1918, 1919. i 1920.," *Naučni skup "Oktobarska revolucija i narodi Jugoslavije,"* vol. 2 (Belgrade, 1967), pp. 1–44.

books removed, and all Bulgar clubs, societies, and organizations dissolved. The Serbianization of family surnames proceeded as before the war, with Stankovs becoming Stankovićes and Atanasovs entered in the books as Atanackovićes. Though there were fewer killings of "Bulgarists" (a pro-Bulgarian source claimed 342 such instances and 47 additional disappearances in 1918–1924), the conventional forms of repression (jailings, internments) were applied more systematically and with greater effect than before (the same source lists 2,900 political arrests in the same period).[29]

The question of Macedonia presented a special problem for Belgrade. Yugoslavia, certain of its territorial claims to the Adriatic coast and the Banat, insisted on plebiscites in territorial demarcations with Italy and Romania. But Pašić thought better of accepting offers of plebiscite in Macedonia. He feared that eventuality so much that he wrote to Protić from the Paris Peace Conference in April 1919 urging that immediate precautionary measures be taken, sparing neither treasure nor effort, to make sure that, if the unwanted plebiscite did come about, it would not turn out badly for Yugoslavia. He noted that the Muslim beys could prove helpful:

[They] can give orders to all Muslims and Arnauts to vote for Serbia, for Yugoslavia. Use our firmest Bosnian Muslims to help us win the Muslims of Macedonia. Also, do not forget the Jews, who, in my opinion, will rather vote for Yugoslavia than for Bulgaria. Send the best teachers and civil servants to all Macedonian counties. The Red Cross and all humanitarian organizations must be sent to Macedonia at once to help the poor. Do not spare any expense to save Old Serbia and Macedonia. Be considerate but quick. Not a word about this in the press or in public. Should there be no plebiscite, [this effort] will still not be a loss.[30]

Pašić's fear and that of Protić's cabinet, which instructed him to refuse any offers of a plebiscite from the Allies, were exaggerated. Still, Pašić did not wish to sign the peace treaty with Austria in September 1919 for fear that the clause on the rights of minorities (including the right to an education in native language) might later be applied to Macedonia.[31] He was sufficiently realistic about Western (especially Italian) reactions to Belgrade's policies in Macedonia to be weary of Pribićević's unitaristic sophisms, the ideologue of the DS having reduced the whole problem to a simple equation: "Even

29. Mihajlov, *Osvoboditelna borba*, p. 680. In the Kratovo area alone, there were 62 killings, 6 disappearances, and 1,107 arrests. It is important to note that during the same period (1918–1924), the repression in Aegean Macedonia was far less intense. In Greece, Mihajlov recorded 33 killings, 3 disappearances, and 724 arrests. Ibid., p. 692.

30. Cited in Desanka Todorović, *Jugoslavija i balkanske države, 1918–1923* (Belgrade, 1979), p. 41.

31. Bogumil Hrabak, ed., "Zapisnici sednica Davidovićeve dve vlade od avgusta 1919. do februara 1920," *Arhivski vjesnik*, vol. 13, p. 28.

according to the [minorities'] convention, the Bulgars would have no right to open schools in Macedonia, because there is no Bulgarian language there; nor do they have a right to their own church, since the Bulgars, too, are Orthodox, though schismatics in Bulgaria.''[32] The fiction of a "Southern Serbia," however, was too costly for Croat and Slovene politicians, who had to worry about the South Slavic minorities in Italy and Austria. Still, any sort of minority status for the Macedonians would have undercut the whole rationale of expansion. Time had to be bought to carry out a slow Serbianization of Macedonia. To that end, Serbian army and gendarmerie, some 50,000 strong in Macedonia, used several methods. Serbian četas, such as the notorious band of Jovan Babunski, who terrorized the Bregalnica and Tikveš districts from September 1919, were under military orders to kill the local leaders, whose work prepared the actions of Bulgar komitas.[33] The population was systematically channeled into forced labor for the army and subjected to intense propaganda.

Like Kosovo, Macedonia was slated for Serb settlements and internal colonization. The authorities projected the settlement of 50,000 families in Macedonia, though only 4,200 families had been placed in 280 colonies by 1940. In addition, various speculators bought the land from emigrating Turkish feudatories. Milan Stojadinović, a leader of the NRS, minister of finance for much of the period after 1922, head of the Belgrade stock exchange, and prime minister (1935–1939), bought 7,413 acres of land, including the whole village of Kruševica in the Tikveš district, in partnership with a group of business associates, who then, having arranged for the tax-exempt status of the estate, proceeded to maintain the same tenurial relationship with their villagers as had existed under the Turks. At the same time, native Macedonians, under economic as well as political pressures, were emigrating to other areas of Yugoslavia (as many as 26,000 in 1938 alone) and abroad (10,244 left for Bulgaria between 1913 and 1920). The state systematically reduced the purchasing prices of agricultural products subject to state monopolies (opium, tobacco, silk cones). For example, though the purchase price of crude opium fell by 77 percent in 1927–1935, its export price during the same period fell by only 42 percent.[34]

The policy of national assimilation also meant that the government would not permit any autonomist or separatist parties in Macedonia, least of all of Bulgar extraction. Even so, in the districts of pre-1914 Serbia, with the exception of eastern Sandžak and one county of Kosovo (Vranište), during the 1920 parliamentary elections, the centralist parties made their worst

32. Ibid., p. 37.
33. Desanka Todorović, " 'Okupacijata na Strumica 1919 godina,' " *Institut za nacionalna istorija: Glasnik*, vol. 10 (1966), no. 1, 50–51.
34. Aleksandar Apostolov, "Specifičnata položba na makedonskiot narod vo kralstvoto Jugoslavija," *Institut za nacionalna istorija: Glasnik*, vol. 16 (1972), no. 1, pp. 46–54.

showing in "Southern Serbia." The NRS did not even put up any lists in southeastern Macedonia (districts of Bregalnica and Tikveš), and the DS, for all its lopsided electoral lists that were full of imported bureaucrats, teachers, and professors, did well only in western Macedonia, notably in predominantly Albanian districts (for example, Debar, 80.72 percent). The chief beneficiary of Macedonian discontent was the Communist party, which won 36.72 percent of all Macedonian votes, doing especially well in the districts of Kumanovo (44 percent), Skopje (44.11 percent) and Tikveš (45.9 percent). But though the Communists certainly were regarded as a party of "motley malcontents," their program in 1920 was anything but autonomist. The party organization in Skopje was headed by Dušan Cekić, an old socialist, though a merchant, who moved to Macedonia from his native Leskovac (Serbia) after the Balkan wars. Serbian Marxists, like Cekić, believed in the autonomous status of Macedonia within the Balkan federation. But despite this asset, the hard opposition to Serbian supremacy in Macedonia had to come through the saplings of Gabriel hounds, the bugbearish *Makedonstvujušči* (Macedonizers) of the Serbian press—the men of the Macedonian organization.

This time, however, the Bulgarian government was no ally. Tsar Ferdinand abdicated in October 1918, and after the parliamentary elections of August 1919 the government was entrusted to the Agrarian party of Aleksandər Stambolijski, an outspoken opponent of Bulgaria's wartime course. He was determined to pursue a policy of peace with Yugoslavia to the extent that Belgrade would accept his friendship. He arrested the leaders of the Macedonian organization in early November 1919, charged them with war crimes, and then proceeded to underwrite the Treaty of Neuilly (November 27), which set the peace terms and Bulgarian frontiers, without the tumult over Bulgaria's territorial losses. On November 13, 1919, after slightly more than a week of incarceration, the Macedonian leaders escaped from Stambolijski's jail. Protogerov was an old vərhovist, who achieved the rank of general in Bulgarian service. His younger fellow escapee, Todor Aleksandrov (1881–1924) of Štip (Vardar Macedonia), soon eclipsed him in the revival of a single Macedonian guerrilla front, now definitively called the Vətrešna makedonska revoljucionna organizacija (VMRO, Internal Macedonian Revolutionary Organization).

Todor Aleksandrov was the last of his kind, a combination of hajduk (outlaw) warlord and politician. His cruelty was not anonymous and his tactics could not be sorted out in classes on guerrilla warfare that came to be taught in regular military academies. He was a schoolteacher by profession, but his work in the Exarchist schools was combined with service to the Internal Organization, whose central committee he joined in 1911. His ideology was rudimentary. He was a Bulgar Macedonian fighting for Macedonia's autonomy. That meant fighting not only against Serbs and Greeks but also against those Bulgars, like Stambolijski, who tried to extinguish the patriot game. Anybody who offered aid to the "cause" was welcome: when necessary, Aleksandrov worked with the Communists and took money from Mussolini. He spent his life on the run, in chase, or in the underground. He was not equally great in the cabinet as in the field. "He who does not have five pounds of lice," he said, "is no komita." Above all, he looked upon himself as an avenger, a protector of the people, and as one with them. His successor wrote, "He forbade anyone to call him 'Mister.' He could be called 'Uncle Todor' or 'Grandpa Todor' or just plain 'Todor.' Among ourselves [komitas], he was mainly the *Stario* [Old Man] and we addressed him as 'Uncle Todor.' . . . When a peasant addressed him as 'Mister Todor,' he would interrupt: 'I am no "Mister"! I do not want you to call me that again! I have a name. The "misters" are those who divided Macedonia on a green table.' "[35]

Aleksandrov's VMRO quickly grew into a formidable organization that not only prevented any fixity of rule in Vardar Macedonia but became an influential source of political power in Bulgaria itself. In fact, during much of the 1920s, the only real government in Pirin Macedonia was that of Aleksandrov's men. The VMRO had several clienteles. In Bulgaria, notably in Sofia, though deriving some of its influence from collaboration with the nationalist, militarist, and court circles that were hostile to Stambolijski, it worked through the powerful Macedonian émigré societies, with their orderly structure that included benevolent associations, clubs, press, and familiar and hometown networks. In Pirin Macedonia, where the VMRO had its principal bases for guerrilla warfare against Yugoslavia and Greece, its people's militias, consisting largely of peasants, became an army of 9,100 men in 1923, with the biggest bases in Gorna Džumaja (now Blagoevgrad, 3,000 men), Petrič (2,100), and Nevrokop (now Goce Delčev, 1,800). Here, the VMRO collected taxes, patrolled the streets, administered justice, promulgated laws. In Vardar Macedonia, where the VMRO commanded 1,675 active komitas in 1923, its chief zones of operation were on the left bank of the Vardar. The central zone (bounded roughly by a triangle delineated by Tetovo, Kjustendil [Bulgaria], and Radoviš) included Aleksandrov's frequent headquarters below Carev vrv (Tsar's Peak) in the Osogovo Mountains.[36] The southern zone, a wide strip from the Plain of Pelagonia (Bitola) to the length of the Pirin frontier, also oversaw the operations in Greece, leaving much of the right bank of the Vardar outside VMRO's regular military organization.[37]

35. Mihajlov, *Osvoboditelna borba*, p. 110.

36. Ivan Katardžiev, *Vreme na zreenje: Makedonskoto nacionalno prašanje meǵu dvete svetski vojni (1919–1930)*, vol. 1 (Skopje, 1977), pp. 176–177, 203.

37. The VMRO, however, had contacts and bases in Albania, from whose territory it staged raids into the western areas of Vardar Macedonia. Gligor Todorovski, "Nekolku podatoci za aktivnosta na vrhovističkata VMRO vo Albanija i Bugarija pomeǵu dvete svetski vojni," *Institut za nacionalna istorija: Glasnik*, vol. 15 (1971), no. 1, pp. 137–156.

The enormous military power of VMRO was based on the allegiance of peasant masses—the urban Exarchists on the whole favoring legal forms of struggle—and, no less important, on the vehemence of VMRO's wrath. According to official Yugoslav sources, from 1919 to 1934, the authorities registered 467 attacks by the komitas, in which 185 Yugoslav officials were killed and 253 wounded. In addition, 268 civilians were killed or wounded by the komitas during the same period.[38] These same official sources state that Yugoslav authorities claimed to have killed 128 komitas in the 1919–1934 period, wounded 13, and captured 151.[39] (VMRO's own sources give a figure of 86 of its men killed in battles with police and army in the years 1921–1924 alone.)[40] Among the more notorious of the VMRO actions was the massacre in January 1923 of some 30 Serb colonists in Kadrifakovo (Ovče Pole) by the četa of Ivan Bərl'o, an action that was designed to intimidate the settlers into leaving Macedonia.[41] In 1926, the VMRO killed Spasoje Hadži Popović, the director of a Serbian newspaper in Bitola. And in 1927 they killed General Mihailo Kovačević in Štip.[42]

The hegemony of VMRO within the Macedonian movement did not exist without difficulties. Perhaps the least dangerous enemies were the Serbian authorities in Vardar Macedonia. Their countermeasures, for example the launching of the Štip-based Association against Bulgar Bandits in 1922 and the indiscriminate terror of its leaders (Kosta Pećanac, Ilija Trifunović-Lune), only strengthened VMRO's hold. Every pogrom, such as the murder of all male villagers from Garvan (Radoviš) on orders of Bregalnica district chief (March 1923), raised popular indignation and helped the VMRO. More serious were occasional challenges by local peasants, who in many cases grew tired of VMRO's highhanded methods, which in some instances bordered on extortion. But inasmuch as the authorities armed the local counter-četas, as in the case of Ilija Kacarski of Bosilovo (Strumica), their effectiveness was forfeited in advance.[43]

The dissident sections of the Macedonian movement presented a far greater challenge. The movement embraced many political tendencies, mainly from the left. It had its social democrats, members of the Bulgarian Communist party (Dimo Hadži Dimov), independent communists, anarchists (Pavel Šatev), and so on. The left was suspicious of Aleksandrov and questioned the sincerity of his autonomism, seeing him as an effective exponent of Bulgarian annexationism. The remnants of the Serres group of the late Jane Sandanski (led by Todor Panica and others) also tended toward the Communist left and

38. Apostolov, "Specifičnata položba," p. 55.
39. Ibid., p. 56.
40. Mihajlov, *Osvoboditelna borba*, pp. 703–708.
41. Ibid., p. 141.
42. Apostolov, "Specifičnata položba," p. 56.
43. Manol Pandevski and Ǵorǵi Stoev-Trnkata, *Strumica i Strumičko niz istorijata* (Strumica, 1969), p. 328.

favored a form of Balkan and Macedonian federalism, which Dimo Hadži Dimov outlined in his pamphlet "Back to Autonomy" (1919).[44] In 1920, the Bulgarian Communist party, dismissing the whole question as a bourgeois problem, withdrew from the Macedonian movement. But some of the other leftists pressed on with the idea of federalism, leading to a split at the Second Congress of Macedonian Fraternities (late 1920). The federalist program, however, with its quixotic idea of a federal Macedonia organized as a vertical union of national communities, led by a council that had to convene abroad (in western Europe or even in America), and united by a neutral language ("Official language of the Federal Republic of Macedonia is Esperanto"), would have been lost in obscurity, if Stambolijski had not been in need of allies against the VMRO.[45] Aleksandər Dimitrov, Stambolijski's minister of defense, started a campaign against the VMRO after his visit to Belgrade (May 1921). During this period, several VMRO leaders were killed by the Bulgarian police. In retaliation, Aleksandrov ordered the liquidation of Gjorče Petrov; a noted Macedonian émigré leader who favored cooperation with Stambolijski. At this point Dimitrov decided upon an anti-VMRO Macedonian guerrilla, entrusting the job to Panica and other federalists. In October 1921, Dimitrov was assassinated by the VMRO.

In the bloody business that followed, Panica's federalists, aided by the Bulgarian government, set out to destroy the VMRO, and Aleksandrov, quick to meet the challenge, scattered the federalist četas and launched an attack on the Stambolijski government. Some of the fleeing federalists (Grigor Ciklev, Stojan Mišev) placed themselves in Serbian service, henceforth pursuing the VMRO on the left bank of the Vardar alongside the Yugoslav army.[46] Still others collaborated with the Greeks.[47] In 1922, the VMRO's militias dislodged the federalists and government troops from Kjustendil (September 4) and Nevrokop (October 7), from which Panica had to flee. He went into emigration in Vienna, where the federalist leadership was reassembled and began seeking foreign contacts—among other targets, Soviet diplomats. The VMRO's successes helped harden Stambolijski's policy, and in March 1923, in consequence of the Yugoslav-Bulgarian agreement reached in Niš, he undertook the obligation of cooperating with Yugoslavia against the VMRO.[48] In June 1923, the VMRO aided the rightist officers in

44. The key excerpt, calling for a Macedonian republic modeled on the Swiss federal state and within the wider Balkan federation, is cited in Ljubiša Doklestić, ed., *Kroz historiju Makedonije: Izabrani izvori* (Zagreb, 1964), pp. 214–215. A further point of the pamphlet was the restatement of the reasons that autonomy was and remained only a Bulgar idea, rejected by the Turks and Greeks. That section is cited in Bulgarian Academy of Sciences, *Makedonija*, pp. 612–615.
45. On the history of the federalist split and the likelihood that Stambolijski had his hand in the affair, see Katardžiev, *Vreme na zreenje*, vol. 1, pp. 152–159.
46. Ibid., p. 167.
47. Mihajlov, *Osvoboditelna borba*, p. 261.
48. Todorović, *Jugoslavija i balkanske države*, pp. 200–202.

overthrowing Stambolijski's government. The premier was hunted down by Aleksandrov's men, cruelly tortured, and hacked to pieces in his native village. Before they killed him, they cut off his right hand, shouting, "With this hand he signed the Agreement of Niš."[49]

The fall of Stambolijski was a great boon to the power of the VMRO. Though the idol of Bulgarian peasants, the hapless premier was no friend of the VMRO's real or potential allies. The court and the political right plotted his overthrow, and the Communist left did nothing to prevent or reverse it; the Communists rose against the new rightist regime of Aleksandər Cankov in September 1923 only after Moscow found the party's passivity a violation of the then current united front line. But though Aleksandrov profited from the new government's cool attitude toward Yugoslavia, he did not mind signing an agreement with the Communists before the September uprising, promising to stay neutral as long as the uprising was not undertaken in Pirin Macedonia. When the Communists violated this agreement in Razlog, some VMRO troops suppressed them and others protected their leaders.[50] The organization vacillated between ideologically disinterested nationalism and political commitment. Aleksandrov personally contemplated an agreement with the Soviet government: an early draft of such an agreement (December 1923) with the clause on how the VMRO "would gratefully accept the material, diplomatic, and moral support of the [USSR]" was found among his papers. Moreover, together with Protogerov and Petər Čaulev, the other members of the VMRO Central Committee, he even signed a declaration disavowing any ties with the Cankov regime and affirming the VMRO's fight for an independent Macedonia in alliance with the Communists (Vienna, April 29, 1924). Under Cankov's pressure, however, he disowned the agreement with the Communists, which was proclaimed from Vienna in the form of a public manifesto on May 6, 1923.[51]

The repudiation of the May Manifesto split the VMRO. Aleksandrov himself was killed on August 31, 1924, perhaps, as the official VMRO communiqué stated, by the men of Aleko Vasilev-Paša, a VMRO leader of pro-Communist tendencies.[52] Leftist accounts have always blamed the court for the "Old Man's" predictable end. In October 1925, ostensibly in continuation of the May Manifesto, the Communists started their own VMRO— the so-called VMRO (*obedinena,* or United), which exercised significant influence over Macedonian leftist intelligentsia through its Vienna headquarters—the center of a sizable publishing effort. Nevertheless, the VMRO (ob.) was no match for the official VMRO, which was increasingly moving

49. Kosta Todorov, *Stamboliski* (Belgrade, 1937), p. 152.
50. Katardžiev, *Vreme na zreenje,* vol. 1, pp. 180–181.
51. Bulgarian Academy of Sciences, *Makedonija,* pp. 676–679, 684–685.
52. "Le chef légendaire du mouvement de libération de la Macédoine Todor Alexandroff assassiné," *Nouvelles Macédoniennes,* Sept. 15, 1924, p. 1.

toward the right under the leadership of Protogerov (assassinated in 1928) and Ivan (Vančo) Mihajlov. The VMRO's absolute hold over Pirin Macedonia was broken by the dictatorship of the Zveno (Link) group (1934), a bloc of reform-minded officers, who, though sympathetic to the Macedonian cause, found irredentism too costly for Bulgaria. But though their measures chimed at the dirge of the official VMRO, the Zvenoists could not prevent the Macedonians' most spectacular assassination. Acting with the backup of Italy and Pavelić's Ustašas (Pavelić having found his allies in the VMRO after the beginning of his emigration in 1929), VMRO's gunman Vlado Černozemski shot King Aleksandar in Marseilles on October 9, 1934. But the end of its greatest enemy was also the end of the VMRO.

The VMRO was part of a generic resistance that helped to tear the fabric of Great Serbianism in the "southern regions." The similarities between the Albanian kaçaks and the Macedonian komitas are real—and indeed, the Albanian and Macedonian oppositionists cooperated with each other, and in November 1920 Protogerov and Hasan Bej Prishtina signed an agreement committing the Albanians to the "liberation of Macedonia in her ethnographic and geographical frontiers," with only Debar being the subject of a projected plebiscite.[53] Both groups had further dealings with Italy, the Montenegrins, and various Croat organizations, first Radić's party and the Frankists, later on the Ustašas.[54] Still, where Azem Bejta is celebrated in socialist Albania and recognized in Kosovo, there are no streets named for Todor Aleksandrov in either Bulgaria or Yugoslavia. Historians in Yugoslav Macedonia admit that the "broad masses of peasants accepted Todor Aleksandrov throughout Macedonia—in Pirin Macedonia, the eastern part of Vardar Macedonia, and to some extent in Aegean Macedonia," but then go to great lengths to show that this was a result of VMRO's factious demagoguery: the VMRO preached Macedonian autonomy, but was in fact a Bulgarian irredentist organization.[55]

This charge is overweighted with parachronistic perceptions. The men of the VMRO certainly considered themselves Macedonians, not by nationality, but as part of a larger multinational region to which the VMRO appealed in its attempts to draw members of all nationalities into the organization.[56] As for the nationality of the Macedonian Slavs, they did not question its Bulgar

53. Mihajlov, *Osvoboditelna borba*, p. 159.
54. Radić had a meeting with Protogerov in 1923 during his tour of Europe, something that alarmed the Yugoslav authorities. Todorović, *Jugoslavija i balkanske države*, p. 203. In 1924, the public prosecutor in Zagreb brought charges of treason against Radić on account of an interview that Radić gave to a VMRO journal. Arhiv Instituta za historiju radničkog pokreta (AIHRPH), ZB-S-9/40: Kraljevski sudbeni stol, I 1702–1924.
55. Katardžiev, *Vreme na zreenje*, vol. I, pp. 171–175.
56. It is difficult to understand how the VMRO's attempts to draw the village poor into the movement's leadership and to treat Turkish members the same as others constitutes demagoguery. Ibid., p. 175.

character. Nor, for that matter, did the members of the VMRO (ob.), whose émigré organs regularly assumed the Bulgar identity of Macedonian Slavs until 1934. The VMRO's negative—and by no means unique—stand on Macedonian nationhood, however, should not be confused with Bulgarian irredentism.

The idea of a separate (Slavic) Macedonian nationhood most certainly had its antecedents before the 1930s—nor is that surprising, considering the political history of the area. Krsto Misirkov (1874–1926), the "first creator of a clear and rounded representation, of argued and systematic conception about the national essence of Macedonian people,"[57] brought arguments in favor of Macedonian "national separatism" in his *Za makedonckite raboti* (About Macedonian Affairs, published in Sofia in 1903 in Bulgarian), but still considered the Macedonian question a part of a larger Bulgar complex, if for no other reason than linguistic. The pattern of Misirkov's national behavior would become rather common among the Macedonian intellectuals of the 1930s. They were Bulgars in struggles against Serbian and Greek hegemonism, but within the Bulgar world they were increasingly becoming exclusive Macedonians: "On the one hand, there was [Misirkov's] pan-Bulgar patriotism, which was based largely on the kinship of language, and his pan-Bulgar positions, which he used, moreover frontally, against the Serbs (and before them the Greeks). On the other, when it concerned the national and cultural differentiation within the framework of the Bulgarophone unit, understood more in a philological than an ethnic way, there were his Macedonian patriotism and his Macedonian positions."[58]

During the 1930s, Macedonians were increasingly accepting the reality of Yugoslavia. Younger generations were moving away from clandestine forms of struggle, affirming Macedonian culture and language, and arguing for a federal status within Yugoslavia. According to a Serbian official, in a report to Prime Minister Stojadinović in May 1938, the "liquidation of the Bulgar revolutionary committee [VMRO], our good relations with Bulgaria, and, finally, our relations with Italy and Austria (ending their aid to Croat separatism)—all of that contributed to a certain reorientation of Macedonians, who are manifesting [preferences for] a certain reformed autonomy without conspiracies, or rather Macedonia for Macedonians. . . . [Their] slogan is: come to the parliament in the greatest possible numbers regardless of the party, and fight there for separatism within the frontiers of Yugoslavia."[59] But despite the intellectual stirrings in Vardar Macedonia, only the Communist move-

57. Dančo Zografski, "Krste Misirkov za nacionalnosta na Makedoncite," in Hristo Andonov-Poljanski et al., eds., *Krste Misirkov: Naučen sobir posveten na 40-godišninata od smrtta* (Skopje, 1966), p. 22.

58. Josip Hamm, "Moj osvrt na K. P. Misirkova," in Trajko Stamatoski, ed., *Krste P. Misirkov i nacionalno-kulturniot razvoj na makedonskiot narod do osloboduvanjeto* (Skopje, 1976), p. 202.

59. Cited in Aleksandar Apostolov, "Manifestacije makedonske nacionalne individualnosti u Kraljevini Jugoslaviji," *Jugoslovenski istorijski časopis*, 1970, nos. 3–4, p. 84.

ment, long respected in the region for its doctrine that a "nation is not merely a historical category but a historical category belonging to a definite epoch, the epoch of rising capitalism" (Stalin), could provide the theoretical underpinnings for separate Macedonian nationhood. According to Dimitar Vlahov, one of the chiefs of VMRO (ob.), that was precisely what happened in Moscow in 1934:

> I mentioned earlier that the Comintern itself wanted the Macedonian question to be considered at one of the consultations of its executive committee. One day I was informed that the consultation would be held. And so it was. Before the convening of the consultation, the inner leadership of the committee had already reached its stand, including the question of Macedonian nation, and charged the Balkan secretariat with the drafting of corresponding resolution. . . . In the resolution, which we published in the *Makedonsko delo* [Macedonian Cause, an organ of VMRO (ob.)] in 1934, it was concluded that the Macedonian nation exists.[60]

A monastic chronicle from Ioannina refers to the depredations of a certain Vonko, who, in 1400, seized Arta. The Greek authors referred to him as a Σερβ-αλβανιτο-βουλγαρο-βλαχος (Serb-Albanian-Bulgaro-Vlach). A Solomon's wise judgment of simpler times or a Solomon-gundy unacceptable to modern monism?

The Communists

> Confused former national romantics—nationalistically oriented in their views and convictions on the question of national unification, children from the prewar [Nationalist] Yugoslav Youth who were perishing as guerrillas on Balkan battlefronts, wild individuals of social-revolutionary orientation who saw no difference between anarchist terror and the mass movement, the rebels of Odessa, anarcho-individualistic literati, old Serbian routineer politicians whose ambitions were disproportionately greater than their subjective capabilities . . . new dissidents of Yugoslav [Nationalist] Youth who were leaving terroristic royalist organizations, a fair number of university trabants from various political groups, and very few proletarians—

60. Dimitar Vlahov, *Memoari* (Skopje, 1970), p. 357. Vlahov, an old VMRO-ist from Kukuš (Aegean Macedonia) who was in the Bulgarian service during the First World War and then became a Communist, noted that the drafting of the resolution was entrusted to a Pole who had no knowledge of the Macedonian question. As a result, Vlahov "acquainted [the Pole] with the [problem] and helped him carry out his task." The Bulgarian Communists had reservations about this procedure and feared that many Macedonian militants would defect to the "Macedonian fascists" (that is, VMRO). Some, such as Vasil Hadži Kimov, did just that—in Kimov's case after the turning of names of all Communist activists to the Bulgarian government. Ibid.

manual workers, those were the elements that made up the first phalanx of our leftist movement.

Miroslav Krleža, 1935

It might seem odd that the members of Yugoslavia's early Communist movement should be grouped alongside the opponents of centralism and unitarism, the Communists being among the most eager supporters of those policies. Nevertheless, no group seethed in greater agitation against the post-1918 Yugoslav system than the Communists, and its large following was mainly among the nationally disaffected.

The history of indigenous communism in Yugoslavia during the first years of the first Yugoslav state is one of great strides and sharp reversals.[1] The Unification Congress of the Komunistička partija Jugoslavije (KPJ, Communist Party of Yugoslavia), or of the Socijalistička radnička partija Jugoslavije (komunista) (SRPJ[k], Socialist Workers' Party of Yugoslavia [Communist]), as the party was called until June 1920, marked the end of the first phase in the consolidation of the Comintern's South Slavic section. Despite its considerable successes, the KPJ was not destined to become a compact entity during its two years of legality. As a result of being forced underground in 1921, the party was decimated. In the next decade and a half, though it increasingly bent to the requirements of Moscow, it was at the same time weakened internally by factionalism. Thus, though it was saddled with the ballast of Russism (less a discredit in Yugoslavia than in the other East European countries), it did not, until Tito's advent in 1937, have anything like the discipline of the Moscow central party.

The KPJ itself was an uneasy combination of independent leftists, many of them, at least in the former Austro-Hungarian territories, from the ranks of the Nationalist Youth, and of Social Democratic groups, whose various traditions and stands on the national question were discussed in Part II. At the Unification Congress (Belgrade, April 20–23, 1919) the party was clearly under the great influence of Srpska socijaldemokratska partija (SSDP, Serbian Social Democratic Party), which joined the new Communist movement en masse and gave it a direction that was wedded to certain orthodox—but not quite Bolshevik—traditions of old Serbian Social Democracy. The centrist faction, at equal distance from the Communist left and the reformist traditions of Social Democracy, was defeated at the Second Congress (Vukovar, June 20–24, 1920), at which point the party largely assumed its familiar ideological contours. Most of its energies were devoted to militant trade-union action, the

1. This section is greatly expanded in my work "The Communist Party of Yugoslavia during the Period of Legality (1919–1921)," in Ivo Banac, ed., *The Effects of World War I: The Class War after the Great War; The Rise of Communist Parties in East Central Europe, 1919–1921* (Brooklyn, 1983), pp. 188–230. This work includes the most up-to-date bibliography of studies on the early history of Yugoslav Communism.

peasant and national questions being largely ignored. Nevertheless, at the elections for the Constituent Assembly in 1920, the KPJ gained 198,736 votes, or fifty-nine seats, ranking fourth, after the ruling Democratic and Radical parties and the oppositional HPSS, in ballots cast.

Most of the Communist votes (see map 3-4) came from Montenegro, Macedonia, Kosovo, and Metohia, the showing in Montenegro being most impressive (37.99 percent of the ballots cast). But in the more industrialized areas, such as Slovenia and Croatia-Slavonia, the KPJ polled 10.29 and 7.13 percent, respectively, below its statewide average of 12.34 percent. Its performance was not exceptional in the major industrial cities (Osijek, 26.73 percent; Zagreb, 24.64; Ljubljana, 17.04; Maribor, 14.03; Sisak, 13.52; Varaždin, 10.54; Celje, 0.75), though it did very well in some other urban centers (Split, 35.7 percent; Subotica, 34.62; Belgrade, 32.25) and overwhelmed certain industrial zones (the Trbovlje mining region in Slovenia, 66.42 percent). On the whole, however, the KPJ's successes cannot be accounted for in terms either of the base that the Communists appealed to or class orientation. In Macedonia and Montenegro, where the KPJ had its most impressive successes, there were no organized national parties that could wage legal struggles against centralism and Serbian hegemonism. The KPJ's good fortune in these areas was an electoral protest against the regime. As an avowedly revolutionary party, the KPJ was the only outlet for the recusant nationalities in these areas. In the other areas of intense national disaffection, such as Croatia-Slavonia, Slovenia, and Bosnia-Hercegovina, the non-Serbs generally voted for the parties that best represented their national and confessional interests: the Croats for Radić's HPSS, the Slovenes for the Slovene People's Party, and the Bosnian-Hercegovinian Muslims for the Yugoslav Muslim Organization. Here the KPJ's showing was less impressive, Nevertheless, the KPJ still tended to discount the strategic potential of the national question and made no attempts to capitalize on this issue. The Communist leaders were overconfident of their ability to ride the continental red wave, and not inclined to reexamine their position.

Subsequent events repudiated the stance of the KPJ leadership. The postwar revolutionary wave in Europe had already reached its peak and was visibly receding. The defeat of the Red communes in Germany and Hungary and Soviet reversals in Poland hastened the stabilization of the anti-Communist governments and the social order that they safequarded. But in Yugoslavia, where peasant insurgency was still seething—as in Croatia in 1920— the KPJ failed to appreciate the importance of national and peasant movements and lost the opportunity to impose itself on the rebel peasants. The Communist deputies in the Constituent Assembly, though seemingly confident, hardly appreciated the resilience of the regime that they continued to attack with an assortment of rhetorical devices. Nor did the KPJ leadership recognize the extent of the party's isolation, widened by the Communist

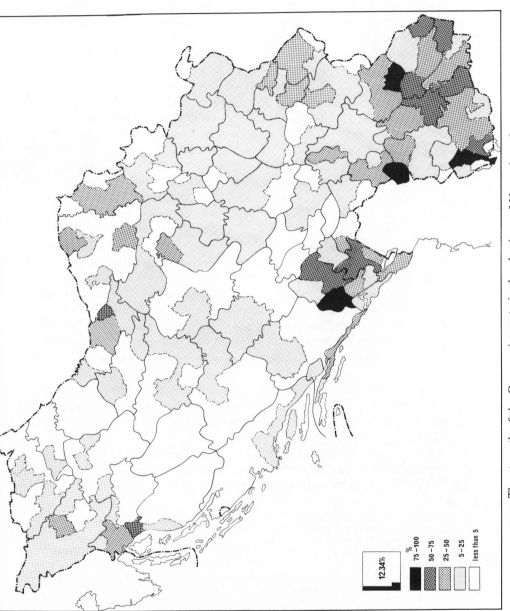

3-4. The strength of the Communist party in the elections of November 28, 1920

	%
12.34%	
	75 – 100
	50 – 75
	25 – 50
	5 – 25
	less than 5

inability to differentiate between the centralist government and the opposition parties. In the long run, the revolutionary bravado, as yet untested in direct conflict, proved counterproductive and exposed the party to governmental reprisals.

At the end of 1920, after a series of Communist-led strikes shut down a number of mines in Slovenia and Bosnia, the government banned Communist propaganda, prohibited the work of party organizations, and in addition to numerous other restrictions ordered the seizure of the KPJ offices and newspapers. On August 2, 1921, after a few Communist gunmen, acting on their own authority, tried to assassinate Regent Aleksandar and actually killed Milorad Drašković, the former minister of the interior, the National Assembly passed a special anti-Communist act, the Law for the Defense of Public Security and Order in the State, which formally banned the KPJ. Known Communist leaders were arrested as initiators of terrorist actions. Within three years of these events, the KPJ's membership dwindled to a mere 688 activists—somewhat less than 2 percent of the membership in 1920.[2]

The KPJ's recovery was slow and painful. Certainly no real gains were possible until the KPJ undertook a careful examination of the causes and the implications of its demise and scrutinized the inherent weaknesses of its stand on the national question.[3] The energies that the KPJ ultimately consigned to the elucidation of its position on the national question had no parallel in any other Comintern section. Under the circumstances, the KPJ's preoccupation with the national question was not in itself extraordinary. What was exceptional was that from 1919 to 1941, as one observer put it, "the KPJ programmatically tested all the viewpoints that are at all possible about Yugoslavia and about the national question in Yugoslavia."[4] And it was equally exceptional that it moved to such an examination from its earlier almost total lack of awareness of the revolutionary potential of the national question.

In the relatively lengthy documents of the Unification Congress the national question is alluded to in only one sentence, in which it is noted that the SRPJ(k) favored "A single national state with the widest self-government in

2. Arhiv Instituta za historiju radničkog pokreta Hrvatske (AIHRPH), Fond Kominterne: KI/69 or 69/II (1924) "Izvještaj o stanju Partije."
3. Among the voluminous literature about the KPJ's evolving positions on Yugoslavia's national question see Dušan Lukač, *Radnički pokret u Jugoslaviji i nacionalno pitanje 1918–1941* (Belgrade, 1972); Janko Pleterski, *Komunistička partija Jugoslavije i nacionalno pitanje 1919–1941* (Belgrade, 1971); Gordana Vlajčić, *KPJ i nacionalno pitanje u Jugoslaviji* (Zagreb, 1974); Gordana Vlajčić, *Revolucija i nacije: Evolucija stavova vodstava KPJ i Kominterne 1919–1929. godine* (Zagreb, 1978); Paul Shoup, *Communism and the Yugoslav National Question* (New York, 1968); Wayne S. Vucinich, "Nationalism and Communism" in *Contemporary Yugoslavia: Twenty Years of Socialist Experiment*, ed. Wayne S. Vucinich (Berkeley, 1969).
4. Jozo Ivičević, "Odrednice unitarističkog nacionalnog programa I i II kongresa KPJ," *Hrvatski znanstveni zbornik*, vol. 1 (1971), no. 1, p. 135.

the regions, districts, and communes."[5] Again in the documents of the Vukovar Congress, the subject is mentioned only briefly, though the tone is more unitarist: "The KPJ will further remain on the bulwark of the idea of national oneness [*nacionalno jedinstvo*] and equality of all the nationalities in the country."[6] Evidently, the KPJ in 1920 did not place any importance on the matter of Yugoslavia's deteriorating national relations. As far as the Communists were concerned, national tensions were a curse of the old regimes, specifically of the Austro-Hungarian Monarchy, and they would be eradicated with the creation of the new "national" state of the South Slavs. As one local SRPJ(k) organ in Croatia noted: "From now on the bourgeoisie in all of its parties will have to conform exclusively to the disposition of the people and its needs here, and not to Vienna or Pest, and that is precisely why we are hoping for the healing of our public conditions. . . . Political equality and the enormous needs of the exhausted people will further contribute to this; national phrasemongering will have to yield to economic and social policy, and Social Democracy [Communists] will also look after that."[7]

The roots of Communist unitarism were disparate. Among others, the South Slavic Social Democratic parties in Austria-Hungary accepted *narodno jedinstvo* as their programmatic approach to the national question in the period before 1918. Thus the Communists in the formerly Austro-Hungarian regions were all in favor of Yugoslavism, and the tenor of certain statements made by the party leaders in those areas was completely out of tune with the decisively defeatist dimension of Leninist reaction to the Great War.

The Croat centrist Bornemissa, for example, spoke glowingly of "our *narodno jedinstvo*, which we won with our blood in arduous and painful struggles,"[8] and no criticism could stir the Communists in Dalmatia as much as the disparagement of their commitment to the unification. Charges of that sort were met with responses to the effect that "If the national and the class consciousness of our working people was not as developed before and during the war as it is now, the fault cannot be laid on it [the people], but on our intelligentsia which did nothing to arouse its awareness."[9] In their wounded pride, the authors of the same protest made much of the claim that "The Communist party firmly embraced national unification, and if some one opposes that, he will not approach [the SRPJ(k)] but the other [*sic*] separatist

5. *Istorijski arhiv Komunističke partije Jugoslavije*, vol. 2, *Kongresi i zemaljske konferencije KPJ, 1919–1937* (Belgrade, 1949), p. 14.
6. Ibid., p. 42. "The phrase 'of all nationalities' means the equality between the Yugoslavs on one side and the Hungarians, Albanians, Germans, and other ethnic groups on the other." Lukač, *Radnički pokret*, p. 49.
7. "Gradjanske stranke," *Radnička straža*, May 1, 1919, p. 4.
8. "Javna pučka skupština u Vukovaru," ibid., Sept. 21, 1919, pp. 1–2.
9. Božidar Radanović, "Povodom jedne radikalske klevete," *Oslobodjenje*, Dec. 18, 1920, pp. 1–2.

parties: the Radicals, Frankists, and the like.''[10] Not only were such positions indistinguishable from vintage unitarist nationalism, but, in isolated instances, the Communists' devotion to Russia had rather a ring of traditional Pan-Slavism. In the years before the fall of tsarism, the Split organ of the SRPJ(k) claimed, "Lenin worked incredibly arduously, with the patience that perhaps nobody but a Slav can understand.''[11]

Heterodox opinions of Communist militants in Yugoslavia's western regions were to a considerable extent a carry-over from the prewar days, when a number of future Communist intellectuals (Djuro Cvijić, Kamilo Horvatin, August Cesarec, Lovro Klemenčič, Miroslav Krleža, and so on) belonged to the revolutionary Nationalist Youth.[12] At the beginning of their political activity they differed from the other unitarist forces in Croatia and Slovenia in that their Yugoslav integralism was revolutionary and uncompromising. It was, therefore, not accicental that these "left Pribićevićists" evolved toward socialism, and that they found fault with the form, but not with the method, of the 1918 unification.[13] Typical of their perceptions were the opinions expressed by August Cesarec in an article published within a week after the unification, but, as Cesarec emphasized, "written even before the [December 5th] events on the Jelačić Square.''[14] The article highlighted the contradiction between Cesarec's positive appraisal of the unification and his growing dismay at the popular dissent to this act. Cesarec blamed the monarchical form of the unification for the Vendée-like passions of the Croat and Slovene republicans:

Having examined the interrelations of the republican and the monarchic current in Yugoslavia, we reach crushing conclusions. The more intelligent and the more progressive current, which seeks unitarism, is actually retrogressive when contrasted to Europe, because it seeks to realize its unitarism by means of a monarchy, [whereas] the more conservative and completely reactionary movement that seeks a republic is in reality, from the European standpoint, more progressive in comparison with its adversaries. But black and egoistic plots are concealed in it, seeking to realize their separatist aims via the vehicle of a republic: *and that is what must be refuted—separatism, and not the republic!*[15]

10. Ibid.

11. "Ko je Lenjin?" ibid., Feb. 2, 1920, pp. 1–2.

12. On this subject see Jaroslav Šidak et al., eds., *Povijest hrvatskog naroda g. 1860–1914* (Zagreb, 1968), pp. 279–284.

13. Ante Ciliga, "Uloga i sudbina hrvatskih komunista u KPJ," *Bilten Hrvatske demokratske i socijalne akcije*, vols. 9–10 (1972), no. 67, p. 3.

14. Cesarec wanted to emphasize that his reaction to the unification was not influenced by the shooting of soldier-demonstrators by the troops of the National Council on Zagreb's main square (December 5, 1918). See August Cesarec, "Povodom najveće i najtužnije slave," *Sloboda*, Dec. 7, 1918, pp. 1–3. This article can also be found in Davor Kapetanić, "Nepoznati Cesarec," *Rad JAZU*, 1965, no. 342, pp. 580–584.

15. Ibid., p. 583.

Consistent in his views, Cesarec called for a voluntary abdication of King Petar. It was singularly unfortunate, in Cesarec's opinion, that the national unification was not brought about by the united revolt of the people themselves. Had it been so, "the problem of a monarchy versus a republic, and even of centralism versus a federation, would have been solved in one stroke in favor of a *centralist republic*."[16]

The concept of *narodno jedinstvo* on which the Communists of the formerly Austro-Hungarian areas based their unitarism was a concept that denied the individuality of the indigenous South Slavic nations and instead, as in the case of Svetozar Pribićević and the Democratic party, insisted on their common nationhood. All the differences among the nationalities were summed up as mere "tribal" idiosyncracies, which would disappear in a unified nation in which they no longer had a historical foundation. The Serbian Communists also adopted the terminology of *narodno jedinstvo*, but their reasons were less ideological—as Nikola Grulović put it, their unitarism was more a matter of temporary expediency than of a total commitment to *narodno jedinstvo*.

Nikola Grulović belonged to the Pelagić Alliance, a group largely made up of former Austro-Hungarian prisoners of war who returned to Yugoslavia from Soviet Russia. The Russian experience implied that the alliance's views on the national question were influenced by the Bolshevik example. Thus the Pelagićists, anticipating smooth sailing for their promotion of the national individuality of the Serbs, Croats, and Slovenes, could logically demand a Soviet-style federalization of Yugoslavia. The SSDP's approach was rather different. A delegation of Pelagićists that came to Belgrade on February 17, 1919, to consult with the SSDP's left on the prospects of the unification of Yugoslavia's pro-Bolshevik factions soon realized how ambiguous the attitude of their Serbian counterparts was to the national question. According to Grulović:

On the national question, Filip [Filipović, one of the leaders of the SSDP and the first head of the SRPJ(k)] expressed himself in a twofold way. He said that he is not opposed to the assertion that the Serbs, Croats, and Slovenes are three peoples, but as far as the Macedonians and the Montenegrins were concerned he said that they were not nations and that he is in favor of centralism, just as the majority [in the SSDP] is. All the rest [of the SSDP participants] also agreed with him and some furthermore stated that it would be unpopular to recognize the existence of several nations. Essentially, the standpoint taken was that all the peoples had accepted *narodno jedinstvo* and that we also must assert the same in our declaration.

After [another Pelagićist] accepted that suggestion, we changed our original

---

16. Ibid., p. 584. My italics.

principled stand about the federative arrangement [of Yugoslavia] and substituted centralism in its place.[17]

The attitude of Filipović and his comrades was in perfect accord with the traditions of the SSDP, a party rooted in an independent and—before 1913—nationally homogenous state. Under Serbian conditions there existed no compelling need for recourse to a supranational Slavic identity, exactly the ideology of *narodno jedinstvo* in the defensive strategy of the unitarist-minded sections of the Croat, Serb, and Slovene opinion in Austria-Hungary. Furthermore, the rigidly orthodox tradition of the SSDP relegated national concerns to the exclusive tutelage of the bourgeoisie. It was part of the SSDP belief that the bourgeoisie had a duty to advance the Serbian national interests, while the socialists were to concern themselves with the imperatives of class struggle. Since the victorious bourgeoisie effected *its* 1918 unification under the banner of *narodno jedinstvo,* and since that fact seemed to have been universally accepted, there was no need—and certainly no obligation—on the part of the Serbian militants to challenge the concept of *narodno jedinstvo,* particularly since the socialists from the other regions seemed to be fully committed to it.

There are many indications that the former SSDP's division-of-labor approach (with the bourgeoisie attending to national concerns and the proletariat to class struggle), so typical of the classic concept of a two-stage revolution, quickly became the common property of the entire nascent SRPJ(k). In numerous party statements throughout the country, *narodno jedinstvo* was repeatedly referred to as the principal "historical task of the bourgeoisie."[18] Nevertheless, since the realities of centralization and the resistance that it provoked increasingly detracted from the nimbus of this presumed mandate, the Communists could claim yet another argument against the regime—that of failing even in an area all its own. The SRPJ(k) Central Party Council's "Manifesto to the Working Class of Yugoslavia," issued in September 1919, was typical of this line of argument: "The general position of the working class in Yugoslavia is all the more difficult and the more complicated inasmuch as the bourgeois government is demonstrating unfitness and evasiveness in executing its historical task in regard to national unification."[19]

If the bourgeois regime was incapable of achieving *narodno jedinstvo,* who could come to the rescue? The fiasco of the centralizing measures found

17. Nikola Grulović, "Jugoslovenska komunistička revolucionarna grupa 'Pelagić,'" *Matica srpska. Zbornik za društvene nauke,* vol. 22 (1959), p. 116.

18. The other "historical tasks of the bourgeoisie" were the "destruction of feudal remnants and the carrying out of social and political reforms." Izvršni odbor centralnog partijskog veća S.R.P.J.(k.), "Manifest radničkoj klasi Jugoslavije!" *Radnička straža,* Sept. 28, 1919, p. 1.

19. Ibid.

the Communist party in the uncomfortable role of being the voluntary retriever of an untenable policy. With a determination that in retrospect defies credence, the Communists made every effort to establish their credit as unflinching champions of unitarism. Since the bourgeoisie had proved that it could not establish *narodno jedinstvo,* the Communist party, claiming that it represented ''one of the strong pillars of national unification,'' took over the task.[20] So infatuated were the Communists with their newly discovered mission that the divisions that had formerly characterized the ideological approaches to *narodno jedinstvo* in Yugoslavia's various regions practically disappeared. Thus, the Serbian Communists became as vocal in the defense of this principle as any of their Croat or Slovene counterparts with a more solid unitarist pedigree.[21]

The Communist defense of *narodno jedinstvo* should not be interpreted as an indication that the KPJ as a whole abandoned its original position that relegated the national question among the secondary (really paltry) concerns. On the contrary, the unitarism of the KPJ was different from that of certain non-Communist politicians (Pribićević) inasmuch as the Communist insistence on the common nationhood of the Serbs, Croats, and Slovenes implied that the entire matter ought not to arouse any further controversy and that they should concentrate on the really important social questions. Nor should the party's increasing accusations of the bourgeoisie's betrayal of *narodno jedinstvo* be seen as merely a matter of expediency. Here also, the key to the Communist attitude lies in the party's accent on the imminence of sharp class confrontations and in the conception of the socialist revolution that the KPJ shared with the entire Communist movement in the immediate postwar period, when victory seemed but a step away.

Expectations of the nearness of the revolution were so high in the party's left wing that this assumption actually cut off a systematic analysis of Yugoslavia's national question. The dominant opinion in the Communist rank and file was that, since the bourgeoisie had failed to achieve *narodno jedinstvo,* not only would this become a task of the proletariat, but it would in fact become an aspect of Yugoslavia's forthcoming socialist revolution: ''Neither federalism nor centralism, nor any other arrangement is in the position to realize *narodno jedinstvo,* or to solve any [other] problem. All of that will remain unsolved and unrealized until the working people take possession of power.''[22]

A paradox, which the KPJ never quite resolved, was implicit in this prognostication. *Narodno jedinstvo* was, after all, a variant of nationalism:

20. Lukač, *Radnički pokret,* p. 35.
21. See, for example, references to the articles of Sima Marković, a leading KPJ theoretician, on the eve of the Vukovar Congress, ibid., p. 45.
22. ''Stjepan Radić,'' *Glas slobode,* Dec. 9, 1920, p. 1.

specifically, the prototype of South Slavic supranationalism. Yet, in Communist perception, it somehow managed to coexist with a different, but no less powerful, strain of decisively Marxist derivation, that is, the concept of internationalist humanity, which, as the liberated entity of the postrevolutionary, genuinely historic epoch, would shed all the elements of the alienation characteristic of class societies, including nationality.[23] Paradoxically, however, although the unitarism of Pribićević contained only attenuated elements of universalism, the KPJ's defense of *narodno jedinstvo* drew much of its inspiration from the universalist/internationalist element of Marxism, which was especially influential during the period under consideration. *Narodno jedinstvo* could not ultimately be reconciled with apocalyptic revolutionary universalism, but it did permit the termination of national pluralism within the KPJ itself, a structural endeavor with far-reaching implications.[24]

The KPJ's unitarism and universalism were not corollaries. The former was rooted in the native soil, whereas the latter was greatly inspired by a dominant strain of Marxism. Yugoslavia's Communist leadership did not yet perceive the implications of the latent tension between these two aspects of the party's national program. With the program of internal centralization, there was no inconsistency. Here, the Comintern's directives perfectly complemented the policy that unitarism also demanded. The Comintern was conceived as a thoroughly centralized international party, with one center and a single global strategy that brooked no local allowances. Although the KPJ's Vukovar statute faithfully reflected all the Comintern's specifications, it was also an offshoot of Yugoslav national unitarism. The Comintern's monolithic aspirations were thus in perfect harmony with the implications of *narodno jedinstvo*. In the case of the KPJ, both policies prescribed centralism. Analogies between the centralizing measures of the Belgrade cabinets and the centralization of the KPJ thus became inescapable; but whereas such correspondence could only dim the Communist luster among the disaffected nationalities of Yugoslavia, it was not immediately apparent that the centralization of the Communist movement necessarily implied still less desirable trends, foremost among which was the preeminence of the Serbian cadres in the party leadership.

Just as the Comintern came to reflect primarily the interests of one party and one state, the rudiments of hegemonism, typical of Yugoslavia's wider national relations, to a great extent were similarly reproduced within the KPJ.[25] The next phase of the KPJ's history would be dominated by the

23. For a detailed analysis of the philosophical foundations of Marxist generic-universalist concept as reflected in the programs of the first two KPJ congresses see Ivičević, "Odrednice," pp. 139–141, 168.
24. Ibid., p. 170.
25. For a detailed and documented discussion of this phenomenon see ibid., pp. 164–167. Drawing from the documents of the Comintern collection in the AIHRPH, Ivičević gives a convinc-

opening of a debate on the national question. The outcome of this exchange would determine the party's altogether different course in the late twenties, when the KPJ advocated a total breakup of Yugoslavia and the independence of Croatia and Slovenia. During the Aleksandrine dictatorship of the early thirties, the KPJ frequently cooperated with Croat and Macedonian nationalists, including the Ustašas, at least in common prison struggles.[26] But it was not until the rise of Nazism in Germany, the hasty retreat from the ultraleftist line of 1928–1933 in favor of the Popular Front with all antifascist forces, the corresponding softening toward the democracies and their East European allies, including Yugoslavia, and Tito's coming to the helm of the KPJ in 1937, that the party adopted a federalist solution to Yugoslavia's national question, a stand that it has pursued, with significant swervings, from the time of its victory in the Second World War. But unlike the other hard oppositionists, the Communists owed allegiance to no particular national base. They could afford to be flexible and build their fortune on the premise that they alone could solve Yugoslavia's national question, solutions of continuity being occasioned by wounds.

---

ing portrayal of the Serbian Communists' preeminence in the KPJ. For example, in one cited document the SSDP's initiative in bringing about the Unification Congress is explained in this way: "This mission [the unification of the party] was assumed by the Serbian Democratic Workers' Party [*sic*], because both by its revolutionary traditions and by its organizational competency it could accomplish this task more easily than others [that is, the other Social Democratic parties in Yugoslavia]. The working masses of Yugoslavia were already aware that the Serbian party always belonged to the left wing of the Second International and that it did not betray socialism in the course of the war, and therefore they related with full confidence to the mandate of the Serbian party in connection with the calling of the First Unification Congress of the Yugoslav proletariat." (Ibid., p. 165). The same tendency is reflected in the other documents. The attitude of the Serbian party leaders had a strong touch of exclusivism, which was bound to strengthen the preeminence of the Serbian organizations of the KPJ.

26. For instances of this fraternity see a revealing KPJ publication: Nikola Rubčić, ed., *Robija: Zapisci hrvatskih narodnih boraca* (Zagreb, 1936), pp. 42–43, 46–47, 78–79.

PART IV

The Autonomist Opposition

Some opponents of centralism, Radić, for example, made occasional concessions to the governments in Belgrade. Even the VMRO tried to bargain with the DS for the language rights in Macedonia. But compromise as a method of gaining political advantage was a prominent feature in the strategy of several other parties that did not evolve in a unilinear fashion. Although these parties fought for the autonomy of their national and confessional groups and therefore tended toward the hard opposition, at the same time they accepted Yugoslavia's state framework and with it the view that their situation could be changed for the better, as could the views of their centralist adversaries.

The Slovene Catholic Populists

> We Slovenes are a people with a distinctive visage; we have a developed language and a distinct spirit. We live in the Alps, approach the Pannonian basin, and, at the same time, we are a maritime people. . . . Two constant qualities, almost without mutual ties, tended to evolve among us. First, the Christian civilization of Aquileia, Bavaria, Saints Cyril and Methodius, Lutheranism, and Catholic Baroque. Second, the post-Renaissance civilization of humanism with its varying accents on subject and object: on the one hand, individuum, maturation, artism, and democracy; on the other, quantity, benefit, and ideology. And still, spontaneity was stronger than voluntarism. We became fantastical realists, tending toward petty skill. We wedded frail spirituality to malicious naturalism. We never solved the contradiction between captivity and imagination, between poverty and ability, between provincialism and lofty insights. . . . We danced all the dances of the macabre and sinned on all our pilgrimages. We were becoming a melancholy and adaptable people, at the same time industrious and inventive, divided in our moods, tragically split apart, and unredeemed.
>
> Edvard Kocbek, 1943

In 1917, on the eve of Austria-Hungary's demise, Janez Krek, one of the founders of the Slovene People's Party (SLS), speaking in Vienna to a fellow Reichsrat deputy from Dalmatia, offered his recipe for making a soup out of a pot of water and a sausage peg that would be so tasty that not a drop would remain after serving. The cook in Krek's story- "took the best lard, various vegetables, and all kinds of seasonings and simmered the soup on the sausage peg. When the party gathered to drink the soup, he dipped two fingers into the pot, took the sausage peg and threw it away. When the guests tasted the soup, they all agreed that it was very choice and said, 'There is nothing quite like the soup on the sausage-peg.' For us," said Krek, "that sausage peg is the Habsburgs."[1]

The SLS had three "K" 's, three unsentimental priests, who went about with sausage pegs as their pilgrim staffs. Krek went to the northern country, entered its elfin Reichsrat, and had his staff anointed to elicit the Habsburg music of pots and pans. Once the Habsburgs were gone, his successor, Anton Korošec, left his library to become the poet of realistic peggery, from which every soup could be made. His pilgrim's staff took him to Belgrade cabinets, and at one particular moment of grave crisis (after the assassination of Stjepan Radić in 1928) Korošec became the first and only non-Serb prime minister of royal Yugoslavia. And when, in 1932, he expressed opposition to Aleksandar's dictatorial centralism, he was merely interned. Radić's successor, Vladko Maček, was sentenced to three years in jail for the same offense. Upon Korošec's death in 1940, the helm of the SLS was given to Franc Kulovec, who was not under the protection of truth-loving owls. He was killed in the German bombardment of Belgrade in April 1941. The fourth "K," Miha Krek, the first SLS chief who did not belong to the sacerdotal estate, was of a somewhat lesser sort. He went into emigration with his Mouse King and together they stirred the stew of émigré politics, the bitterest of the soups on a sausage peg.

As the political arm of the Slovene Catholic movement, the SLS was not the only Slovene party, though it certainly seemed that way. Slovenia was in every respect, including its political culture, a Central European land. Slovenia's economy, though still largely agricultural, was very diversified and, unlike that of Yugoslavia as a whole, clearly in the process of industrialization. Parts of Slovenia, such as Jesenice (Carniola), Štore near Celje (Styria), and Ravne (Carinthia), were among the most industrialized areas of Austria-Hungary and were the most significant centers of the iron and steel industry in Yugoslavia. Not surprisingly, after the unification, Slovenia's political life reflected typically Central European class and ideological cleavages. In addition to the SLS, which controlled some three-eighths of the Slovenian electorate in 1920, Slovenia had its left (Communist and Social Democrat with

1. Marko Kostrenčić, ed. *Zapisi Dra Josipa Smodlake* (Zagreb, 1972), p. 55.

over two-eights of the electorate), left-leaning agrarians (less than two-eighths), and bourgeois liberals (about 8 percent). In the subsequent elections, however, the SLS gained approximately 60 percent of Slovenia's electorate, making it the only important Slovene party and the only genuine voice of Slovene aspirations.[2]

The exigencies of the Slovenes, more than those of any other major South Slavic group, required some kind of Yugoslavia. The malleability of Slovene politicians was due to Slovenia's vulnerability. Without Serbia's help, Slovenia could hardly be expected to withstand the assaults on its territory by Italy and Austria. And Pašić periodically reminded the Slovene leaders that in the course of the war his Serbian colleagues repeatedly urged him to seek a separate peace with Vienna and save at least something for Serbia—the implication being that he could have left Slovenes to Vienna's tender mercies but refused to do so.[3] But though no opponent of centralism could fault such men as Korošec for making a virtue of necessity, many rightly felt that the SLS and other Slovene parties made Slovenia's predicament a kind of security for their dubious virtue. Korošec, especially, was detested by the Croats as a politician who built his fortunes on the permanence of Croat-Serb conflict. In the opinion of Djuro Šurmin, a notable Croat autonomist, who was a member of Protić's cabinet in 1920, Korošec joined the same cabinet as minister of railroads "only to be a minister and to work as a priest against Croat 'separatists,' as he always called us. He was the one who always worked stealthily against the Croats to prevent the agreement with Serbs, because then the Slovenes would be nothing."[4]

Quite understandably, Dr. Anton Korošec did not want to be nothing. But his skill in devising means to ends, in short his political realism, appeared utterly foreign ("German") in a country where national and political programs were seldom judged by their practical bearing upon societal interests and purposes. But whereas the pragmatism of non-Slovene politicians frequently brought scorn upon them, Korošec's maneuvering elicited hilarity and only occasionally derision outside Slovenia. His priestly office was an excuse of sorts, and it was true, as the SLS frequently pointed out, that other parties (and nationalities) also had priest-politicians; but the Catholic clergymen of the DS (Juraj Biankini, for example) never seemed to be using their ecclesiastical influence quite so obviously as did Korošec, who, it was said, wore his Roman collar only in Slovenia. And in Slovenia itself, Slovene

2. Metod Mikuž, "Razvoj slovenskih političnih strank (1918 do zač. 1929) v stari Jugoslaviji," *Zgodovinski časopis*, vol. 9 (1955), pp. 107–139. See also Melita Pivec, "Programi političnih strank in statistika volitev," in *Slovenci v desetletju 1918–1928: Zbornik razprav iz kulturne, gospodarske in politične zgodovine*, ed. Josip Mal (Ljubljana, 1928), pp. 357–373.

3. Ivan Hribar, *Moji spomini*, vol. 2, *Osvobojevalna doba* (Ljubljana, 1928), p. 360.

4. Arhiv Hrvatske, Rukopisna ostavština Dr. Djure Šurmina, Box 5: I-7. Političke bilješke 1906–1936, Notebook 5, p. 50.

Catholicism, on account of its Laodicean alienation, did not find scandal in Korošec's reputation for epicurism and expediency. A political adversary noted that Korošec was forgiven everything because he seemed indispensable. He was a man for every cabinet, and his fierce persecution of the Communists might not have prevented his entrance into Tito's partisan parliament: "Had he lived . . . it would not have been odd to find him in the widened Anti-Fascist Council of the People's Liberation of Yugoslavia [in 1943]."[5]

The SLS's course was to a considerable extent determined by the traditional rivalry between Slovene clericalists and liberals. Through the SLS, the Catholic church in Slovenia waged an uncompromising struggle against the infidelity of the liberal bourgeoisie. After Slovene anticlerical liberals joined the DS in 1919, the SLS and the DS continued the old Carniolan struggle in new guises, the question of centralism versus autonomy becoming the chief point in contention. The widespread affirmation of the SLS, however, can only partly be attributed to any mass disaffection with the liberals' anticlericalism. It was the liberals' economic ascendancy at the expense of the working classes, the petite bourgeoisie, and particularly the peasantry, that permitted the SLS to assume the role of protector of the disadvantaged. That this role was not sham can be discerned by the SLS's proved ability to marshal the church's organizational skills in the formation of numerous cooperative, syndicalist, cultural, youth, and religious organizations. In 1920, the SLS had over 600 party and affiliated organizations and was able to hold as many as 1,500 public meetings in the course of six months.[6] No other political party in Yugoslavia had such an elaborate machinery, the very notion of orderly party structure being largely unfamiliar.

Part of the SLS's appeal to the Slovene lower classes was Catholic populism, based on the social teachings of Leonine *Rerum novarum* (1891). Korošec never failed to note that the SLS was an anticapitalist party.[7] Whereas the SLS equated the policy of the DS with capitalism,[8] the SLS stood not just against Marx but also against mammonism: "A rich man is as abnormal a sight in the SLS, as is a small peasant in the party of capitalist bourgeoisie [DS], or a faithful Catholic in Social Democracy, which in its kernel is today just as materialistic as it was in Marx's time."[9] At the same time it condemned class struggle, stressing the class harmony of the Rule of Love. Hence, it thrived at the expense not only of the liberal DS but of the socialist

5. Dragoljub Jovanović, *Ljudi, ljudi . . . (Medaljoni 56 umrlih savremenika)* (Belgrade, 1973), vol. 1, pp. 427–428.

6. "Zbor zaupnikov Slovenske ljudske stranke," *Slovenec*, April 8, 1920, p. 1.

7. Anton Korošec, "Slovenačka Pučka (Ljudska) Stranka," *Nova Evropa*, vol. 7 (1923), no. 7, p. 216.

8. "Za jugoslovansko misel," *Slovenec*, Feb. 29, 1920, p. 1.

9. "Krekov tabor v Komendi," ibid., Sept. 2, 1919, p. 2.

343

movement as well. Its diligent and highly organized mass action earned the SLS a foremost position in Slovene society, and permitted it to play a decisive role in the consolidation of modern Slovene national consciousness.

As an openly Catholic party, the SLS was genuinely loyal to the Habsburg dynasty while Austria-Hungary appeared irresistible. During the First World War, however, Šušteršič's extreme pro-Habsburg group in the SLS leadership was increasingly shunned, isolated, and finally expelled (December 1917) by Krek-Korošec's populists, whose Yugoslavism—as manifested in the earlier May Declaration of 1917—was decidedly Austro-Slavic and embraced only the Catholic South Slavs.[10] For these reasons, though the exiled Slovene Yugoslavistic unitarists gave Krek-Korošec's SLS a clean bill of health, the party had reason to be apprehensive about its position in the new Yugoslav state.[11] On the eve of his death in 1917, Janez Krek consoled himself with the thought that Serbian hegemony was not likely in the new state, since hegemony could only be wielded by the most capable peoples: "No paragraph and no constitution can save an incapable people from destruction, and since I do not count the Croats and Slovenes among the incapable peoples, I am convinced that they will know how to assume decisive positions in state administration and legislatures."[12] Still, he noted the likelihood of liberal consolidation, which happened when the SLS's traditional liberal opponents, who were solidly in favor of unification, joined the DS on the integralist and centralist platform. Soon, they used Pribićević's patronage in an attempt to curtail the SLS's predominance in Slovenia. Thus the SLS's determination to guard its own position—and that of Catholic clericalism—went hand in hand with its opposition to Belgrade's centralizing measures.

Unlike the Croats, the Slovenes inhabited a relatively compact territory that they shared with no other nation. This, in addition to their language,

---

10. On the struggle between the two wings of the SLS see Momčilo Zečević, "Slovenska ljudska stranka pred stvaranje Kraljevine Srba, Hrvata i Slovenaca 1917–1918.," *Istorija XX veka: zbornik radova,* vol. 9 (1968), pp. 337–379. Šušteršič emigrated after the war and joined forces with his old allies the Frankists. He belonged to the legitimist wing of the Frankist emigration. Manko Gagliardi, *Istina o hrvatskom emigrantskom revolucionarnom komiteu 1919–21: Odgovor na napadaje Stjepana Radića* (n.p., 1919), p. 22. He returned to Slovenia in December 1922, part of Pašić's scheme to put the official SLS on the defensive. Metod Mikuž, *Oris zgodovine Slovencev v stari Jugoslaviji 1917–1941* (Ljubljana, 1965), p. 241.

11. Vladislav Fabjančić, *O Sloveniji i Slovencima* (Geneva, 1917), pp. 30–32. In Fabjančić's appraisal, the SLS was not only quite Yugoslavist after Šušteršič's isolation but quite close to socialism. Fabjančić volunteered in the Serbian army in 1914. After the collapse of Serbia he worked among the JO émigrés in Geneva, went on to become a Communist deputy (1920), edited the chief KPJ newspaper in Slovenia, and was expelled from the KPJ in 1924. Still later, in the 1930s, Fabjančić was in charge of a quasi-fascist veteran group in Slovenia. The relatively benign attitude that a politician of Fabjančić's associations displayed toward the SLS in 1917 would have been unthinkable in any analogous situation among the Croats and Serbs; the vulnerability of the Slovenes produced odd forms of solidarity.

12. Janez Ev. Krek, *Slovenci* (Zagreb, 1919), p. 51.

which perceptively separated them from Croats and Serbs, shielded the Slovenes from the most overt thrusts of Yugoslavist unitarism and Serbian supremacy, which otherwise would have been as challenging to their largely constituted nationhood and would most likely have produced as dramatic defensive responses as in the Croat case. Slovenia was also sufficiently distant from Belgrade to permit the Slovenes a degree of isolation that diminished the impact of centralism, whose limitations were even more obvious in this relatively advanced land with a tradition of efficient administration and rule of law. In addition, unlike Croatia, Slovenia did not experience any significant social upheavals in the 1918–1920 period that could have provided an opening for centralist interventions. Any sort of meddling, under Slovene conditions, could only be harmful.

But meddling there was, particularly in the sensitive area of language and literary activity. Though Slovene unitarists predicted the "full cultural and linguistic unity" of Slovenes and "Serbocroats," they took no immediate initiatives in this direction. The SLS nevertheless noted with alarm the DS's determination to destroy the separate Slovenian language and culture, which would have meant the end of the accepted medium of administration and communication in Slovenia.[13] Even more alarming was the attempt on the part of Momčilo Ivanić, a leading Serbian Radical, to relegate Slovenian to the status of a Serbian dialect. In response, the SLS's polemicists argued that before "our idle hurriers commit their cultural hara-kiri," the Serbs and Croats should be encouraged to establish their own linguistic unity.[14] The SLS noted, too, the Democrats' opposition to the establishment of a university in Ljubljana and the growing signs of neo-Bismarckian *Kulturkampf*, including a drive for a "national Catholic church," that emanated from liberal circles.[15]

Despite these threats to Slovene national individuality, the SLS did not make common cause with the Croat anticentralists. The SLS leaders, notably Korošec, retained the traditional Slovene mistrust of their immediate Croat neighbors, whose aspirations, in their view, were potentially more threatening to Slovene autonomy than the policies of the more distant Serbs.[16] The Slovenes were undoubtedly aware that Supilo and other notable Croats aimed at Croatianizing them, Slovenia being an important area where the concept of Croat "political nationhood" was at its most dubious and where *narodno jedinstvo* offered a chance at Croat assimilationism. Temperamentally, too, the Croats looked upon Slovenes as junior partners. In the words of one Croat

13. "Danes se odloči: ali avtonomna Slovenija ali centralizem," *Slovenec*, Nov. 28, 1920, p. 1.
14. Ivan Mazovec, "'Slovenački jezik,'" ibid., April 1, 1921, p. 1.
15. "Demokrati in ljubljanska univerza," ibid., Jan. 8, 1920, p. 1; Anton Korošec, "Mir in delo," ibid., Dec. 25, 1919, p. 1; "Narodna cerkev na Českem," ibid., Jan. 15, 1920, pp. 1–2.
16. Momčilo Zečević, *Slovenska ljudska stranka i jugoslovensko ujedinjenje 1917–1921.: Od Majske deklaracije do Vidovdanskog ustava* (Belgrade, 1973), pp. 356–358.

unitarist intellectual, "Let us admit: did we not look down upon the Slovenes from on high, or at least fail to care for them? And we had a few phrases as an excuse. We frequently said that they were 'priest-ridden,' forgetting that their 'priest-party' organized the people economically and politically in such a way that today they are more compact and stronger than our people, which were 'enlightened by liberals.' "[17] For their part, the Croats were suspicious of reassertions of Kopitar's teaching that the kajkavian dialect was really Slovenian, leaving always a possibility of a common Sloveno-Serbian front to reduce the Croats to a čakavian minimum.[18]

The lack of a common cause with the Croats had another source. The Croat parties were not in a position to aid the Slovenes in achieving their vital task of extending Yugoslavia's borders to include those compatriots under Italian and Austrian rule. Only support from Belgrade could effect that. Where menaces lurked in an openly oppositional course, not the least among which were Belgrade's stringent repressive measures (which could also be extended against the interests of the church), only benefits could be derived from cooperation with the Serbian parties, including concessions on the question of autonomy. Cooperation with the Democrats became impractical the moment the Slovene liberals joined the DS. Accordingly, the determination of the SLS to safeguard Slovene autonomy as well as its primacy in Slovenia led it to rely on the Radicals, an alliance that, according to Korošec, the SLS's enemies sought to prevent.[19] Though the Radicals continued to express reservations about the clericalists, they did not campaign in Slovenia, where there were no Serbs to begin with. Moreover, the SLS's compromise between centralism and federalism at the same time satisfied the Slovene aspirations and prevented an open confrontation with the Radicals.

It was typical of the SLS's style of work to declare that important issues were not particularly urgent. Since it was obvious that republicanism could only lead the party into the camp of hard opposition, the republican slogans that the SLS experimented with at the end of Austria-Hungary were quietly swept aside with the rationalization that the peoples of Yugoslavia were not yet sufficiently sophisticated for such an admittedly loftier state form: "I am a monarchist," said Korošec, "but every patriot of republican orientation would have to admit that we are not mature enough for a republic."[20] The same attitude was also displayed in reaction to the dispute between the

17. Niko Bartulović, "Kulturno jedinstvo i Slovenci," *Književni jug,* vol. 1 (1918), no. 7, p. 258.

18. Kopitar's thesis found its way into Krek's writings: "The term 'Slovene language' once embraced the Croat kajkavian dialect." Krek, *Slovenci,* p. 27.

19. "Razgovor z dr. Korošcem," *Slovenec,* Oct. 12, 1919, p. 1.

20. Anton Korošec, "Vodilne misli za volilni boj v konstituanto," ibid., Oct. 2, 1920, p. 1. Korošec also stressed that "Slovene deputies are well aware that the current regent [Aleksandar] is a profound, enthusiastic, and sincere friend of the Slovene people." "Razgovor z dr. Korošcem," ibid., p. 1.

centralists and the federalists, which was treated as singularly turgid if not meaningless.[21] But even when tactical circumventions dictated periodic emphasis on one or the other aspect of SLS's autonomism, the principal concerns of the party's program remained remarkably steady.

Though the SLS recognized that the Serbs, Croats, and Slovenes had not yet been nationally fused, it ostensibly embraced the doctrines of state unity and *narodno jedinstvo,* and it used some of the language of Yugoslavist unitarism, saying that Serbs, Croats, and Slovenes were "tribes" of a single Yugoslav people.[22] But because that position, on the face of it, was identical to unitarist theories, the SLS hastened to add that such a state of things did not detract from the historical individuality of Yugoslavia's "economic-cultural communities," whose territorial bounds coincided with the pre-1918 historical frontiers. Since state unity could only be effected by the recognition of differences, Yugoslavia's statesmen, in the SLS's view, would be wiser and above all more practical if their alertness to political realities led them to grant the widest possible autonomy to these "economic-cultural communities."

In fact, the SLS envisaged much more than economic-cultural autonomy, at least in Slovenia. For one thing, the Slovene economic-cultural community was meant to erase the ancient and historically established frontiers among the duchies of Carniola, Styria, and Carinthia, or at least those parts of their frontiers that were within Yugoslavia, thereby definitively uniting the Slovenes within a single political unit. For another, the SLS's definition of autonomy really amounted to full self-government—or indeed, in Korošec's words, to the independence (*samostojnost*) of Slovenia within Yugoslavia: "The autonomy of a province or a land consists of the following: That the supreme provincial authorities have immediate, highest, and supreme power of decision and authority in political, economic, educational, and financial questions. When a state has autonomy, it also has the right to issue regulations for these affairs, to decide in these affairs according to its own considerations and reason, and to have no master over it in these affairs."[23] The SLS wanted it clearly accepted that autonomy meant that the Slovenes "would not be commanded by incompetent and headless Belgrade officials."[24] Moreover, the defense of the "particularities of the [Slovene] tribe that had their roots in history and culture" could be accomplished only when it was recognized that the "unity of the Serb-Croat-Slovene state demands

21. Zečević, *Slovenska ljudska stranka,* p. 263.
22. Some SLS voices expressed a point of view that was more sincerely held by the party: "We are not yet one people, though surely many conditions exist whereby we could slowly become [a single people] by way of evolution." Mazovec, "Slovenački jezik," p. 1. Accordingly, the SLS distinguished between *jugoslovanstvo* (reciprocal Yugoslavism) and *jugoslovenstvo* (Yugoslavist unitarism).
23. "Boj za avtonomijo Slovenije," *Slovenec,* Sept. 15, 1920, p. 1.
24. Ibid.

that the whole Slovene territory be united within its borders" (*da se v njenih mejah združi vse slovensko ozemlje*).[25] Just like the Croat parties that called for the Croatian Sabor, the SLS saw a Slovene regional parliament and government as the highest point of autonomy: "We demand," the SLS leadership stated in its electoral manifesto of October 1920, "the autonomy of Slovenia with an assembly and a provincial government responsible to it— a government that should also manage the state administration in the land. The provincial assembly should have legislative power, inasmuch as it is not retained by the common [central] parliament."[26]

The SLS's autonomist program was somewhat more tolerable to the centralist factors owing to its insistence that economic-cultural communities should not be confused with the federal units based on nationhood (or "tribalism," in unitarist terminology), such as those advocated by the Croat opposition. According to the SLS, the chief problem with the federalist proposals grounded on "tribal" affiliation was that it was impossible to draw a clear demarcation line between Serbs and Croats.[27] Of course, that objection did not obtain in Slovenia, which would remain a distinct unit whether one defined it as the compact homeland of the Slovenes or as a historical economic-cultural area. This advantage was certainly not lost on the SLS leaders when they advocated the superiority of economic-cultural autonomies.

Practical considerations were always hoisted as primary in the SLS's autonomist program. The SLS leaders repeatedly asserted that their opposition to either federalism or unconditional centralism was based on their reading of the current situation and not on principle. Again and again they stressed their uninterest in anything "but a technical device for an improvement of our public administration," noting that nothing could be more commonplace than autonomy.[28] Compromise and moderation inherent in the autonomist program were certainly advantageous to the broadest spectrum of the Slovene population. Cooperation with the NRS could extract yet more danegeld, provided the Radicals were not momentarily in alliance with the DS, since the concentration of centralist parties was certainly not in the SLS's interest. The joint NRS-DS imposition of centralist constitutional solutions met its vigorous resistance. On occasion, the SLS even resorted to blocs with the hard opposition (Radić), but in the long run it felt more secure in an alliance with the Radicals, particularly with those NRS factions that were the exponents of the court. The latter tendency was practically irreversible after 1927.

25. "Velika manifestacija Slovenske Ljudske Stranke," ibid., Oct. 25, 1920, pp. 2–3.
26. "Slovensko ljudstvo!" ibid., Oct. 26, 1920, p. 1.
27. Korošec, "Vodilne misli," p. 1.
28. "Avtonomija in centralni parlament," *Slovenec*, Sept. 10, 1919, p. 1.

348

The SLS was careful not to challenge the centralists in areas that they considered their turf and twig. Its attempts to extend the party's influence outside Slovenia were a hazard of a different sort. The essence of the SLS would have been distorted if it stopped being Catholic, but not if it expanded outside Slovenia. In January 1919, the SLS initiated a drive for the concentration of all the Catholic political groups in Yugoslavia. This action framed the clerical response to the creation of the liberal DS, but it failed to bring the anticipated results. Croat clerical groups loyal to the SLS were started in Bosnia-Hercegovina, Croatia-Slavonia, Dalmatia, and Bačka, leading to the founding of the Hrvatska pučka stranka (HPS, Croat People's Party) in 1919. The parliamentary club of clericalist parties, known as the Jugoslovanski klub (Yugoslav Club) was formed during the same year.

Since the respective showing of the two parties in the 1920 elections was about equal, it can almost be said that the Croat clericalist tail wagged the Slovene SLS dog (see map 4-1). Besides the Slovene base of Catholic parties, the geographical distribution of their vote shows that (in addition to some rural votes in the counties of Varaždin and Medjimurje, both on the Styrian frontier) the HPS scored moderate gains only in the eastern belt of Croat settlement. Indeed, few Catholic Croats lived to the east of the HPS's Catholic corridor, proving the relative strength of religious affiliation (as opposed to purely national) in the areas where Croat national awakening was late in coming (in Hercegovina and among the Bunjevci of Bačka). The showing of the HPS was especially impressive in areas where the Franciscan order forged its own brand of populism during the centuries of Ottoman rule (Imotski and Sinj in Dalmatia, western Hercegovina). At the head of the HPS's electoral list in the district of Mostar (Hercegovina) stood Friar Didak Buntić, the provincial of the Franciscans' Hercegovinian province, the most revered notable of Hercegovinian Croats, who was elected to the Constituent Assembly. And in Dalmatia, the HPS's ticket was headed by none other than Ante Trumbić, though he also headed the Democratic and Agrarian tickets and ran his own independent campaign in the same province.

Nevertheless, the HPS was running against the historical trend of Croat national consolidation, spearheaded by Stjepan Radić, and in its program, the Bosnian part of the HPS envisaged the "gradual leveling of tribal contrasts, confessional contradictions, and historical discordance," leaving this leveling to "natural development," which the authors clearly thought as favoring a sort of Catholic Yugoslavism.[29] For the same reason, the HPS supported the countering of Catholic provinces in Yugoslavia to those of pronounced Orthodox composition. To this end, the clerical bloc's constitu-

---

29. Arhiv Hrvatske, Rukopisna ostavština Dr. Djure Šurmina; I. Politička djelatnost dra Šurmina, Box 3: Fogl. 8: "Jugoslavenska [Hrvatska] Pučka Stranka za Bosnu i Hercegovinu kao sastavni dio Jugoslavenske pučke stranke na čitavom teritoriju S.H.S."

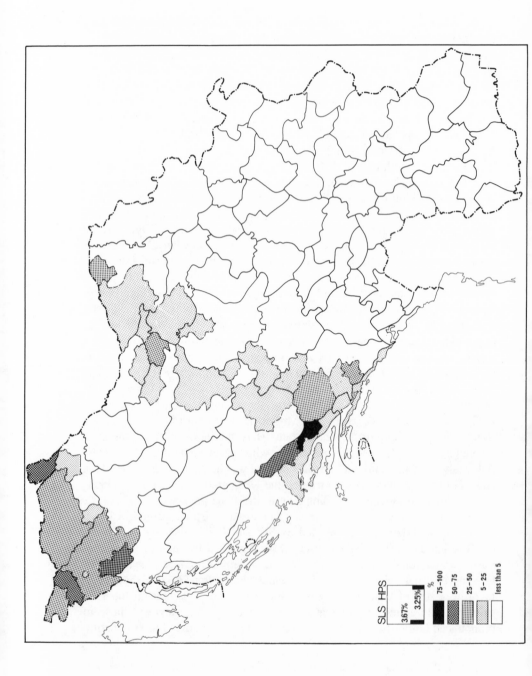

SLS HPS

3.67%

3.25%

%
75–100
50–75
25–50
5–25
less than 5

tional proposals included a provision to set up six autonomous provinces: Serbia, Montenegro, Vojvodina, and their Catholic counterparts, Croatia-Slavonia, Slovenia, and Bosnia-Hercegovina with Dalmatia.[30] With the merger of Bosnia-Hercegovina with Dalmatia, the Catholic element would be numerically superior in the last unit. From the standpoint of strictly Catholic interests, of confessional balancing, such a solution had much to recommend it. Moreover, from the Slovene point of view, which was certainly important in the SLS's calculations, this scheme could also temporarily block the influence of Zagreb in Croat affairs. But from the Croat point of view, the clericalist proposal was unacceptable, particularly since most Croat parties were already on record as favoring the unification of Croatia-Slavonia with Dalmatia. The SLS-HPS, quickly recognizing this problem, obligingly suggested that Dalmatia could also unite with Croatia-Slavonia or remain autonomous in its own right.[31] Nevertheless the HPS, by subscribing to a Slovene-charted national program, was clearly putting confessional interests first, and it therefore had to oppose Radić's party, which it accused of lacking any clear cultural, economic, social, and political principles in inviting all Croats, big capitalists and little people, to join one party.[32]

It would be misleading to leave the impression that the SLS's official course always went unchallenged in the party's base. The analysis of the SLS's characteristic strategic and tactical trends most correctly fits Korošec's wing of the party, admittedly the dominant one. The younger elements in the SLS reflected the more radical disposition of Slovene masses and favored determined steps in the defense of Slovene autonomy and national individuality. Republicanism and Catholic socialism were also persistent hallmarks of the younger generation of Slovene Catholic intelligentsia, to the extent that these sentiments, much to Korošec's displeasure, were frequently voiced in the SLS's trade union section.[33] That does not, however, detract from the overall estimate of the SLS as a temporizing party, which did not utilize its unique position to mitigate centralist excesses, preferring to further Slovene interests, as it saw them. The sin of omission.

The Croat Liberal Bourgeoisie

> The turn of events brought about the conjunction of circumstances whereby our precious "national unification" was carried out *before* the initial uni-

30. "Za nedeljivo in avtonomno Slovenijo," *Slovenec*, June 11, 1921, p. 1.

31. "Sporočilo Hrvatom in Slovencem," ibid., June 17, 1921, p. 1.

32. This was the view of Janko Šimrak, Greek Catholic priest and theologian, longtime secretary of the HPS, and bishop of Križevci (1942), as expressed in his speech in "Zbor zaupnikov Slovenske Ljudske Stranke," ibid., April 8, 1920, p. 3.

33. On this subject see Janko Prunk, *Pot krščanskih socialistov v Osvobodilno fronto slovenskega naroda* (Ljubljana, 1977), pp. 49–86.

fication in the "tribal realm" and before our souls were drained of that
exhilarating effect. That is the deepest reason why the path to full ethnographic [*sic*] integration has not been straightened: the ideology of "tribal" unification has not yet been reconciled to the ideology of national
unification on the higher level. That is why our internal policy wavers
between these two ideologies, the struggle between centralism and autonomy being nothing but a reflection of that contest. This ruinous situation is
exacerbated, on the one hand, by the fact that centralism has the form of the
higher level [of integration], though its motives, however unconscious (and
in fact often consciously plotted), belong to the lower level of unification;
on the other hand, autonomism has the appearance of the lower type,
whereas its spirit in fact derives from the higher type.

Albert Bazala, 1921

The argument of the philosopher Bazala, when lifted from the cant of
unitarism and applied to his fellow Croats, was that even before the Croats
had fully constituted their nationality (lower type of unification) they were
called upon to become Yugoslavs (higher type of unification). Centralism
pretended to be the means toward Yugoslav integration but had in fact
become the tool of the Great Serbs. By contrast, on the face of it, autonomism appeared to be safeguarding Croat nationhood but was in fact fighting for
Yugoslavist unitarism. And, Bazala added, the centralistic manner of reducing Yugoslavia's "tribes" to mere individuals and then attempting to forge
them into "higher" species of Yugoslavs could not work, because atomiza-
tion could only favor the sort of unity that would express the characteristics
of the most numerous and most self-conscious "tribe"—that is, the Serbs.

Croat autonomism was the religion of disenchanted visionaries and the
penance of unrepentant unitarists. Once the nimbus of unitarist ideology lost
its glow, those Croat parties that originally favored immediate unification,
parties that were unitarist by ideology and monarchist by circumstances,
plunged into troubles from which most of them emerged with thoroughly
revised programs. The evolution of the Narodni klub (National Club), the
parliamentary organization most representative of the Croat middle classes,
was typical of the road away from unitarism, via autonomism, and toward
(con)federalism, traversed by marginal Croat groups in the shadow of Radić's movement.

The National Club was the organization of Croat deputies in the interim
parliament of 1919–1920. Its members were heirs of fairly distinct political
traditions, but all opposed Pribićević's brand of centralism. The group included: (1) the Starčevićists of the SSP (Ante Pavelić, Mate Drinković, and
others), who headed the Croat wing of Zagreb's National Council and gave
leave to the unification act of December 1, 1918; (2) Croat dissidents from
the HSK (Ivan Lorković, Djuro Šurmin), some of the leading members of
Masarykist Progressive Youth at the beginning of the century, who left the

HSK in June 1918 over disagreements with Pribićević; (3) Starčevićists from Istria (Matko Laginja, Vjekoslav Spinčić); (4) a few independents, including the former members of the JO. The National Club sat in Protić's first cabinet in 1919, joined Protić's second cabinet in 1920 (during which time Matko Laginja was appointed the Croatian Ban and upon assuming his office released Radić from jail), was in close touch with Ante Trumbić, himself Yugoslavia's nonpartisan foreign minister in 1918–1920, and maintained close ties with the political leaders of Bosnian-Hercegovinian Muslims, who initially participated in its caucus. In May of 1919, the groups of Pavelić, Lorković, Laginja, and a minor organization from Osijek decided to join forces around a single program while retaining their party organizations, and that July, representatives of these groups formed a new political party the Hrvatska zajednica (HZ, Croat Union). At about the same time, the National Club was joined by the Hrvatska težačka stranka (Croat Husbandmen's Party), which though closely allied with the HZ was primarily meant as the organization unifying all the Catholic Croats in Bosnia-Hercegovina, a goal that the HPS effectively spoiled. The National Club therefore consisted of the HZ and the Croat Husbandmen from Bosnia-Hercegovina, whose respective ideologies and programs were nearly identical.[1]

The leaders of the HZ were intellectuals from the free professions, who, in comparison with Pribićević's followers, held negligible interests in Croatia-Slavonia's industry and banking. In addition to the intelligentsia, the urban craftsmen and merchants were the bulk of the HZ's base. Partly on account of its urban-intellectual nature, the HZ never managed to gain the support of the peasantry. By contrast, in the absence of competition from Radić, the Croat Husbandmen of Bosnia-Hercegovina relied largely on the peasant base.

The first president of the HZ was Matko Laginja, whose position as Croatian Ban (February–December 1920) afforded him little authority and less influence in Croatia-Slavonia for as long as Pribićević's men wielded real power in the region. Laginja was more a figurehead on the prow of the Croatian ship than the vessel's commander.[2] The "carnivalesque old man," as the Democrats mockingly called him, could not even prevent the rearrest of Stjepan Radić in March 1920. Much of the popular anger that boiled over in the 1920 revolt against draft-animal registration was also directed against Laginja and the HZ—the party of Croat "top hatters." The masses hardly suspected how little power the HZ really had; as Protić complained, "We [Radicals] took these Croat HZers into the government and they sit with us,

---

1. For an excellent monographic study of the HZ see Hrvoje Matković, "Hrvatska zajednica: Prilog proučavanju političkih stranaka u staroj Jugoslaviji," *Istorija XX veka: zbornik radova*, vol. 5 (1963), pp. 5–136.
2. Hrvoje Matković, "Politički rad Matka Laginje od 1918. do 1920. godine," *Pazinski memorijal*, vol. 3 (1972), pp. 131–142.

but at the same time a narrower ministerial committee was formed, and when these few wretched Croats take their leave from [cabinet sessions], then the military expedition into Croatia is discussed [by Pribićević].''[3] But as long as the HZ hid the truth from the electorate, it was called to account. Laginja, for one, would not even consider a show of protest. When criticized by other HZ leaders for his conduct in the Radić trial, Laginja ''declared that he could cease being a member of the HZ, but would not leave his post [of Ban].''[4]

In the parliamentary elections of November 1920, the National Club, much to its own surprise and that of official Belgrade, which had high hopes for these ''sober Croats,'' demonstrated the extent of its weakness (see map 4-2). The National Club won only eleven seats, of which seven were from Bosnia-Hercegovina. The HZ's bastion in Croatia-Slavonia managed only three seats, including one from Zagreb. On the whole, the Bosnian Husbandmen contributed 59.74 percent of National's vote, including an especially strong vote in the district of Travnik (three seats). Of the two parties that ran under explicitly Croat labels in Bosnia-Hercegovina, the more nationally minded Husbandmen won over the explicitly Catholic HPS by a margin of thirteen to seven. Hence, though religious affiliation was far more important in Bosnia-Hercegovina than in Croatia-Slavonia, it was no longer the decisive element in political behavior. True, Catholic clergymen were also present on the Husbandmen's ticket, but of the twenty-one priests who ran for the Constituent Assembly in Bosnia-Hercegovina, all but five were the candidates of the HPS. The clergy was evidently inclined to the clericalist party, but the Croat Catholic electorate in Bosnia-Hercegovina was not.

Ivan Lorković (1876–1926), who replaced Laginja at the helm of the HZ when Laginja was appointed Ban, was the party's real leader, who guided its slow evolution away from unitarism. The task was especially hard in Lorković's case. Pope Ivan I, as opponents referred to this dignified and authoritative intellectual, was indeed the supreme pontiff of the Progressive Youth, the first generation of Croat political men who gave up on the politics of state right and promoted *narodno jedinstvo*. Moreover, as an inheritor of Croat political tradition, in which ideological pragmatism went against the grain, he was necessarily reticent about making fundamental leaps. In 1919, the HZ stood squarely on the program of *narodno jedinstvo*, but shied away from centralism. The party organ's first editorial proclaimed:

National and state oneness of the Serbs, Croats, and Slovenes was realized by the will, toil, and sacrifice of our people. The program of J. J. Strossmayer, Dr. Ante Starčević, and Jovan Skerlić, has been fulfilled in the most ample way. Out of the bloody and trying years of 1914–1918 the day of liberty has dawned.

3. Ivan Meštrović, *Uspomene na političke ljude i dogadjaje* (Buenos Aires, 1961), p. 148.
4. Arhiv Hrvatske, Rukopisna ostavština Dr. Djure Šurmina; I. Politička djelatnost dra Šurmina, Box 3: Fogl. 3: ''Zapisnik sastanka eksekutivnog odbora Hrvatske Zajednice od 7/VIII. 1920.''

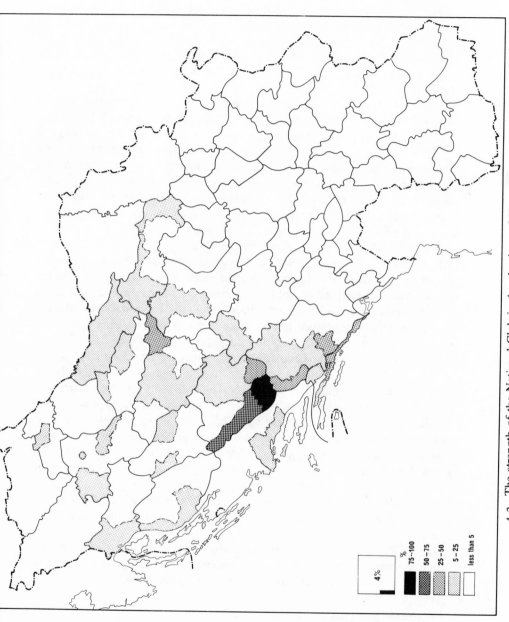

%
75-100
50-75
25-50
5-25
less than 5

4%

4-2. The strength of the National Club in the elections of November 28, 1920

The State of Serbs, Croats, and Slovenes is our national state in which our national political ideal has been realized. We want to build [this state] up so that its edifice will be healthy and strong.[5]

This overpitched appreciation was followed by a moderately phrased criticism of centralism, which, "instead of building the state from below by democratic methods is building it from above [phrase censored, probably 'by force']." This approach, according to the HZ, "endangered the internal agreement of our homogeneous people." Instead, the goal of "E pluribus unum," as practiced in America, would best be realized on the English model of self-government, "both on the local level and in our ancient provinces, which were recognized in our national territory before the Habsburgs. Let each province have its legislature, to which the local government or administration would be responsible. And let the [central] state direct those affairs that are of common or general national interest and concern the state as a whole."[6]

From the HZ's point of view, by doing away with equality between "Yugoslav tribes," the centralist state organization was in fact undermining the estimable prospect of full *narodno jedinstvo*. As Drinković put it in the fall of 1919, "We are led on not by separatism but by prudence, anticipation, and fear that the realization of centuries of effort will be spoiled and ruined." He declared Croat opposition to the "state based on the federation of tribes," not least of all because of the presumed impossibility of drawing a frontier between the Serbs and the Croats. Moreover, he proclaimed the HZ's policy as the "best support of our state."[7] In like manner, Lorković's calls for autonomy were anything but separatist. The autonomy or federal arrangement that he envisaged "was not by form unitaristic, but was so by the function Lorković gave it: according to his conception, [autonomy] had to safeguard the idea of oneness from all attacks and trials; it had to provide time and create conditions for the idea of *narodno jedinstvo* to permeate every [South Slav], so that the internal order of the state would lose its prior significance and would be discussed [in the same way as] in France or Italy."[8] When chided by the unitarists about his supposed betrayal of the common ideal, Lorković would reply, "Wait, we shall meet each other again!"[9]

Lorković was hardly aware that he had already broken the tie that bound him to unitarism. For one thing, if his autonomism were consistent, it could not be advanced under unitarist slogans. The subtle logic of Lorković's

5. Editorial, *Hrvat*, May 16, 1919, p. 1.
6. Ibid.
7. "Spomen skupština Hrv. Zajednice," ibid., Nov. 11, 1919, pp. 1–2.
8. Ivo Politeo, "Ivan Lorković," *Nova Evropa*, vol. 13 (1926), no. 5, p. 130.
9. Milan Ćurčin, "Smrt Ivana Lorkovića," ibid., p. 134.

ideology was lost on the petite bourgeoisie and provincial intelligentsia of the Croat heartland, who saw the HZ as the only respectable Croat party. In Županja (Slavonia), for example, the local HZ organization called for immediate elections for the Croatian Sabor, which should then elect the Ban, who, as the prime minister of Croatia-Slavonia (with Istria and Medjimurje), would head the cabinet that would include the ministries of interior, education, religion, economy, construction, constituent assembly, health, army and navy, finances, and justice. The resolution called upon the assemblies of Dalmatia and Bosnia-Hercegovina to declare their respective disposition toward state unity with Croatia-Slavonia, and it demanded formation of a Croat army.[10] Little was left here for any central government. Moreover, the HZers of Županja stated that in their opinion, the "Croat deputies made their biggest mistake in handing over their authority to the National Council and in dissolving the Croat army [home guards] without the approval of the people"—the very propositions that Ante Pavelić, an HZ leader and the former head of the National Council, continued to defend.[11] Indeed, the HZ was alarmed by the ease with which former Frankists entered the party. These old enemies of Lorković's *narodno jedinstvo* now saluted the HZ's first assembly (October 1919) as a gathering of "Croat fighters."[12] In Zlatar (Varaždin district), a twelve-man temporary committee of the HZ was elected in 1920. "I must tell you," wrote the HZ's local organizer to one of his superiors in Zagreb, "that these are hard-boiled Frankists who place their trust in us because they see us as republicans and radical Croats and our attempts at establishing the organization as a republican movement. So, you can appreciate what difficulties we have here."[13]

There was no question that the HZ's insistence on the autonomous governance of individual regions increasingly could not be defended from the standpoint of one "Yugoslav nation." As a result, the HZ was forced to revise its unitarist ideology. By 1921, the party's statements finally included formulas about the right of the Croat *nation* (no longer *tribe*) to determine its own fate.[14] On the eve of the 1920 elections, Lorković's directive to establish the "closest cooperation with the peasant party [of Radić]," which was not reciprocated, was nevertheless no longer out of joint with the HZ's strategy.[15] In the 1921 debate over Yugoslavia's constitution, without discussing the

10. Arhiv Hrvatske, Rukopisna ostavština Dr. Djure Šurmina; I. Politička djelatnost dra Šurmina, Box 3: Fogl. b.b.: *"REZOLUCIJA* [Hrv. Zajednice u Županji]," Sept. 23, 1919.

11. Ante Pavelić, "Neće Jugoslavije," *Jutarnji list,* April 19, 1921, p. 3.

12. "Pozdravi skupštini Hrvatske Zajednice," *Hrvat,* Oct. 31, 1919, p. 2.

13. Arhiv Hrvatske, Rukopisna ostavština Dr. Djure Šurmina; I. Politička djelatnost dra Šurmina, Box 3: Fogl. 29: HZ leader Cvjetko Štehanec to Djuro Šurmin, Zlatar, Jan. 3, 1920.

14. Matković, "Hrvatska zajednica," pp. 60–61.

15. Arhiv Hrvatske, Rukopisna ostavština Dr. Djure Šurmina, Box 31: VII. Korespondencija: 2. Pisma upućena Šurminu, Fogl. 314: Ivan Lorković to Djuro Šurmin, Budapest (Belgrade?), June 10, 1920.

monarchical system, which its leaders still took for granted, the HZ sought to rally support for its new (con)federalist program, under which the state would be divided into six constituent units. These were (1) Serbia (with Kosovo, Metohia, part of the Sandžak, and Vardar Macedonia); (2) Croatia (that is, Croatia-Slavonia, Dalmatia, Medjimurje, as well as Italian-held Istria and various Adriatic islands); (3) Montenegro; (4) Bosnia-Hercegovina; (5) Vojvodina (as it was then understood; that is, the Yugoslav portions of Baranja, Bačka, and the Banat); (6) Slovenia. The confederative aspect of this proposal was implicit in the stipulation that although the relations between the six provinces would be regulated by the constitution, the constitution could not be changed without the consent of the provinces.[16]

The HZ's constitutional proposals were not accepted. Henceforth, as a minor Croat party, the HZ tied its fortunes to Radić's political powerhouse and did not even participate in elections. The association with Radić, whose treatment of the HZ was none too gentle, imposed new strategic challenges. One of the most substantial was the question of republicanism. Initially, the HZ sought to soften the implications of this cardinal point of Radić's program by interpreting it as not necessarily identical to a specifically nonmonarchical state form. Rather, the HZ preferred to see it as merely a term most attuned to Radić's concept of homeland, which, since it was grounded on the principles of popular sovereignty, could in turn be taken as standing above the concrete questions of state organization. It was not lost on the HZ that constitutional monarchy was also based on popular sovereignty. Where the intricate refinement of this interpretive construction allowed the HZ to coexist with Radić's republicanism, it also prepared the ground for its own abandonment of monarchism.[17]

This tendency was strengthened after Trumbić joined the HZ in the fall of 1924. Once a pronounced monarchist and Yugoslavia's first minister of foreign affairs, Trumbić abandoned his nonpartisan stance and joined the HZ at the time when he was increasingly in agreement with Radić's defense of Croat individuality. After entering the HZ, he steered it further in Radić's direction, and on November 25, 1924, at the annual session of the HZ leadership, he proposed that the party accept republicanism. This motion won, but the HZ, which had always prided itself as a force salubrious to healing the Serb-Croat rift, went one step further and also rejected the politics of compromise with Belgrade.[18] This metamorphosis in the development of the HZ proved to be final. Hence, after Radić's imprisonment and coerced acceptance of the monarchy in 1925, the HZ leaders, their sparse following

16. For a detailed description of these and other constitutional proposals of the HZ see Matković, "Hrvatska zajednica," pp. 73–78.
17. Ibid., pp. 99–100.
18. Ibid., pp. 121–123.

358

notwithstanding, found themselves among those Croat politicians, including some Radić dissidents, who could not bring themselves to accept such a turn. The HZ, therefore, became one of the groups that in 1926 merged within the Hrvatska federalistička seljačka stranka (Croat Federalist Peasant Party), with Lorković as its president, in a vain attempt to capitalize on Radić's compromise.

After Lorković's death, which occurred soon after the merger, the new party was headed by Ante Trumbić. In the 1927 parliamentary elections Trumbić joined forces with the younger Ante Pavelić, the future Ustaša leader, within the new anti-Radić Croat Bloc. They accused Radić of treason and collaboration with the Great Serb government of the same Radical party that the old HZ once collaborated with. Trumbić and Pavelić won the only two seats of the city of Zagreb but failed everywhere else. After the shooting of Stjepan Radić, Trumbić joined Radić's party and remained faithful to it to the end. In 1941, a week after the proclamation of the Independent State of Croatia, Pavelić made Mladen Lorković, his old associate and Ivan Lorković's son, state secretary in the ministry of foreign affairs. In 1944, Pavelić had him arrested as one of the instigators of the attempted pro-Allied coup d'état. Somewhat later, Lorković was executed. Integral Yugoslavs and integral Croats. Fathers and sons.

The Muslims of Bosnia-Hercegovina

Nazvaše me Hamzom	They named me Hamza
Kao što nazvaše hiljadama ljudi	As they named thousands of men
Iz pustinja divljih beduina,	From the deserts of wild bedouin,
. . . . .	. . . . .
I onih s pazarâ visokog Irana	And those from the bazaars of high Iran
Što prodaju ćilime,	Who sell rugs,
Biser, nakit, žene.	Pearls, jewels, and women.
O čudno je to, čudno	And it is strange, queer
Da ovdje	That here
U našoj zemlji kraj Evrope	In our country near Europe
Hamzom zovu mene!	They call me Hamza!
Često mislim na te	I often think of you
Muhamedov striče,	Muhammad's uncle,
O, veliki Hamza.	O, great Hamza.
. . . . .	. . . . .
. . . u bici kod Uhda	. . . at the Battle of Uhud
Ko lav se boriš.	You fight like a lion.

. . . .

O, čudno je to, čudno   O, it is strange, queer

Da ovdje   That here

U našoj zemlji kraj Evrope   In our country near Europe

Hamzom zovu mene!   They call me Hamza!

Hamza Humo, 1924

Kada hotjeh biti—

tagdi i ne bih . . .

When I wanted to be—

Then, too, I was not . . .

Scribe from Kalesija (fourteenth century?)

Yugoslavia was also the midwife of a new political type among the Muslims of Bosnia-Hercegovina. The regime of Benjamin von Kállay, who by reason of his office as the common Austro-Hungarian minister of finance governed Bosnia-Hercegovina from 1882 to 1903, was as efficient and "progressive" a colonial administration as any that Britain could boast of in the Cape Colony or the Gold Coast. In an attempt to suppress Croat and Serb nationalisms, which were considered dangerous for the Monarchy's interests in Bosnia-Hercegovina, Kállay fostered the idea of separate Bosnian nationhood (*bošnjaštvo*), which was meant to prevent the development of separate—necessarily irredentist—national movements on the basis of confessional divisions. Kállay's interconfessional Bosnianism was not, however, a pure contrivance. As the tradition of pre-Ottoman Bosnian statehood was strong among the Catholics of Bosnia-Hercegovina, retained especially by Bosnian Franciscans, so was the history of Bosnian autonomy within the Ottoman state strong among the Muslims. Nevertheless, Kállay's *bošnjaštvo* caught on only among the Muslims, who were the object of Croat-Serb rivalry and, like Kállay, had reason to fear that the unity of Bosnia-Hercegovina would be undermined if significant numbers of Muslims started espousing Croat and Serb nationhood.[1]

The 1890s were the decade of sharpest Croat-Serb clashes over each side's national claims to Bosnia-Hercegovina. After the abdication of Milan Obrenović in 1889, Serbia, newly governed by the Radicals, relaxed its secretly undertaken obligations to Vienna not to pursue a belligerent policy toward Austro-Hungarian rule in Bosnia-Hercegovina. Serbian propaganda, based on the claims of linguistic nationhood, was slowly revived by various nationalist societies but was also nurtured in Serbian schools and textbooks.

---

1. On the national and political orientation of Bosnian communities from the Congress of Berlin to the First World War see Mustafa Imamović, *Pravni položaj i unutrašnji politički razvitak Bosne i Hercegovine od 1878. do 1914.* (Sarajevo, 1976), pp. 69–181.

The words of the Old Bard, nationalist poet Stevan Kaćanski, that "it is time, o Serbdom . . . to save our sad Bosnia," found great response among the nationally conscious Serb bourgeoisie of Bosnia-Hercegovina.[2] From 1896 to 1905, the elite of Bosnian Serbs, big exporters, merchants, and religious leaders, waged a campaign for autonomy in Serb ecclesiastical and educational affairs, seeking at the same time to weaken Austro-Hungarian rule in the province. At the same time, the Catholic Croats in Bosnia-Hercegovina, who were nurtured on the liberal Franciscan traditions of Illyrianism and Strossmayer's Yugoslavism, were increasingly espousing Starčević's integral Croatianism. The Croat elite, economically weaker than its Serb counterpart, consisting mainly of small merchants, civil servants, and clergy, was nevertheless strong enough to lift Kállay's embargo on any manifestations of Croat national sentiment. (Not even glee clubs with Croat appellations were permitted before 1899).[3]

In 1910 the Orthodox (or Serb) population of Bosnia-Hercegovina amounted to 43.49 percent of the province's population; Catholic, 22.87 percent (this was mainly, though not exclusively, Croat population, there being a small immigration of various Austro-Hungarian officials and their families after 1878); Muslim, 32.25 percent.[4] Plainly, neither Serb nor Croat national ideology could advance majority claims to Bosnia-Hercegovina without winning the Muslims—hence the demands for Muslim "nationalization" and arguments, scientistic and historicist, by both sides on behalf of Serb or Croat status of Muslims. As a result, *bošnjaštvo* became the first defensive vehicle of a proud Muslim gentry against the national movements of their former Christian subjects. The *Bošnjak* (Bosnian), the chief voice for Kállay's Bosnianism, but effectively a Muslim journal, warned that the rampart of Islam, which for centuries defended "Bosnians" (that is, Muslims) from the onslaughts of Christianity, might be weakened by Orthodox and Catholic proselytizing in the guise of Serb and Croat nationalism: "Whereas the Croats argue that the Orthodox are our greatest enemies and that Serbdom is the same as Orthodoxy, the Serbs wear themselves out calling our attention to some bogus history, by which they have Serbianized the whole world."[5] For Mehmed-beg Kapetanović of Ljubuški, the founder of *Bošnjak* and chief proponent of Muslim Bosnianism, himself a former Ottoman district administrator (*kaymakam*) of several Hercegovinian districts, as well as mayor of Sarajevo before and after the Austro-Hungarian

2. Stevan Kaćanski, "Mučenica," in *Celokupna dela,* ed. Milan Kašanin (Belgrade, n.d.), p. 150.

3. On the Croat national ideologies and political course in Bosnia-Hercegovina during Austro-Hungarian occupation see Mirjana Gross, "Hrvatska politika u Bosni i Hercegovini od 1878. do 1914.," *Historijski zbornik,* vols. 19–20 (1966–1967), pp. 9–68.

4. For the demographic trends in nineteenth- and twentieth-century Bosnia-Hercegovina see Djordje Pejanović, *Stanovništvo Bosne i Hercegovine* (Belgrade, 1955).

5. Cited in Imamović, *Pravni položaj,* p. 74.

occupation, it was contrary to the dignity of Islamic establishment to be anything but Bosnian and Muslim. And since all establishments expire in dignity, the *Bošnjak*'s dying ditty, penned in 1891 by Safvet-beg Bašagić, a rising Muslim poet of most distinguished ancestry, was: "From Trebinje [the southernmost town in Hercegovina] to the gates of Brod [the northernmost town in Bosnia], there were never any Serbs or Croats." Three years later, Bašagić was an activist of Starčević's party in Zagreb and a declared Croat.[6]

Though the Serb and Croat national ideologies, in their strikingly different ways, certainly posed a danger for Muslim religioethnic particularism, the Westernized Muslim intelligentsia was inclining to go over to the side of their adverse critics, Serbs and Croats, who sought to "awaken" the Muslims to Serb and Croat national movements. Among the Serbs, the antagonism toward Islam and "Turks" and the expectation that the Muslims would "return to Orthodoxy" was so pronounced (Njegoš's "Mountain Wreath" was a fairly typical example of this theme) that they presented a serious obstacle to Serb penetration of Muslim intelligentsia. Individual Serbs, such as Nikola Šumonja, a former editor of a Serb literary journal in Sarajevo, criticized Serb authors on account of their "vindictive rage against 'bloodthirsty' and 'beastly' Turks" and suggested that the Croats were far more sensible in their approach.[7] Indeed, even the most liberal Serbs, such as Jovan Jovanović-Zmaj, the distinguished poet from Novi Sad, who otherwise had no trouble envisioning a harmonious Serb triconfessionalism, did not fail to portray their Muslim characters as sentimentally bound to Orthodox Christianity. Not only is his Muslim hero in the *Devesilje* (Meadow Saxifrage), a cycle published in 1900, in love with an Orthodox girl, but he remembers that as a child he discovered an old icon of Saint George in his grandfather's cabinet and kissed it. Caught in the act by his grandfather, the child is praised instead of being scolded:

> Istog Djurdja ljubili su
> Naši preci kô svečari,
> Pa zar da je djunah ljubnut
> Što ljubljahu naši stari.

> The same George was kissed
> By our ancestors, his devotees,
> So how could it be a sin to kiss
> What the lips of ancients pressed.[8]

6. Muhsin Rizvić, *Književno stvaranje muslimanskih pisaca u Bosni i Hercegovini u doba austrougarske vladavine,* vol. 1 (Sarajevo, 1973), p. 148.
7. Cited in Imamović, *Pravni položaj,* p. 93.
8. Jovan Jovanović-Zmaj, *Sabrana djela,* ed. Jaša M. Prodanović, vol. 8 (Belgrade, 1934), p. 234.

The Orthodox implications of Serbianism certainly lessened the appeal of Serbian national ideologies among Muslims generally. Only a few Muslim intellectuals, such as Osman Djikić, Avdo Karabegović Hasanbegov, and his cousin S. Avdo Karabegović (his adopted initial "S." stood for Serb) espoused Serb nationhood. Moreover, the attraction of Serbianism was lessened by increasingly—indeed preponderantly—political propagation of Serbdom, consisting not so much of appeals to common nationhood (Karadžić's linguistic Serbianism) as of exhortations to become better Serbs by accepting the superiority of Serbian statehood over Habsburg (Catholic) rule or even the Ottoman restoration, the cherished dream of most Muslims. In short, the Serb national movement asked the Muslims to believe that the Ottoman period, from which the conversion to Islam could not be separated, had been a step down. This version of their history was, in fact, accepted by a few Muslim-Serb intellectuals. The meadow nymph of his vision, wrote Djikić,

> Pojala je slavu predja mojih davni',
> I moć Srbinovu Dušanova doba,
> Pojala je hrabrost borioca slavni'
> S' Kosova krvava, — Srbinova groba.

> Sang the glory of my ancestors of old,
> And the Serb's power of Dušan's age,
> Sang the courage of glorious fighters
> From gory Kosovo—the Serb's tomb.[9]

By contrast, Croat national ideologies flattered the Muslims. And though the greatest poetic achievement of the Illyrianist generation, Ivan Mažuranić's "Death of Smail-aga Čengić," ends with the involuntary bowings of the slain aǧa at the Christian cross in a Montenegrin hermitage, the Croats were increasingly oblivious of the spirit of the Catholic bulwark against Islam (*antemurale Christianitatis*) that stamped their self-consciousness in the early modern period. Starčević himself, the founder of modern

9. Osman Djikić, *Sabrana djela: Pjesme i drame*, ed. Josip Lešić (Sarajevo, 1971), p. 56. To a lesser extent, similar tendencies could be found in the works of Muslim-Croats. Musa Ćazim Ćatić, for example, expressed regret over the day when the "Arab's malicious grandson knocked on our door." Musa Ćazim Ćatić, "Slobodi," in vol. 67 of *Pet stoljeća hrvatske književnosti*, ed. Abdurahman Nametak (Zagreb, 1966), p. 437. Ćatić differed from Djikić, however, in recognizing Bosnia's rebirth to greatness within the Ottoman state, when "Sokullus, Piyales, and Tiros [references to Mehmet Paşa Sokullu, Piyale Paşa, and Hasan Paşa Tiro, great sixteenth-century Ottoman officials, all from Bosnia and Croatia] . . . stood at the helm of the greatest empire, shedding the blood of enemies in streams." Ćatić, "Povijest otadžbine," ibid., p. 472. The point that Bosnian Muslims rose to greatness under the Ottomans was later documented by Bašagić in his registry of "Famous Croats—Bosnians and Hercegovinians—in Turkish Empire." See Savfet-beg Bašagić, *Znameniti Hrvati Bošnjaci i Hercegovci u turskoj carevini* (Zagreb, 1931).

Croat nationalism, viewed Bosnian Muslims as the best Croats and was expressly Turcophilic in considering the Ottoman state more tolerant in matters of religion than any European Christian state and Ottoman feudalism more tolerable (free movement of serfs, no military obligation for the non-Muslims) than any Western equivalent. Starčević was convinced that it would be a calamity for Bosnian Christians and Muslims if Bosnia fell to Vienna, and contemplated, in 1853, moving his operations to Sarajevo. His plans included the introduction of a printing house to Bosnia and an educational campaign that would foster Christian loyalty to the Ottoman state at the expense of Habsburg Monarchy and Russia.[10] Somewhat earlier, when he left the seminary in 1848, he even stated that his departure from the clerical estate was a result of his growing conviction that "only the Turkish [faith] is worth something; all the others absolutely nothing."[11]

A conciliatory attitude toward the Muslims was not rare, however, even among Croat churchmen. *Osvit* (Daybreak), "the organ of Croats from Bosnia-Hercegovina," which the Franciscans started publishing in Mostar in 1898, consistently supported religious pluralism, declaring religion a matter of individual conscience, and even went as far as to support the Ottoman cause against the Christian insurgents in Macedonia. And when in 1900 Archbishop Josip Stadler of Vrhbosna (Sarajevo), whose Catholic clericalism was consonant with his non-Bosnian origin, attempted to link Croat nationality with Catholicism, arguing moreover for the conversion of Muslims, the Franciscans of *Osvit* responded by declaring that Catholicism would not be ruined if the Croats disappeared, nor would the Croats be ruined if they ceased being Catholics.[12]

It is typical of Croat national ideologies that their carriers preferred the channels of literature and art for winning over the Bosnian Muslims. Some of the best Croat writers of the realist generation, Josip Eugen Tomić, Eugen Kumičić, and Milan Ogrizović, all adherents of Starčević's party, wrote essays, novels, and plays on Muslim themes; Tomić's novel *Zmaj od Bosne* (The Dragon of Bosnia, 1879), for example, is a glorification of Husejn-beg Gradaščević's Muslim upper-class rebellion for Bosnian autonomy, waged against the Porte in 1831–1832. Typically, Husejn-beg is portrayed as passionately in love with Marija Vidas, a Catholic girl whose father, an exiled Bosnian Croat, is a cavalry major in Habsburg service. Most important, a number of Croat Catholic writers assumed partial or complete Muslim identities in their writings that were aimed in good part at Muslim audiences. Ogrizović and Frane Binički wrote some joint pieces under a half-Muslim

10. Muhamed Hadžijahić, "Jedan neostvareni nacionalno-politički projekt u Bosni iz g. 1853," *Historijski zbornik*, vols. 19–20 (1966–1967), pp. 87–102.
11. Josip Horvat, *Ante Starčević: Kulturno-povjesna slika* (Zagreb, 1940), p. 87.
12. Gross, "Hrvatska politika," pp. 16–19.

pseudonym, Omer and Ivo. Krsto Pavletić wrote under the pseudonym Os-man-beg Štafić, Josip Šebečić was known in Čapljina (Hercegovina) as Jusuf, Ferdo Vrbančić used the pseudonym Ferid Maglajlić, and, in the most significant instance of this practice, two writers from Mostar, Ivan Milićević, a Catholic and the editor of *Osvit,* and Osman Nuri Hadžić, a Muslim, wrote under the joint pseudonym of Osman-Aziz.[13]

This approach was rather fruitful. The overwhelming majority of the first generation of university-educated Muslims considered themselves Croats. Some of them, notably Safvet-beg Bašagić, were contributors to the pages of *Osvit,* testifying to the acceptance of Muslims and Islam within the national and cultural confines of Croatdom.[14] Considering that *Osvit* was published by the Franciscans, it is important to note that some articles by Muslims were on expressly religious Islamic themes. Bašagić himself commented on the integrative aspect of Croat culture in his poem *Čarobna kćeri* (O Magic Daughter, 1896), in which he prayed that he be allowed to weave Eastern melodies into "our songs,"

Jer hrvatskog jezika šum
Može da goji,
Može da spoji,
Istok i zapad, pjesmu i um.

Because the sound of Croatian language
Can nourish,
Can link together,
East and West, song and intellect.[15]

Though Stadler's clericalist Croatianism, coming as it did at the height of Muslim struggle for religious-educational autonomy within the Catholic Habsburg state (with demands for self-governance in the running of religious endowments [*vakıf*] and mosque schools [*mearif*]),[16] a struggle that was waged from 1899 to 1908, deflected the progress of Croat national ideologies among the Muslims and contributed to the cooperation of Serb and Muslim autonomist movements in Bosnia-Hercegovina.

Stadler was unable to block all avenues to Croato-Muslim convergence. The cultural renaissance of the Bosnian Muslims, which began in 1900 with

13. Muhamed Hadžijahić, *Od tradicije do identiteta: Geneza nacionalnog pitanja bosanskih Muslimana* (Sarajevo, 1974), pp. 199–201. Osman Nuri Hadžić later declared himself a Serb. Ibid., p. 230.
14. Rizvić, *Književno stvaranje,* vol. 1, p. 182.
15. Ferid Karihman, comp., *Soj i odžak ehli-Islama: Zbirka pjesama o domu i rodu Muslimana hrvatskog koljena i jezika* (Munich, 1974), p. 43.
16. On this subject see Nusret Šehić, *Autonomni pokret Muslimana za vrijeme austrougarske uprave u Bosni i Hercegovini* (Sarajevo, 1980).

the publication of a journal *Behar* (Blossom) and the establishment of Gajret (Endeavor, 1903), a Muslim cultural society, was directed by Muslims of Croat orientation, notably Bašagić, Hadžić, the novelist Edhem Mulabdić, and Musa Ćazim Ćatić, the tragic lyricist of Oriental modes, who ruined his health in squalid taverns trying to inflame, as he once wrote, the fire of Islam in his breast with the drops of ruddy wine.[17]

Though the ratio of Muslim intellectuals who declared themselves as Croats in the first half of the twentieth century exceeded those who considered themselves Serbs by perhaps as much as ten to one, at least a third of Muslim intellectuals and the overwhelming majority of ordinary Muslims shunned any process of "nationalization." The Bosnian Muslim masses instinctively felt that the demands for nationalization split their community apart, especially since the Croato-Serb contention was uncommonly bitter in Bosnia-Hercegovina. To be a Muslim-Serb meant in fact to be anti-Croat and vice versa. This does not mean that Muslim peasants, urban craftsmen and masses, and lower *ulema* (clergy, Islamic scholarly class) did not have any preferences in the great Bosnian game. Before the annexation, they generally welcomed the cooperation of Serbs in defending the nominal Ottoman sovereignty over Bosnia-Hercegovina, though of course for different reasons from the Serbs, who wanted to deny the province to Vienna, thereby preparing the ground for its incorporation into Serbia.

During this period the Serbs did not press the issue of Bosnia's unequal land tenure, a vestige of Ottoman feudalism, because the Muslims were in firm ownership of most land and would have resented any moves toward change. After the annexation, the Serbs no longer had any incentive to postpone the airing of the agrarian question; Muslim-Serb cooperation ended, and in its place emerged the Croat-Muslim parliamentary coalition of 1911, duly reflected in the political mood of the masses. The Serbian victories over Turkey in the First Balkan War were hardly an occasion for Muslim rejoicing. (Even dedicated Muslim-Serbs, committed to the cause of Balkan allies, could not restrain their tears at the fall of Adrianople, the first Ottoman capital in Europe, which fell to the Bulgarians in March 1913.) Mob violence against Serb businesses and institutions that followed the Sarajevo assassination worsened the Muslim-Serb downturn. Another aspect of the post-1911 political realignment was Muslim and Croat loyalism to Austria-Hungary in

---

17. Despite the individual Croat orientation of its editors, *Behar* espoused an explicitly Croat line only in 1908–1910, when, under the editorship of Ljudevit Dvorniković, a Catholic, it opened its pages to Catholic Croat authors, who then contributed twice as many articles as the Muslims. During that period, many Muslim authors, especially the traditionalist and theologically trained intellectuals, left *Behar* and joined the increasingly Serb-oriented Gajret (which had its own journal). The attraction, however, was not Gajret's Serbianism but the fact that Gajret "intensively nurtured the Muslim popular spirit and was the expression of Muslim mentality, of its ethnic, customary, and communal personality." Muhsin Rizvić, *Behar: Književnoistorijska monografija* (Sarajevo, 1971), p. 370.

the course of the First World War, translated into some ugly attacks on Serb property and numerous cases of "religiously motivated" murders.[18] But in 1918 the Muslims and Croats found themselves part of a state whose topmost leaders were Serbs, and who, moreover, regarded Bosnia-Hercegovina as an integral part of Serbia.

The rebellions of Bosnian Serb peasants against Muslim landholders in the interregnum after the collapse of Austria-Hungary and the anti-Muslim depredations of Serb volunteers after the unification, perpetrated very often with the nodding encouragement of Serb authorities, threatened the life and property of all Muslims, rich and poor. To be sure, landlord-tenant relations in Bosnia-Hercegovina were historically equivalent to confessional differences. According to the 1910 census, Muslims made up 91.15 percent of all landlords whose lands were tilled by customary tenants (the common native term *kmet*, usually translated as "serf," is not altogether appropriate for these sharecroppers). But according to the same census, 73.92 percent of all *kmets* were Orthodox, and 21.49 percent were Catholic. Obviously, the agrarian question in Bosnia-Hercegovina could be solved only at the expense of one confessional community.

It must be remembered, however, that most Bosnian landlords (61.38 percent) owned less than 125.55 acres of land. We do not know what percentage of these landlords were Muslims, but it is likely that the overall Muslim percentage among landlords also obtained among the relatively weak landlords. The point is that the Bosnian Muslim upper crust was not made up of Oriental nabobs living in ostentatious luxury. Only seventeen landlords (not necessarily, though probably, Muslims), or 0.18 percent of all Bosnian landlords, had more than 2,473 acres of land, and they were all from the county of Bosanska Gradiška in the fertile Sava basin of northern Bosnia,

---

18. At the start of the First World War, Austro-Hungarian authorities in Bosnia-Hercegovina arrested and interned perhaps as many as 5,500 prominent Serbs. Between 709 and 2,200 of these hostages died of maltreatment in the camp at Arad (Hungary) during the war. Some 460 additional persons were sentenced to death and executed in Bosnia-Hercegovina for disturbances, treason, espionage, and aid to the enemy (Serbia). The Serbs of the frontier districts in eastern Bosnia and Hercegovina, moreover, suffered because of the policy of resettlement (to northwestern Bosnia) and forcible expatriation (to Serbia—some 5,200 families). See Vladislav Škarić, Osman Nuri Hadžić, and Nikola Stojanović, *Bosna i Hercegovina pod austro-ugarskom upravom* (Belgrade, n.d.), pp. 156–159. The role of the *Schutzkorps*, auxiliary militia raised by the Austro-Hungarians, in the policy of anti-Serb repression is moot. In popular stereotypes, the men of the Schutzkorps were strictly Muslims out to destroy the Serbs. Muslim leaders, however, denied this. According to Sakib Korkut, "Whenever the discussion turns to the Schutzkorps and their misdeeds we hear only of Muslims and Catholics, though many a Serb hid in the Schutzkorps and though most of these units were commanded by Serb gendarmes. When we apply one yardstick, the supposed 'Muslim nature' of the Schutzkorps disappears. . . . One yardstick and [the Serb declarations of loyalty to Austria-Hungary] assume the appearance of the same order as the behavior of Muslims, who found their *Deckung* [shelter] in the Schutzkorps and who thereby saved their lives and did not leave their bones [on some battlefield] in the struggle for hated Austria." "Veliko slavlje naše organizacije u D. Vakufu," *Pravda*, June 24, 1920, p. 2.

one of the few areas in Bosnia-Hercegovina where estate agriculture was at all possible. It is clear, therefore, that the anti-Muslim violence of Christian peasantry in 1918–1919 was only partly due to class antagonisms. But it was unmistakably confessional/national in character, directed not just against the Muslim landlords but against all Muslims, including Muslim smallholders, who represented half of Bosnia's free peasants.[19] In addition, since most of the excesses were committed by Orthodox Serbs, who made up three-quarters of all *kmets*, rural stirrings were viewed as a Serb anti-Muslim movement. Muslim leaders publicly stated that the political system in Yugoslavia "bore the stamp of systematic destruction of Muslims" and characterized the incidence of injustices committed during the first fourteen months of the new state as greater than the wrongs of the preceding forty years under Austria-Hungary.[20] A new exodus of Muslims to Turkey began soon after December 1918.

The alarming threat that hung over them prompted the Muslims into a common defense that united both landlords and smallholders, Westernized intellectuals of Croat and Serb orientation and traditionalist *ulema*, bazaar merchants and urban poor. The organizational form of this resistance was Jugoslavenska muslimanska organizacija (JMO, Yugoslav Muslim Organization), founded in Sarajevo in February 1919. Its adherents, which is to say practically all Bosnian Muslims, were constantly reminded that Muslims could not afford to be caught in the trap of class division: all Muslims, regardless of social standing, had to defend the rights of Muslim landlords, who were hard pressed by the terms of agrarian reform. In the words of Sakib Korkut, a leading JMO activist and the party's most effective public speaker, "There are no class differences. Muslim peasant and Muslim landlord feel the same way because neither has become dead to the demands of justice and will not covet other people's property . . . knowing that usurped goods are cursed [*oteto je prokleto*]."[21]

The JMO sought to extend its organizational refuge to all of Yugoslavia's Muslims, but its candidates actually ran for office only in Bosnia-Her-

19. I am grateful to Prof. Jozo Tomasevich for his calculations in this matter. His reckoning, which I developed further, is based ön the data in Anton Feifalik, *Ein neuer aktueller Weg zur Lösung der bosnischen Agrarfrage* (Vienna, 1916).

20. "Prosvjedna skupština muslimana u Sarajevu," *Pravda*, Jan. 31, 1920, pp. 1–2.

21. "Veliko slavlje," p. 1. On the history of the JMO see three works by Atif Purivatra: *Jugoslavenska muslimanska organizacija u političkom životu Kraljevine Srba, Hrvata i Slovenaca* (Sarajevo, 1974); "Nacionalne koncepcije Jugoslovenske muslimanske organizacije," *Jugoslovenski istorijski časopis*, 1969, no. 4, pp. 141–148; and "Formiranje Jugoslovenske Muslimanske organizacije i njen razvoj do prevazilaženja krize početkom 1922. godine," *Istorija XX veka: zbornik radova*, vol. 9 (1968), pp. 387–445. The latter article is also included in Purivatra's *Nacionalni i politički razvitak Muslimana* (Sarajevo, 1970). See also sections in Salim Ćerić, *Muslimani srpskohrvatskog jezika* (Sarajevo, 1968). For an early appraisal of the JMO by its principal leader see Mehmed Spaho, "Jugoslovenska Muslimanska Organizacija," *Nova Evropa*, vol. 7 (1923), no. 17, pp. 505–506.

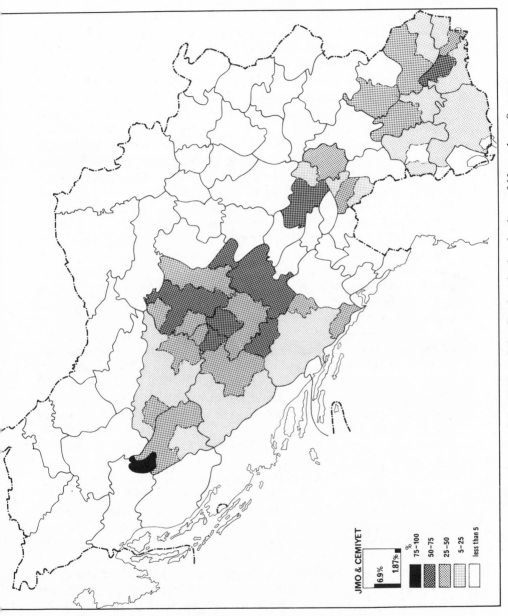

4-3. The strength of the JMO and the Cemiyet in the elections of November 28, 1920

JMO & CEMIYET

6.9% 1.87%

%
75–100
50–75
25–50
5–25
less than 5

cegovina. In the parliamentary elections of November 1920 its performance (see map 4-3, portion for Bosnia-Hercegovina) was in fact greater than the Muslim presence in individual Bosnian districts, which, especially if the age structure of voters (adult males) is taken into account, raises interesting questions about the census of January 1921. Whereas the Muslims constituted 17.08 percent of the population in the district of Banja Luka, the JMO got 18.73 percent of all ballots; in Bihać, 37.24 versus 42.14; in Mostar, 23.08 versus 23.11; in Sarajevo, 44.68 versus 49.57; in Travnik, 26.41 versus 28.63; in Tuzla, 41.18 versus 42.68. The JMO also had pluralities in the four biggest towns of Bosnia-Hercegovina: Sarajevo, 36.16 percent; Mostar, 45.44; Banja Luka, 43.75; Tuzla, 38.35. Moreover, for a party that was repeatedly denounced as the instrument of Muslim landlordism, the JMO had relatively few landlords among its candidates. Of its slate of seventy-eight candidates in all districts of Bosnia-Hercegovina, simultaneous runs by a single candidate in more than one district reducing that number only slightly, fifty-two (or 66.67 percent) were men from the free professions or white-collar occupations, ten (12.82 percent) belonged to the *ulema*, the highest-ranking member of this group being Hadji Hafiz Ibrahim efendi Maglajlić, the mufti of Tuzla and the JMO's first president (1919–1921), six were landlords, five peasants, and four merchants. This does not, of course, mean that some of the candidates from the nonlandlord categories did not simultaneously rent land, but that was not their most important social identification.

In comparison with the JMO, the smaller Muslim parties, which were essentially regional coteries and offshoots of centralist parties, did very poorly. The DS agency's Muslimanska težačka stranka (Muslim Husbandmen's Party), which the JMO punned into oblivion by fashioning the party's unintended acronym of Mutež (turbid, fishy), gained only 1.04 percent of the vote in the district of Mostar and 0.79 in the district of Tuzla. The pro-Radical Muslim List of Šerif Arnautović, a onetime Muslim-Croat and subsequently an exponent of a sort of Muslim Great Serbianism, gained only 0.59 percent of the vote in the district of Tuzla. The Muslim People's Party, also close to the Radicals, which represented the interests of certain Muslim landowners who rejected any compromise on the question of agrarian reform, gained 0.66 percent of the vote in the district of Sarajevo. These parties, denounced as traitorous by the JMO, were in fact the only political alternatives to the JMO in the Muslim community. The Muslims could not be expected to vote for the Catholic clericalists of the HPS or for the Croat Husbandmen, who urged the Muslims to vote for the JMO. None of the candidates of these parties was Muslim. The absence of Muslim candidates from the lists of supposedly secular parties is far more difficult to explain. The Agrarians and Social Democrats run only one Muslim candidate each (1.3 and 1.52 percent of their total list, respectively); the NRS two (2.6 percent), the Communists nine (11.69 percent). The DS, not counting its

Muslim satellite party, ran fourteen (18.18 percent), but in two districts (Banja Luka and Bihać) they had only a token number of Muslims on their ticket, and in three additional districts none at all. Their only strong Muslim ticket was in the key district of Sarajevo, where they ran seven Muslims and five Serbs, and that combination, scorned by Muslims and Serbs alike, gained them only 1.63 percent of the total vote. The Muslims, in short, played the same confessional hand as the other communities of Bosnia-Hercegovina.

The JMO was, of course, the Muslims' only partisan refuge, but the JMO's obviously defensive recognition of its consciously confessional stature reflected an awareness of the increasingly anomalous character of confessional parties in Yugoslav politics. Moreover, despite its total mastery of the Bosnian Muslim community, the JMO could not present itself as the representative of a formed national group, the notion of a separate Bosnian Muslim nationhood being unacceptable not only to the Serbs and Croats but to the Muslim leaders themselves. The JMO spokesmen could only defend their confessional orientation as a necessary answer to the discriminatory policies of centralist administrations. Sakib Korkut readily admitted that the Muslims were organized on the confessional basis but asked the critics of the JMO to consider who was to blame for that development: "What did the national revolution [unification of Yugoslavia] bring us: fraternal forgiveness or savage retribution? I shall not recount all the murders, robberies, and persecutions of Muslims. Even children know about those. I shall only note who committed these things: Orthodox Serbs. Some object, noting that Catholic Croats were also persecuted. That is true. But that only proves that the persecution of Muslims was not a result of our 'anational' circumstances. We were the victims of [organized] religious fanaticism and were, therefore, forced to group ourselves on the religious basis, too."[22]

This stance found a favorable response among the Muslims, especially during the initial phase after the unification when they were systematically excluded from regional and local administrations, were confronted with other obstacles, and were the subject of a well-orchestrated harangue by hegemonist forces, who wished to depict the Muslims as antinational and disruptive elements, synonymous with the Turks. "Bosnia-Hercegovina," the JMO defended itself in an editorial in its central organ welcoming Regent Aleksandar to Sarajevo in September 1920, "is the land in which the word Croats is written in quotation marks and where the Muslim part of our people, its purest branch, is being dispatched from all levels of authority—to Asia. That word, O regent, hurts."[23]

Indeed, not only were the Muslims of Bosnia-Hercegovina demeaned as

22. "Veliko slavlje," p. 1.
23. "Dobro nam došao, Kraljeviću," *Pravda,* Sept. 18, 1920, p. 1.

"Asians," they were also constantly stereotyped as unstable and perverted. According to one Bosnian Serb source, their character was marked by "inertia, every kind of indolence, mendacity and braggadocio, fatalism, [belief in] kismet, ungovernable fancy, and *especially* sensuality, [which when connected] with the claims of biology that homosexuals are weaker than heterosexuals and often without any will for life, [leads to] the incontestable explanation of homosexuality among our Muslims."[24] Their worst characteristic, according to the same source, was, however, the rejection of honest work. Muslims were parasitical, prone to business failures, and found the highest ideal in the cult of *rahatlık* (Turkish, pleasure). A necessary apsect of their rehabilitation was "social deislamization" (p. 168). The most effective but perhaps not the most politic way to accomplish that was by intermarriage with Serbs. Should the process of nationalization fail, "there remains only one solution; short, clear, and inexorable. The singer of folk songs has foretold it and sung about it; he sings about it even today. We shall not repeat it here, because we all know it" (p. 172). That solution was genocide.

Though, after 1918, the Muslims were challenged much more pointedly to define themselves in terms of nationality, their resistance to the sort of nationalization that was expected of them was increasingly substantial. Muslim defensiveness first had to give way to the affirmation of nativeness and national honor: Muslims were not a foreign element. They, perhaps they alone, were autochthonous to Bosnia-Hercegovina.[25] They were pure descendants of Bosnian "Patarins" and King Tvrtko, the purest part of Croat and Serb people.[26] Unlike the Serbs like Pribićević, who was "a refugee from the mountains of Black Wallachia," their blood was pure Slavic.[27] And even if the Muslim masses were not conscious of their national appellation, they were, nevertheless, national.[28] Moreover, some Muslims were not afraid to challenge the bogey of anationality. According to Osman Nurij-beg Firdus, they were "present at the crowning both of Tomislav and of Stefan Dušan, but then lost national sentiment for the sake of faith. . . . They are conscious that their origin is Slavic, that they are the part of the Serbo-Croat body that became anational for the sake of religion. . . . It is impossible to be at the same time a Muslim and have national sentiments. Islam is more important than nationality."[29]

Still others nationalized Islam. No nation, Arab, Turkish, or Persian,

---

24. Čedomil Mitrinović, *Naši muslimani: Studija za orientaciju pitanja bosansko-hercegovačkih muslimana* (Belgrade, 1926), p. 138. (Page numbers that follow are also from this work.)

25. "Prosvjedna skupština," p. 1.

26. [Mustafa] Čelić, "Nedajmo svog sela!" *Pravda*, Jan. 24, 1920, p. 1. "Dobro nam, došao, Kraljeviću," p. 1.

27. Sakib Korkut, "Stanovište bosanskih muslimana," *Hrvat*, Nov. 5, 1919, p. 4.

28. Ibid.

29. Osman Nurij-beg Firdus, "O nacionalnom opredeljenju bosansko-hercegovačkih muslimana," *Nova Evropa*, vol. 11 (1925), no. 10, p. 299.

disappeared in Islam. Neither did the "Bosnian" nation: "The Muslim part of our people is perhaps the best measure of our racial strength. Since our people were stronger and better than the Turks, in a very short time they assumed all the important positions in [the Turkish] state, thereby becoming the leading element in one of the world's greatest empires."[30] There was no Turcification in Bosnia, nor for that matter the assimilation of any other foreign nationality, as happened in the other South Slavic lands, because the "Muslims defended their land from foreign invasion for four hundred years and safeguarded its purest national character."[31] And even those Muslim intellectuals who, like the members of the pro-Serb Gajret, urged the Muslims "to learn from the past only one thing—how to flee from it as far as possible," could not resist pointing out that it was unfair to negate the Islamic heritage of the South Slavs while simultaneously praising their Western affiliations: "When we mention Rudjer Bošković [the great eighteenth-century mathematician, astronomer, and physicist from Dubrovnik], and when we sometimes cite with satisfaction the other great men of Dalmatia who wrote in Italian, why do we not also seek the power of our race in the East, among the Turks and Arabs?"[32]

Bosnian Muslims only lacked a national name. The anti-Muslim character of agrarian strife in Bosnia-Hercegovina made Muslim integration within Serb national ideology well-nigh impossible. To embrace the Croats meant courting a direct confrontation with Belgrade, one that could very possibly result in the partition of Bosnia-Hercegovina, and that was exactly what the JMO—and Muslims generally—wanted to prevent at all cost. The partition, whether arbitrary or otherwise, would have reduced the Muslims to the status of a permanent minority.

Faced with the dilemma of choosing between the two increasingly antagonistic national ideologies, one of them largely unacceptable and the other on the defensive, or else being accused of antinational inclinations, the JMO leadership chose to make the best of the limited refuge offered by Yugoslavist unitarism. In the case of the JMO, however, this choice was devoid of the ideological purport usually associated with unitarist precepts, since the JMO was itself an object of Croat-Serb competition and was clearly the party least likely to be taken in by the unitarist doctrine of Serb-Croat national oneness. The Serbs and Croats simply did not act as a single people in their contention over Bosnia-Hercegovina, and therefore the JMO's unitarism could be only an expedient. In a very important editorial of December 30, 1920, the JMO's organ *Pravda* (Justice) duly accepted the theoretical possibility of Croat-Serb

30. Ahmed Muradbegović, "Problem jugoslovenske muslimanske izolacije," ibid., vol. 3 (1921), no. 4, p. 112.

31. "Naše skupštine u Hercegovini," *Pravda,* July 31, 1920, p. 2.

32. [Šukrija Kurtović], "Gajretov list," *Gajret,* vol. 8 (1921), no. 1, p. 2; and "Pabirci iz prošlosti Bosne," ibid., p. 34.

amalgamation, but, in citing the example of Russo-Polish symbiosis, which failed to produce a new hybrid nationality after a century and a half of coexistence within a single state, strongly suggested that the program of *narodno jedinstvo* was just as unworkable.[33] Moreover, in a continuation of the editorial, a few days later, *Pravda* denounced "Yugoslav nationalism" of the DS as nothing but an Orthodox Serb ideology that "only inflamed and strengthened mutually antagonistic Serb and Croat nationalisms."[34] Clearly, such an ideology, false in both theory and practice, could not become the basis of the JMO's stand on the Muslim national question. But so it did, though only after a fashion, precisely because it offered the Muslims some breathing space. Caught in the agonizing web of demands to nationalize themselves, the Muslims rebelled in still more absurd ways. Some declared themselves neither Serbs nor Croats, but Slovenes.[35] As long as they were obliged to be something more than an Islamic community, their choice of unitaristic riddles (for example, the "bitribal part of our single people") by comparison was the height of good sense. All the weaknesses of Yugoslavist unitarism were evident in their case.

Since unitarism could not end the competition over the status of Muslims, the JMO at least hoped that it could influence the terms of the Bosnian game. The Muslim leadership wanted it understood that the term nationalization was a misnomer. Croat and Serb nationhood could not be inspired by rigorous scholastic proofs; less so by political intimidation: "The factors that have nowadays acquired the strongest role in nation-forming are no longer religion or language, but economic and social relations—that is, material culture in general."[36] The JMO was suggesting that Muslims would hold hard with the group that treated them better: "Should the Muslims feel that they have had their fair chance at economic development, that they can enjoy the same material culture as the Serbs, they will unconditionally and certainly choose the Serb nationhood. But should they continue to observe, as they have hitherto, that chances at economic development are allotted unequally and that in their inequality they are being equated with the Croats, they will as before continue to choose Croat nationality."[37] The JMO leaders did not hesitate to defend the hoary motto of Balkan pragmatism: "Better an inch of power than an ell of right and justice."[38] But as with all pragmatists, they put too much credence in the pragmatism of their adversaries.

The practicality of the JMO was also evidenced by its tolerance of its

33. "Jesmo li Srbi ili Hrvati?" *Pravda,* Dec. 30, 1920, p. 1.
34. "Jesmo li Srbi ili Hrvati?" ibid., Jan. 4, 1921, p. 1.
35. A leftist Muslim law student opted for that solution out of protest in 1927. Yugoslavia's census of 1953 registered 105 Slovenes of Islamic religion in Bosnia-Hercegovina. Hadžijahić, *Od tradicije do identiteta,* p. 227, n. 5.
36. "Jesmo li Srbi ili Hrvata?" *Pravda,* Dec. 30, p. 1.
37. Ibid.
38. "Unakrsna paljba naših prijatelja," ibid., March 24, 1921, p. 1.

membership's more definite national expressions. For example, of the JMO's twenty-four deputies elected in November 1920, fifteen declared themselves as Croats, two as Serbs, five were undeclared, and one opted for the status of a Bosnian. Of the eighteen JMO deputies and their alternates elected in 1923 all but Dr. Mehmed Spaho (1883–1939), the party's president after 1921, declared themselves as Croats.[39] Spaho, a Serb in his student days, later refused to be labeled either a Serb or a Croat. Curiously, his brother Fehim, the *reis ul-ulema* (religious head) of Yugoslavia's Muslims from 1938 to 1942, was a Croat. The third brother, Mustafa Spaho, an engineer, was a Serb.[40] The free expression of nationality persisted throughout the interwar period, but it was never allowed to destroy the party unity. No JMO leader, including those of pronounced Croat or Serb orientation, ever attempted to steer his followers out of the JMO and into the various Croat or Serb parties. This is certainly one of the reasons why Radić failed to draw the Muslims to his movement in any huge numbers and why he repeatedly accused the JMO leaders of alienating the Muslims from Croatdom.[41]

Though the attenuated compromise with unitarism paradoxically contributed to the perpetuation of Muslim particularism, the JMO's insistence on Bosnia-Hercegovina's autonomy and indivisibility remained an open challenge to centralism. Nevertheless, it was the JMO that guaranteed the passage of the 1921 centralist constitution, by providing its pivotal votes to Pašić's draft proposal in exchange for numerous concessions that in effect blunted the edge of centralism in areas of vital Muslim interest.[42] As a result of the JMO's compromise agreement with the centralist parties, Pašić's government formally expressed its determination to protect Islamic regulations and customs. It also moved to include a guarantee of Bosnia-Hercegovina's territorial integrity in Article 135, Subsection 3, of the constitution. Hence, the division of Yugoslavia into small districts (*oblasti*), which the centralists regarded as crucial in stopping the influence of the centrifugal national movements, was not carried out in Bosnia-Hercegovina, or more correctly, the province was divided into districts without the violation of its historically determined external frontiers. No area of historical Bosnia-Hercegovina was adjoined to any neighboring land, as the centralists' original plan intended. The compactness of the province was thereby largely preserved, though Mehmed Spaho argued that no political or historical reasons, but only the needs of good administration, suggested this concession.[43] In

39. Hadžijahić, *Od tradicije do identiteta*, pp. 209–210.
40. Ibid., p. 227.
41. Purivatra, *Jugoslavenska muslimanska organizacija u političkom životu*, pp. 399–400. On Radić's policy in Bosnia-Hercegovina see Tomislav Išek, *Djelatnost Hrvatske seljačke stranke u Bosni i Hercegovini do zavodjenja diktature* (Sarajevo, 1981).
42. "Sporazum postignut," *Pravda*, March 17, 1921, p. 1.
43. Mehmed Spaho, "Prigovori našem sporazumu," ibid., April 2, 1921, p. 1.

addition, Pašić's government also agreed to increase the indemnities that the Muslim landlords demanded in arrear of the lands distributed under the provisions of the agrarian reform.[44]

Despite its specially important aid to the centralists during the vital period of the constitutional debate, the JMO could not join its interests with their in any permanent way. The rise of Mehmed Spaho in 1921 coincided with the beginning of the JMO's purge of those of its founding members who were determined to give their uncritical support to the Belgrade cabinets under any and all circumstances. As long as the status of Bosnian Muslims remained precarious, the JMO would on occasion find the common language with the bloc of oppositional parties under Radić's direction. Nevertheless, the JMO would also not hesitate to enter into further agreements with the centralist factors if it suited the special interests of its Muslim base. Its characteristically tactical interaction between the numerous strategically incompatible forces, so reminiscent of the SLS, was, however, never conducted at the expense of its constant concern for the autonomy of Bosnia-Hercegovina. But it had its price. When Spaho and Korošec joined the remnants of Old Radicals in 1936 to form the Yugoslav Radical Community (JRZ), the regime party that was to afford a modicum of respectability to the authoritarian system of Milan Stojadinović, they bargained away many of the obligations that they could hitherto expect from the hard opposition.

"They took everything from us," sang Hamza Humo in the early 1920s, suggesting that the only homeland of Bosnian Muslims was the wanderer's staff of cornel wood.[45] Indeed, the Muslims of Bosnia-Hercegovina learned that the JMO's gains of 1921 could just as easily be taken away. In 1929 King Aleksandar partitioned Bosnia out of existence between four provinces (banates), in each of which the Muslims were a minority. In 1939, Radić's successor, Maček, underwrote a new partition of Bosnia-Hercegovina, with the thirteen of its counties going to the newly established autonomous Croatia and thirty-eight reserved for the projected Serbian portion of Yugoslavia.[46] The division was accomplished by discounting the Muslims altogether. For example, if in a given county the Catholics constituted 34 percent of the population and the Orthodox 33 percent, the county went to Croatia. The Muslim 33 percent made no difference.[47]

Pavelić's Independent State of Croatia, which included the whole of Bosnia-Hercegovina, was not a great improvement. Under its internal ar-

44. Many Muslim landlords considered the compensation for the lands subjected to the agrarian reform as too small, but Spaho reminded them that it was illusory to expect a better settlement in the future. Not only did the JMO accomplish the best possible arrangement, but its landlord critics were forgetting, according to Spaho, that an "enormous social turnabout took place not only in our country, but throughout the world." Ibid.

45. Cited in Mitrinović, *Naši muslimani*, p. 161.

46. On the JMO's reaction to Maček's arrangement see Ljubo Boban, *Sporazum Cvetković-Maček* (Belgrade, 1965), pp. 258–261.

47. Hadžijahić, *Od tradicije do identiteta*, p. 237.

rangement, a type of integral Croat unitarism, Bosnia-Hercegovina was divided among eleven provinces (grand *župas*), four of which, whose centers were outside historical Bosnia-Hercegovina, acquired thirteen Bosnian-Hercegovinian counties. In all fairness it should be added that three counties from Croatia proper and Dalmatia were added to the *župas* with centers in Bosnia-Hercegovina, but none of these arrangements increased Muslim political influence. Spaho's successor, Džafer-beg Kulenović, figured in Pavelić's hierarchy as part of the requisite Bosnian decor. But despite the official lore on how the Muslims were the "bloom of Croat people," he had no apparent authority.

Where Pavelić did not share power with the Muslims, the Chetniks of Draža Mihailović set out to destroy them and in the process slaughtered not a few ardent Serb-Muslims. In Foča, before killing a Muslim who appealed to his record of Serb patriotism, the Chetniks explained themselves in the following way: "Inasmuch as you were a Serb, you sullied the Serb name, because you are a Turk. And since you helped us, we shall not torture you."[48] They shot him instead of slashing his throat. Is it strange or queer that in Europe there emerged in the second half of the twentieth century a nation that no longer wanted to be anything but incongruously Muslim?

The Cemiyet

The JMO's course was very similar to that of İslam Muhafazai Hukuk Cemiyet (Society for the Preservation of Muslim Rights), usually referred to as the Cemiyet, the party of Muslims from the "southern regions," that is, the Bosnian Muslims of the Sandžak and the Albanians and Turks of Kosovo, Metohia, and Macedonia. Indeed, the Cemiyet's statute was nothing but a translation of the JMO's own by-laws.[1] Like the JMO, the Cemiyet was a confessional party that fought for Muslim religious autonomy and a better deal for Muslim landlords. Its showing in the 1920 elections (see map 4-3, portion for the Sandžak, Kosovo, Metohia, and Macedonia) was relatively impressive, but the Cemiyet was helped by an electoral arrangement with the Radicals whereby in some districts only one party ran for office and the other lent it its candidates and in others both parties ran and mixed their tickets. For example, Nastas Petrović, a Radical minister, was one of the Cemiyet's candidates in the district of Zvečani-Raška, and Puniša Račić, the assassin of Stjepan Radić in 1928, was one of its candidates in Tetovo. In Kosovo, a local mufti was on the NRS's ticket. And in the parts of the

48. Ibid., p. 235.
1. "'Hak' o našoj organizaciji," *Pravda*, July 17, 1920, p. 1. For a brief summary of the Cemiyet's activities see Mihailo Maletić, ed., *Kosovo-Kosova* (Belgrade, 1973), pp. 186–190.

Sandžak, the NRS ran its friends from the Bosnian Muslim community, among them Šerif Arnautović.

The Cemiyet, in short, had a far snugger relationship with the Radicals than anything that the JMO yet accomplished. The Cemiyet was instrumental in helping Pašić push through the centralist constitution in exchange for numerous concessions. These primarily involved favorable indemnities for lands subject to the agrarian reform that, as originally conceived, constituted a serious economic setback to the Muslim notables in the leadership of Cemiyet. The NRS's rivalry with the DS induced Pašić to enter into even closer relations with the Cemiyet. Electoral deals between the two parties were repeated in the 1922 parliamentary elections, and during the 1923 elections the NRS even openly opposed the DS's policy of settlement and colonization of Kosovo and Macedonia, something that could only please the native element, primarily the Albanians.

Nevertheless, after Ferat Bej Draga assumed the Cemiyet's leadership, he persuaded the party's majority to abandon its acquiescence to the continuing national inequality to which the Albanians and Turks were subjected. Political differentiation in the ranks of the Cemiyet, as a result, was brought to completion. The party's moderate wing, which was in favor of unconditional compromises with the Radicals, emerged as a minority tendency, while Draga's dominant group advanced vigorous demands for national equality and for political and cultural rights of Yugoslavia's Muslim southeast. Draga was therefore increasingly drawn toward Radić's Croat movement. Yet another faction of the Cemiyet covertly aided Albania's irredentist efforts in Kosovo and Macedonia. Since the Cemiyet was becoming transformed into a tenacious opponent of centralism and Serbian supremacy, it necessarily clashed with its former allies of the NRS. All cooperation between the two parties came to an end in 1923, and Pašić's electoral terror, which included Draga's arrest, assured the Cemiyet's thorough defeat in the 1925 parliamentary elections.[2] Faced with insurmountable official pressures, the Cemiyet ceased functioning during the same year.

The smaller the political influence of a national group, the greater the pressure on its leaders to conform to the political needs of centralists. The fate of the Cemiyet in many ways was similar to that of the parties of Yugoslavia's German, Hungarian, and Romanian minorities. But these parties were not instrumental in initiating policy on the national question, nor was their role central in the ensuing political clashes, in which the autonomist opposition vacillated between centralism and (con)federalism, between unitarism and national individuality, while simultaneously upholding the faint hope of compromise and reform.

2. "'Ispovest' Ferad-beg Drage," *Reč*, April 10, 1925, p. 1.

PART V

Disenchantment

I am hurt and bored. I expected so much from Belgrade and it disenchanted me so much.

Miloš Crnjanski, 1920

. . . and, moreover, a total decomposition of that certain type of beauty, which we were elevating, fortifying, and which we finally reached. . . . They have all turned their coats, but they are all just as before, even the detectives and spies are the same under the firm of Serbs, Croats, and Slovenes.

Ivo Vojnović, 1919

Che desillusione!

Pero Čingrija, 1920

Even in the quarters where the advent of Yugoslavia was awaited with the most sanguine expectation, the promise turned to disenchantment. The ball-royal of unification took place in an enchanted hall, where even the unmasked players appeared admirable. But soon the plumage of lofty ideals was bartered for old programs. Yugoslav union became a circumstance of language; and Yugoslav politics—a written notation of public affairs, a sort of political choreography.

The Twenty-one Months of the Interim Parliament

According to the agreement between the National Council and the Serbian government, the convening of Yugoslavia's first cabinet, effected by Stojan Protić on December 20, 1918, was to have been accompanied by the convening of a single legislative body. Such an interim parliament was to meet no more than a month after the creation of a joint cabinet. This, however, was not to be accomplished until the end of February 1919. The reluctance to impose restrictions on the Protić cabinet's responsibility was largely the result of willful procrastination on the part of that same body, some of whose leading members, notably Pribićević, were fully cognizant that parliamentary decision-making, which would inevitably be dependent on partisan politics, might slow the pace of the centralizing measures that they sought to establish. The temporary lethargy in the activities of most of the political parties, with the exception of the HPSS, also contributed, albeit to a lesser extent, to the slow process of the normal parliamentary procedures. When the provisional parliament, Privremeno narodno predstavništvo (PNP, Interim National Legislature) was finally called to order in Belgrade in March 1919, the very fact that it was convened on the basis of the regent's decree of February 24 cast a shadow over its ability to prevent further abuses on the part of the centralist forces.[1] Even more foreboding, however, was the character of the selection procedure for its members.

Members of the PNP were delegated, not elected by the voters. The only exception to this fundamental characteristic of the provisional parliament was made in Macedonia and Kosovo, where elections for the twenty-four PNP deputies were held on March 30, 1919. But even there the elections were neither direct (only select electors voted), nor secret.[2] The deputies from Serbia, Montenegro, and Vojvodina were delegated by the respective assemblies of the regions in question, while the deputies from the rest of the country were chosen by the interparty committees, although their mandates were confirmed by the National Council in Zagreb and its equivalents in Split (for Dalmatia) and Sarajevo (for Bosnia-Hercegovina).[3] The undemocratic nature of the selection process was accented not only by the fact that (at least in the formerly Austro-Hungarian areas) the local governments had a decisive say in the selection of the PNP deputies, but even more so by the circumstance that the Protić government itself proceeded to narrow the selection process by imposing its own—highly controversial—proportional key

1. *Stenografske beleške Privremenog narodnog predstavništva Srba, Hrvata i Slovenaca*, vol. 2 (Zagreb, 1919), p. 1.
2. As a result, the deputies from Macedonia and Kosovo were the exponents of centralism and Serbian hegemony, and some were actually employees of the police or born outside the areas they represented. Though such irregularities normally would have disqualified them under electoral procedures, their mandates were, nevertheless, verified. See Aleksandar Apostolov, "Vardarska Makedonija od Prvata svetska vojna do izborite za Konstituantata—28 noemvri 1920 godina," in *Godišen zbornik na Filozofskiot fakultet na Univerzitetot vo Skopje: Istorisko-filološki oddel* (1962), pp. 74–77.
3. The selection process for the mandates of the PNP deputies was challenged by Ante Pavelić, the former vice-president of the National Council, who claimed that the National Council in Zagreb was not asked to submit a list of the candidates for the PNP selected by the Council itself. "Protokol 2. Prethodnog sastanka PNP Ujedinjenog Kr. SHS—držan 4. marta 1919. god. u Beogradu u Kraljevom Dvoru," *Službene novine*, April 26, 1919, pp. 4–5.

for the number of deputies from each region.[4] The government defended itself against charges that it was undermining the autonomy of the parliamentary system by claiming that the PNP's Verification Committee would have the last word on the mandates of the proposed deputies. But since the Verification Committee could only be chosen by a majority vote of the same deputies whose mandates were to be examined, the ultimate verification process was reduced to a double sham.

In internal cabinet discussions, where candor prevailed, the convening of the PNP was viewed as a matter of expediency, as a concession to the democratic spirit of the times. A necessary consequence of this conception was the government's refusal to recognize any legislative authority on the part of the PNP. Its role was to be limited to establishing the procedure for the election of the Constituent Assembly and the fashioning of that body's agenda. Every link in this chain of reasoning could be and was challenged on constitutional and legal grounds. The protest of the HPSS went the furthest. Radić decided to boycott the PNP by refusing to accept the two mandates allotted to his party. The government's last resort, however, was its possession of power, a circumstance that Pribićević for one described as a singularly appropriate argument for the country's revolutionary—and therefore anticonstitutional—phase, which would not stand on formality.

The numerically strongest party in the PNP was the DS. Of the total of 294 deputies, 115 were Democrats. Furthermore, in Protić's cabinet, notwithstanding the prime minister's party affiliation, the Democrats had a clear majority. Eleven out of a total of seventeen ministers were members of the DS. By contrast, the Radicals were in a minority position. Sixty-nine PNP deputies belonged to the NRS, while Protić, in his own cabinet, could count on only two additional ministers from his party. Although the NRS leadership was prepared to tolerate Pribićević's high-handedness with the Croat opposition, it would not tolerate his encroachments on its own political base. Similarly, the Radicals would not accept a minority role for their party, with its considerable tradition of leadership. Contention between the two dominant centralist parties, therefore, hardly extended beyond the bounds of the practical struggle for power and influence, where ideological differences (though they existed) mattered little. Nevertheless, the necessity of changing the relation of forces in their favor caused the Radicals to seek allies among the Croat and Slovene parties—principally the HZ and the SLS—with whom they shared fewer points of agreement than with the DS. This necessarily induced the NRS to become more elastic in its version of centralism, allow-

4. Slovenia was represented in the PNP with thirty-two deputies, Croatia-Slavonia with Rijeka and Medjimurje with sixty, Istria with four, Dalmatia with twelve, Bosnia-Hercegovina with forty-two, Vojvodina with twenty-four, Serbia proper with eighty-four, Macedonia, Kosovo, and Metohia with twenty-four, and Montenegro with twelve.

ing Protić to brand the Democrats as exclusively responsible for the excesses of centralization.[5] Although Protić was personally known to be more attentive to the realities of Yugoslavia's national question than the majority of the NRS leaders, his attempts at a tactical coalition with the HZ and the SLS did not prevent him from continuing to uphold the incontrovertability of monarchism and a modified version of centralism. In fact, hegemonist dominance would only be furthered by a mere modicum of cooperation between a leading Serbian centralist party and sections of the Croat and Slovene opposition.

By early summer of 1919, as the confrontation between the Radicals and the Democrats assumed sharp and—among the two parties' local supporters—even violent contours, a cabinet crisis became unavoidable. Protić covertly sought to strengthen his party's position by attempts to gain the loyalty of the HZ, while Pribićević openly relied on the regent's benevolence. After a visit to Zagreb in late July, Protić felt confident that the time to act had come. Accordingly, he offered a resignation on behalf of his cabinet, claiming that insurmountable differences between the two leading parties on matters of internal policy and agrarian reform made such a step inevitable. The mandate for the composition of a new cabinet was given to the DS leader, Davidović. It quickly became apparent that Protić's aspirations for a cabinet reconstruction on the Radicals' terms were not realistic. Because of the state's precarious external position, the Democrats in fact succeeded in gaining political advantage by representing Protić's initiative as the height of irresponsibility. In addition, Davidović's refusal even to consider the removal of his party's ministers, Pribićević (Interior) and Franjo Poljak (Agrarian Reform), from his projected cabinet necessarily forestalled the possibility of a DS-NRS coalition, or, for that matter, a coalition with the Croat and Slovene parties. Davidović's intransigence thus augmented Protić's determination not to participate in a cabinet dominated by the DS. Although the Radicals could not yet effect a working plurality in a bloc with the HZ and the SLS that would enable them to repulse the Democrats, Protić wanted to advance that hour by fighting the DS from the opposition benches. Confronted by a coalition of the strongest Serbian and Slovene parties, in which the most powerful Croat party in the PNP also participated, the DS turned to Korać's Social Democrats. Davidović's DS-Social Democrat cabinet was installed on August 16.

From the beginning the new cabinet's position was most vulnerable. The government parties controlled only 126 votes in the PNP, while the opposition amounted to 134 deputies. Without a parliamentary plurality, Davidović was forced to rely on certain PNP grouplets that did not participate in his

5. *Stenografske beleške PNP*, vol. 4, pp. 104–105.

cabinet. The ruling DS continually sought to undermine the oppositional bloc, but its internal policies, which were still under Pribićević's sway, could only have the opposite result. In fact, Protić's efforts to bolster the compactness of the opposition were much more successful. The government continued its efforts to widen the cabinet, which merely furthered the crisis atmosphere. It was under these conditions that Davidović's cabinet resigned for the first time within a month of its initiation.

Although his cabinet was quickly reconstructed, any dénouement remained impossible. Protić's mandate for the creation of a new cabinet was proved to be unworkable because the DS-Social Democrat bloc denied it its cooperation. Confident that his ally Marko Trifković, a leader of a grouplet of independent Radicals, would succeed where he failed, Protić secured a strong NRS-HZ-SLS bloc, known as the Parliamentary Union, which was effected only through further compromises with centralism on the part of the HZ. The Radicals, however, also compromised and promised that the HZ adherents would dominate Croatia's regional government after the Democrats were ousted from power. In fact, the reasons for the regent's refusal to install Trifković's proposed cabinet are to be sought in more than Aleksandar's collusion with the DS. The regent's decision was principally motivated by the opposition's ability to unite behind a common strategy that would have removed the most repellent features of centralism. Such concessions, however attenuated and far removed from the maximum demands of the Croat opposition, were sufficient to provoke charges of separatism from the DS ranks. Aleksandar clearly shared the Democrats' aversion to even the slightest retreat from the course outlined by Pribićević.

Although the DS-Socialist government continued functioning while the opposition tried its hand at finding a workable alternative, its position was considerably strengthened on October 16, when Aleksandar gave Davidović a mandate to organize a new cabinet. More important, however, the prime minister also received carte blanche to dissolve the PNP and carry out the elections if the government failed to receive parliamentary support. Armed with such broad authority and counting on Aleksandar's continued support, the Democrats and their socialist partners decided not only to ignore any demands that would detract from their policy of stringent centralism but also to undertake a new wave of centralization. Serbia's military laws were thus immediately extended statewide, and new regulations were promulgated permitting the dismissal of the county and municipal civil servants in Croatia-Slavonia whenever the higher authorities deemed it necessary.[6] Local autonomy in Croatia-Slavonia was further undermined through new communal electoral regulations, which included the obligatory oath of allegiance to the

6. "Uredba o premeštivosti opštinskih činovnika u Hrvatskoj i Slavoniji te o skraćenju karnosnog postupka proti njima," *Službene novine,* Nov. 19, 1919, p. 1.

monarch, while in Slovenia the Davidović cabinet succeeded in installing a regional government free of SLS influence.[7]

The cabinet's heavy-handed domestic measures only added to Yugoslavia's already seriously impaired external position, which was accented by D'Annunzio's seizure of Rijeka, and the government's decision to impose a two-month recess on the PNP did not improve matters. Davidović was therefore forced to negotiate with the opposition. When these contacts failed to resolve the substantive matters, the DS decided that it could improve its position only by dissolving the PNP altogether and undertaking of an electoral campaign for the Constituent Assembly. This gamble was in large part based on the Democrats' conviction that their electoral success was assured because their party had managed to establish a nucleus in the civil administration during its period of rule. Aleksandar, however, refused to approve this course. Accordingly, Davidović's cabinet resigned on February 15, 1920. Several days later, after a failure to organize a concentrated cabinet, Protić succeeded in composing a government of his Parliamentary Union bloc.[8]

Protić's assumption of power constituted the first tangible relaxation of the collision-ridden national question. The massive dissatisfaction in Croatia and elsewhere finally convinced the Court that nominal concessions to decentralism could only alleviate the protracted state crisis. The fact that Pribićević, the symbol of centralism, was finally eased out of the Ministry of Interior after fourteen months of arbitrary rule could only improve the political climate in the disaffected areas. With him went some of his key followers in the regional administrations of Croatia and Slovenia. For example, Matko Laginja of the HZ was appointed the new Croatian Ban, and he took immediate steps to lift the repressive measures that previously had been inflicted on the HPSS. But presence of both the HZ and the SLS politicians in Protić's cabinet and in the regional administrations was not indicative of a shift from centralism, mainly because the court, which was certainly not pleased with concessions to Radić, kept interfering with Protić's initiatives through its confidants.

A more serious obstacle confronting the government of the Parliamentary Union was the inability of the Protić cabinet, like its Democratic predecessors, to muster a majority in the PNP. In fact, the DS-led opposition was successful in paralyzing the governing coalition by denying it the necessary parliamentary quorum. Protić was therefore persuaded to go back on his promises that he would rule by legislative consent. Confronted with the opposition's obstructionism, he reverted to the DS's practice of rule by edict.

---

7. "Uredba o izboru općinskih odbora za upravne općine Hrvatske i Slavonije," ibid., Nov. 23, 1919, p. 1.

8. Ibid., Feb. 22, 1920, p. 1.

Protić's position was further undermined by the Democrats' attempts to regain the footing they had lost in Croatia. The DS was certainly adroit in spreading alarmist rumors about the alleged collusion between the Croat dissidents and the revisionist neighboring countries. Foreign complications and a wave of Communist-led strikes were, however, serious enough to prompt yet another attempt at a bipartisan cabinet. The regent, therefore, mandated an NRS leader, Milenko Vesnić (1863–1921), with the task of bringing about a coalition government.

Although Vesnić, Serbia's—and later, Yugoslavia's—ambassador to France, stood above the current partisan clashes owing to his prolonged absence abroad, this advantage was offset by his association with Pašić's strictly centralist wing of the NRS. It is difficult to judge how much Vesnić's political allegiance had to do with his success in reaching a compromise with the Democrats. The concentrated cabinet that he headed after Protić's resignation on May 17 conceded to several DS demands. Vesnić agreed to a speedy completion of the PNP's sessions after the passage of an electoral law and certain other measures and promised to carry out the elections for the Constituent Assembly. The DS was also assured of proportional representation in the regional governments. For their part, the Democrats modified their platform on the question of agrarian reform. Besides the Radicals and the Democrats, Vesnić's cabinet also included representatives of the HZ, the SLS, and some smaller parties. The sensitive Ministry of Interior was assigned to Davidović, although Pribićević's compulsive centralism found ample outlet in his capacity as the new minister of education. Protić was for the moment allowed to head the crucial *ressort* in charge of preparations for the Constituent Assembly.[9]

The DS's participation in the Vesnić cabinet contributed to the Democrats' tactical fluidity but not at the expense of their strategic goal—a manifestly centralist constitution. The concessions that the DS was prepared to make regarding the agrarian reform were meant as the necessary remuneration for bringing over the NRS to the DS's vision of an unreservedly centralist Yugoslavia. It was not lost on DS leaders that the success of this expedient would bring about yet another dividend, the breakup of the NRS-HZ-SLS partnership that Protić had welded earlier. Since the consensus that bound this partnership together was embodied in Protić's draft constitutional proposal, the DS leaders found it necessary to undermine Protić's standing in the Radical councils, leading to his removal from the cabinet.

It soon became obvious that the Democrats had a tacit partner in Vesnić, whose failure to support Protić's constitutional proposals was a consequence of an understanding that Vesnić reached with the DS leaders. Both Pašić and the court encouraged the reconciliation of the two leading centralist parties at

9. Ibid., May 18, 1920, p. 1.

the time the outlines of the opposing constitutional proposals were already crystallizing. Protić had to draw certain conclusions from the isolated position in which he suddenly found himself in the NRS leadership. Accordingly, he resigned from the cabinet. On August 18, during a cabinet reshuffle, he was replaced by an NRS deputy, Lazar Marković, while Davidović's Interior *ressort* was filled by another prominent Democrat, Milorad Drašković.[10]

The DS was not satisfied merely to get rid of Protić. Its next goal was to compel the HZ and the SLS to agree on the government's joint constitutional proposal, which, because of the relation of forces in the Vesnić cabinet, could only be clearly centralist. After some hesitation the two parties did indeed accept such a step, though with some reservations. It is clear, however, that the HZ-SLS leaders did not go back on their opposition to any unmistakably centralist constitution, as the DS imputed for strictly political purposes. Rather, the two parties continued to hope that the Constituent Assembly would arrive at a compromise constitutional formula that could satisfy their aspirations.

The Vesnić cabinet, however, pushed through two regulations that further restricted the autonomy of the Constituent Assembly. The law that regulated the election of the Constituent Assembly's deputies, passed by the PNP on September 3, not only denied the franchise to women and military personnel but also set the minimum age of male voters at twenty-one and stipulated that every district electoral list must have at least two "qualified" candidates, that is, university graduates. The electoral units were also derived on the basis of the 1910 census, thus favoring Serbia, which had sustained great population losses from wartime casualties and epidemics. The law, however, went beyond the normal concerns for purely electoral legislation by imposing certain restrictions on the Constituent Assembly's prerogatives. For example, it specified that the Constituent Assembly would frame a constitution and other *related* laws as well as financial regulations. The wording by its omission suggested that the Constituent Assembly had no right to arrive at any additional legislation. This impression was strengthened by an imposition of a two-year limit for the Assembly's deliberations. Certainly the most serious encroachment on the Assembly's sovereignty was the law's offhand reference to the ukase that would dissolve the Assembly. Although the originator of such a ukase was not designated, it was clear that only the regent was invested with such power. In this way the court was in fact arbitrarily protected from any constitutional decisions that it could deem unfavorable to its interests.[11]

The second regulation that the Vesnić cabinet arrived at—which was not

10. Ibid., Aug. 20, 1920, p. 1.
11. "Zakon o izboru narodnih poslanika za Ustavotvornu Skupštinu Kraljevine Srba, Hrvata i Slovenaca," ibid., Sept. 6, 1920, pp. 1–6.

even passed by the PNP—amounted to a government edict establishing the Constitutional Assembly's standing orders. This edict was promulgated on December 8, 1920, ten days after the elections for the Constituent Assembly and the termination of the PNP's legislative mandate. It specified that the elected deputies could not serve before they had taken an oath of allegiance to the court, thus in effect precluding the deputies from exercising their option to arrive at a republican form of government. The edict further limited parliamentary initiative by providing that the government was principally responsible for proposing constitutional drafts. Countermotions and amendments could be considered only if they were backed by at least twenty deputies. The prerogatives of the elected deputies were also abridged by a rule limiting speeches to one hour. More significantly, the edict circumvented the National Council's 1918 demand that the constitution be reached only by a two-thirds majority. Instead, it designated a simple plurality as sufficient for this purpose.[12]

The regulations promulgated by the Vesnić cabinet were decidedly political; their aim was to assure the advantage for the centralist constitutional proposals. Such manipulations signaled a momentary halt in the NRS-DS collision. In the fierce electoral campaign for the Constituent Assembly, raging throughout October and November 1920, political divisions were principally crystallized along the lines of support or opposition to centralism, demonstrating afresh the continuing salience of Yugoslavia's national question.

The 1920 Elections

Both the centralists and their opponents pinned their hopes on the elections of November 28, 1920, confident that the voters would bolster their respective positions. When the results of the elections were tabulated (see tables 5-1 and 5-2), it became clear that the two main centralist parties (the DS and the NRS) gained only a relative majority, and this in spite of numerous electoral irregularities perpetrated by these government parties.[1] One of these irreg-

12. "Privremeni poslovnik za Ustavotvornu Skupštinu," ibid., Dec. 10, 1920, pp. 1–4.

1. Statistical tabulations for the tables were performed by the author on the basis of statistical tables in *Statistički pregled izbora narodnih poslanika Kraljevine Srba, Hrvata i Slovenaca* (Belgrade, 1921). Electoral irregularities were described by the minority groups of the Constituent Assembly's Verification Committee. See *Stenografske beleške Ustavotvorne skupštine Kraljevine Srba, Hrvata i Slovenaca* (Belgrade, 1921), pp. 14–16. For an analysis of the elections see Vasilij Melik, "Izidi volitev v Konstituanto leta 1920," *Prispevki za zgodovino delavskega gibanja*, vol. 2 (1962), no. 1, pp. 3–61.

Table 5-1. Regional contributions by political party, November 28, 1920, elections for Yugoslavia's Constituent Assembly

Region	DS		NRS		HPSS		KPJ	
	Number	Percent	Number	Percent	Number	Percent	Number	Percent
Serbia	103,465	32.39	111,597	39.21	0	0.00	50,385	25.40
Macedonia, Metohia, Kosovo, and the Sandžak	75,512	23.64	20,790	7.31	0	0.00	49,449	24.93
Bosnia-Hercegovina	18,500	5.79	59,443	20.89	0	0.00	18,074	9.11
Croatia-Slavonia	78,406	24.54	39,050	13.72	230,590	100.00	31,281	15.77
Dalmatia	5,189	1.62	6,008	2.11	0	0.00	8,074	4.07
Montenegro	7,955	2.49	3,837	1.35	0	0.00	10,869	5.48
Slovenia	12,288	3.85	0	0.00	0	0.00	16,289	8.21
Banat, Bačka, and Baranja	18,133	5.68	43,850	15.41	0	0.00	13,955	7.03
Total	319,448	100.00	284,575	100.00	230,590	100.00	198,376	100.00

Region	National Club		SLS & HPS		JMO		Cemiyet	
	Number	Percent	Number	Percent	Number	Percent	Number	Percent
Serbia	0	0.00	0	0.00	0	0.00	0	0.00
Macedonia, Metohia, Kosovo, and the Sandžak	0	0.00	0	0.00	0	0.00	30,029	100.00
Bosnia-Hercegovina	38,380	59.74	20,774	18.67	110,895	100.00	0	0.00
Croatia-Slavonia	22,950	35.72	11,871	10.67	0	0.00	0	0.00
Dalmatia	2,917	4.54	13,947	12.53	0	0.00	0	0.00
Montenegro	0	0.00	0	0.00	0	0.00	0	0.00
Slovenia	0	0.00	58,971	53.00	0	0.00	0	0.00
Banat, Bačka, and Baranja	0	0.00	5,711	5.13	0	0.00	0	0.00
Total	64,247	100.00	111,274	100.00	110,895	100.00	30,029	100.00

Region	Social Democrats		Agrarians		Others	
	Number	Percent	Number	Percent	Number	Percent
Serbia	0	0.00	45,121	29.76	14,782	24.88
Macedonia, Metohia, Kosovo, and the Sandžak	0	0.00	0	0.00	6,296	10.60
Bosnia-Hercegovina	2,784	5.95	55,108	36.35	7,000	11.78
Croatia-Slavonia	7,611	16.27	4,055	2.68	12,985	21.85
Dalmatia	0	0.00	10,636	7.02	3,198	5.38
Montenegro	0	0.00	0	0.00	5,951	10.01
Slovenia	29,541	63.13	33,010	21.77	8,166	13.74
Banat, Bačka, and Baranja	6,856	14.65	3,673	2.42	1,048	1.76
Total	46,792	100.00	151,603	100.00	59,426	100.00

Table 5-2. Regional votes and percentage cast for each political party, November 28, 1920, elections for Yugoslavia's Constituent Assembly

Region	Total vote	Parties					
		DS	NRS	HPSS	KPJ	National Club	SLS & HPS
Serbia	325,350	31.80	34.30	0.00	15.49	0.00	0.00
Macedonia, Metohia, Kosovo, and the Sandžak	182,076	41.47	11.42	0.00	27.16	0.00	0.00
Bosnia-Hercegovina	330,958	5.59	17.96	0.00	5.46	11.60	6.28
Croatia-Slavonia	438,799	17.87	8.90	52.55	7.13	5.23	2.71
Dalmatia	49,969	10.38	12.02	0.00	16.16	5.84	27.91
Montenegro	28,612	27.80	13.41	0.00	37.99	0.00	0.00
Slovenia	158,265	7.76	0.00	0.00	10.29	0.00	37.26
Banat, Bačka, and Baranja	93,226	19.45	47.04	0.00	14.97	0.00	6.13
Total and averages	1,607,255	19.88	17.71	14.35	12.34	4.00	6.92

Region	Total vote	JMO	Cemiyet	Social Democrats	Agrarians	Others
Serbia	325,250	0.00	0.00	0.00	13.87	4.54
Macedonia, Metohia, Kosovo, and the Sandžak	182,076	0.00	16.49	0.00	0.00	3.46
Bosnia-Hercegovina	330,958	33.50	0.00	0.84	16.65	2.12
Croatia-Slavonia	438,799	0.00	0.00	1.73	0.92	2.96
Dalmatia	49,969	0.00	0.00	0.00	21.29	6.40
Montenegro	28,612	0.00	0.00	0.00	0.00	20.80
Slovenia	158,265	0.00	0.00	18.67	20.86	5.16
Banat, Bačka, and Baranja	93,226	0.00	0.00	7.35	3.94	1.12
Total and averages	1,607,255	6.90	1.87	2.91	9.43	3.69

ularities, though contrary to the Treaty on the Defense of National Minorities that was signed between the Allied powers and Yugoslavia at Saint-Germain (1919), was in fact a part of electoral legislature: that is, the denial of the vote to those citizens who by virtue of their nationality had a right to opt for foreign citizenship. This provision was used to exclude most Germans, Hungarians, and Jews from the electoral process. According to *Židov* (Jew), the Zagreb organ of the Zionist movement, the county authorities in Srijem (Slavonia) sent oral and later written instructions to their subordinates informing them that "Germans, Hungarians, and Jews, though citizens, had no right to vote.''[2] As a result of such practices, the Radicals gained an edge in the Banat, Bačka, Baranja, and parts of Slavonia. Most distressing, the ratio between the number of registered voters and the number of deputies allotted to each province was quite inequitable. Whereas 3,301 registered voters elected a deputy from the Banat, Bačka, and Baranja, many more than twice that number (8,092) were needed to elect a deputy from Dalmatia.[3] The following tabulation lists the number of registered voters per elected deputy:

> Banat, Bačka, and Baranja—3,301
> Montenegro—4,337
> Slovenia—5,381
> Metohia, Kosovo, and the Sandžak—5,600
> Serbia—5,662
> Macedonia—5,990
> Croatia-Slavonia—6,849
> Bosnia-Hercegovina—7,495
> Dalmatia—8,092

The tabulation obscures additional inequities. For example, the three principal cities of Belgrade, Zagreb, and Ljubljana, each a separate electoral district, were highly favored in electoral power over the rest of the country. But again, whereas 2,737 registered voters elected a deputy in Belgrade, 4,954 did so in Zagreb. In some parts of Yugoslavia, where unequal distribution was even below the regional average, the Radicals stood to gain (in Subotica, 2,312; in Srijem, 5,791). Elsewhere, as in the Serb enclaves of Croatia, where the number of registered voters per deputy was above the already discriminatory regional average, the Democrats stood to lose (in Modruš-Rijeka, 7,682; in Lika-Krbava, 8,467). Both tendencies betrayed the hand of the NRS in shaping a system that fitted the party's electoral strategy. Nevertheless, in parts of western Serbia, western Macedonia, and in Kosovo, the Democrats profited from the system. Last, when the actual number of votes cast in the elections of November 1920 is divided by the number of elected deputies, an additional bias in favor of centralist parties and their allies evidently holds in most cases. The following tabulation shows the number of all votes cast for the cited parties per every elected deputy:

> NRS—3,127
> KPJ—3,420
> Cemiyet—3,753
> DS—3,472
> Agrarians—3,887
> SLS-HPS—4,121

2. ''Izbori za ustavotvornu skupštinu,'' *Židov*, Oct. 11, 1920, p. 3.

3. I am grateful to Prof. Jozo Tomasevich for his information on this question. His calculations, part of an ongoing study of war and revolution in Yugoslavia, were extremely suggestive for my inquiry on the worth of the ballots cast in 1920 per region and party.

HPSS—4,611
JMO—4,620
Social Democrats—4,679
National Club—5,840

The electoral results showed that out of 2,480,623 eligible voters, only 1,607,255 (or 64.79 percent of eligible voters) actually exercised their right to vote. In fact, balloting was somewhat above the statewide average only in Slovenia (73.52 percent), Bosnia-Hercegovina (70.08), and Croatia-Slavonia (68.88). The following tabulation shows voter abstention by region:

Dalmatia—43.87
Serbia—43.67
Macedonia,
    Metohia, Kosovo, and
    the Sandžak—42.54
Banat, Bačka, and Baranja—35.83
Montenegro—34.03
Croatia-Slavonia—31.12
Bosnia-Hercegovina—29.92
Slovenia—26.48

Though the two main centralist parties made substantial gains in Serbia, jointly polling 66.10 percent of all Serbian votes, the Radical showing was less impressive than in 1912 and the Democratic vote was below the amount won in 1912 by those Serbian parties that merged into the DS. The centralists also did very well in the Banat, Bačka, and Baranja. There the Radicals were leading the Democrats by 47.04 as opposed to 19.45 percent of the total vote.

The ratio between the DS and the NRS was reversed in Macedonia, Metohia, Kosovo, the Sandžak, and Montenegro. In these southern borderlands the Democrats were leading the Radicals by 41.47 and 27.80, as opposed to 11.42 and 13.41 percent of all votes, respectively. The local population in the "southern regions" was evidently wary of the Radicals' Great Serbianism, a situation from which the liberal-unitarist DS could only gain. The Radical standing was, however, augmented by the Cemiyet's gains. In the final analysis, despite considerable electoral abstentionism in these nationally disaffected areas (with a record high of 44.62 in Macedonia), the centralists won the majority in Metohia, Kosovo, and the Sandžak, two-fifths of all votes in Montenegro, and only slightly more than a third in Macedonia, and then mainly in western Macedonia. Moreover, in Bosnia-Hercegovina, the two ruling centralist parties managed to gain only 23.55 percent of all votes and were seriously outflanked by the autonomists of the JMO. Centralist showing was even lower elsewhere in Yugoslavia. In Croatia-Slavonia, the Democrats won 17.87 percent of all votes, mainly among the Serb population of Lika, Kordun, and Banija, and the Radicals trailed far behind with 8.90 percent of all ballots cast, with their best showing among the Serbs of Srijem. The two leading centralist parties attracted 22.40 percent of voters in Dalmatia, with slightly more than a half that figure for the NRS ticket. In Slovenia, where the Radicals did not even run, the DS scored a paltry 7.76 percent of all votes cast.

The showing of anticentralist and autonomist parties was impressive. The HPSS in particular demonstrated its remarkable strength in Croatia-Slavonia, the only area where the party ran a ticket. Before the elections, the government revoked all previous prohibitions against public meetings in Slovenia and Croatia-Slavonia, and in the same vein, Radić was released from prison on November 28, 1920, the day of the elections. It is not likely that this latter action had any significant impact on the electoral results, however, since the Croat countryside, particularly in northwestern Croatia, was already irrevocably committed to the HPSS; Radić's party attracted 230,590 votes—that is, over half the votes cast in Croatia-Slavonia—winning a clear majority. This accomplishment gains in weight when it is noted that no other party in any other region succeeded in becoming majoritarian. The elections thus confirmed the HPSS's claims to leadership of the Croat opposition. This coveted status was all the more legitimate in light of the poor performance of the other Croat parties. For example, the autonomists of the HZ won only 5.23 percent of all votes in Croatia-Slavonia and the Frankists a mere 2.48 percent. In Bosnia-Hercegovina, the JMO won 33.50 percent of all votes. The electoral results of the autonomist parties were even better in Slovenia, where the SLS attracted 37.26 of the Slovene vote. This showing, nevertheless, disappointed the clericalist leaders, who had legitimate grievances against the inequalities of the electoral system. Last, in Macedonia, Metohia, Kosovo, and the Sandžak, the Cemiyet won 16.49 percent of all votes, which was, however, much below the overall strength of Muslim nationalities in these areas.

Elections for the Constituent Assembly undermined the standing of the two principal centralist parties. Jointly, the DS and the NRS polled 604,023 votes, while those parties that were opposed to centralism in one way or another (such as the HPSS, the SLS and its allies, the JMO, the HZ and its Bosnian appendage, the HSP and Trumbić), gained 534,467 votes. If one excludes the Cemiyet, which despite its anticentralist proclivities was in alliance with the NRS as well as the Agrarians and the Marxist parties (which generally disparaged the importance of the national question despite their commitment to varying shades of centralism), it would seem that Yugoslavia's electorate was divided fairly evenly on the question of state organization. But instead of mitigating the government's haste for a firm centralist constitution, the elections contributed to the growing reconciliation between the Radicals and Democrats, who became all the more determined to beat back the anticentralist forces.

The Centralist Bloc Masters the Constituent Assembly

Even before the elections, both the DS and the NRS were greatly dissatisfied with the attitude of the HZ-dominated local administration in Croatia-Slavonia in regard to the September 1920 peasant revolt against draft-animal registration. In the opinion of the centralist majority in Vesnić's cabinet, the HZ, despite its participation in the government, behaved disloyally during this crisis. Laginja's reluctance to suppress the revolt with all the means at his disposal was viewed as a serious omission. Unanimity of the DS and the NRS on the need to utilize stern measures against the HPSS was strengthened after Radić's electoral victory and the subsequent actions initiated by the HPSS leadership.

Despite the unmistakably conciliatory tone of Radić's behavior in the aftermath of the November 28 elections, made possible by the confidence engendered by his party's electoral showing in Croatia-Slavonia (or, perhaps, precisely because of the HPSS's newly acquired political legitimacy) Radić's actions remained an open challenge to the centralist parties. On December 7, 1920, Radić presided over a massive open-air rally at the Zagreb fairgrounds (Sajmište). In an assertive speech to some 100,000 assembled supporters, he made it plain that he spoke as the leader of a triumphant movement, but he also stressed that impulsive rejection of union with Serbia must give way to a more thoughtful stand: "When we recall the terrible violence, tortures, beatings, jails, etc., especially during Pribićević's rule ([Shouts:] Down with him!; Radić: He is already down!), each one of us says with feeling: I shall traffic neither with Serbia nor with the Serbs, but when we deliberate [on this], we see that it is best that we be our own masters among ourselves, and they their own, but that, despite everything, we [both] remain brothers."[1]

Unwilling to yield on the point of a thoroughly self-governed Croatia, although "within the international borders of the South Slavs," nor on the question on a republican polity, Radić promulgated a change in his party's name during the December 8 rally. Henceforth, the HPSS would be called Hrvatska republikanska seljačka stranka (HRSS, Croat Republican Peasant Party).[2] He also stressed that the HRSS would not participate in the Constitu-

1. "Izvanredna glavna skupština Hrvatske Republikanske Seljačke Stranke dne 8. prosinca u Zagrebu," *Slobodni dom*, Dec. 10, 1920, pp. 1–2.
2. Radić and his followers continued to refuse any oaths of loyalty to the king. Had they gone to the Constituent Assembly, the HRSS deputies probably would not have submitted to the required oath of allegiance to the monarchy, the stance that they maintained in similar situations. For example, as an elected member of Zagreb's city council, Radić refused to swear his allegiance to the king on December 29, 1920, and again on May 6, 1921. In both cases Radić invoked the results of the elections for the Constituent Assembly and claimed that as a sovereign institution, the assembly alone had the right to determine what state form the country should adopt. Arhiv Instituta za historiju radničkog pokreta Hrvatske (AIHRPH), 1921, Sig. VI C, Box 1: Iz predsjedničkog spisa broj 6951/Pr. Kr. Hrv.-slav. zemaljske vlade.

ent Assembly, although he announced that his party would prefer "to achieve [its program] in *agreement* [my emphasis] with the neighboring national brothers . . . without any outside interference." In other words, Radić served notice that although he was not necessarily hostile to compromises with Serbia (provided the Croat aspirations to self-rule were respected), he would not allow his party to participate in a parliament where decisions would be reached by majority vote rather than by mutual agreement. In rejecting majoritarianism, Radić, in fact, rejected the centralists' method and their raison d'être for the forthcoming Constituent Assembly and put the DS and the NRS on the defensive, a position not necessarily mitigated by his simultaneous exclusion of any forcible means of effecting his and his party's policies.

The centralists had correctly foreseen that Radić's announced December 8 rally would add to their political difficulties, and they had sought to prevent it. Mate Drinković, an HZ member of Vesnić's cabinet, recalled that the issue was considered at a cabinet meeting. During the deliberations, Pavle Marinković of the DS "turned toward me [Drinković] and threateningly exclaimed that they would strangle and shoot us (Croats) on the streets."[3] Permission was granted only after contingency plans were laid that would have allowed Ban Laginja to disperse the rally in case Radić took a sharply radical stand. The centralists thought Radić's deportment at the rally had warranted the implementation of the cabinet's contingency plan, and they vented their indignation at Radić on Laginja, who allowed Radić to go on with his speech. On December 11, Vesnić's cabinet dismissed Laginja, and shortly afterward (December 23) two HZ cabinet ministers were dismissed.[4] This change abruptly concluded the NRS-HZ alliance. But the immediate cause of the break—the disagreement on policy toward the HRSS—was only symptomatic of the larger drawing apart. More than anything, the alliance was a natural victim of the emerging DS-NRS partnership, forged in the common struggle against the opposition in the Constituent Assembly.

The Constituent Assembly was convened on December 12, 1920, without the participation of the HRSS and the HSP. The following tabulation shows the deputies that had been elected from each party:

> DS—92
> NRS—91
> KPJ—58
> HRSS—50
> Agrarians—39
> SLS & HPS—27
> JMO—24
> Social Democrats—10

3. Mate Drinković, *Hrvatska i državna politika* (Zagreb, 1928), p. 18.
4. Hrvoje Matković, "Pad bana Matka Laginje," *Historijski pregled*, vol. 8 (1962), no. 1, pp. 39–50.

Cemiyet—8

National Club   Croat Husbandmen's Party—7
                 HZ—4
Republican Party—3
HSP—2
National Socialist Party (Slovenia)—2
Nonparty lists (Trumbić)—1
Liberal Party (Serbia)—1
           Total   419

From the beginning, preliminary sessions of the Constituent Assembly were marked by intense clashes between the two centralist parties on the one hand and the various oppositionists on the other. Initially, the issue of the government instituting temporary, standing orders (*Privremeni poslovnik*), which included a provision on the required oath to the king, dominated the procedures. At the center of the debate was the question of the Constituent Assembly's sovereignty. Speaking in the name of the Communist Club, Sima Marković was the first to demand that the government's standing orders be suspended and new ones, more in keeping with the spirit of parliamentary sovereignty, instituted.[5] Marković's demand was echoed by the representatives of the Yugoslav Club (the SLS and HPS), the National Club, the Republican party, the JMO, and the Social Democrats, all of whom denounced the standing orders as illegal (pp. 4–7). A representative of the Agrarians stated that his group would prefer a revision of the standing orders, although it accepted them for a fortnight for the sake of facilitating the assembly's work (p. 5). Despite these protests, the centralists succeeded in exacting the oath of allegiance to the king from all the assembled parties, and then proceeded to elect Ivan Ribar, a noted DS member, as president of the Constituent Assembly, by applying the procedure established in the temporary standing orders.[6]

The debate on the standing orders, which commenced on December 22, was resumed on January 12, 1921, but under rather different circumstances. Vesnić's cabinet resigned on December 23, 1920, leaving the DS and the NRS free to reconstruct a cabinet that would meet their specifications. Both sides were conscious that a centralist constitution was possible only if their mutual rivalries were temporarily relinquished. As the principal leader of the NRS, Pašić was well aware that under existing conditions the Radicals could cooperate only with the DS. Accordingly, he urged the Protić-led minority of his party to subordinate its differences with the leadership "to the common goal, a creation of one joint constitution."[7] While the negotiations between

5. *Stenografske beleške Ustavotvorne skupštine*, Dec. 13, 1920, p. 4. (Page numbers that follow refer to this source.)

6. Ibid., Dec. 22, 1920, p. 20. Ribar won 192 votes out of 243 cast.

7. Quoted in Branislav Gligorijević, *Demokratska stranka i politički odnosi u Kraljevini Srba, Hrvata i Slovenaca* (Belgrade, 1970), p. 202.

the two parties were still going on, Vesnić's caretaker government promulgated a series of anti-Communist measures, banning Communist agitation and public activities, thereby dealing a determined blow to the KPJ, a demonstrably troublesome oppositional party, as evidenced by its behavior in the Constituent Assembly.[8] Then on January 1, 1921, the new DS-NRS cabinet, headed by Nikola Pašić, was confirmed by the regent.

Homogenous in its support of centralism, Pašić's cabinet was free of all the encumbering debts that the NRS had owed its autonomist partners under Protić and—to some extent—Vesnić. Stern measures against the KPJ, which provoked hardly any opposition outside the Communist ranks, encouraged the new centralist cabinet in its peremptory treatment of other oppositional parties. Nevertheless, though the NRS-DS coalition in Pašić's cabinet divided the twelve major *ressorts* evenly between themselves, they chose to keep the other four cabinet posts vacant, holding them in reserve as a lure to the other parties, particularly the JMO and the Agrarians. This tactic, coupled with persistent negotiations with the SLS and the HZ, undertaken with the aim of drawing off their anticentralist fire, seriously damaged the oppositional ranks, already debilitated by Radić's boycott of the Constituent Assembly. But although the government's handling of the opposition was marked by some resourceful maneuvering, the attitude of the cabinet as a whole remained unyielding. The centralists' failure to accommodate increasingly vociferous demands for a revision of the standing orders bears out this contention. Eschewing compromises, a committee dominated by the centralists went through the motions of drafting a new version of parliamentary procedure but in the end only produced several alterations that, in the opinion of some, "were not changes of essential provisions . . . but only modifications of secondary provisions."[9]

During the debate on the slightly altered standing orders, deputies from the government coalition made no secret of their views on the limited prerogatives of the Constituent Assembly. Ljuba Jovanović, an old guard Radical, who was extremely close to the court, invoked a principle of Roman law (*Nemo plus juris ad alium transfere potest quam ipso habet*) to claim that the people itself had no right to topple the monarch, to choose a new one, or to abolish the monarchy. Therefore, according to Jovanović, "the question of an eventual change of [monarchical] rule cannot be within the competence of

8. On the attitudes and initiatives of the KPJ deputies in the Constituent Assembly see Neda Engelsfeld, "Rad Kluba komunističkih poslanika u plenumu Ustavotvorne skupštine (u prosincu 1920. i u siječnju 1921.)," *Radovi Instituta za hrvatsku povijest,* 1972, no. 2, pp. 181–262.

9. *Stenografske beleške Ustavotvorne skupštine,* Jan. 28, 1921, pp. 18–19. The speaker, Mehmed Spaho, was also quite right in adding that "except for questions of interpellations, which are extremely limited, all the provisions, against which voices were heard here at the beginning, have remained almost completely unchanged." For the committee's report see ibid., Jan. 25, 1921, pp. 13–15.

this house.''[10] An NRS minister, Momčilo Ninčić, was even more explicit. After denouncing any liberalization of the standing orders, he concluded with a ringing denunciation of those deputies who demanded the abolition of the oath to the king: ''[The oath] is an expression of a special understanding, an understanding adopted by the PNP and held by the majority of the present Constituent Assembly. It is an expression of an understanding that the Constituent Assembly is *not sovereign* [my emphasis].''[11]

An ultimately more important matter than the issue of the oath to the monarch—though that dominated the debate on the standing orders—was the question of what constituted a ''qualified majority'' necessary for the passage of the constitution. The Corfu Declaration, Pribićević's urgent proposal to the Croatian Sabor of October 29, 1918, which became the basis for Croatia's separation from Austria-Hungary, and the National Council's directives of November 24, 1918, to its Belgrade-bound delegation were all examples of solemn declarations that envisaged a constitution based on the vote of a ''numerically qualified majority,'' that is, of more than a simple majority of 50 percent plus one. The Croat autonomists considered these declarations as binding agreements; their Serbian counterparts seemed less interested in arriving at a mutually agreed consociational democracy than in obtaining a constitution, however unsatisfactory, dictated by the ability of the largest group to impose its will on the others. Ninčić reflected the centralists' stand when he declared that no existing law defined the nature of a qualified majority; that definition had to depend on political expediency. Therefore it was better to opt for the lowest possible numerical definition and gain a constitution that was less than perfect than to search for a possibly unworkable agreement.[12] The autonomists were unable to reverse this strategy of the centralist bloc. The insignificantly revised version of the old standing orders was adopted by the Constituent Assembly on January 28.

After the termination of the debate on the standing orders, the Constituent Assembly turned its attention to its principal task, the drafting of a constitutional document. On January 31 the assembled deputies elected a Constitutional Committee in which the majority (52.38 percent) belonged to the NRS-DS coalition. The committee was charged with entertaining and canvassing various constitutional proposals, but, from the beginning, only one proposal, that of the Pašić government, was taken as the point of departure and the standard by which the other proposals were judged. Pašić's constitutional draft was relatively brief (eleven parts with a total of eighty-six paragraphs), and it was in many ways inspired by Serbia's 1903 Constitution. Without entering into a detailed analysis of all its provisions, some of its more important aspects should be noted.

10. Ibid., Jan. 28, 1921, pp. 20–22.
11. Ibid., pp. 23–24.
12. Ibid., p. 24.

In line with the government's centralist conceptions, decision-making in all state affairs was entirely relegated to the three central powers: the king, the parliament, and the government. Of the three, the king was decidedly the beneficiary of most prerogatives. There were numerous provisions limiting his initiatives; nonetheless, it was specified that the legislative and the executive powers were vested in the royal personage, in the first case, in conjunction with the parliament, and in the second, through his ministers. Judicial powers were left to the nominally independent courts, though all verdicts were to be announced and executed in the name of the king. The king's authority was particularly accented in regard to the parliament. Though no royal act was valid without the signature of the responsible minister, the laws passed by the legislature were equally invalid without the king's sanction. In fact, the king's law-making responsibilities were clearly defined: "The king confirms and promulgates all laws, appoints all state officials, and establishes military ranks in accordance with the law. The king is the supreme commander of all continental and naval military forces."[13] Moreover, the cabinet was not only responsible to the parliament, it was also responsible to the king. It is therefore valid to claim that Pašić proposed a "centralistically ordered monarchy with limited parliamentarianism."[14] Indeed it was a purposed indignity directed against the sensibilities of the republican and decentralist opposition.

The administrative provisions of the proposal could only increase decentralist fears. There was to be no national or regional autonomy: the only administrative units sanctioned in the proposal were districts (*oblasti*), counties (*srezovi*), and communes (*opštine*). The number of districts was not to exceed thirty-five, with between 200,000 and 600,000 inhabitants in each. The negative phrasing of this provision could not conceal the centralists' aim, that is, the parceling of local administrative units so as to destroy their prestige and political initiative and prevent the buildup of regional opposition. Nor were local administrative initiatives limited only in regard to their territorial competence: Pašić's proposal further specified that the head of each district (*načelnik*) would be appointed by the king. The draft contained a detailed list of subjects that were "confided" to the local administrative organs (by implication, other matters were not within their competence); in case these limitations were not heeded, it was noted that centrally appointed district prefects could invalidate the decisions of local legislative agencies (*oblasne skupštine*) and prevent the application of other local decisions. Appeals could be lodged with the State Council or contested in special administrative courts. No protection was provided against the inevitable

13. "Nacrt Ustava," ibid., Jan. 25, 1921, p. 3.
14. Ferdo Čulinović, *Jugoslavija izmedju dva rata*, vol. I (Zagreb, 1961), p. 322.

violations of the conflict of interest that were bound to arise in the final decisions of these central instances.[15]

The constitutional project of the Pašić government did not undergo any major changes on its path to full codification as Yugoslavia's constitution. Its slightly revised version—different from the original draft inasmuch as bicameralism was abandoned, numerous sections (especially those dealing with social programs) expanded, and the projected *oblasti* defined in terms of a somewhat larger population (800,000)—was adopted by the centralist-dominated Constitutional Committee as the Constituent Assembly's constitutional project. Though the centralist coalition did make some minor concessions (mainly in social and religious matters) in order to attract the Agrarians, Social Democrats, and the JMO, its stand on the key questions of state organization was not significantly altered despite the vociferous opposition of the decentralists and the development of a dissident faction, headed by Stojan Protić and Momčilo Ivanić, within the NRS itself. Protić was increasingly vocal in his opposition to the government's uncompromising tactics and resigned from the NRS's parliamentary club on April 8, 1921. Ivanić voted against the final version of the constitution.[16]

Frustrated by the government's unwillingness to accommodate their demands, the various decentralist parties had to decide whether to remain in the Constituent Assembly, knowing they would repeatedly be outvoted, or to deny the legitimacy of the proceedings and boycott any further sessions. The HZ was the first party to opt for a walkout. On May 12, before the crucial vote on the acceptance of the government's constitutional proposal in general, the HZ's spokesman, Drinković, read a statement of his club, which said in part:

> Until the [Constituent] Assembly arrives at the established standpoint of an agreement [with the representatives of the peoples formerly within Austria-Hungary], which excludes the majorization of the Croats, the National Club is forced to negate, as it expressly does, the legality of this Assembly (Clamor) and its right to reach a Constitution valid for Croatia and the Croat people (Shouts, voices: You have no right to say that, there are only three of you). In the case that such a Constitution would be, nevertheless, adopted, it would be null and void, as if it did not exist and without any legal importance (Clamor).[17]

Drinković's protest and the HZ's abrupt departure made no difference: the Constituent Assembly (minus the ninety-nine who had walked out or did not

---

15. "Nacrt Ustava," *Stenografske beleške Ustavotvorne skupštine*, p. 7.
16. Djordje D. Stanković, "Kriza radikalsko-demokratske koalicije 1921. i hrvatsko pitanje," *Jugoslovenski istorijski časopis*, 1972, nos. 1–2, pp. 79–91.
17. *Stenografske beleške Ustavotvorne skupštine*, May 12, pp. 14–15.

participate) adopted the government's constitutional proposal in principle with a vote of 227–93.[18] Subsequently, when the centralists proceeded to submit individual sections of the constitutional project for final votes, the remaining oppositionists were confronted with the choice already made by the HZ. On June 11, after six sections of the constitution had been adopted, the Communists announced that they were leaving the Assembly. Speaking on behalf of the Communist Club, Filip Filipović declared their intentions:

> The ruling bourgeoisie wants to reach a Constitution after rendering impossible every criticism, not only on our part [that of the KPJ] but on the part of the entire opposition. . . . Departing from the Constituent Assembly, after all activities of the KPJ were thwarted in [our] country, *we are going to the masses of the working people, to inform them about the misdeeds of the government and its so-called majority* (V[alerijan]. Pribićević: and on whose expense?!) *and to prepare them for the moment, which is not distant, when led by the Communist party and relying on its own forces,* [the masses] *will succeed in overthrowing the present brutal, violent, and bloody regime.*[19]

Two days later, representatives of the SLS's Yugoslav Club rose to protest against the government's decision (allowed by the Assembly's President Ribar) to postpone the discussion of Section VIII of the Constitution—the key section dealing with the prerogatives of central and local administration—and instead to proceed to the subsequent sections of the majority's proposal. When Ribar dismissed the protests of the Yugoslav Club, the SLS and its allies finally walked out of the Constituent Assembly.

Radić was the undisputed leader of most sections of the decentralist opposition that left the Assembly. On May 21 the elected deputies of the HRSS, HSP, and HZ drew up a message to the Croat people. This message was largely based on the HZ's statement read by Drinković on May 12, which called for an agreement with Serbia based on the decisions of the Croatian Sabor of October 29, 1918, but it went beyond that to deny that the rump Constituent Assembly had any right at all to reach a constitution valid for Croatia and the Croats.[20] Though publication was blocked by the censors, the drawing up of the message was important in that it prepared ground for the long-awaited coalition of the Croat oppositional parties in the struggle against centralism. Immediately after the adoption of the centralist constitution, Hrvatski blok (Croat Bloc), composed of the three parties, succeeded in emerging as the product of the search for unity.

In a sense, the coalition of Croat parties was built on the groundwork

18. Ibid., May 12, 1921, p. 18.

19. Ibid., June 11, 1921, pp. 3–5.

20. For a description of this document, which exists only in manuscript, see Hrvoje Matković, "Hrvatska zajednica: Prilog proučavanju političkih stranaka u staroj Jugoslaviji," *Istorija XX veka: zbornik radova,* vol. 5, pp. 78–80.

prepared in Radić's criticisms of the centralists' constitutional proposal. As early as February 11, 1921, elected deputies of Radić's HRSS sent a message to Regent Aleksandar demanding that the HRSS be allowed to exercise administrative authority in Croatia-Slavonia and that all attempts to reach a centralist constitution be halted.[21] When these demands failed to elicit any response (and certainly no concessions), Radić proceeded to draft his own Constitution of the Neutral Peasant Republic of Croatia. This draft constitution, which was discussed among the HRSS leaders in March and April and finally adopted on May 14, 1921, restricted the territory of the Croat republic to the eight counties of Croatia-Slavonia (with Medjimurje), although it detailed a procedure for an extension of state territory to the adjoining lands (especially those inhabited by the Croats). It also made specific mention of Croatia's desire to join a confederated Yugoslavia. The exact nature of this confederation was left within the competency of the Constituent Assembly, elected on November 28, 1920, provided the deputies from the other parts of Yugoslavia declared themselves in favor of an agreement and in opposition to any majorization. The prerogatives reserved for the joint organs of the confederation were, however, extremely attenuated and included only common external representation, while all other functions (finances, home guard, taxation, and so on) were reserved for the agencies of the Croat republic and, by implication, the corresponding agencies in the other confederated lands. The proposal's other sections reflected Radić's social philosophy and repeatedly stressed Croatia's desire to remain free of monarchism, militarism, and the other institutions that Radić associated with arbitrary rule.[22]

As a result of the HRSS's dissemination of its draft constitution, a new wave of peasant unrest rippled over the Croatian countryside in the spring of 1921. The party's constitutional proposal, which was discussed at village gatherings, aroused so many hopes that the authorities found it difficult to cope with the peasantry's revitalized confidence. In a report to the district prefect in Bjelovar it was noted that "during the last several days reports are coming from some of the communes in the district that the HRSS's adherents are holding secret nocturnal meetings, and, in connection with this, rumors are circulating that an uprising will take place."[23] Though the HRSS's representatives almost certainly did not incite rebellion (their stance was instead rather self-assured and mildly contemptuous of the troubled central authorities), the party's activities seemed threatening enough to the insecure

21. Stjepan Radić, *Politički spisi*, comp. Zvonimir Kulundžić (Zagreb, 1971), pp. 357–358.

22. Ibid., pp. 366–398. There is some question whether the text of this draft constitution as cited by the editor of Radić's political writings is the last version of the document. For a discussion of this possibility see Tomislav Išek, "Stjepan Radić kao politički mislilac," *Časopis za suvremenu povijest*, vol. 4 (1972), no. 1, pp. 187–199.

23. AIHRPH, 1921, Sig. VI C, Box 1: Predsjedništvo kr. hrv. slav. zemaljske vlade (Broj 3319 Pr. 1921), March 4, 1921.

Pašić government, prompting a temporary ban on HRSS's public meetings.[24]

Within the Constituent Assembly, even though the atmosphere was hostile and the opposition was concentrated outside the parliament, isolated voices continued to speak out against the majority's constitutional proposal. Momčilo Ivanić excoriated the government's failure to adopt even one of the opposition's forty-four proposals on the question of administrative authority: "Because Stjepan Radić, perhaps, wants a separation of Croatia and independence, you [the centralist majority] want to trample down [Serbia's] whole previous life, you want to perform a vivisection on our people. I can tell you this: what Stjepan Radić wants is not good, but what you want cannot be good either. May we all live long to see the effects."[25]

One of the strongest condemnations of the draft constitution was uttered by Ante Trumbić on the eve of the final vote. Speaking as the last notable Croat autonomist politician who still remained in the Constituent Assembly, Trumbić denounced the government's proposal as a "diktat of several club notables and often a product of negative compromises between them." Trumbić was particularly vocal in his remarks on the likely effects of the constitution on Yugoslavia's national question: "A centralist system is pushed through under the guise of unity. . . . This system represents a danger to peace and harmony among the people and to the pacification of conditions in the state. . . . This constitution will sharpen the tribal conflicts all the more, even though they are today exacerbated more than under Austria-Hungary."[26]

The Pašić government was still confident of obtaining the majority in the final vote, but this confidence was seriously shaken by the centralist Agrarians' announcement that they would vote for the centralist proposal only if certain preconditions were met. These included consistent and immediate implementation of agrarian reform, the cabinet's responsibility to the parliament, and the division of the state into districts that were to be determined "exclusively on the basis of a healthy economic-geographic principle without regard for numerical standing of the population."[27] The Agrarians evidently resented the NRS's horsetrading with the JMO, a party opposed to the agrarian reform and the dismantling of Bosnia's territorial unity, whose leaders were persuaded to join the centralist bloc in exchange for a lenient application of agrarian reform in their home province and for the maintenance of what amounted to historical Bosnia. Faced with Agrarian opposition to this course, Pašić went for the policy that the Agrarians feared most. In a flurry of last-minute political maneuvering with two smaller groups, one of them from within the Agrarian fold, he succeeded in gaining the support of

24. Ibid. (Broj 813, Res. 1921), May 31, 1921.
25. *Stenografske beleške Ustavotvorne skupštine*, June 22, 1921, pp. 11–16.
26. Ibid., June 27, 1921, pp. 25–28.
27. Ibid., p. 21.

Ivan Pucelj's ten Slovene Agrarians, who were until then the members of the Agrarian Club, in exchange for certain concessions, including the Prague ambassadorship for Bogumil Vošnjak, one of the faction's leaders. Pašić also ensured the vote of the Cemiyet on terms similar to the deal made with the JMO. Turkish and Albanian landlords among the Cemiyet's leadership and following were relieved of the immediate threat of agrarian reform. The centralist sportsmen had bagged the necessary catch.

The Tragedy of the Vidovdan Constitution

June 28, the feastday of Saint Vitus in this century's reading of the Julian calendar, is sacred in Serbian history. The cult of the Sicilian martyr who exorcized the evil spirit out of Diocletian's son was especially active among the South Slavs, perhaps because the church substituted the worship of the pagan Slavic god Svantevid for this gentle patron of pharmacists and cop-persmiths. The feast became especially revered among the Serbs after the fourteenth century, because on Saint Vitus's Day (Vidovdan) of 1389 the Ottoman Turks defeated the Serbs in the Battle of Kosovo and reduced the Serbian state to vassalage. Before the battle was over, however, it was said that the legendary Serbian hero Miloš Obilić slaughtered the Ottoman Sultan Murat.

Through the centuries, Serbian folk imagination had transformed the temporal defeat at the Field of Kosovo into a source of spiritual strength. The revenge of the 1389 defeat and the restoration of the fallen Serbian state had become the elementary aspect of all Serb national programs. It was thought that Kosovo was avenged in the Balkan wars. And it was perhaps not accidental that Princip's assassination of Archduke Franz Ferdinand in Sarajevo also occurred on this fateful feast day (June 28, 1914). On Saint Vitus's Day of 1921, Yugoslavia's centralist constitution was finally adopted. Of the 285 attending deputies, 223 voted in favor of the Constitutional Committee's draft. The opposition mustered 35 votes, those of the Social Democrats, official Agrarians, Republicans, the NRS dissidents, and Trumbić; the 161 deputies who boycotted the procedures (by walking out or failing to participate) could have raised the opposition's numerical standing to 196. Yugoslavia's first constitution, unofficially referred to as the Vidovdan Constitution, was thus passed by a majority of only thirteen votes (over the required 210). The associations invoked by the historical Vidovdans could not have been more unfortunate for the subsequent fate of the new charter, since an impression was made that the constitution represented the final triumph of Serb national ideology.

Though the passage of the Vidovdan Constitution would still have been possible if either Pucelj's Agrarians or the Cemiyet (but not both) had abstained or voted against the centralist proposal, its passage was not possible without the support of the JMO. An autonomist party thereby contributed to the slim centralist victory. As it was, the 223 votes cast for the Vidovdan Constitution were still far short of the "qualified" two-thirds majority proposed by some autonomists and enshrined in several preunification documents.

It has been claimed that the DS's contribution to the passage of the centralist Vidovdan Constitution surpassed that of the NRS—not because of numerical plurality (which was insignificant in relation to the NRS) but because of its unitarist ideology, which rendered systematic opposition to centralism more difficult; not least in importance, eleven Croats, three Slovenes, and six Muslims of various nationalities (one of them a Bosnian Muslim from the Sandžak) in the ranks of the Democrats "permitted an outward appearance, especially to the foreign public, that this Constitution was accepted by the representatives of almost all South Slav peoples."[1]

The Vidovdan Constitution sanctioned the untenable centralist solution of Yugoslavia's national question. Reached without the participation—and against the will—of most of the non-Serb parties, it bore the seeds of further rancor. As a historical threshold, it marked a dividing line between two key phases of nascent Yugoslavia's parliamentarianism. The period before the adoption of the Vidovdan Constitution, therefore, can be considered as the testing ground for administrative practices that were legalized in this document. Before June 28, 1921, despite a systematic introduction of centralism, the national question was still susceptible to other—more equitable and pluralistic—solutions. After this date, such solutions were less likely and would become inseparable from open challenges to the constitution itself. Various anticentralist blocs, in which Radić's party always took the lead, continued to base their action on the demands for a revision of the Vidovdan Constitution. As these movements gained strength, the partisans of centralism, King Aleksandar notable among them, themselves started viewing the constitution as an unnecessary obstacle. They finally abolished it, aiming to preserve centralism by extraparliamentary means. Their reaction, in turn, led to still more unfortunate turns.

Two days after the passage of the Vidovdan Constitution, an editorial in the *Samouprava* (Self-Administration), the organ of the NRS, showed how far the Vidovdan system had been designed as a directory of Serbian obligation: "This year's Vidovdan," the editorial said, "restored an empire to us."[2] The restored empire was small and short-lived, like the terrestrial

---

1. Branislav Gligorijević, *Demokratska stranka i politički odnosi u Kraljevini Srba, Hrvata i Slovenaca* (Belgrade, 1970), , p. 218.

2. "Vidovdanski Ustav," *Samouprava*, June 30, 1921, p. 1.

empire that, according to the Serbian folk epic, Prince Lazar abjured on the eve of the first Vidovdan in exchange for the celestial empire that is always and forever.

PART VI

The Building of Skadar

Three full brothers were building a city,
Three full brothers, three Mrljavčevićes:
The first brother was King Vukašin,
The second was Voivode Uglješa,
The third was Mrljavčević Gojko;
They were building Skadar on the Bojana,
They were building for full three years,
For three years with three hundred masons,
But they could not lay the fundament,
Much less raise up the turreted city:
What the masons built by the day
The highland oread destroyed by night.
Upon the dawn of the fourth year,
The oread cried from the mountain:
"Do not torment yourself, King Vukašin,
Torment yourself and waste your treasure;
You cannot, O king, lay the fundament,
Much less raise up the turreted city,
Until you find two kindred names,
Until you find Stoja and Stojan,
One a sister and the other brother,
And wall them up in the fundament,
So that the fundament will be maintained,
So that you will build your turreted city."

From a Serbian epic song

Yugoslavia's national question was the expression of the conflicting national ideologies that have evolved in each of its numerous national and confessional communities, reflecting the community's historical experiences. These ideologies assumed their all but definite contours well before the unification and could not be significantly altered by any combination of cajolery or coercion. The divisions inherent in the national movements of the Serbs, Croats, and Slovenes, the three principal nationalities of Yugoslavia, were not, however, sufficient to forestall the rise of a single South Slavic state. The credit for this feat must be ascribed to the ideology of unitaristic Yugoslavism. It captured the imagination of the South Slavic intelligentsia in Austria-Hungary and could be accepted by the Serbian elite without any significant departures from all the traditions and trappings of Serbian statehood.

After the unification, the denial of the national individuality of each South Slavic nation, a position inherent in the precepts of unitaristic Yugoslavism, greatly facilitated the introduction of centralism. Under the conditions that prevailed, with all the institutions of the former Serbian state virtually intact, centralism was the system least likely to foster national equality. Instead, it furthered the goals of Serbian supremacy, reflected in the dominant position of the Serbs in all spheres of public affairs. Hence, contrary to the wishes of some high-minded unitarists, integral unitarism became regarded as an implement of Serbian hegemony and therefore discredited.

Yet, though the demise of unitarism was hastened by the concept's debasement and misuse, integralist prospects were slim in any case owing to a fundamental weakness: unitarism was plainly opposed to the reality of Serb, Croat, and Slovene national individuality and moreover in contradiction to the empirically observable fact that these peoples were fully formed national entities of long standing. Each of Yugoslavia's three principal national groups had one or more developed national ideologies. If anything, the national movements against centralism—particularly prominent among the Croats—merely completed the process whereby each group's national individuality was firmly set. To act as if that were not the case, to ignore the fact that the South Slavs were not one nation, one culture, and one loyalty, or to insist that they could acquire these unitary characterisics in due course, only weakened the already fragile state and diminished the prospects for good-neighborliness based on the rejection of all forms of assimilationism and on respect of Yugoslavia's multinational character, the only policy that could strengthen the Yugoslav polity. But it was precisely the integralist forces, best represented by Pribićević and his followers, who provided the ideological groundwork for the construction of a centralist state system that did not reflect the multinational peculiarity of Yugoslavia. Their efforts aided the Great Serbian forces (the dynasty, its military and bureaucratic apparatus, and the Radical party), whose policy of centralism was an expression not of unitaristic commitments but of Serbian national ideology. The Vidovdan Constitution of 1921 represented the compromise between the ideologies of Yugoslavist unitarism and Serb nationalism. The struggle for the revision of this solution could not but express the distinguishing features of non-Serb national ideologies.

There have been other ways of looking at the origins of the national question in Yugoslavia. Ever since the time of Sima Marković (1888–1938), the secretary and leading theoretician of the KPJ in the 1920s, various economic interpretations have been advanced, whereby the class purport of national ideologies (and of the national conflict itself) has been vulgarized in the most extreme fashion. According to Marković, the "basis of national struggle was *the struggle for the marketplace* and *state power*." As a result, he denied the objectiveness of any historically rooted conflict among the nationalities, viewing such conflicts as nothing but "external labels that masked the most varied class interests" of the bourgeoisie.[1] And since modern national struggles were nothing except conflicts between the bourgeoisie of various nations, it followed that the case of Serbs, Croats, and Slovenes was no exception. Marković saw the whole question as strictly a post-1918 phenomenon, whereby the Serbian bourgeoisie, which had suffered great material losses during the First World War, pursued the policy that would favor the improvement of its economic standing:

> Holding all the real power in the state in its hands, the Serbian bourgeoisie assigned itself *the principal goal of restoring itself economically as a class at least at the level of its Croat and Slovene competitors.* But this goal impinged not only on the interests of the Serb, Croat, and Slovene proletariat, but also on the interests of Croat and Slovene bourgeoisie. . . . This is the *basic economic cause,* which brought the Serbian bourgeoisie into conflict with the Croat and Slovene bourgeoisie. . . . *Hegemonistic policy of the Serbian bourgeoisie is an expression of its economic backwardness, a condition of its class restoration, and the indispensable necessity for its affirmation in competitive struggle against the more progressive Croat and Slovene bourgeoisie.*
>
> The Croat and Slovene bourgeoisie would have an interest in keeping Serbia a purely agrarian country with its industry in infancy, as was the case before the war, because, according to the law of capitalist production, the contradiction between the more progressive and industrially developed Croatia and Slovenia, on the one hand, and the capitalistically backward Serbia, on the other, would mean the unquestionable predominance of Croat and Slovene bourgeoisie over the Serbian.[2]

The strength of Marković's theory was precisely its extreme vulgarization. Since Marković had no doubt about the outcome of actual national conflict, he simply transplanted it into the mythical battlefield among the rival bourgeois factions, notwithstanding the illogic of the loss by the "more progressive" side. Moreover, to the extent that every ideology is nothing but a mask and a plaything for demagogic manipulation of the masses, it makes little difference that nationally constituted Croat and Slovene bourgeoisie did not even exist. The bourgeoisie, after all, could assume any national mask. Most of Croat and Slovene industry was in fact owned by foreign capital, and,

1. Sima Marković, *Nacionalno pitanje u svetlosti marksizma* (Belgrade, 1923), p. 34.
2. Ibid., pp. 112–113.

though Šlovene commerce was largely owned by native merchants, Croatian-Slavonian commerce to a great extent was controlled by Jewish commercial houses.[3] The archetypical representatives of Croatia-Slavonia's Jewish elite and of Marković's Croat bourgeoisie were Šandor D. Alexander and his brother Šandor A. pl. Alexander Sesvetski, who transformed their father's fortune in the export of cereals into a base for new industrial endeavors. Šandor D. took over the breweries of Sisak and Zagreb, founded Zagreb's oil factory, and had extensive interests in coal, cement, chemical industry, and Zagreb's German-language press (*Agramer Tagblatt, Morgenblatt*). He was the honorary president of Zagreb's Association of Industrialists, the Center of Industrial Corporations in Belgrade, and the vice-president of the Zagreb Trade Fair. Šandor A. was the honorary president of the Zagreb Chamber of Commerce, president for life of the commercial association Merkur and also of the Alliance of Merchants of Croatia-Slavonia, and the founder of Prehrana, a charitable society for the feeding of urban poor.[4] And though the brothers surely had reason to resent any number of politically motivated fiscal measures promulgated by the Belgrade governments, they were certainly not known for promotion of Croat nationalism with the aim of putting pressure on their Serbian competitors.[5] In fact, both Alexanders had a fair collection of Aleksandrine medals on their chests.

Only one major Croat capitalist, Milan Prpić, the founder of several textile industries centered around Oroslavlje, north of Zagreb, and an entrepreneur with significant interests in petroleum and lumber, had any special connection with the Croat opposition, being a political associate of Stjepan Radić. Moreover, Marković himself noted that the "Croat and Slovene bourgeoisie, as capitalistically more developed, wanted a more extensive marketplace for their industrial products; they have the most lively interest in seeing to it that

3. On the role of foreign capital on the territory of Yugoslavia see Jože Šorn, "Nacionalno poreklo velikega kapitala v industriji, rudarstvu in bančištvu na slovenskem ozemlju," *Jugoslovenski istorijski časopis*, 1969, no. 4, pp. 136–141; Slobodan Ćurčin, *Pénétration économique et financière des capitaux étrangers en Yougoslavie* (Paris, 1935); Sergije Dimitrijević, *Das ausländische Kapital in Jugoslawien vor dem zweiten Weltkrieg* (Berlin, 1963); Dimitrijević, "Vladavina stranog kapitala u staroj Jugoslaviji," in Sergije Dimitrijević et al., eds., *Iz istorije Jugoslavije 1918–1945: Zbornik predavanja* (Belgrade, 1958), pp. 279–298; L. Berov, "Le capital financier occidental et les pays balkaniques dans les années vingt," *Études balkaniques*, 1965, nos. 2–3, pp. 139–169.

4. "Markantne ličnosti u životu Trgovačke i obrtne komore u Zagrebu," *Narodno bogatstvo*, vol. 5 (1927), nos. 13–17, pp. 7–11; Ivan Malinar, "Privredni prvoborac," *Jugoslovenski Lloyd*, July 13, 1937, p. 1.

5. Šandor D. Alexander, in his report to Djuro Šurmin, a leader of the HZ, noted that although he to an extent recognized the need to tax wartime profits (realized mainly in Croatia-Slavonia and Slovenia), a policy on which the ministry of finances in Belgrade insisted, he did not believe that one should go so far as to kill the goose that laid golden eggs nor cut the branch on which the minister was sitting. This was typical of his middle-of-the-road attitude, which belied his leadership of Croat capital in opposition to Serbian supremacy. Arhiv Hrvatske, Rukopisna ostavština Dr. Djure Šurmina; I. Politička djelatnost dra Šurmina, Box 3: Fogl. 12: Š. D. Alexander to Djuro Šurmin, Zagreb, Aug. 17, 1919.

the state territory, as a *single* customs zone, be as large as possible."⁶ Yet neither Marković nor any of the reductionist historians who shared the elements of his economic interpretation ever bothered to reconcile the (con)federalist politics and ideology of Croat opposition with the expansive interests of the chimerical Croat bourgeoisie.⁷ Their flawed argument was multiplied in economic interpretations of national conflict in socialist Yugoslavia, where the economic reductionists have substituted the interests of the "bureaucracies of the industrially developed republics" (Slovenia and Croatia) for that of the long-expropriated Slovene and Croat bourgeoisie in order to reach conclusions very similar to those of Sima Marković. The positivistic distortionists of the Marxist method are always oblivious of the fact that Marx's *Capital* was a "critique of political economy," in which Marx explained, among other matters, why the "relation of the producers to the sum total of their labour is presented to them as a social relation, existing not between themselves, but between the products of their labour."⁸ The fetishism of commodities can indeed be found in the least expected quarters.

Though hardly a theory, the focus on the implications of Yugoslavia's marked confessional cleavages has been another significant tendency in interpretive discourse on the origins of the national question. The moral doctrine of modern materialism, among the South Slavs no less than elsewhere, assumes the antipopular drift of religion. Once this premise is accepted, it is only a matter of detail whether the rival churches damaged South Slavic unity by dividing the homogeneous South Slavic mass into separate communities, which then evolved into separate nationalities, or by preventing the symbiosis of separate religions, which could have evolved into a uninational community. In either case, the preoccupation with the religious roots of Yugoslavia's national question is typical of unitaristic attitudes and tends to exaggerate the admittedly harmful effects of religious bigotry.

The truth is that, except for the clash of Christianity and Islam, and then in an attenuated form, South Slavic interconfessional relations never occasioned religious wars on the scale of those fought in Western Europe after the Reformation. For all the tensions between Orthodoxy and Catholicism, the religious commitments of Serbs and Croats were not expressed in anything remotely similar to the "Spanish fury" that was inflicted on Dutch Calvinists in 1576 or the frightening vehemence of Cromwell's soldiery in Ireland, not to mention the concentrated violence of the Thirty Years' War. Moreover,

6. Marković, *Nacionalno pitanje*, p. 118.

7. Vaso Bogdanov's category of a "class state apparatus" that was dominated by the "united Croat-Serb, or 'Yugoslav,' exploiters of the people," as the source of national conflict between the Serbs and Croats in interwar Yugoslavia was merely a reductionist attempt to square the circle—this despite the far more compelling empirical evidence in his study of the origins of the Serbo-Croat conflict, with its emphasis on the pre-1918 period. See Vaso Bogdanov, "Historijski uzroci sukoba izmedju Hrvata i Srba," *Rad JAZU*, 1957, no. 311, esp. pp. 419–422, 457–477.

8. Karl Marx, *Capital*, vol. 1 (Moscow, n.d.), p. 72.

there were periods of communal cooperation between the two churches that reached an apex in the crisis of 1848–1849, as well as significant ecumenical endeavors, notably Križanić's and Strossmayer's work on the lifting of the schism.

For all that, the outspoken proponents of South Slavic unification, especially from the turn of century onward, believed that religious differences presented an insurmountable obstacle to any Serb-Croat symbiosis. In Skerlić's view, the "first step toward our *narodno jedinstvo* is religious indifference, a temporary comprehensive decline in religious feelings. . . . The Yugoslav idea . . . will either be anticlerical or it will not exist."[9] Given the history of its struggle against indifferentism, the Catholic church was acutely aware that in the eyes of the latitudinarian Yugoslavist unitarists it stood condemned, whatever its attitude toward South Slavic unity might be or whatever its contributions to ecumenism. Moreover, whereas Catholicism was condemned as anti-Slavic, the unitarists and Great Serbs viewed Orthodoxy as native and national, and this attitude fueled Catholic defensiveness and attempts on the part of Slovene and Croat clericalists to limit South Slavic unity to their Catholic flock.

Despite grave forebodings, the Catholic church accepted the establishment of Yugoslavia as an irreversible development and honestly sought to turn its temporary discomfort into an opportunity. Some leaders of Catholic Action believed that life in a single state would erase suspicions between the churches and ultimately lead to their reunification.[10] In a move to advance that hour, the Catholic episcopacy in 1918 called upon the Holy See to extend the use of Church Slavonic liturgy to all Catholic dioceses in Yugoslavia. In the areas under Italian occupation, members of the hierarchy, notably Bishop Anton Mahnič, spoke out against Italianization and called for accession to Yugoslavia.[11] Moreover, Mahnič, himself one of the founders of Slovene clericalist movement before he became the bishop of the Croat diocese of Krk (Istria), saw the establishment of Yugoslavia as a divine action against which there was no recourse: "In His wise providence, God gathered us within one body in a truly miraculous way. The great day has begun, and in the heavens a sign appeared with the inscription S.H.S. [Serbs, Croats, Slovenes]. My people, you will conquer in that sign. Croats, Serbs, Slovenes! It is God's will that you remain indissolubly united forever. Providence has assigned to you a great purpose. Your salvation and your future is only in your unity. Where is the traitorous hand that would dare destroy this unity? What God has joined together, let no man rend asunder!"[12]

But for all its blessings of the Yugoslav nuptials, the Catholic church

9. Cited in Milorad Ekmečić, *Ratni ciljevi Srbije 1914* (Belgrade, 1973), p. 117.
10. Ivan Mužić, *Hrvatska politika i jugoslavenska ideja* (Split, 1969), p. 191.
11. "† Dr Antun Mahnić," *Katolički list,* Dec. 16, 1920, pp. 390–391.
12. "Besede biskupa dr. Antona Mahniča o Jugoslaviji," *Slovenec,* Nov. 14, 1920, p. 1.

encountered numerous challenges. Unitaristic forces openly encouraged the schism with Rome, calling for a Catholic national church.[13] In February 1919 a group of clerics initiated a reform movement within the church that called for permission to grow beards, abolition of celibacy, Slavonic liturgy transcribed in Cyrillic script rather than in Roman as the Catholic bishops requested, and church congresses, consisting of laymen and clerics, to administer the church.[14] The reformers denied imputations of collusion with Pribićević or that they constituted a "peril for Croatdom."[15] But after their excommunication and the founding of the Croatian Old Catholic church in 1923, they became the favorites of all anti-Catholic forces.[16] Some Catholic apostates did not hesitate to promote Orthodoxy as the better alternative to Catholicism.[17] And Orthodox chruchmen themselves promoted the separation of Yugoslavia's Greek Catholics from the Holy See and aided dissenters among Ruthenian Greek Catholics in Czechoslovakia in their schism with Rome.[18] Moreover, the Serbian Orthodox church encouraged the National Czechoslovak church (a product of a schism with Rome by a Czech reform movement similar to that of Croat reformers) in its attempts to accept Orthodox practices and, in 1921, helped found the Czechoslovak Orthodox church from among a group of reformers, consecrating one of their leaders a bishop according to the rites of Serbian Orthodoxy.[19] The Catholics, inured to state protection in Austria-Hungary, tried to win state support to stem these reversals. Instead, they encountered indifference and even hostility, much of which they blamed on the influence of Masonic lodges. But this was a conditioned reaction against the group that had only conditional influence among the centralist parties.[20] Catholicism and Islam were opposed not

13. Such calls were raised in parts of Dalmatia immediately after the coming of the Serbian army. See *Srpska vojska i francuska mornarica u Dubrovniku 13. novembra 1918.* (Dubrovnik, 1918), p. 17.

14. For excerpts from the demands of the reformers see R. M. Pavić, "Savremene želje katoličkog nižeg klera, god. 1919," *Krug*, vol. 1 (1938), no. 4, pp. 74–76.

15. Stjepan Vidušić, "Odgovor 'Obzoru,'" *Preporod*, vol. 3 (1922), no. 1, pp. 3–4.

16. Ivan Mužić, *Katolička crkva u Kraljevini Jugoslaviji: Politički i pravni aspekti konkordata izmedju Svete Stolice i Kraljevine Jugoslavije* (Split, 1978), p. 38.

17. Božo Milanović, *Moje uspomene (1900–1976)* (Pazin, 1976), p. 60.

18. "Povratak u Sv. Pravoslavlje," *Vesnik*, Feb. 14, 1921, p. 1.

19. Ludvik Nemec, *The Czechoslovak Heresy and Schism: The Emergence of a National Czechoslovak Church* (Philadelphia, 1975), pp. 27–59.

20. The obituaries in interwar Freemasonic bulletins, *Šestar* (Compass) and *Neimar* (Builder), covering the period from 1915 to 1939, when Masons were banned, cite only a few noted politicians who were Freemasons, among them Lazar Paču and Joca P. Jovanović of the NRS, Kosta Stojanović of the DS, Franko Potočnjak and Hinko Hinković, who were close to the DS, Vilim Bukšeg of the Social Democrats, and various veterans of pre-1914 unitarist youth movement, such as Ljuba Jovanović-Čupa. From other sources it is certain that Miroslav Spalajković and Momčilo Ninčić of the NRS and Juraj Demetrović and Hinko Krizman of the DS were Masons. See Nadežda Jovanović, *Politički sukobi u Jugoslaviji 1925–1928* (Belgrade, 1974), pp. 162–163. It has been asserted that Svetozar Pribićević belonged to a Masonic lodge, but there is no firm evidence to support this claim. The point is that Freemasons tended toward centralist (notably unitarist) factions, and that there was no evident Masonic presence in oppositionist parties. This should hardly surprise. European Masons were by definition members of the establishment.

because they were more obscurantist than Orthodoxy, but because they were not the spiritual homes of the Serbs.

This being the situation, it is hardly surprising that relations between the churches deteriorated after the unification. But that is not the same as defining a general disposition from goaded responses. The failure of unitarism called for *un bouc émissaire:* "Clericalism in our country is an organized danger, which poisons the broad masses. . . . It stirred up the revolt among the masses, claiming that they would fall under the heretical Serbs and would no longer be allowed to be Catholics. It sowed discontent in our lands, roused the masses (priest Tomas in Vojni Križ) against the Serbian army and thereby helped Italians to grab our Istria. After all, the Italians are Catholics."[21] But in addition to scapegoating this was an ideological statement. Here, too, it is far more useful to proceed from national ideologies to determine the conceptual structure in the encounter between a nationalism that saw Catholicism as ever in tension with the joyous Slavic blood (the phrase belongs to Jovan Dučić, Serb poet and diplomat), and a local church that saw Orthodoxy as especially worthy of conversion because it was predominantly Slavic.

A corollary to the overemphasis on confessional cleavages has been the preoccupation with the mutual unacquaintance of the South Slavs. And indeed, there was (and continues to be) a certain spiritual deadness in South Slavic stereotypes that speaks volumes about how little the South Slavs, notably (and paradoxically) the run-of-the-mill intellectuals, wish to know about the other South Slavs. But this was only a secondary manifestation of extreme segmental cleavages, to borrow a phrase of political theorists, that accompanied far more elementary diversities in Yugoslavia's national, linguistic, religious, cultural, regional, and developmental components. Moreover, Yugoslavia's political parties, cultural associations, press and other means of communication, were themselves organized along those very lines of segmental cleavages. A modicum of stability in such a state of affairs was dependent not so much on the abolition of mutual ignorance as on the cooperation among the accepted leaders of—at the very least—the main national communities.

Since Yugoslavia's national question was, more than anything, an expression of mutually exclusive national ideologies, the chances for its internal stability were not very good. Worse still, the chances for a workable democratic system in such a polity also were very slim. Arend Lijphart, a Dutch political scientist, recently detailed the conditions that favor the functioning of democracy in multinational states. His "consocietal democracy" is based above all on "elite cooperation and stable nonelite support."[22] For

21. Zagrepčanin [pseud.], "Jezuitska gimnazija u Zagrebu," *Demokratija,* Nov. 27, 1920, p. 2.
22. Arend Lijphart, *Democracy in Plural Societies: A Comparative Exploration* (New Haven, 1977), p. 54. (Page numbers that follow refer to this work.)

the leaders of each community to be committed to cooperation while retaining the loyalty of their own group, five conditions should be met. (1) The given society must consist of more than two groups, since a multiple balance of power is more stable than dual balance or the hegemony of one group. In this respect, it is a good thing that the political parties in a multinational state ''are likely to be the organized political manifestations of the segments. They can act as the political representatives of their segments, and they provide a good method of selecting the segmental leaders who will participate in grand coalitions'' (pp. 61–62). (2) The country must be relatively small and indeed vulnerable to outside threats. The exposure to imminent outside peril tends to promote internal solidarity, but only if the peril is perceived as dangerous by all the groups. (3) Certain overarching loyalties or basic principles of unity, possibly a form of nationalism, should moderate the potential for conflict among the communities. (4) A ''consocietal democracy'' should be fragmented, that is, federated, with each ''segmental group'' isolated from the others, since ''clear boundaries between the segments of a plural society have the advantage of limiting mutual contacts and consequently of limiting the chances of ever-present potential antagonisms to erupt into actual hostility'' (p. 88). If necessary, that means the splitting of historical units to promote isolation, as the Swiss have done with the cantons of Unterwalden, Appenzell, and Basel. (5) A consocietal democracy would also profit from an existing tradition of elite cooperation and certainly from a political culture that favors pluralism and political accommodation or is at the very least not inured to forms of absolutism and, presumably, centralism.

When Yugoslavia's situation of 1918–1921 is examined in light of Lijphart's conditions it is readily apparent that the country was entirely unprepared for evolving into consocietalism, or for that matter into any form of democracy or even stability. Cooperation was not the aim of political leaders, nor could it be as long as the centralist bloc refused to respect a principle of concurrent majority in each national community. Instead, the centralists sought to impose a patchwork majority, consisting of Serb parties and their tactical allies, onto the parties that represented most of the non-Serb groups. A pretense was made that such parties as the DS were ''multitribal,'' though in fact the Croat and Slovene Democrats had no stable support in their communities. Yugoslavia was indeed a highly diversified multinational state, but multinationalism could not promote consocietalism while the national ideologies of the principal group encouraged the notion that domination through assimilation was imminent. Paradoxically, the emergence of various political parties as spokesmen of specific groups (HPSS for the Croats, JMO for the Bosnian Muslims, SLS for the Slovenes) was not sufficient for the growth of consocietalism as long as the Serbs were politically fragmented. Despite the impressive national solidarity among the Serbs, there was no overall Serb party. Indeed, practically all the parties that were self-evidently

Serb aspired to a non-Serb base. In these circumstances, the prospect for cooperation was not a bright one.

As for the other conditions, Yugoslavia was indeed relatively small and, with the exception of Albania, the Balkan country that was most vulnerable to outside threats. But as long as Italian irredentism was seen as a Croat and Slovene problem and the maintenance of the frontier with Bulgaria something that was in fact a liability to these groups, imminent outside perils were not a stabilizing factor. Moreover, Croats especially nursed resentment for the way their understandable concern about Italian expansionism was turned into a disadvantage that was not reciprocal. The overarching function of Yugoslavism could not be developed as long as the concept implied national amalgamation and the final destruction of the existing groups. And a Yugoslavism that accepted and reconciled the national ideologies of the Serbs, Croats, and Slovenes was not in evidence, nor could it ultimately, even had it emerged, be acceptable to the non-Slavic minorities or the Macedonians. The isolation of each national group was unworkable without exchanges of population, and a federal agreement based on the historical provinces was rejected by the Serb parties. This standstill logically precluded the possibility of autonomous self-rule within each of the historical provinces, for example an autonomous district for the Serbs of Croatia or for the Croats of Bačka. One group would not have it because it violated the integrity of historical provinces, the other because it rejected the status of a minority for its conationals. Finally, neither the Austro-Hungarian nor the Ottoman and post-Ottoman models of statecraft favored the development of a pluralistic political culture, least of all an accommodating one. Small wonder that the national question, particularly its Croat aspect, remained the "point round which every problem of the Jugoslav home and foreign policy has revolved ever since the Union."[23]

Indeed, despite dictatorships and attempts at democratic renewal, occupations and wars, revolutions and social changes, after 1921 hardly any new elements were introduced in the set pattern of South Slavic interactions. The game was open-ended, but pawns could proceed only one square at a time except on their first move, bishops always moved diagonally and were nearly always fianchettoed in Indian defenses, knights were always least effective in the endgame, kings slowly advanced or retreated within their narrow square, and castling was permitted only if the king in question was not in check. And some kings fell.

The national question permeated every aspect of Yugoslavia's public life after 1918. It was reflected in the internal, external, social, economic, and even cultural affairs. It was solved by democrats and autocrats, kings and

23. Robert William Seton-Watson, "Jugoslavia and the Croat Problem," *Slavonic Review*, vol. 16 (1937), no. 2, p. 102.

communists. It was solved by day and unsolved by night. Some days were particularly bright for building, some nights particularly dark for destroying. One horn of the dilemma was that a single solution could not satisfy all sides. Was the other that a firm citadel could be maintained only by human sacrifice?

Selected Bibliography

The following references exclude cited sources that do not have a large bearing upon the subject of this study and include important works in Western languages not cited previously.

BOOKS

Apostolski, Mihailo, and Dančo Zografski, eds., *Istorija makedonskog naroda*. Vol. 3, *Period izmedju dva svetska rata i narodna revolucija (1918–1945)*. Belgrade: Zavod za izdavanje udžbenika SR Srbije, 1970.

Avakumovic, Ivan. *History of the Communist Party of Yugoslavia*. Vol. 1. Aberdeen, Scotland: Aberdeen University Press, 1964.

Balcanicus [Stojan Protić]. *Albanski problem i Srbija i Austro-Ugarska*. Belgrade: Knjižarnica Gece Kona, 1913.

Bartulović, Niko. *Na prelomu*. Belgrade: Srpska književna zadruga, 1929.

Bašagić, Savfet-beg. *Znameniti Hrvati Bošnjaci i Hercegovci u turskoj carevini*. Zagreb: Matica Hrvatska, 1931.

Behschnitt, Wolf Dietrich. *Nationalismus bei Serben und Kroaten 1830–1914: Analyse und Typologie der nationalen Ideologie*. Munich: R. Oldenbourg Verlag, 1980.

Belić, Aleksandar. *Srbi i Bugari u balkanskom savezu i u medjusobnom ratu*. Belgrade: Knjižara S. B. Cvijanovića, 1913.

Bićanić, Rudolf. *Ekonomska podloga hrvatskog pitanja*. 2d ed. Zagreb: Vladko Maček, 1938.

Bihiku, Koço. *A History of Albanian Literature*. Tirana: 8 Nëntori, 1980.

Bilandžić, Dušan, et al., eds., *Komunistički pokret i socijalistička revolucija u Hrvatskoj*. Zagreb: IHRPH, 1969.

Boban, Ljubo. *Sporazum Cvetković-Maček*. Belgrade: Institut društvenih nauka, 1965.

———. *Svetozar Pribićević u opoziciji 1929–1936*. Zagreb: Sveučilište u Zagrebu—Institut za hrvatsku povijest, 1973.

Bogdanov, Vaso, Ferdo Čulinović, and Marko Kostrenčić, eds. *Jugoslavenski odbor u Londonu*. Zagreb: JAZU, 1966.

Božović, Todor, and Jovan Djonović. *Crna Gora i napredni pokret*. Belgrade: Nova štamparija "Davidović," 1911.

Brković, Savo. *O postanku i razvoju crnogorske nacije*. Titograd: Grafički zavod, 1974.

Bulgarian Academy of Sciences. *Makedonija: Sbornik ot dokumenti i materiali*. Edited by Dimitər Kosev et al. Sofia: Izdatelstvo na BAN, 1978.

Ćatić, Musa Ćazim. *Pjesme*. Vol. 67 of *Pet stoljeća hrvatske književnosti*. Edited by Abdurahman Nametak. Zagreb: Matica Hrvatska and Zora, 1966.

Ćerić, Salim. *Muslimani srpskohrvatskog jezika*. Sarajevo: Svjetlost, 1968.

Ciliga, Vera. *Slom politike Narodne stranke (1865–1880)*. Zagreb: Matica Hrvatska, 1970.

Ćirković, Sima. *Istorija srednjovekovne bosanske države*. Belgrade: Srpska književna zadruga, 1964.

——, ed. *Istorija srpskog naroda*. Vol. 1, *Od najstarijih vremena do maričke bitke (1371)*. Belgrade: Srpska književna zadruga, 1981.

Ćorović, Vladimir. *Istorija Jugoslavije*. Belgrade: Narodno delo, 1933.

Čubrilović, Vasa. *Istorija političke misli u Srbiji XIX veka*. Belgrade: Prosveta, 1958.

——, ed. *Jugoslovenski narodi pred prvi svetski rat*. Belgrade: Naučno delo, 1967.

Čulinović, Ferdo. *Državnopravna historija jugoslavenskih zemalja XIX i XX vijeka*. Zagreb: Školska knjiga, 1954.

——. *Državnopravni razvitak Jugoslavije*. Zagreb: Školska knjiga, 1963.

——. *Jugoslavija izmedju dva rata*. 2 vols. Zagreb: JAZU, 1961.

——. *Odjeci Oktobra u jugoslavenskim krajevima*. Zagreb: IP "27. srpanj," 1957.

——. *1918 na Jadranu*. Zagreb: Glas rada, 1951.

Ćurčin, Slobodan. *Pénétration économique et financière des capitaux étrangers en Yougoslavie*. Paris: Editions Pierre Boussuet, 1935.

Cvijić, Jovan. *Balkansko poluostrvo i južnoslovenske zemlje: Osnovi antropogeografije*. 2d ed. Translated by Borivoje Drobnjaković. Belgrade: Zavod za izdavanje udžbenika SR Srbije, 1966.

Damjanović, Pero, et al., eds. *Uchastie iugoslavianskikh trudiashchikhsia v Oktiabr'skoi revoliutsii i grazhdanskoi voine v SSSR: Sbornik dokumentov i materialov*. Moscow: Nauka, 1976.

Dedijer, Vladimir. *Sarajevo 1914*. Belgrade: Prosveta, 1966.

Délégation du Royaume des Serbes, Croates et Slovènes à la Conférence de la Paix. *Rapport sur les Dommages de Guerre causés à la Serbie et au Monténégro présenté à la Commission des Réparations des Dommages*. N. p.: 1919.

Despalatović, Elinor Murray. *Ljudevit Gaj and the Illyrian Movement*. Boulder, Colorado: East European Quarterly, 1975.

Dimitrijević, Mita. *Mi i Hrvati: Hrvatsko pitanje (1914–1939); Sporazum sa Hrvatima*. Belgrade: Author, 1939.

Dimitrijević, Sergije. *Das ausländische Kapital in Jugoslawien vor dem zweiten Weltkrieg*. Translated by Martin Zöller. Berlin (GDR): Rütten & Loening, 1963.

——; Hasanagić, Edib, Jovan Marjanović, and Pero Morača, eds. *Iz istorije Jugoslavije 1918–1945: Zbornik predavanja*. Belgrade: Nolit, 1958.

Direkcija državne statistike u Beogradu. *Prethodni rezultati popisa stanovništva u Kraljevini Srba, Hrvata i Slovenaca 31. januara 1921. godine*. Sarajevo: Državna štamparija, 1924.

Djikić, Osman. *Sabrana djela: Pjesme i drame*. Edited by Josip Lešić. Sarajevo: Svjetlost, 1971.

Djodan, Šime. *Ekonomska politika Jugoslavije*. Zagreb: Školska knjiga, 1970.

Djonović, Jovan. *Govori Jovana Djonovića, narodnog poslanika*. Belgrade: Author, 1921.

_____. *Ustavne i političke borbe u Crnoj Gori 1905–1910*. Belgrade: K. I. Mihailović, 1939.

Djurdjev, Branislav, Bogo Grafenauer, and Jorjo Tadić, eds. *Historija naroda Jugoslavije*. Vol. 2. Zagreb: Školska knjiga, 1959.

Djurović, Milinko, ed. *Istorija Crne Gore*. 3 vols. Titograd: Redakcija za istoriju Crne Gore, 1967–1975.

Doklestić, Ljubiša, ed. *Kroz historiju Makedonije: Izabrani izvori*. Zagreb: Školska knjiga, 1964.

_____. *Srpsko-makedonskite odnosi vo XIX-ot vek do 1897 godina*. Skopje: NIP "Nova Makedonija," 1973.

Dragićević, Risto J. *"Tajni ugovor Crne Gore s Austrijom."* Cetinje: Author, 1968.

Drinković, Mate. *Hrvatska i državna politika*. Zagreb: Author, 1928.

Drljević, Sekula. *Balkanski sukobi 1905.–1941*. Zagreb: Naklada Putovi, 1944.

Dubrovčanin, L. G. [Lujo Vojnović]. *Srpsko-hrvacko pitanje u Dalmaciji: Nekoliko iskrenijeh riječi narodu*. Split: Štamparija Karla Russo, 1888.

Dvorniković, Vladimir. *Karakterologija Jugoslovena*. Belgrade: Geca Kon A.D., 1939.

Dzhurich, Momchilo M. *Obrazovanie mnogonatsional'nogo gosudarstva Iugoslavii (1918–1921gg.)* Moscow: Izdatel'stvo Moskovskogo universiteta, 1970.

Ekmečić, Milorad. *Osnove gradjanske diktature u Evropi izmedju dva svjetska rata*. 2d rev. ed. Sarajevo: Zavod za izdavanje udžbenika, 1967.

_____. *Ratni ciljevi Srbije 1914*. Belgrade: Srpska književna zadruga, 1973.

Fabjančić, Vladislav. *O Sloveniji i Slovencima*. Geneva: Štamparija jugoslovenske kulture, 1917.

Faure-Biguet, J.-N. *Le roi Alexandre Ier de Yougoslavie*. Paris: Plon, 1936.

Feifalik, Anton. *Ein neuer aktueller Weg zur Lösung der bosnischen Agrarfrage*. Vienna: F. Deuticke, 1916.

Freidzon, V. I. *Bor'ba khorvatskogo naroda za natsional'nuiu svobodu*. Moscow: Nauka, 1970.

Gagliardi, Manko. *Istina o hrvatskom emigrantskom revolucionarnom komiteu 1919–21: Odgovor na napadaje Stjepana Radića*. N.p.: 1919.

Gavrilović, Slavko. *Vojvodina i Srbija u vreme Prvog ustanka*. Novi Sad: Institut za izučavanje istorije Vojvodine, 1974.

Georgevitch, T.-R. *La Macédoine*. Paris: Bernard Grasset, 1919.

Georgevitch, Vladan. *Die Albanesen und die Grossmächte*. Leipzig: Verlag von S. Hirzel, 1913.

Giurati, Giovanni. *Con D'Annunzio e Millo in difesa dell' Adriatico*. Florence: G. C. Sansoni, 1954.

Gligorijević, Branislav. *Demokratska stranka i politički odnosi u Kraljevini Srba, Hrvata i Slovenaca*. Belgrade: Institute za savremenu istoriju, 1970.

Grafenauer, Bogo. *Zgodovina slovenskega naroda*. Vol. 5. Ljubljana: Kmečka knjiga, 1962.

Graham, Stephen. *Alexander of Yugoslavia: The Story of the King Who Was Murdered at Marseilles.* New Haven: Yale University Press, 1939.

Gross, Mirjana, ed. *Društveni razvoj u Hrvatskoj (od 16. stoljeća do početka 20. stoljeća).* Zagreb: Sveučilišna naklada "Liber," 1981.

———. *Povijest pravaške ideologije.* Zagreb: Sveučilište u Zagrebu—Institut za hrvatsku povijest, 1973.

———. *Vladavina Hrvatsko-srpske koalicije 1906–1907.* Belgrade: Institut društvenih nauka, 1960.

Grulović, Nikola. *Jugosloveni u ratu i Oktobarskoj revoluciji.* Belgrade: Prosveta, 1962.

Hadžijahić, Muhamed. *Od tradicije do identiteta: Geneza nacionalnog pitanja bosanskih Muslimana.* Sarajevo: Svjetlost, 1974.

Hadži-Vasiljević, Jovan. *Kumanovska oblast.* Vol. 2 of *Južna stara Srbija: Istorijska, etnografska i politička istraživanja.* Belgrade: Zadužbina I. M. Kolarca, 1909.

Herceg, Rudolf. *Die Ideologie der kroatischen Bauernbewegung.* Introduction by Stjepan Radić. Zagreb: Verlag Rud. Herceg und Genossen, 1923.

———. *Seljački pokret u Hrvatskoj.* Zagreb: Author, 1923.

Hikec, Ante. *Radić: Portrait historijske ličnosti.* Zagreb: Author, 1926.

Horvat, Josip. *Ante Starčević: Kulturno-povjesna slika.* Zagreb: Antun Velzek, 1940.

———. *Frano Supilo.* Belgrade: Nolit, 1961.

———. *Hrvatski panoptikum.* Zagreb: Stvarnost, 1965.

———. *Ljudevit Gaj: Njegov život, njegovo doba.* Zagreb: Sveučilišna naklada "Liber," 1975.

———. *Politička povijest Hrvatske.* Zagreb: Binoza, 1936.

———. *Politička povijest Hrvatske 1918–1929.* Zagreb: Binoza, 1938.

———. *Supilo: Život jednog hrvatskog političara.* Zagreb: Binoza, 1938.

Horvat, Rudolf. *Hrvatska na mučilištu.* Zagreb: Kulturno-historijsko društvo "Hrvatski rodoljub," 1942.

Hribar, Ivan. *Moji spomini.* Vol. 2, *Osvobojevalna doba.* Ljubljana: Author, 1928.

Imamović, Mustafa. *Pravni položaj i unutrašnji politički razvitak Bosne i Hercegovine od 1878. do 1914.* Sarajevo: Svjetlost, 1976.

Išek, Tomislav. *Djelatnost Hrvatske seljačke stranke u Bosni i Hercegovini do zavodjenja diktature.* Sarajevo: Svjetlost, 1981.

Istorijski arhiv Komunističke partije Jugoslavije. Vol. 2, *Kongresi i zemaljske konferencije KPJ, 1919–1937.* Belgrade: Istorijsko odeljenje Centralnog komiteta KPJ, 1949.

Ivić, Pavle. *Srpski narod i njegov jezik.* Belgrade: Srpska književna zadruga, 1971.

Janković, Dragoslav. *Jugoslovensko pitanje i krfska deklaracija 1917 godine.* Belgrade: Savremena administracija, 1967.

———. *Srbija i jugoslovensko pitanje 1914–1915. godine.* Belgrade: Institut za savremenu istoriju, 1973.

———; and Krizman, Bogdan, eds. *Gradja o stvaranju jugoslovenske države.* 2 vols. Belgrade: Institute društvenih nauka, 1964.

Janković, Milivoj B. [Milivoj Blažeković]. *Hrvatksi seljak u novoj državi: Razgovori za seljački puk.* Zagreb: Pučka prosvjetna knjižnica, 1919.

Jareb, Jere. *Pola stoljeća hrvatske politike: Povodom Mačekove autobiografije.* Buenos Aires: Knjižnica Hrvatske revije, 1960.

Jelavich, Charles, and Barbara Jelavich. *The Establishment of the Balkan National States,*

1804–1920. Vol. 8 of *A History of East Central Europe*. Seattle: University of Washington Press, 1977.

Jovanović, Dragoljub. *Ljudi, ljudi . . . (Medaljoni 56 umrlih savremenika)*. 2 vols. Belgrade: Author, 1973–1975.

Jovanović, Ilija, Stevan Rajković, and Veljko Ribar. *Jugoslovenski dobrovoljački korpus u Rusiji: Prilog istoriji dobrovoljačkog pokreta (1914–1918)*. Belgrade: Vojno delo, 1954.

Jovanović, Nadežda. *Politički sukobi u Jugoslaviji 1925–1928*. Belgrade: Rad, 1974.

Jovanović, Slobodan. *Vlada Aleksandra Obrenovića*. 3 vols. Belgrade: Geca Kon A.D., 1934–1936.

———. *Vlada Milana Obrenovića*. 3 vols. Belgrade: Geca Kon A.D., 1934.

Kaćanski, Stevan. *Celokupna dela*. Edited by Milan Kašanin. Belgrade: Narodna prosveta, n.d.

Kadić, Ante. *From Croatian Renaissance to Yugoslav Socialism: Essays*. The Hague: Mouton, 1969.

Kalić, Jovanka, ed. *Istorija srpskog naroda*. Vol. 2, *Doba borbi za očuvanje i obnovu države (1371–1537)*. Belgrade: Srpska književna zadruga, 1982.

Karadjordjević, Djordje. *Istina o mome životu*. Belgrade: Prosveta, 1969.

Karadžić, Vuk Stefanović. *Pismenica serbskoga iezika, po govoru prostoga naroda*. Vienna: J. Schnürer, 1814.

Karaulac, Miroslav. *Rani Andrić*. Belgrade: Prosveta, 1980.

Karihman, Ferid, comp. *Soj i odžak ehli-Islama: Zbirka pjesama o domu i rodu Muslimana hrvatskog koljena i jezika*. Munich: Knjižnica Hrvatske revije, 1974.

Katardžiev, Ivan. *Vreme na zreenje: Makedonskoto nacionalno prašanje meǵu dvete svetski vojni (1919–1930)*. 2 vols. Skopje: Kultura, 1977.

Kessler, Wolfgang. *Politik, Kultur und Gesellschaft in Kroatien und Slawonien in der ersten Hälfte des 19. Jahrhunderts: Historiographie und Grundlagen*. Munich: R. Oldenbourg Verlag, 1981.

Klaić, Nada. *Povijest Hrvata u razvijenom srednjem vijeku*. Zagreb: Školska knjiga, 1976.

Kovačić, Matija. *Od Radića do Pavelića*. Munich: Knjižnica Hrvatske revije, 1970.

Krek, Janez Ev. *Slovenci*. Zagreb: Znanstvena knjižnica "Narodne prosvjete," 1919.

Križanić, Juraj. *Politika ili razgovori o vladalaštvu*. Translated by Mate Malinar. Zagreb: Matica Hrvatska, 1947.

Krizman, Bogdan. *Ante Pavelić i ustaše*. Zagreb: Globus, 1978.

———. *Raspad Austro-Ugarske i stvaranje jugoslavenske države*. Zagreb: Školska knjiga, 1977.

Krleža, Miroslav. *Sabrana djela*. 27 vols. Zagreb: Zora, 1953–1972.

Kulundžić, Zvonimir. *Atentat na Stjepana Radića*. Zagreb: Stvarnost, 1967.

———. *Politika i korupcija u kraljevskoj Jugoslaviji*. Zagreb: Stvarnost, 1968.

Kvaternik, Eugen. *Politički spisi*. Compiled by Ljerka Kuntić. Zagreb: Znanje, 1971.

Lederer, Ivo J. *Yugoslavia at the Paris Peace Conference: A Study in Frontiermaking*. New Haven: Yale University Press, 1963.

Lijphart, Arend. *Democracy in Plural Societies: A Comparative Exploration*. New Haven: Yale University Press, 1977.

Lorković, Mladen. *Narod i zemlja Hrvata*. Zagreb: Matica Hrvatska, 1939.

Lovrenčić, Rene. *Geneza politike "novog kursa."* Zagreb: Sveučilište u Zagrebu— Institut za hrvatsku povijest, 1972.

Lukač, Dušan. *Radnički pokret u Jugoslaviji i nacionalno pitanje 1918–1941.* Belgrade: Institut za savremenu istoriju, 1972.

Macan, Trpimir. *Miho Klaić.* Zagreb: Matica Hrvatska, 1980.

MacDermott, Mercia. *Freedom or Death: The Life of Gotsé Delchev.* West Nyack, N.Y.: Journeyman Press, 1978.

Maček, Vladko. *In the Struggle for Freedom.* Translated by Elizabeth and Stjepan Gazi. University Park: Pennsylvania State University Press, 1957.

Maletić, Mihailo, ed. *Kosovo-Kosova.* Belgrade: NIP Borba and Ekonomska politika, 1973.

Marjanović, Milan. *Genij Jugoslovenstva Ivan Meštrović i njegov hram.* New York: Jugoslovenska biblioteka, [1915?].

———. *Londonski ugovor iz godine 1915: Prilog povijesti borbe za Jadran 1914–1917.* Zagreb: JAZU, 1960.

———. *Narod koji nastaje: Zašto nastaje i kako se formira jedinstveni srpsko-hrvatski narod.* Rijeka: Knjižara G. Trbojević, 1913.

———. *Obnova: Zbornik za inicijativu i diskusiju poratnih problema.* Valparaiso: Jugoslovenska Narodna obrana, 1918.

———. *Savremena Hrvatska.* Belgrade: Srpska književna zadruga, 1913.

———. *Stjepan Radić.* Belgrade: Jugo-istok, 1937.

Marković, Lazar. *Jugoslovenska država i Hrvatsko pitanje (1914–1929).* Belgrade: Geca Kon A.D., 1935.

Marković, Sima. *Nacionalno pitanje u svetlosti marksizma.* Belgrade: Grafički institut "Narodna misao," 1923.

Marmullaku, Ramadan. *Albania and the Albanians.* Translated by Margot and Boško Milosavljević. London: C. Hurst, 1975.

Matković, Hrvoje. *Svetozar Pribićević i Samostalna demokratska stranka do šestojanuarske diktature.* Zagreb: Sveučilište u Zagrebu—Institut za hrvatsku povijest, 1972.

Matoš, Antun Gustav. *Sabrana djela.* 20 vols. Edited by Vida Flaker and Nedjeljko Mihanović. Zagreb: JAZU, Liber, and Mladost.

Meštrović, Ivan. *Uspomene na političke ljude i dogadjaje.* Buenos Aires: Knjižnica Hrvatske revije, 1961.

Mihajlov, Ivan. *Spomeni.* Vol. 2, *Osvoboditelna borba, 1919–1924 g.* Brussels: Author, 1965.

Mikuž, Metod. *Oris zgodovine Slovencev v stari Jugoslaviji 1917–1941.* Ljubljana: Mladinska knjiga, 1965.

Miladinov, Dimitər, and Konstantin Miladinov. *Prepiska.* Edited by N. Trajkov. Sofia: Izdatelstvo na BAN, 1964.

Milanović, Božo. *Moje uspomene (1900–1976).* Pazin: Istarsko književno društvo sv. Ćirila i Metoda and Kršćanska sadašnjost, 1976.

Milenković, Toma. *Socijalistička partija Jugoslavije.* Belgrade: Institut za savremenu istoriju, 1974.

Mitrinović, Čedomil. *Naši muslimani: Studija za orientaciju pitanja bosanko-hercegovačkih muslimana.* Belgrade: Biblioteka "Društvo," 1926.

Mitrović, Andrej. *Jugoslavija na konferenciji mira: 1919–1920.* Belgrade: Zavod za izdavanje udžbenika SR Srbije, 1969.

Mitrović, Živan. *Srpske političke stranke.* Belgrade: Politika A.D., 1939.

Morača, Pero, Milinko Djurović; and Dragan Marković, eds. *Četrdeset godina: Zbornik sećanja aktivista jugoslovenskog revolucionarnog radničkog pokreta.* Vol. 1. Belgrade: Kultura, 1960.

Mužić, Ivan. *Hrvatska politika i jugoslavenska ideja.* Split: Author, 1969.

_____. *Katolička crkva u Kraljevini Jugoslaviji: Politički i pravni aspekti konkordata izmedju Svete stolice i Kraljevine Jugoslavije.* Split: Crkva u svijetu, 1978.

Nemec, Ludvik. *The Czechoslovak Heresy and Schism: The Emergence of a National Czechoslovak Church.* Philadelphia: American Philosophical Society, 1975.

Nikitin, S. A., and Vaso Čubrilović, eds. *Pervoe serbskoe vosstanie 1804–1813 gg. i Rossiia: Kniga pervaia: 1804–1807.* Moscow: Nauka, 1980.

Očak, Ivan. *Vojnik revolucije: Život i rad Vladimira Ćopića.* Zagreb: Spektar, 1980.

Palavestra, Predrag. *Dogma i utopija Dimitrija Mitrinovića.* Belgrade: Slovo ljubve, 1977.

_____. *Književnost Mlade Bosne.* 2 vols. Sarajevo: Svjetlost, 1965.

Pandev, Konstantin. *Nacionalno-osvoboditelnoto dviženie v Makedonija i Odrinsko 1878–1903.* Sofia: Nauka i izkustvo, 1979.

Pandevski, Manol, and Ǵorǵi Stoev-Trnkata. *Strumica i Strumičko niz istorijata.* Strumica: Opštinski odbor na Sojuzot na združenieto na borcite od NOB—Strumica, 1969.

Pano, Nicholas C. *The People's Republic of Albania.* Baltimore: Johns Hopkins University Press, 1968.

Paulová, Milada. *Jugoslavenski odbor.* Zagreb: Prosvjetna nakladna zadruga, 1925.

Pavelić, Ante. *Putem hrvatskog državnog prava: Članci, govori, izjave, 1918–1929.* Madrid: Domovina, 1977.

Pavelić, Ante Smith. *Dr. Ante Trumbić: Problemi hrvatsko-srpskih odnosa.* Munich: Knjižnica Hrvatske revije, 1959.

Paver, Josipa, comp. *Zbornik gradje za povijest radničkog pokreta i KPJ 1919–1920: Dvor, Glina, Ivanić-Grad, Kostajnica, Kutina, Novska, Petrinja, Sisak.* Sisak: Historijski arhiv, 1970.

Pavlović, Kosta St. *Vojislav Marinković i njegovo doba (1876–1935).* Vol. 1. London: Author, 1955.

Pejanović, Djordje. *Stanovništvo Bosne i Hercegovine.* Belgrade: Naučna knjiga, 1955.

Petrović, Rastislav V. *Adam Bogoslavljević.* Belgrade: Rad, 1972.

Petrovich, Michael Boro. *A History of Modern Serbia.* 2 vols. New York: Harcourt Brace Jovanovich, 1976.

Petrović-Njegoš, Nikola I. *Pisma.* Cetinje: Obod, 1969.

_____. *Pjesme.* Cetinje: Obod, 1969.

Petrović-Njegoš, Petar II. *Gorski vijenac.* Belgrade: Jugoslovenska knjiga, 1947.

Pleterski, Janko. *Komunistička partija Jugoslavije i nacionalno pitanje 1919–1941.* Belgrade: Komunist, 1971.

Polić, Martin. *Ban Dragutin grof Khuen-Hedervàry i njegovo doba.* Zagreb: Anonymous "Croat Patriot," 1901.

Pollo, Stefanaq, and Aleks Buda, eds. *Historia e popullit shqiptar.* 2 vols. 2d ed., rev. Priština: Enti i tekszeve dhe i mjeteve mësimore i KSA te Kosovës, 1969.

Popović, Miodrag. *Vuk Stef. Karadžić*. Belgrade: Nolit, 1964.

Popović, Nikola, comp. *Jugoslovenski dobrovoljci u Rusiji, 1914–1918: Zbornik dokumenata*. Belgrade: Udruženje dobrovoljaca 1912–1918, 1977.

Prepeluh, Albin. *Kmetski pokret med Slovenci po Prvi svetovni vojni*. Ljubljana: Kmetijska matica, 1928.

Preradović, Petar. *Die Kroaten und ihre Bauernbewegung*. Vienna: Adolf Luser Verlag, 1940.

Pribićević, Adam. *Moj život*. Toronto: Lazar Jovanović and Katica Savić, 1982.

Pribićević, Svetozar. *Diktatura kralja Aleksandra*. Edited by Sava N. Kosanović; translated from the French by Andra Milosavljević. Belgrade: Prosveta, 1952.

Pribojević, Vinko. *De origine successibusque Slavorum*. 2d ed. Zagreb: JAZU, 1951.

Prica, Bogdan. *Hrvatsko pitanje i brojke*. Belgrade: Author?, 1937.

Prijatelj, Ivan. *Slovenska kulturnopolitična in slovstvena zgodovina: 1848–1895*. 5 vols. Ljubljana: Državna založba Slovenije, 1955–1966.

Protić, Stojan. *Oko Ustava: Kritika i polemika*. Belgrade: Izdavačka knižarnica Gece Kona, 1921.

Prunk, Janko. *Pot krščanskih socialistov v Osvobodilno fronto slovenskega naroda*. Ljubljana: Cankarjeva založba, 1977.

Purivatra, Atif. *Jugoslavenska muslimanska organizacija u političkom životu Kraljevine Srba, Hrvata i Slovenaca*. Sarajevo: Svjetlost, 1974.

_____. *Nacionalni i politički razvitak Muslimana*. Sarajevo: Svjetlost, 1970.

Radić, Stjepan. *Devet seljačkih zastupnika izabranih prvi put po proširenom izbornom pravu u banskoj Hrvatskoj: Pogled na politički njihov rad*. Zagreb: Slavenska knjižara, 1912.

_____. *Gospodska politika bez naroda i proti narodu: Govor predsjednika hrvatske seljačke stranke nar. zast. Stjepana Radića na noćnoj sudbonosnoj sjednici Narodnog Vieća dne 24. studena 1918*. Zagreb: Slavenska knjižara, 1920.

_____. *Korespondencija Stjepana Radića*. Compiled by Bogdan Krizman. 2 vols. Zagreb: Sveučilište u Zagrebu—Institut za hrvatsku povijest, 1972–1973.

_____. *Politički spisi*. Compiled by Zvonimir Kulundžić. Zagreb: Znanje, 1971.

_____. *Uzničke uspomene*. 3d ed. Zagreb: Matica Hrvatska and Zora, 1971.

Radosavljević-Bdin, Steva J. *Istorija bugarizma na Balkanskom poluostrvu: Narodnost i jezik Makedonaca*. Belgrade: Štamparija Kr. Srbije, 1890.

Radošević, Mijo. *Osnovi savremene Jugoslavije: Nova Politika*. Zagreb: Author, 1935.

Raïkovitch, Bogomir A. *L'avancement et le traitement des fonctionnaires publics du Royaume des Serbes, Croates et Slovènes*. Paris: Université de Paris—Faculté de Droit, [1929?].

Rakočević, Novica. *Crna Gora u Prvom svjetskom ratu*. Cetinje: Istorijski institut, 1969.

Report of the International Commission to Inquire into the Causes and Conduct of the Balkan Wars. Washington, D.C.: Carnegie Endowment for International Peace, 1914.

Ritter, Vitezović Pavao. *Croatia rediviva; regnante Leopoldo Magno Caesare*. Zagreb, 1700.

Rizvić, Muhsin. *Behar: Književnoistorijska monografija*. Sarajevo: Svjetlost, 1971.

_____. *Književno stvaranje muslimanskih pisaca u Bosni i Hercegovini u doba austrougarske vladavine*. 2 vols. Sarajevo: Akademija nauka i umjetnosti Bosne i Hercegovine, 1973.

Rogel, Carole. *The Slovenes and Yugoslavism, 1890–1914*. Boulder, Colorado: East European Quarterly, 1977.

Rubčić, Nikola, ed. *Robija: Zapisci hrvatskih narodnih boraca*. Zagreb: Author, 1936.

Šafařík, Pavel Josef. *Slovanský národopis*. 4th ed. Prague: Československa akademia věd, 1955.

Šarinić, Ivo. *Ideologija hrvatskog seljačkog pokreta*. Zagreb: Publications Committee, 1935.

Šaulić, Novica. *Crna Gora*. Belgrade: Narodna misao, 1924.

Šehić, Nusret. *Autonomni pokret Muslimana za vrijeme austrougarske uprave u Bosni i Hercegovini*. Sarajevo: Svjetlost, 1980.

———. *Četništvo u Bosni i Hercegovini (1918–1941)*. Sarajevo: Akademija nauka i umjetnosti BiH, 1971.

Šepić, Dragovan. *Italija, Saveznici i jugoslavensko pitanje, 1914–1918*. Zagreb: Školska knjiga, 1970.

———. *Supilo diplomat: Rad Frana Supila u emigraciji, 1914–1917 godina*. Zagreb: Naprijed, 1961.

Seton-Watson, Hugh et al., eds. *R. W. Seton-Watson and the Yugoslavs: Correspondence 1906–1941*. 2 vols. London: British Academy, 1976.

Shoup, Paul. *Communism and the Yugoslav National Question*. New York: Columbia University Press, 1968.

Šidak, Jaroslav. *Kroz pet stoljeća hrvatske povijesti*. Zagreb: Školska knjiga, 1981.

———. *Studije iz hrvatske povijesti XIX stojeća*. Zagreb: Sveučilište u Zagrebu—Institut za hrvatsku povijest, 1973.

———. *Studije iz hrvatske povijesti za revolucije 1848–49*. Zagreb: Sveučilište u Zagrebu—Institut za hrvatsku povijest, 1979.

———. Gross, Mirjana, Igor Karaman, and Dragovan Šepić. *Povijest hrvatskog naroda g. 1860–1914*. Zagreb: Školska knjiga, 1968.

Šišić, Ferdo, comp. *Dokumenti o postanku Kraljevine Srba, Hrvata i Slovenaca, 1914.–1919*. Zagreb: Matica Hrvatska, 1920.

Skendi, Stavro. *The Albanian National Awakening, 1878–1912*. Princeton, N.J.: Princeton University Press, 1967.

Skerlić, Jovan. *Svetozar Marković: Njegov život, rad i ideje*. Belgrade: Nova štamparija "Davidović," 1910.

Škerović, Nikola P. *Crna Gora na osvitku XX vijeka*. Belgrade: Naučno delo, 1964.

Skok, Petar. *Dolazak Slovena na Mediteran*. Split: Jadranska straža, 1934.

Slijepčević, Djoko. *Istorija Srpske pravoslavne crkve*. Vol. 2, *Od početka XIX veka do kraja Drugog svetskog rata*. Munich: Iskra, 1966.

———. *Srpsko-arbanaški odnosi kroz vekove sa posebnim osvrtom na novije vreme*. Munich: Iskra, 1974.

Smodlaka, Josip. *Zapisi Dra Josipa Smodlake*. Edited by Marko Kostrenčić. Zagreb: JAZU, 1972.

Srpska vojska i francuska mornarica u Dubrovniku 13. novembra 1918. Dubrovnik: Naklada nacionalističke omladine, 1918.

Stamać, Ante. *Ujević*. Zagreb: Biblioteka Kolo, 1971.

Stančić, Nikša. *Hrvatska nacionalna ideologija preporodnog pokreta u Dalmaciji: Mihovil Pavlinović i njegov krug do 1869*. Zagreb: Sveučilište u Zagrebu—Odjel za hrvatsku povijest, 1980.

Starčević, Ante. *Misli i pogledi*. Compiled by Blaž Jurišić. Zagreb: Matica Hrvatska, 1971.

———. *Politički spisi*. Compiled by Tomislav Ladan. Zagreb: Znanje, 1971.

Statistički pregled izbora narodnih poslanika Kraljevine Srba, Hrvata i Slovenaca. Belgrade: Izdanje Ustavotvorne Skupštine, 1921.

Stemmatografïa: Izobraženïe oružïj Illÿričeskihъ. Vienna: Thomas Messmer, 1741.

Stenografske beleške Privremenog narodnog predstavništva Srba, Hrvata i Slovenaca. 4 vols. Zagreb: Zemaljska tiskara, 1919.

Stenografske beleške Ustavotvorne skupštine Kraljevine Srba, Hrvata i Slovenaca. 2 vols. Belgrade: Državna štamparija, 1921.

Stojković, Andrija B. *Razvitak filosofije u Srba 1804–1944.* Belgrade: Slovo ljubve, 1972.

Strossmayer, Josip J., and Franjo Rački. *Politički spisi.* Compiled by Vladimir Košćak. Zagreb: Znanje, 1971.

Strugar, Vlado. *Socijaldemokratija o stvaranju Jugoslavije.* Belgrade: Rad, 1965.

_____. *Socijalna demokratija o nacionalnom pitanju jugoslovenskih naroda.* Belgrade: Rad, 1956.

Stulli, Bernard. *Revolucionarni pokreti mornara 1918.* Zagreb: IHRPH, 1968.

Südland, L. v. [Ivo Pilar]. *Die südslawische Frage und der Weltkrieg.* Vienna: Manzsche k.u.k. Hof-, Verlags- u. Universitäts Buchhandlung, 1918.

Šufflay, Milan. *Srbi i Arbanasi (Njihova simbioza u srednjem vijeku).* Belgrade: Biblioteka za arbansku starinu, jezik i etnologiju, 1925.

Sugar, Peter F. *Southeastern Europe under Ottoman Rule, 1354–1804.* Vol. 5 of *A History of East Central Europe.* Seattle: University of Washington Press, 1977.

_____, and Ivo J. Lederer, eds. *Nationalism in Eastern Europe.* Seattle: University of Washington Press, 1969.

Swire, J. *Albania: The Rise of a Kingdom.* London: Williams & Norgate, 1929.

Terzić, Velimir, Dragić Vujošević, I. Jovanović, and Uroš Kostić, eds. *Operacije crnogorske vojske u Prvom svetskom ratu.* Belgrade: Vojno delo, 1954.

Todorov, Kosta. *Stamboliski.* Belgrade: Jugo-istok, 1937.

Todorović, Desanka. *Jugoslavija i balkanske države, 1918–1923.* Belgrade: Institut za savremenu istoriju, 1979.

Tomašević, Jozo. *Novac i kredit.* Zagreb: Author, 1938.

_____. *Peasants, Politics, and Economic Change in Yugoslavia.* Stanford: Stanford University Press, 1955.

_____. *War and Revolution in Yugoslavia, 1941–1945: The Chetniks.* Stanford: Stanford University Press, 1975.

Tomić, Jaša. *Rat na Kosovu i Staroj Srbiji 1912. godine.* Novi Sad: Električna štamparija dra Svetozara Miletića, 1913.

_____. *Rat u Albaniji i pod Skadrom 1912. i 1913. godine.* Novi Sad: Električna štamparija dra Svetozara Miletića, 1913.

Tucović, Dimitrije. *Srbija i Arbanija: Jedan prilog kritici zavojevačke politike srpske buržoazije.* Belgrade: Izdanje Socijalističke knjižare, 1914.

Turczynski, Emanuel. *Konfession und Nation: Zur Frühgeschichte der serbischen und rumänischen Nationsbildung.* Düsseldorf: Pädagogischer Verlag Schwann, 1976.

Valev, L. B., G. M. Slavin, and I. I. Udal'tsov, eds. *Istoriia Iugoslavii: Tom II.* Moscow: Akademiia nauk SSSR, 1963.

Verković, Stefan I., ed., *Narodne pesme makedonski Bugara.* Belgrade: Pravitelstveno knjigopečatanie, 1860.

Vince, Zlatko. *Putovima hrvatskoga književnog jezika.* Zagreb: Sveučilišna naklada "Liber," 1978.

Vlahov, Dimitar. *Memoari*. Skopje: Nova Makedonija, 1970.

Vlajčić, Gordana. *KPJ i nacionalno pitanje u Jugoslaviji*. Zagreb: August Cesarec, 1974.

———. *Revolucija i nacije: Evolucija stavova vodstava KPJ i Kominterne 1919–1929. godine*. Zagreb: Centar za kulturnu djelatnost SSO Zagreb, 1978.

Vošnjak, Bogumil. *U borbi za ujedinjenu narodnu državu: Utisci i opažanja iz doba svetskog rata i stvaranja naše države*. Ljubljana: Tiskovna zadruga, 1928.

Vrčinac, Julijana. *Naša najnovija istorija: Pregled (1919–1945)*. Belgrade: Zavod za izdavanje udžbenika SR Srbije, 1967.

Vucinich, Wayne S. ed. *Contemporary Yugoslavia: Twenty Years of Socialist Experiment*. Berkeley and Los Angeles: University of California Press, 1969.

———. *Serbia between East and West*. Stanford: Stanford University Press, 1954.

Vujović, Dimitrije-Dimo. *Crnogorski federalisti, 1919–1929*. Titograd: Crnogorska akademija nauka i umjetnosti, 1981.

———. *Ujedinjenje Crne Gore i Srbije*. Titograd: Istorijski institut NR Crne Gore, 1962.

Vukićević, Milenko M. *Kralj Petar od rodjenja do smrti*. Belgrade: Narodno delo, 1922.

Vukojević, Stjepan F. *Aleksandar I: Tvorac države i ujedinitelj*. Belgrade: Štamparija "Soko" Milivoja J. Trajkovića, 1937.

Vuković-Todorović, Ljubica. *Hrvatski seljački pokret braće Radića*. Belgrade: Izdavačka zadruga Politika i društvo S.O.J., 1940.

Wilder [Vilder], Većeslav. *Bika za rogove*. London: Demos, 1957.

———. *Dva smjera u hrvatskoj politici*. Zagreb: Author, 1918.

Zbornik Dokumenata i podataka o Narodnooslobodilačkom ratu jugoslovenskih naroda. Tome 1, vol. 19, *Borbe na Kosovu 1941–1944*. Belgrade: Vojnoistorijski institut, 1969.

Zečević, Momčilo. *Slovenska ljudska stranka i jugoslovensko ujedinjenje 1917–1921.: Od Majske deklaracije do Vidovdanskog ustava*. Belgrade: Institut za savremenu istoriju, 1973.

Žeželj, Mirko, *Veliki Tin: Životopis*. Zagreb: Znanje, 1976.

Živanović, Milan. *Solunski proces*. Belgrade: Author, 1955.

Zwitter, Fran, in collaboration with Jaroslav Šidak and Vaso Bogdanov. *Les problemes nationaux dans la monarchie des Habsbourg* [*sic*]. Belgrade: Comité National Yougoslave des Sciences Historiques, 1960.

ARTICLES

Apostolov, Aleksandar. "Manifestacije makedonske nacionalne individualnosti u Kraljevini Jugoslaviji." *Jugoslovenski istorijski časopis*, 1970, nos. 3–4:71–88.

———. "Revolucionarne prilike u Makedoniji u godinama 1918, 1919. i 1920." In vol. 2, *Naučni skup "Oktobarska revolucija i narodi Jugoslavije,"* 1–44. Belgrade: Zajednica institucija za izučavanje radničkog pokreta i SKJ, 1967.

———. "Specifičnata položba na makedonskiot narod vo kralstvoto Jugoslavija." *Institut za nacionalna istorija: Glasnik* 16 (1972), no. 1:39–62.

———. "Vardarska Makedonija od Prvata svetska vojna do izborite za Konstituantata—28 noemvri 1920 godina." *Godišen zbornik na Filozofskiot fakultet na Universitetot vo Skopje: Istorisko-filološki oddel*, 1962, no. 13:27–90.

Banac, Ivo. "The Communist Party of Yugoslavia during the Period of Legality (1919–1921)." In *The Effects of World War I: The Class War After the Great War; The*

Selected Bibliography

Rise of Communist Parties in East Central Europe, 1918–1921, edited by Ivo Banac, 188–230. Brooklyn, New York: Brooklyn College Press, Social Science Monographs, 1983.

––––. "Main Trends in the Croat Language Question." In *Aspects of the Slavic Language Question,* 189–259, vol. 1, *Church Slavonic—South Slavic—West Slavic,* edited by Riccardo Picchio and Harvey Goldblatt. New Haven: Yale Concilium on International and Area Studies, 1984.

Bartulović, Niko. "Kulturno jedinstvo i Slovenci." *Književni jug* 1 (1918), no. 7:257–261.

Berov, L. "Le capital financier occidental et les pays balkaniques dans les années vingt." *Études balkaniques,* 1965, nos. 2–3:139–169.

Bikar, Fedora. "Razvoj odnosa izmedju hrvatske i srpske socijalne demokracije i pokušaji uskladjivanja njihovih koncepcija o nacionalnom pitanju od 1909. do. 1914." *Putovi revolucije* 3 (1965), no. 5:165–192.

Bogdanov, Vaso. "Historijski uzroci sukoba izmedju Hrvata i Srba." *Rad JAZU,* 1957, no. 311:353–477.

––––. "Hrvatska i srpska prošlost u interpretaciji S. Pribićevića." In *Likovi i pokreti,* 223–235. Zagreb: Mladost, 1957.

Bogdanović, Milan. "O srpskoj književnosti izmedju dva rata." *Rad JAZU,* 1954, no. 301:25–34.

[Bonifačić, Ante]. "Les idées du mouvement paysan croate: Antoine et Étienne Radić." *Le monde slave,* 15 (1938), no. 1:342–369.

"Borba srpskih junaka—ustaša u Staroj Srbiji i Makedoniji i izginuli junaci." In *Vardar: Kalendar za redovnu godinu 1907,* 78–84. Belgrade: Izdanje društva "Kola srpskih sestara," 1906.

Božović, Grigorije. "Braća Drage." *Savremeni pregled* 1 (1926), no. 1:1.

––––. "Kačaci." *Policija* 7 (1920), nos. 13–14:559–567.

Brozović, Dalibor. "Hrvatski jezik, njegovo mjesto unutar južnoslavenskih i drugih slavenskih jezika, njegove povijesne mijene kao jezika hrvatske književnosti." In *Hrvatska književnost u evropskom kontekstu,* edited by Aleksandar Flaker and Krunoslav Pranjić, 9–83. Zagreb: Zavod za znanost o književnosti Filozofskog fakulteta Sveučilišta u Zagrebu and Sveučilišna naklada "Liber," 1978.

Ciliga, Ante. "Uloga i sudbina hrvatskih komunista u KPJ." *Bilten Hrvatske demokratske i socijalne akcije* 9–10 (1972), no. 67:1–68.

Ćorović, Vladimir. "Za književno jedinstvo: Pitanje narečja i pisma." *Književni jug* 1 (1918), nos. 3–4:89–100.

Ćurčin, Milan. "Ko je izdao Crnu Goru." *Nova Evropa* 13 (1926), nos. 10–11:341–347.

––––. "Naš Gledston, i naš Gandi." *Nova Evropa* 12 (1925), no. 2:52–57.

Daković, Marko. "O padu Crnogorske Države i njene Dinastije." *Nova Evropa* 13 (1926), nos. 10–11:315–333.

Deanović, Mirko. "Naša umjetnost u Rimu." *Jug* 1 (1911), no. 5:136–139.

Djonović, Jovan. "Crna Gora u novoj Evropi." *Nova Evropa* 13 (1926), nos. 10–11:301–306.

Dostian, I. S. "Plany osnovaniia slaviano-serbskogo gosudarstva s pomoshch'iu Rossii v nachale XIX v." In *Slaviane i Rossiia,* edited by Iu. V. Bromlei, V. G. Karasev, V. D. Konobeev, I. I. Kostiushko, and E. P. Naumov, 98–107. Moscow: Nauka, 1972.

Džambazovski, Klime. "Stojan Novaković i makedonizam." *Istoriski časopis* 14–15 (1963): 133–154.

Engelsfeld, Neda. "Rad Kluba komunističkih poslanika u plenumu Ustavotvorne skupštine (u prosincu 1920. i u siječnju 1921.)." *Radovi Instituta za hrvatsku povijest*, 1972, no. 2:181–262.

Fancev, Franjo, ed. "Dokumenti za naše podrijetlo hrvatskoga preporoda (1790–1832)." *Gradja za povijest književnosti hrvatske* 12 (1933):i–xlvi, 1–320.

Firdus, Osman Nuri-beg. "O nacionalnom opredeljenju bosansko-hercegovačkih muslimana." *Nova Evropa* 11 (1925), no. 10:293–300.

Freidzon, V. I. "Sotsial'no-politicheskie vzgliady Antuna i Stepana Radichei v 1900-kh godakh i vozniknovedenie khorvatskoi krest'ianskoi partii (1904–1905)." *Uchenye zapiski Instituta slavianovedeniia* 20 (1960):275–305.

Gaković, Milan. "Osnivanje Saveza zemljoradnika i njegov program (1919–1921)." *Godišnjak Društva istoričara BiH* 21–27 (1976):199–218.

Gaži, Stjepan. "Stjepan Radić: His Life and Political Activities (1871–1928)." *Journal of Croatian Studies* 14–15 (1973–1974):13–73.

Gligorijević, Branislav. "Demokratska i Radikalna stranka prema revolucionarnim pokretima u Jugoslaviji 1919–1929." *Istorijski glasnik*, 1969, no. 2:95–106.

———. "Organizacija jugoslovenskih nacionalista (Orjuna)." *Istorija XX veka: zbornik radova* 5 (1963):315–396.

———. "Razlike i dodirne tačke u gledištu na nacionalno pitanje izmedju Radikalne i Demokratske stranke 1919–1929." *Jugoslovenski istorijski časopis*, 1969, no. 4:153–158.

———. "Srpska nacionalna omladina (Srnao)." *Istorijski glasnik*, 1964, nos. 2–3:3–38.

———. "Uloga vojnih krugova u 'rešavanju' političke krize u Jugoslaviji 1924. godine." *Vojnoistorijski glasnik* 23 (1972), no. 1:161–186.

Grol, Milan. "Savremeni nacionalizam." *Jugoslovenska demokratska liga*, 1919, no. 1:9–16.

Gross, Mirjana. "Die 'Welle'. Die Ideen der nationalistischen Jugend in Kroatien vor dem I. Weltkrieg." *Österreichische Osthefte* 10 (1968), no. 2:65–86.

———. "Hrvatska politika u Bosni i Hercegovini od 1878. do 1914." *Historijski zbornik* 19–20 (1966–1967):9–68.

———. "Nacionalne ideje studentske omladine u Hrvatskoj uoči I svjetskog rata." *Historijski zbornik* 21–22 (1968–1969):75–143.

———. "Socijalna demokracija prema nacionalnom pitanju u Hrvatskoj 1890–1902." *Historijski zbornik* 9 (1956):1–27.

Grulović, Nikola. "Jugoslovenska komunistička revolucionarna grupa 'Pelagić.'" *Matica srpska. Zbornik za društevene nauke* 22 (1959):108–128.

Hadri, Ali. "Kosovo i Metohija u Kraljevini Jugoslaviji." *Istorijski glasnik*, 1967, nos. 1–2:51–84.

———. "Nacionalno ugnjetavanje šiptarske narodnosti i stav i borba KPJ za nacionalna prava Šiptara za vreme stare Jugoslavije." *Gjurmime albanologjike*, 1965, no. 2:145–168.

Hadžijahić, Muhamed. "Jedan neostvareni nacionalno-politički projekt u Bosni iz g. 1853." *Historijski zbornik* 19–20 (1966–1967):87–102.

Hamm, Josip. "Moj osvrt na K. P. Misirkova." In *Krste P. Misirkov i nacionalno-kulturniot razvoj na makedonskiot narod do osloboduvanjeto*, edited by Trajko Stamatoski, 199–207. Skopje: Institut za makedonski jazik "Krste Misirkov," 1976.

Hercigonja, Eduard. "Društveni i gospodarski okviri hrvatskog glagoljaštva od 12. do polovine 16. stoljeća." *Croatica* 2 (1971), no. 2:7–100.

Hrabak, Bogumil. "Dezerterstvo i zeleni kadar u jugoslovenskim zemljama u prvom svetskom ratu." *Zbornik Historijskog instituta Slavonije i Baranje* 16 (1979):1–131.

———. "Reokupacija oblasti srpske i crnogorske države s arbanaškom većinom stanovništva u jesen 1918. godine i držanje Arbanasa prema uspostavljenoj vlasti." *Gjurmime albanologjike*, 1969, no. 2:254–297.

———, ed. "Zapisnici sednica Davidovićeve dve vlade od avgusta 1919. do februara 1920." *Arhivski vjesnik* 13 (1970), no. 13:7–92.

Išek, Tomislav. "Stjepan Radić kao politički mislilac." *Časopis za suvremenu povijest* 4 (1972), no. 1:187–199.

Ivičević, Jozo. "Odrednice unitarističkog nacionalnog programa I i II kongresa KPJ." *Hrvatski znanstveni zbornik* 1 (1971), no. 1:135–179.

Ivšić, Stjepan. "Etimologija i fonetika u našem pravopisu." *Hrvatski jezik* 1 (1938), no. 1:3–13.

Janković, Dragoslav. "Društveni i politički odnosi u Kraljevstvu Srba, Hrvata i Slovenaca uoči stvaranja Socijalističke radničke partije Jugoslavije (komunista): 1.XII.1918—20.IV.1919." *Istorija XX veka: zbornik radova* 1 (1959):7–147.

———. "Niška deklaracija (Nastajanje programa jugoslovenskog ujedinjenja u Srbiji 1914. godine)." *Istorija XX veka: zbornik radova* 10 (1969):7–111.

———. "Ženevska konferencija o stvaranju jugoslovenske zajednice 1918. godine." *Istorija XX veka: zbornik radova* 5 (1963):225–262.

Jeremić, Dragan M. "O filozofiji kod Srba." *Savremenik* 13 (1967), no. 12:487–500.

Korošec, Anton. "Slovenačka Pučka (Ljudska) Stranka." *Nova Evropa* 7 (1923), no. 7:215–218.

Koščak, Vladimir. "Formiranje hrvatske nacije i slavenska ideja." *Kritika*, 1971, no. 17:267–279.

———. "Mladost Stjepana Radića." *Hrvatski znanstveni zbornik* 1 (1971), no. 2:123–164.

Krizman, Bogdan, ed. "Izvještaj D. T. Simovića, delegata Srpske vrhovne komande kod vlade Narodnog vijeća SHS g. 1918." *Historijski zbornik* 8 (1955), nos. 1–4:123–132.

———. "Jadransko pitanje na pariškoj mirovnoj konferenciji (od 28 juna 1919—9 decembra 1919)." *Istorija XX veka: zbornik radova* 7 (1965):257–343.

———. "Pitanje granice Vojvodine na Pariškog mirovnoj konferenciji 1919 god." *Matica srpska. Zbornik za društvene nauke*, 1959, no. 24:31–72.

———. "Pitanje medjunarodnog priznanja jugoslavenske države 1919 godine." *Istorija XX veka: zbornik radova* 3 (1962): 347–386.

———. "Stjepan Radić i Hrvatska pučka seljačka stranka u prvom svjetskom ratu." *Časopis za suvremenu povijest* 2 (1970), no. 2:99–166.

———. "Stranke u Hrvatskom saboru za vrijeme I svjetskog rata." *Zgodovinski časopis* 19–20 (1965–1966):375–390.

———. "Vanjskopolitički položaj Kraljevine Srba, Hrvata i Slovenaca godine 1919." *Časopis za suvremenu povijest* 2 (1970), no. 1:23–60.

Krstić, Viktor D. "Uzroci rdjave bezbednosti u Južnoj Srbiji i vladina 'Objava.'" *Policija* 8 (1921), nos. 5–8:324–326.

Kulundžić, Zvonimir. "O vezama frankovaca i radikala od god. 1918. do 1941." *Historijski zbornik* 17 (1964):311–317.

[Kurtović, Šukrija]. "Gajretov list." *Gajret* 8 (1921), no. 1:2–5.

———. "Pabirci iz prošlosti Bosne." *Gajret* 8 (1921), no. 1:33–34.

Kušan, Vladislav. "Moderna skulptura u Hrvata: Geneza i prvi tokovi razvoja." *Forum* 19 (1980), nos. 1–2:282–308.

L. and M. "Seljačka buna u Hrvatskoj." *Nova Evropa* 1 (1920), no. 2:71–78.

Lampe, John R. "Unifying the Yugoslav Economy, 1918–1921: Misery and Early Misunderstandings." In *The Creation of Yugoslavia 1914–1918,* edited by Dimitrije Djordjević, 139–156. Santa Barbara: Clio Books, 1980.

Loboda, Anton. "Za kulturno zedinjenje Jugoslovanov." *Književni jug* 1 (1918), nos. 8–9:297–301.

M. "Rimska izložba i hrvatski umjetnici." *Jug* 1 (1911), no. 4:101–106.

M. M. "Triumf smjelosti i karaktera." *Jug* 1 (1911), no. 5:133–135.

Mamuzić, Ilija. "Ilirizam i Srbi." *Rad JAZU,* 1933, no. 247:1–91.

"Markantne ličnosti u životu Trgovačke i obrtne komore u Zagrebu." *Narodno bogatstvo* 5 (1927), nos. 13–17:7–11.

Marković, Božidar [Boža]. "Unutrašnje uredjenje Jugoslavije." *Jugoslovenska demokratska liga,* 1919, no. 1:4–8.

Matković, Hrvoje. "Djelovanje i sukobi gradjanskih političkih stranaka u Šibeniku izmedju dva svjetska rata." *Radovi Instituta za hrvatsku povijest* 2 (1972):263–282.

———. "Hrvatska zajednica: Prilog proučavanju političkih stranaka u staroj Jugoslaviji." *Istorija XX veka: zbornik radova,* 5 (1963):5–136.

———. "Odnos Aleksandra Karadjordjevića prema političkom djelovanju Matka Laginje." *Časopis za suvremenu povijest* 6 (1974), no. 3:39–51.

———. "Pad bana Matka Laginje." *Historijski pregled* 8 (1962), no. 1:39–50.

———. "Politički rad Matka Laginje od 1918. do 1920. godine." *Pazinski memorijal* 3 (1972):131–142.

———. "Stjepan Radić i Svetozar Pribićević u jugoslavenskoj politici od ujedinjenje do šestojanuarske diktature." *Jugoslovenski istorijski časopis,* 1969, no. 4:148–153.

———. "Veze izmedju frankovaca i radikala od 1922–1925." *Historijski zbornik* 15 (1962):41–59.

Melik, Vasilij. "Izidi volitev v Konstituanto leta 1920." *Prispevki za zgodovino delavskega gibanja* 2 (1962), no. 1:3–61.

Meštrović, Ivan. "Povodom osnivanja Jugoslovenske demokratske lige." *Jugoslovenska demokratska liga,* 1919, no. 1:iii.

Micić, Ljubomir. "Delo zenitizma." *Zenit* 1 (1921), no. 8:2–3.

Mikuž, Metod. "Razvoj slovenskih političnih strank (1918 do zač. 1929) v stari Jugoslaviji." *Zgodovinski časopis* 9 (1955):107–139.

Milenković, Toma. "Socijalreformistički pravac u radničkom pokretu jugoslovenskih zemalja (od sredine 1917. do 2. avgusta 1921)." *Istraživanja Instituta za izučavanje istorije Vojvodine* 2 (1973):195–287.

———. "Socijalšovinistička grupacija u Bosni i Hercegovini—Zvonaši (1919–1921. godine)." *Istorija XX veka: zbornik radova* 7 (1965):407–451.

Milković, Zvonko. "Za ekavštinu." *Književni jug* 1 (1918), nos. 8–9:349–350.

Mirdita, Zef. "Problem etnogeneze Albanaca." *Encyclopaedia moderna* 5 (1970), no. 13:30–39.

Muradbegović, Ahmed. "Problem jugoslovenske muslimanske izolacije." *Nova Evropa* 3 (1921), no. 4:107–116.

Novaković, Relja. "Još o nekim pitanjima teritorijalnog prostranstva Srbije i Hrvatske sredinom X stoljeća." *Historijski zbornik* 19–20 (1966–1967):265–293.

Obradović, Milovan. "Agrarni odnosi na Kosovu 1918–1941. godine." *Jugoslovenski istorijski časopis*, 1978, nos. 1–4:442–455.

Pavić, R. M. "Savremene želje katoličkog nižeg klera, god. 1919." *Krug* 1 (1938), no. 4:74–76.

Pavlović, Teodor. Editorial note in "Domaći ili narodni istočnicy drevne slavenske istorie." *Novyj serbskij lětopisъ* 11 (1837), no. 41:29.

Petrović, Radomir M. "Na frontu smrti." *Učiteljska iskra* 1 (1922), nos. 5–6:57–58.

Pijade, Moša. "Teze o nacionalnom pitanju." In *Peta zemaljska konferencija KPJ (19–23. oktobar 1940)*, edited by Pero Damjanović, Milovan Bosić, and Dragica Lazarević, 375–400. Belgrade: Izdavački centar Komunist, 1980.

Pirraku, Muhamet. "Kulturno-prosvetni pokret Albanaca u Jugoslaviji (1919–1941)." *Jugoslovenski istorijski časopis*, 1978, nos. 1–4:356–370.

Pivec, Melita. "Programi političnih strank in statistika volitev." In *Slovenci v desetletju 1918–1928: Zbornik razprav iz kulturne, gospodarske in politične zgodovine*, edited by Josip Mal, 357–373. Ljubljana: Leonova družba, 1928.

Plamenac, P[etar]. "Uzroci crnogorske kapitulacije." *Nova Evropa* 13 (1926), nos. 10–11:348–367.

Pleterski, Janko. "Komunistička partija Jugoslavije i nacionalno pitanje u prvoj jugoslavenskoj državi." *Nastava povijesti*, 1969–1970, no. 2:10–19.

———. "Nacionalno pitanje u Jugoslaviji u teoriji i politici KPJ-KPS." *Jugoslovenski istorijski časopis*, 1969, nos. 1–2:28–68.

Politeo, Ivo. "Ivan Lorković." *Nova Evropa* 13 (1926), no. 5:129–132.

Popović, Dušan J. "Sava Tekelija prema Prvom srpskom ustanku." *Zbornik Matice srpske: Serija društvenih nauka*, 1954, no. 7:118–125.

Pravoljub, S. D—ć [Ivan Frano Jukić]. "Potomci hàrvátah i sèrbaljah u ilirskih dèržavah." *Danica ilirska* 8 (1842), no. 29:113–116.

"Privremena pravila Jugoslovenske demokratske lige." *Jugoslovenska demokratska liga*, 1919, no. 1:i–ii.

Purivatra, Atif. "Formiranje Jugoslovenske Muslimanske organizacije i njen razvoj do prevazilaženja krize početom 1922. godine." *Istorija XX veka: zbornik radova* 9 (1968):387–445.

———. "Nacionalne koncepcije Jugoslovenske muslimanske organizacije." *Jugoslovenski istorijski časopis*, 1969, no. 4:141–148.

Radica, Bogdan, ed. "Supilova pisma Ferrerovima." *Hrvatska revija* 7 (1957), no. 4:365–405.

Radojević, Danilo M. "Problemi crnogorske historije oko prvoga svjetskog rata." *Kritika* 4 (1971), no. 16:65–87.

Rakočević, Novica. "Politička aktivnost knjaza Mirka Petrovića u toku austrougarske okupacije Crne Gore." *Istorijski zapisi* 23 (1970), nos. 3–4:251–298.

Ravlić, Jakša. "Povijest Matice hrvatske." In *Matica Hrvatska, 1842–1962*, 9–270. Zagreb: Matica Hrvatska, 1963.

Rojc, Milan. "Prilike u Hrvatskoj." *Nova Evropa* 2 (1921), no. 2:46–71.

Seton-Watson, Robert William. "Jugoslavia and the Croat Problem." *Slavonic Review* 16 (1937), no. 2:102–112.

Šidak, Jaroslav. "Počeci političke misli u Hrvata—J. Križanić i P. Ritter Vitezović." *Naše teme* 16 (1972), nos. 7–8:1118–1125.

Šimić, Antun Branko. "Juriš." *Juriš* 1 (1919), no. 1:4–6.

———. "Nazorova lirika." *Vedrina* 1 (1923), nos. 3–4:76–83.

Simplex. "Ličnost Nikole Pašića." *Nova Evropa* 13 (1926), no. 12:410–416.

Šičić, Ferdo. "Hrvatska historiografija od XVI do XX stoljeća." *Jugoslovenski istoriski časopis* 1 (1935), nos. 1–4:22–51.

Škerović, Nikola. "Crna Gora u Svetskom Ratu." *Nova Evropa* 13 (1926), nos. 10–11:306–315.

Šorn, Jože. "Nacionalno poreklo velikega kapitala v industriji, rudarstvu in bančništvu na slovenskem ozemlju." *Jugoslovenski istorijski časopis*, 1969, no. 4:136–141.

Spaho, Mehmed. "Jugoslovenska Muslimanska Organizacija." *Nova Evropa* 7 (1923), no. 17:505–506.

Stančić, Nikša. "Hrvatska nacionalna i državna misao Mihovila Pavlinovića." *Encyclopaedia moderna* 6 (1971), no. 16:75–80.

———. "Problem 'Načertanija' Ilije Garašanina u našoj historiografiji." *Historijski zbornik* 21–22 (1968–1969):179–196.

Stanković, Djordje D. "Kriza radikalsko-demokratske koalicije 1921. i hrvatsko pitanje." *Jugoslovenski istorijski časopis*, 1972, nos. 1–2:79–91.

———. "Neuspeh Stojana Protića u okupljanju političkih snaga radi rešavanja hrvatskog pitanja 1921. godine." *Istorijski glasnik*, 1971, no. 1:7–34.

Stipetić, Vladimir. "Jedno stoljeće u brojčanom razvoju stanovništva na današnjem području Jugoslavije." *Forum* 12 (1973), no. 12:885–915.

Stiplovšek, Miroslav. "Slovenske politične stranke in njihovi kmečki programi 1918–1920." *Jugoslovenski istorijski časopis*, 1973, no. 304:191–206.

Stranjaković, Dragoslav. "Kako je postalo Garašaninovo 'Načertanije.'" *Spomenik SKA* 91 (1939):63–115.

Stulli, Bernard. "'Idemo u bunu!'—'U Sv. Ivanu Zelini treba reda delati!'" *Kaj* 4 (1971), nos. 7–8:44–48.

Todorović, Desanka. "'Okupacijata na Strumica 1919 godina.'" *Institut na nacionalna istorija: Glasnik* 10 (1966), no. 1:45–59.

Todorovski, Gligor. "Nekolku podatoci za aktivnosta na vrhovističkata VMRO vo Albanija i Bugarija pomeǵu dvete svetski vojni." *Institut za nacionalna istorija: Glasnik* 15 (1971): no. 1:137–156.

Tudjman, Franjo. "Uvod u historiju socijalističke Jugoslavije." *Forum* 2 (1963), no. 2:292–352; no. 3:530–564; no. 4:702–741.

Vasić, Milan. "Etnička kretanja u Bosanskoj krajini u XVI vijeku." *Godišnjak Društva istoričara Bosne i Hercegovine* 13 (1962):231–250.

Vasiljević, Jovan. "Stvaranje ratne mornarice Kraljevine Jugoslavije (oktobar 1918–septembar 1923)." *Istorija XX veka: zbornik radova* 11 (1970):121–229.

Vidmar, Josip I., comp. "Prilozi gradji za historiju radničkog pokreta i KPJ 1919. god." *Arhivski vjesnik* 2 (1959), no. 2:7–227.

———. comp. "Prilozi gradji za povijest 1917.–1918. s osobitim obzirom na razvoj radničkog pokreta i odjeka Oktobarske revolucije kod nas." *Arhivski vjesnik* 1 (1958), no. 1:11–173.

Vidoeski, Božo. "Osnovi dijalektni grupi vo Makedonija." *Makedonski jazik* 11–12 (1960–1961), nos. 1–2:13–31.

Vidušić, Stjepan. "Odgovor 'Obzoru.'" *Preporod* 3 (1922), no. 1:3–4.

Vigil. "Kosta Strajnić i nacionalna umetnost." *Vedrina* 1 (1923), no. 1–27.

Vujović, Dimitrije-Dimo. "Gradjanske političke stranke u Crnoj Gori u periodu formiranja KPJ." *Istorijski zapisi* 22 (1969), nos. 2–3:189–222.

———. "Oslobodjenje Skadra 1918 godine i stanje na crnogorsko-albanskoj granici." *Istorijski zapisi* 13 (1960), no. 1:93–128.

———. "Učešće dr Vukašina Markovića u oktobarskoj revoluciji i njeni odjeci u Crnoj Gori." *Prilozi za istoriju socijalizma* 5 (1968):490–514.

Vukićević, Milan. "O uzrocima nemira u kosovskoj i podrimskoj Srbiji." *Novi život* 2 (1921–1922), no. 7:161–166.

Zaninović, Vice. "Mlada Hrvatska uoči I. svjetskog rata." *Historijski zbornik* 11–12 (1958–1959):65–104.

Zečević, Momčilo. "Slovenska ljudska stranka pred stvaranje Kraljevine Srba, Hrvata i Slovenaca 1917–1918." *Istorija XX veka: zbornik radova* 9 (1968):337–379.

Zografski, Dančo. "Krste Misirkov za nacionalnosta na Makedoncite." In *Krste Misirkov: Naučen sobir posveten na 40-godišninata od smrtta,* edited by Hristo Andonov-Poljanski, Blaže Ristovski, and Trajko Stamatoski. Skopje: Institut za makedonski jazik "Krste Misirkov," 1966.

Žugić, Gojko M. "Javna bezbednost u Crnoj Gori." *Policija* 8 (1921), nos. 5–8:300–311.

Zwitter, Fran. "Narodnost in politika pri Slovencih." *Zgodovinski časopis* 1 (1947), nos. 1–4:31–69.

———. "Slovenski politični preporod XIX stoletja v okviru evropske nacionalne problematike." *Zgodovinski časopis* 18 (1964):75–153.

ENCYCLOPEDIAS AND REFERENCE MATERIALS

Enciklopedija Bəlgarija. 2 vols. (others forthcoming). Sofia: BAN, 1978–1981.

Enciklopedija Jugoslavije. 8 vols. Zagreb: Jugoslavenski leksikografski zavod: 1955–1971.

Enciklopedija Jugoslavije. 2 vols. (others forthcoming). Zagreb: Jugoslavenski leksikografski zavod, 1980–1982.

Enciklopedija Leksikografskog zavoda. 2d ed.; 6 vols. Zagreb: Jugoslavenski leksikografski zavod, 1966–1969.

Hrvatska enciklopedija. 5 vols. Zagreb: Konzorcija Hrvatske enciklopedije, 1941–1945.

Ko je ko u Jugoslaviji. 2d ed. Belgrade: Jugoslovenski godišnjak, 1928.

Narodna enciklopedija srpsko-hrvatsko-slovenačka. 4 vols. Zagreb: Bibliografski zavod d.d., 1929.

Slovenski biografski leksikon. 3 vols. plus 1 copybook. Ljubljana: Zadružna gospodarska banka, 1925–1933; SAZU, 1960–1980.

Vojna enciklopedija. 7 vols. Belgrade: Redakcija Vojne enciklopedije, 1958–1969.

Zbornik plemstva u Hrvatskoj, Slavoniji, Dalmaciji, Bosni-Hercegovini, Dubrovniku, Kotoru i Vojvodini. 2 vols. Zagreb: Viktor Anton Cte Duišin, 1938–1939.

UNPUBLISHED DISSERTATIONS

Gazi, Stjepan. "Stjepan Radić and the Croatian Question: A Study in Political Biography." Ph.D. dissertation, Indiana University, 1965.

Livingstone, Robert G. "Stjepan Radić and the Croatian Peasant Party, 1940–1929." Ph.D. dissertation, Harvard University, 1959.

ARCHIVAL SOURCES

Arhiv Hrvatske (The Archive of Croatia), Zagreb.
> Narodno vijeće SHS, Sekcija za organizaciju i agitaciju (The National Council of the Slovenes, Croats, and Serbs; Section for Organization and Agitation).
> Narodno vijeće SHS, Središnja kancelarija NV SHS (The National Council of the Slovenes, Croats, and Serbs; Central Office of the National Council of the Slovenes, Croats, and Serbs).
> Odjel za unutrašnje poslove Zemaljske vlade (Department of Internal Affairs of the Land Government [of Croatia-Slavonia].)
> Rukopisna ostavština Dr. Djure Šurmina (Private papers of Dr. Djuro Šurmin).
> Rukopisna ostavština Dr. Milana Šufflaya (Private papers of Dr. Milan Šufflay).

Arhiv Instituta za historiju radničkog pokreta Hrvatske (AIHRPH, Archive of the Institute for the History of the Workers' Movement of Croatia), Zagreb.
> Fond Kominterne (The Comintern Collection).
> Sig. VI/C: Gradjanske stranke, HPSS-HRSS (Bourgeois Parties, HPSS-HRSS).
> Sig. XXI: Politička situacija (Political Developments).
> Sig. ZB-S: Zbirka arhivskih sudskih predmeta (Collection of Archival Court Documents).

Hoover Institution Archives, Stanford, California.
> Charles W. Furlong Collection.

NEWSPAPERS

Balkan (Belgrade), daily close to Narodna radikalna stranka (NRS).
Demokratija (Belgrade), main organ of Demokratska stranka (DS).
Epoha (Belgrade), independent daily.
Glas slobode (Sarajevo), organ of Socijalistička radnička partija Jugoslavije (komunista) (SRPJ[k]).
Glas Slovenaca, Hrvata i Srba (Zagreb), forerunner of the DS's unofficial Zagreb organ.
Hrvat (Zagreb), main organ of Hrvatska zajednica (HZ).
Hrvatska riječ (Split), "organ of Dalmatian Croats."
Hrvatska sloboda (Zagreb), electoral organ of Hrvatska stranka prava (HSP).
Jadran (Buenos Aires), publication of the Yugoslav National Defense.
Jedinstvo (Novi Sad), organ of the DS.
Jug (Osijek), organ of the Yugoslav Democratic Club (DS).
Jugoslovenski Lloyd (Zagreb), newspaper for "economic policy and general welfare."
Jutarnji list (Zagreb), independent daily.
Karlovac (Karlovac), organ of the DS.
Katolički list (Zagreb), weekly of the Archdiocese of Zagreb.
Montenegrin Press Bureau (Rome), bulletin of the Montenegrin government-in-exile.
Narodna riječ (Cetinje), unofficial organ of the DS.
Neimar (Belgrade), organ of "Yugoslavia," the Grand Lodge of the Serbs, Croats, and Slovenes.
Nouvelles Macédoniennes (n.p., probably Sofia), organ of Vətrešna makedonska revoljucionna organizacija (VMRO).
Novi Srbobran (Zagreb), organ of the Serb Independent party in Croatia-Slavonia.

Selected Bibliography

Novosti (Zagreb), daily close to the DS.

Obzor (Zagreb), prestigious daily of Croat liberal intelligentsia, close to the HZ.

Oslobodjenje (Split), organ of the SRPJ(k)-KPJ.

Politika (Belgrade), prestigious daily of Serbian liberal intelligentsia.

Pravda (Sarajevo), main organ of Jugoslavenska muslimanska organizacija (JMO).

Pravda: Dnevnik (Belgrade), unofficial organ of the DS.

Radikal (Belgrade), daily owned by Stojan Protić.

Radnička straža (Vukovar), organ of the SRPJ(k)-KPJ.

Razvitak (Bitola).

Reč (Belgrade), organ of Pribićević's Independent Democratic party.

Republika (Belgrade), organ of the Republican Democratic party.

Riječ Srba-Hrvata-Slovenaca (Zagreb), unofficial organ of the DS.

Samouprava (Belgrade), main organ of the NRS.

Sloboda (Zagreb), socialist organ.

Slobodni dom (Zagreb), main newspaper of Hrvatska republikanska seljačka stranka (HRSS).

Slovenec (Ljubljana), "political newspaper for the Slovene people," main organ of Slovenska ljudska stranka (SLS).

Službene novine (Belgrade), state official gazette.

Smotra (Belgrade).

Srpska riječ (Sarajevo), organ of the NRS.

Srpsko kolo (Zagreb), organ of the DS's Serb peasant councils in Croatia-Slavonia.

Stara Srbija (Skopje).

Šestar (Zagreb), organ of the freemasonic lodge "Justice."

Tribuna (Belgrade), daily close to the NRS.

Vesnik (Belgrade), "ecclesiastical-political and social newspaper" of the Orthodox church.

Vrelo (Dubrovnik), monthly of the secondary school youth.

Zastava (Novi Sad), organ of the NRS.

Židov (Zagreb), "organ for the questions of Jewry."

Život (Split), organ of the DS.

Index

Index

Croatia-Slavonia (cont.)
  Dalmatia, 92, 98, 182, 351, 357; Serbian
  policy in, 110; in First World War, 125–28,
  261; disorders in 1918, 129–30; in elections
  of 1920, 156, 175, 191, 197, 227, 241,
  263, 266, 330, 354, 390–92; in Yugoslavia,
  215–16, 218, 220, 353, 357; mentioned
  passim. See also Croatia; Croats
  Croats: their identity, 13, 23; settlement of,
  33–34; their early medieval state, 34–35,
  161–62; in medieval period, 35–37; in
  Bosnia, 38–39; early modern migrations,
  42, 47; their number, 49, 53, 58, 81; of
  Orthodox religion, 58, 88, 164; Christianization of, 61; culturally divided, 61–62;
  pass into Serbian church, 66; and Catholic
  universalism, 66; their political culture, 69,
  354, 415; their national ideologies, 70–79,
  85–91, 93–95, 98–99, 100–106, 108, 111,
  115, 406–7; their national revival, 75–79;
  as "linguistic Serbs," 79–80, 161; and
  Yugoslavist unitarism, 101–3, 184, 207;
  and unification, 117–24, 128, 135, 138,
  170, 260; disenchantment with Yugoslavia,
  147–48, 151–52, 259, 379; anti-Serb sentiment, 147, 236, 257n; in Yugoslav army,
  150–53; in Pribićević's ideology, 182–83;
  art among, 203–7; insurgency among,
  215–16, 239, 242, 244–47, 248–54,
  257–58, 301, 330; in Belgrade cabinets,
  216–17; and Slovenes, 345–46; mentioned
  passim
Croat-Serb Coalition. See Hrvatsko-srpska
  koalicija (HSK)
Cuce, tribe, 271, 285, 287
Curri, Bajram, 302, 304–6
Cvijić, Jovan, 67, 117, 201, 311–13
Cyril (Constantine), Saint, 61, 312, 340
Cyrillic script: devised in Macedonia, 61; Bosnian recension, 62; recommended to Croats,
  79; among Serbs, 211–13; mentioned,
  151–52, 183
Czechoslovakia, 96, 127, 132, 219, 412
Czechs: influence Croats, 96; their national
  movement, 96, 105; mentioned, 49, 71

Daković, Marko, 277–79, 285
Dalmatia: Roman and Byzantine province, 36,
  61; Romance idiom of, 36; and Croatia, 36;
  and Venice, 36, 73; in Habsburg Monarchy,
  37, 73, 82, 91, 185n, 293; migrations to,
  42; Serbs in, 45, 50, 93, 98, 187, 221;
  dialects in, 47; Catholic Serbs in, 58,
  107–8; center of Croatian literature, 61–62,
  77; unification with Croatia-Slavonia, 92,
  98, 182, 267, 351, 357; liberal Starčevićism
  in, 96–97; Serbian policy in, 110; and col-

lapse of Habsburg Monarchy, 127–28; re-
  puted unitarism of, 172, 177; in elections of
  1920, 175, 191, 194, 390, 392; mentioned
  passim. See also Croatia; Croats
D'Annunzio, Gabriele, 265, 267–69, 384
Danube River, 33, 34, 37–38, 43, 47, 65, 80,
  87, 91, 109, 311
Danubian principalities, 46, 82, 314. See also
  Moldavia; Wallachia
Davidović, Ljubomir (Ljuba), 173–75,
  177–78, 186, 192, 197, 202, 221, 291,
  304–5, 382–85
"Death of Smail-aga Čengić, The" (Ivan
  Mažuranić), 205–6, 363
Debar (Dibër), 107, 303, 313, 317, 326
Dečani, monastery of, 291–92
Delčev, Goce, 314–17
Delvina, Sulejman Bej, 247, 302
Demetrović, Juraj, 172, 412n
democracy, 31, 143, 153, 169, 188, 195, 225,
  233, 239, 340, 397, 413–15
Democratic Party. See Demokratska stranka
  (DS)
Demokratska stranka (DS, Democratic Party):
  and Slovene liberals, 113–15, 173, 192,
  343–44, 346; and monarchism, 153,
  179–80, 184, 188, 192, 194–95; origins of,
  173, 189; its unitarism, 170–85 *passim*,
  189, 192, 194–95, 207, 213, 225, 335,
  374, 391; and NRS, 173–75, 177–78,
  188–89, 192, 378, 381–83, 385–87,
  393–97; and political left, 174; in elections
  of 1920, 175–77, 191–92, 321, 330, 349,
  370–71, 387, 390–92, 393–97; turns
  hegemonistic, 177–78; ideology of, 178–88
  passim, 319; and historical provinces,
  179–80, 185, 415; and centralism, 186–89,
  192, 385; totalitarian tendencies in, 187–88;
  and democratic centralists, 192–95, 197,
  199, 202; and Constituent Assembly, 193,
  385–87, 393–97, 404; in PNP, 381–87 *passim;* mentioned, 169, 291, 300, 303, 340,
  342, 345, 348–49, 353, 412n, 414
Dibra, Zija, 302, 305–6
Dimitrijević-Apis, Dragutin, 133n, 193,
  174–75
Dimov, Dimo Hadži, 323–24
Djakovica (Gjakove), 47, 271, 298, 301–2
Djalski, Ksaver Šandor (Ljubo Babić),
  88–89
Djikić, Osman, 363
Djonović, Jovan, 194, 278–79
Djordjević, Vladan, 293–94
Dobrudža, 122, 311, 317
Doclea (Duklja), later Zeta, 23, 35, 44, 63,
  75, 88, 274, 291
Dostoevsky, F. M., 208, 212

Index

Yugoslav Club. *See* Jugoslovanski klub
Yugoslav Committee. *See* Jugoslavenski odbor (JO)
Yugoslav Democratic League. *See* Jugoslovenska demokratska liga (JDL)
Yugoslavia: census of 1921, 49–58; frontiers of, 50; national structure, 58; plans for its unification, 98, 103–4, 115–20, 123–24, 128, 130, 132–38, 172; unification, 105, 138, 371; Constituent Assembly, 124, 134, 137, 172, 197–99, 236, 330, 349, 381, 384–87, 393–404 *passim;* Serbian institutions extended in, 142, 147–48, 150–53, 194, 216, 218, 249, 383, 407; elections of 1920 in, 156, 172, 175, 177, 189, 191–94, 196–98, 227, 241, 263, 266, 287, 320–21, 330, 341–42, 349, 354, 370–71, 377–78, 389–92; Vidovdan Constitution (1921), 169, 193, 216, 357–58, 375, 403–4, 407; its economy, 222–225, 320, 341; Privremeno narodno predstavništvo (PNP, Interim National Legislature), 239, 262, 359, 379–387 *passim;* its political culture, 342–343, 354, 415; mentioned *passim*
—projected state organization: general aspects, 123–24, 132, 134, 137, 200–202, 392; federalism, 124, 138, 165–67, 179, 195, 201, 215, 231, 235–36, 239, 289–90, 336, 339, 348, 357, 397–99; centralism, 124, 144, 160, 163–64, 166–70, 182, 186–89, 195, 199–201, 212–15, 225–26, 232, 248, 329, 335, 338, 343, 345, 352, 356, 378, 381–83, 385–86, 392, 396, 402, 404, 407; autonomism, 124, 167–69, 182, 192, 195, 198, 201, 235, 289, 340, 343, 347–48, 351–52, 356, 375–76; confederalism, 135–36, 200–201, 215, 226, 231, 335, 352, 357–58, 378
Yugoslav Muslim Organization. *See* Jugoslavenska muslimanska organizacija (JMO)

Zach, František A., 83–84
Zadar, 39, 109, 267
Zagreb, capital of Croatia: mentioned *passim*
Žefarovič, Hristofor, 74–75
zelenaši (Greens), 285–291 *passim*, 298, 303, 308
zeleni kader (green cadre), 127, 129, 249
Zeta. *See* Doclea (Duklja)
Zogu, Ahmet Bej (Zog I), king of Albanians, 302, 305–6
Žujović, Jovan, 174, 193, 201
Zvono (Bell): Bosnian social patriotic faction, 196, 199–200

Library of Congress Cataloging in Publication Data

Banac, Ivo.
  The national question in Yugoslavia.

  Bibliography: p.
  Includes index.
  I. Nationalism—Yugoslavia.   2. Yugoslavia—Politics and government—
1918–1945.   I. Title.
DR1295.B36   1984   949.7′02   83–45931
ISBN 0–8014–1675–2